LANCIA

LANCIA
PIRELLI
MAGNETI MARELLI
Lombard
RAC rally
3
HF

LANCIA

Compiled from the archives of

Autocar

by Peter Garnier

Hamlyn
London · New York · Sydney · Toronto

This edition published in 1981 by
The Hamlyn Publishing Group Limited
London · New York · Sydney · Toronto
Astronaut House, Feltham, Middlesex, England

ISBN 0 600 34934 9
Phototypeset by Tradespools Ltd., Frome, Somerset
Printed in Great Britain

The publishers are grateful to the following individuals and organisations for additional illustrations used in this book:
Hugh Bishop; Neill Bruce; Peter Garnier;
Robert Harding Associates; David Hodges; Leigh Jones;
The Lancia Division of Fiat Auto (UK) Ltd.;
John Millham; Charles Pocklington; Colin Taylor

CONTENTS

LANCIA THROUGH THE YEARS

Background to Present Range

"Cast not aside the things upon which the eyes of your fathers have rested, for these are the links that unite one generation with another".

WHETHER consciously or unconsciously, Joubert's dictum—loosely translated above—must have been a guiding force in Turin through the years, for there can be few manufacturers with such a comprehensive record of their products—even to a personal museum. Whether, in the purely venal sense, there was anything to be gained from these links with the past may have been questionable 20 years ago. But now, with old car values soaring auction by auction, motoring history has assumed a sudden importance. Any manufacturer who, in exchange for an engine and chassis number, can produce full details of the car together with working drawings of ancient components and accessories—if not even the parts themselves—and who can offer for scrutiny the model in question (however old) in original and mint condition, is worth his weight in gold. There is something, too, about the lasting pride in his products that all this implies.

Currently responsible for the cars and records at the Museo Vincenzo Lancia in Turin is Architetto Luigi Ferraresi—a remarkable person in many ways. During a visit to the Museum earlier this year I mentioned I was rebuilding a 1939 Aprilia, and he asked whether I needed any parts, drawings, instruction book, workshop manual and so on. Nave plates and hub nuts were my principal problems, I told him; plus paperwork of which I had virtually none. We had dinner together, and parted for bed at around 10.30. Next morning I visited his office at noon, and there on a groaning table were all the things I had mentioned. What's more, he had driven 600 km to Bellinzona, Switzerland, and back to collect some of them.

Though the year of the Lancia

On show in the Museum is a page of Vincenzo Lancia's "doodles" while establishing the marque's badge. The centre, top design was chosen—and continues today. Left: Beta steering wheel with knurled ignition control, which was incorporated in the badge

Top right: The 3,120 c.c. Beta, introduced in 1909, followed the Alpha and Dialpha and had a top speed of 90 kph

Bottom right: Museo Vincenzo Lancia—with Lambda, Dilambda, Aprilia, Ardea, Appia, B24 Spider and B20 Aurelia stretching away into the distance

Alpha (1908) — Beta (1909) — Theta (1913) — Trikappa—Lancia's first vee-8' (1922) — Lambda (1922-1931); 3rd Series

company's birth is generally reckoned as 1907, it was in fact founded—and legalized by a 1 *lira* stamp—on 29 November 1906, when Vincenzo Lancia was 25 years old. As a Fiat "works" driver, under Cav. Giovanni Agnelli, Vincenzo had embarked upon a motor racing career with a win at Padua in July 1900. His last race was at Modena in 1910 when, in a car bearing his own name, he set a mile record at 70.2 mph. The car was a racing version (the Alpha Corse) of the four-cylinder, side-valve, 2,543 c.c. type 51, the 18-24 h.p.—or, as it was finally designated, the Alpha, Lancia's first car, which had appeared on its first road test in September 1907. It was revolutionary in that the engine revved up to 1,450 rpm, very fast by current standards; that it was shaft-driven, instead of by the almost ubiquitous chain; and that it started the Lancia tradition of naming the cars after characters in the Greek alphabet.

It is interesting that the metaphorical wheel has turned full circle, with the Fiat-Lancia association now a permanent one under the chairmanship of the present-day Giovanni Agnelli.

Only 13 months after his first car had taken the road, Lancia began exporting to England. At the Olympia Show in October 1909, W. L. Stewart of Shaftesbury Avenue, London, Lancia's first UK concessionaire, exhibited a six-cylinder, 3,815c.c., 30h.p. Dialpha landaulet and a four-cylinder, 20 h.p. Beta chassis; the type 53, or Dialpha had followed the Alpha in the summer of 1908, and the 3,120 c.c. Beta, with monobloc four-cylinder engine, had appeared in 1909.

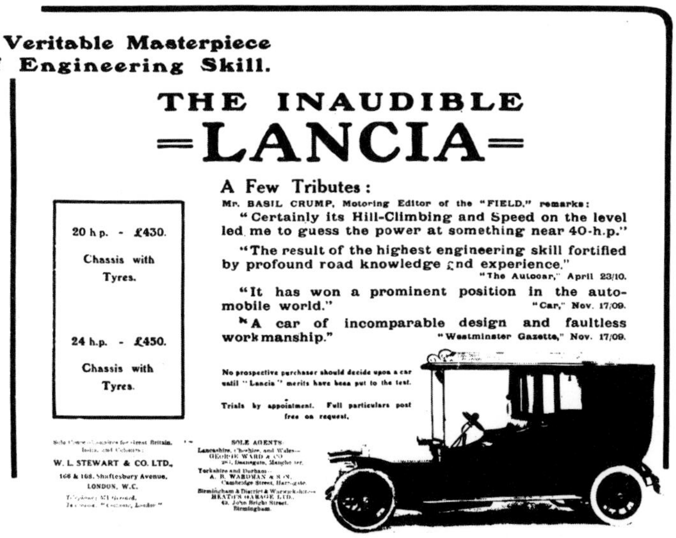

A Veritable Masterpiece of Engineering Skill.

THE INAUDIBLE =LANCIA=

A Few Tributes:

Mr. BASIL CRUMP, Motoring Editor of the "FIELD," remarks:

"Certainly its Hill-Climbing and Speed on the level led me to guess the power at something near 40-h.p."

"The result of the highest engineering skill fortified by profound road knowledge and experience." "The Autocar," April 23/10.

"It has won a prominent position in the automobile world." "Car," Nov. 17/09.

"A car of incomparable design and faultless workmanship." "Westminster Gazette," Nov. 17/09.

20 h.p. - £430. Chassis with Tyres.

24 h.p. - £450. Chassis with Tyres.

No prospective purchaser should decide upon a car until "Lancia" merits have been put to the test.

Trials by appointment. Full particulars post free on request.

W. L. STEWART & CO. LTD., 166 & 168, Shaftesbury Avenue, LONDON, W.C.

SOLE AGENTS:

W. L. Stewart and Co. Ltd.—Lancia's first British concessionaire—advertised what looks like a Beta as the "Inaudible Lancia" in 1910, with a quotation from The Autocar *to support the claims*

To publicise the name, Stewart ran Alphas and Betas in sporting events in England, and well-known British coachbuilders began fitting special bodywork to Lancia chassis. During the first year of the Alpha's production, 108 were sold—the first 16 of which were road-tested personally by Vincenzo Lancia.

The original workshop on the Via Ormea was by now bursting at the seams. This was enlarged, and a second factory set up in the Corso Dante where the 3,460c.c. Gamma (another monobloc four-cylinder) was produced in 1910; more than 250 examples of this car were built in the enlarged factory, but even this soon proved too small. On 14 January 1911 the original Via Ormea workshops were moved to the Via Monginevro where the new factory, on a floor area of 26,500 sq. metres, proved sufficient for many years and the Company's main offices are still housed there.

First new cars to come from the Via Monginevro factory were the 4,080c.c. Delta and Didelta (of which very few were made), and the 5,030c.c. Epsilon and sporting little Eta which would do 75mph. In 1911 and 1912, no fewer than 1,145 of these three new models were built. The Theta came next, in 1913, and was noteworthy for the fact that it was Europe's first car to have the electrical system designed into it, rather than added afterwards as a sort of "bolt-on goodie" (or, more probably "baddie"). The car made its debut at the Paris and London shows of 1913, with a production run that eventually reached 1,700.

The factory's car production was interrupted by the Great War, when military vehicles were produced—such as the IZ, and the Iota and Diota, some of which went to the British Army; but just before Italy entered the war, patents had been taken out (on 5 June, 1915) for a narrow-angle, 45-degree vee-8. This was joined, after the war, by a 30-degree vee-12—and then by a narrower, 20-degree vee-12. Thus began Lancia's famous line of narrow-angle vee engines that has lasted right through to the currently produced Fulvia coupé.

The car for which the vee-12 was designed appeared at the Paris and London shows of 1919; both engine and car (particularly the lovely engine) were enthusiastically received. But the post-war era of austerity was no time for launching super-cars, and it soon went out of production. An example of the engine (7,837 c.c.) still exists in the Lancia Museum—as a tribute to the compactness of the Lancia layout and to the artistry of Vincenzo Lancia. One can scarcely believe the capacity to be anything near its 7.8 litres. The museum specimen has its valve gear laid bare beneath a Perspex cover; the long, single camshaft with its 24 lobes is an incredible device and one wonders how its designer coped with torsional stiffness problems—even at half its modest crankshaft speed of 2,200 rpm; its 150bhp would have been well worth having, though, a few years later in the age when big, powerful cars sold well to the nobility and gentry.

Weymann-bodied Lambda saloons, and open cars, in production

Dilambda
(1928-1932)

Artena
(1931)

Augusta—1st Series
(1933)

Aprilia—1st Series
(1937)

Ardea—1st Series
(1939)

The life-span of the 12-cylinder car seems to have been so short that it was not even given its *niche* in the Greek alphabet. Its contemporary the Kappa was Lancia's first true post-war car, a development of the pre-war Theta with a specification that included such tremendous advances as an adjustable steering column, central gear lever, and electric starter—interesting enough in itself, but the more so for the fact that the pinion wás engaged mechanically with the flywheel before the current was turned on. The sporting Dikappa followed in 1921, with 87 bhp at 2,300 rpm, a handsome torpedo body with lightweight wooden frame and aluminium skin, spoked wheels and a maximum of 81 mph. Having passed through the Diota stage, the Iota commercial vehicle chassis progressed via the Triota to the Tetralota in 1921.

The following year—1922—the Trikappa was introduced, with the vee-8 engine making a reappearance in the first production vee-8-engined Lancia. With bore and stroke of 75 by 130 mm, and capacity of 4,594 c.c., the engine developed 98 bhp at 2,500 rpm—the Trikappa in some way taking over the luxurious, large-car role that would have been fulfilled by the anonymous vee-12.

Whatever may have gone before—or followed since, for that matter—it is the immortal and utterly unmistakable Lambda that *still* comes to mind, so far as my own generation is concerned, at the mention of the name Lancia. It was never a pretty car. At a time when the term "short wheelbase" in the specification usually suggested the more desirable, sporting version of a particular model, it was *very* long. What's more, only a small proportion of its overall length was bonnet—at a time when a long bonnet was essential on cars that mattered, however short and insignificant the engine beneath, for it *implied* a big, big engine . . . and the speed and power that went with it. Yet Vincenzo Lancia flouted these conventions—and the Lambda looked "right" in its own peculiar way; but it certainly wasn't anybody else's way, and it wasn't only in looks that it was unique.

The car was launched in the autumn of 1922 at the Paris and London shows—with the first-ever integral body-chassis construction, and fully independent suspension at the front, incorporating a hydraulic type of telescopic dampers since the old friction-type were useless with the new suspension. So low was the floor level that a tunnel was needed in which to house the propeller shaft—and the gear-lever linkage, since the narrow-angle vee-4 engine was so short that the gearbox was located beneath the bonnet.

The Lambda progressed through nine series during its eight-year run from 1923 to 1930, and 13,000 examples were produced. The engine capacity started at 2,170 c.c., increasing to 2,370 with the third Series and again to 2,570 with the fifth—while the power output rose from 49 bhp via 59 to 69, and the maximum speed from 71 to 78 mph. Though the model was never intended as a sports car, a few were used in competitions, and in 1928 nine cars were fitted with Pirotta cylinder heads specially produced by Nardini, in England. One of these, driven by Strazza and Gismondi, would have taken second place in the 1928 Mille Miglia, behind Campari's Alfa Romeo, had it not been involved in a minor accident just before the finish. One of these cars, No. 8602, still exists in France, owned by F. V. G. Bird.

Asturas, Artenas and Augustas receive final attention from the retouchers before being released to the public

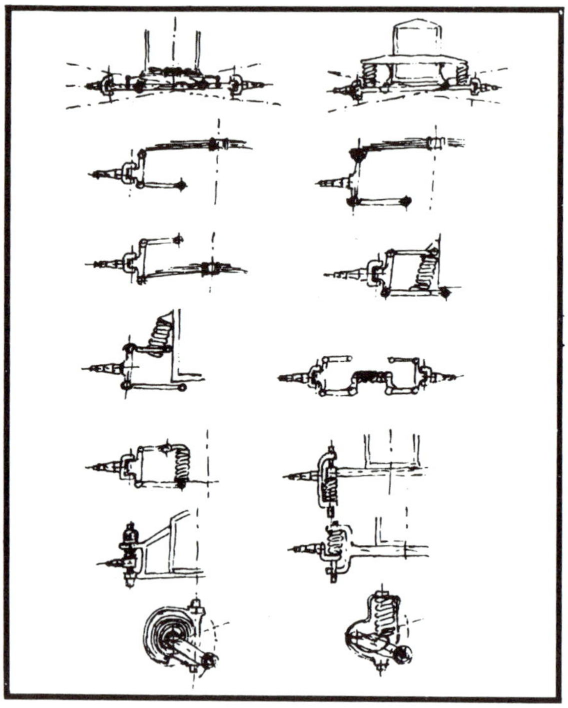

This page from an ancient notebook shows Vincenzo Lancia's original "doodles" when designing the independent front suspension of the Lambda. The sixth from the top in the left-hand column was eventually adopted

Following the Lambda years came the Artena and Astura (which ended the Greek alphabet connections, these two being respectively a town and an ancient castle), and the super-luxury Dilambda, with ifs along the lines of the Lambda. The integral body-chassis layout was not suited to a saloon with its wide door-openings—that is to say, the Lambda's layout wasn't—so a special cruciform frame was developed with boxed side-members and the fuel tank strengthened to form a large-section "tubular" cross-member at the rear. The narrow-angle, 24-deg. ohc 3,960 c.c. vee-8 gave 100 bhp at 4,000 rpm, and had almost steam-like flexibility with a range of 0-20 kph in top gear, pulling smoothly and strongly right through. In all, 1,685 Dilambdas were produced. The Artena had a narrow-angle 2-litre vee-4 engine and the Astura a 2.6 vee-8, both cars fitted with very similar saloon bodywork by the factory though the Astura was subsequently to carry the creations of some of Europe's top coachbuilders—and to make a name for itself in competition with strikingly modern sports-racing two-seater bodywork, an example of which recently sold for over £7,000 at one of Christie's auctions in Geneva. The Artena, in turn, earned fame for its durability, being capable of upwards of 60,000 without overhaul.

Just like today's motorists, those of the slump-ridden 1930s were acutely conscious of the cost of motoring, and Lancia was quick to appreciate the commercial value of a small saloon with reasonably high performance and good fuel economy. He went to work on such a car during 1930, and late in 1932 the Augusta emerged—a beautifully balanced small saloon with much of the high-stepping poise and beauty of the Zagato-bodied 1750 Alfa Romeo two-seaters of the same period. Again, the combined body-chassis method of construction was used—which, in saloon car form, was to be the first of its kind in motoring history. As ever, the engine was a narrow-angle vee-4 cylinder—this time of only 1,194 c.c., developing 35 bhp at 4,000 rpm. The same sliding-pillar independent front suspension was used; and, very unusual, pillarless construction of the four-door saloon body, with the front and rear doors hinged at their front and rear edges respectively. Between 1933 and 1935 the Augusta ran into three series, and a special edition with a separate chassis was developed for the specialist coachbuilders—the March Special open car being a product of Kevil Davis and March in this country.

Last of Vincenzo Lancia's creations was the little Aprilia, with which road testing began in the

Appia—2nd Series (1956) | B20 Aurelia (1950) | B24S Aurelia (1955) | Flaminia Coupé (1962)

summer of 1935. With its integral construction, inboard rear brakes, independent rear suspension with torsion bars and tranverse leaf spring, independent (sliding pillar) front suspension, pillarless body-work, and an incredible dry weight of under 16 cwt, it was (and still is) a fascinating design. The standard "streamlined" saloon was about as "unexpected" (never ugly) as the Lambda; yet, beauty being in the eye of the beholder, it had (and still has) as many ardent admirers as the Lambda. Very few good examples remain—partly because of the car's apalling propensity for rusting away, and partly because it naturally appealed to the competition drivers of its time, with the inevitable early demise of a great many examples.

It was tragic that Vincenzo Lancia, who died on 15 February 1937, did not live to enjoy the car's tremendous success, for it continued in production (with an interuption for the war years) from 1937 until 22 October 1949, when the last car came off the line at the Via Monginevro factory. For those readers who are not familiar with the *marque*, this final Aprilia had, secluded in its boot, the following message—which still exists, written in a childish, stilted hand: *"Dear Aprilia, in saying goodbye I greet you with respect. Your famous name is known in all the great capitals—just reward for the great pioneer who has gone from us, but whose name lives on. The workers in this factory hope and expect that your little sister soon to be born* (the Appia), *will give as much glory and even more understanding for the good of all'.*

Fascinating and different cars continued to spring from the Via Monginevro plant in Turin and from the newer factory in the industrial centre of Bolzano

Above: Vincenzo Lancia's first car—the 4-cylinder 2,543 c.c. "18-24" which was subsequently named the Alpha and started the tradition of naming models after letters in the Greek alphabet

Below: Appia: This model was introduced at the Turin Show in 1953, and retained the traditional shield-shaped radiator grille until the Geneva Show of 1959, where the horizontal grille took its place

Pininfarina's handsome bodywork for the open two-seater B24 Spider

right up to the day in 1969 when Lancia teamed up with their giant neighbour Fiat. The narrow-angle (13-deg) vee-4 survived in the Fulvia range, which consisted of an oddly perpendicular, square-cut saloon and the very much prettier coupé, a delightful car in its more powerful forms spoiled only by far too low-geared steering; the finest of all was the late-flowering 1600HF coupé, a most gentlemanly boy-racer which was real fun. The engine came in gradually increasing size, starting as an 1100, progressing to 1200, and then to 1300—the most common version—and finally to 1.6 litres.

The Flavia was the Fulvia's medium capacity bigger brother, originally a 1500, then an 1800 and in its final form dropping the Flavia name for the less alluring number only, becoming the 2000, which survived well into the first five years of the Fiat hegemony, in spite of—perhaps because of—its totally old-style Lancia mechanicals; the engine, still a four, was horizontally opposed, which kept the centre of gravity low and made some maintenance jobs a little cumbersome. On the first examples, it helped when changing a sparking plug if one removed a front wheel.

It was the Fulvia coupé which survived the Fiat's absorption of Lancia longest, continuing in production well into the 1970s and deservedly so. The old Flaminia range was much less fortunate: distinguished from the Flavia and Fulvia by being front-engine, rear-drive—the Lancia attachment to front-drive had otherwise been firm throughout the 1960s—it was technically interesting like all the Lancia Lancias, with a 2.8-litre 60-deg vee-6, a de Dion rear axle and its entire transmission from the clutch onwards mounted at the back in unit with the final drive—a salutary reminder that the same design's adoption by Porsche and Alfa Romeo today is not new—not of course that it was new in Lancia's Flaminia, since AC were doing the same thing in the early 1920s. In spite of its sophistication, and a variety of special coachwork versions—open, coupé and limousine—by such names as Touring, Pininfarina and Zagato, the Flaminia had disappeared by 1970.

The Lancia company was not healthy financially, and the partnership with Fiat was undoubtedly a lifesaver. The first Fiat

Lancia appeared three years after the merger, and seemed at first sight to confirm the worst fears of the marque's devotees—the Beta had a Lancia name, but its engine range (1.4, 1.5 and 2-litres) was entirely Fiat. However, suspicions were pleasantly allayed by the discovery that the Beta was—and still is—very much a Lancia, with front-drive, a distinctive fastback body with better than average room inside (for an Italian car), excellent road manners for its type; and, Fiat or not, the engines were in all cases excellent performers, in spite of being technically much more 'ordinary' than the old Lancia units. The Beta replaced the Fulvia range comprehensively, being in fact a much better car overall, and the range was expanded in June 1973 with the very pleasing coupé, an entirely delightful car of excellent character. A 1.3-litre economy version was announced at the Turin Show in 1974, followed by the Beta Spider, a T-bar-topped open car. The current cars remain basically the same but with improved interior details.

Based on the Beta but considerably different in various ways were the Lancia Beta H.P.E. and the Beta Monte Carlo. The H.P.E. was a two-door hatchback distantly recalling the Ogle-designed Reliant Scimitar GTE in its strongly sporting character. It was one of the first cars to offer a split folding rear seat, which allowed one to seat a person in the back and use the other side of the car as full length load space. The Monte Carlo was originally a Fiat suggestion, a bigger version of the Fiat X1/9 of 1972. Announced at Geneva three years after the X1/9, it was an ingenious mid-engined car using Beta 2-litre components, taking advantage of the compact transverse front-drive power unit adapted to mounting behind the driver. It got off to a middling start, with an arguable reputation in some quarters for unduly easy front-brake locking. It was re-launched in 1980 with modifications and improvements, and deserves to do well as it is practical and great fun to drive.

After the Beta family, the Gamma of 1976 came as a tremendous surprise. There was nothing very Fiat about this car, for it was a big, prestige saloon, with a Citröen-like fastback (not a hatchback) roomy body of simple grace. It was powered by an astonishing engine, the largest flat four of recent times, a zestful 2½-litre which gave excellent performance but understandably lacked smoothness. This and some other curious failings in refinement caused a little disappointment—discernible scuttle shake is out of place

in any car today—but the way the car goes and, in particular, the way it corners, are exceptional for a large front-drive model, and have endeared the Gamma to many. The most beautiful of all Gammas is the marvellously restrained Pininfarina-styled coupé, which appeared at the same time as the saloon.

Space permits only a brief mention of the sensational Stratos, an early product of the Fiat days, with a 2.4-litre 65-deg vee-6 Dino engine originally giving 190 bhp from amid a very short, stubby shape; it was really a competition car and is better dealt with on subsequent pages.

The most recent issue of the Fiat/Lancia combine is the Delta, Car of the Year for 1979, and an interesting attempt to capitalise on a market which is very much Lancia's—the small, luxurious, refined car, in this case based on the mechanicals of Fiat's Ritmo (Strada) 1.3 and 1.5, but owing nothing recognisable to the Ritmo in its arrestingly different shape.

This clear difference in character and design, in spite of the common power unit and transmission, bodes well for the future of the marque bearing Vincenzo Lancia's name, for it shows that Fiat understand the difference between wasting the hard-won reputation of a famous old company in a painful charade of pure badge-engineering, and of taking over something valuable and using it carefully and sensibly. For this reason, Lancia look in much better shape in the 1980s than they did at the end of the 1960s, thanks to rather than in spite of Fiat—a most happy state of affairs which is all too often not the case elsewhere.

Now back in Italian hands and immaculately restored (although British-registered and not yet in its original colours), this is the Lancia Aurelia GT which won the 1953 Liége-Rome-Liége Rally in the hands of Johnny Claes (see page 90 for contemporary photograph). The event was always one of the very toughest in motor sport, the organisers striving to select a route and a schedule which would result in only one finisher. The whole rally was run virtually non-stop and Claes' victory was particularly notable, for he drove the last 1,700 miles single-handed after his co-driver, Trasenster, became ill. This victory was one of many enjoyed by Aurelias, which by 1953 had grown to 2.5 litres and produced 118 bhp. The following year saw Louis Chiron win the Monte Carlo Rally in another Aurelia.

Sporting Tradition

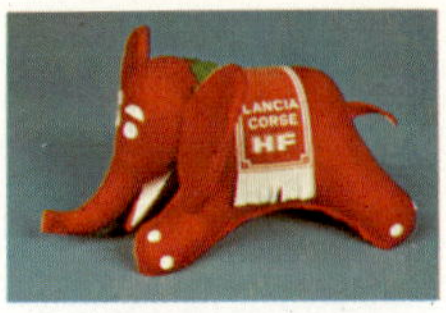

Lancias in Competition

AHOUGH VINCENZO LANCIA had earned fame and popularity as a Fiat works driver, he gave up motor racing completely almost directly he became a manufacturer—aware, from experience, of the demands made by an official racing department upon factory time and resources. Inevitably, however, the Lambda (and later the Augusta, Aprilia and Aurelia) were entered by private owners in sporting events, the Aprilia dominating the 1,500 c.c. saloon car category.

Vincenzo Lancia's first competition car—and his only one—the racing Alpha Corse version of the Alpha, in which (in 1910) he made his final sporting appearance, setting up a mile record at over 113 kph at Modena

Fortunately for the factory, Vincenzo's son Gianni (who succeeded him on his death as head of the company) possessed a great enthusiasm for racing, and although he managed to uphold his father's principles for a few years, he was eventually swayed by the successes in private hands of the Aprilias between 1946 and 1950, the B10 Aurelias in 1950 and subsequently the B21 Aurelia. Particularly significant was the success achieved by a team of privately-entered B21s in the 1951 Tour of Sicily for it was this that specifically triggered-off Gianni Lancia's decision to set up a works competition department.

It so happened that the 2-litre vee-6 B20 Aurelia, with engine designed by De Virgilio, was undergoing its final development stages at the time, so that there was a ready-made competition car almost immediately available, beautifully bodied by Pininfarina, and subsequently credited with being the first-ever true Grand Tourer. First unveiled at the 1951 Turin Show, the car made its competition debut in the 1951 Mille Miglia in which a team of four was entered. Bracco.s finished second at 73.9 mph (to the 75.6 mph of Villoresi's winning 4-litre Ferrari—twice the engine size), and the others took fifth, seventh and sixteenth places. During these formative years, Pasquarelli was Competition Manager.

Other B20 successes included Ascari's and Villoresi's win in the 1951 Sestriere Rally, Bracco's in the Pescara Six Hours, and class wins in the Tour of Tuscany, Le Mans 24 Hours and Tour of Sicily. The following year, 1952, brought another Sestriere win, team prize in the Tour of Sicily, another Le Mans class win, and overall victory in the Targa Florio for Bonetto. In 1953 Claes won the Liège-Rome-Liège, after a fantastic, almost single-handed 4-day drive, Bracco the Biella-Oropa, Palmieri the Tour of Calabria, and Amendola the Stella Alpina Rally. Greatest of all was perhaps Louis Chiron's outright win in the 1954 Monte Carlo Rally—and it was on the 1952 factory cars that Lancia's little red elephant emblem first appeared.

Above and above right: Under Pasquarelli's management, the 3,284 c.c., 265 bhp D24 sports-racing cars, later named the Carrera after its Carrera Panamericana win, scored a formidable list of successes, including wins in the Targa Florio, Mille Miglia and Tour of Sicily, and second place in the Sebring 12 Hours, in the hands of such "names" as Fangio, Taruffi and Castellotti

Right: Setting the pattern for the little Fulvia's long run of successes, this car won the 1972 Monte Carlo Rally in the hands of Munari and Mannucci; it started from Almeria

D24 Carrera (1953)

D50 Formula 1 GP car (1954)

In November 1952 a supercharged version of the B20 Aurelia, giving 150 bhp at 5,800 rpm (compared with the unblown version's 100 bhp) ran in the Carrera Panamericana, finishing fourth overall—while a completely new competition car was being developed at Turin. This, the D20 sports coupé, had a 60 deg vee-6 engine designed by Zaccone Mina (Vittorio Jano was in charge of products at the time)—similar to the Aurelia's except that it had twin overhead camshafts per bank and the capacity was 2,962 c.c. Power output was up to 217 bhp at 6,500 rpm (73.5 bhp per litre), and the top speed was around 155 mph.

The new car made its debut in the 1953 Mille Miglia, taking third place after teething troubles. At Le Mans none of the four cars finished the race; but after this the car's luck changed, with wins almost wherever it ran, including the Targa Florio. In the meantime, the D24 had been completed—an open sports-racing car with engine enlarged to 3,284 c.c. and power output up to 265 bhp at 6,500 rpm. Four cars were entered for the Carrera Panamericana (Fangio, Bonetto, Taruffi and Castellotti). Outright victory went to Fangio, with Taruffi second and Castellotti third.

Still under Pasquarelli, the factory D24s—now referred to as the Carrera—ran in every major event open to them, placing second in the Sebring 12 Hours, and winning the Tour of Sicily, Targa Florio and Mille Miglia as well as many more events. It was inevitable that Gianni Lancia, Jano, Zaccone Mina, Pasquarelli and indeed the whole competitions department should start thinking in terms of formula 1 Grand Prix racing. The decision to build cars was taken in the summer of 1953, when the formula stood at 2½ litres unsupercharged; by February 1954 the first car was ready for testing.

The D50, as it was called, had a 90 deg vee-8 engine of 2,486 c.c., giving 255 bhp at 8,000 rpm (102.5 bhp per litre). With its "saddle tanks" mounted outboard, between the front and rear wheels on either side, and the driver's very low seating position achieved by angling the engine/transmission across the frame, the car was unique in appearance and it produced a tremendous stir when it made its debut during practice for the Spanish GP in October 1954. On race day, Ascari's car led from the start, increasing its advantage by 2sec a lap—until, when it was some 20sec ahead of Mike Hawthorn's Fer-

The very purposeful D50 Lancia Grand Prix car, which made its first appearance in the Spanish GP of 1954—and its last in the 1955 Monaco GP. After this, Ascari was killed in a different make at Monza and Lancia handed over the cars to Ferrari—lock, stock and barrel

rari in second position, the clutch went sick and the car was out of the race.

Similar disappointments continued, though the D50s finished third and fourth in the Valentino Grand Prix. In the 1955 Monaco GP, when leading the race with only a few laps to go, Ascari shot out of the tunnel, through the *chicane* . . . and into the harbour; Castellotti took second place in what could have been a 1-3 victory for Lancia. Very shortly after this race, while still recovering from the shock (though he was uninjured), Ascari took over the wheel of a Ferrari sports car that Castellotti was testing at Monza—and inexplicably crashed, suffering fatal injuries.

Lancia decided, then and there, to discontinue the competitions department, and abandon motor racing. On 26 July 1955, the formula 1 D50 Lancias, together with their transporters and all spares, were handed over to Ferrari—and the distinctive-looking, extremely promising scarlet cars left Turin for Maranello . . . to win for Ferrari the 1956 World Championship. Their luck had turned, though not for Lancia, for whom all interest in motor sport ceased until 1963. The HiFi Club was formed in 1959 for customers who, through High Fidelity to the *marque,* had bought and owned at least six Lancias from new. This figure was later increased to eight, in the interests of exclusivity, and then to 10—but even at this figure there are 8,000-plus members. When, in February 1963, the company resumed active participation in competitions, the name HiFi was given to the works racing team, Lancia Corse.

It was with the Appia Zagato (last car to use the Lancia sliding-pillar ifs) and Flaminia Zagato that the comeback was made, though the Appia (which had been used since 1959) ceased production in 1963. During the period 1959 to 1963, factory cars had been lent to private entrants for use in rallies. The outstandingly successful Fulvia coupé—last car to use the narrow-angle vee engine—was first campaigned in the 1966 Monte Carlo Rally and finished fifth. The following year, Andersson's Fulvia coupé took second place in the Monte to Aaltonen's Mini-Cooper S by only 8 sec, with Lancias also third, and fifth overall.

In 1969 and 1970 they won the RAC Rally of Great Britain, with Harry Kallstrom as the driver on both occasions. The team's best year with the Fulvia, however, was 1972, when Sandro Munari rather unexpectedly won the Monte Carlo Rally. The Fulvia 1600HF went on to take second place in Sweden and win in Morocco and Greece (the Acropolis), and a second on the San Remo in Italy clinched the 1972 World Rally Championship for Lancia.

This achievement (particularly the Monte win) gave Cesare Fiorio, then head of the Competitions Department, the opportunity to expand his department and, ultimately, to embark on the Stratos programme. Meanwhile, however, the Fulvia remained thoroughly competitive and still played a major role in helping Lancia win a second world title in 1974. The little front-drive car did remarkably well for the marque, especially when one remembers the relatively heavy, mildly performing production car on which it was based.

Appropriately, the Stratos was born from an idea first based on Fulvia running gear. Bertone had shown a special at the 1970 Turin motor show with a Fulvia engine/gearbox subframe mounted at the rear instead of the front. The following year, they threw out the 1.6-litre Lancia twin cam and inserted a 2.4-litre Ferrari Dino vee-6 unit, and this later car became the Stratos. Fiorio wasted no time in turning the show car into a purpose-built competition car and the first example was tested at Lancia's Chivasso proving grounds in 1972, after which it underwent trials on unsurfaced Italian roads and French mountain passes.

The competition debut of the Stratos came on the Tour of Corsica in December 1972, when it retired, and Munari won the Firestone Rally in Spain early the following year. The car was still not homologated as a production model, so that events in which it could be entered were few and far between, but it would surely have won the 1973 Targa Florio but for a broken oil seal which dropped Munari to second; on the Tour de France there were no such mistakes and the Stratos won its first event.

Since then, the career of the Lancia Stratos has been nothing short of amazing, with successes far too many to list in full. It won the Monte Carlo Rally four times (1975, 1976, 1977 and 1979), the last time in the hands of a private team; it gained for Lancia the World Rally Championship in 1974, 1975 and 1976, the European Drivers' Championship in 1973, 1976, 1977 and 1978 . . . and it was still winning in private hands in 1980. Light, powerful, tricky to handle but offering tremendous traction and extraordinary acceleration on every kind of surface, this car won rallies on snow, sand, gravel, tarmac and mixtures of all four – and it made a noise which no one who heard it will ever forget.

Despite their results, the Competitions Department under Fiorio was never a large organisation, with less than 20 mechanics on the payroll. In charge of development was the Englishman Mike Parkes, who had driven and then worked as an engineer for Ferrari; he was brought in by Lancia to undertake two projects, the Stratos

Right: Destined to fly the colours of Lancia Corse—and Marlboro—in dirt-road rallies, and to replace the Fulvia . . . the new Beta coupé

Below: Turbocharged, and developing 350 bhp—the Marlboro-sponsored Stratos projectiles under preparation at the Competitions Department for such main road events as the Tour de France

and the rallying Beta Coupé. The latter car was intended for use on the rougher events where it was believed that the Stratos might prove too fragile, but when the mid-engined special proved so completely versatile and, at the same time, there were tremendous problems in making the front-engine Beta handle with up to 200 bhp at the front wheels, this part of the plan quietly fizzled out.

At the end of 1978, Lancia's new Fiat overlords ceased to see any logic in having Lancias competing against Fiats on rallies, and 15 years of international rallying by Lancia came to an end. Their interest in motor sport continued, however, with attention turning to sports car racing, a field in which they had already been involved when turbocharged versions of the Stratos (producing up to 350 bhp) had been used on such events as the Tour de France.

In December 1978, Lancia announced the Beta Monte Carlo programme, with its mid-mounted four cylinder engine reduced in size to 1,425 c.c. and turbocharged, the equivalency formula allowing this combination to run in the up-to-2-litres class of the Manufacturers' World Championship. With the help of a KKK turbocharger and Bosch fuel injection, this device produced an immediate 370 bhp at 8,000 rpm and—driven by Formula One driver Riccardo Patrese and rally driver Walter Rohrl—it won its category in 1979. For 1980 the team ran two factory cars and sold a number of others to private teams. Further development raised the power output to 400 bhp at 8,800 rpm and one of the factory cars, again driven by Patrese and Rohrl, actually won outright the opening European race of the 1980 season, the Brands Hatch 6 Hours, with Monte Carlos also placing second and fourth.

Examples from three decades of Lancia's sporting heritage.
Left: an airborne Flaminia during the 1953 Gran Premio Internacional di Turismo, one of the hugely popular Argentine road races.
Centre: Claudio Maglioli driving a Flavia Sport on the tortuous closed-road Mugello circuit in 1966.
Bottom: Lancia's latest sports racer—this is Patrese testing the turbocharged Beta Monte Carlo in 1979.

THE LANCIA CARS.

A 15 H.P. FOUR-CYLINDER AND 30 H.P. SIX-CYLINDER ENGINED CHASSIS, BUILT TO THE DESIGNS OF THE CELEBRATED ITALIAN DRIVER, V. LANCIA.

If only for the racing fame attached to the name of the great Italian driver, Lancia, attention would be drawn to any cars so distinguished, but when it is known, as is not generally the case, that Vincenzio

Fig. 1.—The substantial appearance of the Lancia front axle will be gathered from a glance at this illustration.

Lancia is not only a great driver but holds a prominent position in Italian engineering circles, and has enjoyed a long mechanical experience, which, combined with his racing knowledge, he has brought to bear upon the car named after him in an unmistakable and praiseworthy manner, his cars are certain to interest the automobile public. Photographic illustrations can hardly do adequate justice to this excellent and in parts original design, but drawings being unavailable photographs must content.

Fig. 2.—The Lancia chassis viewed from the back.

The Frame.

Fig. 3 gives an excellent view of the lines of the chassis, which shows character and distinction. The side members are as usual of pressed cambered channel steel, inswept forward of the dashboard and upswept and outswept over the back axle. The cross member immediately in rear of the dashboard is formed to support the brake fittings, etc., that immediately in the rear being well splayed and gusseted, while the rear member itself is of special and unusual design, as shown in fig. 2. It is formed and splayed to take the rear ends of the side members, and produced outwards to carry and anchor the ends of the laminated spring

Fig. 3.—Plan of the Lancia chassis illustrating the clean and substantial design.

dumb irons. This arrangement makes for exceptional strength and stiffness, while keeping the frame itself narrow. In addition to the cambering of the side members, the flanges, it will be seen, are widened to afford the greatest sections at the points of the greatest stresses.

The Engine.

Both the engines of the 15 h.p. four-cylinder and the 30 h.p. six-cylinder Lancias have their cylinders cast and set in pairs upon the crank chamber. They are 90 mm. in bore, and have a stroke of 100 mm.—practically 3½ × 4in. The valve chambers are all on the left, thus necessitating one camshaft only. Off this camshaft the H.T. magneto is driven. The

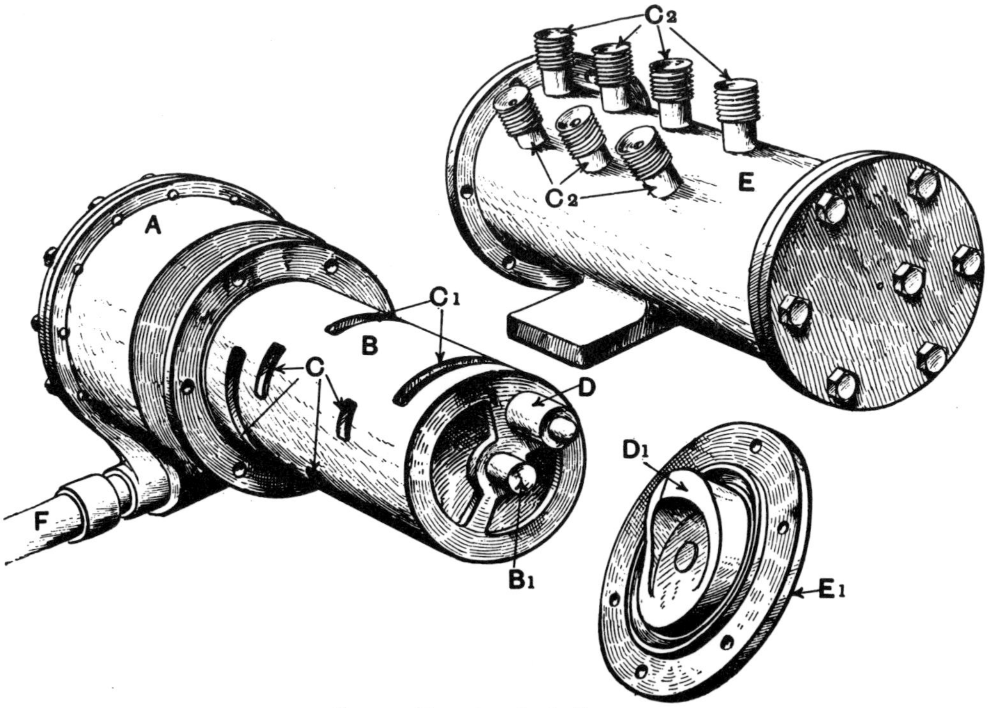

Fig. 4.—The rotary feed oil pump.

A, oil chamber
B, rotating barrel with delivery ports
C C1, oil delivery ports
D, pump plunger
E, cylindrical casing over rotating barrel B carrying delivery unions
D1, pump plunger cam
E1, end plate with cam for actuating force pump plunger
F, oil delivery to oil chamber
C2 C2, unions for attachment of oil delivery pipes
B1, barrel spindle

crankshaft, which is formed from a special solid forging, runs in three bearings of large dimensions. All the distribution gear is enclosed forward in a special casing, and is easily accessible. Ignition is by Bosch magneto in the usual way. The accessibility of those parts of the magneto which occasionally require attention is praiseworthy.

The engine is oil fed by means of the cylindrical oil pump shown by sketch (fig. 4), which is driven off the distribution gear. This method of engine lubrication is a special feature of Lancia design, a unique, interesting, and ingenious rotating force-feed oil pump being fitted for the purpose. Its construction and method of operation can be very easily gleaned by reference to fig. 4. This neat little apparatus is fitted on the crank chamber in such wise that the ported barrel B can be rotated from the distribution gear. The means provided for performing this operation are not shown in the sketch. The drawing shows the right-hand outer portion of the casing E carrying the delivery unions C_2C_2 and the end cam plate E_1, withdrawn from around the rotating barrel B for the purpose of showing the graduated delivery ports C C_1 and the head of the plunger force pump carried therein. Now it will be seen that when the outer cylindrical casing E, as shown in the sketch, is replaced over the rotating barrel B and secured to the flange on the oil chamber A, the barrel B, being rotated as above described, will bring the variously cut ports CC_1 under their respective deliveries C_2C_2 in the casing E. Also that as the barrel rotates within this casing the nose of the pump plunger pressing on the path of the cam D_1, which is of course stationary, will cause the plunger to travel up and down the barrel of the pump within the rotating barrel B. Now the chamber A and the interior of the barrel B are kept full of oil, upon which pressure is exerted by the operation of the pump plunger D as already described. The result of this is that oil is forced through the ports in C C_1 in the barrel B, and also into their respective delivery pipes, as long as the open port is travelling beneath them. The quantity of oil delivered to each bearing at each revolution of the barrel is apportioned by the length of the slot, and as the speed of the barrel is exactly proportionate to the speed of the engine the feed of oil is always in the set and due proportion to the requirement of the bearing and the engine revolutions per minute.

The Carburetter.

The Lancia carburetter presents several interesting features, illustrated in the accompanying sketch. It has two jets, the smaller remaining open alone up to 200 r.p.m., and both it and the larger coming into effect from that speed up to 1,500 r.p.m.

Its design and construction and operation can be readily understood by reference to the accompanying

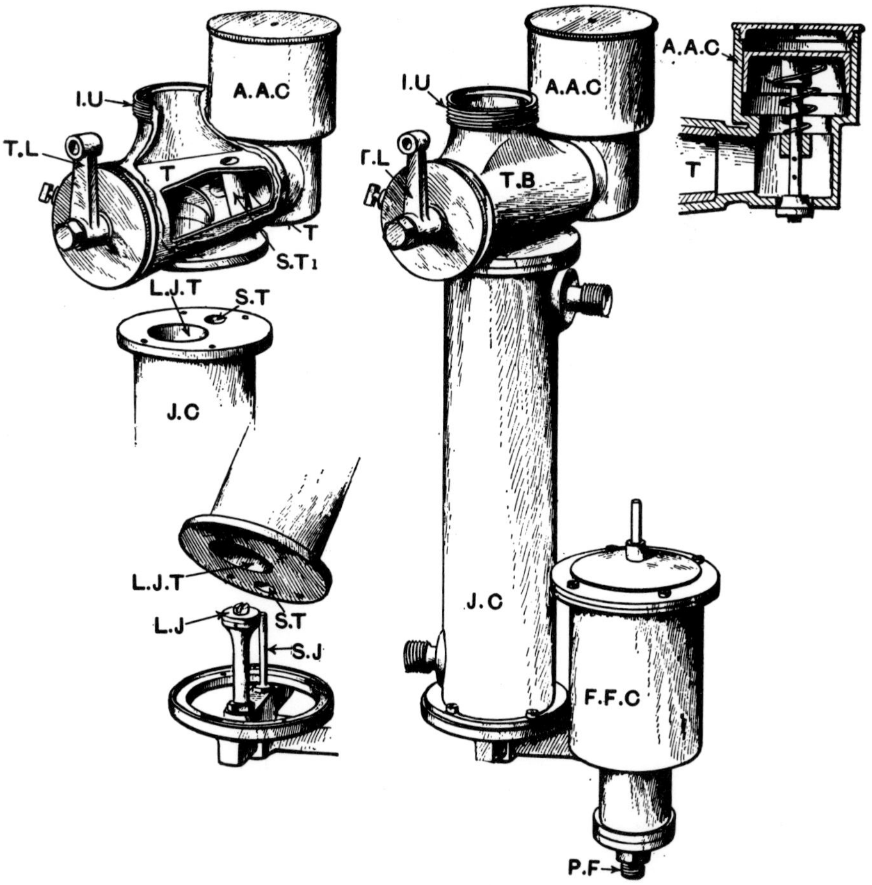

Fig. 5.—Details of the Lancia carburetter.

P F, petrol feed
F F C, float feed chamber
J C, jet column
T B, throttle barrel
T L, throttle lever
A A C, automatic air valve case
T, rotary graduated throttle
S T, small jet tube
L J T, large jet tube
I U, induction pipe union
L J, large jet
S J, small jet
S T1, small jet tube in throttle

dissected sketch (fig. 5). The float feed chamber is of the usual type, but the petrol supply pipe therefrom communicates with two jets, one small S J and the other the larger or main jet L J, both having their own mixture tubes S T and L J T formed in the jet hot jacketed column J C. These tubes run upwards to the tapered graduated throttle valve T, set above and across the jet column as shown.

Now the operation of the apparatus is as follows: When it is desired to start up the engine the throttle

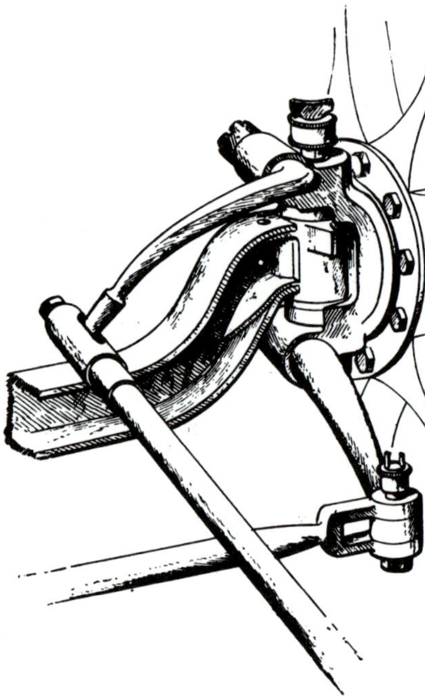

Fig. 6.—Steering pivot and arms.

is so manipulated from the steering wheel that the small tube S T seen traversing the throttle shell in a perpendicular direction is brought immediately over the upper end of the hole S T in the jet tube J C. The engine can then draw gas from the small jet S J, no part of the larger opening being free. Further movement of the throttle opens the large orifice in the valve to the upper end of the mixture tube L J T, when both large and small jets come into operation up to the maximum opening of the throttle. When the throttle is quite closed its movement can be extended until the small tube S T_1 is brought opposite an orifice in the outer casing, and, both the larger and smaller mixture tube outlets being closed, fresh, cold air is delivered to the cylinders in response to the engine suction. The additional pure air supply is obtained in response to the requirements of carburation by the automatic operation of the dash pot valve contained in the casing A A C and shown in section in the sketch.

The clutch is of the ordinary multi-disc type, very sweet and flexible, and absolutely oil-retaining. The drive passes from the engine through this clutch to a gear box formed in a V-shaped aluminium casting, which provides a pot for the encasement of the flywheel, and is bolted rigidly up to the crank chamber. This brings the gear box directly under the footboards and much closer to the flywheel than is the usual practice. The gear box, too, is extremely short; indeed the gearing is very compact, and the gearshafts are kept shorter than we ever remember to have seen them in cars of similar type. By the solidity of the box with the V-shaped aluminium casting and its shortness perfect alignment and extraordinary stiffness of the shafts are secured, while weight is reduced. Leakage is impossible. The gear affords four speeds forward, with direct drive on top speed. Immediately in rear of the gear box is found a large diameter brake drum mounted on the forward portion of the universal. Thence a propeller-shaft of a length rendered much above the average by the above cited position of the gear box transmits the drive to the rear axle. By the fact of its length the angular movement of this propeller-shaft is reduced to a minimum—a very excellent feature. The outward construction of the back axle can be realised from figs. 2 and 3. The differential gear casing is of robust design, well ribbed, and formed with sockets of considerable length to take the live axle casing. The road wheels run on ball bearings in the casings, as in all the best types of live axle drive. A pressed steel webbed and flanged steel torque member is interposed between the back axle and the frame to relieve the springs of the drive and the thrust of the brakes. In the absence of suitable drawings fuller details are not impossible, but we think enough has been said to show that the Lancia cars are well worth attention.

June 19th, 1909.

November 6th, 1909.

A 20 h.p. Lancia car for which a specially designed Maythorn body has been made. The car is the property of Mr. Arthur Forbes, the well-known blood-stock owner of Shoombie, Cape Colony.

The 15 h.p. Lancia car (90 x 100), fitted with Rudge-Whitworth detachable wire wheels, which won Class 3 at the Modena meeting with an average speed of 66½ miles an hour for the flying mile. At the wheel is Mr. Rodice

The 24 h.p. Four-cylinder Lancia.

A Great Name and a Good Car.

Several Unique and Interesting Points of Design.

Fig. 1.—The chassis of the 24 h.p. Lancia car.

FROM the first moment of its presentation in this country the Lancia car showed distinctly that its design was the result of the highest automobile engineering skill, fortified by profound road knowledge and experience. Before Signor Lancia gained renown by his many successes in automobile races he had enjoyed a thorough engineering training in the best Italian school. That training and his practical experience have been centred on the production of the Lancia chassis, and no one with any knowledge of the subject will deny that it does the greatest credit to both.

Lancia cars are being handled in this country by Messrs. W. L. Stewart and Co., Ltd., 166 and 168, Shaftesbury Avenue, London, W.C.

As seen in figs. 1 and 3, the side members are of the usual channel section pressed steel suitably cam-

Fig. 2.—A front view of the Lancia chassis, showing the pressed steel axle.

bered as to depth, but also graduated as to flange widths in order to present the greatest sectional areas where strength is most required. The forward cross members are generously swept where they make junction with the sides, while the rear member is specially formed with curved angles, the flanges being continued to serve as plate brackets to take the butt ends of the rear springs.

The front axle is also formed of channel section steel, with the web of the member facing forwards and forming a very strong but light front axle. The radiator, as seen in the front view, is of the true honeycomb type, and is carried entirely upon the forward front member of the frame. The four-cylinder engine is of the *moteur bloc* order, the unit, however, being cast with considerable width between the pairs of cylinders (100 mm. bore by 110 mm. stroke), affording opportunity for a central crankshaft

Fig. 3.—A rear view of the Lancia chassis.

bearing of excellent length. The valves are all set upon the left-hand side, so that one camshaft suffices. The pistons are of more than average length, and while but two piston rings are fitted, these are kept quite

Fig. 4.—The right-hand side of the Lancia engine, showing the peculiar arrangement of the water connections. The pump is carried in the body of the engine bracket.

close up to the piston head. A groove is formed lower down on the outside of the piston in the plane of the gudgeon pin, which, as shown in the longitudinal section (fig. 6), is hollow. These grooves in the pistons lessen the possibility of oil passing into the combustion space and causing a smoky exhaust.

The system of lubrication adopted in connection with the Lancia engine is so excellent that we venture to describe it in detail, and give diagrams which show the scheme very clearly.

The lower portion of the base chamber A (figs. 7, 8, and 9) serves as an oil reservoir, the level of the oil therein being determined by the overflow cock P. When lubricant has been introduced into the crank chamber in sufficient quantity through the filler B, the geared oil pump C, which is driven off the camshaft, lifts the oil from a suction chamber D (in which is fitted a large wire gauze filter F) through the suction pipe R, and forces it through the elbow G to the main lead H running along the inside of the crank chamber. From this lead ducts J formed in the end and central webs of the crank chamber conduct the oil to the interior of the hollow crankshaft, whence it flows through the ducts shown to the big end bearings of the connecting rods, and by the pipes L lying alongside the rods themselves to the interior of the hollow gudgeon pins. There it lubricates the small end bearings and flows outwards to the groove formed in the centre of the piston, so lubricating the walls of the cylinder, the latter also receiving oil thrown from the big ends. A pressure gauge is fitted on the dashboard, and a bypass valve M permits any excess of oil above a predetermined pressure to return to the crank chamber

Fig 5.—The left-hand side of the Lancia engine, showing the valve stem cover plates, the position of the magneto, and the oil filler cap.

through the pipe N. The sump can be emptied and cleansed through the plug S.

A Bosch magneto is fitted, which is gear driven off the camshaft, and is most accessibly placed, as shown in fig. 5.

A twin jet Lancia carburetter is in position on the off side of the engine (fig. 4), having small and a large sized mixture tubes, which communicate with the additional air chamber in such wise that for starting and slow running the small jet alone comes intc

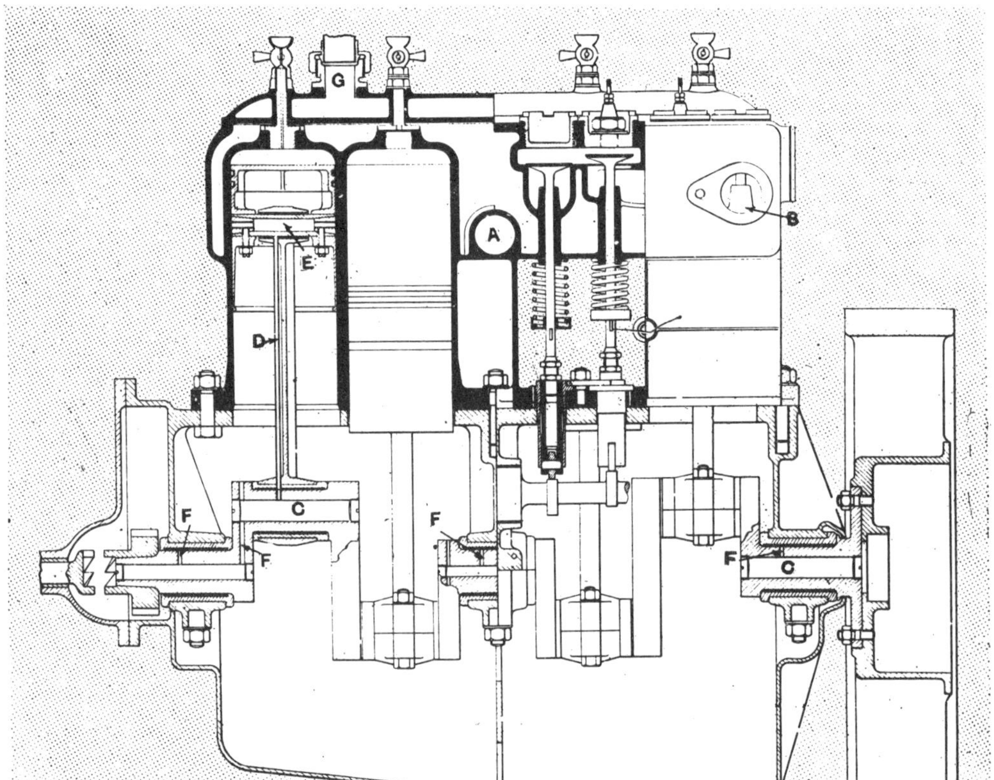

Fig. 6.—Vertical longitudinal view of the Lancia engine, part section.

A, induction passage in cylinder casting
B, exhaust outlet
C, hollow crankshaft
D, tube conveying oil to gudgeon pins
E, hollow gudgeon pins
F, oil ducts
G, outlet from water jackets

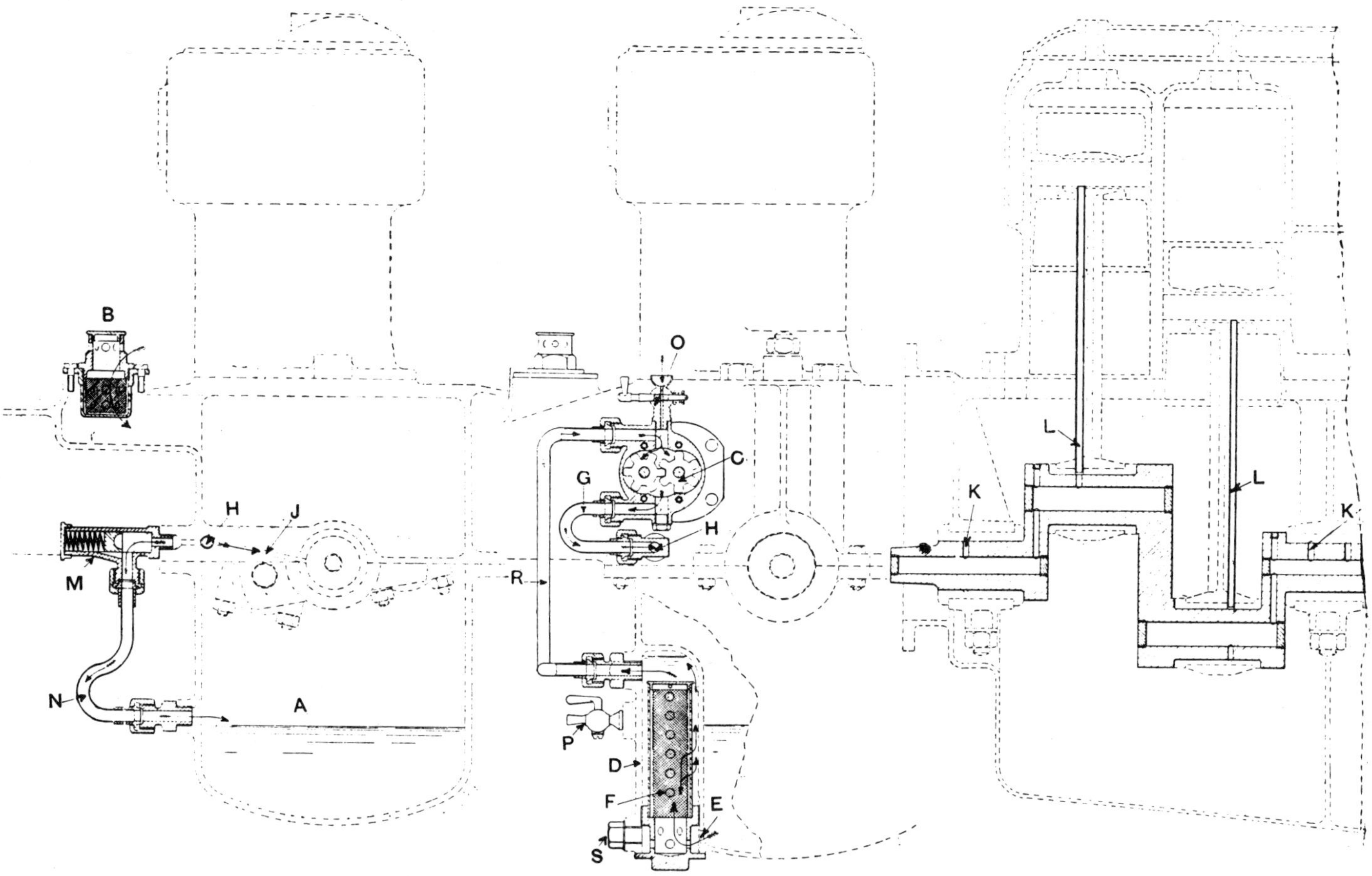

Figs. 7, 8, and 9.—Forced lubrication system of the 24 h.p. Lancia engine.

A, oil sump in crank case
B, filler pipe
C, gear pump
D, suction chamber
E, oil passage from sump
F, filter
G, oil pipe to main lead
H, main lead
J, ducts in crank case webs
K, oil ways in crankshaft
L, oil leads to gudgeon pins
M, bypass valve
N, return pipe to sump
O, cock to relieve air lock
P, overflow tap
R, suction pipe
S, drain plug

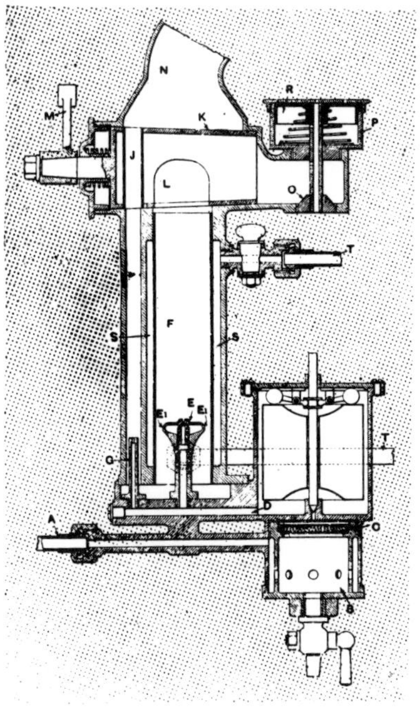

Fig. 10.—The Lancia carburetter vertical section.

A, petrol supply pipe
B, silt chamber
C, gauze filter
D, petrol lead to jets
E, main jet
E_1, petrol outlets of main jet
F, main jet tube
G, auxiliary jet
H, auxiliary jet tube
J, auxiliary throttle opening
K, throttle
L, main throttle opening
M, throttle lever
N, induction pipe
O, additional air valve
P, vacuum chamber
R, vacuum piston
S, water jacket
T, hot water leads

operation, while at further opening of the throttle the big jet performs. For maximum speed and hill-climbing the small jet again comes into effect in aid in the last open position of the throttle.

The design of the main jet, which is shown at E in fig. 10, is worthy of notice. It will be seen that petrol, instead of issuing from a hole in the top of the jet, finds exit from holes E_1 drilled through the side of the mushroom top shown; the contour of this top forms a choke tube or passage. The silting chamber beneath the gauze filter is of ample dimensions, and readily removable for cleaning. The design of the additional air valve is also unusual; as will be seen from the drawing, the valve itself does not actually find a seating in the casing when at rest, but, although shaped somewhat as a mushroom valve, acts rather as a piston valve, its movement being damper-controlled by reason of its connection with the piston R in the vacuum chamber P. The mixture is warmed by hot

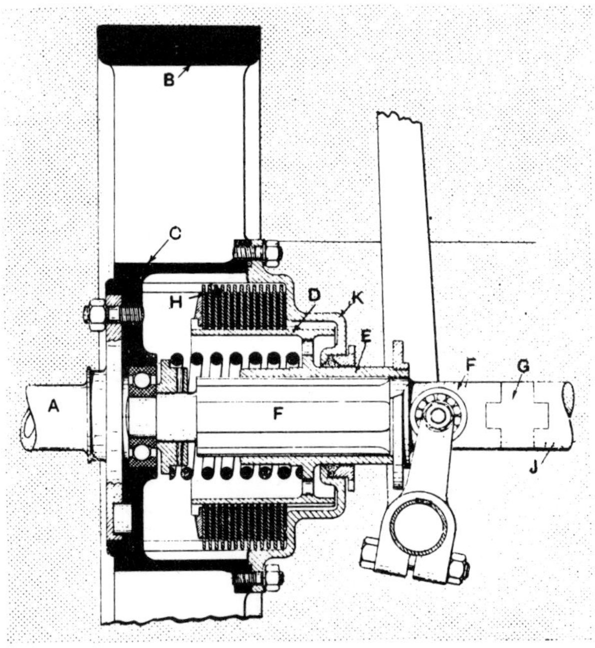

Fig. 11.—Vertical section of multi-disc clutch.

A, crankshaft
B, flywheel
C, driving drum of clutch
D, driven drum of clutch
E, clutch sleeve
F, clutchshaft
G, flexible joint
H, clutch discs
J, primary gearshaft
K, oil retaining cover

water circulation through the jacket S, which surrounds the main tube. The gas passes to the inlet valves through passages formed in the cylinder water jacket casting, as shown in figs. 4 and 6.

A simple but effective form of multi-disc oiltight clutch (fig. 11) conveys the drive from the engine.

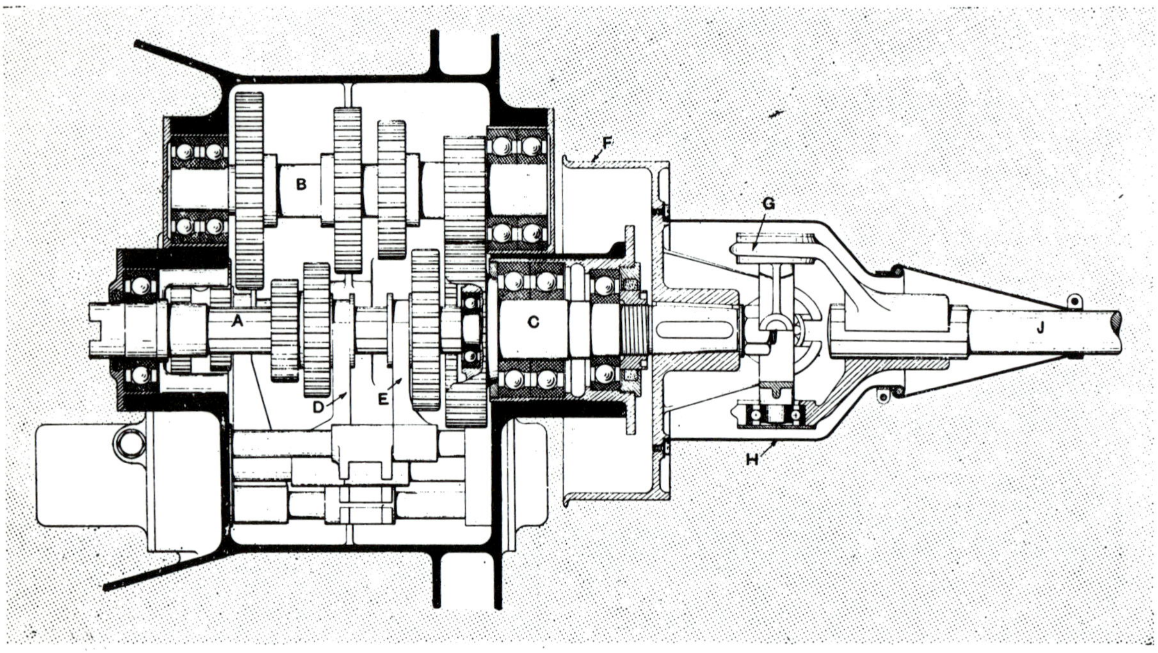

Fig. 12.—Plan of gear box.

A, castellated primary shaft
B, secondary shaft
C, intermediate gear sleeve
D, striking fork of first and second speeds
E, striking fork of third and fourth speeds
F, brake drum
G, ball bearing universal joint
H, universal joint casing
J, propeller-shaft

The clutchshaft F is carried at its forward end in a ball bearing set in the end of the crankshaft, and connects with the gearshaft by a flexible joint G. It will be seen that as this clutch is entirely self-contained, there is no end thrust on either crank or clutchshaft, and consequently no thrust bearing is required. The thrust bosses of the clutch striking fork take the form of ball bearings, as shown—a refinement in producing smoothness of clutch manipulation which, although not unique, is rarely used.

The gear box, which may be said to form part of the crank case by means of the stiff splayed brackets bolting it thereto, has its shafts set in the horizontal plane also; they have been kept very short and correspondingly stiff. The primary-shaft is castellated, and runs in large single ball bearings, while the secondary-shaft rotates in double ball bearings of equal diameter. The ends of the gear-striking rods and the shafts are carefully capped and provided with felt washers to obviate oil leakage. The gearing affords four speeds forward, with direct drive on top speed, operated by an easily manipulated gate change.

The drum of the pedal-applied brake is of unusual width, and is carried directly upon the rearward keyed and tapered end of the intermediate gear sleeve.

The universal joint deserves particular attention from the point of view of its design. It will first be seen from fig. 12 that the pivotal centre lines bisect each other, and that the jaw ends of the brackets where they attach to the pivot spindle do so through the medium of ball bearings. The rearward bracket is made to slide upon the octagonal end of the propeller-shaft J, so that the necessary universal and plunging motions are all obtained at the forward end of the propeller-shaft itself.

As can be seen from the rearward view of the chassis (fig. 3), the propeller-shaft is of much greater length than ordinarily, this being due to the position and shortness of the gear box. When the car is loaded this shaft closely approaches a horizontal position, so that the minimum amount of work is thrown upon the universal and plunging joints.

The driving bevel pinion B (fig. 13) is carried directly at the end of the propeller-shaft, and is formed with a sleeve extension, which rotates in further large double ball bearings. At its rearward end the bevel is further supported by a single row ball bearing.

A bevel type of differential gear is used, and, contrary to the general practice obtaining to-day, the road wheels are carried on the well-proportioned tapered and feathered ends of the driving shafts, which rotate in ball bearings. The differential gear casing is very stiffly webbed, and the back axle as a whole is strengthened by tension rods.

The flanged plate torque member seen in fig. 3 deserves remark. It is particularly designed as to section, and also as to suspension at its forward end.

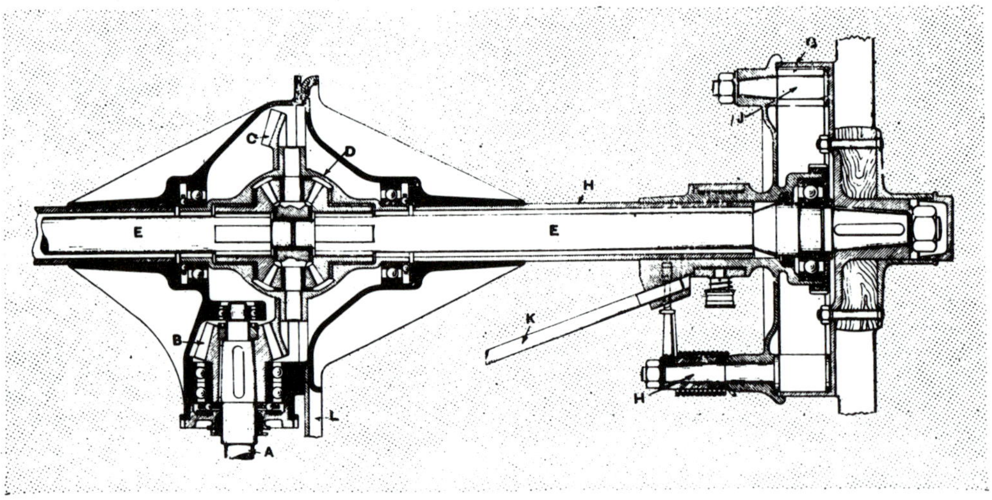

Fig. 13.—Part horizontal, part vertical section back axle.

A, propeller-shaft
B, driving bevel pinion
C, driven bevel crown wheel
D, differential gear
E, driving shafts
H, brake cam spindle
J, brake pivot
K, tension rods
L, torque member

The 24 h.p. Four-cylinder Lancia.

The chassis is made in three sizes—9ft., 9ft. 8in., and 10ft. 6in. wheelbases, all the wheels being 820 mm. by 120 mm.

The front wheel hubs have their steering pivots set so that a line produced downwards through their centres will impinge upon the road at its point of contact with the tyre. This, of course, makes for easy steering and long tyre life. The dashboard is innocent of any fittings except the oil pressure gauge and the ignition switch.

We think it will be found impossible to peruse the foregoing description or to scrutinise the accompanying drawings and illustrations without concluding that the Lancia chassis has received the closest attention in every detail, and that its design has proceeded from the brain of a man who is, above all, a trained and practical automobile engineer.

The owner of a Lancia car is particularly blessed when it comes to the necessity for ordering a spare of any part of his car. A catalogue has been prepared containing no fewer than sixteen sheets of photographs, in which representations of every single part, from the smallest screw upwards, are given, numbered and indexed, with price and the code word for wiring. We have never seen anything of the kind more completely or more satisfactorily done. The possession of such a ready means for ordering spares without trouble and with the utmost certainty should be a great comfort to every Lancia car owner though he may not often need to avail himself of the convenience.

The 24h.p.

A NEW LANCIA CAR. It will be noticed that both the brake and gear change levers are enclosed, the only fittings on the outside bodywork being the brackets for the spare wheel.

A "Yarborough" limousine-landaulet by Maythorn on a 24 h.p. Lancia chassis. The side windows behind the doors are of the same width as the doors and the windows behind the driving seat, and operate similarly to those of a railway carriage.

A handsome 24 h.p. Lancia car, long type chassis, with raked steering, which has been supplied to Mr. Hubert Arundel, of Gatley, near Manchester, by Messrs. Jevons and Broomhall, Cheadle, near Manchester. The fittings include Bosch dual ignition, speedometer, dash clock, Klaxon horn, a double folding luggage grid, concealed tool boxes under the running boards, spare tyre brackets in conjunction with a well in the step ; also Lucas acetylene head lights, electric side and tail lamps, electric light to the interior, and a polished mahogany cabinet under the scuttle dash.

Another view of Mr. Arundel's 24 h.p. Lancia car, the body of which has been built by Messrs. J. Rothschild et Fils, Ltd., Westminster, S.W. The leather hood is rendered very compact when folded, as it is double japanned, thus dispensing with the usual cloth lining. The driving seat has been made specially comfortable, and is of the armchair pattern. The seat next to the driver is also of the armchair pattern, but is arranged to fold up to the side of the body, and the back is made to open like a door so that access may be obtained from the central door to the driver's seat. The interior is trimmed with green leather ; the outside finish is white body colour with apple green mouldings and fine gold lining.

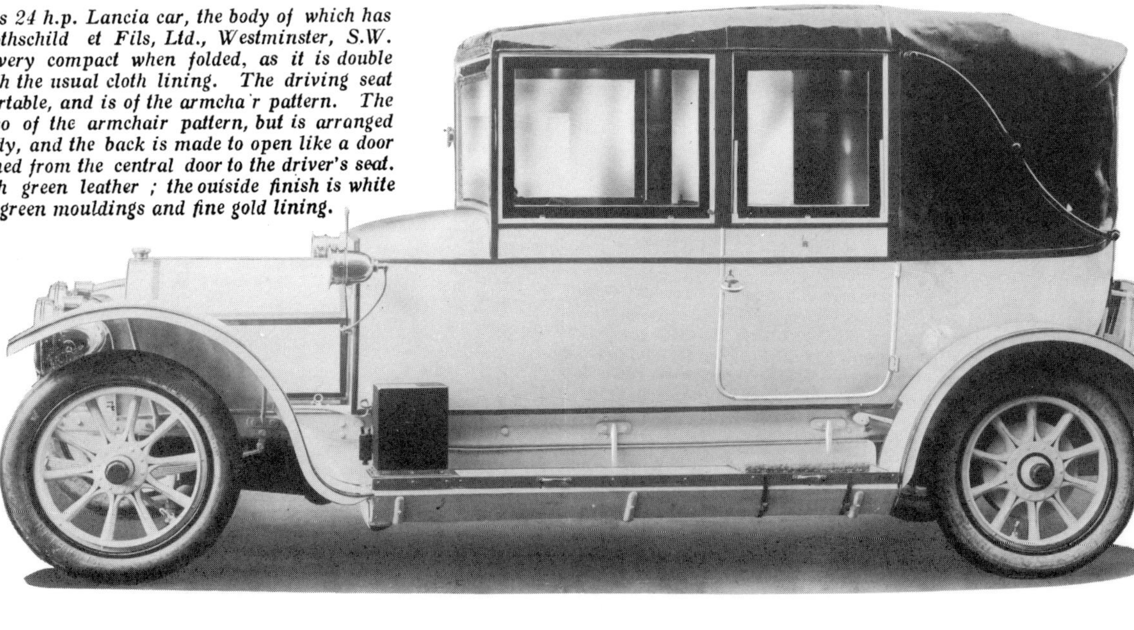

Olympia.

AT OLYMPIA. A 24-40 h.p. four-cylinder Lancia four-seater shown by Messrs. W. L. Stewart and Co., Ltd. The body, which is by Maythorn, of Biggleswade, possesses practically all the points desirable in a well designed car. The main body line is the same height as the bonnet, there is no visible filling in strip between the bottom of the body and the chassis frame, and the side panels are well proportioned. The hood folds neatly and the screen is well placed, but the charm of the whole design lies in the scuttle. An examination of the engravings shows that this has been beautifully moulded to recede from the truncated V-shaped bonnet to merge into the body lines, the moulding being all the more creditable, as the V-shaped bonnet is, with perhaps the exception of the cylindrical bonnet, the most difficult for the body-builder to deal with. It will be noticed that the side view of the car shows that a re-entrant or double curve occurs in the scuttle, a design which was to be seen on a few other cars in the Show and which seems to us to be a solution of many scuttle design difficulties. The only points we can criticise, and those are minor ones, are the position of the side lamps, which would have been less obtrusive if placed in line with the screen, the wire leads being taken through short tubular brackets, and the front wings would be better both in appearance and usefulness if they curved down a little in front. Taken all round it is one of the smartest designs for an open body we have seen, as it keeps clear of all extremes and yet is quite up-to-date It possesses the rare virtue of looking handsome from whatever angle it is viewed.

Two views of a 24 h.p. Lancia fitted with a coupé landaulet body by Maythorn and Son, Biggleswade. Comfortable seating accommodation is provided for two persons, but there is room for three on the driver's seat in an emergency. The front doors are so designed and the gear and brake levers are so placed that exit or entry can be made from either side. As shown in the photographs the head is made to open entirely and half the front glass can be hinged forward. The space behind the seat is primarily intended for carrying luggage, but when not in use for this purpose the lid opens and two spare seats are then available

The 15 h.p. Lancia.

Water-driven Fan. Gear-box on Back Axle. Two Direct Speeds. Spring Drive.

WE have always held that to approach perfection in automobile design a combination of engineering knowledge and road driving experience is a necessity. This combination is assuredly found in Signor Lancia, who is responsible for the design and output of the highly attractive cars which bear his name, and whose driving repute in the great road contests of the past is still fresh. In the 15 h.p. Lancia at present under review, there will be observed many special and interesting points of design all making for the improvement of the automobile.

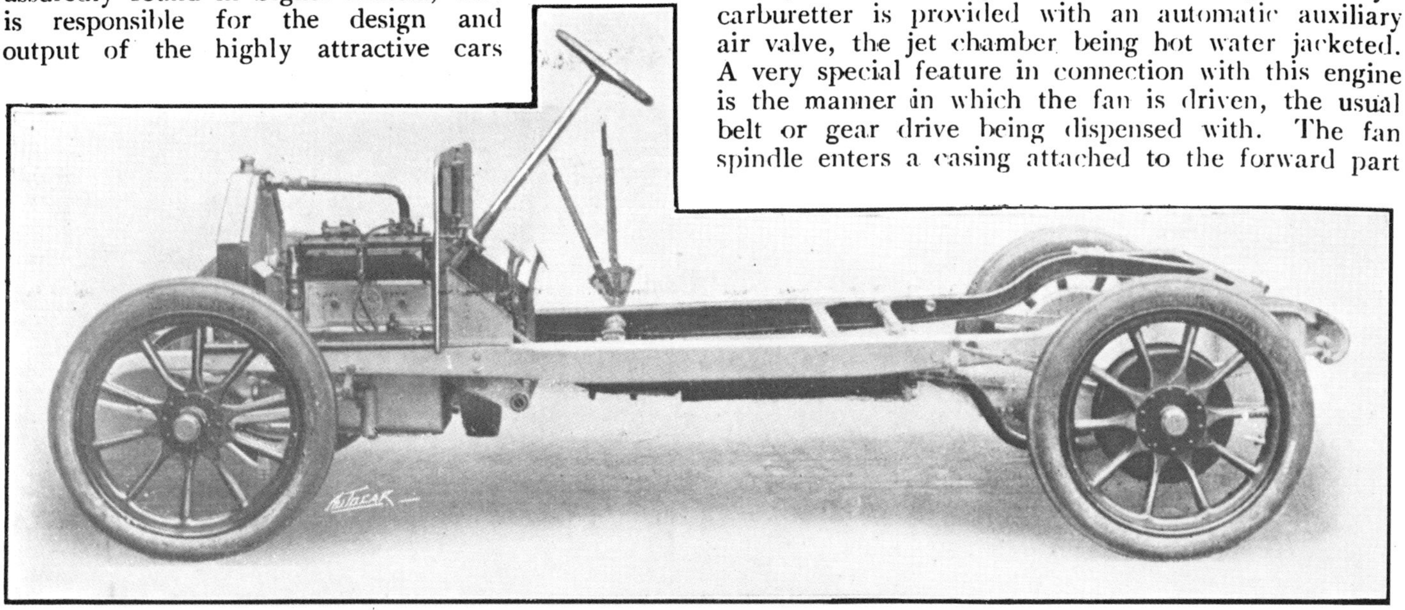

Fig. 1.—The 15 h.p. Lancia chassis.

The keynote of originality is at once struck in the frame. The side members, which are throughout of generous section, are flared in quite an unusual manner before the insweep at the dashboard, while the V-member at the rear of the frame is formed to take the butt ends of the threequarter elliptical springs, and stiffen the rear of the frame.

The engine has its four cylinders cast *en bloc* with integral leads. The flanged exhaust trunk is, however, bolted to the casting. The valves, stems, and tappets are enclosed by one cover plate, and are remarkably accessible, as seen in the near side view of the engine. Compression taps are very properly placed over the combustion heads.

The crank chamber is carried directly from the side members, and the rear brackets are swept round to embrace and partially enclose the flywheel, and to continue in depending brackets which carry the clutch, brake, and throttle pedals. A well-designed two-jet carburetter is provided with an automatic auxiliary air valve, the jet chamber being hot water jacketed. A very special feature in connection with this engine is the manner in which the fan is driven, the usual belt or gear drive being dispensed with. The fan spindle enters a casing attached to the forward part of the cylinder block in which is contained a turbine rotated by the water on its passage from the pump to the water jackets. By this arrangement, as we have already suggested, the necessity for fan belt or other driving gear is non-existent.

Fig. 2.—Rear view of the 15 h.p. Lancia chassis.

The drive is transmitted from the engine to the propeller-shaft through a multi-disc clutch in combination with a special design of spring drive contained within the flywheel. The drive is conveyed from the flywheel to the shoes seen in figs. 2 and 4, embracing the driving drum of the multi-disc clutch (which in the case of this arrangement is not part of the flywheel), through the medium of the helical springs. A gradual and shockless take up is thus provided even though the clutch be carelessly engaged.

The propeller-shaft runs through the large tubular fork-headed torque column to the intermediate gear sleeve in the four-speed gear box bolted to and forming part of the differential gear case. The fork head of this torque column is pivoted where it connects up to the crank chamber arms to allow of vertical axle play. The gear striking rods pass down the inside of the torque column, and are therefore packed very neatly away. Within the gear box is gearing giving four speeds with direct drive on third and fourth

Fig. 3.—Near side view of the 15 h.p. Lancia engine, showing the water lead from the pump to the water-driven fan. It will be noticed that the water entering the cylinder jacke behind the fan at the front ascends to the top of the radiator by one tlead from over the third and fourth cylinders.

speeds, and upon examination and comprehension of the methods by which these direct drives are obtained, the extreme ingenuity displayed in their arrangement will be admitted. By reference to fig. 4 it will be seen that the gear changing lever A racks and traverses in the gate B, and in so doing racks and traverses the gear-changing sleeve C, which is provided at its inner end with the segmental gripping cap D. Mounted on the spindle which runs from side to side of the frame are the two sleeves E and F, having studs formed on them which engage with the slots in the gripping cap D, as it is moved transversely by the similar movement of the gate lever. Attached to these two sleeves are the levers G and H, connected by means of double links, the second of which in each case passes back through the forked head of the torque tube to the half tube striking rods enclosed within the torque tube J. One of these half tube striking rods is shown marked K in the gear diagram fig. 5 with the propeller-shaft L running through it. The half tube connected to the lever H (fig. 4) operates the first and second speeds, while the opposite half tube connected to the lever G operates the direct third and fourth speeds.

With this arrangement understood it is possible to follow the gear change by reference to the gear diagrams reproduced in figs. 5, 6, 7, 8, and 9. In the case of fig. 5 all the gears are shown in the neutral position, which position is necessarily occupied by the gear changing lever. Now by moving this lever into the first speed slot the intermediate driving wheel 1 is brought forward into mesh with the driven intermediate gear wheel 2, and the first speed driving wheel 3 into mesh with the driven first speed wheel 4 as shown in fig. 6. Then the drive passes from the propeller-shaft through the wheels 1 and 2, the wheels 3 and 4 and the bevel pinion and crown wheel 5 and 6, to the differential casing and road wheels. To obtain the second speed (fig. 7) the gear lever is moved into the second speed slot, with the result that, while the intermediate gear wheels remain engaged, the wheels 7 and 8, being the driving and driven wheels of the second speed, are brought into mesh, and the drive then passes through 1 and 2 to 7 and 8, and so by 5 and 6 again to the road wheels. In the matter of the third speed (fig. 8) the movement of the gear changing lever disengages the wheels 1 and 2 and also 7 and 8, but thrusts and locks the wheel 1 into engagement with the internally toothed clutch 9, which is an extension of the sleeve on which the driving bevel pinion 5 is formed. The drive then passes directly from the propeller-shaft to this pinion in mesh with the crown wheel 6, and so the road wheels are rotated in the ratio of the third speed and directly through from the engine.

For the top direct fourth (fig. 9) the movement of the gear-changing lever carries the toothed wheel 1 farther back and engages it with the internally toothed clutch 10, which is fast on the forward end of the shaft carrying the bevel pinion 11 at its opposite end and meshed with 12. Thus the road wheels are rotated in the ratio of the fourth speed, the bevels 5 and 6, and the internally toothed clutch 9 running idle the while. It will also be noticed that the

***Fig. 4.**—The amidships portion of the 15 h.p. Lancia chassis In this view is seen the spring drive within the flywheel, also the arrangement of the forked end of the propeller-shaft casing, and the gear striking sleeves, dogs, and levers.*

A, gear lever. B, gate. C, gear lever sleeve. D, gripping cup on gear lever sleeve. E and F, gear striking sleeves. G and H, gear striking levers. J, propeller-shaft casing.

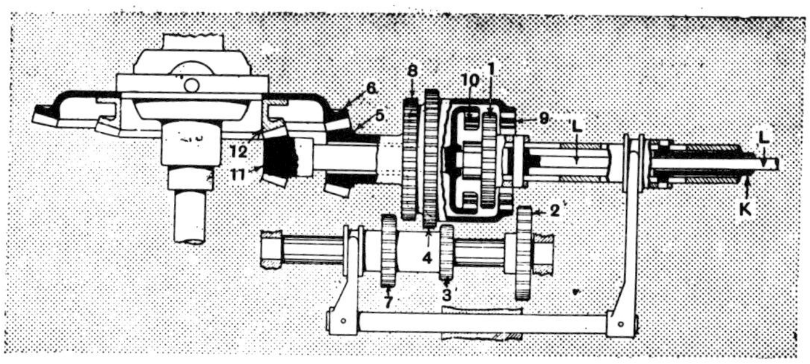

Fig. 5.—Diagram of the Lancia gears in the neutral position.

K, half tube gear-striking rod
L, propeller-shaft
1, driving wheel of intermediate and direct third and fourth gears
2, driven wheel of intermediate gear
3, driving wheel of first speed
4, driven wheel of first speed
5 and 6, bevel pinion and crown bevel taking the drive on all gears except fourth
7, driving wheel of second speed
8, driven wheel of second speed
9, internally toothed clutch of direct third speed
10, internally toothed clutch of direct fourth speed
11, bevel pinion of direct fourth speed
12, crown bevel of direct fourth speed

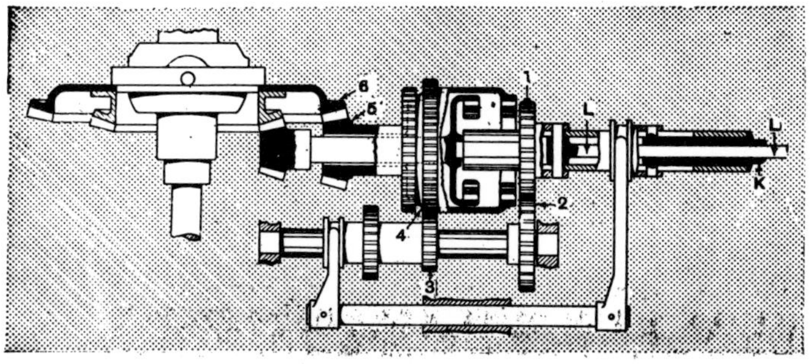

Fig. 6.—Diagram of the Lancia gear showing the positions of the gear wheels of the first speed. References to the index numbers will be found under fig. 5.

secondary shaft carrying the driven intermediate wheel 2 and the first and second speed driving wheels are disengaged and idle when either the third or fourth direct speeds are engaged.

The road wheel driving shafts within the axle casing rotate the road wheels only, the hubs running on ball bearings carried on the axle tubes. In the latest model both the pedal and side lever applied brakes, with internally expanding shoes, take effect upon the internal peripheries of the brake drums, and are placed side by side on the wheels and not concentric as in the model here illustrated. This re-arrangement has resulted in greatly lessening the weight of the brake drums themselves.

The control of the engine is by throttle operated from a reel on the steering wheel instead of by the

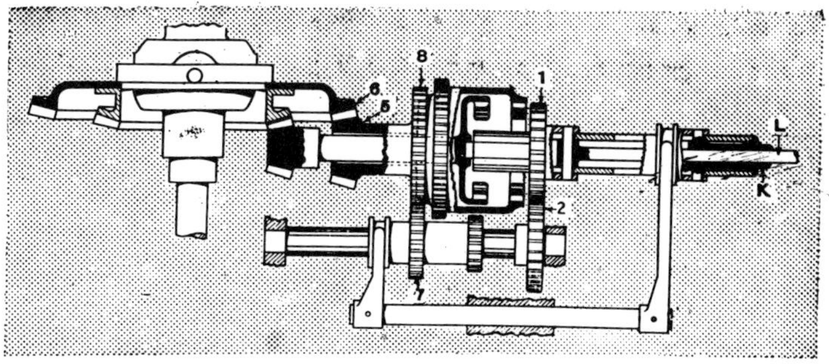

Fig. 7.—Diagram of the Lancia gear, second speed position. References to the index numbers will be found under fig. 5.

usual lever or the small pedal seen in fig. 4. The steering standard can be had at either of two rakes 50° and 38°. The wheels are 815 mm. × 105 mm. back and front, Michelin detachable rims being fitted, and a spare rim supplied together with the Jones speedometer and mileage recorder. The wheelbase is 9ft. 4in., and the wheel gauge 4ft. 7in.

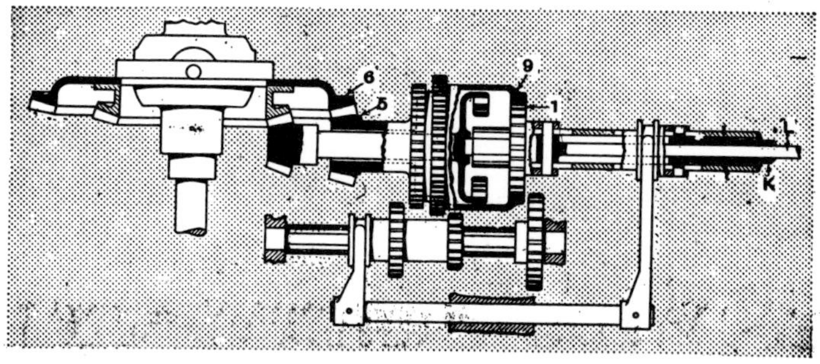

Fig. 8.—Diagram of the Lancia gear with the third speed direct engaged. It will be seen that the drive of the direct third speed is conveyed through bevel wheels 5 and 6. References to the index numbers will be found under fig. 5.

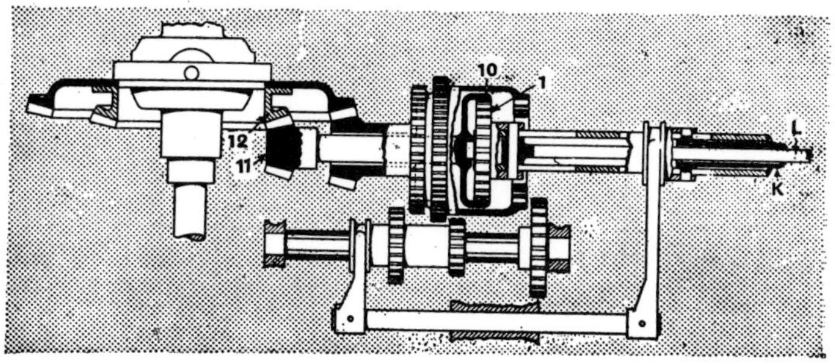

Fig. 9.—Diagram of the Lancia gear in fourth speed direct. The drive in this case is conveyed through bevel wheels 11 and 12. References to the index numbers will be found under fig. 5.

THE AUTOCAR, March 23rd, 1912.

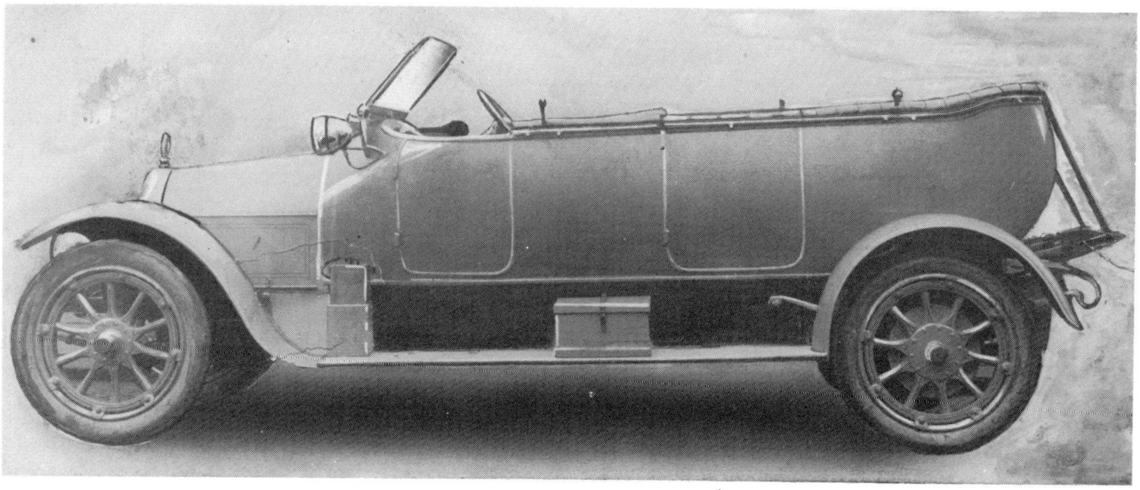

A high flush-sided body by Mr. E. S. Myers, Bradford, on a 24-40 h.p. Lancia.

The 1914 Lancia Cars.

A New Model with Electric Lighting and Engine Starting.

THE Lancia programme will in 1914 comprise three models : the current 15 h.p. four-cylinder, 80 × 130 mm., with the four-speed gear box giving two direct top gears ; the current 30 h.p. four-cylinder, 100 × 130 mm., which will in future be known as the 20-30 h.p. model ; and an entirely new type to be known as the 35 h.p. model. The 15 h.p. and 20-30 h.p. models remain exactly the same as before, except for a slight modification in cylinder design in the case of the 15 h.p. model, which will be listed at £380 chassis price.

The 20-30 h.p. model will still have four speeds, and will still carry as standard a Rushmore dynamo, electric lamps, Klaxon horn, wire wheels with Vinet detachable rims, and speedometer, the inclusive chassis price to be £495.

With regard to the new 35 h.p. model, this will, without doubt, occasion great interest, as it embodies as an integral part of the design an electric engine starter and lighting dynamo. This is the Rushmore set, with which the Lancia firm has had considerable experience extending over twelve months in the case of the 1913 lighting dynamo. Moreover, most of the controls are mounted on the steering wheel. That is to say, a control in the centre, when pressed, sounds the Klaxon, turned to the left the engine is switched off, central the engine is switched on, and to the right the dash lamp is illuminated. A knurled centre boss is arranged to control the lamp switches, and engine starting is effected by means of a pedal.

The new model has a bore and stroke of 110 × 130 mm., four cylinders, and four speeds ; also the steering rake adjustable to any one of three positions, tapered bonnet, and aluminium dash. It is fitted with the new intermediate sized 835 × 135 mm. tyres.

Its 10ft. 10in. wheelbase gives the exceptionally long body platform of 9ft. 6in. The gear box brake embodies chain-applied shoes giving, it is claimed, very even braking pressure.

All the models have the Lancia carburetter. The direct gear ratios of the three models are for the 15 h.p. 3.5 to 1 and 4.8 to 1 on the direct fourth and third gears, for the 20-30 h.p. model 3.26 on top, and for the new 35 h.p. model either 3.26 or 3.06.

A 30 h.p. Lancia car with an all-enclosed body built by Messrs. Lookers, Ltd., Manchester, in which all unnecessary joints and pillars have been eliminated. The front pillars are entirely done away with, and the windows at the front are carried in brass rims at the back of the wind screen permanent fittings.

Another view of the 30 h.p. Lancia. The centre pillars as shown above fold out of sight when the car is open. The two rear pillars are secured to the cant rail, so that the whole folds perfectly flat, and there are no loose pillars to rattle.

A 35 h.p. Lancia with a special type of sporting body built by Messrs. Chas. Grimshaw and Sons, Sunderland. The body has been designed to present the minimum of wind resistance, whilst providing four comfortable seats. The bonnet line has been emphasised and carried right through to the back panel. The peculiar shape of the wings is a feature of note.

Some Recent Patents.

By Eric W. Walford, F.C.I.P.A.

A Spring Universal Joint.

The plate clutch is located within a casing A, carried by the shaft B, and arranged within the fly-wheel C. The clutch casing is provided with a number of projecting arms D, and these lie in slots

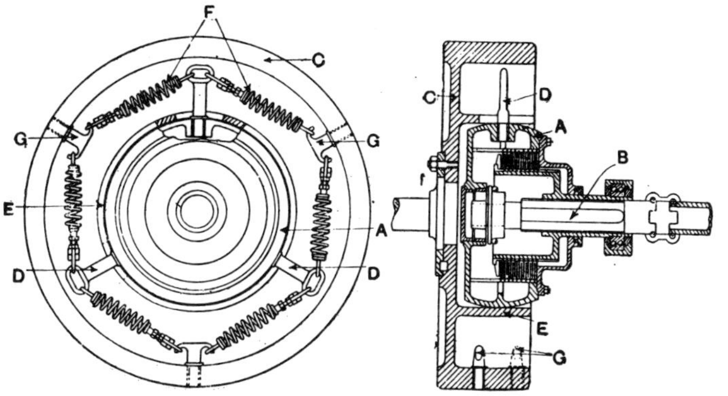

in a web E carried by the flywheel. The arms D are connected by springs F to brackets G on the flywheel, but the brackets do not all lie in the same plane. The springs take the drive, but permit of tilting of the clutch casing in relation to the flywheel.—Lancia and Co., No. 12,492, 1912.

An Adjustable Steering Column.

The steering gear box is formed with a hollow boss A having conical surfaces which take a bearing inside the conical box B, which is attached to the car frame C. When the nut D is slackened the pillar can be adjusted to any angle, whilst the dashboard carries a curved guide to which a bracket on the steering column is bolted. Means are also provided for varying the length of the rod connecting the steering wheel to the steering gear when the rake of the steering pillar is changed and renders such alteration necessary.—Lancia and Co., No. 26,083, 1913.

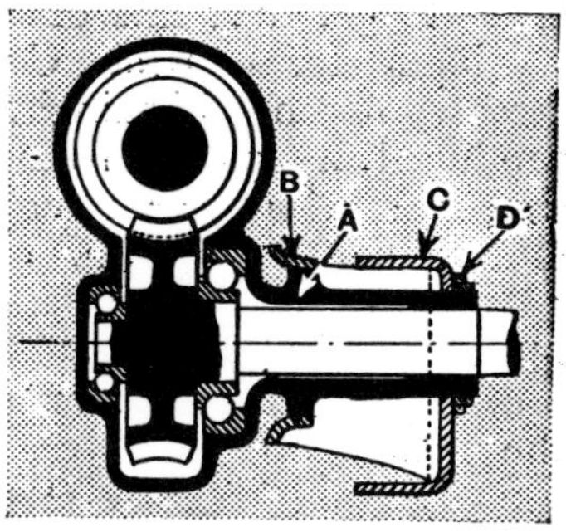

A threequarter front view of the 35 h.p. Lancia shown at the bottom of page 29. This view gives a good idea of the manner in which the scuttle dash and body sides merge into the taper bonnet.

A 35 h.p. Lancia with a limousine body by Messrs. H. J. Mulliner and Co., recently supplied to a customer by Messrs. Curtis, Arthur, Campbell and Co.

A 35 h.p. Lancia with a flush-sided body built by Mr. William Arnold, Manchester. A feature of the car is the concealed hood, which is carried within the top of the rear panel.

THE AUTOCAR, November 17th, 1917.

Correspondence.

SECOND-HAND CARS.

[24431.]—Looking over the advertising columns in *The Autocar* of October 20th I observe under "Second-hand Cars Wanted" that several of the advertisers (trade and others) employ some such terms or conditions as "not earlier than 1914," "not older than 1914," "models earlier than 1914 not entertained," and so on. This seems to me a foolish limitation.

All the motoring world knows that during the last three years practically no new models have been introduced—at least, none of any striking variation in the *tout ensemble*. Presumably a number of buyers assume that a car dating further back than 1914 must necessarily be of old-fashioned pattern, or otherwise out of date. Nothing could be more erroneous. There are hundreds of thoroughly efficient, smart, and most modern looking cars on the road which were built and bought four or five or even six years ago. I myself own a handsome 24-30 h.p. Lancia car, which was built in the autumn of 1912, and I can, if desirable, pass practically any car on the road, excepting a Rolls-Royce or an out-and-out racing equipment; and only a few weeks ago, when driving some officers to a distant camp, I was asked by a garage owner if my car was a new one—a new model!

Everything depends not on the age of the car, but on the mileage it has done, and the way it has been treated. A careful owner-driver, who knows how to get the best out of his car without punishing it, and has kept it "as fit as a fiddle" over a number of years, will have better value to offer than he who has fouled and cut his gears, neglected his differential, etc., in even a few months' reckless or ignorant service. The number of cars which are ruined by crazy manipulation, overheating, gear bashing, under lubrication, etc., in the first year or two of ownership must be a heavy aggregate.

I would not exchange my car (which has been driven over some 28,000 miles) for any model, simply because the latter may be offered as built only last year. "Last year" might be eloquent of gross abuse and rotten value. To bar a car because it is four or five years back dated is, therefore, surely folly, and, as mine is not for sale, I cannot be accused of personal interest in my modest protest.

ALFRED BRACEWELL.

The 24-30 h.p. 1912 Lancia car referred to by Mr. Alfred Bracewell.

November 30th, 1918.

The 35 h.p. Post-war Lancia.

THROUGHOUT the war the Admiralty made full use of Lancia cars for official work, and the post-war Lancia will not differ materially from the model that the Government has had in service during the past four years. It is the intention of the manufacturers, whose concessionnaires in this country are Messrs. W. L. Stewart and Co., Ltd., 26b, Albemarle Street, London, W.1, to produce only one model of touring car—a 35 h.p. four-cylinder—of which the main characteristics will be those embodied in the 1913 chassis, though slight modifications resulting from war experience will naturally be made. The chassis will be sold complete with electric equipment, lamps, speedometer, horn—in fact, with everything but the coachwork.

February 22nd, 1919.

The Lancia Post-war Programme.

MR. W. L. STEWART, who, for many years past, has conducted the business of Messrs. W. L. Stewart and Co., Ltd., British concessionnaires for Lancia cars, writes to us from the Lancia Company's works in Turin, informing us that the only 1919 model will be the 35 h.p. chassis, which, as a post-war production, will be but little different from the pre-war pattern. Mr. Stewart states that, save in quite small and unimportant points, it has not been found necessary to vary the specification to meet present-day requirements.

Lancia's first post-War design was the 35hp Kappa, with a conventional four-cylinder engine of 4,940cc producing 70bhp at 2,200rpm and giving a top speed of over 70mph.

The 35 h.p. Lancia.

A Powerful Italian Car of Sturdy and Clean Design.

DURING the War the Navy and the Royal Naval Air Service possessed a fleet of Lancia cars for use as tenders or anti-aircraft gun cars. Many of these cars went abroad during 1915 and were driven over the awful Belgian roads, had to be left in the open and, generally, were tried most severely. Later the cars underwent still more strenuous testing because the quality of the drivers became very much worse, and every part of the car, therefore, was misused. In spite of these handicaps, the Lancias stood up very well to the hard work and gave service which could hardly have been bettered.

SPECIFICATION.

35 h.p., four cylinders, 110 × 130 mm. (4,941.74 c.c.)
Detachable head.
Special ignition starting system.
Dry multi-disc clutch.
Four-speed gear box. Central control.
Full floating, bevel driven rear disc axle.
Semi-elliptic springs.
Tyres, 895 × 135 mm. on Michelin disc wheels.
Wheelbase, 11ft. 1¼in. Track, 4ft. 4½in.

Detail Improvements.

For this year there are not a great number of alterations to the 35 h.p. chassis, but certain details have been altered in conformity with the present fashion in design or in order to improve minor points. The engine now has a detachable cylinder head, while an auxiliary vibrator has been fitted to the ignition circuit and comes into action when the engine-starter is used, giving that ease of starting associated with battery and coil ignition.

We are informed that the 1919 engine gives no less than 90 h.p. at 2,300 r.p.m. The crankshaft has three bearings of ample width, and the pistons for this year's engine are much lighter. There is a single camshaft at the side of the crank case, driven by helical-tooth gears from the crankshaft, which gearing also drives a cross shaft having the magneto at one end in such a position that its contact-maker and distributer are quite accessible. A large centrifugal pump, of which the casing is part of the crank case, supplies water to the jackets, air being sucked through the honeycomb radiator both by the action of vanes on the flywheel and by a belt-driven fan. A Zenith carburetter now is used, and is placed on the side of the cylinders opposite to the valves, the gas passing to the ports through passages cast with the cylinder block.

Starting the Engine at Slow Speeds.

The ignition system is of special interest, because the magneto is supplemented by an auxiliary battery and a trembler or vibrator. The battery circuit is broken by the magneto contact-maker, and the high-tension current is led through the magneto distributer, both magneto windings being used. In action the device is automatic, the vibrator being put into circuit when the starting motor is used; thus the engine can be started at lower speeds than is desirable when a magneto only supplies the current.

Oil is forced both to the big ends and to the gudgeon pin bushes, as well as to the crank bearings, by a spur pump driven from the camshaft, the amount of oil passing to these bearings being varied in accordance with the position of the throttle pedal and, therefore, directly with the engine load. As before, there is a safety valve which deals with any untoward rise of pressure due to the oil congealing in winter. Incidentally the sump holds one and threequarter gallons of oil.

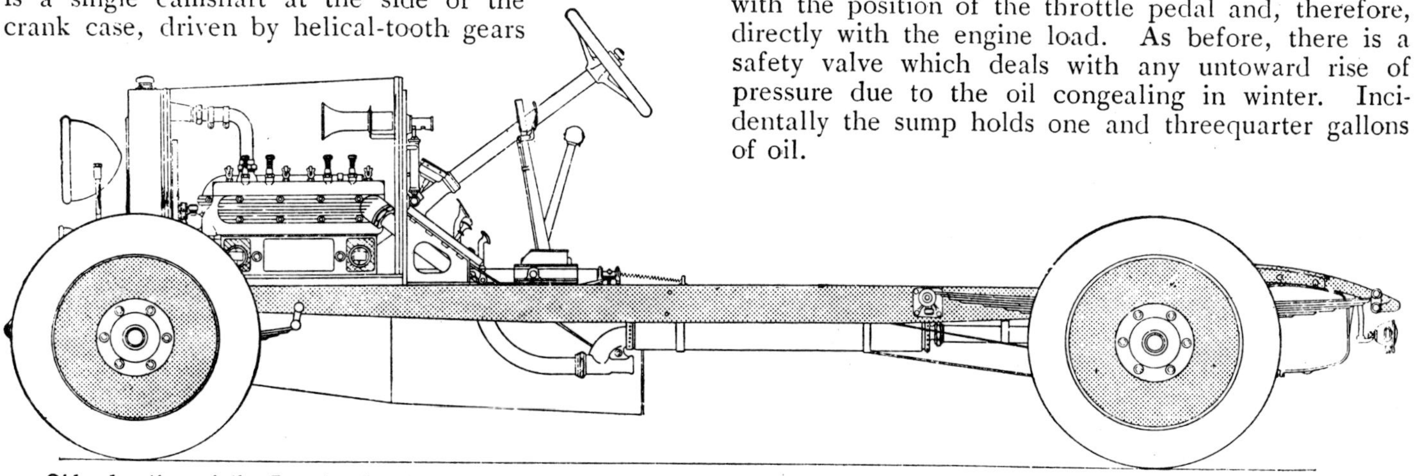

Side elevation of the Lancia chassis showing electric horn concealed under the bonnet and the arrangement of exhaust cut-out.

The six volt electric starter actuates the flywheel through teeth cut in the rim of the latter and disengages automatically when the engine starts. A dynamo, placed on the left side of the engine, is driven from the distribution gearing, the 120 amp. 6 volt battery being carried on steel slats attached to the frame. All the leads for this dynamo are in armoured cables. There is a multi-disc clutch, which requires no lubricant whatever, the discs being alternately steel and composition.

Gear Box : Rear Axle : Brakes and Springs.

A four-speed gear box, giving ratios of 3.45 to 1 on top gear, 4.8 to 1 on third, 7.0 to 1 on second, and 10.6 to 1 on first, is fitted, and is a single aluminium casting formed with two side arms bolted to the frame and two forward arms which are secured to the engine crank case in familiar Lancia fashion. The oil level is set by a tap in the side of the box.

This year, the gear and brake levers are on the left of the driver, and on quadrants in the centre of the gear box, thus allowing the body-maker more scope, while the driver can reach his seat from a door on the off side. At the rear of the gear box is the chain-actuated contracting band brake peculiar to this chassis, and behind this again the covered single universal joint for the open propeller-shaft.

In the central casing of the rear axle is a bevel gear, a single pressed steel torque arm being bolted to this centre and transmitting the torque to a frame cross member through a special link.

Both sets of brakes are compensated, the expanding shoes controlled by the central hand lever being housed in drums on the rear wheel hubs, while a pedal actuates the propeller-shaft brake already mentioned. As one would expect in an Italian chassis, the total brake surface is very great. For this year Michelin detachable disc wheels are used. As heretofore, the front axle is of pressed steel in section like a U with the flanges horizontal, and is fitted with semi-elliptic springs, which type is used for the rear axle, in which case they serve also to take the drive.

Neatly Arranged Instrument Board.

At the rear of the chassis is the twenty-two gallon petrol tank having a level indicator, petrol being forced to the carburetter from this tank by an air pump actuated by the camshaft. Incidentally, there is an outer shield protecting the tank against damage caused by stones flung up by the wheels. The column of the worm and worm wheel steering gear can be set in any one of the three different angles to suit the requirements of the coachwork. On the aluminium cast dashboard is an instrument board containing petrol and oil gauges, the switches for the head, side, and tail lamps, together with their ammeter and voltmeter, while, for inspection purposes, a portable electric lamp with cable is supplied, the cable being long enough to allow the light to be carried to the tyres if necessary. The speedometer drive is simplified, shortened, and protected by being arranged on the gear box layshaft.

When one remembers that the car is born in Turin and tested among the mountain passes, the reason for the great strength of the chassis and its large and powerful brakes becomes apparent. In England we have no such testing ground, for around Turin one can pick almost any gradient, even any length of gradient, whereon to test, on the one hand, the power and cooling of the engine, on the other the similar qualities of the brakes. Italian chassis are all stamped with the mark of this testing, and, because of it, one is certain that the car can deal with any hills even after a prolonged burst of speed. For Great Britain, the car is handled by Messrs. W. L. Stewart and Co., Ltd., of 26, Albemarle Street, London, W.

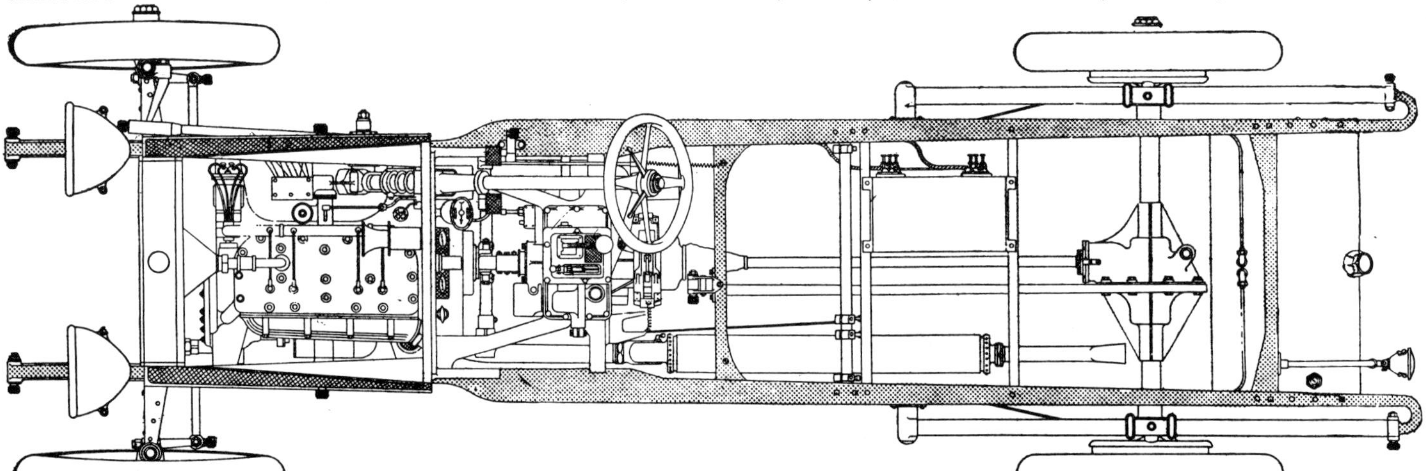

The 1919 Lancia chassis is fitted with central control for the gears and rear brakes.

The Twelve-cylinder Lancia.

A Remarkable 22° V Engine installed in a Chassis equipped with an Interesting System of Rear Suspension.

Nothing could well be neater than the external appearance of the new twelve-cylinder Lancia engine and three-speed gear box

In addition to the four-cylinder 35 h.p. model supplied during the war to most of the Allied Powers, and continued with detail improvements, the Lancia factory is producing for next year, and exhibiting at the Paris and London shows, a most interesting twelve-cylinder car.

Probably nine motorists out of every ten brought face to face with this new Lancia engine would pronounce it a six, with double ignition. Such a mistake would be quite excusable, for the block is of quite normal dimensions; there are no visible moving parts, there are no external oil pipes, and at first sight there appears to be no exhaust. On one side of this block there is a carburetter, and, inserted at an angle of 45° along each side, are six spark plugs.

SPECIFICATION.

Twelve cylinders, 80 × 100 mm. bore and stroke (6,032 c.c.)

Three speeds and reverse gear box, forming unit with engine.

Semi-elliptic front and combined cantilever and semi-elliptic rear springs.

Electric lighting and starting.

R.A.C. rating 48 h.p.

The explanation of this apparent mystery is that the twelve cylinders are a single casting in V form, with an angle of 22° between the two rows. Further, one line of cylinders is offset in relation to the other, but as the water jacket is common to the twelve, this offset is not visible externally. This construction, naturally, implies offset throws of the crankshaft, for the connecting rods are not forked, as in practically all twelve cylinders built up to the present, but are mounted side by side. The result is a wonderfully neat and compact engine, for this new Lancia, with its twelve cylinders of 80 × 100 mm. bore and stroke (6,032 c.c.), is very little longer than the 35 h.p. four-cylinder, the actual overall length being thirty-five inches.

The inlet side of the twelve-cylinder Lancia. To the front lies the magneto, and to the rear the starter motor is carried. The centrally placed exhaust pipe is seen projecting to the rear of the cylinder block. The absence of external piping renders the engine extraordinarily neat.

The block casting has a single detachable head for the whole of the twelve cylinders. In this head are mounted the twenty-four vertical valves, which are operated by a single central camshaft running in oil, and by rocker arms. The studs and nuts by which the head is held down to the cylinder block are inside the valve stem chamber, and as this latter is covered by an aluminium housing, a very neat external appearance is secured. On the majority of engines the cylinder barrels are visible below the bottom of the water jacket; but on the twelve-cylinder Lancia this portion of the casting is covered by an aluminium plate, which adds to the neat appearance of the whole. Incidentally, this gives the impression that there are valves on opposite sides, and that these covers are used to enclose the stems. In reality, they do nothing more than add to the neat appearance of the engine, and need never be detached.

This arrangement of overhead valves in a detachable head has the advantage of allowing a valve spring to be changed with the greatest ease. When a valve has to be taken out the head has, of course, to be removed, as is the case with all detachable head engines.

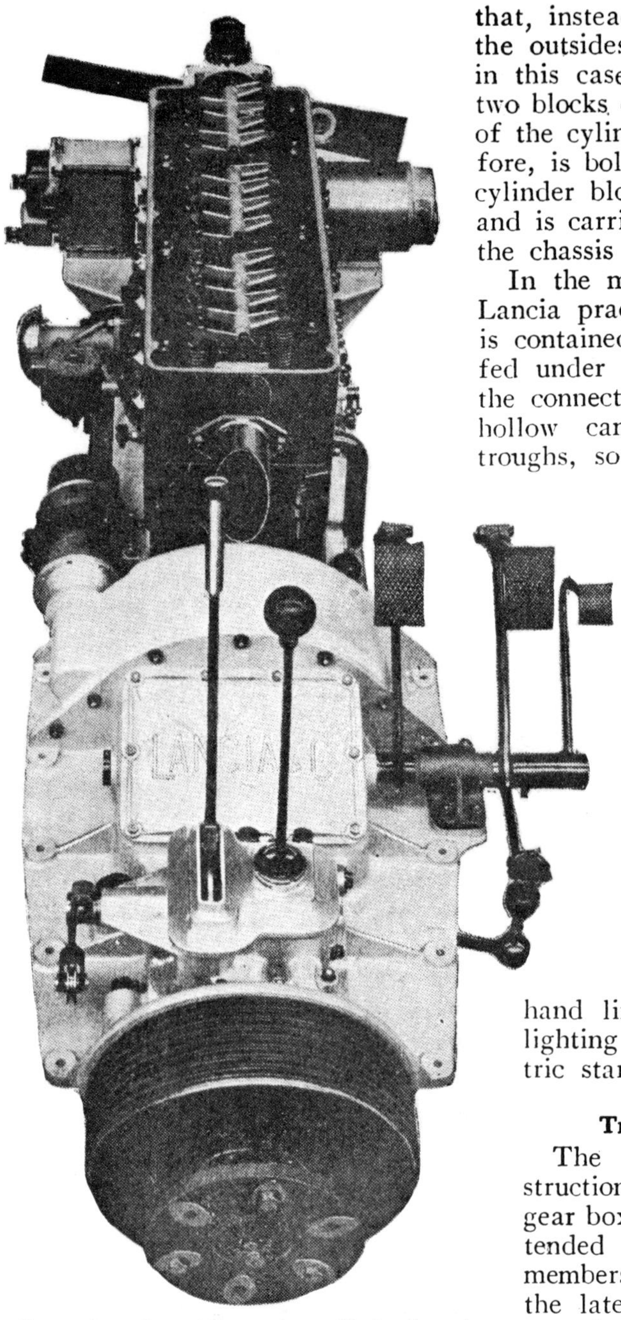

Semi-plan view of the twelve-cylinder Lancia power unit and gear box. The valve rocker arrangement, magneto, carburetter, lighting dynamo and starting motor are all shown. To the rear of the gear box is the large foot-operated shaft brake, and behind this the fabric universal joint.

Driving the Components.

The crankshaft is carried in four plain bearings, or one between each pair of cylinders. At the front end of the engine there is a bevel pinion, which drives an enclosed vertical shaft operating the overhead camshaft through a pair of bevel gears. The vertical shaft is divided, and has a screwdriver type connection which allows the head to be removed without interfering in any way with the gears. At the base of the vertical shaft there is an oil pump very readily detachable, together with its filter, and higher up there is a cross-shaft, from one end of which is driven the magneto, and from the other the electric generator. A separate helical gear drives the water pump, which is just below the magneto cross-shaft. The inlet water pipe runs through the full length of the crank case, emerging near the rear to enter the bottom of the water jacket, between the fifth and sixth cylinders on the right-hand side. The water outlet is by means of a single pipe at the front end of the engine.

It has already been mentioned that at first sight no exhaust pipe is visible. This is owing to the fact that, instead of collecting the exhaust on the outsides of the cylinder casting, it is in this case in the angle formed by the two blocks of cylinders, and forms a part of the cylinder casting. The pipe, therefore, is bolted up to the rear face of the cylinder block, just under the dashboard, and is carried away to the exhaust box in the chassis with a minimum of curves.

In the matter of lubrication the usual Lancia practice is followed. All the oil is contained in the base chamber, and is fed under pressure to the main bearings, the connecting rod ends, and also to the hollow camshaft. The cams run in troughs, so that, whatever the inclination of the engine, an adequate supply of oil is delivered to the overhead mechanism. As in the case of the four-cylinder Lancia, the whole of the oil delivered by the pump is sent through the bearings when the throttle reaches its full open position. The magneto is a Dixie, running at engine speed, and the carburetter is a horizontal Zenith, bolted up to the left-hand side of the engine. Internal gas passages lead the mixture through the cylinder casting to the right-hand line of cylinders. While the lighting system is six volts, the electric starting system is twelve volts.

Transmission Accessibility.

The engine, which is a unit construction with the clutch housing and gear box, is mounted directly to the extended webs of the channel frame members. This, of course, fills in all the lateral space and makes unnecessary the use of a sheet metal underpan.

The clutch housing and gear box form a single casting bolted up to the rear face of the engine housing. There are two very big covers giving easy access to both clutch and gears, the latter being three in number. The change-speed lever and the hand brake are mounted on the top of the gear box, and are controlled by the left hand, for steering is on the right. The electric starting motor is placed on the left-hand side of the gear box, and engages, in the usual way, with a ring gear cut on the flywheel. All the mechanism is fully enclosed. There is a positive speedometer drive from the gear box.

The rear axle construction has been changed, for the axle housing and propeller-shaft casing now form a T with a spherical end through which the drive is taken. This naturally abolishes the separate torque member.

A New System of Suspension.

Undoubtedly the most interesting feature of this car, after the engine, is the rear suspension. This consists of a combination of cantilever and semi-elliptic with a single leaf. The cantilever is mounted directly under the main frame members, and also passes under the axle. The forward and the central attachments of the axle spring follow accepted practice in general. The rear end of the spring, however, is not rigidly shackled to the axle, but is connected to it by a short heavy steel cable, the two ends of which terminate in hardened steel balls fitting into sockets respectively on the axle housing and on the spring ends. Instead of the usual rigid connection, there is thus a thoroughly flexible attachment between the end of the cantilever spring and the rear axle. But in addition to the cantilever there is a single leaf semi-elliptic. This spring is not a single length, but is in two halves, which are bolted respectively to a seating on the front and the rear of the axle casing. A further peculiarity is that the width is variable. At the axle end the spring measures 4 inches across; at the shackle end its width is 2.3 inches.

Provision for Shackle Lubrication.

Up to the present there has been only one method of attaching the springs to the axle or to the frame, this being by forming an eye on the end of the main

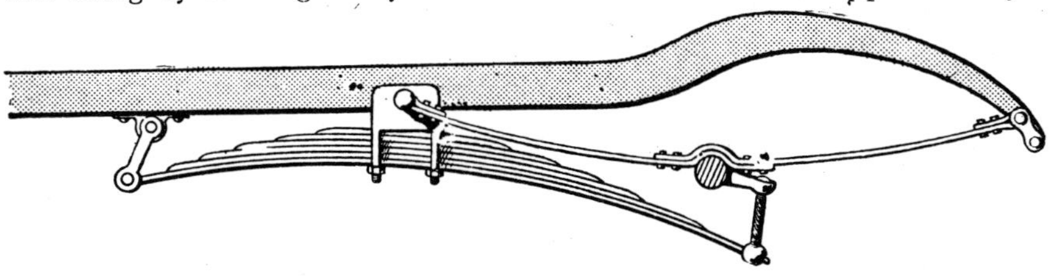

A feature of the design in the new Lancia is the suspension which consists of a combination of cantilever and semi-elliptic springs as shown in this diagram.

leaf. Sometimes this eye is forged out of the solid, but more often it is formed by turning the end of the spring over on itself, and then boring out accurately. On the new Lancia there are no spring eyes. The ends of the main leaves are drilled with from two to four holes, and are bolted to quite special shackles. With this design it is possible to secure a shackle which can be thoroughly lubricated, which gives a big bearing surface, and which is immune from wear owing to lateral motion. It is common practice now to bush spring eyes, but this does not prevent wear taking place on the inner faces of the shackles owing to side motion, and this wear can only be taken up by inserting thin washers. On the Lancia the shackle is bushed in both planes, and, in addition, there is a helical spring to take up automatically, and also to prevent, wear owing to side motion. This arrangement is applied not only to the rear springs, but to those at the front. As a consequence, the rear shackles of the front springs (the most neglected part of all cars) can be fed with oil by lubricators under the bonnet.

On most cars when wear takes place on shackles and shackle bolts, repair is a most unsatisfactory matter, particularly if the eye is not bushed. Even in this latter case the wear, owing to side motion, cannot be readily taken up. With the Lancia design, the spring can be disconnected from the shackle by taking out two bolts; and the entire shackle, or, rather, the complete dumb-iron, can be changed in a very short time, and at very little cost.

This system of suspension has been under test for two years. The dominating idea has been to get all the advantages of the cantilever without certain inherent disadvantages, most prominent among them being the tendency of the car "to wag its tail" at very high speeds. With the Lancia combination, the cantilevers are free to damp out vibrations, while the semi-elliptics form an anchorage between axle and frame. The result is that the car "holds the road" in a remarkable manner, there being no tendency when cornering at speed for the rear end to sway or skid.

Another advantage of this combination is that a supplementary compensated suspension is obtained. The car on which experiments have been carried out for the last two years carries nine passengers in three rows of three. It is as comfortable with its full load as with a driver and a single passenger on the rear seat. The explanation is that, when running lightly loaded, the semi-elliptic absorbs the shocks, and when under full load the cantilever also comes into play. The arrangement is clearly shown in the accompanying illustration.

Completely Equipped Chassis Supplied.

The practice inaugurated by the Lancia Co. of supplying chassis complete in every respect is being continued with improvements. A standardised scuttle dash, which will suit all types of bodies, has been adopted. This is complete with dashboard and aluminium instrument board, with tool lockers under the scuttle, and even with hinges. The result is that the body-builder merely has to build a body from the scuttle rearwards, and does not have to drill the chassis at any place. The chassis are also supplied with a special spare wheel carrier at the rear, this being designed to receive the Michelin disc wheels now adopted as standard, whether the tyres are fully inflated or deflated.

At the Paris Salon there is also being exhibited a Lancia-built touring car, which, within five minutes, can be stripped of all its seats and upholstery, and washed down internally with a hose pipe.

October 18th, 1919

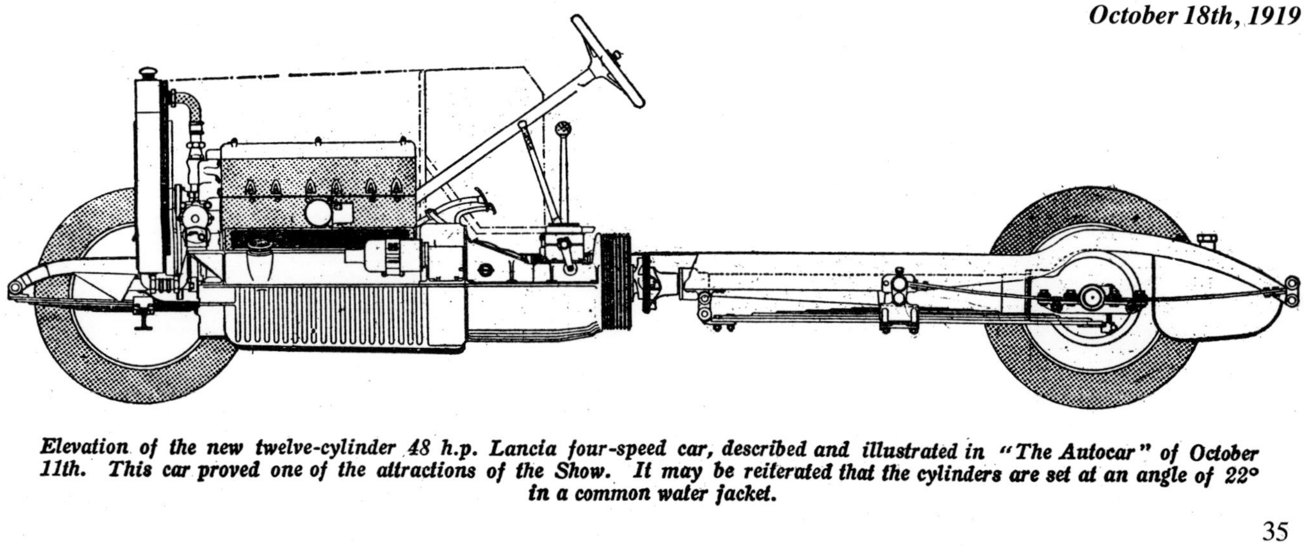

Elevation of the new twelve-cylinder 48 h.p. Lancia four-speed car, described and illustrated in "The Autocar" of October 11th. This car proved one of the attractions of the Show. It may be reiterated that the cylinders are set at an angle of 22° in a common water jacket.

A Frameless Car.

Some Details of a Very Novel Design patented recently by the Lancia Company.

FOR years past designers have aimed at reducing the height of the mean centre of gravity of the car, and for years also the difficulties of obtaining sufficient axle and ground clearances, together with unhampered movement for the rear axle and transmission when the seats are low down, have baffled their aims and stultified their efforts. It, therefore, becomes a matter for some comment when a firm of the reputation of the Lancia Co. takes out patent specifications for a design in which the body actually forms the frame, and is so arranged as to allow an unusually low centre of gravity.

In the two illustrations given herewith, an attempt has been made to visualise the idea set forth in the original patent specification. The body consists of a stamped sheet steel shell, and it combines the function of a body with that of a frame. At the front of this shell is attached horizontally a form of stirrup, to which in turn is attached a semi-elliptic transverse spring, shackled at each end to the forks of a straight front axle. Fore and aft location of the front axle relative to the body is obtained by the use of a radius rod on each side, running from the bottom of the axle back to the body. Suspension for the rear axle consists of long quarter-elliptic springs, the butt ends of which are attached to the body at a point where a channel rib, forming part of the front seat support, crosses and stiffens the body.

An essential feature of this specification is the use of a channel section rib or tunnel running longitudinally from the front portion to the back, and forming also a compartment open at the bottom in which the propeller shaft or tube can rise or fall, this tunnel, of course, coming between the seats. Clearance for the rear axle is given by a similar tunnel running transversely across the back of the body. These channels may be made by stamping the sheet metal forming the lower portion of the shell to form a longitudinal member, thus improving the stiffness of the body without, to any extent, reducing the foot room capacity of the seating accommodation. By this construction it becomes possible to lower the body shell, and, therefore, at the same time the plane of the seats, very considerably, and also to bring the base of the shell as near to the ground as is possible consistent with safety.

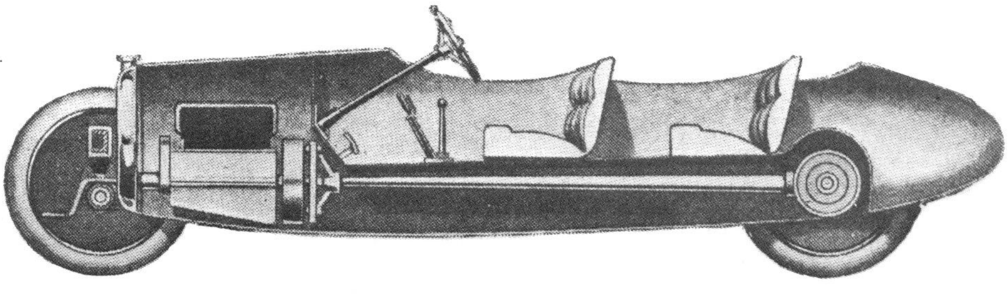

What a car, constructed on the Lancia frameless principle, would look like when completed.

Sectional sketch of a Lancia design in which no frame is used, and a sheet steel body takes its place. An essential feature of this design is the use of channel section tunnels in the bottom of the body to give stiffness, and to accommodate the transmission and the rear axle.

In the original specifications and drawings, from which the accompanying sketches have been prepared, no mention is made of the gear box, nor is one shown. It may possibly have been incorporated in the rear axle.

It will be recognised that this is a highly interesting patent, and not only should it have a very great effect upon improving the stability, the road-holding qualities, and the suspension of a car so designed, but it conceivably would have the effect of reducing weight to a very great extent. There are, of course, a number of points in this design about which one would like to know more, such as, for example, what steps are to be taken to render the engine itself accessible from outside the car? Lastly, the wind resistance of a car made on these lines would be very materially less than that of present-day types, wherein the under gear is usually completely exposed.

November 15th, 1919

A striking touring body with bevelled edges on a 35 h.p. Lancia chassis.

The 35h.p. Four-cylinder

INSPIRATION FROM NAUTICAL DESIGN. The tumble-in gunwale tops of the sides of this extraordinarily attractive coachwork on a 1920 35 h.p. Lancia chassis are reminiscent of the shape of a modern motor launch. The coachbuilders, Messrs. Park, Ward and Co., 473, High Road, Willesden, N.W.10, who have built this coachwork for Major Skelton, deserve great credit for the evolution of such a graceful design, which embodies a cleverly concealed hood.

This picturesque scene shows a Lancia car at Cortina, in what had recently become the Italian Alps (they had been part of Austro-Hungary before the War). The occupants appear to be members of the local constabulary.

A LANCIA SPORTING MODEL.

A Fast and Powerful Four-seater, with a Four-cylinder Overhead Valve Engine, Capable of Developing over 90 b.h.p.

MANY motorists have kindly recollections of the 35 h.p. Lancia, a car which, unchanged for many years, gave yeoman service in private hands and in the armies of various countries.

This year, the same chassis has been fitted with an overhead valve engine, developing some ninety odd horse-power, and a light four-seated body, the combination appealing especially to sportsmen, particularly for Continental work. The famous 35 h.p. touring model is retained, of course, and this new car is a sporting model most worthy of the name. Some details of the design are interesting.

The valve seats, plugs, and ports are all in a cast-iron detachable head, while the camshaft is in the crank case and operates the valve rocking levers by means of push rods which are concealed within passages cast in the cylinders, and, therefore, are heated sufficiently to prevent a rapid increase of valve clearance. On the cross-shaft, which drives the magneto, is an automatic advance, additional to the hand lever on the steering wheel. A special Zenith carburetter is used, having its jet and compensator arranged at one side of the choke tube instead of beneath, as is usual. Certain alterations also have been effected to the water pipes, as a result of the adoption of a detachable head, but otherwise the engine is exactly the same as for the touring model. Apart from the engine, the radiator is of altered shape, a mudguard is placed between the front dumb irons, and three tool compartments are provided, one placed between the instrument board and the dash. A useful item of the standard equipment is a large suitcase at the rear of the car, to augment the otherwise rather scanty luggage accommodation.

DATA FOR THE DRIVER.

35 h.p., four cylinders, 110 × 130 mm. (4,941 c.c.). Treasury rating, 30 h.p. Tax, £30.
Weight of complete car less passengers, 1 ton 15 cwt. 3 qrs.
Weight per c.c., 7 lb.
Gear ratios: 1st, 10.6 to 1; 2nd, 7 to 1; 3rd, 4.8 to 1; and top, direct, 3.46 to 1.
Bevel final drive.
Semi-elliptic springs, front and rear.
895 × 135 mm. tyres.
Wheelbase, 11ft. Track, 4ft. 7½ n.
Fuel consumption, 12 m.p.g.
Tank capacity, 21 gals.

In actual fact, the car placed at our disposal by the courtesy of Mr. W. L. Stewart, of Lancia and Co., 45, Albemarle Street, London, W.1, in whose care is the British representation of the Lancia firm, was one of the experimental cars—not that it differed radically from standard, but was one which had not been tested to the full, and lacked several detail modifications which will appear on the standard model. Nevertheless, it was something of a revelation in sheer power, notwithstanding the quite large four-cylinder engine from which it is natural to expect a great deal.

Acceleration and Hill-climbing.

Despite a top gear of which the ratio is unusually high for a modern car, there was no difficulty whatso-

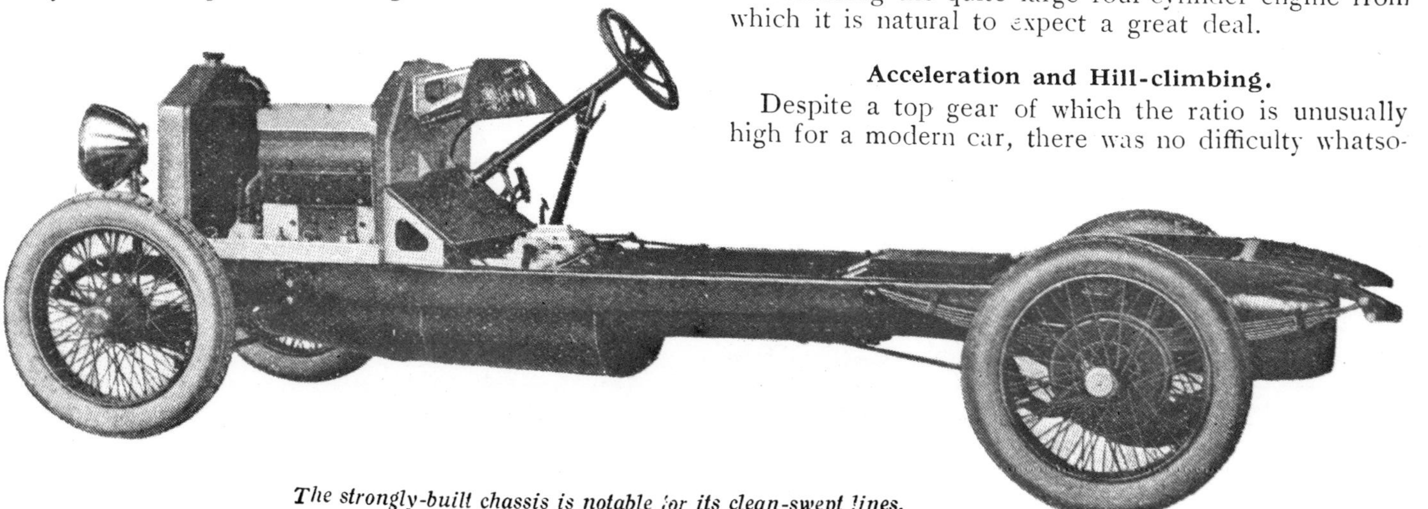

The strongly-built chassis is notable for its clean-swept lines, so characteristic of the best Italian craftsmanship.

ever in negotiating traffic in swift yet silent progress, very fascinating to experience. An easy change to third places at one's disposal a tremendous power of acceleration, which is extremely useful should an opening in the traffic permit, and this acceleration is an immediate response to the movement of the throttle, without trace of hesitation or flat spot in the mixture. Using the gears intelligently, and taking full advantage of this acceleration, the driver can enjoy a sense of control unusual with this particular type of car, in the densest traffic that London can normally provide.

LUGGAGE FOR TOURING.

A trunk case to accommodate two suit cases is a standard fitting, and two spare wheels may be carried, one on each running board.

In the open country this car sweeps along at quite deceptive speed, each hill being met by a corresponding alteration of throttle, but if it is desired to make a really fast climb an early and rapid change down is necessary. For example, the climb to Newlands Corner is best accomplished by using third speed just after the cross-road, and top about 200 yards above the double corner. Handled thus, the car can make a very fast climb. Another hill, Pebblecombe, is really a third-speed climb, but on the occasion of our test certain road repairs necessitated the car's speed being reduced until second gear was required, on which the machine accelerated the whole way up to the top. Allowed full throttle, the speed over a timed mile on the track was 67.67 m.p.h., during which the engine showed no more harshness than is to be expected from a four-cylinder of large bore when the crankshaft is rotating at high speed. On the test hill the Lancia climbed at 16.92 m.p.h., from a standing start, with three passengers—a quite good performance.

Typical neatness of Italian craftsmanship is exemplified in the design of the new Lancia engine. The whole of the valve-operating mechanism is enclosed in the head, and all exterior fitments are easily accessible for cleaning or adjustment.

Brakes and Suspension.

This particular car, it may be mentioned, was suffering from the brake shoes rubbing on their drums—a singularly annoying trouble, but, this apart, the power of the brakes independently is all that one could wish for, and is, of course, to be expected on a big Italian car. Either pair of shoes will bring the car etasily to rest on the 1 in 4 grade of the Brooklands test hill, while, on the road, their power is equally apparent. As it happened, the hand brake shoes could be applied more smoothly than those of the foot brake, which, by reason of the maladjustment aforementioned, were apt to cause chatter.

At present the front springs are a trifle hard, but, as a whole, the suspension is very good, particularly in that it allows the car to corner without side sway. Partly for this reason, the machine holds the road beautifully, no jar or shock throwing it off its course, no matter at what speed it may be travelling. Something of this is due to the steering, which is just right, the wheel moving freely even when the car is crawling, yet not becoming too free when it is running fast, while the caster action is sufficient, neither too powerful to be tiring, nor insufficient to cause the wheels to lack a sense of direction. Since the car, completely equipped with two spare wheels and a large kit, is comparatively heavy, the sensitiveness of the steering is a feature well worth having, particularly on a long run.

The ventilators for the cowl might be larger with advantage, though the driving compartment does not become extremely hot, even if the engine is working hard on a real summer's day; just a slight increase in area, however, would keep the temperature normal, a thing much to be desired. Possibly one is tempted to be ultra-critical on this matter on account of the tropical weather of this summer, but proper ventilation of the driver's compartment is a matter that deserves serious attention. We make further allusion to this matter this week in " Notes."

Details of Control and Bodywork.

Both the gear lever and the brake lever are placed in the central position of the driving seat, the former working in an unusually small gate, which is a little disconcerting until one is accustomed to the range of movement, but the brake lever might well be placed nearer to the driver. The steering wheel is well placed, and the levers on the wheel are black so that they do not reflect light, but, as a personal matter, we prefer that the ignition and throttle controls should not move with the wheel. A rather interesting feature is that the starter pedal first switches current through a trembler and the magneto armature coils, then engages the starting motor pinion with gearing on the flywheel, and, finally, switches current to the motor armature. Sometimes the action of the trembler alone is sufficient to start the engine if one of the pistons happens to be in the firing position.

All fillers are placed conveniently, the brake adjustments are handy, and the auxiliaries in positions where they can be attended to, while the rear axle is provided with a block so that the jack can be put in position without trouble—a thing necessary because the rear tank naturally is somewhat in the way.

To aid the driver to inspect any part during darkness, a plug is fitted to the rear of two of the lamps to receive the adapter on a flex for an inspection lamp, the flex being long enough to go round the car. All four seats have good leg room, though the body is purposely kept short, and the front seats are more commodious than those at the rear, while, as the body has but two doors, one on the near side of the driving compartment and one on the off side for the rear, the places where usually there are other doors are used to accommodate the spare wheels.

A Fascinating Car.

Speaking generally, the latest Lancia sporting model is comfortable, well fitted out, and possesses that sense of power which is best realised when, in obedience to a movement of the throttle, the seat presses hard upon one's back as the powerful car rapidly gathers way. Naturally, one expects a good deal for the price, which, inflated by the import duty, is £1,550, but, even so, the car grows upon one with almost every mile, even as a few miles brings a general feeling of being one with the machine and able to make it do just what is desired.

An open-bodied touring example of the 1922 28–80 hp Lancia.

THE AUTOCAR, May 15th, 1920.

Luxurious Road Travel.

This superb vehicle has just been completed to the order of a well-known racehorse owner. On a 1½ ton Lancia commercial chassis, Messrs. The London Improved Motor Coachbuilders', Ltd., 149, Lupus Street, London, S.W., have built a special interior drive saloon, and the passenger compartment has, in addition to the usual back seat for three, four armchairs and a card-table. When not in use the card-table folds up and fits into a well under the floor-boards. Even with the table in place there is plenty of leg-room for all seven passengers in the interior, which is trimmed in grey Bedford cord. The driver's compartment seats three abreast and is finished in dark blue leather. The proportions of the body are particularly good, and on first glancing at the photographs one may not appreciate the enormous size of this luxurious vehicle.

THE AUTOCAR, January 15th, 1921.

COVERED COACHWORK.

Designs in which Quiet Good Taste, Comfort, and Elegance are Blended.

Mr. R. E. Donkin, of Cottingham, Hull, is the owner of this substantial and cosy Lancia saloon. Observe the luxurious occasional chairs and the neat stowage of the spare wheels.

(George Maddox, Hartford Road, Huntingdon.)

NOVEL LANCIA LIGHT CAR.

Remarkable Power Obtained from V-Type Four-cylinder Engine. Efficient Suspension and High Road Speed.

PRESSED STEEL CONSTRUCTION.

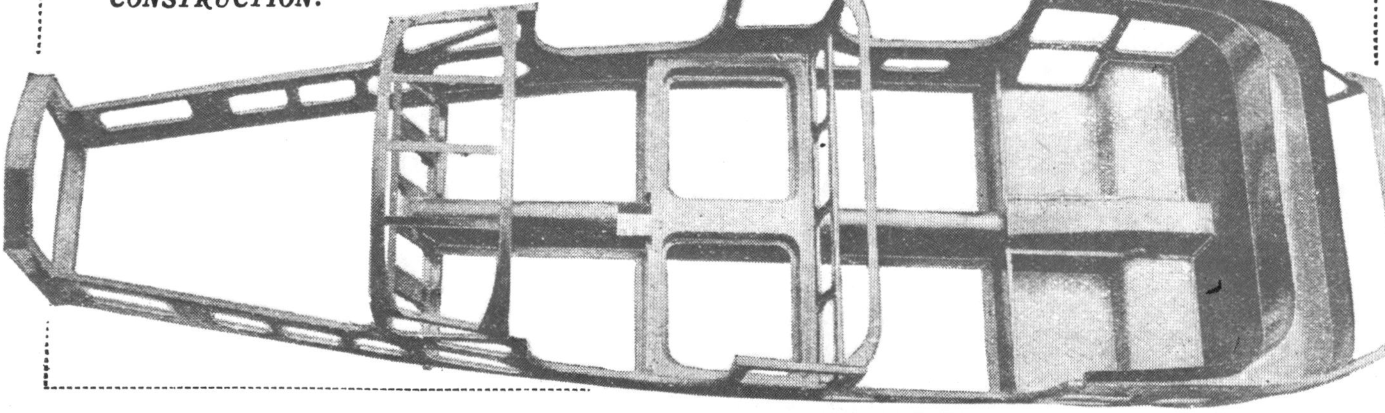

Extremely clever pressed steel work forms the basis of the new Lancia, the frame and foundation for the body being built up as a single unit. The engine is mounted on two steel tubes (not shown) running from the base of the two main dashboard struts to the front cross member at the base of the radiator, while the whole chassis is stiffened by the arched pressing running from the dashboard to the back of the rear seats. This tunnel accommodates the propeller-shaft.

IN the last analysis all the virtue of any car lies in the one word "performance." Admitting this, the new model just produced by the Lancia Company, of Turin, after several years of research work, is one of exceptionally high value. With a 13.9 h.p. four-cylinder engine only very slightly exceeding two-litres piston displacement—the bore and stroke are 75×120 mm. (2,120 c.c.)—more than 45 h.p. are available; a very commodious four-passenger body is provided, for the wheelbase is 10ft. 2in. and the track 3ft. 7in.; the total weight with radiator and tanks filled, spare wheels, tools, etc., does not exceed 15 cwt.; the speed on the level is guaranteed by the makers to be 70 to 75 m.p.h.; petrol consumption is 26 miles to the gallon; and, as we have experienced, the car holds the road in an extraordinarily efficient manner.

It is doubtful if there is any car on the market of this seating capacity, speed and road ability which approaches the low weight of the Lancia. This weight reduction has not been obtained by the use of costly alloy steels and lacework construction, but by a radical change in design. This new production has been termed a frameless car, and, although the expression is somewhat confusing, it is really quite accurate.

Lancia builds the carcase of a special type all-metal body; he covers this carcase with thin sheet steel; he garnishes it internally with leather and fits into it movable seats and back rests; inside the housing forming a forward portion of this rigid carcase he fits the radiator; immediately behind it, on a couple of steel tubes which in ordinary automobile parlance we would call a subframe (in reality there cannot be a subframe when there is no main frame), he mounts an unusually compact engine and gear box; at the rear he attaches a live axle by means of springs and shackles to the carcase; power plant and axle are united by a propeller-shaft, with universal joints; and a car is produced minus frame members and without a removable body bolted on to them.

In the case of an unusual construction such as this, illustrations are more eloquent than words; and we show the carcase laid on its left-hand side, and again after the sheet metal panelling has been added. This carcase is made of 2 mm. steel pressings riveted and welded together. As is evident, there are no heavy body stills, and the entire structure, while possessing great strength, has the advantage of being very much lighter than a normal type body built in the usual way of wood and metal.

It will be noticed that there is a central tunnel for the propeller-shaft and a transverse tunnel for the rear axle. This central tunnel, while having the slight disadvantage of dividing the lower part of the

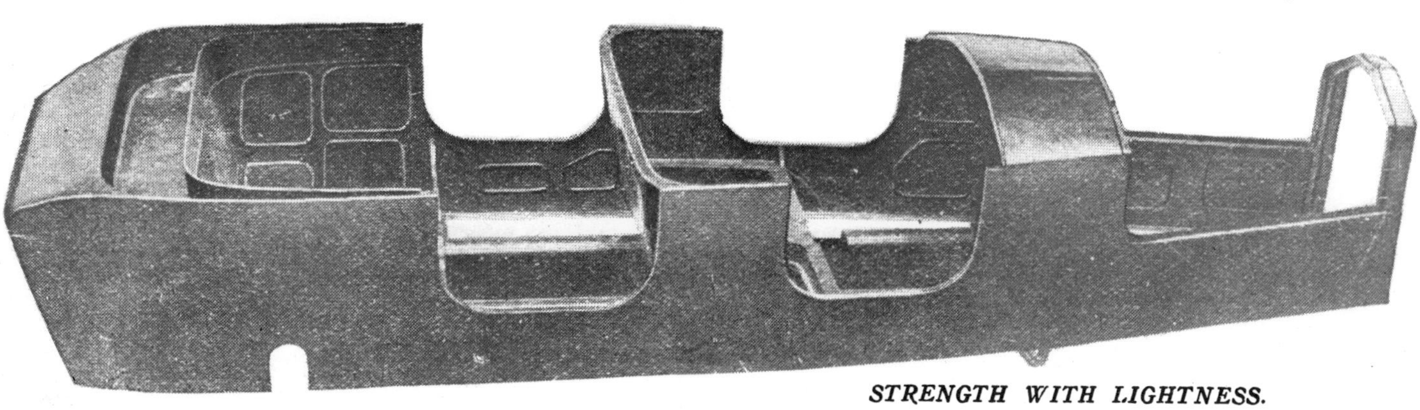

STRENGTH WITH LIGHTNESS.

After the skeleton chassis has been built up the body is formed by the attachment of metal panelling to the pressed steel foundation.

body into two parts, serves to give it strength and enables the centre of gravity to be brought much lower than would be otherwise possible. On the touring model the clearance is 7⅘in., while the height from the ground to the top of the scuttle dash is 43in., and to the top of the radiator about 40in. It is probably largely owing to this exceptionally low centre of gravity that the car literally clings to the road. As a demonstration, the writer was taken over the most twisty mountain road to be found within thirty miles of Turin. When the driver took the turns, both uphill and downhill, at the highest possible speed, the writer almost instinctively placed his arm around the back of the front seat, but it was soon realised that the absence of swing at the rear end was so complete that one could sit with folded arms even when travelling fast on a corkscrew road, without any tendency to be thrown from side to side. While the general suspension is good, the steadiness of the car on the road at high speeds is really remarkable.

Although the cylinders are set V-fashion, the engine is narrow. A highly efficient wooden air screw is employed.

The position of the engine is clearly shown in the illustration of the body, but there is nothing to indicate how it is attached. From the dashboard frame to the front cross piece forming the base of the radiator two steel tubes are fitted, and on these the engine rests.

Like the body, the four-cylinder engine is quite special. It is a V type with the cylinders set at the very small angle of 20 degrees, each two forming a pair, staggered in relation one to the other. In general design it is similar to the eight-cylinder Lancia which has been on the market for about a year. The advantage of this construction is compactness and low weight; the overall length of the cylinder block is 16½in., and the total length, including fan and flywheel, 22in. It is hardly necessary to say that it is impossible to get down to such dimensions with the usual "line ahead" construction.

It would not be quite correct to describe the engine as one having aluminium cylinders with liners, for in reality it has iron cylinders around which the aluminium jacket and crank case is cast. The iron cylinders are cast with a flange on the upper end of the barrel, and are roughly machined before being set in the mould for the aluminium to be cast around them. There is the usual type of copper and asbestos joint between the cylinder block and the detachable head, but there is contact of cast-iron cylinder barrel against cast-iron cylinder head.

The valves are mounted vertically in the cylinder head, and are operated by an overhead camshaft which receives its movement from a vertical shaft within the cylinder casting and by helical gears. When the cylinder head is detached, the upper portion of the vertical shaft comes away, but not the helical gears.

Although a V-type engine, the staggering of the cylinders avoids the use of forked connecting rods. The rods, which are tubular, have white metal split bearings, with a crank pin for each, while the crank-

THE LANCIA POWER UNIT.

The carburetter is mounted at the rear of the block and receives the benefit of the heat from the exhaust pipe. The skew gear driving the overhead camshaft, the disposition of the electric generator and distributer, and the extremely accessible position of the water pump, driven in the same line as the generator, are other features of this attractive power unit.

shaft has circular webs, and is carried in three plain bearings. The pistons are die cast aluminium alloy with plenty of metal in the heads, but with very thin skirts. Three steel compression rings only 2 mm. in depth are used, and in addition there are a couple of special scraper rings designed with no thought of assisting compression, but of preventing excess oil reaching the combustion chamber. Double springs are fitted on the valves. The rocker arms have rollers in contact with the cams, and at the opposite end a hardened adjustable stud for contact with the valve stem cap.

Engine and Transmission.

On the right-hand side of the engine there is nothing but the combined oil filter and breather; on the opposite side is the water pump and the Bosch combined generator and distributer. A wooden aeroplane type propeller, belt driven, and running on a ball bearing shaft, assists in cooling the engine. Lubrication is under pressure, with all the oil in the crank case. The carburetter, a latest type Zenith, is in the unusual position at the rear of the cylinder block, within the fork of the two exhaust leads. The exhaust pipe is swung to the left and carried away to the rear in the usual manner. The Lancia engineers state the horse-power of the engine as 45; in reality the normal type runs up to 48 h.p. at 3,000 revolutions, and it appears quite possible to get 50 h.p. from this compact little power plant.

The unconventional method of suspension provides an extremely distinctive front appearance to the new Lancia.

Immediately behind the engine, and carried on the same pair of tubes, is an exceedingly small three-speed gear box. The gear set is not a unit with the engine, but is mounted very closely to it, and both engine and gear box are contained under the bonnet. After the water connections have been broken, only four bolts have to be withdrawn to lift the engine out of the frame, and the gear box is removed in the same way after withdrawing two bolts.

The part of the car which adheres most closely to standard practice is the rear axle, which is built up of a central housing and steel tubes, and contains a differential and spiral bevel gears. Semi-elliptic springs are employed, and are made use of to take both the drive and the torque. The propeller-shaft is of the open type, being provided with two universal joints.

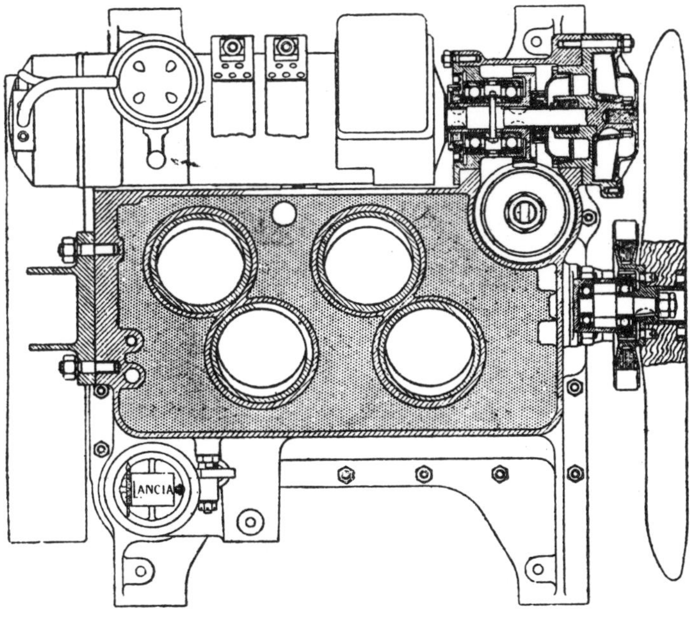

The arrangement of the staggered cylinders which are set in a narrow V is apparent from this line drawing.

At the front there are no visible springs, and nothing approaching the usual type of front axle. Suspension is provided by a system of coil springs and a hydraulic shock absorber, the cylinder of which constitutes the housing for the springs. The springs work under the very best conditions, being inside a dustproof and oil-tight casing, and the big area available has made it possible to produce a hydraulic shock absorber of a very effective nature.

What might be termed the front axle is a 35 mm steel tube with lugs enabling it to be bolted to the base of the radiator housing, but which in reality only forms part of a triangular structure, the other members of which are a tube going from the top of the open jaw type steering head to the top of the radiator housing, and a tube of similar diameter going from the bottom of the steering head to a point on the body just at the rear of the bonnet. The front wheels are carried on double radial ball bearings, with double-thrust bearings between them. With a car of this low weight and high-speed ability, it is necessary to take advantage of the total adherence for braking. One of the features of the front wheel brakes is that the drums are inside the road wheels, the centre of the brake band being less than half an inch out of the centre of a vertical line passing through the tyre. The pedal operates all four brakes, while the lever in the centre controls the rear wheel brakes only. The brake shoes are of aluminium, with Ferodo lining. A detail, but one having its importance to the owner, is that the brake camshafts have ball bearings, experience having shown that this part is never lubricated, and that plain bushings may seize as a result of neglect.

Finish.

The finish of the body follows more or less normal lines. The four doors are, of course, separate attachments. The body is upholstered in the usual way, except that the upholstery is detachable, while the floor boards are fixed permanently in position, for there is nothing under them to need attention. A polished wood instrument board is fitted under the scuttle dash. Behind the rear seats a well is provided for the folding hood, and behind this is a locker, the full width and height of the body, to which access is obtained by a hinged rear panel. This locker carries the petrol tank and a trunk for personal effects, the trunk being furnished with the car.

On the rear of this hinged panel is a carrier for a couple of spare wire wheels fitted with 765 × 105 mm. tyres. The tyres are carried externally as a matter of convenience, but it is not necessary to remove the wheels from the carrier when the trunk compartment has to be opened. In addition to the open touring model, the new Lancia is also built with a closed body.

ON THE ROAD WITH THE 13·9 h.p. LANCIA.

A Trial Run on a Most Unconventional Chassis which has just arrived in this country, and which Possesses an Exceptional Performance.

DATA FOR THE DRIVER.

- 13·9 h.p., four cylinders, 75×120 mm. (2,120 c.c.). Tax, £14. Magneto ignition.
- Tested weight of complete car, less passengers, 21 cwt.
- Weight per c.c., 1·1 lb.
- Gear ratios: 11·6, 6·65, and 4·16 to 1.
- Straight bevel final drive.
- Semi-elliptic rear and coil front suspension.
- 375×105 mm. tyres on detachable wire wheels.
- Wheelbase, 10 ft. 2 in. Track, 4 ft. 5½ in. Price £625.

A feature of the Lancia is its very low build which gives it a speedy appearance.

WHEN the latest Lancia chassis appeared at the Paris Salon it was at once apparent that it was entirely unconventional as regards not only the actual components but also the main layout of the parts and the design generally. This car had been subjected to a great deal of experimental work, and had been on the road for some years before it was officially included in the Lancia programme. The idea underlying so novel a design was to obtain a strong rigid chassis and body, which should at the same time be light and capable of a performance that would be something out of the ordinary.

Our readers may remember that the engine has four cylinders of 75 x 120 mm., and that, though the cylinders are, to outward appearances, vertical, they are, in actual fact, arranged as a V, while the frame and body (except the panels) constitute a unit, the whole being formed from pressings bolted or welded together. Coil springs are used for what is usually the front axle, though in this case the axle is really a part of the frame, and the wheels are sprung independently. The brake drums are so deeply housed in the wheel hubs that they are almost invisible, and all four wheels have brakes.

Owing to the design, the car is extremely low, especially when used as an open four-seater. There is, however a detachable top, which can be supplied for converting the car into a saloon if necessary.

Four wheel brakes, which prove remarkably efficient, and the unusual front axle and suspension system are other prominent features of an unorthodox design.

On the Road with the 13.9 h.p. Lancia.

A car as unconventional as this must have some exceptional points to justify its existence, a mere departure from standard lines not being in itself sufficient or desirable. A trial run is thus particularly interesting.

After taking over the wheel, and as soon as one moves off, the Lancia gives that curious feeling which very few cars have, and which makes the driver thoroughly at home at once. The steering is exceptional, giving absolute certainty without effort—a very valuable attribute. Unlike some other steering gears, it possesses an ease of control which remains undisturbed whatever may be the speed of the car, for at 70 m.p.h. the Lancia can be held easily with one hand, and at road speed its corner work is magnificent. The gear change presents no difficulties, though at first it is not easy to realise that so short a lever can possibly be the gear control, while the absence of a clutch stop, though no disadvantage for touring, is noticeable if the car is handled racing fashion. It might be expected that a V engine would be harsher than one of normal design, yet few engines are smoother, and it can attain a crankshaft speed well above average.

An Excellent Suspension.

With an almost perfect suspension, the car, when driven at ordinary speeds, gives no indication of the state of the road surface, good, bad, and indifferent surfaces being alike immaterial; the springs can deal with quite alarming obstacles, as was proved when we drove deliberately over a series of deep pot-holes and ruts and on the grass border at the side of the road at a speed of 30 m.p.h. One realises from tests with coil suspension how much can be gained from using this type of spring, but before handling the Lancia it was difficult to realise that the combination of coil and leaf suspension could give such good results and yet keep the car steady on corners. It is a direct outcome of this suspension that the car is extremely comfortable, both in the front and in the back seats.

The result of reducing the weight carried by the engine is amply apparent, for the car has a remarkable liveliness, and its sustained speed is quite out of the common. Over a measured mile, for example, with three passengers on board and a stiff adverse wind, the average speed was 66.42 m.p.h., which is extremely good and better than that of many other larger cars. During this time the car was travelling at over 70 m.p.h. for a while, and it is possible that when the carburetter is exactly right the average speed would be 70. On Brooklands hill, from a standing start, the average speed was 17.40 m.p.h., as against the 12 m.p.h. usual for cars of this class.

The Advantages of Power.

Such a great reserve of power is of the utmost value, as it is possible to carry the full load at 20 m.p.h., with no throttle to speak of, and at higher speeds with extremely little. In this the Lancia is exactly like very much larger cars. To those drivers who are enthusiastic, the machine will reveal quite unsuspected powers and give that wonderful feeling of high speed without effort which has to be experienced to be believed. A drop to second gear will send the car up long hills very fast, yet with throttle in reserve. On the other hand, the same hill can be climbed slowly, and on the level the car can run at 5 m.p.h. on top gear and pick up without difficulty.

Another feature of the chassis, which is invaluable to those who understand how to use it, is the brake system, which allows a hitherto unthought-of range of speed in perfect safety. In fact, the more one handles a good four-wheel brake set, the more certain does it become that this is the system of the future. It is practically impossible to give an accurate idea of the brake power, but the Lancia can be allowed to run at 12 m.p.h. down a 1 in 4 gradient, and will then stop in its own length *plus* 2ft. Moreover, the brakes are absolutely decided; they do not interfere with the steering on corners, and do not lock the wheels unless the driver wishes it.

As regards the general care of the chassis, the various adjustments to the engine can be effected easily, while there is an oil filler of ample size. The brakes have a good adjusting mechanism, the batteries are easy to get at, there is an elaborate tool kit, and ample space for luggage in a special boot at the rear of the car. The hood is concealed, the whole switchboard can be locked and rendered unusable, while the upholstery is very good.

A large compartment at the rear of the back seats provides accommodation for tools and spares and for a large suit case, which forms part of the equipment, in the upper portion. The petrol tank is below the suit case. The spare wheel is carried on the hinged door of this compartment, and the hood is enclosed.

Taken as a whole, the design is entirely justified, and the car is altogether exceptional in its performance.

The agents in this country, The Curtis Automobile Co., Ltd., 18, Berkeley Street, London, W.1, state that the weight of the chassis is 20 cwt., and inform us that in the near future a modified and improved version of the saloon top which was shown at Olympia will be available.

Front wheel brakes, coil spring suspension and steering of the 13.9hp Lancia.

THE LANCIA ON TEST.

A Long Run with One of the most Unconventional of Cars, and some Hints on its Running.

To anyone who drives many different cars it soon becomes apparent that in one or two cases a machine possesses something akin to what in a human is termed a soul. How otherwise is it that one can sit down at the wheel, and at once feel in sympathy with the car, at once know that it will do exactly what one wants it to do? Such a car, undoubtedly, is the Lancia Lambda

Speed and Controllability.

Straightway is one intrigued by its appearance, since body and chassis are one, and there are no dumb irons in front, only the coil springs and frame of the suspension. Handsome it may not be, but, like many things unusual, it grows on one as time passes. Being a thoroughly unconventional car it is fitting that it should have a most unusual performance. On a long straight road the maximum speed by speedometer would be about 70 m.p.h. Acceleration, together with a set of excellent brakes, enables one to average a surprising speed if need be, and to demonstrate this it may be mentioned that the car can be driven at 30 m.p.h. on a wet, slippery surface to where four roads cross. In three seconds the speed can be reduced to 10 m.p.h., six seconds afterwards, using second speed, 30 m.p.h. is attained once more. This entails neither skid nor side-slip, nor exceptional skill in handling. Should it be necessary to do so an average of over 30 m.p.h. can be kept up in perfect safety. The engine is very smooth, has a most healthy power of "revving" on second, and a slight peculiarity of exhaust note due to the V set of the cylinders. Hills of 1 in 8 or 1 in 10 gradient are best tackled on second, yet top will suffice for long and reasonably steep gradients, as, for example, from Swiss Cottage up Fitzjohn's Avenue to Hampstead Heath, and that with due respect to the 10 m.p.h. limit near the top of the climb.

DATA FOR THE DRIVER.

14–60 h.p., four cylinders, 75 × 120 mm. (2,120 c.c.). Tax £14.
Tested weight of complete car, less passengers, 22 cwt. 2 qrs. 14 lb.
Gear ratios : 4·16, 6·65 and 11·6 to 1.
Brakes on all four wheels.
Spiral bevel final drive.
Spiral front and semi-elliptic rear springs.
Detachable wire wheels with 765 × 105 mm. tyres.
Wheelbase, 10 ft. 2 in. Track, 4 ft. 4⅜ in.
Fuel consumption, 22 to 26 m.p.g. Tank capacity, 14 galls.
Price, £725.

Road Holding Qualities.

But it is more than the engine that makes the car fascinating. The steering is exceptional, inclined, on the particular car tested, which had been in use for a considerable time, to develop slight wheel wobble at certain speeds, but beautifully decisive at high speed and always light to handle with a good automatic return. It would be difficult to improve the driving position, the gear change is easy, and becomingly sensitive, though a clutch stop is needed for good changing up, and it takes time to make the back, through the gate, forward, movement from first to second automatic. Best of all, the Lancia holds to the road at any speed. Where it is desired to place it there it will go, and never does the driver feel a moment's uncertainty. For this reason the car was tried on really slippery asphalt, and when made to side-slip could be controlled to an inch. Some wheel spin there is, inevitably, in such circumstances, especially if the rear seats are unoccupied.

Exceedingly powerful brakes are expected on a car of this nature, nor will the purchaser be disappointed, and in the whole 240 miles which the car was driven never once was it possible to provoke a side-slip with the brakes only, though they were used on purpose at full power on wet tar, wood, macadam, and asphalt, wet in this case meaning really slippery. On four occasions the car slid forward, even then not far, and it was steerable in each instance. From the feel of the wheel it is impossible to tell whether the brakes are on or off, and, be it remembered, they were not used touring fashion, but hard on.

Another marked good feature is the suspension, which enables the Lancia to travel a good 10 m.p.h. faster than many other fast cars on really bad roads. For demonstration, one wheel was taken over a four-inch kerb once, and over a tree root another time, on both occasions at 30 m.p.h. The shock to the wheel was felt, but the body scarcely moved. All four seats are comfortable, dry when the hood is up, and provide a natural position. It would be better if the wings were modified; at present they look well, but do not guard against mud effectively when a very strong head or side wind is blowing on a really wet day.

Last, but not least, an exceptionally small turning circle allows the car to run round in an ordinary main road on one lock, a very great advantage which is demonstrated even better if it is necessary to manœuvre in a garage entailing a somewhat complicated series of movements.

FORE AND AFT FEATURES.

***(Top)** Each front wheel being sprung independently, it is possible to surmount even large obstacles without affecting the body. In the photograph the tie-rod between the two stub axles shows the height to which one wheel has mounted, and the lower tube of the frame gives the inclination of the body, which has scarcely moved from the horizontal.*

***(Bottom)** In the tail of the car is the petrol tank and a large felt-lined compartment for luggage. This compartment is accessible when the tail itself is unclipped and lowered.*

In detail, as in general, the car is more than usually interesting. Access to the clutch and gear box is obtained by lifting the bonnet, and all three main components can be withdrawn from above after dropping the under-shield to get at some of the bolts. Vacuum Arctic oil in winter, and A in summer, suit the engine, C or BB is used for the gear box and axle. No fan belt adjustment has been found necessary. The clutch withdrawal ball races should be well lubricated. On one side of the crank case is a pointer used when timing the engine from marks on the flywheel, the correct setting, when No. 1 cylinder is on top dead centre, being assured by a pin in the camshaft drive which registers with a slot in the vertical shaft. Rocker clearance with the engine hot should be .002in.

A carburetter setting of 24 choke, 100 main, 100 compensator suits the engine best, but there is one small flat spot in very cold weather. With this setting the engine can be started at once by the starting motor on a cold morning. For slow running the ignition should be full retard, and its setting is 38° at full advance.

For brake adjustment both axles should be jacked. The two cables for the front brakes, though compensated, have separate adjustments where the cables end inside the bonnet. First unlock the smaller nuts, then the larger one at the jaw, and then turn the screwed body. For the rear brake the cable clips under the car must be released, and the cables pulled up. The rear brakes are set to engage first, then the front brakes.

It is necessary to fit the peg on the front seat cushions into a hole in the seat frame, otherwise the cushion may push the gear lever into neutral. Facilities are provided for stowing the hood conveniently in a special recess provided. The adjustment of the hood is good.

Inside the luggage compartment is the petrol tank and its filler cap, for which there is a special spanner. The vent pipe is at the back, and should not be muffled by parcels, while the clips holding the tail in place have each little locking levers which are important. On a straightaway run, even at speed, the car will average 28 m.p.g., but in town more fuel is consumed. We are informed by the concessionaires, Curtis Automobile Co., Ltd., 18, Berkeley Street, London, W.1, that these cars are now being delivered in quantities.

A FOUR-SPEED LANCIA— —LAMBDA.

New Model of the Famous Italian Car Now Available either as a Two- or Four-seater.

The Lancia Lambda is now obtainable as a smart and speedy two-seater.

THE Lambda type Lancia is in many respects unconventional, having a frame as part of the body, an engine with cylinders arranged in a very sharp V, and coil spring suspension for the front axle. Moreover, the open four-seater can be converted to a saloon by the addition of a special top which can be fitted in a comparatively short time.

The car has always had an excellent performance, even with three speeds, but the addition of a fourth gear to the latest model has made a considerable difference, as may be readily imagined.

Speed on Hills ; Improved Accelleration.

Maximum on top remains the same, 74 m.p.h., but on third the car will run up to 51 m.p.h., on second 38 m.p.h., and on first 23.75 m.p.h., while on a long hill such as Wrotham, on the London-Folkestone Road, which has a gradient of one in ten to one in eleven, the car is five miles an hour faster than it was before, and gives a most exhilarating sense of speed and power. Second is also improved and the speed of the car on that gear increased.

As regards acceleration, it takes 14 seconds to attain 30 m.p.h. on top gear from a steady 10 m.p.h., and 8 seconds on first with three speeds, whereas with the additional gear the increase of speed is effected in 6⅘ seconds on second gear and 8⅖ seconds on third, which very considerably increases the total acceleration when the gears are used in quick succession. The gear change is easier than that of the three-speed type, and much quicker to operate.

There have been one or two minor chassis changes, the steering arm on the front axle being increased in length and the brackets holding the shackles for the rear springs considerably strengthened, but these do not make much difference from the driver's point of view, since the car always had very good steering and excellent suspension.

A New Two-seater Model.

As a matter of interest the brakes of this particular car were tested, and from 40 m.p.h. the Lancia was stopped in 63 feet, showing that the extreme brake power noticeable in the first cars is being maintained.

Incidentally, a two-seater model has now been introduced, a number of these having been received by the concessionaires, Curtis Automobile Co., Ltd., Curtis Buildings, Abbey Road, Park Royal, N.W.10, the price of the new four-speed model with either four- or two-seated coachwork being £625.

Laid bare: the chassis and basic running gear of the four-seater Lancia Lambda.

LANCIA LAMBDA DEVELOPMENTS.

A Six-seater Touring Model with Lengthened Wheelbase and Many Detail Refinements Now Available.

With a longer wheelbase the rear compartment of the latest Lancia is sufficiently roomy to take four passengers, two being accommodated on occasional seats which can be folded up when not in use. The low, rakish lines of the car form a striking contrast to the big Lanchester saloon beside it.

THE advent of a six-seater Lancia Lambda is an interesting development in the progress of one of the most unconventional chassis to attain success.

The original car was a four-seater, and Signor Lancia, wishing to make a 2-litre car with an exceptionally light yet rigid chassis, constructed the body and frame in one. At the same time he designed the engine with its cylinders set V-wise at a slight angle, making the crank case and cylinder block so short that the gear box is under the bonnet and thus extraordinarily accessible. Furthermore, coil spring suspension was adopted for the front axle.

Accommodation for Six.

The latest car is practically the same as its forerunners, but two roomy seats can be unfolded from the rear panel of the front seat, and give accommodation for additional passengers, the result being a six-seater with comfortable room for everybody. At the same time the steering has been revised and, of course, the frame has had to be lengthened to take the body.

The performance of the new model is almost equal to that of the four-seater, though it was a little difficult to judge definitely, as the car we tested was the first of its series and several points had already been marked for improvement. It would appear that a typical machine of this series may be about 3 m.p.h. slower, if anything, than the four-seater, and the four-seater's maximum is 74 m.p.h. On the gears the same maximum speeds are available, 50 m.p.h. on third, 38 m.p.h. on second, and 24 m.p.h. on first. In general touring, however, it pays to change up when 30 m.p.h. has been reached on second, and 40 m.p.h. on third gears, as beyond those speeds the engine is being needlessly revved, which is no good for any engine and should not be indulged in.

DATA FOR THE DRIVER.

13·9 h.p., four cylinders, 75 × 120 mm. (2,120 c.c.), overhead valves and camshaft. Tax, £14.
Tested weight of complete car, less passengers, 2½ cwt.
Weight per c.c., 1·2 lb.
Gear ratios: 13·3, 7·9, 6·02 and 4·16 to 1.
Spiral bevel final drive.
Spiral front and half-elliptic rear springs.
775 × 145 mm. tyres on detachable wire wheels.
Brakes on all four wheels.
Wheelbase, 11ft. 2¼in. Track, 4ft. 8¼in.
Fuel consumption, 22-26 m.p.g. Tank capacity, 15 gallons.
Price, £695, with six-seater body.

The new steering is extremely satisfactory, and one most interesting feature is that at no point in the car's range of speed is there any wheel flap or unsteadiness of the front wheels. Since the new Lancia has low pressure tyres it would seem that the special design of stub axle has something to do with the elimination of a defect apparent in quite a number of cars. It would be very difficult to say that low pressure tyres really make the car much more comfortable. That they must have an effect may be granted, but the springing of the car is so good that the added effect of the tyres is not readily appreciable. Certainly the steering is not heavier with balloons. Very rough roads may be traversed at 30-40 m.p.h. without the body being disturbed at all, which gives a good idea of the excellence of the springs and tyres combined.

Effect of Four Speeds.

Four speeds, embodied in both models during the early part of this year, have had a great effect, and on a hill of about two miles in length with a section of about 1 in 5 the Lancia never fell below the legal limit, nor, by the way, did it show any signs of overheating, though this, after all, is only what is to be expected from an Italian car built to tackle Alpine passes. At first the four-speed gear box is a little tricky when changing up, but the driver soon becomes accustomed to the "feel" of the gears, and certainly this particular box seemed to be a little more difficult than the similar box on the four-seater which we tested previously.

The brakes are exceptionally good; they are every bit as powerful as those of the four-seater, which arrest the car in 63ft. from 40 m.p.h.—an exceedingly good figure—and there is not the slightest suggestion of the brakes interfering with the steering, handle the car how one will.

AN IMPROVED LANCIA LAMBDA.

ORIGINALITY IN CHASSIS DESIGN.

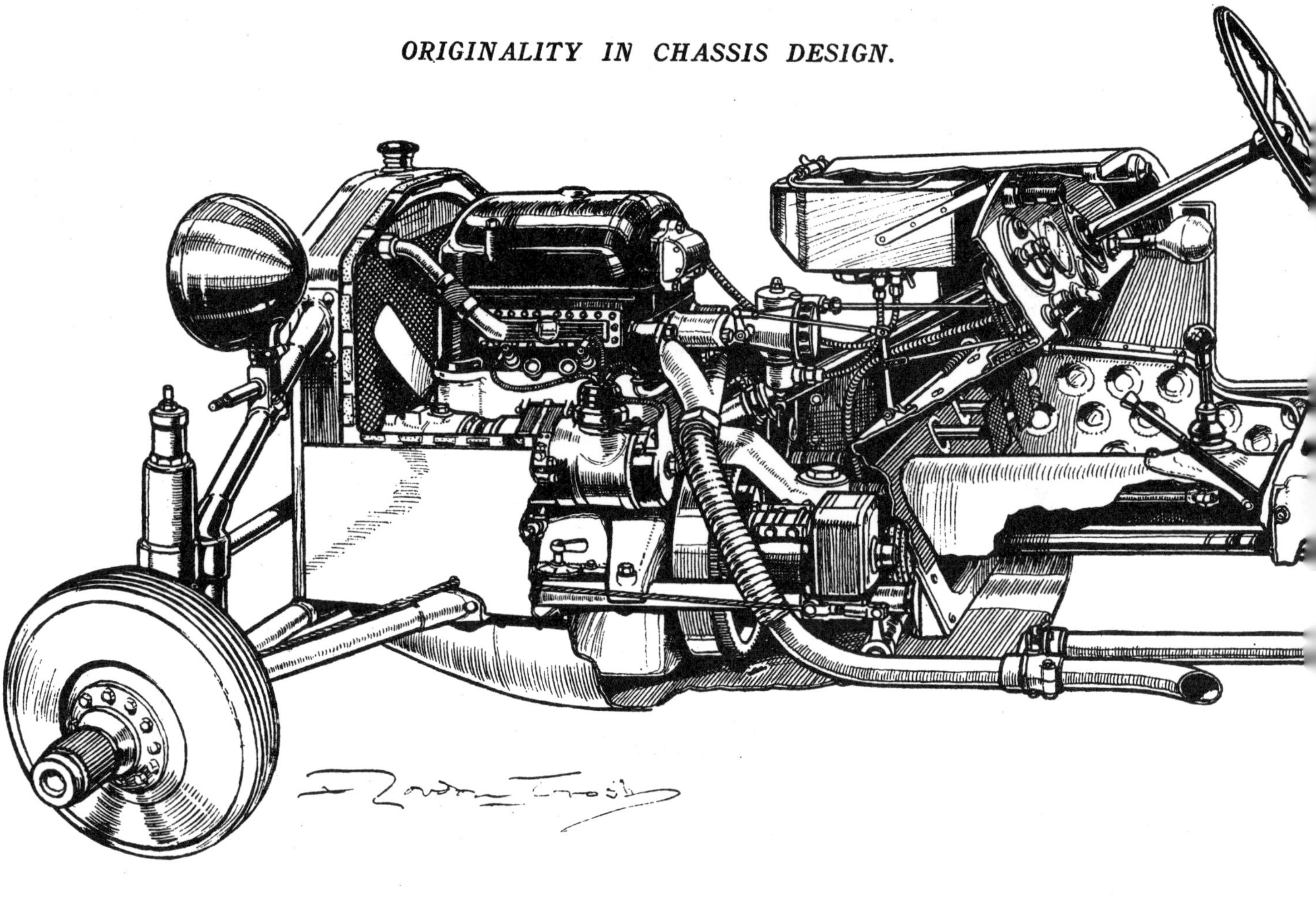

THE latest Lancia Lambda model differs considerably from its predecessors. The engine is still a V-type four-cylinder, an arrangement which allows the power unit to be remarkably compact and brings the gear box under the bonnet, but the bore is now 79 mm. and the stroke 120 mm., giving a capacity of 2,352 c.c. instead of 2,121 c.c.

The overhead valve gear of the Lancia Lambda. The camshaft is balanced by the provision of extra valve springs operated by special cams.

The increase has greatly benefited the car, as would be expected. The larger engine does its work with less effort, even though the chassis length has been increased, which entails a corresponding increase to the weight of the car generally. The new engine is smoother, the comparatively slight intermediate period having been eliminated entirely, so that there is no suspicion of rough running until the engine is at the limit of its useful range of revolutions on the intermediate gears.

This is due partly to the introduction of a camshaft balancing device, which consists of extra valve springs operated by a special cam on the shaft in such a manner that the torque and effort of the camshaft are maintained at a certain definite figure instead of fluctuating.

Improving the Mixture.

There are other minor changes. The carburetter ha[s] been provided with a pipe extending from the rear o[f] the cylinders, so that the instrument is free from th[e] exhaust pipe, it having been found in hot climates tha[t] the float chamber fuel tended to become unduly warm. Water pipes are now at the side, while the lubricating system has been revised and now comprises a supplementary, separate tank on the dashboard next to the vacuum feed tank. On the camshaft end is a pump which slowly augments the contents of the engine base sump from this auxiliary tank, the idea being that th[e]

The unconventional layout of the Lancia Lambda is clearly portrayed in this part-sectioned drawing, which indicates how by ingenious use of pressings, a light yet very rigid structure to carry the coachwork is obtained. The V-cast four-cylinder engine saves overall space to such an extent that the gear box is brought under the bonnet.

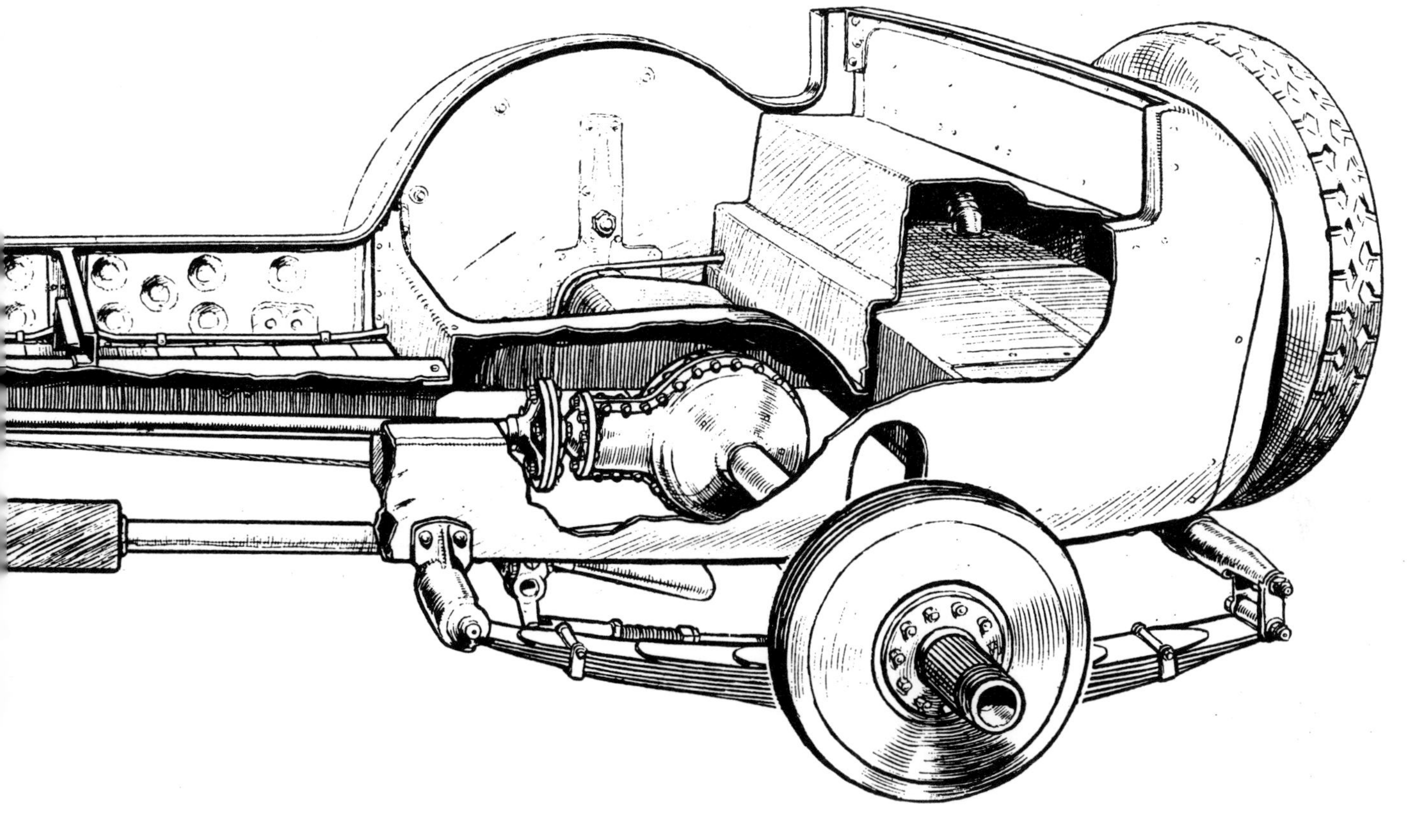

level of oil in the gear box is kept approximately constant and the driver need therefore fill only the auxiliary tank, which is higher and therefore more conveniently placed for the purpose. The feed of oil depends upon the speed of the camshaft, and as a consequence increases with the revs.

Driver and Car in Unity.

As was the case with previous models, the car is very pleasant to handle, the driver having that feeling that he has entire command of the machine almost in the first few yards. The steering is very light indeed, the ratio having been altered so that the wheel makes more turns from lock to lock than it did before. This has balanced, as it were, the low pressure tyres, which are now standard, and at no point in the car's range of speed is there any sign of wheel wobble or uncertainty in the steering. Furthermore, castor action automatically returns the wheels to the straight after a sharp corner.

The steering lock is admirable, and there must be relatively few vehicles of this length which can turn in so small a circle.

As before, the gears—speaking now, of course, of the four-speed gear box which was introduced last year—are easy to handle, and are an immense improvement over the three-speed box, greatly enhancing the range of the car's speed, especially in hilly country.

Something also of an improvement is noticeable in the brake gear, as the drums have been made very much stiffer, the shoes being more of racing type, and the effort on the pedal is slightly less than hitherto. While reversing, incidentally, the front wheels do not tend to swing over to full lock even at speed, an alteration that has been effected by the reduction in the steering gear ratio.

At the rear of the Lancia engine is the carburetter, which is connected to the engine by an extended inlet pipe.

Continental Cars for 1927.

Coil forward suspension is, as before, a feature of the car, and a very valuable one, since no vehicle rides better than the Lancia over really bad roads and yet adapts itself to the good, modern, smooth surface. From the trick point of view, it is almost possible to drive over a sharp kerb or obstruction without the effect being noticeable to the occupants of the car.

Another improvement which those familiar with the older type Lancia will notice at once is that the whole car is very considerably quieter. And to show what the increased size of engine can do, the acceleration from 10 to 30 m.p.h. on top takes no more than $12\frac{4}{5}$ seconds, while on third the elapsed time is $8\frac{2}{5}$ seconds, and on second 6 seconds. The speedometer, incidentally, is optimistic, a correction having to be made for this reason. A timed flat mile was covered at 69 m.p.h.

On the instrument board in front of the driver is a warning notice giving a maximum speed for each of the gears. This maximum speed seems to be well within the range in each instance, for the figure appears to be well within the engine's limit, as it can be exceeded quite easily without reaching the rough speed in the engine's running. Nevertheless, the makers have evidently placed the information there for a definite purpose, and it should be regarded seriously.

Next year's range of cars has been very greatly amplified, for a chassis can be supplied, as has been the case for the last few months of this year. In addition, there are now two models, short and long; the latter chassis costs £570—chassis being a relative term, since the wings, lamps, scuttle, dashboard, tail, valances, running boards, floor boards, and tool boxes are all included.

The Lancia Lambda chassis is obtainable in two lengths. (Top) The short-wheelbase type for open bodies and (bottom) the long for saloons.

It is now possible to obtain an English-built Weymann saloon at £795, a coachbuilt saloon at £850, and a four-five-seater at £725, all on the long chassis. On the short chassis there is a coupé at £795, a two-seater with dickey at £725, and the production Italian four-seater at £675. The Weymann saloons, by the way, are fitted with pneumatic upholstery.

NEW MODEL LANCIA "LAMBDA."

July 9th, 1926

Chassis Now Offered to which it is Possible to Fit Coachwork to the Customer's Choice.

The Lancia "Lambda" is now available as a chassis, which in this case includes wings, running boards and spare wheel. (Top) A commodious Weymann saloon can now be supplied on this chassis.

THE range of Lancia "Lambda" cars has been considerably increased by the provision of a chassis to which any type of coachwork can be fitted. The chassis and body of this car were originally one, but as a number of customers preferred to have special bodies a chassis is now supplied for this purpose. As a matter of fact, it is rather more than a chassis, as the photograph shows. The side members have been reinforced by deep, welded linings, each formed as a box girder of U section, the whole being remarkably stiff. The pressings which formed the front seat and sides of the body have been cut away, but the scuttle remains in position, and the stern portion of the chassis has a superstructure which contains the petrol tank and a large locker for luggage.

Both front and rear wings, the running boards, and spare wheel carrier are included with the chassis, and, therefore, a great deal of material which otherwise is supplied at the coachbuilder's charge is included in the price of £595, while, in regard to detail, the tool boxes, battery box, and all floor boards, together with the framings for the seats, are also provided. The only other modification to this model is that the front brakes have been increased considerably in size with a narrow shoe, like that of a racing car.

As a direct result of this innovation, a Weymann fabric saloon is now offered at £795. The saloon illustrated is one built in Italy, and is notable for its big window area and narrow uprights.

All the models have low pressure tyres, and these cars are handled by the Curtis Automobile Co., Ltd., from their showrooms at 18, Berkeley Street, Piccadilly, W.1. The works and large, specially equipped service station are at Curtis Buildings, Park Royal, N.W.10.

CARE and MAINTENANCE of the LANCIA LAMBDA

Part I.—Notes to Assist Owners of an Unconventionally Designed Italian Car to Keep it in the Best Possible Condition.

BEING unconventional in design the Lancia "Lambda" must be understood if repairs or adjustments are to be effected without waste of time and consequent needless and irritating expenditure of money.

Probably the first operation which will be necessary is to decarbonise the engine, for which operation the water should be drained from the radiator. It holds 4¾ gallons, and there is a drain tap in the pipe leading from the water pump. The water pipes from the head to the radiator should be uncoupled, the nut holding the exhaust pipe to the exhaust branch unscrewed, and the carburetter removed. Lift off the valve cover plate, exposing the valve and the upper camshaft driving gear, undo the nut in the centre of the skew gear and remove the skew gear from its shaft, first noting that on the teeth of the driving skew gear there are two timing marks, as shown in the accompanying sketch, indicating the teeth which fit over a single marked tooth of the driven skew gear. This is necessary in order to reassemble the timing gear correctly.

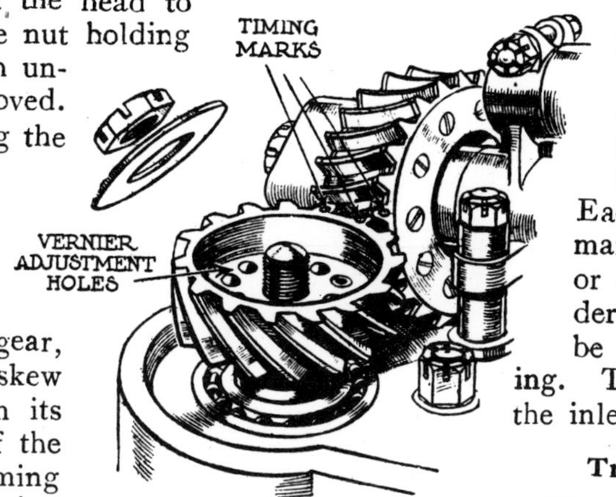

Timing marks to be found on the teeth of the overhead camshaft drive.

On the driven skew gear is a vernier coupling, and the gear flange has a series of small holes in one of which is a pin. The pin engages also with one of another series of holes in a flange below the gear. By removing the pin a fine adjustment of the gear can be obtained, the gear being locked when in the required position by replacing the pin.

Assuming that the whole of the valve gear has then to be removed, although this is not absolutely necessary for decarbonisation, the rocking lever axis pin can be driven out lengthwise, freeing all the rocking levers, the pedestal bearing nuts undone and the camshaft lifted out of place, leaving the valves and valve springs exposed. The hexagon nuts which hold the head to the cylinder can then be unscrewed and the head itself lifted off the engine, the utmost care being taken not to damage the gasket in the process.

Decarbonisation can then be carried out in the ordinary manner with scrapers, precautions being taken after the process to clean the head thoroughly, allowing no speck of dirt or carbon to remain. This is a most important part of the operation and should on no account be neglected.

If the valves have to be removed, their retaining collars must be unscrewed from the valve stems after the lock nuts have been released. Each valve has etched on its head marks showing whether it is an inlet or exhaust valve, and to which cylinder it belongs, but the valves should be kept in proper order notwithstanding. The etched marks are A 1 to 4 for the inlets, and S 1 to 4 for the exhausts.

Treatment of the Valve Guides.

If the valve stems have much play in their guides, which is unlikely, the guides can be driven out from the combustion space side and replaced. Broken valve springs should, of course, be renewed at once, as also any spring which shows obvious signs of weakness. Carborundum paste, obtainable at any garage, is the best medium for grinding in the valve seats, but particular pains must be taken to remove every trace of grinding paste from the valves, ports and guides after the operation is completed.

When the head is replaced the gasket should be handled carefully, smeared with goldsize and seated properly, it being particularly necessary to see that no dirt has got into the joint. Goldsize should also be smeared on the head itself, but before this operation is effected the small water passage holes in the head should be cleared of deposit. When the head is back in position the nuts should be tightened down so

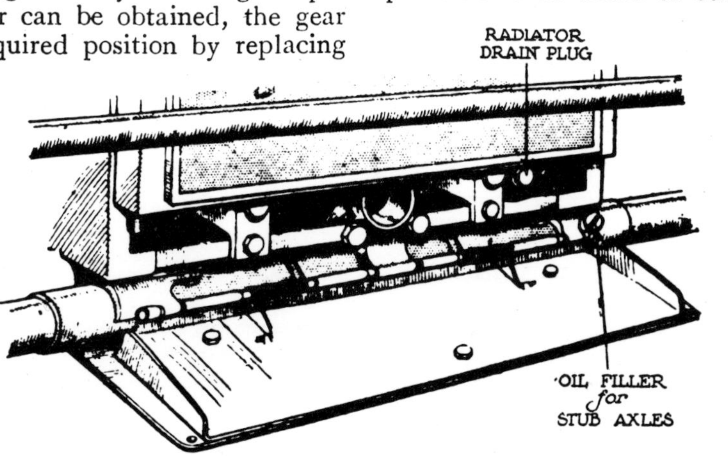

When the number plate is moved down in the manner shown, the oil filler plug for the stub axles is exposed, together with the radiator drain plug.

as to give an even pressure, and should be re-tightened after the car has had its first run on the road.

In re-assembling the valve gear be careful that the rockers are replaced in the correct order, and that the timing marks on the camshaft gears match. The timing can be checked because the top and bottom dead-centres are marked by a line with the cylinder numbers on the rim of the flywheel, the line being brought opposite to a special pointer provided on the end of the crank case. Note, by the way, that the full advance position of the magneto is also marked by an arrow and A on the flywheel rim, and this must not be confused with the top dead-centre mark. The valve timing is given in the accompanying diagram, the clearance between the end of the valve and the rocking lever being 0.002, to check which a feeler gauge should be used. If the clearance is not correct the lock nut holding the adjusting screw on the rocking lever should be released and the adjustment moved to correct the clearance, the actual clearance being checked when the lock nut has been tightened home once more. This operation should be carried out for each pair of valves with the corresponding piston at top dead-centre firing point.

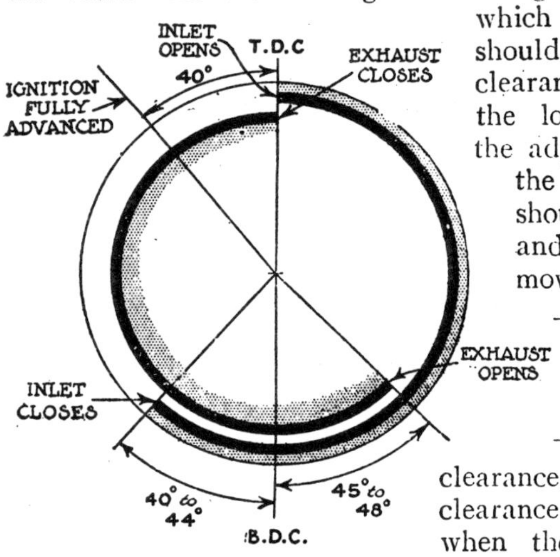

Valve timing diagram for the engine.

If the carburetter flange washer has been damaged it must be replaced, and it is well to have spare water-pipe joints handy in case of need, as these often become damaged when being removed.

It will be noticed that on the under face of the head there is a peg which must fit precisely in its orifice. The gasket itself cannot be replaced in an incorrect position. Should it be necessary to remove the pistons and connecting rods, the crankshaft will have to be removed first, as it is not possible to take out the pistons from underneath. The pistons are marked on the crown with the number of the cylinders to which they belong. The connecting rod bearings are marked also, and in later engines it is essential that the big-ends are replaced the right way round.

Removing the Engine.

The engine itself can be lifted from its tubular frame by disconnecting the gear box, and, of course, the engine piping and controls, undoing the four bolts on the engine arms, and lifting the unit clear away. Apart from this, however, the sump can be dropped from underneath if necessary, and bring with it the oil pump and oil filler tube. The oil pump is housed in a separate chamber and can be withdrawn when a cap underneath the crank case has been unscrewed. The main oil pipes are cast in the sump and cannot, therefore, be detached.

Care should be taken to make a good joint between the lip of the sump and that on the crank case, while the sump is located by two snugs, one in the crank case and one in the sump, which must fit exactly back into position. There is a gauze in the filler tube through which oil passes on the way to the sump, another at the bottom of the filler tube from which oil is sucked to the pump, and on the later models there is, in addition, a pressure filter made up of four columns of small brass discs in a special chamber on the outside of the crank case. If at any time the oil pressure falls below the 10 lb. which is set as standard, it is possible that these filters need cleaning, more especially the suction and pressure filters. The filters can be withdrawn when the filler cap is off, and the four units of the pressure filter are very accessible, when the nut in the centre of the pressure filter cap is unscrewed and the lid lifted off. Oil reaches the pressure filter chamber and then passes through the spaces between the brass discs to pipes in the centre, afterwards being led down a tube in the centre of the filter chamber to the bearings. All dirt will, therefore, be on the outside of the discs, and can be washed away with petrol.

Marking on the flywheel to show, by means of a corresponding indicator on the crank case, when the crankshaft is at top dead-centre.

Adjustment of Oil Pressure.

In one side of the filter chamber is a release valve underneath a plug with a screwdriver head. This consists of a small piston controlled by a spring, and should not be altered. It can, however, be removed if there is any question of the spring being broken. On the crank case, close to the filter chamber, is a pressure-adjusting valve and a sleeve which rises against the coil spring. A weak spring allows more oil to by-pass and therefore reduces the pressure from the pump, and a strong spring increases the pressure. Alteration, therefore, can be made by pulling out the spring a little, or by cutting off a coil if it is too strong.

The oil recommended for the engine is Vacuum A or BB. The sump holds $1\frac{1}{3}$ gallon, and its correct level is indicated by a rod at the side of the crank case, close to the filler. If the lubricant is too high it can be drained by means of a tap on the same side of the crank case, the tap also serving to empty the sump at need. With a new engine the oil should be drained away after a matter of 750 miles, the filters cleaned and fresh oil inserted.

The magneto is bolted to the casing of the dynamo and

CYLINDER ARRANGEMENT.

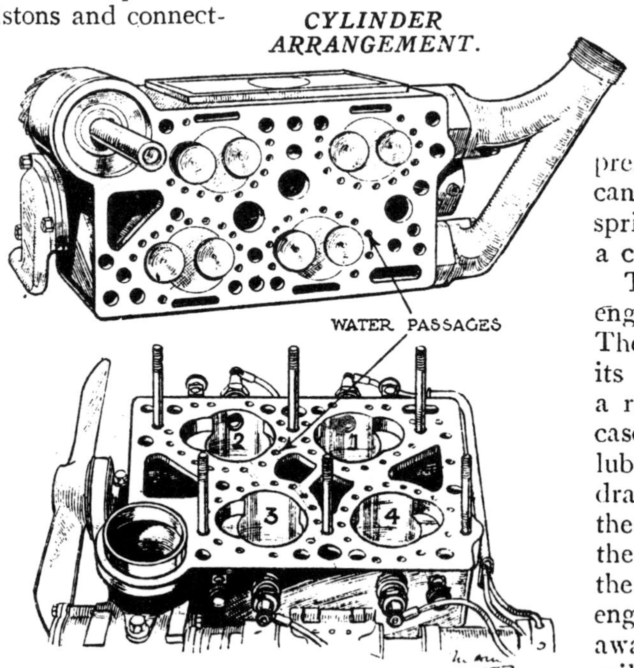

The cylinder block and head. The numbering of the cylinders is unusual and the small, circular holes allow water to pass from the jackets to the head.

driven through the armature shaft of the latter, which is in turn driven from the distribution gear through a flexible coupling. When timing the magneto, therefore, the mark A on the flywheel should be put opposite the indicator on the crank case, and the valve cover plate removed to see that the valves of No. 1 cylinder are both on their seats, with the rockers having their correct clearance. The ignition lever should then be placed at full advance, and the magneto contact points should just separate. If there is a small error this can be corrected by loosening the clamps holding the dynamo and partly rotating the dynamo, which carries with it the magneto, a movement of about 30 degrees. The correct position of the magneto is indicated by red arrows on the outer casing of the dynamo and on the dynamo platform.

Stops on the crank case limit the amount of rotation possible. A periscopic mirror is necessary to see the magneto points of the Marelli instrument. With the new type Bosch, removing the cover exposes the distributor and contact-breaker at once. If the magneto is being replaced care should be taken that the distributor arm is on the segment for No. one cylinder when setting the timing.

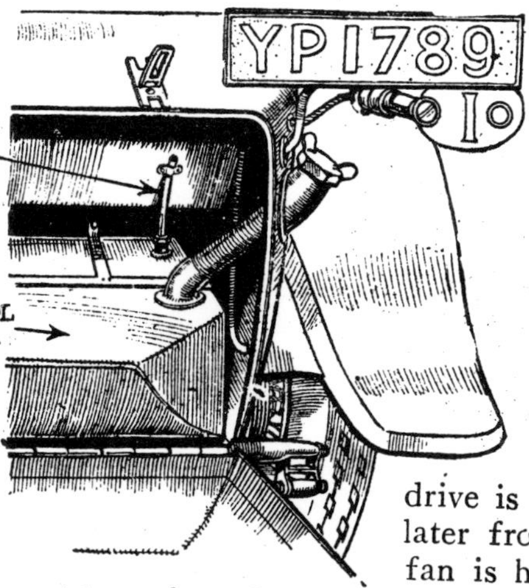

Vent pipe on the petrol tank, which must not be damaged when luggage is placed in the stern compartment.

Unlike most engines, the inlet pipe passes between the two cylinders, as the engine is really a V with two cylinders on one side and two cylinders almost opposite to them. This brings the carburettor at the back near the exhaust pipe. The setting usually recommended is 26 choke, 120 main, 105 compensator, 70 slow runner. The only jet likely to become blocked is the slow runner, which can be removed almost instantly and very easily cleaned, but care should be taken that the filter for the petrol is cleaned at frequent intervals, as a deposit of foreign matter may accumulate rapidly.

The vacuum fuel tank, by the way, has a cork float, though experience suggests that this is not affected, as might be expected, by benzole, and the only difficulty likely to be experienced at any time is the sticking of the valve in its guide, which is easily remedied by undoing the cap over the valve and working the latter up and down. If the fuel pipe and suction pipe are disconnected from the vacuum tank, it is, of course, necessary to see that they are put back in the right place.

The latest tanks have a filler cap for priming purposes, as the main fuel tank is in the luggage compartment in the tail of the car. It is possible that the air vent, a copper tube, may be damaged by a suit case hastily put in. This pipe should be inspected, therefore, from time to time, as it must allow the air to pass freely. In replacing the filter, below the carburetter, great care should be taken not to strain the nipple or the petrol pipe, at the same time doing up the nut holding the filter casing tight enough to prevent leakage. Benzole mixture is not recommended by the makers of the car.

Water is circulated by a centrifugal pump bolted to the front of the timing case with its gland within the casing. Leakage through the gland may affect the crank case lubricant.

During the general overhaul, therefore, the pump casing should be unbolted, the gland nut, which has a left-hand thread, unscrewed, and the gland carefully remade with Palmetto to ensure its being tight after the pump is replaced. The pump is best dismounted when the radiator is removed. To do this the water-pipe should first be uncoupled, then the nuts under the radiator withdrawn.

The Cooling System.

Cooling is assisted by a belt-driven fan. In the older models the fan-drive is taken from the camshaft, and in the later from the crankshaft, in which case the fan is held by a bracket bolted to the front of the cylinders, and the bolt holes are slotted. The four bolts should be slackened a little until the bracket can be moved upwards.

As the cylinders are liners cast in aluminium and, moreover, are at an angle to one another, regrinding should only be effected by highly experienced personnel. The service station of the concessionaires, the Curtis Automobile Co., Ltd., Abbey Road, N.W.10, is fitted out for this work. Oversized pistons can be supplied, if absolutely necessary. Should certain of the earlier cars fitted with aluminium pistons tend to over-oil after a good many thousand miles of hard running, cast-iron pistons can be provided with a special form of oil-retaining ring, and available at the service station. Later pistons are of different design altogether. Pistons, if obtained singly as a replacement, should be brought down to the same weight as the three remaining pistons of any one engine by taking a little metal from the lip at the bottom of the skirt.

A series of Care and Maintenance articles dealing with well-known and popular cars has been for a considerable time an exclusive and widely appreciated feature of "The Autocar." The graphic illustrations which accompany the notes render the necessary adjustments easily understood by all owner-drivers. This is the thirtieth article of the series. Cars previously dealt with are as under :—

A.C.—Sept. 25/25, Oct. 2/25.
Armstrong Siddeley.—July 20/23.
Austin, 12 *h.p.*—July 30/26.
Bean, 11·9 *h.p.*—Feb. 15/24.
Bentley.—May 21/26, May 28/26.
Bugatti, 1½-*litre.*—July 2/26, July 9/26.
Citroën.—Aug. 31/23, Sept. 7/23.
Clyno.—Jan. 28/27, Feb. 4/27.
Crossley, 14 *h.p.*—Jan. 7/27, Jan. 14/27.
Essex.—March 26/26, April 2/26.
Fiat, 10-15 *h.p.*—Dec. 14/23, Dec. 21/23.
Ford.—May 27/22, June 3/22, June 10/22.
Hillman.—Dec. 12/24, Dec. 19/24.
Humber.—Aug. 3/23, Aug. 10/23.
Jowett, 7-17 *h.p.*—Nov. 21/24.
Lagonda.—April 18/24, April 25/24.
Morris-Oxford and Morris-Cowley.—June 29/23, July 6/23, July 13/23.
Renault, 8·3 *h.p.*—Nov. 12/26, Nov. 19/26.
Riley, 12 *h.p.*—Jan. 22/26, Jan. 29/26.
Rover Eight.—Feb. 16/23, Feb. 23/23.
Rover, 12 *h.p. and* 14 *h.p.*—Jan. 11/24.
Singer, 10-26 *h.p.*—Aug. 7/25, Aug. 14/25.
Standard, 14 *h.p.*—March 28/24, April 4/24.
Star, 12-25 *h.p.*—May 30/24, June 6/24.
Swift, 10 *h.p.*—May 8/25.
Talbot, 10-23 *h.p.*—July 10/25, July 17/25.
Vauxhall, 14 *h.p.*—Aug. 22/24, Aug. 29/24.
Vulcan, 12 *h.p.*—Dec. 11/25.
Wolseley, 14 *h.p.*—July 18/24, July 25/24.

Owing to the extraordinary popularity of this series of articles, the great majority of the issues containing them are out of print.

CARE and MAINTENANCE of the LANCIA LAMBDA

Part II.—Notes to Assist Owners of an Unconventionally Designed Italian Car to Keep it in the Best Possible Condition.

THE Lancia clutch is a multi-disc, the steel discs being secured by splines to the clutch-shaft, the discs lined with fabric secured by similar means to the flywheel, the coil spring being right inside the clutch with a thrust washer next to the flywheel. No part of the clutch can be adjusted, and to reach the plates the whole component must be dismounted, first sliding back the gear box. There is no likelihood of the clutch needing attention for very many thousand miles. The fabric-lined discs are $7\frac{1}{2}$ mm. thick, when new.

On the outside of the casing, enclosing the clutch, is a single lubricator. This lubricator is liable to be overlooked, but is most important, as it supplies oil to the clutch spigot. The rollers which withdraw the clutch should be kept covered with grease, otherwise they may become noisy in course of time.

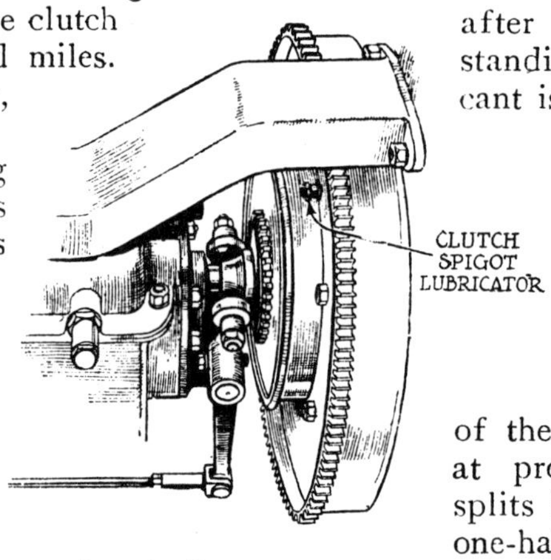

Clutch spigot lub-icator which might conceivably be overlooked when the car is receiving attention. The rollers for the clutch withdrawal mechanism should be given plenty of grease.

Gear Box, Back Axle, Brakes.

In the gear box, which is an entirely separate component and is easy to dismount, the shafts are all on ball races in gun-metal housings, the clutch spigot bearing also being a ball race. Locking gear, holding the gears in mesh and consisting of a plunger backed by a spring, is enclosed in small, cylindrical, nickel-plated projections. The oil filler is in the top, and every 6,000 miles the level indicator should be removed, cleaned, and replaced, and Vacuum C added if the level is not high enough. There is a drain plug underneath the gear box itself.

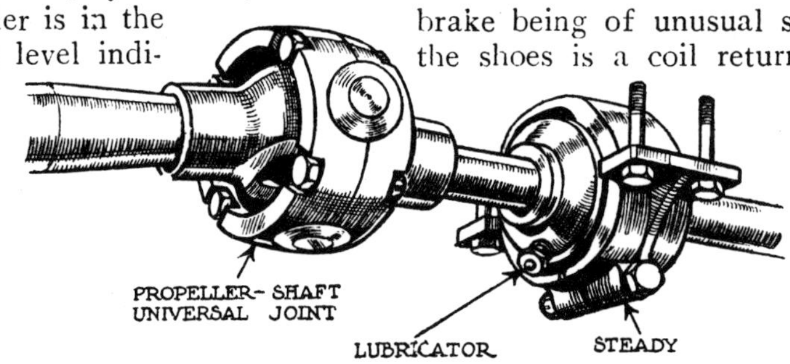

The universal joint and steady bearing of the Lancia open propeller-shaft.

The gear lever is aft of the gear box, with a special control running forward from it to the box. The selector forks and selector arm are, however, in the box itself. Immediately behind the driven shaft is a fabric universal joint, then the propeller-shaft extension piece with the usual coupling spider and a steady bearing consisting of a ball race in a casing contained in a housing bolted to the frame. The shaft slides in the centre race of the ball bearing. Immediately behind the steady is a ball bearing universal joint, with races that can be removed and replaced easily, then come the propeller-shaft proper and the rear fabric joint. The steady bearing and the universal joint should be kept lubricated.

The back axle is of straightforward design, and should be kept full of Vacuum C, inserted through the filler, which is accessible when the rear cushions and rear seats have been removed, oil only being put in immediately after a run and not when the car has been standing still for some time until the lubricant is solidified. The bearings and housings of the differential should only be dealt with at properly equipped works. The casing splits in the centre, and each side tube, with one-half of the bevel casing, can be withdrawn separately, carrying with it the brake.

As regards the rear brakes, each shoe is of aluminium alloy with fabric lining $\frac{5}{32}$ in. thick when new. The fulcrum point is in front, and the end of the shoe is provided with a hardened roller, the cam operating the brake being of unusual shape. Across the cam ends of the shoes is a coil return spring held in position by a bolt passed through the shoe. The cam-operating shaft has bearings which can be replaced.

The system of brake operation is that the pedal brings into action all four brake shoes through cables, and the lever is connected to the same cables through a system of three pulleys to allow compensation. These three pulleys are underneath the brake lever itself and up inside the shaft tunnel. The rear brake cables terminate in adjustments in a place which is rather difficult to get at, but can be seen by looking in front of the rear wheel under the frame. Similar adjustments are provided for the cables passing to the front brakes but these are visible when the bonnet is raised. Thes four adjustments set the positions of each pair of shoes.

There is a second adjustment for the front brakes, where the cable is carried round the cam-operating arm, the cable being looped through the eye of a stud and pinched by a nut. This adjustment, which is the setting to be used when new linings have been riveted on, is set by slackening off the cable-pinching device and pulling the cable through or letting it out until the shoes are right.

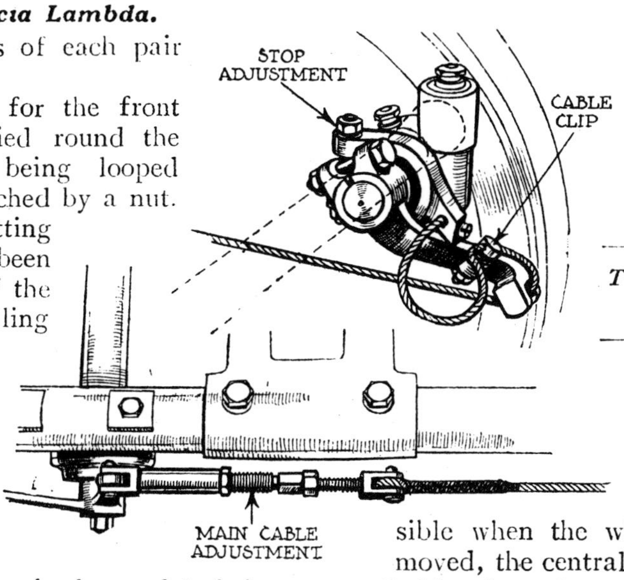

Two of the cable adjustments for the front wheel brakes.

All four wheels should be jacked up to adjust the brakes, the front wheels being in a straight ahead position, and each shoe should be brought close to the drum by the cable adjustment without actually touching it, the brake pedal being brought back along its slot so as to take advantage of its full range of movement.

The front brakes are compensated, and if the adjustment has been properly effected, all four wheels should lock together. If one wheel runs free and the other three lock, the cable adjustment should be taken up until the fourth wheel is braked equally with the others. There is a certain tendency for the fabric to vary in consistency, and if one wheel brakes harshly, a little lubricating oil should be put on the fabric of that particular brake. The Lancia brakes are very powerful, and when properly set should pull the car up from 40 m.p.h. in 63ft. or thereabouts.

The rear brake shoes are accessible when the wheel and hub cap have been removed, the central nut undone, and the wheel puller supplied by the makers screwed on to the hub and its central bolt screwed in until the hub and drum come off.

There are no bearings in the hub itself, but in the centre of the axle, when the hub and drum have been removed, will be seen a C spanner nut, behind which is the ball race, and behind the ball race are Palmetto oil-retaining washers. The front brake drums are removed in the same way, but each hub contains three races, two

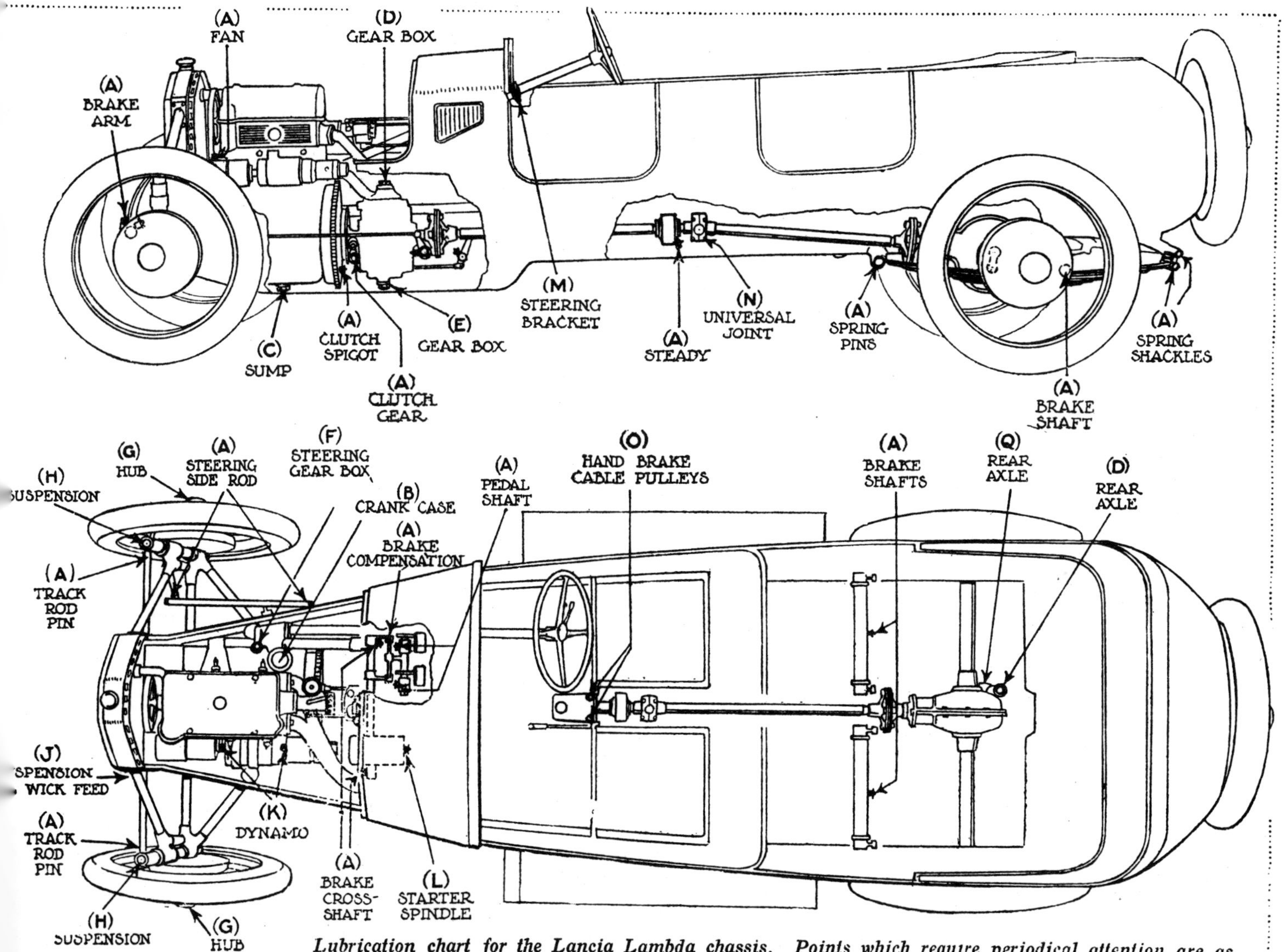

Lubrication chart for the Lancia Lambda chassis. Points which require periodical attention are as follow: A, grease every 1,000 miles; BC, empty oil from engine, clean filters and refill every 750 miles; DE, check oil level every 6,000 miles; F, refill steering gear box during general attention; G, ditto, lubricate hubs; H, every 3,000 miles verify oil level in front suspension system; J, lubricate suspension wick feed every 1,000 miles; K, lubricate dynamo every 1,000 miles; L, oil starter spindle every 3,000 miles; M, oil steering bracket during general attention; N, dismantle and fill universal joint with oil during general attention; O, oil hand brake cable pulleys every 1,000 miles; Q, check oil level every 6,000 miles.

journals and one thrust. In course of time these bearings will need replacement, and to do this is a perfectly simple operation.

The hub should be withdrawn, the C spanner locking ring undone from the back, and one ball race can then be removed. Another C spanner nut, when undone, releases the thrust bearing and finally the outer ball race, all three of which can be renewed and then reassembled, care being taken to put them together accurately.

The front suspension of the Lancia being one of its most unconventional features, it follows that no part should be dismantled by anyone who is not conversant with the general arrangement of the components, or who does not possess the necessary special implements. This will be realised when it is mentioned that the very strong coil spring which carries the weight of the car on each side will come out with considerable violence if the prescribed routine is not followed during its removal.

Dealing with Front Springs.

The front suspension consists of coil springs on either side, there being no separate front axle. In the base of the stub axle is an oil damper equivalent to a shock absorber, and the lubricant in this damper will have to be replenished at intervals after, say, 3,000 to 4,000 miles. To do this, remove the cover plate which seals the special orifice in the front wing. With a small adjustable spanner hold the end of the central rod, which has flats on it for the purpose, and, keeping this firm, unscrew the small nut which locks the upper casing and unscrew and remove the upper casing itself. Using the special box spanner provided, unscrew the gland nut and fish it out of the casing with a piece of bent wire. It is then possible to insert a metric rule and take a measurement from the top of the casing to the mouth of the central cylinder in which is the oil. Further movement downwards of 40 mm. from this position the lower end of the rule should just touch the oil, and if it does not do so more oil should be added.

To make sure that this lubricant has reached the damping cylinder, screw the tool provided with the car, and termed a dismantling tool, on to the end of the central rod, and by means of the handle on the tool work the central rod up and down, verifying the oil level again when this has been done.

It is then possible to dismantle the spring itself. First unscrew the hexagon nut A until the sleeve to which it is attached shows about one inch of thread. The inner rod of the dismantling tool is still screwed on to the end of the central rod, and the central rod, with the aid of the handle provided, should be pulled up as far as possible. The outer portion of the dismantling tool must then be screwed down until it pinches tightly the slotted washer, provided for the purpose in the tool kit.

The locking ring shown in the sketch should then be unscrewed by means of the pin spanner provided, remembering that there is a small locking snug which holds this ring in position, and must be removed entirely before the ring can be turned. Let the locking ring fall down as far as it will go. Now unscrew the nut A until its sleeve is off the thread and can be removed. The long main spring will then be seen and can be drawn out intact through the hole in the mudguard. In the earlier models the spring has to be bent to one side to clear the mudguard.

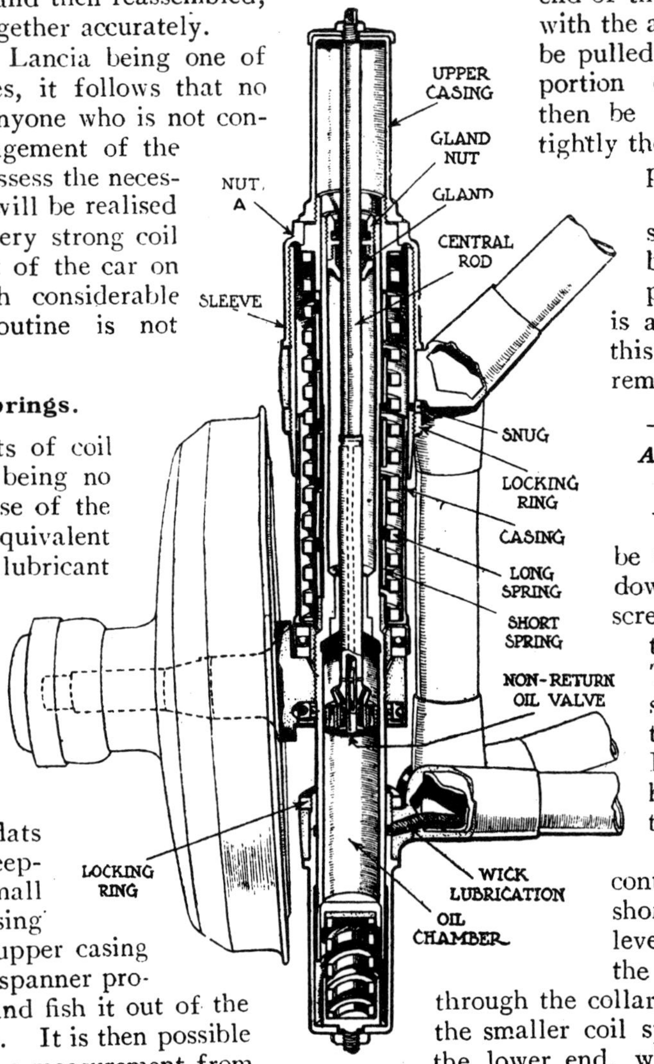

A full sectional view of the unusual system of Lancia front suspension.

Inside the casing which has contained the spring will be seen a shorter coil spring which can be levered out with a screwdriver, and the casing itself will then come away through the collar on the tubular frame. Note that the smaller coil spring is slightly tapered, because the lower end, which is of smaller diameter than the other, must be replaced exactly as found, or this spring will rattle. Do not remove the locking ring without making certain which side should be uppermost. The central spindle should be coated with grease, and, incidentally, it is a good plan on the latest cars to drill two more holes in the locking ring for the pin spanner, as this makes the spindle easier to remove in future whenever such an operation becomes necessary.

A series of Care and Maintenance articles dealing with well-known and popular cars has been for a considerable time an exclusive and widely appreciated feature of "The Autocar." The graphic illustrations which accompany the notes render the necessary adjustments easily understood by all owner-drivers. This is the thirty-first article of the series. Cars previously dealt with are as under:—

A.C.—Sept. 25/25, Oct. 2/25.
Armstrong Siddeley.—July 20/23.
Austin, 12 *h.p.*—July 30/26.
Bean, 11·9 *h.p.*—Feb. 15/24.
Bentley.—May 21/26, May 28/26.
Bugatti, 1½*-litre.*—July 2/26, July 9/26.
Citroën.—Aug. 31/23, Sept. 7/23.
Clyno.—Jan. 28/27, Feb. 4/27.
Crossley, 14 *h.p.*—Jan. 7/27, Jan. 14/27.
Essex.—March 26/26, April 2/26.
Fiat, 10-15 *h.p.*—Dec. 14/23, Dec. 21/23.
Ford.—May 27/22, June 3/22, June 10/22.
Hillman.—Dec. 12/24, Dec. 19/24.
Humber.—Aug. 3/23, Aug. 10/23.
Jowett, 7-17 *h.p.*—Nov. 21/24.
Lagonda.—April 18/24, April 25/24.
Morris-Oxford and *Morris-Cowley.*—June 29/23, July 6/23, July 13/23.
Renault, 8·3 *h.p.*—Nov. 12/26, Nov. 19/26.
Riley, 12 *h.p.*—Jan. 22/26, Jan. 29/26.
Rover Eight.—Feb. 16/23, Feb. 23/23.
Rover, 12 *h.p.* and 14 *h.p.*—Jan. 11/24.
Singer, 10-26 *h.p.*—Aug. 7/25, Aug. 14/25.
Standard, 14 *h.p.*—March 28/24, April 4/24.
Star, 12-25 *h.p.*—May 30/24, June 6/24.
Swift, 10 *h.p.*—May 8/25.
Talbot, 10-23 *h.p.*—July 10/25, July 17/25.
Vauxhall, 14 *h.p.*—Aug. 22/24, Aug. 29/24.
Vulcan, 12 *h.p.*—Dec. 11/25.
Wolseley, 14 *h.p.*—July 18/24, July 25/24.

Owing to the extraordinary popularity of this series of articles, the great majority of the issues containing them are out of print

Care and Maintenance of the Lancia Lambda.

The lower portion of the suspension, which contains the oil damper and another coil spring, is removed by unlocking the circular pin spanner nut which retains the parts in position and can be withdrawn quite simply, but the tie-rod and brake cable should be disconnected. The thrust bearing below the spring casing should be inspected carefully, and, if such inspection should reveal signs of wear in the race, it should be replaced by a new one.

In replacing the parts, assemble the lower spring and its casing first, then slide the thrust race for the main springs into position the right way up, followed by the spring casing. Before going further it is convenient to replace the gland nut, which need be only fairly tight, and not extremely tight, or it will be difficult to remove next time. Make sure that the locking ring, incidentally, is put on the right way up, put the smaller spring in position with its smallest diameter downwards, insert the larger spring, place the sleeve with nut A on the top of the main spring, attach the dismantling tool once more, with the slotted washer tight between the outer portion and the nut, screw down the handle gradually until the sleeve attached to the nut already referred to can be engaged with the threaded portion of the body, taking great care throughout the job.

As this body moves gradually down into position, centralise the casing, which should slide into it. When the nut A can be turned no more, lock it hard home, remove the dismantling tool, and screw up the locking ring. All that then remains is to replace the cover and its locking nut, and while the latter is being done up the central rod should be held again by means of the flats provided for the purpose.

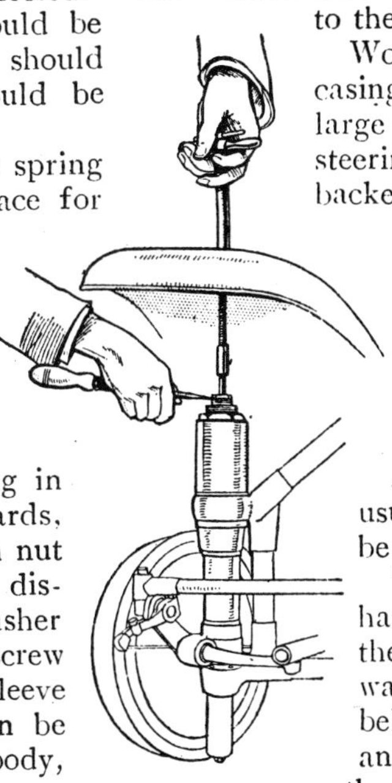

Using the special dismantling tool in the process of verifying the oil level in the front suspension system.

It is well to remember, because it is very easy to overlook, that there is a lubricator for the lower end of the stub axle underneath the hinged number plate and directly below the radiator, oil being inserted at this point on both sides and finding its way through the tubular structure to the bearings.

Worm and segment steering is provided, and the casing should be kept full of lubricant through the large filling orifice. The joints on the tie-rod and steering rod consist of cups on either side of a ball backed by springs, the outer spring being retained by a cap screwed into tubes and locked. The springs automatically take up any adjustment that is required.

At the rear the half-elliptic springs have the usual detachable bushes and pins which should be renewed when wear is apparent.

The battery is kept in a casing on the left-hand running board. Care should be taken that the plates are covered with the liquid, distilled water being added whenever the level has fallen below this point. The wiring is single-pole with an earth return through the chassis, and the fuses are on the switchboard.

With the older type tyres the pressure front and rear should be 55 lb. and 50 lb. respectively. In the later cars, with low pressure tyres, it should be 32 lb. in front and rear. When it is necessary to remove a Rudge-Whitworth wheel the ears of the retaining caps should be undone with a wood mallet, remembering that to unscrew the retaining nut it should always be turned in the direction in which the road wheel normally rotates.

April 20th, 1928

The Lancia-Lambda "Airway" saloon in its latest standardised form

The curious bodywork on this 1928 Lambda was built by the Albany Carriage Company for show purposes—but created such a stir that several examples were ordered. Aircraft influence was evident throughout, with front seats almost identical to those of an Imperial Airways airliner, airspeed and altitude indicators, and an "astrodome" over the single rear seat. A contemporary writer said that the acute angle of the windscreen took some getting used to!

NEW 8-CYLINDER LANCIA

Dilambda Model as Distinctive and Interesting as the Well-known Lambda Type.

THE Lancia Company is just about to place on the market its Dilambda model, an entirely new type just as distinctive and outstanding as the well-known Lambda introduced seven years ago and still much in demand. As the name indicates, the Dilambda is a development of the earlier type, and embodies several of its outstanding features, notably independent front wheel springing and a compact type of engine.

The chassis, however, does not constitute a revision of old ideas. It is new from beginning to end, embodying all the advanced features—and they are many—suggested by research work of the last seven years. Briefly, the Dilambda is just as much an advance over current design as was the Lambda when it first appeared.

This new model from the famous Italian factory has an eight-cylinder engine of 79.37 x 100 mm. bore and stroke, giving a piston displacement of 3,960 c.c., and a Treasury rating in England of 31.2 h.p. It develops more than 100 h.p. at 4,000 r.p.m.

Improved Appearance.

In a car so full of originality it is almost impossible to select any one feature for special attention. The front appearance is changed by reason of the modern radiator design, which is higher, narrower and more graceful.

The general principle of construction of the car is unchanged, but the horizontal and the vertical tubes, the former fulfilling the function of an axle and the latter containing the hydraulic and coil spring suspension, are very much greater in diameter than on the earlier type. As is well known, with this system each wheel is free to rise and fall independently, and the unsprung weight is reduced to a minimum, with the result that wonderful road-holding is secured and wheel wobble and shimmy troubles are eliminated. Detail improvements in the suspension make it impossible for water and dust to enter the working parts or for oil to escape. By reason of the stronger construction of the front end, the two tubes going in a horizontal plane from the main cross-tube to the chassis members have been rendered unnecessary. At the rear long, broad, half-elliptic springs are used, the pivots and shackles being bushed with Silentblocs, which require no lubricant.

Practically all cars have channel-section side members united by either channel-section or tubular cross-members, the various parts being riveted together. According to the height and section of the frame members a chassis of this type has more or less flexibility, and this flexing under road inequalities is transmitted to the body and sets up squeaks and rattles. Lancia has sought to produce a perfectly rigid chassis in which no rivets are used, the various parts being welded together and constituting an indeformable whole.

Front end of the Lancia eight-cylinder engine.

The side members have the extraordinary depth on the portion from the radiator to the dashboard of $15\frac{3}{4}$in., while from that point to the rear, which constitutes the body-carrying portion of the chassis, the depth is slightly over 7in. These side members are double, with very narrow horizontal flanges, and are welded together. Where they have been built up the two side members are united by a cross-member in front, serving as engine support, and by an X-member the centre of which forms a rectangular box through which the propeller-shaft passes.

Petrol Tank as Cross-member.

Even the petrol tank adds rigidity to the frame. Obviously this could not be welded in position, for it might have to be dismounted for cleaning or for repairs, but it is formed with a flange on its two ends and is attached to the side members by a series of bolts, thus constituting a very big diameter tubular cross-member.

The engine is as interesting and original as the chassis. It is a small angle V-type eight, no longer than a four of equivalent bore; indeed, it might be mistaken by the uninitiated for a four-cylinder with sparking plugs on either side. The two lines of cylinders are staggered in relation to one another, so that each connecting rod has its own crankpin, thus avoiding the more delicate construction of forked rods and their attendant lubrication problems.

The crankshaft is carried in five bearings in the cylinder casting. The head, which is detachable and held to the casting by twenty studs, carries

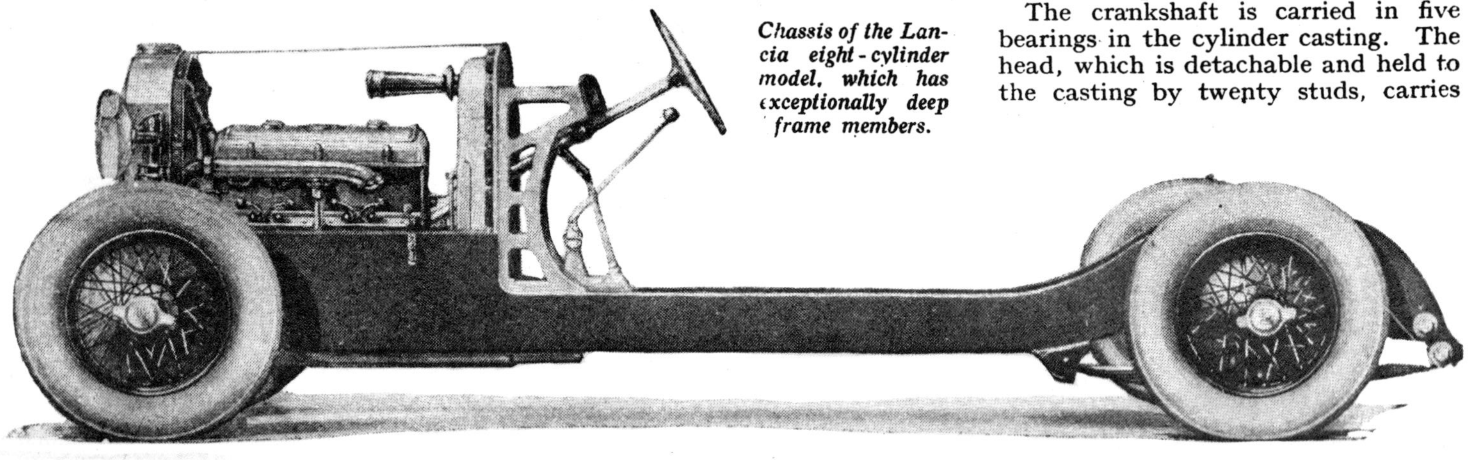

Chassis of the Lancia eight-cylinder model, which has exceptionally deep frame members.

two vertical valves per cylinder and the two rocker shafts. The camshaft is on the cylinder casting in the angle formed by the two rows of cylinders. Above the camshaft are the tappet guides, the whole of this portion being held down by the ten central cylinder head bolts. When the cylinder head is lifted the camshaft and the tappet guides remain undisturbed, although exposed to view. An advantage of the design is that short, and consequently light, push rods are used.

The exhaust is on either side of the head and is led down from the front. The carburetter is a double American Zenith mounted on the left-hand side, with an exhaust-heated mixing chamber. On the right of the engine are the electric starting motor, the dynamo and coil, and the distributor. There is a detachable water cover on each side of the cylinder block, allowing the water space to be verified, while on the left hand of the crank case there is a detachable cover plate through which the connecting rod bearings can be examined.

Few people would judge this new Lancia engine to be an eight-cylinder.

The Lubrication System.

The main supply of oil is contained in the one-piece cast aluminium sump fitted with longitudinal cooling ribs on each side. There are two oil pumps, one taking the lubricant from the sump and delivering it to the main bearings, the connecting rods and the overhead-valve gear, the second pump drawing oil from the reserve tank under the cowl and maintaining a constant level in the base chamber. There is a detachable filter on the left-hand side of the cylinder block.

After the initial filling of the crank case it is not necessary to open the bonnet to add oil, replenishment being effected through the dashboard tank and the supply pump. The dashboard oil tank is also made use of for supplying the Bijur chassis lubricating system. An interesting feature of the oiling system is the arrangement made for cooling the lubricant. The sump has a very shallow false bottom with transverse divisions extending nearly all the way across and with a height equal to the depth of the bottom. In consequence, the oil, returning to the sump at one end, has to describe a zig-zag path from the front to the rear, in contact with the coolest portion of the base-chamber, before it is aspired by the pump. This results in lowering the temperature of the oil.

Front of the new Lancia chassis.

Two double roller chains are used, one driving the water pump and the pinion operating the inclined shaft for the distributor and oil pump, and the other driving the camshaft. The six-blade fan is positively driven off the end of the camshaft. There is a thermostat on the water outlet.

Transmission Details.

A single-plate clutch is fitted. The gear box provides four speeds and reverse, with central change-speed lever. The drive shaft is in two parts, the first portion being rigid and going from the clutch to a central support in the box construction, thus forming a chassis cross-member, and the rear portion having a fabric and a metal universal joint. The rear axle is in two pressings welded together and contains hypoid gears, which are silent and enable a very low body line to be adopted.

The brakes on the four wheels have a diameter of 16½in. While there is a single pair of shoes in each rear drum, there are two brake camshafts and two entirely independent sets of controls, thus meeting with the legal requirement in certain countries. In

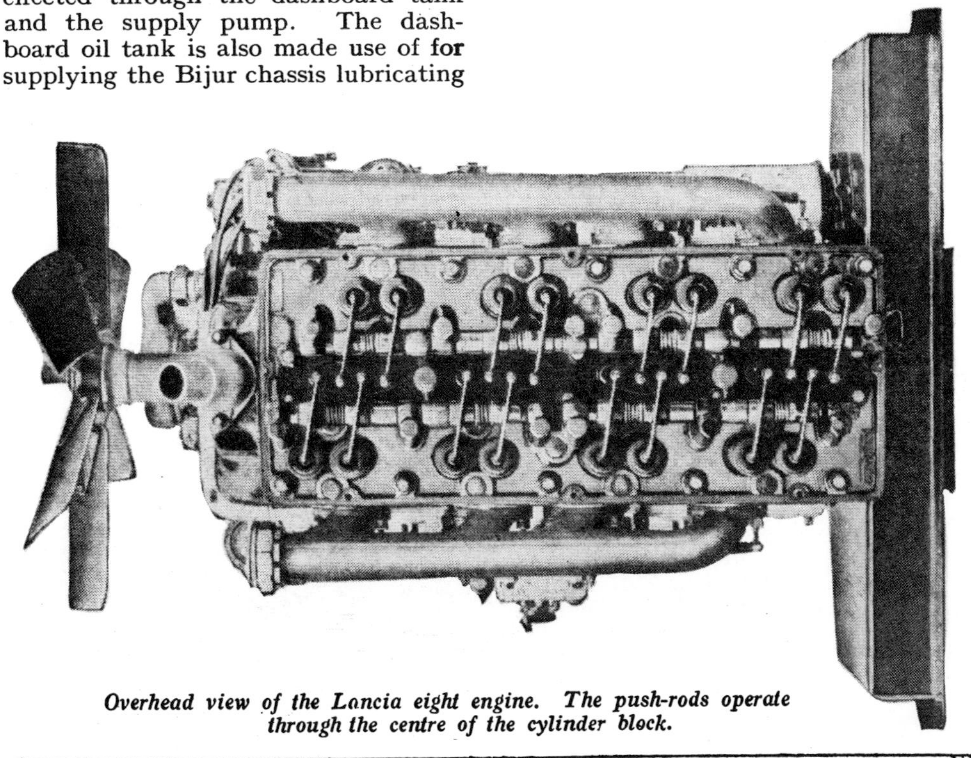

Overhead view of the Lancia eight engine. The push-rods operate through the centre of the cylinder block.

One form in which the new Lancia model will appear.

the forward portion of the gear box, and thus completely protected, is an equaliser acting between the two front brakes and a differential between the front and the rear sets. Connections are by cable, and no working part is exposed.

The chassis has a wheelbase of 11ft. 5in., a track of 4ft. 9½in., and a total length of 14ft. 10¾in. The weight of the chassis, with Rudge-Whitworth wheels and 16 by 50 tyres, is 23 cwt. The spare wheel carrier is at the rear and goes through the petrol tank, thus serving to give it extra rigidity in its function as a cross-member, and also acting as a baffle plate. The ratio of horse-power to weight is very favourable, thus providing a car which, in addition to a high maximum speed (it will maintain 75 m.p.h. with full load), is also exceptionally lively on hills and rapid in its acceleration on top gear.

An immaculately preserved 1929 example of the Lancia Lambda. Production ended the following year, by which time some 13,000 had been made.

"THE AUTOCAR" ROAD TESTS

17 h.p. LANCIA WEYMANN SALOON

Controllability and Responsiveness Keynotes of Fast and Exceptionally Well-sprung Cars.

THE main appeal of the Lancia is, and always has been, difficult to express in words, because there is no phrase to indicate at once that it is the car as a whole, rather than a summary of its performance or a description of its details, which attracts.

The only way to deal with the question is to say that it is one of those rare machines over which the driver knows that he has full and complete control from the very moment that the car moves away from rest. Really there is more in the matter than that alone. One's natural feeling is that the car can be made to do exactly what one wishes, can, as the phrase goes, "be steered over a halfpenny" at any speed, and that it will obey instantly and effectively the slightest desire of the man at the wheel.

Part of this personality, as it were, is due to an unusually comfortable driving seat, and to the fact that the brake and gear levers and the pedals all seem to be in exactly the right places. The seat itself is firm and rigid, giving ample support to the driver when the car is cornering fast; this in itself is a much more important matter than many people realise.

Recently *The Autocar* was enabled to try two cars, both of the same type. One was the ordinary touring model and the other had been adapted for use in last year's Italian 1,000-mile race, in which event it performed extraordinarily well. In the case of the ordinary car the best test of its capabilities was provided when an opportunity arose to take it really fast up a long zig-zag gradient, with a very bad surface, at a time when the road was slippery. In such circumstances it is necessary for a car to answer exactly to all its controls, to "broadside" on the least acute of the curves, and to get round the sharper hairpin included in this road even if the front wheels skid, as they did. The gears have to be changed rapidly and often to enable the best results to be obtained. There are not many cars that would undertake this particular climb as well as did the Lancia on this occasion.

As to whether the longer gear lever now used is better than the earlier shorter design it is difficult to say. There were attractions in the shorter lever, though the longer one undoubtedly makes it easier to feel the gears, but the gear change at speed is, in any case, extremely good, and one would not imagine that anyone, however prejudiced in this connection, could object to the left-hand control in this car. A gradient of 1 in $6\frac{1}{2}$ was

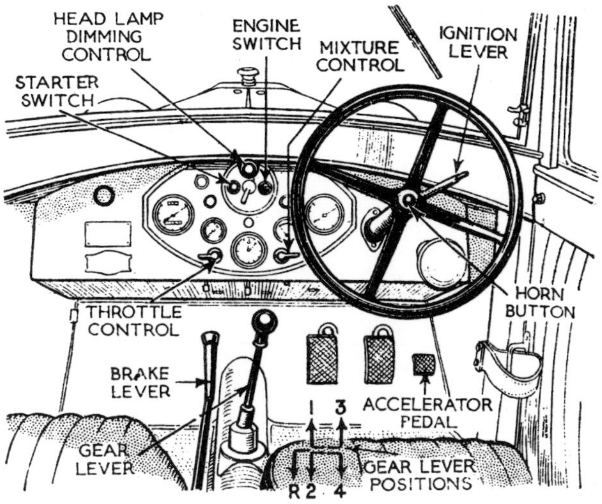

DATA FOR THE DRIVER.

17 h.p., four cylinders, 82.5 × 120 mm. (2,570 c.c.).
Tax, £17.
Wheelbase 10ft. 2in., track 4ft. 7in.
Overall length 13ft. 5in., width 5ft. 6in., height 5ft. 4in.
Tyres: 14 × 50 on detachable wire wheels.

Engine—rear axle gear ratios.	Maxima (m.p.h.).	Acceleration (10–30 m.p.h.).
13.3	25	—
7.9	44	$6\frac{1}{5}$ sec.
6.02	57	$8\frac{1}{5}$ sec.
4.16	70	13 sec.

Tank capacity 15 gallons, fuel consumption 20–22 m.p.g.
12-volt lighting set cuts in at 12 m.p.h.
Weight 27 cwt. 2 qr.
Price, with Weymann saloon body, £895.

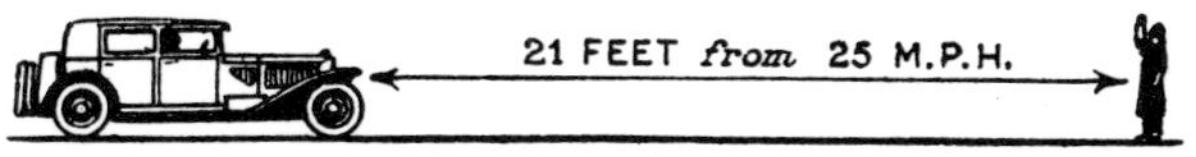

"THE AUTOCAR" ROAD TESTS—*(continued).*

climbed easily, at a good speed, on third gear, and although it was not possible to obtain an accurate maximum on top, 70 m.p.h. is about the figure.

The Lancia front suspension has been one of the great features of the design from its inception. Experience over a period of years with different models goes to confirm the fact that the suspension is exceptionally good, far better, in fact, than that of most cars. The steering has ample caster action, giving the automatic return of the wheels after a sharp corner which is so valuable, and ensuring that the car holds the road as though glued to it either when cornering or at speed on the straight.

Curiously, from the driving seat the ordinary model does not seem to be low, although in actual fact, as the illustration shows, it is low enough. This feeling is due to the presence of a frame cross-member just below the seat; when the seat is made adjustable, as in the touring model, it has to be placed higher than would be the case with a rigid seat. There is another interesting point. The deep wells in the driving compartment, and on either side of the gear box, give the occupants of the front seats a normal seating position, that is to say, the seat cushion is not on the floorboards but is relatively high. Provided the seat is comfortable, this is an easier position than any other for long-distance driving.

Power with Flexibility.

The four-cylinder engine has the hard feeling which comes of power and is more flexible than one would expect, though the car as a whole is not designed to do all its work on top gear. The gradual rise in the standard by which the silence of a car is judged has had one interesting effect in that, compared with other machines of to-day, the Lancia engine is not quiet, though it must be said in its favour that in a very short time the engine noise is forgotten.

On the touring model tested the brakes were very good, certain and effective, while the 1,000-mile race car was better still, in that the stopping distance from 25 m.p.h. was 17ft. The brake adjustment is not too convenient.

The tool box is carried on the running board, and is, therefore, exposed to the weather; it has an ingenious combination lock. Fresh oil is fed slowly by a pump to the engine sump from a separate oil tank. This arrangement, incidentally, makes replenishment an easier matter, since only the separate tank need be filled. The standard car carries one spare wheel at the rear behind the big luggage container; the single-panel front screen can be raised to ventilate the interior of the saloon, the instrument board is illuminated and contains a revolution counter; the switchboard fuses are accessible.

The speedometer is now provided with a trip, as well as with an ordinary, mileage recorder, and the contents of the main fuel tank are shown by a gauge on the instrument board. The saloon body of the car tested, shown in the illustration overleaf, is shorter than usual, but even so it has been possible to provide comfort for the two rear passengers, while at the rear an additional spare wheel has been fitted as an extra.

Not a Racing Car.

By comparison with the ordinary car, the 1,000-mile race machine accelerated slightly better, the times from 10-30 m.p.h. on the four gears being respectively 6, 7, 9⅘, and 12 seconds, while the maxima on those gears were higher, 32 m.p.h. on first and 65 m.p.h. on third being examples. The maximum it was possible to obtain on top when the car was tried was 75 m.p.h. This car is not, of course, a racing machine, but is simply an ordinary car slightly faster than usual and equipped for high speeds over long distances.

This type has an interesting system of double vacuum fuel feed to the carburetter, either tank or both being brought into operation by a combination of taps, so that there shall be no fear of the carburetter being starved on long runs up the mountains of the 1,000-mile race course. The whole of the tail compartment is taken up by the fuel tank, luggage space being deleted in favour of this component; a big tank filler projects through the top of the tail.

With such a machine it should certainly be possible to keep up a high average speed on any course composed mainly of curves and sharp corners. The special vacuum feed tank is illustrated on another page in this issue under the heading "Innovations."

New 11.9 h.p. four-cylinder Lancia.

The Olympia Show 1932

LANCIA SPECIFICATIONS

11.9 h.p., 4 cyls., 69.85×78 mm. (1,194 c.c.), tax £12, magneto ignition, pump cooling, disc clutch, 4-sp. unit gear box, spiral bevel drive, spiral front and ½-E. rear springs, hydraulic brakes, disc wheels. Prices: Saloon, £390.

15 h.p., 4 cyls., 82.5×90 mm. (1,924 c.c.), tax £17, coil ignition, disc clutch, cable-operated brakes, 14×45 tyres on wire wheels. Prices: Chassis, £425; saloon, £585.
Other details as in 11.9 h.p.

20 h.p., 8 cyls., 69.8×85 mm. (2,604 c.c.), tax £25, 15×45 tyres. Prices: Chassis, £625; saloon, £785.
Other details as in 15 h.p.

30 h.p., 8 cyls., 79.3×100 mm. (3,960 c.c.), tax £32, 16×50 tyres. Prices: Chassis, £895; saloon, £1,145.
Other details as in 15 h.p.

No. 718 (*Post-War Series*).—15 h.p. LANCIA SALOON

SOME few cars stand alone by reason of their special qualities, and cannot be identified as belonging to any particular class. The Lancia in the past has been a machine of this order, and the latest 15 h.p. four-cylinder model gives precisely the same impression, being thoroughly pleasing and satisfactory as a whole, and utterly different from the general run of cars of a similar engine size.

Beyond that, the car possesses several individual features, among them its independent front wheel springing. Basically, the 15 h.p. two-litre car follows the famous Lambda, though the engine is smaller; the arrangement of the front axle is broadly the same, but simplified, and the engine still has cylinder bores which are not in line but are staggered, so giving a short engine from front to back. But in the mounting of the engine in the frame a very great departure for Lancia has been made, in that the unit is held flexibly at four points in rubber and coil spring bearers, there being, in addition, laminated springs running fore and aft between each pair of mountings. The result is that the engine is free to move sideways against crankshaft torque, whereby vibration is very largely damped out.

It is no exaggeration to say that any experienced driver would be deceived into believing that this car had at least six cylinders, and even at quite low speeds and in picking up, when it is true that the engine can be felt to a slight extent, it is not the feel of a four that is suggested; the effect is soft and might be produced by any number of cylinders.

A car of this nature can be tested adequately only by giving it a quite strenuous run, allowing it to show its special capabilities to advantage. Thus, in two days more than 700 miles were covered, the final result being that the highest possible esteem existed for the effortless, tireless way in which the machine can be kept moving at a high average speed. At the end of the run the speed and the exhaust note of the engine were exactly as in the beginning, and, still more remarkable, the oil level had not fallen at all.

So smooth and deceptive is the engine that a speed automatically reached on the open road is 50, and, not only is the maximum exceedingly useful, but it can be held, if need be, without effort. The speedometer recorded 74 during the timed test. The engine will pull as slowly as 4 m.p.h. on top gear, and main road gradients can be climbed without changing down, but third speed is so valuable as to be worth bringing in frequently by anyone who appreciates such a car as this, for a reading of 60 is possible, and 50 is perfectly normal.

The car is started smoothly from rest on second gear as an ordinary procedure, and a reading of 40 is possible on this ratio, which deals with the steepest of main road gradients, while first, though not unduly low, is in the nature of an emergency gear. Third is a good silent ratio, the other gears are not unduly

15 h.p. LANCIA SALOON

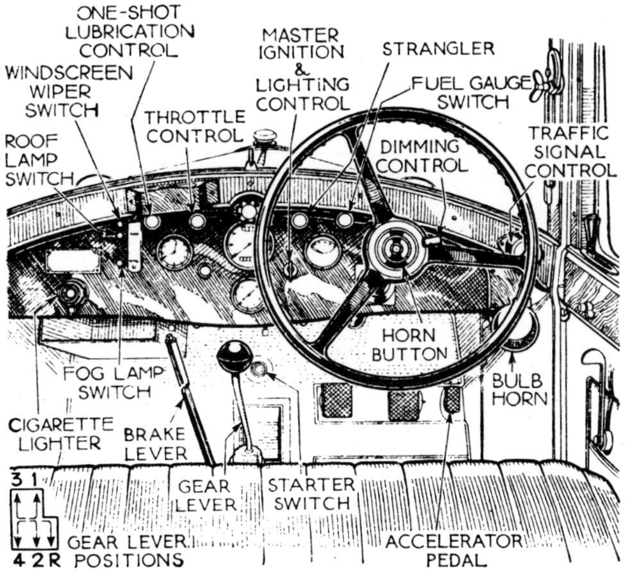

DATA FOR THE DRIVER

15 h.p., four cylinders, 82.55 × 90 mm. (1,924 c.c.).
Tax £17.
Wheelbase 9ft. 9½in., track 4ft. 7½in.
Overall length 14ft. 2in., width 5ft. 4½in., height 5ft. 8½in.
Tyres: 14 × 45 on detachable steel disc wheels.

Engine—rear axle gear ratios.	Acceleration from steady 10 to 30 m.p.h.	Timed speed over ¼ mile.
16.4 to 1	—	
10.3 to 1	6 sec.	
6.09 to 1	8⅘ sec.	
4.71 to 1	13 sec.	70.86 m.p.h.

Turning circle: 33ft. 6in.
Tank capacity 13 gallons, fuel consumption 22 m.p.g.
12-volt lighting set; constant voltage system.
Weight: 24 cwt. 2 qr.
Price, with Dorset saloon body, £675.

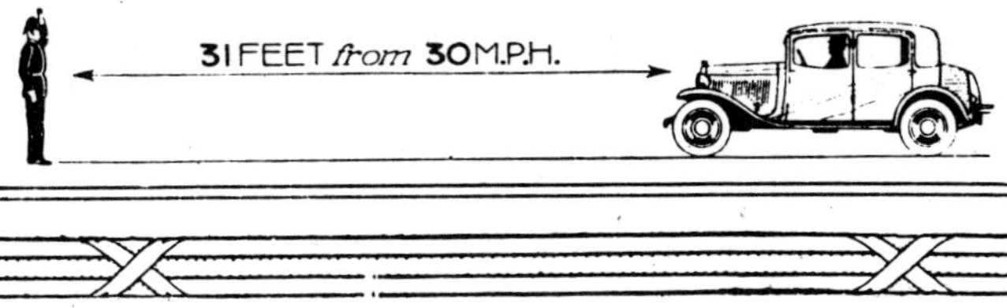

noisy, and the change, particularly between top and third and back again, is quick and decidedly easier than usual.

Exceptionally light pressure operates the clutch pedal, the brakes respond at once to normal pressure, being not only powerful but pulling the car up without deviation from the straight; the hand brake, as would be expected, is a real brake. Steering, too, is very light even for to-day, which, coupled with the outstandingly good lock, makes for the easiest possible manœuvring in confined spaces. There is some caster action, but even more would probably be an advantage, while at round about 50 a slight but not really troublesome tremor made itself apparent in the steering, due, it is understood, to the disc wheels not lending themselves to thorough balancing, though wire wheels would normally be fitted.

The opinion of passengers is that the suspension for the back seat is one of the best in existence, and the car can be cornered fast without side sway, though for still faster corner work additional damping of the springs would be beneficial, this being possible since frictional shock absorbers are provided at the back.

The body fitted is a four-door saloon by James Young, British-built coachwork being standardised. Thus on a chassis of exceptional merit one has the advantages of specialist bodywork, with first-class soft leather upholstery, and items making for luxury such as detachable roll arm-rests at the centre of both back and front seats, the one-piece front seat being adjustable easily for position.

Though relatively short, and with the seats within the wheelbase, the body has plenty of room at the back for tall passengers, soft side arm-rests adding further to the comfort. The driver's window has a quick-action lever control, recessed into the sides of the body at the back are useful direction indicators, safety glass is fitted all round, whilst above the windscreen, inside, are anti-glare visors which can be lowered. The screen has a double-blade electric wiper, and the instruments include a clock as well as an accurate fuel gauge.

Points applying to the chassis are the one-shot lubrication system, which deals with every bearing not provided with Silentbloc bushings; each time the starting motor switch is pressed a disc filter in the engine is partly rotated and thereby cleaned, the engine as a whole being characteristically clean, with a beautiful finish, and all the components are laid out in a businesslike way, as well as accessibly. Oil is poured in through an orifice in the top of the overhead-valve gear cover, the tools are carried in compartments under the bonnet, the carburetter is on the down-draught principle, and two sparking plugs are placed at either side of the cylinder block, each accessible. Ignition advance and retard is automatic. Shutters for the radiator are opened and closed according to variations of engine temperature.

Bumpers are fitted, and the luggage container at the back is of a really useful size and not unsightly.

June 3rd, 1932

USED CARS ON THE ROAD

No. 72. Lancia Lambda Saloon: Car No. 20200

Price, new - - - £745	**Second gear - - 8¼ sec.**	**Fuel consumption 22 m.p.g. (approx.)**	**Brake test figure from 30 m.p.h. - - - 55ft.**
Second-hand - - £275	**Third gear - - 11¼ sec.**	**Oil consumption 600 m.p.g. (approx.)**	
Acceleration - 10-30 m.p.h.	**Top gear - - 16½ sec.**		**First registered January, 1930.**

WHAT one felt about the Lancia Lambda saloon offered by Alpe and Saunders, Providence Court, North Audley Street, W.1, was that the mileage covered, which appeared to be in the neighbourhood of 20,000, had made little impression upon the car mechanically.

The design, of course, was an advanced one in its time; everything felt solid in the proper sense, and everything worked as it should, the performance being pleasing, though the brakes could well have had more power for the speed of the car.

Chief of the impressions on the road were a feeling of effortless running round about 45 m.p.h., mechanical noise and vibration increasing appreciably above 50, and the exactness of the controls, including the steering—which gave a remarkably good lock—and the quick, sensitive gear change, with its rigid, short central lever—incidentally, one of the first of this now popular type. There was a suggestion of looseness in the engine when running slowly, probably due in part to the valve gear, but no noise anywhere of a suspicious nature. The exhaust was slightly smoky with the oil level high.

On Brooklands track a speedometer reading of 72 was reached, 50 was possible on third, and 36 on second, with 20 on first. The speedometer was one mile an hour *slow* at 30 m.p.h., but the mileage recorder was not working, which made it difficult to give accurate figures for oil and fuel consumption. No ammeter is provided with the Bosch electrical system, but judging by the power of the excellent horn note and the ease with which the engine started from cold, the dynamo was charging well.

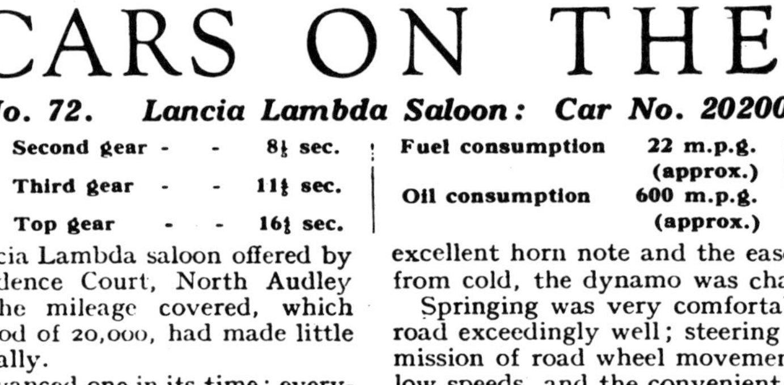

Springing was very comfortable indeed, yet the car held the road exceedingly well; steering was accurate, with slight transmission of road wheel movement through the steering wheel at low speeds, and the convenient hand brake worked really effectively. The clutch took up the drive smoothly, and none of the indirect gears was at all noisy. At low speeds the back axle was mildly audible.

The body was a four-door Weymann, of which the fabric generally was in a good state; the wings were scratched but not dented, and in the main the paint was bright, and the chromium plating on the radiator was not tarnished. The leather upholstery and the floor coverings were slightly damaged here and there, but not to an extent noticeable except under close scrutiny.

The instruments included a rev counter, which was working, but the clock was out of action. There was an accurate fuel gauge; the illumination for the instruments was intermittent. The double-blade electric screenwiper was working properly, also the roof lamp and a fog lamp.

None of the tyres was in at all bad condition, and there were two spare wheels. The driving position was good, with most comfortable armchair type seats, though it would have been better for some people if the adjustable driving seat could have been secured nearer the wheel.

An Excellent Small Four

Details of an Interesting Italian Design, the 11.9 h.p. Lancia

The 11.9 h.p. Lancia is neat in appearance.

THOUGH it appeared at the Paris Salon and the Olympia Show in 1932, the 11.9 h.p. four-cylinder Lancia model known as the Augusta has not been heard of very much in this country until just recently. Now, however, it is being actively handled here by Lancia (England), Ltd., Alperton, near Wembley, London, who state that the car is attracting a considerable amount of favourable attention.

It is a car so full of interesting features in its design, and so efficient in its performance on the road—as described in the Road Test published in *The Autocar* of April 20th—that it is worth while referring to its principal characteristics, by way of addition to the general information given about this model when it first came out.

As would be expected from the famous Turin firm of Lancia, it has many features which are distinctly individual, following in the footsteps of the famous old Lambda and the later, existing, V eight-cylinder Lancia Dilambda; in fact, the arrangement of the cylinders is the same in principle as that in the Lambda, the Augusta having a V-type four-cylinder unit, though this is scarcely apparent since the bores are staggered at an acute angle.

Two Plugs Each Side

The valves are operated by an overhead camshaft, which is driven at the front end by a chain. The arrangement of the cylinders results in two of the four sparking plugs being placed at each side of the engine, and ignition is by coil and distributor, the latter being driven by a vertical shaft, operated in turn by skew gears from the camshaft, and mounted high up at the back of the engine. The electrical gear is of Bosch manufacture.

In the four-speed gear box, which has behind its main housing a free wheel, a constant-mesh helical-toothed third speed is used, and engine and gear box form a neat, compact, and businesslike-looking unit, the sumps of both engine and gear box being ribbed for cooling. It is stated that at a peak of 4,000 r.p.m. the engine develops 35 b.h.p. The actual engine dimensions are: bore and stroke 69.55×78 mm., 1,194 c.c., tax £12.

Transmission is by an open propeller-shaft, with fabric universal joints, and the spiral-bevel-driven back axle is normal, except that it is of what is termed hypoid type, in which the driving bevel on the tail of the propeller-shaft is off-set at a point below the centre line of the crown wheel. The front suspension is independent, enclosed coil springs being used, following well-tried Lancia practice.

The usefully big luggage container at the rear of the car has a lid which hinges backwards against two light coil springs, so that a sufficiently wide opening is given to allow baggage to be put in or taken out, and here there is a clever, though small, point. Owing to the position of the number plate and tail lamp the lid of the container would foul the plate when opened, so the number plate is pivoted on its bracket, and the luggage-container lid is connected to it by a short section of chain, and when the lid is opened the plate swings round sufficiently to be out of the way.

A very interesting point is that the pillarless pressed-steel body is, in effect, also the frame of the car, for there is no ordinary chassis. This is a form of construction in which Lancia have had previous experience with the earlier Lambda.

The six-volt battery is in a compartment under the bonnet, and can be removed for attention when a bar held by a wing nut, and supporting, incidentally, the horn, has been swung to one side; the fuses, six of them in all, are very well placed, on the near side of the scuttle. The tyres are Michelin low pressures of the size known as 140×40, running at a pressure of 20 lb. per square inch. The price of the standard four-door saloon in this country is £390.

A good point of the electrical system is the Bosch master switch which, when pushed in at the first position, switches on the ignition, and its successive positions give the side and tail lamps, a flat-topped anti-dazzle beam, and the full head lamp beams. The switch is so arranged that, even though it may be moved rapidly from the "bright" to the "dim" position, one cannot inadvertently pass back to the side lamp position, thereby robbing oneself altogether of useful driving light. It is necessary to push in the switch lightly before it can be turned back to the side lamp position.

A chassis of normal character, upon which special bodies can be mounted in the ordinary way, is to be available as an alternative, but not to supplant the standard saloon, the chassis price being £325.

The engine is neatly laid out, and the auxiliaries are accessible.

The interior of the pillarless saloon is roomy and comfortable

"THE AUTOCAR" ROAD TESTS

11.9 h.p. LANCIA AUGUSTA SALOON

No. 856 (Post-War Series)

Extremely Efficient Engine and a Reasonably High Gear Ratio Give an Exceptionally Easy Performance

A SURPRISE is in store for anyone who tries the 11.9 h.p. four-cylinder Lancia Augusta, expecting it to be just another twelve horse-power car, perhaps good in view of the name of Lancia, but not necessarily outstanding. That, however, is exactly what the car is.

It has an extraordinarily efficient engine of just under 1,200 c.c., and carrying a £12 tax, and throughout the car there are clever and practical features of design at once endearing it to a driver who is interested in engine and chassis layout and in an efficient performance in relation to engine size, as opposed to someone who demands little more of a car than that it shall be a means of conveyance.

The Augusta was introduced, incidentally, at the Paris and Olympia Shows in 1932, but has only lately come on to this market actively. It is essentially a type of car produced by Italian and Continental conditions generally, which have the effect of moulding cars on certain well-defined lines; and in addition Lancia is a firm which has never been afraid to turn out something individual, in fact very largely different in important components from the majority of existing cars. This smaller model follows in many respects the design of the bigger cars, notably in the arrangement of the cylinder bores in an acute V formation giving a very compact engine, and in the use of the thoroughly well-tried Lancia system of independent front wheel suspension by means of coil springs at either side.

There are three main features which make this Lancia different from the average, ordinary car—first, that the power developed by the overhead camshaft engine is exceedingly useful; secondly, the car runs on high gear ratios, and therefore achieves its performance, easily and without fuss; and, thirdly, the weight of the complete car is not by any means high, though the saloon body is a good four-seater with plenty of space inside.

The maximum speed figure given in the table shows what the car can do, and it is to be remembered that the figure in question is a mean of several runs with and against the wind, the highest reading over the quarter-mile under favourable conditions of wind, but still on the level, being 67.16 m.p.h.

These are exceptionally good figures for a saloon car of this size and not of what is generally regarded as sports type; but even more important is the fact that the engine does not feel stressed at the maximum speed—due, no doubt, to the high gear ratio, whilst the car will keep up 50 m.p.h. on almost any kind of road with a delightful sense of ease, the engine running smoothly and ready the whole time to go faster if the driver chooses and traffic conditions permit. This it can do, too, with four people and luggage on board, just as easily as with the driver alone.

In spite of the fairly high top gear ratio, which has such marked advantages in giving an effortless high-speed performance, the car holds its speed well on the ordinary kind of main road hill, especially if a good steady swing is maintained.

There is, too, the very considerable asset to the experienced type of driver who is likely to be interested in a car such as this that the lower gears are remarkably useful for accelerating.

Top, third, and second are fairly close in ratio, third giving a genuine 50 m.p.h., second 38 m.p.h., and even first the quite high figure of 23 as a limit. Since the gear change is a rapid, very light-acting one, excellent results can be obtained by accelerating through the gears or by a quick drop down to third, whilst there is no sense of the engine becoming too "busy," and it remains smooth.

Third gear is very quiet indeed, barely distinguishable from top, in fact; the two other ratios are by no means noisy. By ordinary methods the gears almost fall in, so straightforward is the change; in addition, there is a free wheel, put in or out

11.9 h.p. LANCIA AUGUSTA SALOON

DATA FOR THE DRIVER

11.9 h.p., four cylinders, 69.55×78 mm. (1,194 c.c.). Tax £12.
Tyres: 140 × 40 on bolt-on wire wheels.

Engine—rear axle gear ratios.	Acceleration from steady speed. 10 to 30 m.p.h.	20 to 40 m.p.h.	30 to 50 m.p.h.	Timed speed over ¼ mile.
15.5 to 1	—	—	—	
9.9 to 1	6 1/5 sec.	—	—	
7.21 to 1	9 3/5 sec.	10 1/5 sec.	14 sec.	
4.87 to 1	16 sec.	17 3/5 sec.	21 1/5 sec.	65.22 m.p.h.

Acceleration from rest through the gears to 50 m.p.h., 22 3/5 sec.
Speed up Brooklands Test Hill from rest (1 in 5 average gradient), 17.16 m.p.h. (on first gear).
Acceleration up 15 yards of 1 in 5 gradient from rest, 4 3/5 sec.
Turning circle: 34ft.
Tank capacity 10 gallons, fuel consumption 30 m.p.g.
6-volt lighting set; automatic dynamo output control.
Weight: 16 cwt. 1 qr.
Price, with pillarless four-door saloon body, £390.

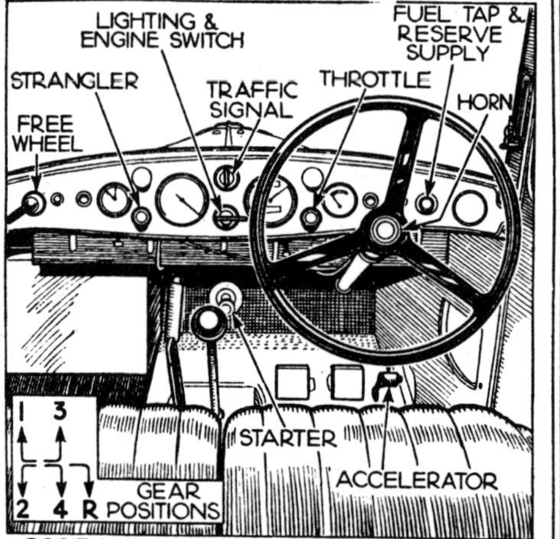

POSITIONS OF THE VARIOUS CONTROLS

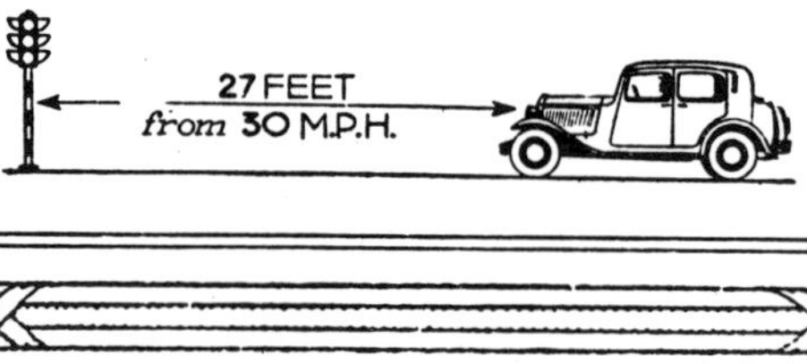

11.9 h.p. LANCIA AUGUSTA SALOON

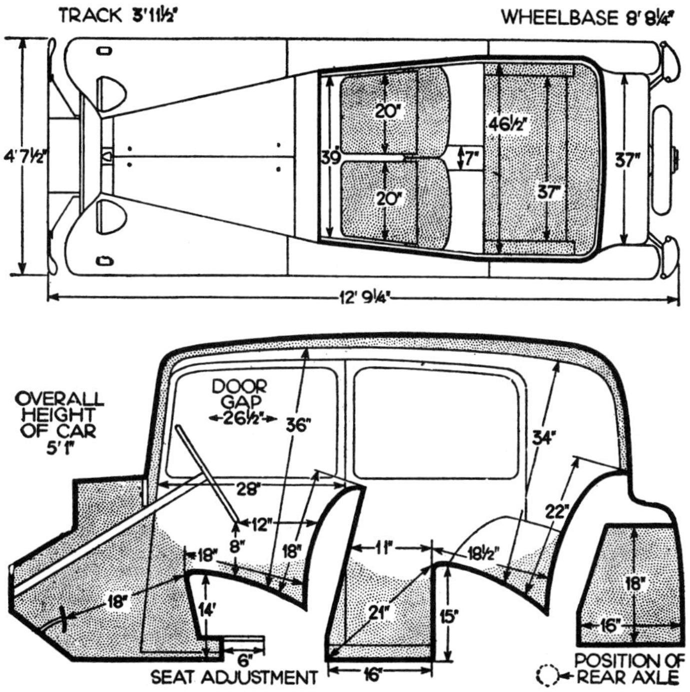

of action by means of a control within easy reach of the driver, and with the free wheel in use changing becomes a dead-easy matter without employing the clutch at all.

High average speeds are easily obtained on this car—in fact, exceptional figures are possible if full use is made of the acceleration. Control of the car as a whole is very light, and it has exceedingly powerful hydraulically operated brakes; a light touch on the pedal gives all the deceleration that is ordinarily needed.

The engine is notably quiet mechanically; there is a certain amount of carburetter intake roar. This car rides comfortably; there is some appreciable up and down movement over certain types of road surfaces, but it is soft movement, and over really badly pot-holed roads, of which several stretches were sought out during the test, it can travel without direct shock at speeds which would be impossible with a normally sprung machine.

There is some light movement noticeable through the steering wheel even on a good road, but never amounting to severe kick-back, as that term is understood. The car has an extremely good steering lock.

The body, of pressed-steel construction but very nicely finished, is of pillarless construction, with four doors. It has cord upholstery, the separate front seats are immediately adjustable and are set fairly high, giving a good driving position, and affording excellent vision.

The instruments are remarkably well illuminated at night; the speedometer, incidentally, proved accurate within decimal points up to 50 m.p.h., and did not exceed a reading of 67 during the fastest timed run mentioned.

There are semaphore arm traffic signals recessed into the rear quarters of the body, the instrument board, in addition to a clock, has a big fuel gauge, and at the right-hand side of it is a tap which besides, when pulled out, shutting off the supply from the under-bonnet tank, also, in an intermediate position, brings in the fuel reserve. At the back of the car is a useful size of luggage container.

A Berlina-bodied example of the 1934 Augusta 11.9 hp.

The AUTOCAR ROAD TESTS

Haymaking in Kent: the Lancia intrudes.

No. 961 (Post-War Series) 12.1 h.p. LANCIA AUGUSTA SEMI-SPORTS FOUR-SEATER

The Smallest Model of a Famous Italian Make Mildly Supercharged for Acceleration Purposes : Quiet, Flexible Running

BECAUSE it gives a lively road performance for its size, handles well, and feels right in the essentials, the 12.1 h.p. four-cylinder Augusta model Lancia created an excellent impression from the commencement when it was introduced in this country eighteen months or so ago. Weight has been kept down, the overhead camshaft, four-cylinder engine is of an efficient type, but quiet and easy running, and the saloon model last tried produced exceptionally good results as regards test figures.

Now it is an open model fitted with a supercharger to give a mild boost which has been tested. The engine being as useful as it is, it was clear that with some assistance as possible by a forced induction effect an already good performance could be still further improved, notably as regards top gear running and acceleration as a whole.

The conversion is carried out for the London and Home Counties distributors of Lancia cars, Kevill-Davies and March, Ltd., by whom this car was provided for test. As an extra, a Centric supercharger is added to the engine.

There is no intention of giving an exceptional maximum speed or of entirely altering the characteristics of the car. A maximum "blow" of 3.5-4 lb. per sq. in. is all that is developed, neither noise nor harshness is produced, and, deliberately, stronger valve springs and other similar modifications have not been introduced.

For a great part of the car's running, indeed—at cruising speeds and with the throttle at a steady opening—no "blow" is indicated on the supercharger pressure gauge. It is only when the throttle is opened wide that a boost is developed and the desired assistance to acceleration provided, but still the engine remains quiet and altogether smooth. It appears to be a sane application of a blower to a standard car, fulfilling the purpose of more effectively filling the cylinders with mixture than is possible under atmospheric pressure alone—the prime function of a supercharger.

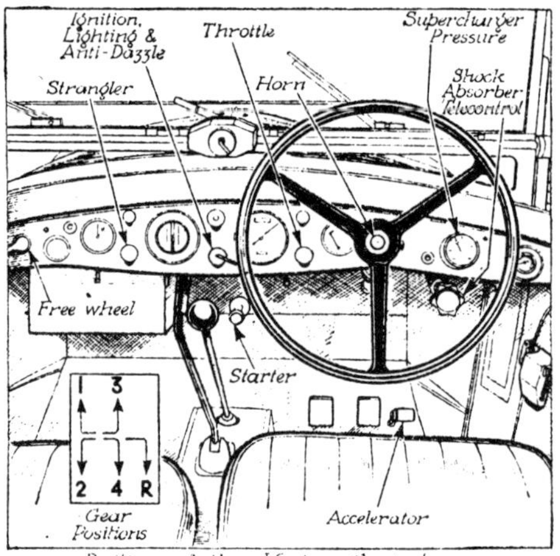

Positions of the Various Controls

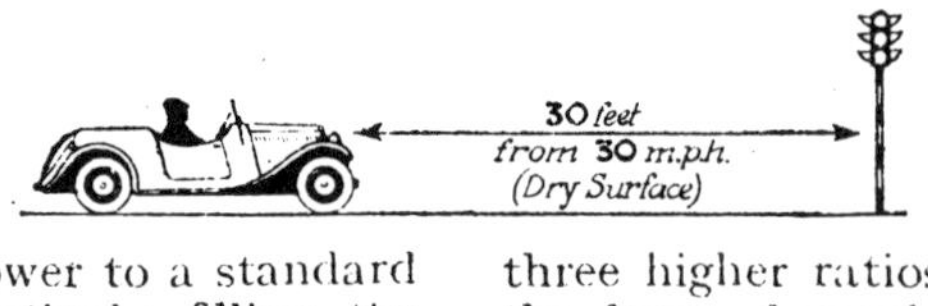

Also, as has been noticed with other supercharged machines, the low-speed running is smoothed out to a remarkable degree. Good in this as the Augusta is for its size in the ordinary way, this blown example seems still better, and has altogether exceptional capabilities on top gear for an engine of its capacity.

There is no immediate impression of the car having a supercharger. It is outstandingly quiet, and top gear can be used down to quite low speeds without snatch or jerk becoming apparent. When a leisurely method is preferred, it can be taken slowly up gradients, perhaps following other vehicles, without need for changing down, and so easily as to suggest that the engine is happy.

Whilst the maximum "blow" is not high, as already mentioned, this system is valuable for its particular purpose in that the supercharger will show pressure if the throttle is opened fully at speeds between 15 and 20 m.p.h. on top gear. If the driver listens, a faint whir, hardly a whine, can be detected at the lower speeds, but at higher speeds there is no added noise. The drive of the blower, by a belt, is, of course, silent, but any noise could not but be noticed, for the engine itself is very quiet.

This Lancia Augusta possesses a most attractive kind of performance, for it has adequate speed, quickly gets up to 55 or 60 m.p.h., and will run there without the least fuss or bother, at the same time being not at all a "gear-box" car except as a means to increasing the performance from the enthusiastic driver's point of view. Actually, the limits on the gears are fairly high, and most effective use can be made of third and second in sports machine fashion, though this is not essential for a good performance.

There is the further advantage that the gears are quiet and pleasing to handle. The lever is long, the action is light, and with quite ordinary methods of clutch control the gears almost fall in when changing upwards, especially between second and third, whilst with very mild speeding-up of the engine in changing down, quiet, certain movements are obtained, the three higher ratios being close. There is no assistance in the form of synchromesh, and it seems hardly necessary, though a free wheel is fitted and can be used to give a dead-easy, clutchless change, or be locked out of use.

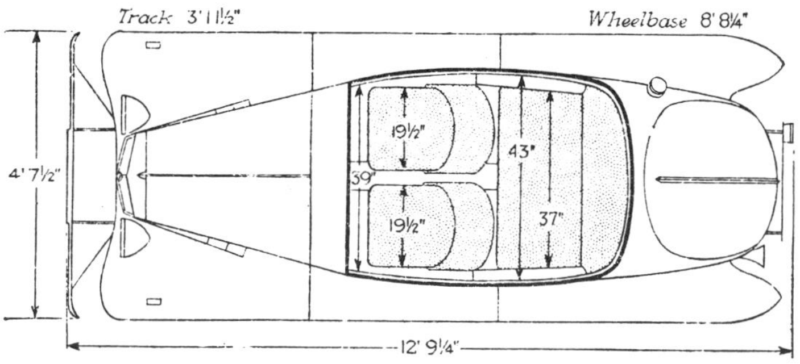

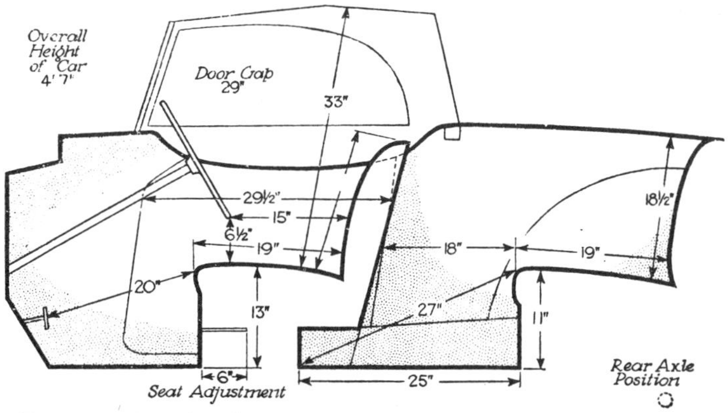

The steering is exceptionally light, though fairly high-geared so that control over the car is immediate, and a comparatively small turn of the wheel will change the car's course abruptly. The steering lock is remarkably good, which makes the car very handy to manœuvre.

In common with the larger Lancia models, the Augusta has the special system of front-wheel suspension utilising enclosed oil-damped coil springs at each side. This gives unusually comfortable riding, not only on good roads, but on pot - holed and ridged surfaces as well, without permitting roll or side-sway on corners. As has been noticed before, there is a slight tremor transmitted back to the steering wheel, more so on some surfaces than on others, and more noticeably at low speeds than at high, but never to an extent that requires the wheel to be held rigidly.

The Lancia with March body

Low-pressure tyres are fitted, running only at about 24 lb. per sq. in., and no doubt increase the comfort, besides which they do not make the steering heavy, but on corners and under fairly hard braking they "squeal."

This particular car had Telecontrol shock absorbers for the rear axle, which is normally sprung by half-elliptics, and these, as usual, permit a firmer effect for fast cornering, and can be supplied, if desired, at £9 5s. extra.

The hydraulically operated brakes have fine power suitable to the performance, but conceal this, as it were, behind a light operation. In emergency a firm push on the pedal brings the car up all-standing, but it still remains in a straight line.

The speedometer proved to be only 1.2 m.p.h. fast at 30, and less than 1 m.p.h. fast at 50, showing a reading of 77 at the best timed speed of 76.27 m.p.h., which was taken with the windscreen lowered. With the screen raised a best timed speed of 72.58 m.p.h. was recorded, the speedometer showing 75, and the mean of several readings over different quarter-miles on Brooklands thus was 70.59 m.p.h.

The body is a March open sports tourer, an English-built body, of course, fitted on the standard chassis. This is intended as a two-four-seater, with exceptionally comfortable separate front seats, immediately adjustable on Leveroll slides. A fairly high position is given, so that vision out of the car is better than is often the case nowadays, the edge of the near-side wing being visible to the driver without leaning forward, as well as a proper view of the off-side wing. The thin-rimmed steering wheel is set nearly vertical, and the right arm comes naturally inside the body without cramping when a passenger is carried.

Deep, wide wells at both front and rear give an unusual amount of leg room. The back seat has a comfortable cushion, but is intended really for emergency accommodation and as luggage space, the room afforded being exceptional. Access to the back compartment is by means of a step built into the near side of the body, emphasising the emergency nature of the seat, and the hood, of roll-up type, folds down behind the front seats and is only a two-seater hood, the back compartment being enclosed by a tonneau cover. If needed, a four-seater hood can be supplied at £9 10s. extra. There are side curtains for the front compartment.

The engine does not seem to have been made inaccessible for ordinary attention by the addition of the supercharger, which goes in neatly on the off side.

Starting was on every occasion found to be easy, and the engine had a regular tick-over, with no tendency to soot or oil its sparking plugs. It is not necessary to add oil to the fuel for the supercharger, a separate supply fed to the blower by suction being carried in a tank, which also is under the bonnet. The oil consumption for the supercharger seemed to be in the order of 2,000 m.p.g.

It is worth mentioning that the car tried showed 12,000 miles on its speedometer. Unsupercharged, the price of this model is £450.

A car which feels solid and safe, exceptionally easy in its running, and which makes a most decided appeal.

DATA FOR THE DRIVER

12.1 H.P. LANCIA AUGUSTA SEMI-SPORTS FOUR-SEATER.

PRICE, with March semi-sports four-seater body (with supercharger), £487 10s. Tax, £9 15s.

RATING : 12.1 h.p., four cylinders, o.h.v., 69.85 × 78 mm., 1,196 c.c.

WEIGHT, without passengers, 16 cwt. 3 qr. 10 lb.

TYRE SIZE : 140 × 40 on knock-off wire wheels.

LIGHTING SET : 6-volt ; automatic voltage control.

TANK CAPACITY : 10 gallons ; fuel consumption, 22-26 m.p.g.

TURNING CIRCLE (L. and R.) : 32ft. GROUND CLEARANCE : $6\frac{3}{4}$in.

ACCELERATION

Overall gear ratios	From steady m.p.h. of 10 to 30	20 to 40	30 to 50
4.87 to 1	12 sec.	$12\frac{3}{5}$ sec.	$14\frac{2}{5}$ sec.
7.21 to 1	8 sec.	$7\frac{1}{5}$ sec.	$8\frac{2}{5}$ sec.
9.90 to 1	$5\frac{3}{5}$ sec.	—	—
15.50 to 1	—	—	—

From rest to 50 m.p.h. through gears, $15\frac{1}{5}$ sec.

From rest to 60 m.p.h. through gears, 25 sec.

25 yards of 1 in 5 gradient from rest, $5\frac{3}{5}$ sec.

SPEED

	m.p.h.
Mean maximum timed speed over ¼ mile	74.53
Best timed speed over ¼ mile ...	76.27
Speeds attainable on indirect gears—	
1st	22
2nd	33-35
3rd	48-51
Speed from rest up 1 in 5 Test Hill (on 1st and 2nd gears)	19.69

Performance figures of acceleration and maximum speed are the means of several runs in opposite directions.

(Described in "The Autocar" of June 1st, 1934.)

All Independently Sprung Lancia

New 13 h.p. Four-cylinder Model with an Excellent Power-Weight Ratio

THERE is a new four-cylinder Lancia model built on the main principles of the design of this make for some years past in that there is no normal chassis frame, the body being of special steel construction and combining the functions of frame and coachwork, whilst the established Lancia feature of a narrow V arrangement of the cylinder bores is employed. This is known as the Aprilia, and is rated at 12.9 h.p., with a bore and stroke of 72 by 83 mm. (1,352 c.c.), the tax being £9 15s., and the unit giving the useful power output of 46 b.h.p. at 4,000 r.p.m. It is provided with a four-speed gear box.

Four-door pillarless saloon model of the new Lancia.

Drop-head cabriolet on the separate chassis available.

The front suspension is broadly similar to that found on Lancia cars, including the famous Lambda, for some years past, incorporating an oil-damped spring enclosed in a cylinder at each side, but there is a departure on this new Aprilia in that the rear wheel suspension is independent, too. At the rear is a transversely placed leaf spring, in conjunction with two torsion bars. Lockheed hydraulically operated brakes are employed, there is an 11-gallon fuel tank, and the electrical equipment is 6-volt.

Owing to the nature of the design, the car's total weight in relation to the power output is particularly favourable, and an unusually good performance is to be anticipated.

So far the standard saloon has been mentioned. This is priced at £345, having a wheelbase of 9ft. 0¼in., a track of 4ft. 2in., an overall length, including bumpers, of 13ft. 7½in., a width of 4ft. 10in. and height of 4ft. 9½in., the weight of the complete car being quoted as 15¾ cwt. This car runs on the quite high top gear ratio of 4.1 to 1.

Then, to meet the needs of those who require different types of bodywork, there is a long wheelbase version of the Aprilia, for which is used a separate chassis in the orthodox way, built up of box-shaped members to give an extremely rigid construction, low in relation to the road at the same time. A feature is that a completely smooth underside is secured. This separate chassis also has four-wheel independent springing, but runs on a lower top gear ratio of 4.55 to 1, and the wheelbase is 9ft. 4½in. This chassis carries a drop-head foursome cabriolet body priced at £495 complete, or will take larger styles of coachwork, including even one of six- or seven-seater accommodation with occasional seats. The chassis price is £280.

Death of Brilliant Designer

February 19th, 1937.

Vicenzo Lancia, Famous Italian Driver and Engineer

IT would be difficult to over-estimate the ability of Commendatore Vicenzo Lancia, who died in Turin last Monday. The design of the cars for which he became so famous, though unorthodox, was always sound and in advance of the times. Also in pre-War days, between 1904 and 1908, he was one of the most famous drivers of Fiats in races.

Lancia began his career in 1902 as a tester at the Fiat factory in Turin. His outstanding mechanical ability was recognised by Vaccarossi, of Michelin's, and Fogolin, of Fiat's, who formed a separate company for him in 1907. His first car was destroyed by fire in that year, but another 15 h.p. model was prepared and exhibited at Brussels and Turin in 1908. This has been regarded by many as the pioneer light car.

After the War came his four-cylinder Lambda model, a 1921 car with independent front wheel suspension and the chassis forming part of the body! There followed the eight-cylinder Dilambda, the little Augusta, and more recently the Aprilia. An unusual feature of their engines was the slightly staggered arrangement of the cylinders in the block.

Lancia leaves a widow and three children. He died aged fifty-seven and a rich man. Although he rose to fame from humble parentage he had a profound knowledge on many subjects, including history and photography. He drove in the Gordon Bennetts of 1904 and 1905, was third in the Florio Cup, 1905, fourth in the Vanderbilt Cup the same year, drove the second Fiat home behind Nazzaro in the first of all Grands Prix, being fifth in general classification, was second in the 1906 Vanderbilt Cup Race, and second in the 1907 Targa Florio. He won the first Kaiserpreis eliminating race in 1907, and came in second in the 1908 Targa Florio.

The AUTOCAR ROAD TESTS

No. 1,122.—12.9 h.p. LANCIA APRILIA PILLARLESS SALOON

New Four-cylinder Model Shows an Exceptional Turn of Speed, and is Remarkably Easy Running and Very Comfortable

ALWAYS this make provides interest on the road, and displays a clever mechanical layout. The Aprilia is the latest successor to the small four-cylinder Lancia Augusta, a car which made friends in this country for its lively performance and pleasing manner of handling. This new model has an engine of 12.9, against 11.9 h.p., rating, and also four-wheel independent suspension—a still somewhat rare feature.

Its overhead-camshaft-and-valve engine—arranged in the traditional Lancia fashion with "staggered" cylinder bores—does not appear to be of a highly tuned or specially high-compression type, but it gives the car a thoroughly interesting performance, by virtue of a favourable power-to-weight ratio. The figure of 17½ cwt. for a saloon that can be a five-seater is astonishingly low, being achieved by special construction of the body, which eliminates the ordinary chassis frame.

This car travels on the open road in a fast stride, at 60 m.p.h. or more, with a remarkable absence of fuss. Indeed, then, the engine might well be judged to be larger than it is, and be taken for a six-cylinder, so smooth is it. The acceleration is decidedly brisk if the gears are used fairly freely at the lower speeds. Absence of wind "shriek" no doubt has much to do with the suggestion of particularly easy fast running. There is the impression of the little car sweeping along with hardly a sound of mechanism working; it seems impossible to over-drive it.

A result, in conjunction with high-speed cornering capabilities and good brakes, is that a distinctly high average speed can be held. A point of considerable value in this same connection is that the car is of just the right size on present-day roads. On a route reasonably free from traffic 45 miles were achieved in an hour without exceeding 70 m.p.h., and this with four up.

The engine can be taken up and up in revs on the gears, the speed increasing progressively and the engine showing no distress, not altering its characteristics, in fact, until the valve bounce point is reached. It is worth while using the lower gears on the Aprilia, for the maxima they give are decidedly useful, and the extra power afforded for acceleration or hill-climbing is of considerable value when any attempt is being made to hurry. Speed on the quite high top gear will fall off fairly rapidly against normal gradients approached comparatively slowly, though the car will swing over these when travelling fast at the commencement. Engine "flutter," as well as slight transmission judder sometimes, will come in below about 15 m.p.h. on top gear.

DATA FOR THE DRIVER

12.9 H.P. LANCIA APRILIA PILLARLESS SALOON.

PRICE, with four-door pillarless saloon body, £298. Tax, £9 15s.
RATING: 12.9 h.p., four cylinders, o.h.v., 72 × 83 mm., 1,352 c.c.
WEIGHT, without passengers, 17 cwt. 2 qr. 4 lb.
LB. (WEIGHT) PER C.C.: 1.45.
TYRE SIZE: 140 × 40 low pressure on bolt-on steel disc wheels.
LIGHTING SET: 6-volt. Automatic voltage control (no ammeter).
TANK CAPACITY: 11 gallons; approx. normal fuel consumption, 25-28 m.p.g.
TURNING CIRCLE: (L. and R.) 34ft. **GROUND CLEARANCE:** 7½in.

ACCELERATION

Overall gear ratios	From steady m.p.h. of 10 to 30	20 to 40	30 to 50
4.10 to 1	14.6 sec.	15.5 sec.	16.3 sec.
6.10 to 1	8.9 sec.	8.7 sec.	9.9 sec.
9.21 to 1	5.6 sec.	6.5 sec.	—
14.42 to 1	—	—	—

From rest to 30 m.p.h. through gears, 6.2 sec.
To 50 m.p.h. through gears, 15.4 sec.
To 60 m.p.h. through gears, 25.2 sec.
To 70 m.p.h. through gears, 45.2 sec.
25 yards of 1 in 5 gradient from rest, 6.1 sec.

SPEED

	m.p.h.
Mean maximum timed speed over ¼ mile	76.92
Best timed speed over ¼ mile...	81.08
Speeds attainable on indirect gears (normal and maximum):—	
1st	21-23
2nd	36-41
3rd	55-61
Speed from rest up 1 in 5 Test Hill (on 1st gear)	19.22

BRAKE TEST: Mean stopping distance from 30 m.p.h., 33.5ft. (Dry concrete).

Performance figures for acceleration and maximum speed are the means of several runs in opposite directions.

(Described in "The Autocar" of October 9th, 1936.)

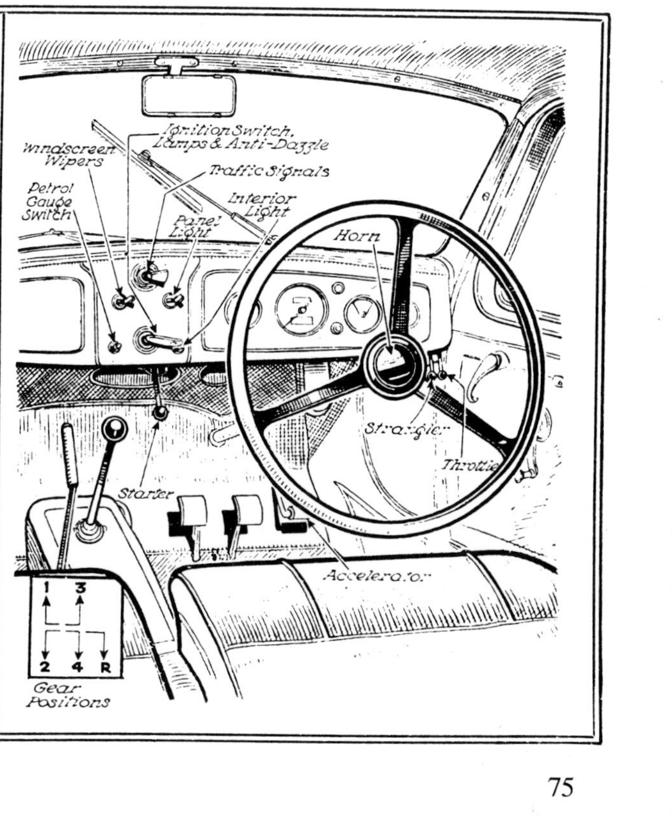

A "plain" gear change is fitted, meaning that there is no aid to changing. However, the movements are exceptionally light and quick and satisfactory. The travel of the lever between gear and gear is short. Third is so quiet as hardly to be distinguishable from top, and second is not at all conspicuous. Certainly there is a fascination in climbing fast on a quiet third with an efficient little engine turning over rapidly but effortlessly. On second gear the car was making a fine climb of the usual 1 in 6½ hill, when it was completely baulked by other traffic, and first gear had to be used.

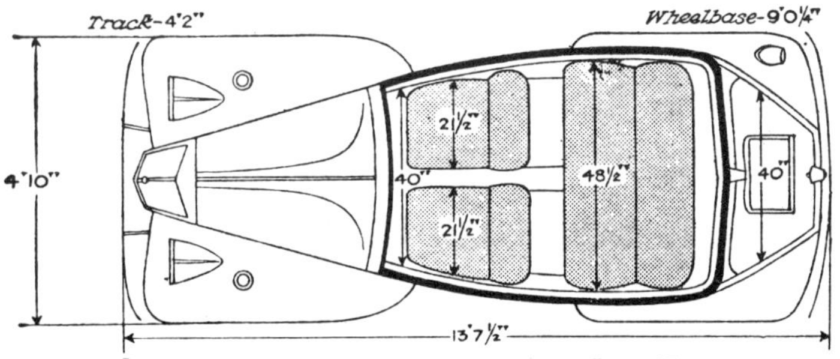

Much of the unusual "feel" of this car on the road comes from its special suspension, which embodies the customary Lancia enclosed vertical coil spring at each side in front, and the new feature of a single transverse leaf spring mounted low at the rear, in conjunction with a torsion bar, for independent suspension of the back wheels.

There is an essential softness about this system. No impression of tautness from a rock-firm springing is experienced, but the car is most satisfactorily safe-feeling at speed both on the straight and around corners. Also, the comfort of riding is quite exceptional for rear seat as well as front passengers. Normal variations in surface are scarcely noticed. When a more extreme deflection is caused by a specially bad surface, definite and fairly hard wheel movement is apparent, though this is not transmitted in shock to the car's occupants.

The whole control is light, the steering being no exception. The easiest possible movement of the hands keeps the car on a normal course. There is good caster action, and, curiously, the steering gear ratio feels higher than it is, about three and a third turns actually being needed from lock to lock. A "shake" set up in the steering at times on certain road surfaces, at around 20 m.p.h. This did not become extreme, and was not actually uncomfortable, while no trace of it was ever encountered at higher speeds. The steering lock is outstandingly good for manœuvring and taking sharp corners.

Hydraulically operated brakes give fine power; a certain, all-square emergency pull-up can be made, and for ordinary slowing down the driver needs scarcely to do more than brush the pedal with his foot. The hand-brake lever is not too convenient, and required to be pulled hard on to hold the car on any appreciable gradient. An adequate re-start is made on 1 in 4 in spite of a high first gear ratio.

In driving position this car strikes the right note from the commencement of a stranger's experience of it, the wheel being almost vertical, the pedals well placed, and the gear lever within comfortable reach. Also, there is proper room for the feet. Another point is that the driving seat has an unusually fine-adjustment range of movement, and this is very easily made. There is the impression of a short bonnet which falls away to the front, hence giving forward vision near to the car. The top of the steering wheel tends, however, to come into the line of sight, and neither wing is visible, though this is not of such importance as applies with a bigger car. The windscreen is of good breadth and depth. In general appearance the car is slightly unusual, more particularly at the rear.

Immediately in front of the driver are the instruments, which include an interesting kind of petrol gauge, a reading being illuminated in red when a button is pressed. A British type of speedometer was fitted to this particular car, and proved to be fractionally slow at 30 and 40, only fractionally fast at 50, and 4.1 m.p.h. fast at 70, while the highest reading shown was 84 at the excellent, and even unexpected, best timed speed of 81.08 m.p.h. achieved by this 13 h.p. car. The lighting of the instruments at night is weak. The beam provided by the Bosch head lamps is capital in spite of a six-volt set, and the anti-dazzle system is found to be most effective.

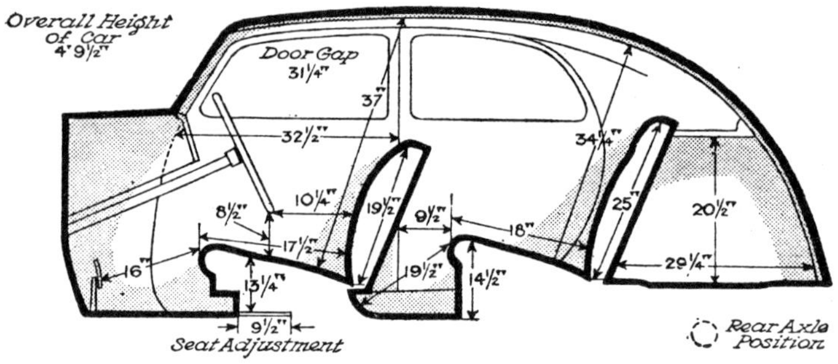

Seating dimensions are measured with cushions and squabs uncompressed

Cloth upholstery is used, and, though outwardly possessing no special features, the seats prove comfortable for two hours or so at a stretch. The interior is plainly finished in English eyes, but the essential fittings are provided, including a driver-operated control for the rear window blind and twin windscreen wiper blades working from the bottom, which, however, do not go down out of sight. The windscreen is fixed, and there is no special provision for ventilation apart from louvres over the door windows, nor is a sliding roof fitted. The rear compartment gives excellent leg room, wide but not deep foot wells being employed, and getting in and out is easy. The mirror view is fairly good.

In a tail locker two wide, shallow suitcases are provided, and the lid of this compartment has to be opened to reach the petrol filler. The engine is neat and surprisingly compact, with a good external finish. From cold it seems advisable to make minimum use of the mixture control, otherwise an instantaneous start may not be secured. Automatically operated radiator shutters are fitted behind the decorative grille, and in this space, too, are the dynamo, the steering box, and some electrical auxiliaries.

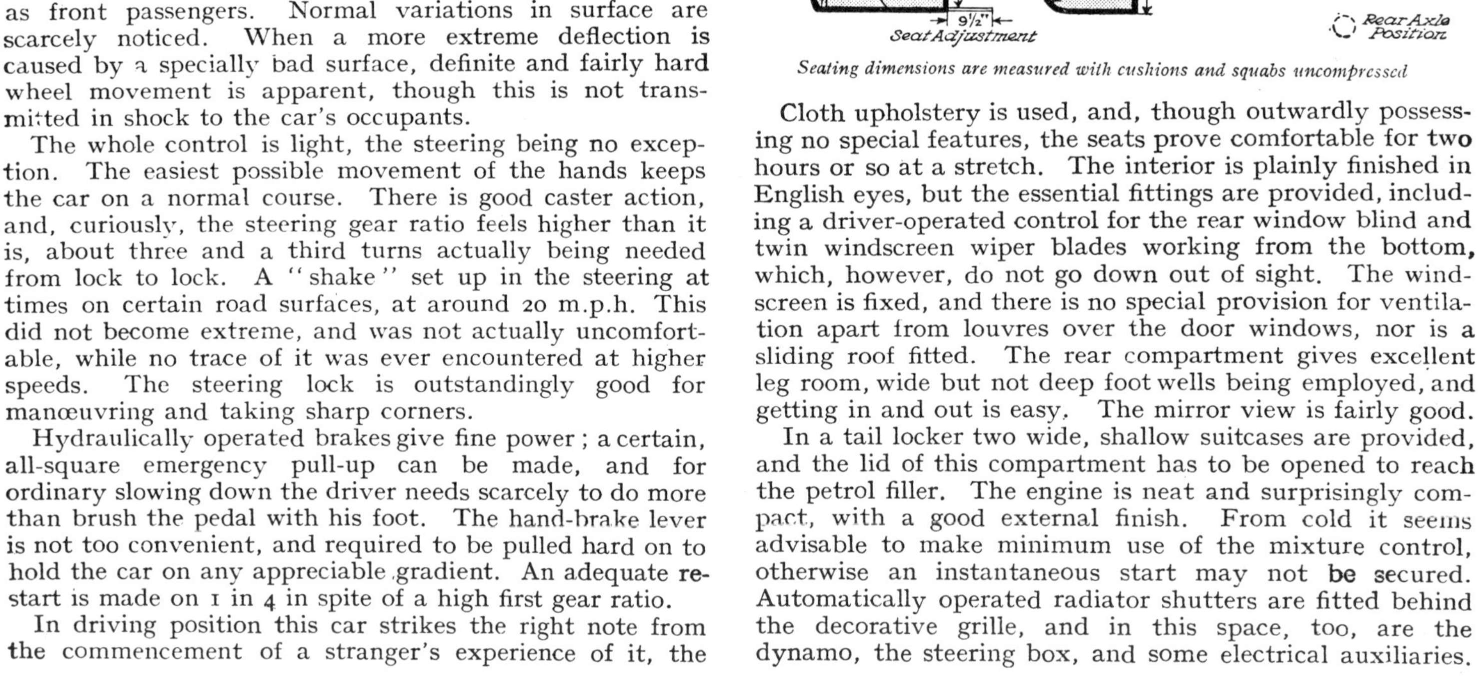

Visibility test chart for the Lancia Aprilia saloon.

New Lancia Aprilia Chassis

Introduced to Take Special Coachwork to Reinforce the Standard Saloon

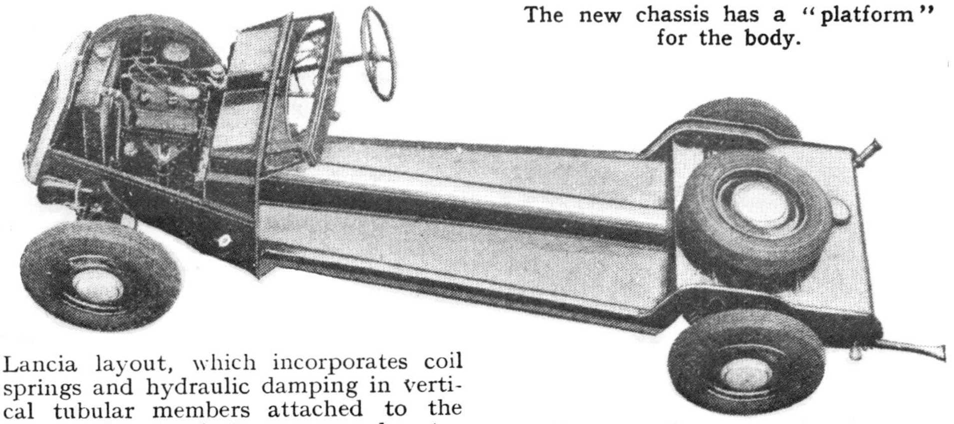

The new chassis has a "platform" for the body.

SINCE its introduction a year ago the Lancia Aprilia has earned an excellent reputation for its combination of comfort and high performance. It has many points of interest, for it is of chassisless construction, the streamlined steel body shell also serving as the chassis.

At the time of its introduction it was announced that it would appear in a conventional chassis form also. Whereas the standard pillarless saloon model has a wheelbase of 9ft with a track of 4ft. 2in., the chassis has a wheelbase of 9ft. 4½in. The frame is of pressed-steel boxed and welded construction, and its upper surface presents a flat floor or platform for the reception of the coachwork, broken only by the propeller shaft tunnel which helps to stiffen the frame.

At the rear of the frame is mounted the hypoid final drive and differential, for the rear wheels are independently sprung and the drive to them is by universally jointed shafts. The wheels are carried by pivoted levers or radius rods which locate them, and the levers are splined to torsion rods which have their other ends anchored to the chassis. There is also a transverse half-elliptic spring with a trunnion mounting at its centre. The front suspension is also independent and follows the well-known Lancia layout, which incorporates coil springs and hydraulic damping in vertical tubular members attached to the frame. Steering is by worm and sector and a transverse drag link is now used.

Quite unorthodox is the four-cylinder engine, as the cylinders may be described as set in pairs slightly staggered in narrow V formation. The bore and stroke are 72 by 83 mm. (1,352 c.c.), treasury rating 12.9 h.p., tax £9 15s. The overhead valves are set in hemispherical combustion chambers in which the sparking plugs are mounted centrally, and the valves are operated by push-rods and rockers. A Zenith carburettor supplies the mixture.

A single-plate clutch and four-speed gear box with silent third form a unit with the engine, which is mounted in the frame on four short quarter-elliptic springs, two at each side, while there is a steady mounting behind the gear box in addition. Lockheed hydraulic brakes are used.

Foursome drop-head cabriolet, price £465.

Four types of coachwork are offered on the chassis, and the six-light, four-door saloon is of particularly graceful appearance, having wide doors, ample seating accommodation, adjustable single-piece front seat, and wide rear seat with centre arm-rest and foot-rests. The upholstery is in leather and the equipment includes built-in traffic indicators and a large rear luggage boot in which is also carried the spare wheel. The price is £495, and at the same figure is offered a four-door, four-light close-coupled saloon with sliding roof.

A foursome drop-head cabriolet with two large doors and four drop windows costs £465, and at the same figure is offered a semi-sports open tourer with separately adjustable front seats and a rear seat which can be enclosed.

Incidentally, the price of the chassis, known as Model 239, is £270, and the standard five-seater streamlined saloon with a 9ft. wheelbase, known as Model 238, is, of course, continued, its price being £330.

Standard five-seater saloon, which costs £330.

Six-light, four-door saloon, price £495.

September 1st, 1939. *The Autocar.*

SOME QUERIES AND REPLIES

READERS' EXPERIENCES

No. 13293.—Lancia Aprilia

ON the advice of knowledgeable friends I purchased, in July, 1938, an Aprilia which had then done 6,000 miles. I ran it, with unvarying satisfaction, a further 10,000 miles and part-exchanged it for a latest type 1939 on February 1st, 1939.

The car first referred to had a Brooklands outer-circuit speed of 78.73 m.p.h. and a maximum of about 82 m.p.h. During my ownership its petrol consumption was 28-29 m.p.g., driven hard—using Shell.

It was decoked at 10,000 miles and had, at the same time, new piston rings fitted; subsequently no oil was used between sump emptyings every 1,000 miles. On one occasion over sixty miles were accomplished in one hour on the road in England, and the car would always, when called upon, do an extraordinary average speed.

The 1939 car has now done 16,000 miles at 30.2 m.p.g., its speed is slightly higher than that of its predecessor and its road-holding even better, perhaps by reason of the Broadbase Michelin tyres with which it is fitted as standard.

I cruise at 70 m.p.h. when circumstances permit, but am not afraid of speeds of 80 m.p.h., for as long as they can be held in this country. Of troubles I have had none with either car, and as with its predecessor, I find no need to "top up" with oil between sump drainings every 1,000 miles.

I know no car which will do a better average or which is less tiring to drive at continued high speeds. This is my 68th car in 35 years of ownership and I would not exchange it for any I know. I have no interest in the *marque* save gratitude for such good service.—LIONEL MARTIN.

Introduced in 1937, the Aprilia was Vincenzo Lancia's final creation. With independent torsion-bar rear suspension, an all-up weight of about 1,800lb and a 1,352cc engine producing 47bhp, even the 1st Series model (left) *could top 80mph. On the 1939 model* (below)*, several detail improvements were introduced and the engine capacity was increased to 1,486cc.*

(Opposite top:) *saloon versions of the Astura were the recognised mode of transport for dignitaries in Mussolini's Italy during the late 1930s, but the 2.9 litre V8-engined chassis also attracted the attention of the country's famous coachbuilders, among them Pinin Farina, who produced this elegant version in 1938.*

(Opposite lower:) *introduced just before the war in 1939, the Ardea was a miniature version of the Aprilia, with a 903cc engine producing just 29bhp. By 1949, on the 4th series model shown here, engine power had risen to 30bhp and there was a five-speed gearbox to help it along.*

Earl's Court 1949

The Autocar,
September 30, 1949

LANCIA [182]

Lancia (England), Ltd., Lancia Works, Ealing Road, Wembley, Middlesex.

BEFORE the war the Lancia Aprilia saloon set such a high standard in performance and road holding that it was often wrongly regarded as a sports car. The post-war model, now seen in England for the first time, is unchanged in general design, but has a larger engine of 1,485 c.c., which makes it one of the fastest small family cars available. Weight is saved by using an integral body-chassis structure, and the fine handling qualities are helped by concentrating weight within the wheelbase and eliminating overhang at front or rear. The engine is a V-four, shorter than a four in line. Also shown here for the first time is the little Ardea, a scaled-down version of the Aprilia, which has an equal reputation for performance and handling. Specially interesting is the five-speed gear box, fifth being a geared-up overdrive ratio for economical main road cruising.

Specification

Ardea.—4 cyl, 65×68 mm (903 c.c.) o.h.v.; 5-speed, synchromesh (14.57, 5.10, 7.3, 11.25 and 19.9). Central change. Wheelbase 8ft, track (front) 3ft 9¾in, (rear) 3ft 10½in. Length 12ft 1½in; width 4ft 6¼in. Ground clearance 6¾in. Suspension, independent front, ½-elliptic rear. Tank capacity 6½ gallons.

Aprilia.—4 cyl., 74.61×85 mm (1,486 c.c.), o.h.v; 4-speed, synchromesh (4.1, 6.1, 9, 14.41). Central change. Wheelbase 9ft 0¼in; track (front) 4ft 1¾in, (rear) 4ft 2½in. Length 12ft 10¾in; width 4ft 11in. Ground clearance 7½in. Suspension, independent front, torsion bar rear. Tank capacity 10½ gallons.

No British price quoted.

Lancia Aurelia

V-SIX ENGINE AT FRONT

SINCE the Lancia Aprilia went out of production a few months ago, after a career extending over 14 years, the arrival of its successor has been awaited with great interest, and the new car, the Aurelia, is being revealed to the public at the Turin Motor Show which opened this week.

Technically, the Aurelia is one of the most interesting cars evolved in post-war Europe, yet the requirements of present-day motorists have been met without abandoning the traditional features of Lancia design and the unique character which has made the *marque* famous. It is a fine example of the way in which Italian designers have been taking a detached look at the automobile as at present known, and seeking new solutions to old problems without resorting to freakish experiments.

The Aprilia could no longer meet the current demand for more body space, better visibility, greater luggage capacity and more graceful body lines, but Ing. Jano has succeeded in providing these features in the new car without sacrificing the Lancia qualities of lightness, liveliness, good acceleration, high cruising speed and economical operation. It was a difficult task, and has called for bold innovations in engine design, mechanical layout, transmission and suspension. Yet the car still has the integral construction and vertical coil spring front suspension which have been seen on Lancias since 1923 and, like its predecessors, it is offered as a pillarless four-door saloon which is exceptionally easy to enter.

For the first time, Lancia introduce a

SPECIFICATION

Engine.—Six cylinders, V formation at 60 deg. 70×76 mm, 1,754 c.c. Overhead valves inclined at 52 deg in hemispherical combustion chambers. Operation by push-rods and rockers from single camshaft. Compression ratio 6.85 to 1. 56 b.h.p. at 4,000 r.p.m. Maximum torque 78 lb ft at 3,000 r.p.m.

Transmission.—Two-piece propeller-shaft driving dry single-plate clutch and four-speed gear box at rear in unit with differential. Steering column change. Synchromesh for second, third and top. Geared-up top. Overall ratios: 13.44, 8.65, 5.82 and 4.05 to 1. Reverse 17 to 1.

Suspension.—Coil springs in vertical slides at front enclosed in oil bath with integral hydraulic dampers. Independent at rear by single wishbones and coil springs with double-acting piston-type dampers.

Brakes.—Sabif hydraulic on all four wheels. Rear brakes inboard on differential casing. Hand brake operates shoes in rear drums.

Wheels and Tyres.—Perforated steel discs with tyres 165×400 mm on wide-base rims. 5.50×16in tyres for export.

Electrical Equipment.—Coil ignition. 12 volt, 48 ampere-hour battery.

Steering.—Worm and sector.

Structure.—Integral body-chassis in steel for saloon. Box-section platform for special coachwork.

Dimensions.—Saloon, wheelbase 9ft 4 7/16in. Track (front) 4ft 2 3/8in, (rear) 4ft 3 1/8in. Overall length 14ft 5 7/8in, width 5ft 1 3/16in. Height 4ft 11 1/16in. Ground clearance 6in. Weight (dry) 2,380 lb. Cabriolet on separate chassis has wheelbase 9ft 6 1/2in, length 15ft 6 31/32in, width 5ft 4 15/16in, and dry weight 2,490 lb.

Fuel Tank.—13 gallons with 2 gals in reserve.

Price.—Not available in England. Price in Italy, 1,830,000 lire at 1,700 to £1=£1,075 (saloon). Cabriolet 2,600,000 lire=£1,530. Chassis 1,240,000 lire=£730.

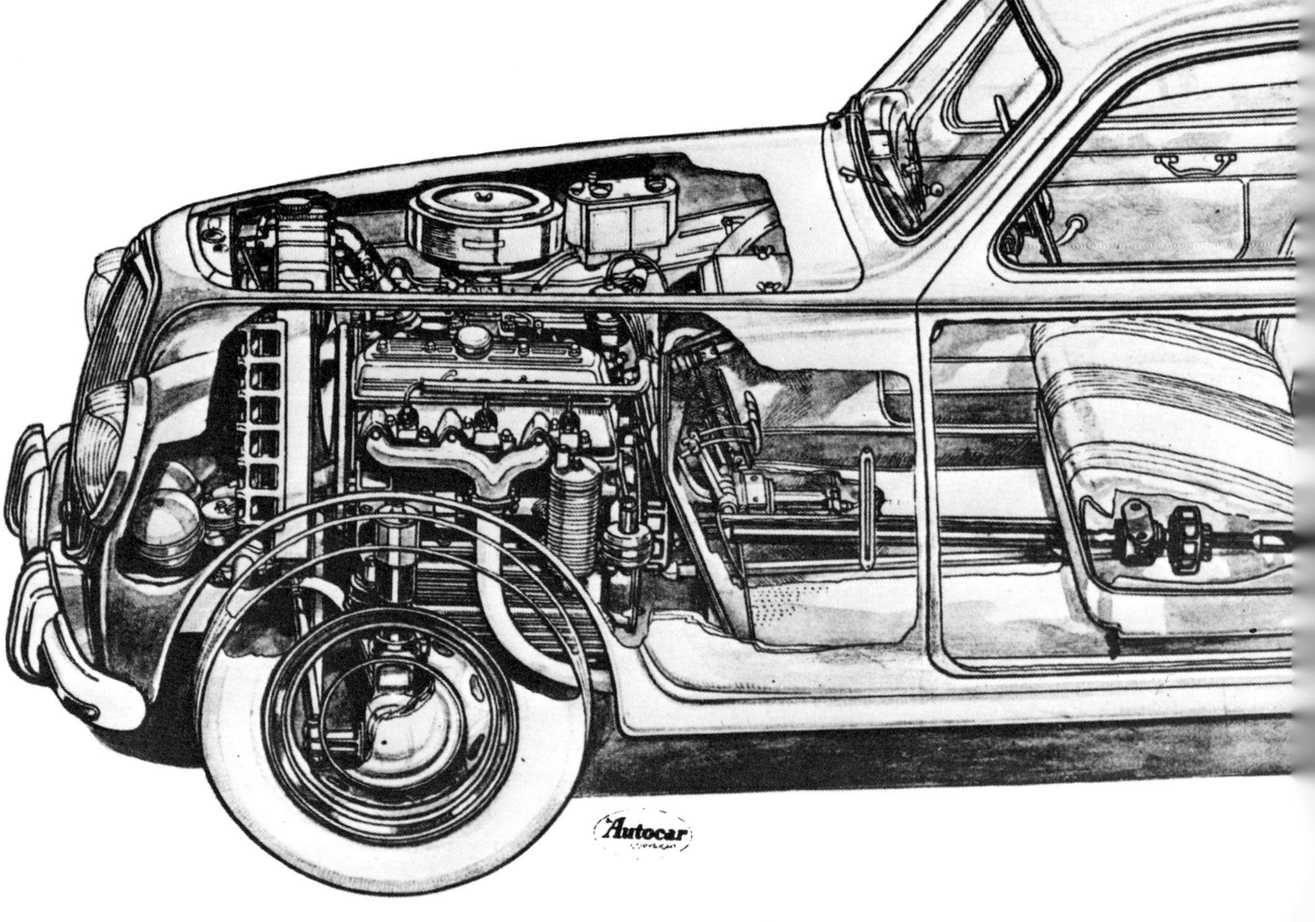

CLUTCH, GEAR BOX AND FINAL DRIVE AT REAR : INDEPENDENT SUSPENSION ALL ROUND

six-cylinder engine, but it maintains their record of compactness in power units, being a V-six with a cleverly designed valve gear operating inclined valves in hemispherical heads from a single camshaft in the crankcase.

Equally startling is the removal of clutch and gear box to the rear of the car, where they are attached to the body structure as one unit with the differential. This clears the front toe-board of obstructions and cuts the propeller-shaft tunnel down to the minimum. All the gears are indirect and the propeller-shaft takes up so little space that it has been possible to build a roomy five-six-seater saloon having adequate ground clearance and head room, with an overall height of under five feet. The body line is more graceful than on previous Lancias, but it remains quite simple, and the wing panels, both front and rear, can be removed for repair.

Besides the saloon, there is a separate chassis with slightly longer wheelbase and box section platform frame, which is available to coachbuilders, and three models—two cabriolets by Pinin and Stabilimenti Farina, and a station wagon by Viberti—will be offered as models in the standard range.

Body and chassis structures are of steel, but a great deal of weight has been saved on engine and transmission by the use of aluminium castings. The two cylinder blocks are cast in one with the top half of the crankcase, and another casting forms the sump and lower half of the crankcase, with fins on the outside to assist in cooling the oil. Heads and rocker boxes are cast in aluminium and the cylinders are hardened liners dropped into the blocks. They seat on faces at the top and the water passages at the base of each liner are sealed by twin rubber rings.

On the four-cylinder Lancia engines built on the narrow V principle, the cylinders are cast in one block with their centre lines converging at a point below the crankshaft centre line, so that they are all slightly offset, but the new engine has two separate banks of cylinders at an angle of 60 degrees, and the centre lines of the cylinders converge exactly on the centre line of the shaft. There are four main bearings carrying the six-throw crankshaft, which is counterbalanced and, owing to the short stroke of the engine, has substantial overlaps between main and big-end journals. All the bearings have Hoyt 11 linings on centrifugally cast bronze shells, the mains being 54mm in diameter and the big-ends 44mm.

The camshaft lies centrally in the crankcase above the crankshaft and is driven by a double chain. The valves are operated through hollow aluminium push rods which work rockers set fore and aft over each cylinder head rather as on a motor cycle cylinder. The valves are inclined to each other at an angle of 52 degrees.

There is only one carburettor, a Solex with twin chokes mounted centrally between the cylinder blocks. It has two separate throttles synchronized by gears and feeding into two manifolds which are completely water-jacketed and warmed

Lancia's oil-immersed telescopic front suspension with built-in hydraulic dampers and forward mounted steering gear box. Below : The gear lever is very neatly mounted on the steering column. Full visibility of the instruments is ensured by the three-spoked steering wheel.

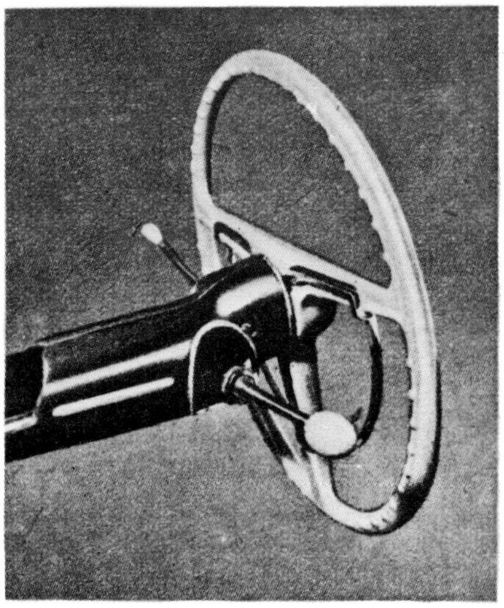

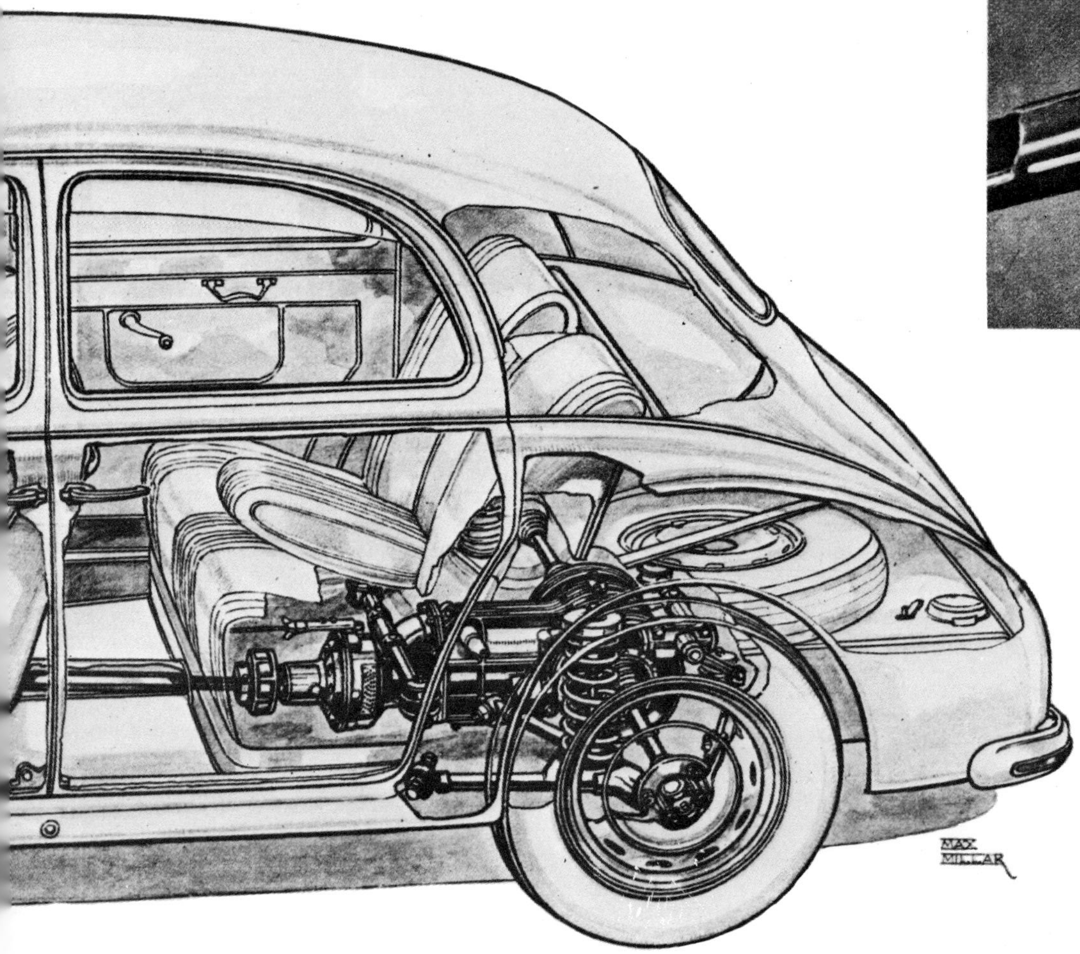

The short V engine and the removal of clutch and gear box to the rear of the car provide an exceptional amount of body space, with unobstructed floors having very shallow transmission tunnels in both front and rear compartments. The overhangs at front and back are exceptionally short.

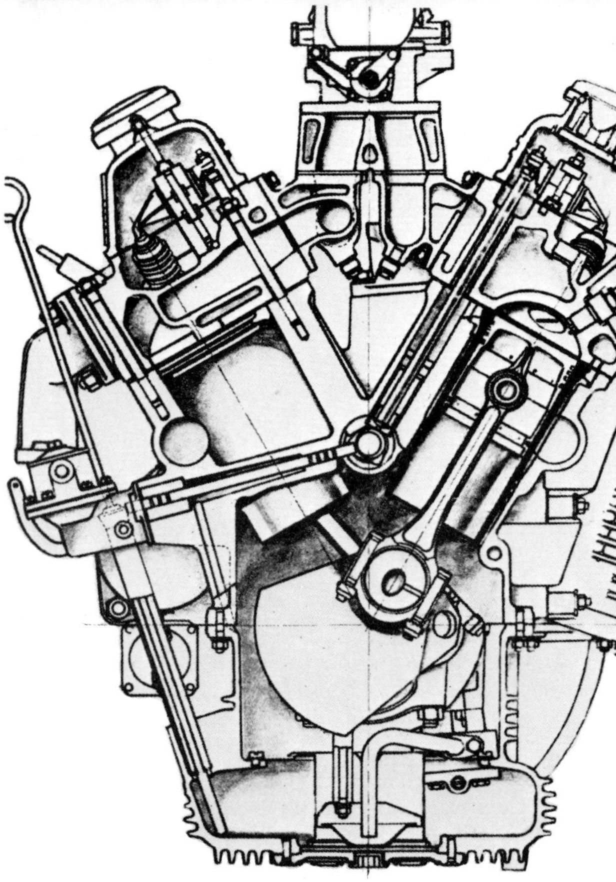

The V-six Lancia engine in section. With cylinders of the right bank numbered 1, 3, 5 and those of the left bank 2, 4 and 6, the firing order is 1, 4, 3, 6, 5, 2. Below : The crankshaft and connecting-rods. The crankpins are set at 60 degrees to each other—an equal division of 360 degrees—and the shaft runs in four main bearings.

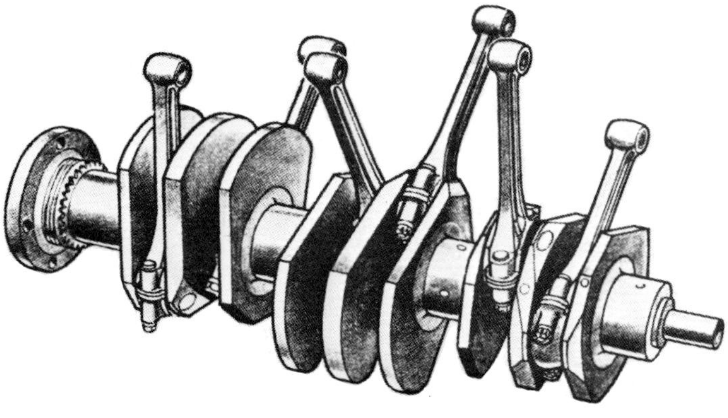

Lancia Aurelia — continued —

by water rising from the cylinder heads. Three-branch exhaust manifolds are mounted on the lower sides of the cylinder blocks and lead into twin exhaust pipes with separate silencers suspended by rubber strips beneath the floor of the car.

The water pump has a bronze centrifugal impeller in an aluminium housing and is mounted on a pedestal between the banks of cylinders. Water from the radiator enters round the cylinder barrels at each side of the engine and is drawn off past the heads by the pump, via the inlet manifolds. There is one thermostat in the riser to the header tank and another inside the tank operates a set of radiator shutters. Rapid warming up in cold conditions is thus assured and some protection is offered against freezing of the radiator when starting out on very cold days.

Lubrication of the engine is by a gear-type pump which passes all its output through a big filter with a washable element contained in an external aluminium housing. The relief valve is located in the filter housing and has an easily accessible external adjustment. Distributor and fuel pump are both driven from the camshaft.

Immediately behind the flywheel at the rear of the engine is a flexible rubber coupling with aluminium spiders to which is splined a small-diameter propeller-shaft running at engine speed. The shaft is in two sections, with an intermediate bearing which is mounted in soft rubber and is self-aligning. There is a second rubber coupling at this point and a third in front of the clutch on the nose of the transmission casing.

Although the clutch is of the usual dry single-plate type the diameter has been kept small by careful design and it is engaged by compound spiral springs.

All the gears are indirect as the clutch shaft is at the bottom of the box and the output shaft at the top. There are four forward speeds, the upper three having baulk-ring synchromesh, and top is geared up. One remarkable feature of the gear box is that it incorporates an arrangement also seen on the Fiat 1400, whereby the second gear pinions and their synchromesh unit are carried outside the main casing, thus producing a compact assembly with well-supported shafts. The transmission unit has its own vane-type oil pump which lubricates all bearings under pressure.

Brakes on all four wheels are Italian Sabif hydraulic, with single-leading shoes all round; the brakes for the rear wheels are carried directly on the differential casing to cut down unsprung weight.

The design of the rear suspension and drive assembly is extraordinarily interesting and reflects the considerable experience gained with independent rear suspension on the Lancia Aprilia. Special care has been taken to ensure reliable operation over long periods of the universal joints on the drive shafts. Dogs on the stub shafts from the differential engage with cast iron cylindrical members of pot-type universals. The drive shafts carry forks riding in needle roller bearings in steel blocks which slide in channels cut in the iron drive members. Angular movement of the shaft is accommodated by the spherically ground outer faces of the steel blocks working against the inside of an aluminium pot surrounding the whole assembly. The housing is filled with oil and if, after considerable mileage, the section in contact with the steel blocks becomes worn it can easily be turned to bring a new section into use.

An important factor in ensuring a long life for the universal joints on the drive shafts on an independent rear suspension system lies in making the shafts as long as possible so that for a given vertical deflection of the road wheels the angular movement of the universals is kept to the minimum. Lancia's solution of this problem is bold and original; the drive shafts have been taken right through the rear hubs, and the outer universals are carried *outside* the rear wheels, where they are concealed only by the garnish plates covering the wheel nuts. The hub itself consists of a steel cylinder with a flange carrying the wheel studs, and it runs in a double-row roller

Valve and overhead rocker gear of the engine. The hardened cylinder liners seat on the upper face of the cylinder block barrel and are held in position by the cylinder head.

bearing in a steel housing carried on the end of the semi-trailing wishbone.

There has been several modified swing axle layouts carrying the wheel hubs on single wishbones with pivots inclined to the centre line of the car, but a patented feature of the Lancia layout is that the wishbone pivots do not line up at all. They are set at a slight angle to each other to ensure that the rubber is always stressed in torsion, and no endwise movement can arise which would tend to produce a shearing load on the rubber bushes.

Rubber mountings are extensively used to prevent noise and vibration from power unit and transmission reaching the body structure. The engine rests on four large rubber cushions and the transmission housing hangs on two cross tubes attached to the underside of the body structure by four rubber mountings.

Assembly procedure is simplified by mounting the front suspension and steering units on an ordinary axle beam which is then attached to the box section extensions on the front of the body structure by four bolts.

There are many interesting ideas on the car to make it easy to maintain and, therefore, promote long periods of trouble-free service. Under the bonnet is a large thumbscrew to adjust the pendant hand brake linkage, and at the rear, under the car, is another equally large one to adjust the clutch control cable, but made in brass to resist the effects of weather. Mounted accessibly under the bonnet, adjacent to fuse box and battery, is a double oil reservoir with plungers and dipsticks. One side replenishes the hydraulic brakes and the other side is fitted with a selector cock to replenish the oil supply in left or right front suspension units, as required. A further refinement is an external adjustment on the top of each front suspension unit, which regulates a valve in the damping system and enables the owner to compensate for changes in oil viscosity caused by climatic conditions in any part of the world.

The steering column gear change is an innovation for Lancia, and in this case is justified, for both front and rear seats, both bench types, are wide enough to take three abreast. The back rest of the front seat can be let down so that it joins up front and rear seats to form a comfortable bed.

Interior lights are illuminated when the doors are opened and automatic lights also illuminate engine and luggage locker. The petrol filler is concealed in a trapdoor under the floor of the luggage locker, and other openings give access to transmission, oil filler and rear brake connections. Bonnet and luggage locker are locked from inside the car, so that they are safe from interference when the doors are locked.

Production plans have been severely disorganized by a serious strike at the Lancia factory in Turin which has lasted several months. Only about a dozen prototypes have as yet been built, but a run in one of these in the hills above Turin quickly showed that this is a car out of the ordinary. The engine is very conservatively rated in producing only 56 b.h.p. from 1,754 c.c., and should have exceptionally good wearing qualities while providing really good acceleration and hill-climbing virtues, by reason of the low total weight of the car.

The body space in the Aurelia is quite surprising, in view of its handy and compact proportions, and visibility all round is unusually good, with an excellent view forward over a short, sloping bonnet which allows both wings to be seen. Interior finish, in cloth and plastic, is simple to the point of austerity, but the seats are well-shaped and comfortable.

The engine is remarkably smooth, and the revs go soaring with real eagerness when the throttle is opened. Ventilation is ensured by cold air intakes alongside the radiator which feed air in through pedal-controlled intakes on each side above the front toe-board. A Smiths heater on the scuttle warms air from inside the car and recirculates it to the toe-board or through de-mister slots to the windscreen.

When the labour troubles are finally settled, production of the Aurelia should quickly increase up to about 300 cars a month. At the price of 1,820,000 lire, it is only about £23 dearer in Italy than the Aprilia, which it replaces. In view of the many attractive and original features it offers, this seems to be a modest increase and should ensure a firm demand for the car from Lancia enthusiasts throughout the world.

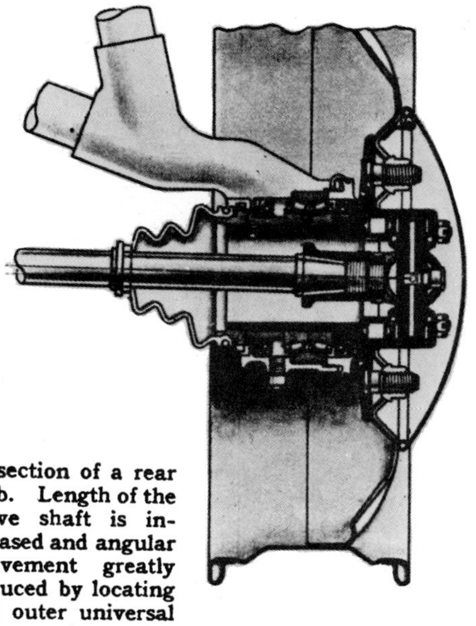

A section of a rear hub. Length of the drive shaft is increased and angular movement greatly reduced by locating the outer universal joint on the outside of the hub.

Section of the rear transmission unit. The clutch is mounted in front of the gear box and the drive is taken through the gears to the upper shaft and thence to the bevel gear and rear drive shafts.

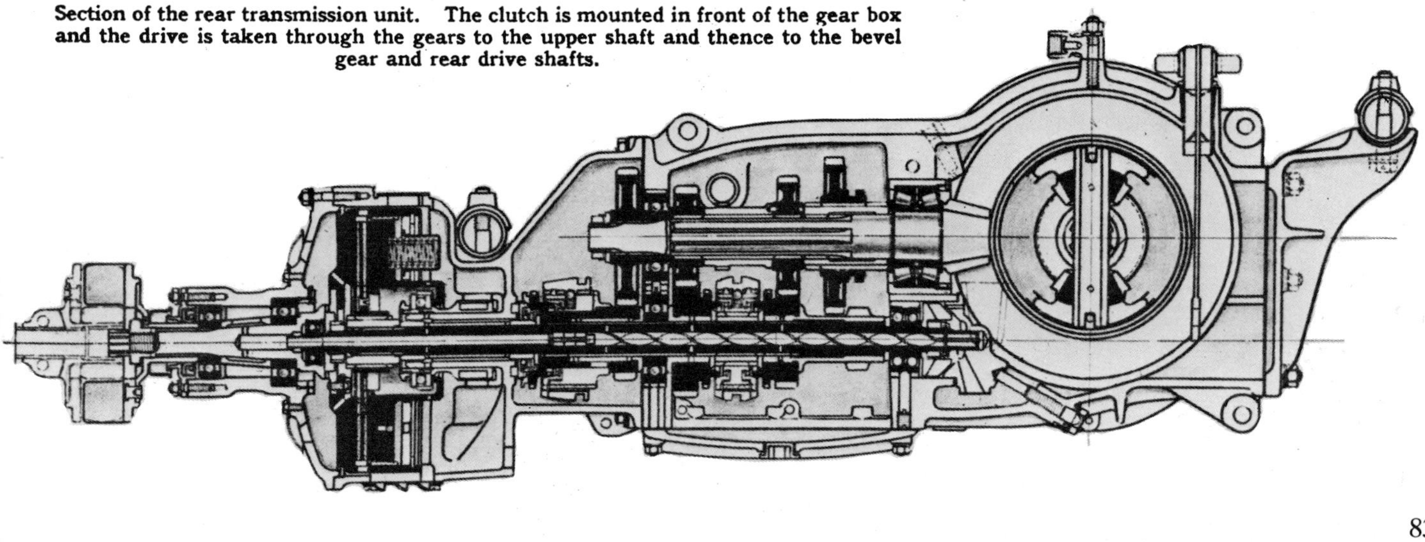

NEW CARS DESCRIBED

Externally the new Appia closely resembles the larger Aurelia, having a full width front with head lamps mounted in the wings, and a sloping rear panel.

SMALL FOUR-DOOR, FOUR-SEATER SALOON IN WHICH NOVEL FEATURES ABOUND

V-Four LANCIA APPIA

FOR many years the productions of the famous Italian concern, Lancia, have been distinguished by certain unorthodox features. The newly introduced Appia saloon, a full four-seater on a wheelbase which only just exceeds 8ft, is no exception, for it continues the unusual design characteristics which have become traditional of the *marque*. Thus the steel body shell acts also as the chassis and has the mechanical units attached to it, and the independent front wheel suspension is of the type which has for so long been associated with the name Lancia. The power unit also has the unique Lancia arrangement of the four cylinders in a narrow-angle V form in a single casting.

Little Brother

In appearance the Appia is almost a scaled-down Aurelia; it is, in fact, difficult to distinguish between the two models at a distance. This argues that its appearance is well-balanced, as indeed it is, and it does not look "a small car." The utmost use has been made of the wheelbase and track dimensions, and by clever design it has been possible to provide a rear seat cushion 4ft 1in wide, the headroom above it being 2ft 9in. The separate adjustable front seats have a similar width across them, and 3in more headroom. These measurements are without compressing the cushions, so that the effective headroom is rather more, and the car really is a full four-seater with adequate space for comfort.

Another body feature which adds considerably to passenger convenience is the pillarless construction. The two doors give a combined door gap of 5ft 3in, and the absence of a centre pillar makes ingress and egress a matter of ease for all occupants. Luggage space in the sloping tail is also generous for a car of this size, despite the fact that the spare wheel is accommodated in an upright position on the right-hand side of the locker.

The basis of the body shell is the floor, which incorporates box-section side rails. The scuttle, engine compartment sides, floor, wheel arches and roof are steel pressings—the roof being a single pressing—and form the stressed portion of the body shell. The unstressed portions, i.e., doors, bonnet top, wings and luggage locker lid, are of aluminium, in order to reduce weight.

It is largely owing to the compact design of the engine that so much space is available for passengers. The engine is, in fact, almost as wide as it is long, for its four cylinders, although formed in a single casting, are set at an included angle of 10 deg 14 min, and, seen in plan, overlap one another. Cylinders 1 and 3 are on the left side of the car, and cylinders 2 and 4 on the right. The firing order is the conventional 1, 3, 4, 2, and therefore cylinders 3 and 4 have their crankpins at 180 deg, as do cylinders 2 and 1. In order to obtain regular firing intervals it is, however, necessary for the crankshaft to be "given a twist," as it were, of 10 deg

Access to all seats is facilitated by the absence of a centre pillar. Upholstery is in cloth piped with leather in a plain style which nevertheless suggests comfort.

14 min between crankpins 2 and 3. This adjustment of the crankpin spacing is actually made in the machining of the shaft, which is an ordinary steel forging.

This typical Lancia design results in the engine being extremely compact, the block being only about 9½in long. The crankshaft is correspondingly short, very sturdy, and accordingly is provided with a main bearing only at each end, these being indium-coated bronze shells. The shaft is counterweighted and accurately balanced on a Gisholt electronic balancer.

Aluminium Crankcase

The cylinder block is in cast iron, has ample water passages and—an unusual feature in these days—is bolted to a separate aluminium crankcase, generously ribbed for cooling. The bottom plate, which encloses the crankcase, and with it forms the sump, is also plentifully ribbed. At the centre of the crankcase there is a robust transverse strengthening rib in which is a circular hole that just clears the shaft. In this rib are formed the centre bearing housings for the two three-bearing camshafts, that on the right side operating the inlet valves through push rods and rockers, and the other on the left similarly operating the exhaust valves. The push rods pass through holes in the cylinder block. The camshaft bearings are bronze bushes.

A single light alloy casting forms the head for all four cylinders and has bronze inserts for the overhead seats. Valve guides are of cast iron. Seats and guides are inserted when the head has been moderately heated, being driven into place with a hammer and drift in a very simple manner. The metal of the head close to the inserts is then rolled or spun so that it is forced into slight recesses in the inserts, thus securing them. Combustion chambers are approximately hemispherical and the 14mm sparking plugs are inclined at a slight angle.

The integral chassis - body is of pressed steel and the floor is an important unit, box section side rails being a feature. Wings, doors, bonnet top and locker lid are of aluminium.

Also unusual is the arrangement of the duplex chain drive for the camshafts. The lower run of the chain passes over the crankshaft sprocket while the upper run passes beneath a tensioning sprocket controlled by oil pressure acting on a plunger. The two small sprockets, therefore, run on the back of the chain. The attachment of the camshaft sprockets provides a simple vernier adjustment for timing. From the inlet valve camshaft an inclined shaft is driven by skew gears and drives the gear-type oil pump submerged in the sump, also the ignition distributor, which is accessibly located on a level with the cylinder head.

Steel connecting rods have bronze shells lined with anti-friction metal for the big-end bearings, and bronze bushes for the floating gudgeon pins, which are retained in the light alloy pistons by circlips. Pistons are of normal full-skirted type, and carry three pressure and two oil-control rings above the gudgeon pin. The piston crowns are slightly curved, and the pistons are longer in the skirt on their outer sides, in order to compensate for the angle of the cylinders. A single Solex Type 30 BI downdraught carburettor is bolted to the water-jacketed inlet manifold, on the right side of the engine, which feeds siamesed ports. It is supplied by a mechanically operated petrol pump immediately below it, driven off the inlet camshaft. On the left side the four exhaust ports discharge into a manifold. Also on the left side are the dynamo, forming an adjustable third point in the belt drive of the fan, and the starting motor. The two-bladed cast aluminium fan is mounted on the spindle of the centrifugal water pump. The cooling system includes radiator shutters controlled automatically by a thermostat in the header tank.

Accessibility of auxiliaries is a good point, and the oil filler is on the top of the cylinder head between the valve rocker covers at the front of the engine. The dipstick is unusually long, as it projects from the cylinder head at the rear of the engine. Oil is circulated to all bearings under pressure, and also passes through the hollow camshafts and valve rocker spindles to lubricate all the valve gear.

Transmission

Dry single-plate clutch and four-speed gear box form a unit with the engine. The bell housing and gear box casing are of aluminium, ribbed for strength and to prevent drumming. Synchromesh mechanism is provided for second, third and top gears, the layout of which is such that the shafts are unusually short and rigid. Gear changes are effected by a steering column gear lever projecting to the left with right-hand drive, which is normal on Lancia cars. If left-hand drive is specified the gear lever projects to the right. The gear change is remarkable for the precision of movement of the gear

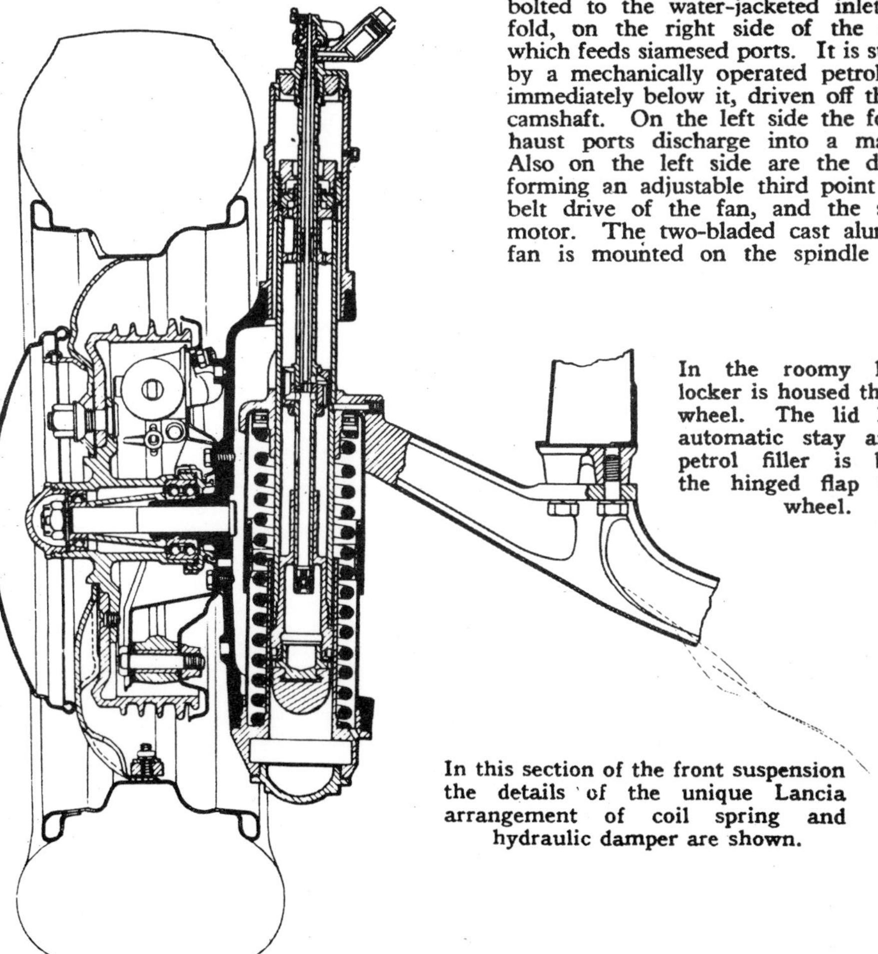

In this section of the front suspension the details of the unique Lancia arrangement of coil spring and hydraulic damper are shown.

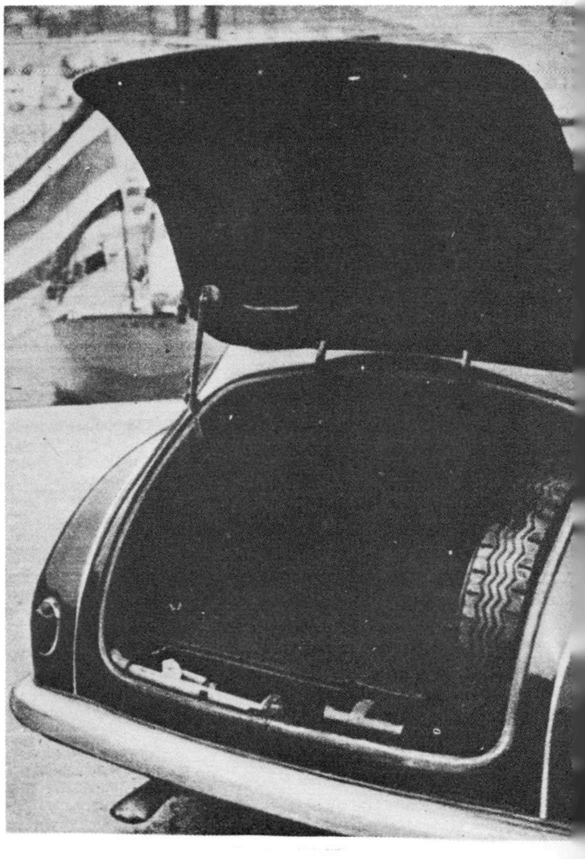

In the roomy luggage locker is housed the spare wheel. The lid has an automatic stay and the petrol filler is beneath the hinged flap by the wheel.

Plainly finished to match the exterior the facia has a locker in front of the passenger and the instruments and controls are grouped in front of the driver.

number of chassis points requiring lubrication to a minimum. There is, indeed, only one grease nipple, which is located on the shaft carrying the clutch and brake pedals.

Brakes are hydraulic, with a leading and trailing shoe in each drum. The drums have a diameter of 9¼in, and are ribbed for cooling and to increase their rigidity. The shoes in the rear drums are applied by a pistol-grip handbrake beneath the scuttle, which is turned through 90 deg to release the ratchet.

In the finish of the body considerable attention to detail is observable. The fixed single-panel curved screen gives excellent visibility as the screen pillars are of narrow section. The rear window also is large, well-curved, and gives a good view of the road astern through the centrally placed interior mirror. Door windows have winders, and the front doors also have ventilating panels, which are a

Through the large curved rear window a wide field of vision is obtained.

necessity in the warm Italian climate. Upholstery is in cloth with piped edges, and the squabs of the front seats have a simple adjustment for rake. The style is plain but pleasing, and conveys an impression of comfort. Very practical is the use of rubber floor covering in the front compartment, whilst carpet is used at the rear. The four doors carry useful pockets

V-Four LANCIA APPIA . . . continued

lever, there being no backlash or lost motion.

To the rear of the gear box proper the tail shaft is extended in a casing, so as to reduce the length of the open propeller-shaft. The end of the extended casing forms the third engine mounting as it is suspended on rubber bushes from a cross-shaft above it. The main engine mountings are located at each side towards the rear of the crankcase; brackets extend upwards to a point approximately in line with the crankshaft, and are received on rubber blocks containing a coil spring. There is thus no metallic contact between the power unit and the body shell. At each end of the propeller-shaft there is a Saga rubber joint, consisting of a hexagonal-shaped moulded rubber ring into which project three-armed spiders, one on each end of the propeller-shaft and the others on the gear box tail shaft and final drive shaft respectively. These joints are sufficiently flexible to cope with slight variations in the length of the drive as the axle moves on its springs, so that no sliding joint is necessitated, and therefore a lubrication point is avoided. The hypoid bevel final drive has an aluminium housing for the pinion on a conventional double-banjo axle casing.

Half-elliptic springs are mounted below the axle casing and the forward portion of the spring is shorter than the rearward portion. Double-acting telescopic dampers are fitted, and project slightly through the forward corners of the floor of the luggage locker. These projections are covered by rubber cups which, on removal, disclose adjusters for the damper action. Front suspension is by coil springs and built-in hydraulic dampers, in units which slide vertically on fixed pillars carried by the ends of an axle beam. The suspension units carry the stub axles and the axle beam is bolted rigidly to the body shell. Rubber buffers for both bump and rebound are incorporated in the units, and while the vertical movement is somewhat restricted in this design a total deflection of about 4in is available.

Steering

Steering is by worm and sector, with a two-spoked steering wheel of 16¼in diameter, the steering gear ratio being such that it takes three turns of the wheel to pass from lock to lock. The steering wheel carries a central button from which extensions pass along the two spokes, forming a very convenient method of horn operation. Rubber bushes are used in the steering linkage, and also for the rear spring shackles, thereby reducing the

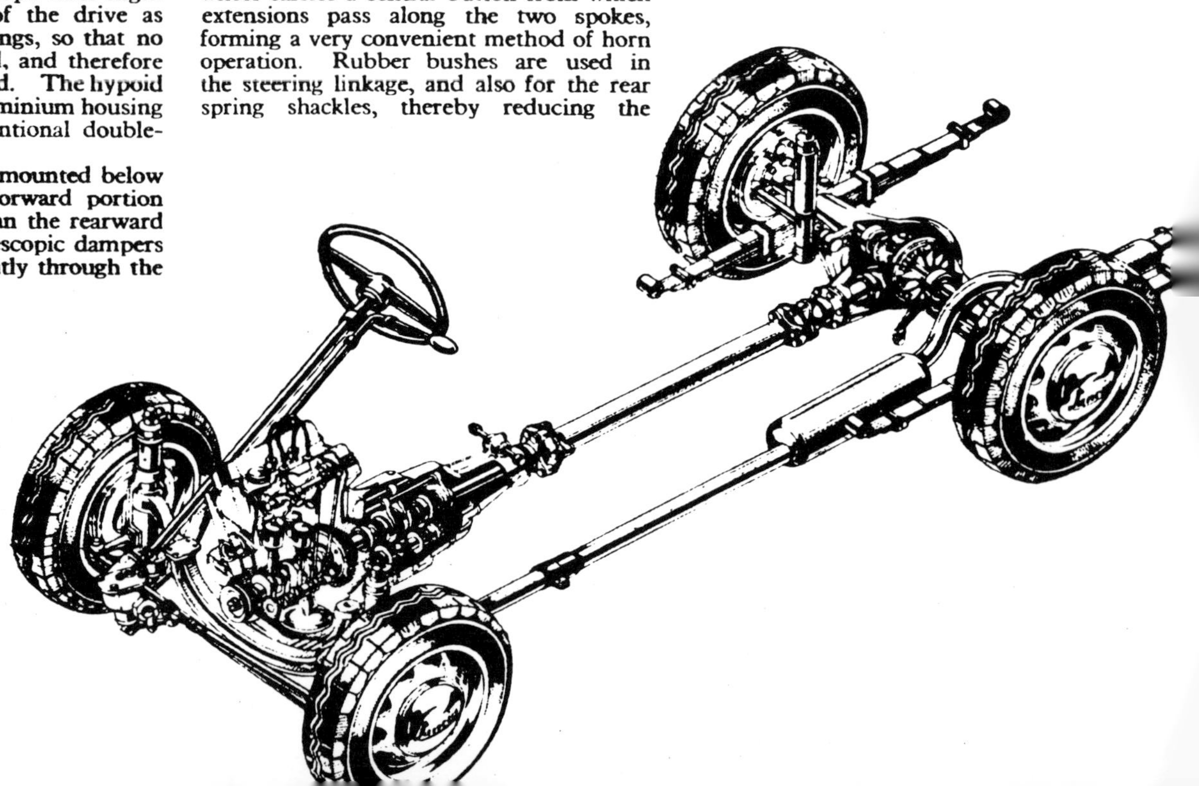

The mechanical units shown here are attached to the body shell, but they take up little of the space which passengers could use.

This view of a partly dismantled engine gives some idea of its compact design and of the unique arrangement of the cylinder bores. The block is only 9½in long from front to back. A single casting in light alloy forms the cylinder head and carries the inlet valves on the right-hand side and the exhausts on the left side.

and have interior handles at the waistline; sun visors are fitted in the roof peak. The facia is a steel pressing, finished to match the exterior colour, and has a glove locker in front of the passenger, with the instruments and subsidiary controls neatly grouped in front of the driver, who has a clear view of the dials through the top half of the steering wheel.

Internal Releases

The one-piece bonnet top is hinged at the rear and is provided with a simple automatically operating stay, as also is the locker lid. The bonnet is released by a lever beneath the scuttle, and has the normal type of safety catch. The locker lid is released by a lever behind the rear squab. Jacking points are provided in the body side rails.

Electrical equipment is of 12-volt type, with a 35 ampère-hour battery carried beneath the floor of the locker on the left side, so that it counterbalances the weight of the spare wheel in its well on the right. A trap in the floor gives ready access to it.

The petrol tank, with a capacity of 8 gallons, lies between the battery and the spare wheel well, and its filler cap projects through the edge of the locker floor, being covered by a hinged flap. The tool kit also is accommodated at the rear edge of the locker floor.

Heating and defrosting equipment is standardized, the heater being centrally placed beneath the scuttle. An electric screenwiper having two blades is provided, and is controlled by a switch on the facia. Winking indicators are also controlled by a facia switch which incorporates a tell-tale light. A small steering column lever controls the head lamps for dipping or flashing a warning at night, apart from the separate facia switch. A warning light indicates when the reserve petrol supply of just over a gallon is in use.

Altogether the new Appia is a typical Lancia product, not only as regards its technical specification, but also in the quality of its general finish. Both the character of the Italian climate, with its hot summers and cold winters, and of the average Italian driver, who has at his disposal many miles of fast *autostrade*, have obviously been taken into account in the design of the car, which with a maximum speed in the neighbourhood of 75 m.p.h. is likely to be asked to maintain a cruising speed but a few miles below that figure.

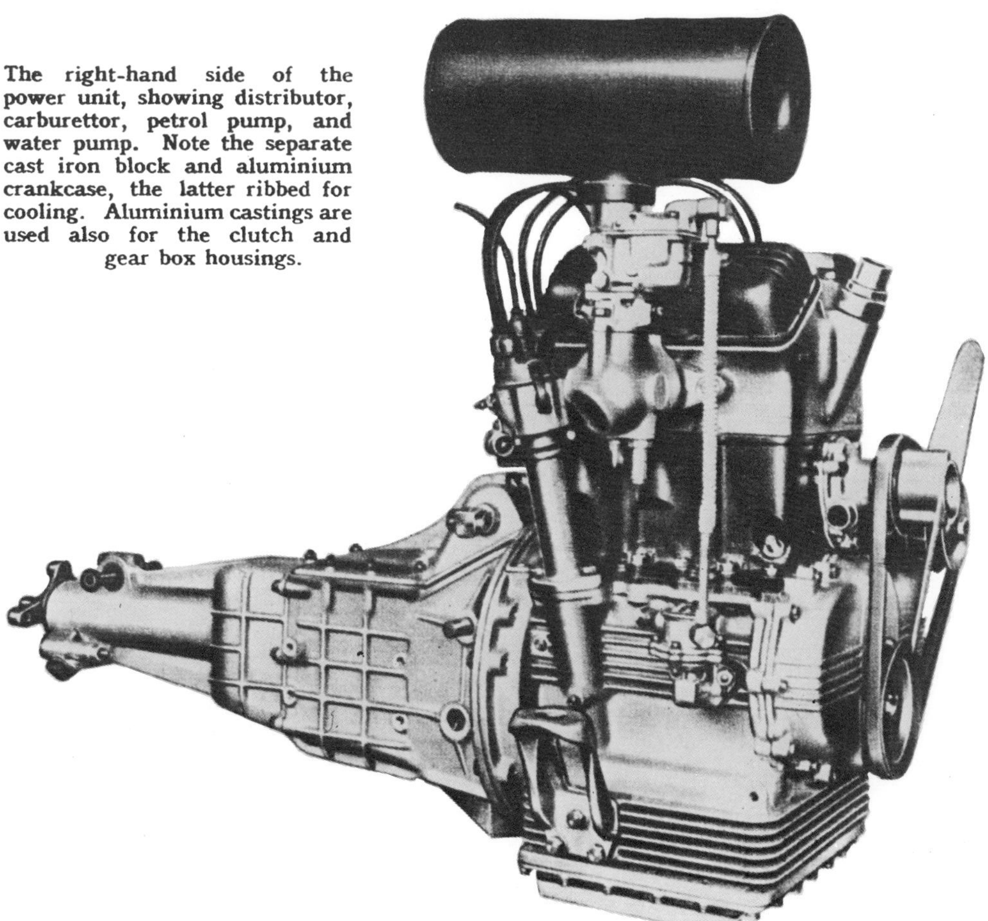

The right-hand side of the power unit, showing distributor, carburettor, petrol pump, and water pump. Note the separate cast iron block and aluminium crankcase, the latter ribbed for cooling. Aluminium castings are used also for the clutch and gear box housings.

SPECIFICATION

Engine.—V-4-cyl, included angle 10 deg 14 min, 68 × 75 mm (1,090 c.c.), o.h.v. push-rods. Compression ratio 7.4 to 1, maximum b.h.p. 38 at 4,800 r.p.m., maximum torque 51.96 lb ft at 3,000 r.p.m. Two-bearing crankshaft.

Transmission.—Dry single-plate clutch and four-speed synchromesh gear box in unit with engine; open propeller-shaft with two rubber couplings, hypoid bevel final drive. Overall gear ratios: top 4.56, third 6.46, second 9.92 and first 17.8 to 1.

Suspension.—Independent front by coil springs and vertical guides, with direct-acting built-in hydraulic dampers; rear half-elliptics with adjustable telescopic hydraulic dampers.

Steering.—Worm and sector, with 16¾in diameter two-spoke wheel.

Brakes.—Hydraulic, in 9⅞in diameter drums, friction lining area 138 sq in.

Wheels and tyres.—Steel disc, with 5.60-15in tyres.

Main dimensions.—Wheelbase 8ft 1⅝in, track, front, 3ft 10⅜in, rear, 3ft 10½in. Overall length 12ft 8 3/16in, width 4ft 7⅞in, height 4ft 8in, ground clearance 6 5/16in. Weight, with water and oil, no petrol, 16 cwt 14 lb (1,806 lb).

The Lancia Appia bears a family resemblance to the Aurelia in its lines and proportions. The windscreen and rear window have curved glasses.

APPIA on the ROAD

Impressions of a Quality Small Lancia, a Recently Introduced Model with a Lively Performance and Excellent Road Holding

IN describing the new Lancia Appia in *The Autocar* of May 22, it was stated that in appearance it resembles a scaled-down Aurelia. The same may be said of its performance, which it has recently been possible to sample in Italy by the co-operation of its manufacturers; it is now possible to give a general impression of the car's behaviour.

In view of the Appia's low weight—only just over 16 cwt with water and oil but no petrol, and as tested with two adult passengers 19¼ cwt—and the engine output of 38 b.h.p. at 4,800 r.p.m., it has an excellent power-weight ratio for a small car. This is reflected in its acceleration, which is decidedly brisk, particularly on the indirect ratios.

Again, in view of the engine's capacity for high rates of r.p.m.—it peaks at 4,800 r.p.m.—the performance on the well-chosen indirect gear ratios is such as to make the maintenance of a high cruising speed a matter more of the capacity of the driver and of the suitability of the road than of the capability of the car. Without forcing the engine beyond the peak of its power curve maxima on first gear of 18 m.p.h., on second of 33, and on third of 52 m.p.h. are available. On top gear, timed over kilometre distances, a figure of 30 sec was repeatedly obtained, corresponding to a speed of 74 m.p.h.

It is, however, in the manner in which such speeds are provided that the charm of the car lies. The engine remains smooth and free from vibration throughout its range, and it seems, indeed, to run the more smoothly the faster it is driven. It is also a quiet running unit. The fact that it is mounted at three points on rubber, and that the propeller-shaft has a rubber joint at each end, so that there is no metal-to-metal contact between the engine and the steel body-chassis unit, doubtless plays a considerable part in preventing the transference of noise and vibration.

The clutch is smooth in action, does not object to gear changes under power—although these are by no means necessary in view of the general liveliness of performance—and needs only light pedal pressure. The synchromesh mechanism provided on second, third and top gears is also well up to its work, gives quite swift as well as noiseless changes, and the clean precision with which the steering column gear lever operates is remarkable, a point which has been commended previously on other Lancia cars. The gear box itself is commendably quiet.

The brakes are hydraulically operated and need only comparatively light pressure on the pedal in order to produce optimum results, 100 lb pressure producing efficiencies of nearly 80 per cent. An emergency test stop locked all four wheels so that the car slid to rest, meanwhile maintaining

To give increased protection, the rear bumper wraps well round the wings. The sloping rear panel is in keeping with the well-balanced look of the car.

APPIA on the ROAD . . . . . continued

The one-piece bonnet top has an automatically operated stay and gives easy access to the engine and auxiliaries.

Right : Although the spare wheel is carried in the locker, there is generous luggage space for the size of the car. The petrol filler cap is covered by a hinged flap.

a perfectly straight course with front and rear tyre marks overlapping. There was no suspicion of brake fade during a number of successive stopping tests in rapid succession. The hand brake is operated by a pistol grip beneath the scuttle, and to bring the ratchet into play to hold the pull-out handle in the "on" position it is turned through 90 degrees; a similar turn in the opposite direction releases the ratchet.

Suspension of the Appia follows what has long been Lancia practice for the front end, and it combines firmness with comfort very successfully. Particularly is this apparent in traversing really rough road surfaces at speed. Even over pot-holes the car rides with a surety that engenders comfort of mind as well as bodily comfort in both driver and passengers. The range of movement of the front wheels is somewhat less with this design of suspension than when the more orthodox wishbone linkage is used, but even on full bump or rebound, when rubber buffers incorporated in the suspension units come into play, there is no actual discomfort and no loss of stability.

In such conditions also the two-spoked steering wheel remains free from road shocks. The steering is light and direct, has sufficient caster angle, and a nice degree of understeer so that the car can be held into a fast bend with confidence. The road-holding resulting from these good qualities of the suspension and steering is of an unusually high order for such a small and light vehicle. As a consequence its performance on a winding road of give-and-take character makes it the equal of a more powerful and much faster car unable to utilize its speed in such conditions. Indeed, for a cross-country run over the winding roads of Great Britain it would be difficult to imagine a more suitable car and one capable of putting up a better performance.

Pillarless

Of the body one of the most important features from the point of view of the user is the absence of centre door pillars. This results in the access to both compartments being virtually unrestricted when both front and rear doors are open, as they obviously would be if the family were loading up for a day's journey or if elderly passengers were being carried. The width of opening across the two doors is 5ft 3in. As the front seat squabs also hinge forward, access to the rear seats can be made particularly easy.

The seating is comfortable and has cloth upholstery in plain style piped with leather. The rear seat cushion measures 4ft 1in across, and 20in from front to back, and has a squab 24in high. The separate adjustable front seats have a similar width when placed side by side and also measure 20in from front to back, although the squabs are 3in shorter. Head room is 3ft above the front seats and 3in less above the rear seat. An important dimension for comfort is the knee room between front and rear seats, which is approximately 7in with the front seat in the mid-position of adjustment. Foot room is ample, as it extends beneath the front seats.

Useful pockets are formed in the trim of all four doors, which have metal pull handles below the waist rails, of a type which normally lies flat against the trim. The window winders are well placed so that they do not cause an obstruction. Ventilator panels are fitted to the front windows. Rubber floor covering is used at the front, which is likely to get the most wear, and carpet at the rear. Sun vizors are hinged in the roof peak.

Instruments are grouped in a single dial in front of the driver, flanked by switches for lights and screenwipers on the left and for flashing indicators and ignition on the right. Beneath the scuttle are small lever controls for fresh air, one each side, for starter motor and choke, for the hand throttle, and, on the extreme right, for bonnet release. Also on the steering column is a small lever for controlling the head lamp beam, a normal Continental fitting. Thus the driver has all controls within easy reach. Centrally placed on the bulkhead is the heater unit, which also supplies demister slots. Altogether the style of the interior gives the impression of comfort, good finish and quality.

Through the wide curved windscreen and rear window the driver has excellent visibility; the rear view mirror, mounted centrally above the screen, gives a good view astern without obstructing forward vision. A useful locker is formed in the facia in front of the passenger seat. Luggage space is generous even though the spare wheel is carried in the locker in a vertical position; an unobstructed platform at the side of it is approximately 2ft 6in square. Through its forward corners project the upper ends of the telescopic dampers carrying adjusters for their action. These are concealed by moulded rubber caps. The luggage compartment lid and bonnet both have automatically operating stays.

Access to the engine when the one-piece bonnet is lifted is a good point, the oil filler cap and dipstick being on top of the cylinder head. Ignition coil, brake fluid reservoir and distributor are also readily accessible. Altogether, the Lancia Appia ranks as a quality small car as regards both its general finish and its performance.

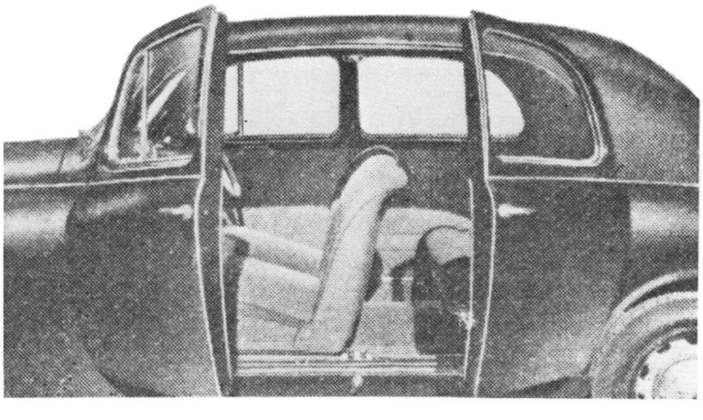

Owing to the pillarless construction, access to both front and rear seats is unobstructed. The cloth upholstery is in plain style and gives an air of comfort.

THE SPORT 1952-1953

For the 1952 Mille Miglia, Lancia entered a 2-litre version of the Aurelia GT coupé. One of these, in the hands of 54-year-old Luigi Fagioli, finished third overall and first in class.

The 1953 Carrera Panamericana was run over 1,912 miles of ordinary roads in Mexico and the four-day race proved a major triumph for Lancia, whose 3.3-litre cars finished 1-2-3, third place going to Castellotti.

A famous rallying victory for the Aurelia GT: this 2½-litre saloon won the 1953 Liége-Rome-Liége in the hands of Claes and Trasenter.

The 1952 Targa Florio was another triumph for Lancia, with Umberto Maglioli winning outright. This is Taruffi's Lancia being chased by an Alfa Romeo on the seventh lap.

THE LAMBDA WAS A FAMOUS MID-PERIOD ENGINE FROM TURIN

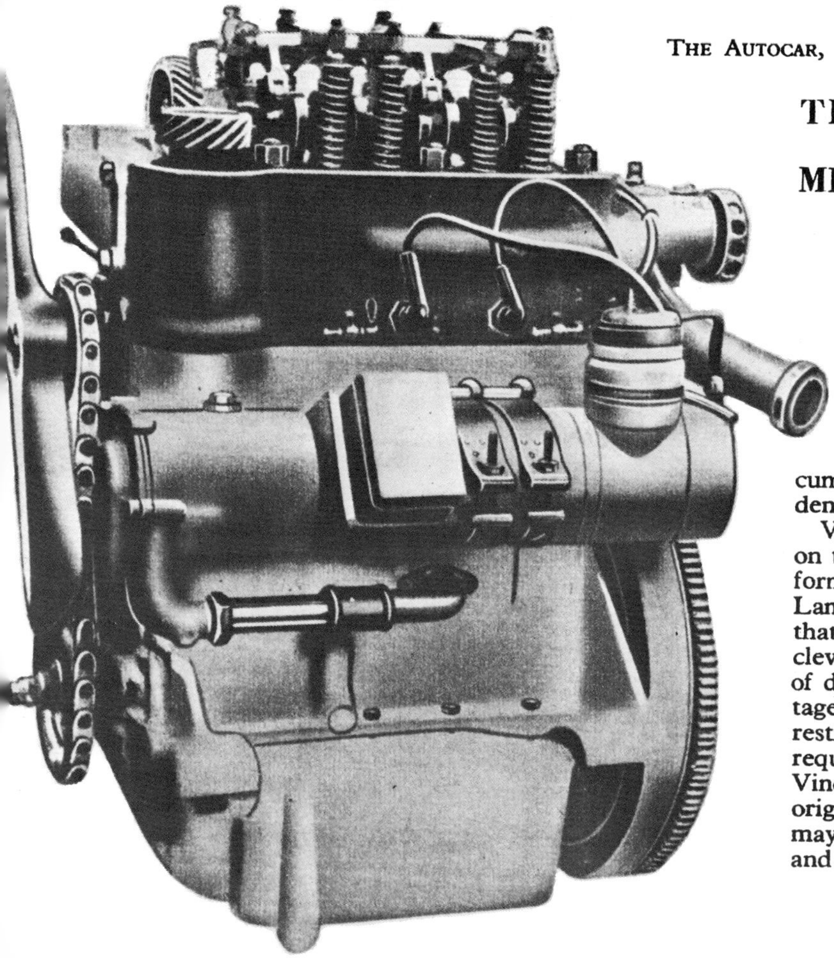

Left side of the 1922 Lambda power unit. The water pump, dynamo and magneto were tandem gear driven from the vertical drive to the camshaft.

Between ALPHA and OMEGA

By MAX MILLAR

WHEN one comes to trace the history of design in the world of cars few names stand out over the years with such remarkable brilliance as that of Vincenzo Lancia, unless it be Henry Ford. But whereas Ford designed and built vehicles on a vast scale on an avowedly commercial basis with an enterprise that is unlikely to be surpassed in the future, Lancia broke new ground and struck out in an entirely different manner in a sphere of design which resulted in achievements that must rank similarly, the ultimate fruition of which can be seen in the individuality of the Lancia today.

Up to the period of the first world war the firm of Lancia produced a series of well-made but very conventionally designed cars, conforming with standards which, at that time, were considered to be classic all over the world. In 1919 Lancia built a 12-cylinder V-type engine, 80 × 100 mm bore and stroke, and of 6,032 c.c. capacity, as the first breakaway from the earlier in-line type of engine, but few were made and the design was not proceeded with because of the unsettled conditions prevailing at the time.

The main direction of Lancia design technique changed almost violently when the firm produced a new car, the Lambda*, which was in many major respects not only completely different from previous models, but which also was to innovate three important departures in design, namely, a narrow angle V-type engine, a stressed body-cum-chassis construction and the famous Lancia independent front suspension.

Vincenzo Lancia was a racing driver before embarking on the manufacture of cars and demanded superlative performance from the creations of his own brain; indeed, the Lambda represented such a transformation in design policy that one can think of him as being not only one of the cleverest, but also one of the boldest men in the sphere of design. Like Royce and Bugatti, Lancia had the advantage of instituting and developing his own ideas without restriction, coupled with a knowledge of road performance requirements which were on a very high level. Although Vincenzo Lancia died in 1937 the influence of his early originality in the Lancia concern persists to this day, as may be witnessed by the specialized design, performance and workmanship of present-day Lancia cars.

The earliest Lambda engine produced in 1922. Sparking plugs and main accessories were exceptionally accessible.

In discussing the Lambda engine some preliminary remarks must be made as to the aim of Lancia in designing a four-cylinder unit with the very narrow angle between the banks of cylinders; in order to assess the value of such a cylinder arrangement it is necessary to refer to the alternatives of a conventional in-line engine and a 90-degree V-type power unit. In his quest for a very short and rigid engine Lancia immediately dismissed the conventional in-line arrangement on account of the irreducible fore and aft dimensions of a unit having a given cylinder bore dimension, while the 90 deg four-cylinder V-type, although offering a much shorter crankshaft and overall length, exhibited too many disadvantages in respect of the immoderate width of the engine, long induction pipes, inaccessibility of certain components and general untidiness.

In planning the narrow angle power unit Lancia aimed at building an engine of the shortest possible length, and to do this he staggered one pair of cylinders at 13 deg from the other in his first engine, the angle being governed by the selected positions of the connecting rods on the crankshaft and the location of the cylinder bores in relation to each other. Various factors such as the bore and stroke of the engine, degree of connecting rod swing, length of piston, and suchlike affected the disposition of the cylinders, the centre lines of which met at a point well

* The Greek letter λ : Lancia used the Greek alphabet as a source of model names before and after the 1914-18 war.

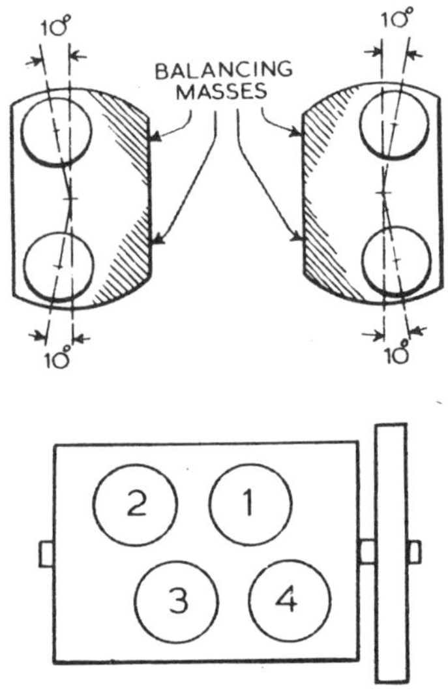

Above are the setting of the crankpins in pairs, with the approximate balancing masses, and the numbering of cylinders in the Lambda, No. 1 cylinder being at the flywheel end. The firing order was 1, 2, 3, 4.

Between ALPHA and OMEGA . . . continued

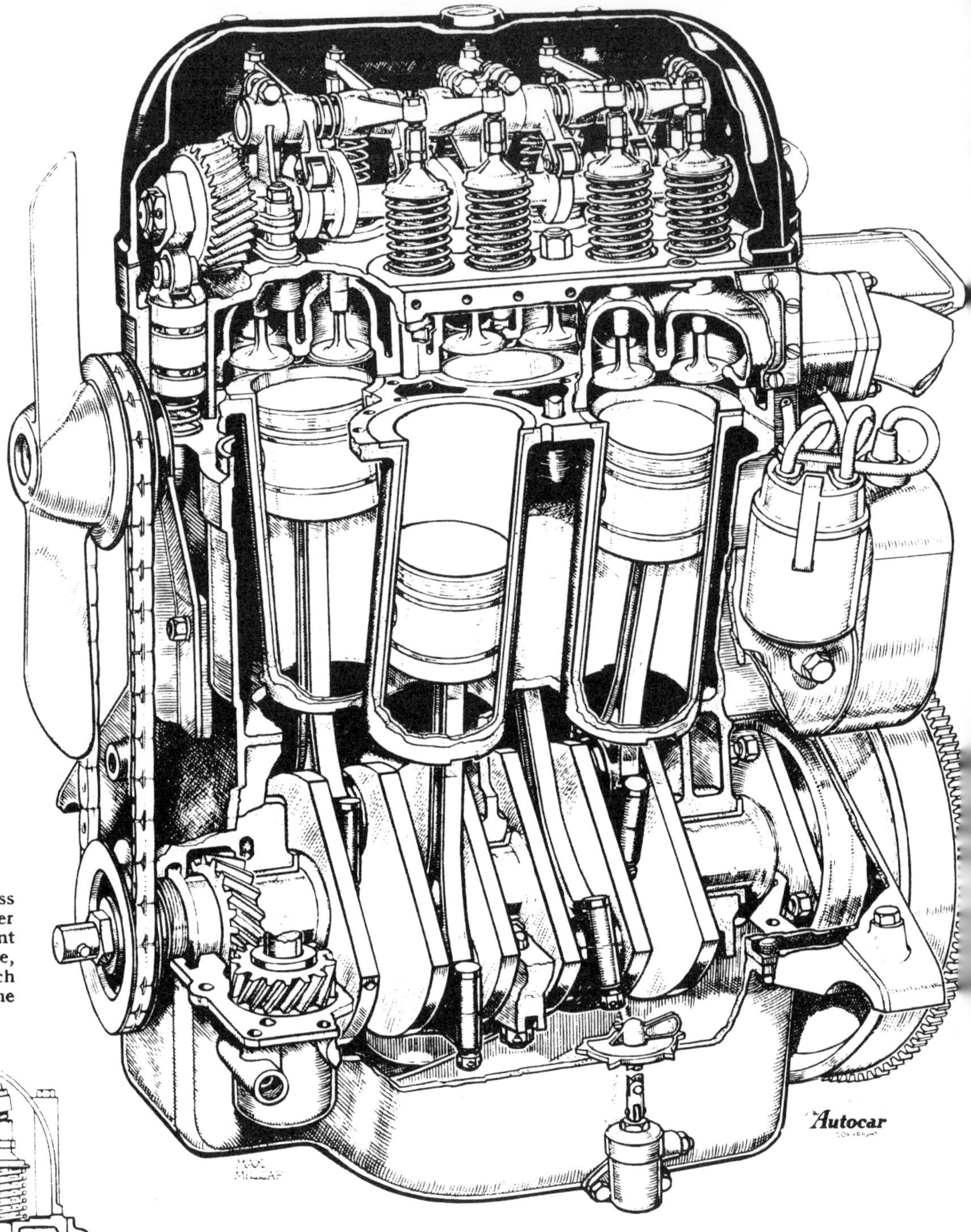

The 2½-litre four-cylinder Lambda power unit of 1928 and a forerunner of the long series of highly successful Lancia engines. Exceptionally sturdy in build, the cylinders were set at an angle of 13 deg in a block only 15½in long.

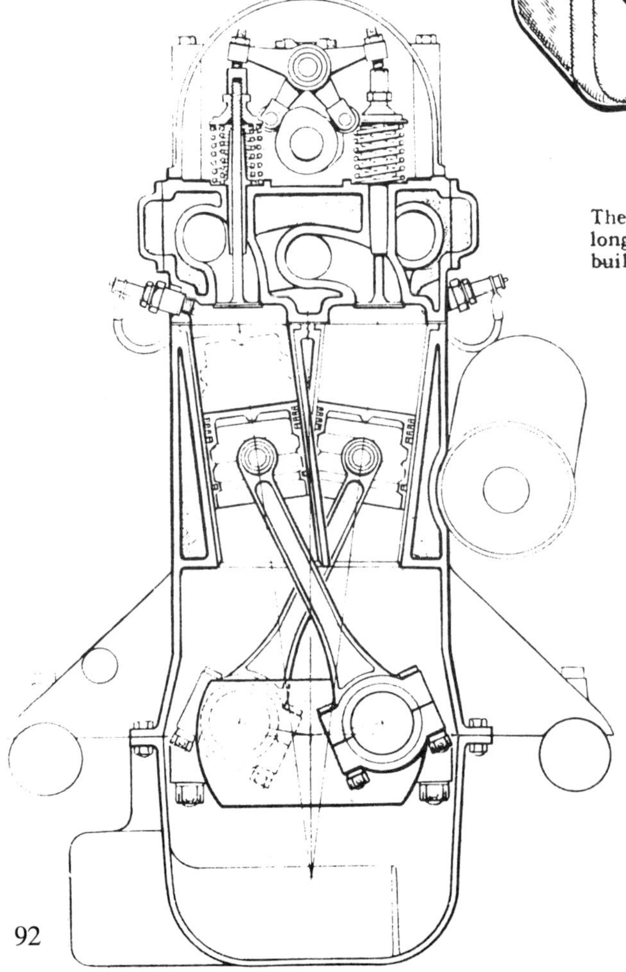

The Lambda engine in cross section, to show the cylinder centre lines meeting at a point well below the crankshaft centre, and the connecting rods which have offset shanks to clear the cylinder bores.

below the centre line of the crankshaft, giving an inclusive angle of 13 deg, 14 deg and 13 deg 40 minutes according to the particular series of Lambda engine. In general it may be said that the engine is more readily visualized as a staggered four-cylinder unit rather than a V-type as ordinarily known.

Lancia, in adopting this design, immediately achieved some potent advantages, and it is not surprising that Lancia engines have been based on similar lines up to the present day. The short rigid crankshaft, located in a stiff box-like crankcase, well dispersed combustion chambers and the absence of external induction and exhaust manifolds are consequent advantages of such a design. Not only do the square cylinder block and head permit freer circulation of cooling water, but a single camshaft with rockers can be used in place of two separate sets of mechanism as would be required on a 90 deg V-type engine, while, of course, the Lancia valve gear is infinitely more accessible for maintenance.

Because the cylinder centre lines in the Lambda did not meet at the crankshaft centre, both banks of cylinders, right and left, were eccentric; the right bank had the piston side thrusts increased by this setting while the left had the piston thrusts reduced. A further effect of this cylinder arrangement was the contra-balance effect between the two groups of pistons and connecting rods, but, in order to produce an approximately even period between power impulses, the crankpins were offset in pairs at 10 deg from the crankshaft vertical centre line. Thus there were two crankpins offset to the left for one pair of cylinders as seen in V formation and the other pair of crankpins were offset to the right. Despite the non-conformity between the cylinder and crankpin angles, the general smoothness of the engine did not seem to be impaired.

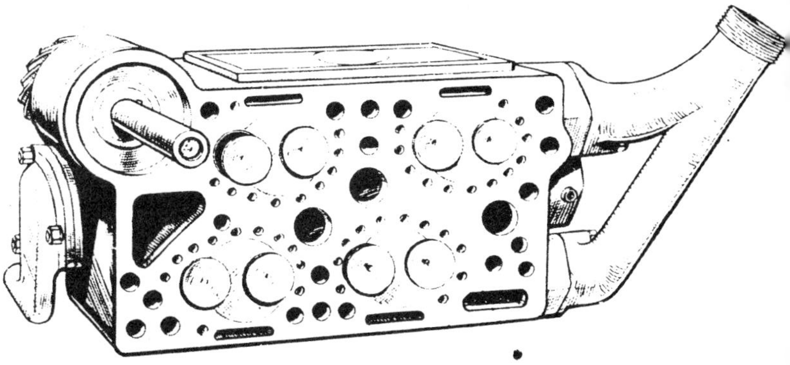

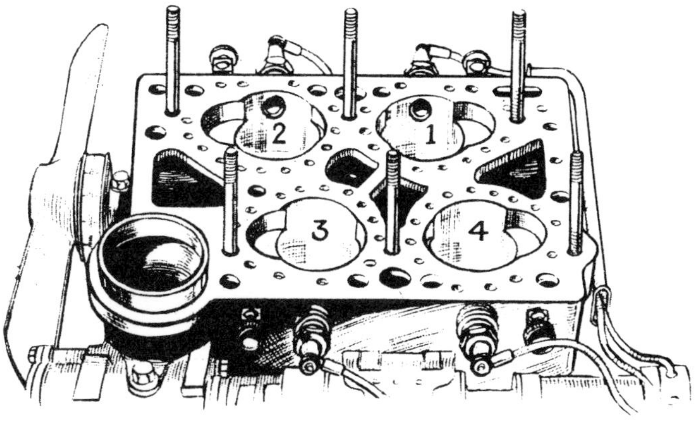

The cylinder head lifted off the block of the early Lambda. The head was flat underneath, while the combustion chambers were located at the top of the cylinders with recesses formed on either side for valve clearance.

Firing Order

Lancia numbered the cylinders of the Lambda (and all other engines) from the rear of the cylinder block, commencing with No. 1 on the right side. The firing order of the Lambda was Nos. 1 and 2 on the right side and thence to Nos. 3 and 4, No. 3 being the forward cylinder on the left side. The order, therefore, went anti-clockwise around the block, two cylinders firing on one side of the engine, followed by the pair on the other side.

The earliest Lambda 67 engine was produced in 1922, having a bore and stroke of 75 × 120 mm with a capacity of 2,120 c.c., and a short description of it was published in *The Autocar* of September 29, 1922. The engine, which developed 49 b.h.p., was manufactured, with various modifications, in nine series up to 1931.

In the drawing opposite is depicted the Lambda of about 1928, the 8th series of this famous engine, an earlier version

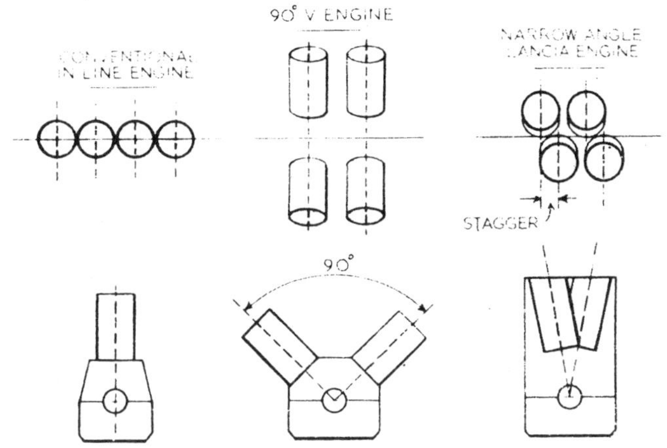

Three types of four-cylinder engines shown diagrammatically to emphasize the gain in length by the Lancia and in particular its advantage over the 90 deg V power unit. The amount of stagger of the cylinders is largely imposed by the angle of the V.

not being available for accurate illustration purposes. This later engine had a bore and stroke of 82.55 × 120 mm, the capacity being 2,570 c.c., and observation of the cross-section of the unit will reveal the extraordinary compactness and inherent rigidity of the crankcase and cylinder block, as well as the novelty of the valve and port arrangement in the head and the overhead camshaft and rocker gear. The aluminium cylinder block measured only $15\frac{1}{2}$in long by $9\frac{1}{4}$in wide, which is remarkable for an engine of above $2\frac{1}{2}$-litre capacity, but the cast iron cylinder liners were cast in position, with the top flanges extended and shaped to conform with the contour of the offset combustion chambers. Undoubtedly, the possession of a first-class foundry in his own works greatly assisted Lancia in the production of these unconventional components, and, it may be noted that the Lancia reputation for beautiful castings, especially in iron, has continued throughout the years.

The crankshaft, running in three substantial main bearings, had six crankwebs to accommodate the four offset crankpins, and was machined all over as well as being drilled for the normal pressure lubrication. Owing to the long stroke of the pistons, and the fact that one edge of the cylinder barrels is nearer the crankshaft than the other, the shafts of the connecting rods were set over in a very unconventional manner in order that they could clear the cylinder bores. In the first series engine the cylinder liners protruded from the water jackets to an extent which permitted the liners to be cut away to give clearance to the connecting rods, which were tubular and not set over as in the later power unit.

The staggering of the cylinder bores in the square cylinder block and the three crankshaft bearings ; the centre bearing cap is very heavily braced to the crankcase by four widely spaced studs and nuts.

Between ALPHA and OMEGA . . . continued

The unconventional Lancia connecting rod with offset shank.

LAMBDA ENGINES

	1st–6th series 1923–1925 engine 67	7th series 1926–1927 engine 78	8th–9th series 1928–1931 engine 79
Bore and stroke	75 × 120 mm	79.37 × 120 mm	82.55 × 120 mm
Cubic capacity	2,120 c.c.	2,370 c.c.	2,570 c.c.
V angle of cyl.	13 deg	14 deg	13 deg 40 min
Compression ratio	5.1 to 1	5.15 to 1	5.15 to 1
Max. b.h.p.	49	59.4	69
at r.p.m.	3,250	3,250	3,500
Connecting rods	Straight, tubular	Offset	I section
Diameter of valve	42.5 mm	42.5 mm	42.5 mm
Valve lift	11.5 mm	11.5 mm	11.5 mm
Carburettor	Zenith	Zenith	Zenith
Ignition	Magneto	Magneto	8th series: Magneto 9th series: Coil 12-volt

Lancia located the valves vertically with ports leading to manifolds cast within the iron cylinder head. In the eighth series engine the combustion chambers were of conventional design, with a slight irregularity in shape created by the flat tops of the aluminium pistons at t.d.c., but in the prototype the combustion chambers were formed by lateral extensions of the cylinder barrel, the head being flat underneath. Both the single carburettor and twin exhaust pipe branch were bolted to the rest of the head, thus providing an unobstructed cylinder block on both sides with free access to the four sparking plugs. No hot spot for the induction system was provided, the engine being designed many years before such a feature was introduced, but the location of the exhaust manifolds must have provided local warmth to the centrally disposed induction feed in the head.

The Lambda valves were nearly 8in long and threaded at the upper ends to take the cups for the double valve springs and the hexagon cap. The overhead-valve gear was designed on very generous lines, the rockers having ball-bearing rollers working against cams of large diameter. A four-lobed cam on the front end of the camshaft engaging an upright spring-loaded plunger in the cylinder head acted as a camshaft vibration damper, while the vertical shaft at the front end of the engine which drove the camshaft from the crankshaft had skew gear wheels of liberal proportions to give long life. On the left-hand side of the cylinder block the water pump, dynamo and magneto were driven in tandem from similar gears on the vertical shaft, the units being high mounted and readily accessible.

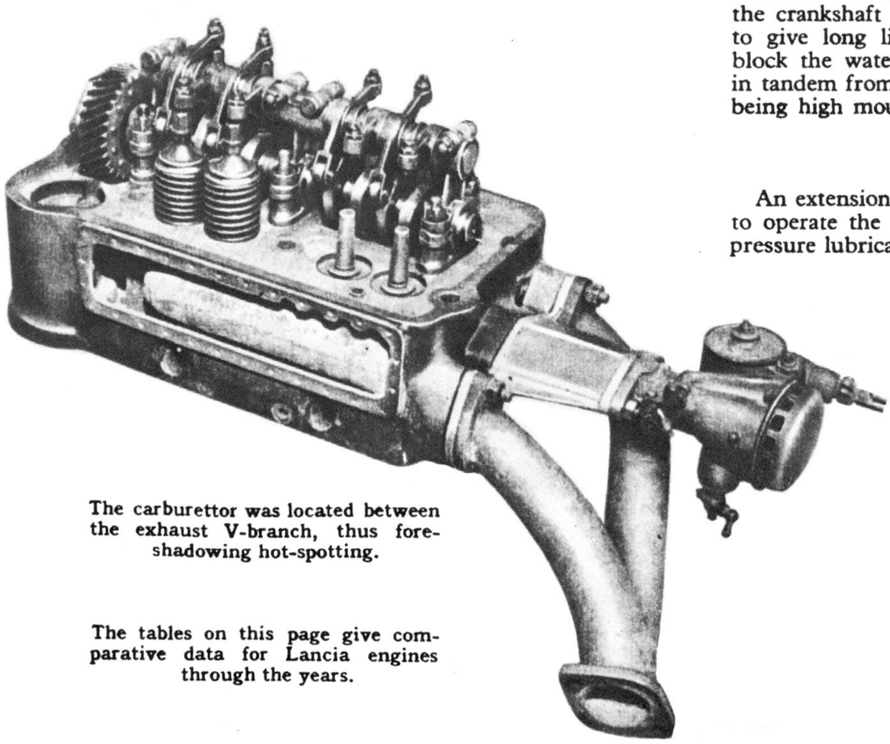

The carburettor was located between the exhaust V-branch, thus foreshadowing hot-spotting.

The tables on this page give comparative data for Lancia engines through the years.

Lubrication

An extension of the vertical shaft drive was carried below to operate the oil pump in the sump, but a feature of the pressure lubrication system was the enormous oil filter fitted in an elevated position on the left side of the cylinder block where it could easily be dealt with. Near the filter was the tell-tale indicator for oil level in the sump, and at the rear of the valve gear a very small pump (driven by its own worm gearing from the tail end of the camshaft) metered oil from a small gravity tank under the bonnet to maintain the level in the sump.

The general arrangement of the engine and all its details reflected the master mind of Vincenzo Lancia and his eminently practical approach to design, backed by his earlier racing experience. Many of the Lambda cars are still in existence, and the owners, almost without exception, have high praise for their exceptional general qualities. Similar tribute has also been paid by those owning Aprilia, Augusta and other Lancia cars.

	DILAMBDA	ASTURA 1-2 series	ASTURA 3-4 series	ARTENA	AUGUSTA	APRILIA 1st series	APRILIA 2nd series	ARDEA
Bore, mm	79.37	69.85	74.61	82.55	69.85	72	74.61	65
Stroke, mm	100	85	85	90	78	83	85	68
Cubic capacity	3,960 c.c.	2,604 c.c.	2,972 c.c.	1,925 c.c.	1,196 c.c.	1,351.6 c.c.	1,486 c.c.	903 c.c.
V angle of cyl.	24 deg	19 deg	17 deg 30 min	17 deg	18 deg 15 min	18 deg 6 min 40 sec	17 deg 40 min	19 deg 54 min
B.h.p.	100	73	82	55	35	47.8	48	29.2
Max. r.p.m.	3,800	4,000	4,000	4,000	4,000	4,300	4,300	4,600
Year of introduction	1928	1931	1934	1931	1933	1937	1939	1939

	AURELIA B10	AURELIA B21	AURELIA B22	AURELIA Gran Turismo B20 1st series	AURELIA Gran Turismo B20 2nd series	AURELIA G.T.2500	APPIA
Bore	70	72	72	72	72	78	68
Stroke, mm	76	81.5	81.5	81.5	81.5	85.5	75
Cubic capacity	1,754 c.c.	1,991 c.c.	1,991 c.c.	1,991 c.c.	1,991 c.c.	2,451 c.c.	1,090 c.c.
V angle of cyl.	60 deg	60 deg	60 deg	60 deg	60 deg	60 deg	10 deg 14 min
B.h.p.	56	70	90	75	80	118	38
Max. r.p.m.	4,000	4,500	5,000	5,000	5,000	5,300	4,800
Year of introduction	1950	1951	1952	1951	1952	1953	1953

THE SPORT 1954

THE long-awaited Lancia formula 1 Grand Prix car is in the news again, and this time it would really seem that this hush-hush vehicle is very nearly ready to race. In the course of tests at Monza last week, Ascari was unofficially timed to lap in 1m 56s (121.49 m.p.h.), which is Very Fast Indeed (the official lap record, set up during the 1951 Italian G.P., stands at 1m 56.5s, to the credit of Giuseppe Farina and a supercharged 1½-litre Alfa Romeo). Villoresi then took the new Lancia round in 1m 58s; the fastest lap in practice for this year's Italian G.P. was Fangio's 1m 59s in the streamlined G.P. Mercedes-Benz. Since then the Lancias have been out for tests on the Ospedaletti circuit, near San Remo, where they have also been very fast, but Villoresi had a crash and severely damaged one car, though happily not himself. It is still not certain whether or not these cars will make their first competition appearance at Barcelona on October 24; Mercedes, Ferrari, Gordini and Maserati teams are already entered, as is the Vanwall Special, so that this last major 1954 G.P. may be very interesting.

Initial testing of the D50 Grand Prix car was very encouraging (see paragraph at right). The car is seen here during testing on the Ospedaletti circuit with Luigi Villoresi at the wheel. The car appeared at the Spanish Grand Prix in 1954.

THE AUTOCAR, 29 OCTOBER 1954

THE new Lancia is an example of weight saving; parts of the front and rear suspensions look almost flimsy and must obviously have been the subject of much careful stresswork. Double wishbones of tubular construction are used at the front with ball joints in place of a king pin; the end of the main leaf of the narrow little transverse leaf spring pushes into a slot in the lower wishbone outer end, no shackle being used. At the back a de Dion layout is used; the brakes are outboard all round, Lancia having now abandoned the inboard front and rear brakes which caused a sensation on their sports-racing cars two years ago. One notable feature of the new car is the use of the wide V-eight power unit to brace and stiffen the chassis frame.

The D50 was powered by a 2,487cc, four overhead camshaft V8 with two sparking plugs per cylinder and four double-choke Weber carburettors. It produced 260bhp at 8,200rpm. The independent front suspension (above) used double wishbones, while the rear employed a de Dion axle layout inherited from the D24 sports racer.

THE SPORT 1954 Continued

Despite their involvement in Formula 1 (see previous page), Lancia continued to compete in sports car races. Alberto Ascari transferred his allegiance from Ferrari to Lancia at the start of the season and went on to win the most prestigious race of all, the Mille Miglia (below)—his number indicates that he started the race at 6.02 am. Lancias also won that year's Targa Florio and Giro di Sicilia.

The Lancia has very smooth, classic lines and is almost completely free from ornamental attachments.

The curved glass of the rear window neatly follows the smooth lines of the main body. The rear number plate is mounted on the luggage locker lid, and twin lights illuminate it. A very strong V-section bumper protects the back of the car, and extends round almost as far as the rear wheel arches to protect the rear quarters.

The Autocar ROAD TESTS

No. 1540:

LANCIA AURELIA GRAN TURISMO 2500 SALOON

THE introduction of the Lancia Aurelia saloon in 1950 caused a very considerable interest because of its somewhat unconventional layout and its very advanced design. A close examination of the car showed that in a number of ways it continued the line of development initiated by previous models; items such as the layout of the front suspension and the V formation of the cylinders illustrate this point. Although the Lancia company has produced narrow-angle V engines in the past, they have all been either four or eight-cylinder units, perhaps one of the best known being the Lancia Aprilia, which had a narrow angle V-four. For the Aurelia, however, a V-six arrangement was used, providing a compact six-cylinder engine with an overall length shorter than that which could be obtained with a six-in-line engine having a similar bore and stroke. The arrangement of the transmission and rear suspension was also unusual, and instead of the clutch and gear box being placed in unit with the engine, these components were grouped to form a single unit with the final drive gear and with the rear brakes, which were mounted inboard and coupled to the independently sprung wheels by means of two short shafts.

The Gran Turismo Lancia, which first appeared in 1951, was developed from the Aurelia saloon, a number of the major basic components being used, but whereas the standard Aurelia is a four-door saloon, the Gran Turismo is a two-door sports saloon with a low streamlined body having what is known in America as "a fast back"; in fact, as the performance figures show, it is not only the back that is fast!

Since the Gran Turismo was introduced its engine capacity has been increased to nearly $2\frac{1}{2}$ litres, and, earlier this year, a fundamental modification was made to the rear suspension. Indeed, this alteration applies to both the Aurelia and the Gran Turismo models, and in place of a fully independent rear suspension both cars now have a de Dion axle with half-elliptic leaf springs, and a Panhard rod to provide transverse location.

Normally, when a car is submitted for road test purposes it is in a fully run-in condition with several thousand miles on the speedometer, but the example of the Gran Turismo submitted for test, at the factory in Italy, was brand new. It was possible, therefore, to observe the performance of the car from the word "go." It was recommended that the maximum speed in top gear should not exceed 140 kilo-

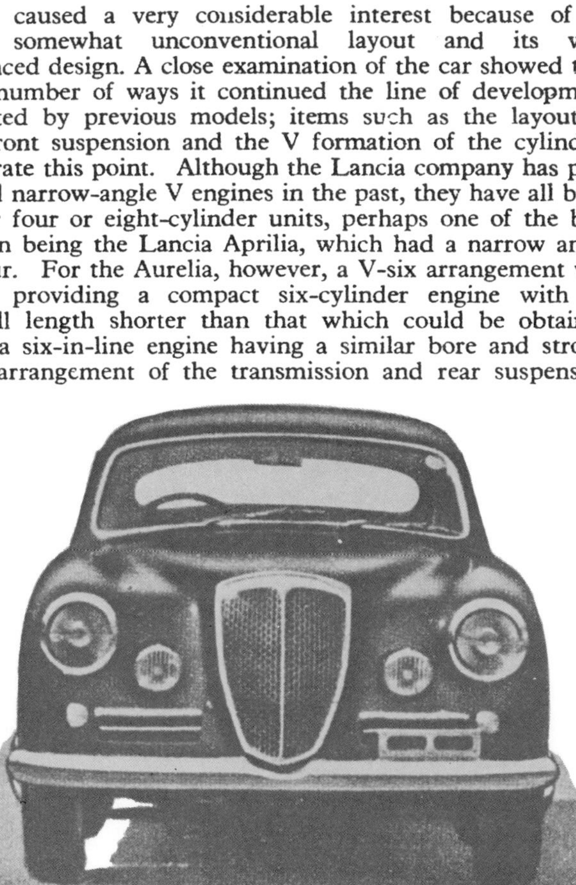

The Gran Turismo retains a small version of the familiar Lancia radiator grille. Six light units are fitted to the front of the car; below the main head lamps, small units contain the side lamps and direction indicators, while twin fog lamps are placed one on each side of the grille. The number plate bracket is placed on the left side of the bumper.

metres per hour for the first 2,000 km, and with this limit, which is equivalent to 87 m.p.h., the running-in process could in no way be described as tedious, and was in fact completed in two days, during which time it was possible to obtain an accurate impression of the car's handling qualities at medium speeds and to see how they varied, if at all, when the car was driven really fast.

Now, the Gran Turismo is very much a dual purpose car, for although it has a top speed and general performance which would satisfy most enthusiasts, it also has very many other qualities which are perhaps even more important to the majority of would-be purchasers. For example, outwardly it looks like a two-seater, but in fact three persons can be comfortably carried on the front seats, and in addition the upholstered area at the back of the front seats can provide occasional accommodation for two extra persons for short distances, or alternatively it can be used to carry a considerable quantity of luggage. In keeping with all this, the engine provides very good power output throughout its entire range, although the maximum torque does in fact occur at between 3,000 and 4,000 r.p.m. The engine is very smooth generally and the car can be accelerated in top gear from a speed as low as around 12 m.p.h. up to its maximum of around 112 m.p.h. A slight degree of roughness was noticed as compared with a six-in-line engine, but this was in no way excessive.

Folding pull handles are attached to the insides of both doors; they are conveniently placed and do not get in the way when not in use. There are two ash trays, one at each end of the facia. The floor is covered with rubber.

The body interior is neatly trimmed. Although the rear compartment can provide occasional accommodation for additional passengers, it is chiefly intended as an extra luggage compartment. A metal protective strip can be seen midway along the rear squab.

Placing the clutch and gear box in unit with the final drive necessitates the use of remote controls to operate both these components, and although the mechanism required to operate the clutch is very straightforward, the arrangement of the steering column gear change presents one or two problems; however, these have been solved in a satisfactory way and the gear change mechanism has an easy action and can be operated quickly, but there is a slight amount of flexibility in the mechanism as compared with a central remote control change, for example. Synchromesh is provided on top, third and second gears; it is effective and not easily beaten by fast gear changing. The clutch is smooth and perfectly satisfactory for all normal driving, although slight slip was experienced under the severe conditions imposed during performance testing.

The general roadholding qualities of the Gran Turismo are very good indeed, and the change over from an independent to a de Dion type rear suspension has no doubt been responsible for the improvement in general directional stability, and has eliminated the tendency to oversteer which was displayed by previous models. In fact, the car now has a slight tendency to understeer and feels very stable. There is a negligible amount of roll on corners and the handling characteristics do not vary appreciably when passengers are carried in the rear seat and the locker is full of luggage.

High-speed Suspension

The springing is soft enough to iron out all the bumps yet the car does not feel floppy; there was slight damper fade after it had been driven fast for a long distance over roads where the suspension system was really working. At speeds of over 110 m.p.h. there was some tendency for the car to weave very slightly, and this effect may well be produced by the slight changes in position between the sprung and unsprung masses at the rear of the car brought about by the action of the Panhard rod as the rear wheels move up and down.

The steering is light and accurate, although some road shocks are transmitted back through the mechanism to the driver's hands. The system gives a very good sense of road feel and there is a moderate amount of self-centring action. It is also satisfactorily light for manœuvring the car in confined spaces; 3¾ turns are required from lock to lock.

Hydraulically operated leading and trailing shoe brakes are used at front and rear; those at the front are mounted close to the wheels, while the rear ones are inboard on either side of the final drive casing. On the road no fade whatsoever was experienced and the brakes remained nicely balanced and could be relied on to stop the car in a dead straight line. During performance testing, which requires frequent brake application, some judder was experienced, but it is possible that the brakes may not have become fully bedded in in the comparatively short mileage covered by the car. A pendant hand brake lever is conveniently placed under the scuttle, and is mechanically coupled to the rear brakes.

The Lancia is a pleasantly quiet car to drive or ride in; there is very little road excited body noise, and the interior does not boom; it is also quiet as regards wind noise when the windows are closed. There is a certain amount of engine noise, and the gear box can be heard when it is in the lower speeds.

The driving position is very well arranged. The steering wheel is in a convenient position, and although the column extends some distance back from the facia, the wheel is well forward in relation to the driver, providing a typically Italian style of driving position which is very comfortable and provides maximum control. To assist three-abreast seating in the front, the steering wheel is well over to the right of the car, so the driver's right arm is very close to the door. The relative positions of the steering wheel and pedals are also well arranged, and the rubber covered organ-type of throttle pedal is sufficiently close to the brake pedal to allow both these controls to be operated together if required. The absence of a bell housing and gear box right behind the engine results in plenty of room to the left of the clutch pedal for the driver's foot, and it is necessary to provide only a small tunnel in the floor to clear the transmission shaft.

The driver has very good all-round vision, and the tops of both front wings can just be seen. The windscreen pillars are quite small, and because of the curvature of the glass they are fairly well back and do not cause a serious blind spot. The side windows extend back as far as the front of the rear wheel arch, and these, in conjunction with the large rear window, provide good three-quarter rear visibility. The rear view mirror, which can be dipped to prevent glare from following traffic at night, is suspended from the top of the windscreen in a position where it provides good rearward vision but does not obstruct a large area of the glass. The windscreen wiper blades overlap in the centre so that a single large area is swept; they are also self-parking.

All the instruments are housed in two circular dials conveniently placed in front of the steering wheel. They are well recessed in the facia and are provided with small cowls to prevent reflections in the windscreen at night. The main dial in the left-hand instrument is the speedometer, while a similar dial on the right is the tachometer.

LANCIA AURELIA GRAN TURISMO 2500 SALOON

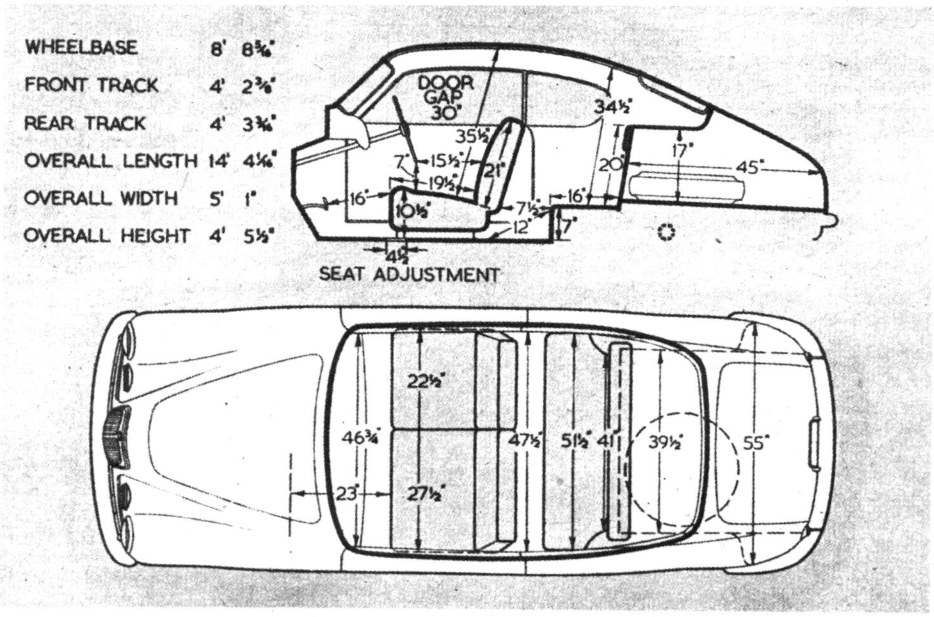

Measurements in these $\frac{1}{4}$in to 1ft scale body diagrams are taken with the driving seat in the central position of fore and aft adjustment and with the seat cushions uncompressed.

PERFORMANCE

ACCELERATION: from constant speeds. Speed Range, Gear Ratios and Time in sec.

M.P.H.	3.68 to 1	5.34 to 1	7.85 to 1	12.2 to 1
10—30 ..	13.5	7.9	5.3	3.5
20—40 ..	11.9	7.3	4.7	—
30—50 ..	11.4	7.0	4.7	—
40—60 ..	12.7	6.7	—	—
50—70 ..	12.4	7.3	—	—
60—80 ..	12.6	—	—	—
70—90 ..	15.8	—	—	—
80—100 ..	22.5	—	—	—

From rest through gears to:

M.P.H.	sec
30	4.0
50	8.4
60	12.3
70	15.8
80	22.2
90	31.4
100	44.7

Standing quarter mile, 19.1 sec.

SPEEDS ON GEARS:

Gear		M.P.H. (normal and max.)	K.P.H. (normal and max.)
Top ..	(mean)	111.5	179.44
	(best)	112	180.25
3rd		65—78	105—126
2nd		40—50	64—80
1st		22—30	35—48

TRACTIVE RESISTANCE: 24.5 lb per ton at 10 M.P.H.

TRACTIVE EFFORT:

	Pull (lb per ton)	Equivalent Gradient
Top	200	1 in 11.1
Third	315	1 in 7.0
Second	465	1 in 4.8

BRAKES:

Efficiency	Pedal Pressure (lb)
89 per cent	100
80 per cent	80
51 per cent	50

FUEL CONSUMPTION:

19 m.p.g. overall for 300 miles (14.9 litres per 100 km).

Approximate normal range 17–22 m.p.g. (16.6–12.8 litres per 100 km.)

Fuel, Italian first grade (80–83 octane).

WEATHER: Dry surface; wind negligible.

Air temperature 80 deg F.

Acceleration figures are the means of several runs in opposite directions.

Tractive effort and resistance obtained by Tapley meter.

SPEEDOMETER CORRECTION: M.P.H.

Car speedometer:	10	20	30	40	50	60	70	80	90	100	110	115
True speed:	8	18.5	29	39	49	59	69	78.5	88	97.5	107	112

DATA

PRICE (in Italy), with two-door saloon body, 2,828,000 lira = £1,620 at 1,750 lira = £1. Not available in Great Britain.

Extras: Radio 95,000 lira.
Heater, standard equipment.

ENGINE: Capacity: 2,451 c.c. (149.1 cu in).
Number of cylinders: 6.
Bore and stroke: 78 × 85.5 mm (3.071 × 3.366in).
Valve gear: Overhead; push rods and rockers.
Compression ratio: 8 to 1.
B.H.P.: 118 at 5,000 r.p.m. (B.H.P. per ton laden 88).
Torque: 134 lb ft at 3,500 r.p.m.
M.P.H. per 1,000 r.p.m. on top gear, 22.

WEIGHT: (with 5 gals fuel), $23\frac{1}{2}$ cwt (2,633 lb).
Weight distribution (per cent): F, 48.5; R, 51.5
Laden as tested: $26\frac{3}{4}$ cwt (3,003 lb).
Lb per c.c. (laden): 1.23.

BRAKES: Type: F, Leading and trailing; R, Leading and trailing.
Method of operation: F, Hydraulic; R, Hydraulic.
Drum dimensions: F, 11.81in diameter; 2.76in wide. R, 11.02in diameter; 2.76in wide.
Lining area: F, 130 sq in. R, 117 sq in (185 sq in per ton laden).

TYRES: 165—400 mm.
Pressures (lb per sq in): F, 26; R, 27 (normal).

TANK CAPACITY: 17 Imperial gallons (including $1\frac{1}{4}$ gallons reserve).
Oil sump, $8\frac{3}{4}$ pints.
Cooling system, 18 pints.

TURNING CIRCLE: 32ft 0in (L and R).
Steering wheel turns (lock to lock): $3\frac{3}{4}$.

DIMENSIONS: Wheelbase: 8ft $8\frac{5}{16}$in.
Track: F, 4ft $2\frac{3}{8}$in; R, 4ft $3\frac{3}{16}$in.
Length (overall): 14ft $4\frac{1}{16}$in.
Height: 4ft $5\frac{1}{2}$in.
Width: 5ft 1in.
Ground clearance: 6in.
Frontal area: 18.2 sq ft (approximately).

ELECTRICAL SYSTEM: 12-volt; 50 ampère-hour battery.
Head lights: Double dip; 45–40-watt bulbs.

SUSPENSION: Front, Independent; coil springs. Rear, de Dion axle; half-elliptic leaf springs and Panhard rod.

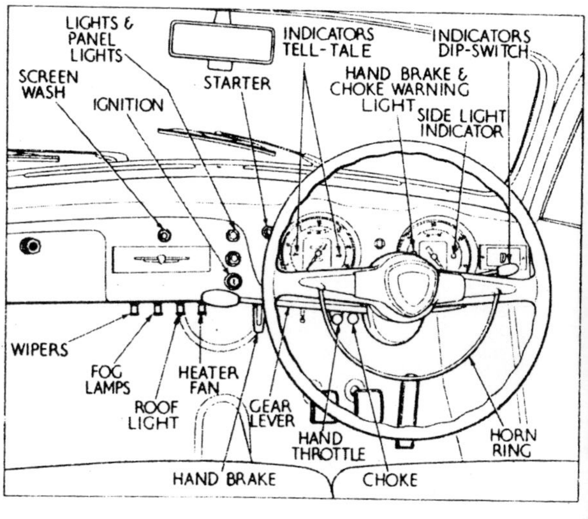

The left-hand instrument also contains the fuel gauge, warning lights for the direction indicators, and the ignition warning light. The right-hand one also houses the oil pressure gauge, and warning lights to show when the side lights are on; if the choke has been left out too long; or the driver has forgotten to release the hand brake, while yet another light indicates low oil pressure. The instruments are nicely illuminated and there is a rheostat in the circuit to enable the brightness of the lighting to be adjusted; the control for this is built into the side and head-lamp switch, which is pulled to operate the side lights, pulled again to bring on the head lights, and rotated to operate the instrument light rheostat.

The two wide doors are hinged at their leading edges and it is very easy to get in and out of the front seats. To provide access to the rear seats, the front seat back rest is split and hinged but the division is offset towards the

The floor of the luggage locker is covered with rubber, and the spare wheel is held in place by means of a strap. It is necessary to open a cover in the floor of the compartment to gain access to the fuel tank filler.

ROAD TEST . . . . continued

driver's side, and a folding central arm rest is built into the larger portion of the back rest on the passenger side. This arrangement enables passengers to get in and out, or luggage to be stowed in the rear compartment, without disturbing front passengers. There are ample head room and leg room for driver and passengers, and the front seat cushion and back rest are very nicely proportioned and give good support, with the result that very long distances can be covered without the driver feeling tired. The seat is upholstered in cloth, a feature which tends to reduce the sideways movement of both driver and passengers when the car is cornered quickly.

In the rear compartment the seat cushion is quite low in order to give as much head room as possible, and no upholstery is provided for the squab except a strip about 6in wide at shoulder height. The cushion itself is trimmed in leather, the remainder of the upholstery being in cloth; the reason for this, no doubt, is to provide greater durability when the compartment is used for carrying luggage. There is a large parcel tray behind the rear squab as well as a lockable glove box on the facia. To protect the trim, metal strips are fixed to the tray and also round the sides and back of the rear compartment.

Pockets are fitted to the insides of both doors, and the door pulls and window winders fold flat. Ten turns of the winder are required to open or close a side window completely. The rear sections of the side windows are hinged on their leading edges and can be opened to increase ventilation; owing to their shape, they tend to provide an extractor effect which assists the heating and ventilating unit.

The rear luggage locker is of moderate proportions but is of a convenient shape, although it also houses the spare wheel. For normal fast touring, with only two persons, a very considerable quantity of baggage can be carried behind the front seats. The fuel tank is placed below the luggage locker floor, and it is necessary to open a trap door in the floor to gain access to the fuel filler cap. No petrol fumes were noticed inside the car, but with this type of fuel filler there is always a possibility that a not-too-careful service station attendant may spill fuel on the luggage. The fuel tank has both main and reserve pipes, which are controlled from a tap located below the passenger seat.

The double dip head lights have a very good main beam range, together with a very good spread of light in the dipped position. A lever type dip switch and direction indicator control is mounted on the steering column; it is moved around the column to operate the flashing type indicators, and moved up and down the column to operate the main and dipped beams. With the side lights switched on, moving the lever up towards the steering column enables the head lights to be flashed for a warning signal at night.

The horns are controlled by a D-shaped ring, and they have a powerful, penetrating note. A two-point jacking system is provided, with one socket on each side of the car midway along the wheelbase; this is enclosed by a small metal cover. The chassis has eleven points that require attention with a grease gun, five of these at intervals of approximately 2,000 miles. An oil reservoir is provided under the bonnet for manual lubrication of the sliding members of the front suspension, and this has a two-way tap to enable the oil to be fed to either the left- or the right-hand unit as required.

The Lancia Aurelia Gran Turismo 2500 is a very satisfying car to drive; it has a fine performance and very good roadholding, both qualities being of an order that would satisfy the enthusiastic driver. Also it has a very large number of refinements and a high degree of detail finish, features which are apparent whenever the car is driven.

The engine compartment is well filled by the V-six engine and its auxiliaries. A thermostatically controlled shutter is built on to the front of the radiator and is operated by means of a spring- and temperature-operated unit built into the right-hand side of the radiator header tank. The battery, housed on the left side of the bulkhead, is neatly enclosed by a cover. The unit on the right-hand side of the bulkhead, by the side of the electrical equipment, contains two tanks, one to lubricate the sliding joints of the front suspension, and the other, which is provided with a visual level indicator, forming the brake fluid reservoir.

Left: No external frills spoil the simple and businesslike lines of the Series II Aurelia. Below: There is plenty of wing clearance for the wheels. The bumpers protect each corner of the car and the flashing indicators can be seen from the side as well as from front and rear

The Autocar ROAD TESTS

No. 1563

LANCIA AURELIA SALOON

FROM the Turin factory of the Lancia company come three models, the 1,090 c.c. Appia, the bigger (2,266 c.c.) Aurelia, and the 2½-litre Gran Turismo Aurelia. They have in common the well-tried coil spring, sliding pillar front suspension, and cylinders set at a narrow V-angle in the block.

To the uninitiated the Aurelia, which is the subject of this road test, has nothing extraordinary in its external appearance, except that the bonnet is notably short in comparison with the overall length of the car; at a second glance there will be seen a certain determination about the styling. The 60 degree V six-cylinder engine has an aluminium block, fitted with detachable cylinder liners. The oil sump is deeply and amply finned. The clutch, gear box and differential are in one unit, located on the body structure at four points. The rear brakes are inboard, and the de Dion rear axle is located laterally by a Panhard rod.

There is always something intriguing, to the motoring enthusiast's mind, about a car which is built in a country whose road conditions and the nature of whose populace demand a car out of the ordinary. With its method of construction and sporting background the Aurelia comes into this category, and experience of it left one with a longing for more, much more.

The engine starts immediately after a night in the open with the temperature below freezing point. The test car did not use an anti-freeze mixture, and it was filled with cold water; the system is simple to drain by means of the one tap connected to a long T handle; it warms up quickly, the thermostatically operated radiator shutters remaining closed until the water in the header tank is quite warm. Slight use of the choke control is necessary at first, and then the hand throttle can be set for a fast tickover. A light in the instrument panel warns when the choke is in operation. Strangely enough for a car of this nature, there is no temperature gauge.

One of the features of the Aurelia is the mechanical smoothness of the engine, and the dual exhaust system plays its part in helping the flow of gases and also assists towards the unobtrusiveness of the car. The engine is very quick to answer the throttle, and revs heartily and cheerfully. With the mountains of Northern Italy on the manu-

Good forward vision is provided by the wide windscreen. Twin fog lamps are built in and despite modern styling, the car is still unmistakably a Lancia

All trimming and seat covers are of good quality cloth. There is an armrest on each door and a small shelf behind the seat for parcels

ROAD TEST . . . . continued

facturer's doorstep as a testing ground, the power unit as produced does its work in a most efficient manner. Since last tested by *The Autocar* in 1952, the Aurelia engine has been slightly increased in size from 1,991 c.c., the previous bore and stroke being 72 × 81.5 mm and b.h.p. 70 at 4,500 r.p.m. as against 86.5 of the model now tested. The earlier car was also some two hundredweight lighter.

Although there is no increase in maximum speed with the slightly larger engine, there is a valuable improvement in acceleration times over the earlier car which, incidentally, was tested in its native country with the temperature in the seventies. The new car takes 1.4 sec less from 0 to 50 m.p.h., 5.2 sec less to 80 m.p.h., and shows an improvement over the standing quarter mile of nearly a second.

In these days of increasing congestion on the roads, acceleration is more valuable than maximum speed. As well as an ability quickly to overtake slower moving traffic, and its seemingly natural cruising speed of between 75 and 80 m.p.h. when conditions permit, one of the outstanding performance features of this Lancia is the enthralling behaviour in third gear.

Here is no under-geared car for the driver who wishes to use the change lever as little as possible. It is advisable to use first gear when starting from rest on nearly every occasion, and one can then change almost immediately into second with its useful maximum of over 50 m.p.h., and then into third.

This is obviously a ratio which has been designed for mountain passes, and the long, climbing gradients that are associated with them. It can be used when driving through built-up areas when the car does not feel comfortable in top gear, and it is valuable to carry the speed up again rapidly after an enforced delay. It is most useful when following other traffic along a winding road, the driver happy in the knowledge that when the opportunity occurs he is ready to take advantage of it. Up to a genuine 80 m.p.h. is available in this gear without the engine protesting, and it is part of the character of the car.

Remote Control

The steering column gear change is good of its type, but one was left with a desire for a more definite feeling, perhaps because of the necessarily long linkage. There was also the possibility of moving the lever into the reverse position when changing from third to top, and even when top gear was engaged there was some noise from the gear box.

The clutch is light and, during normal road driving, works well, but showed a tendency to slip slightly after repeated acceleration tests from a standing start. Standing out even more than the performance in third gear is the steering and road holding. The former is light—one driver said even too light—and the car can be controlled directionally by two fingers; the lock is taxi-like. Although there are four turns of the wheel from lock to lock, it does not appear undergeared, and control is precise.

There is the tremor which is associated with all Lancias, and which becomes pronounced when the car is driven very hard round a corner. And driven very hard round a corner it can be indeed. Dry roads, wet roads—it seemed to make no difference. The Aurelia just went round, with

One could not wish for easier entry to a car, than is allowed by the Lancia pillarless construction. Rubber mats cover the floor of the front compartment and there is a carpet in the rear. The angle of the front seat backrest is adjustable

very little heeling over, no tyre scream (Michelin X were fitted to the test car) and no fuss. There is understeer at high cornering speeds, the throttle is used all the way, and the experience is well worth having.

One double bend on a familiar test route, which can be relied upon to find steering faults if there are any, was taken faster than in any other car, and the performance immediately repeated to make sure that it was so. On a fine wide road with a series of very fast open bends, a following car, a fast 2½-litre, was seen in the mirror to be in a controlled slide while the Aurelia went through in a clean line from which there was no tendency to deviate.

The suspension is the equal of the cornering abilities; on smooth main roads the Lancia gives the normally expected comfortable ride, and on by-roads with a not-so-good surface, little bumps are felt which would not be so with cars having conventional suspension, but it is on what can be described as appalling, bumpy surfaces that it is especially good. Unmade roads covered with loose granite and crossed by small ruts can be traversed at 60-65 m.p.h. without the occupants being aware that the car is not on a tarmac surface.

The design of the Lancia rear axle gives a reduction in unsprung weight compared with the conventional design of transmission, and there is no doubt this plays its part in the high quality of the suspension. There is little, if any, road noise transmitted to the body interior. As one member of *The Autocar* road test team remarked, the harder the car is driven and the worse the road conditions become, the better it behaves.

Like the engine, the size of the brakes has been increased since the Aurelia was last tested, and the front drums have an extra ¾in of diameter, while the width of front and rear drums has been increased from just over 2¼in to 2⅞in.

LANCIA AURELIA SALOON

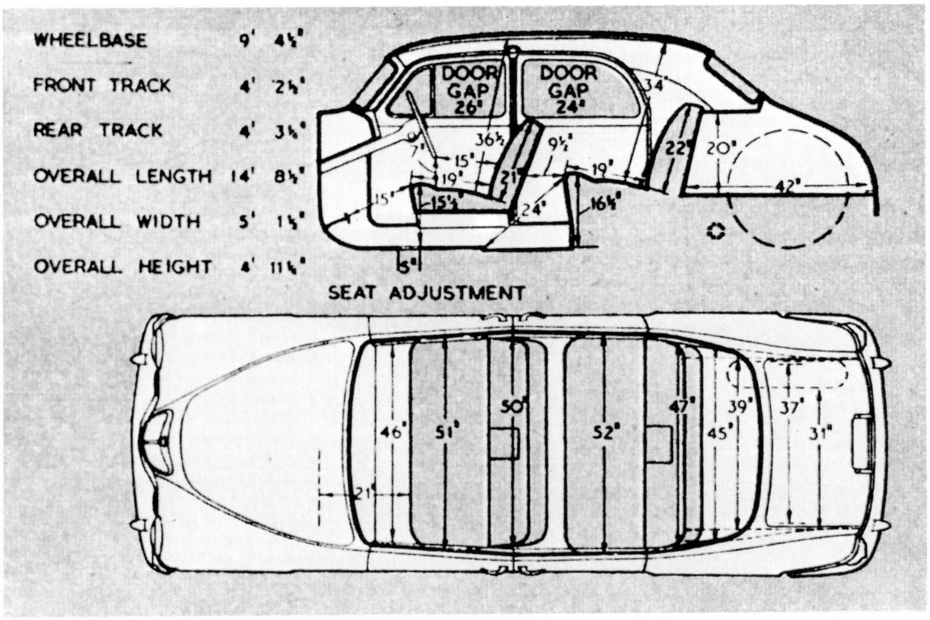

Measurements in these ¼in to 1ft scale body diagrams are taken with the driving seat in the central position of fore and aft adjustment and with the seat cushions uncompressed

PERFORMANCE

ACCELERATION: from constant speeds. Speed Range, Gear Ratios and time in sec.

M.P.H.	3.86 to 1	5.57 to 1	8.26 to 1	12.84 to 1
10—30	—	7.5	5.0	3.7
20—40	11.9	7.2	5.7	—
30—50	12.4	7.4	—	—
40—60	13.5	8.2	—	—
50—70	14.2	10.8	—	—
60—80	17.3	—	—	—

From rest through gears to:

M.P.H.	sec.
30	5.0
50	11.8
60	17.9
70	24.7
80	33.2

Standing quarter mile, 20.5 sec.

SPEEDS ON GEARS:

Gear		M.P.H. (normal and max.)	K.P.H. (normal and max.)
Top	(mean)	90.5	145.6
	(best)	92.0	148.0
3rd		70—80	112—128
2nd		40—54	64—87
1st		30—36	48—58

TRACTIVE RESISTANCE: 10 lb per ton at 10 M.P.H.

TRACTIVE EFFORT:

	Pull (lb per ton)	Equivalent Gradient
Top	204	1 in 11.0
Third	335	1 in 6.6
Second	450	1 in 4.9

BRAKES:

Efficiency	Pedal Pressure (lb)
84 per cent	100
75 per cent	75
52.5 per cent	50

FUEL CONSUMPTION:

22.8 m.p.g. overall for 473 miles (12.35 litres per 100 km.).

Approximate normal range 21—25 m.p.g. (13.5—11.3 litres per 100 km.).

Fuel, First Grade.

WEATHER: Dry surface, light breeze.

Air temperature 45 deg F.

Acceleration figures are the means of several runs in opposite directions.

Tractive effort and resistance obtained by Tapley meter.

SPEEDOMETER CORRECTION: M.P.H.

Car speedometer:	10	20	30	40	50	60	70	80	90
True speed:	9	19	29	38	47	55	65	74	84

DATA

PRICE (basic), with saloon body, **£2,020.** British purchase tax, **£842 15s 10d.** Total (in Great Britain), **£2,862 15s 10d.**

ENGINE: Capacity: 2,266 c.c. (138 cu. in). Number of cylinders: 6. Bore and stroke: 75 × 85.5 mm. (2.97 × 3.36in). Valve gear: overhead, push rods and rockers. Compression ratio: 7.4 to 1. B.H.P.: 86.5 at 4,300 r.p.m. (B.H.P. per ton laden 60.7). Torque: 117.5 lb ft at 2,900 r.p.m. M.P.H. per 1,000 r.p.m. on top gear, 19.4.

WEIGHT (with 5 gals fuel): 24¼ cwt (2,716 lb). Weight distribution (per cent): F, 50; R, 50. Laden as tested: 28½ cwt. (3,193 lb). Lb per c.c. (laden): 1.4.

BRAKES: Type: F, Two-leading shoe; R, Two-leading shoe. Method of operation: F, Hydraulic; R, Hydraulic. Drum dimensions: F, 11⅞in diameter; 2⅞in wide. R, 11in diameter; 2⅞in wide. Lining area: F, 137.5 sq in. R, 126 sq in (153.2 sq in per ton laden).

TYRES: 5.50—16in. Pressures (lb per sq in): F, 21; R, 21 (normal). F, 23; R, 23 (for fast driving).

TANK CAPACITY: 12 Imperial gallons. Oil sump, 8 pints. Cooling system, 19 pints.

TURNING CIRCLE: 35ft. (L and R). Steering wheel turns (lock to lock): 4.

DIMENSIONS: Wheelbase: 9ft. 4½in. Track: F, 4ft 2½in; R, 4ft 3½in. Length (overall): 14ft 8½in. Height: 4ft 11½in. Width: 5ft 1½in. Ground clearance: 6in. Frontal area: 20.4 sq ft (approximately).

ELECTRICAL SYSTEM: 12-volt; 50 ampère-hour battery. Head lights: Double dip; 45-40 watt bulbs.

SUSPENSION: Front, Independent coil springs and sliding pillars. Rear, De Dion half-elliptic springs and Panhard rod.

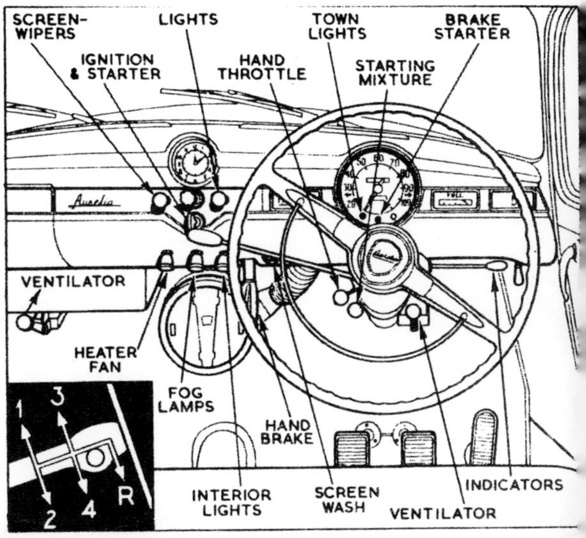

Pedal pressure required for maximum braking is less than on the earlier model. In practice the brakes cannot be faulted. They stand up to hard driving, and pulled the car up fair and square with no suspicion of fade after repeated stops during testing. The hand-brake lever projecting vertically below the facia is awkward to reach. The choke warning light on the instrument panel also serves as a warning when the hand brake is on.

The well-placed, thin-rimmed, ribbed steering wheel, short bonnet and curved windscreen combine to give a good driving position. The front seat has easily adjustable fore and aft movement, and the seat back is adjustable for rake. There is a folding central arm rest. The left-hand wing is not seen by a driver of medium height, and the screen pillars are on the thick side. Tinted safety glass is used in all windows. The double-dipping head lamps are powerful and enable maximum speed to be used at night. The electrical system is comprehensive, and separate fuses are provided for each circuit.

A neat control on the right of the steering column housing gives a choice of dip, full head, or enables the lamps to be flashed in built-up areas. The main lighting switch also controls the panel light rheostat and, unlike the usual state of affairs, the light was not bright enough. Turning

A good luggage locker is provided in the Lancia. The spare wheel is held in position by a quick release strap. The fuel tank filler has a hinged cover

ROAD TEST . . . . continued

the switch hard over switched off the head lamps unexpectedly, and a fault also developed in the windscreen wiper circuit. A windscreen washer is included in the equipment, and the horn note is worthy of the car. There are also two lights in the engine compartment, which are useful for checking oil level and the like at night. A reversing light is fitted below the middle of the rear bumper.

Lancia is almost alone these days in producing pillarless saloon coachwork, and there cannot be a car of similar carrying capacity which is easier to get into or out of. At speeds over 70 m.p.h. wind noise becomes very apparent, chiefly from the rubber sealing joint between the doors. The cloth-covered upholstery of the seats, which are well within the wheelbase, is very comfortable, and there is room for three adults on the rear seat; three can be accommodated in front for comparatively short distances, but for the sort of motoring for which this car is designed the front seat should be regarded as being for two occupants only.

The floor, divided by the propeller-shaft tunnel, is covered with thick moulded rubber matting in the front compartment, and carpeting in the rear. The interior finish is quiet but very well executed. A recirculating system heater is fitted as standard equipment. Very hot air can be directed to the windscreen, and into the front compartment; the blower fan is rather noisy. There are 11 greasing points to attend to every 2,000 miles, and provision is made for a starting handle although one is not supplied in the kit.

As an indication of the manufacturing methods, Lancia advise owners not to exceed 74 m.p.h. in top gear for the first 1,250 miles.

The engine compartment is almost completely filled and the workmanship is impressive. There are individual fuses for each circuit, the battery is enclosed and wiring is metal ducted. The bonnet lid is self-supporting and noise is suppressed by felt treatment of the underside

The Sport

1955

THE AUTOCAR, 15 JULY 1955

FEELING the pinch for the second time recently is Enzo Ferrari who, you will recall, threatened to retire from Grand Prix racing last year unless somebody managed to round up enough money to keep him going in this exceedingly expensive game. With things as they are, and Mercedes, probably retiring at the end of this season, it would be a tragedy if another of the Continental teams were to stop racing —particularly as next year looks like being a prolonged Ferrari versus Maserati contest.

However, Fiat and Lancia have come to the rescue, Fiat volunteering to supply something in the region of £28,500 a year for the next five years. What is even more cheering is that Lancia appears to be handing over the fast and beautiful formula 1 cars which, in the one race in which they competed as a works team this season, showed great promise. At Monaco Ascari put up equal fastest practice lap with Fangio's Mercedes and, at Spa, Castellotti's lone Lancia put up fastest lap in practice. Whether Ferrari will run the cars in their present state, or combine the best of his and Lancia's designs remains to be seen, but one can't help hoping that the good looking Lancias will appear again.

During their first full season in Formula 1, the Lancia D50 (top, driven by Castelloti) proved fast but fragile. Its full potential was shown at Monaco in May (centre), when Ascari, seen here leading team-mate Chiron up the hill towards Casino, led the race until he crashed into the harbour. Just one week later, Ascari was killed in an accident at Monza, which took all the heart out of the team; Lancia, already in financial trouble, sold all the GP cars and spares to Ferrari, as predicted by Autocar *that summer (see story at left). Towards the end of the year, in September, British fans had a rare chance to see the D50 at the International Gold Cup at Oulton Park (below); here the Lancias of Castelloti and Hawthorn lead at the end of lap one, soon to be overhauled by Stirling Moss' Maserati.*

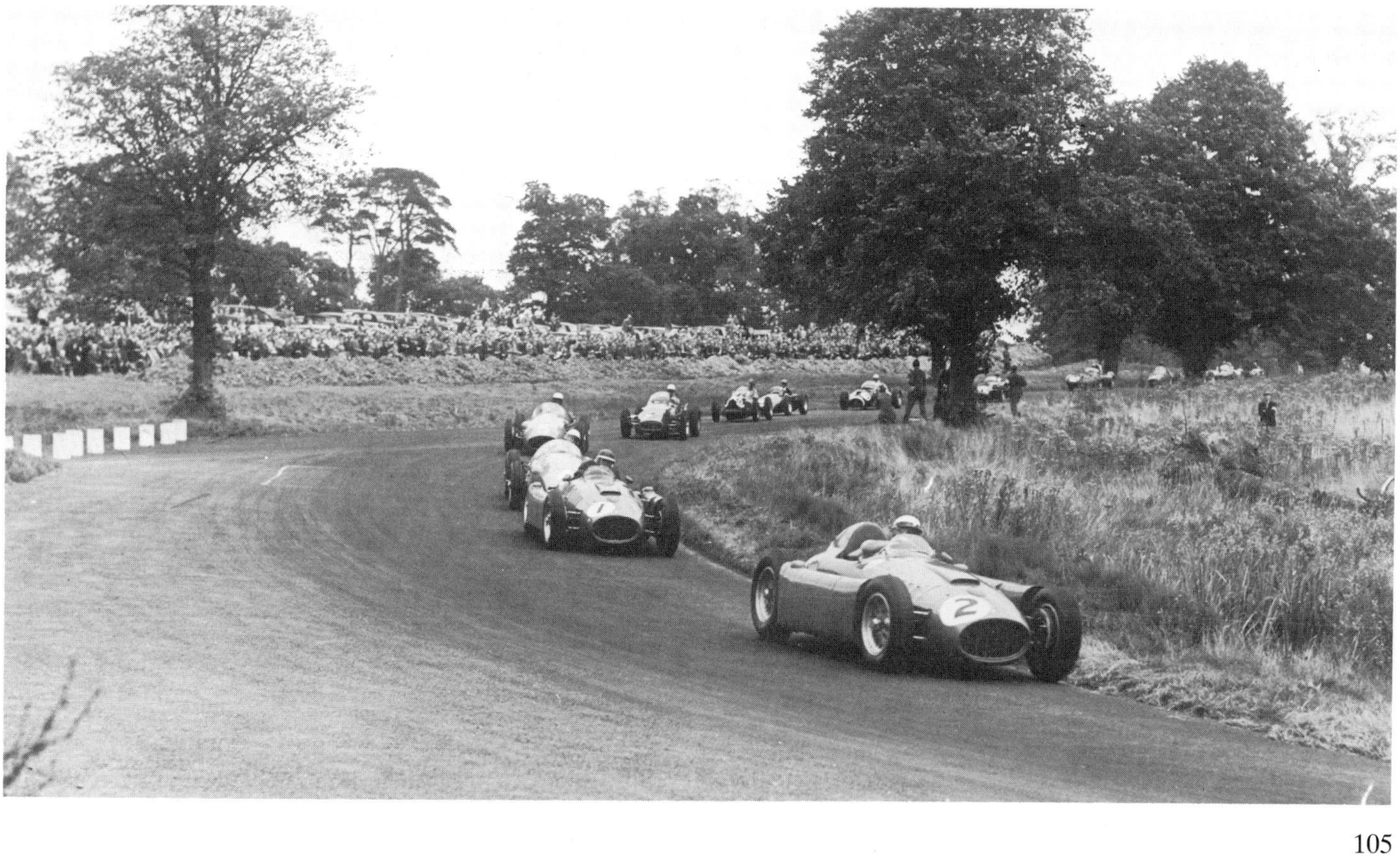

CONNOISSEUR'S CARRIAGE

Road Impressions of the Latest Aurelia

ONE of the cars about which one very seldom hears a bad word is the Lancia Aurelia. An estate agent might refer to it as "much sought after" and, probably for the first time in his working life, he would be telling the truth. Perhaps it is because Lancias have always managed to be sensibly different that they have a special appeal. Particularly have they been noted through the years for advanced suspensions and, as a result, outstanding roadability.

Today one of the traditional features of the marque is the V engine layout. The little Appia has a unique (12 deg) narrow angle V4 of only 1,090 c.c. capacity; the Aurelia has a 2,266 c.c. V6 (60 deg angle) and the Gran Turismo Aurelia (particularly "much sought after" by enthusiasts) a basically similar 2½-litre V6. The Aurelias (and the Sports Spyders) have independent front suspension and de Dion plus half elliptics at the back. This layout replaced a fully independent one of two to three years ago.

It may be recalled that the clutch, gear box and final drive—including rear brakes—are grouped together at the back; the makers say that this gives an advantageous weight distribution. The absence of a propeller shaft between clutch and final drive gives the car slow-speed transmission characteristics comparable with those of a rear-engine design. This entails extra care to obtain a smooth drive. The vee engine and absence of forward gear box and clutch account for the short nose and clear but short floor space for the front seats.

It is difficult to place the Aurelia in any particular class. It has a decidedly sporting performance, yet the power output of the 2¼-litre engine could easily be higher. The road-holding qualities match those of the best sports cars, yet the steering and suspension have no suggestion of harshness. The light-weight, pillarless coachwork is that of a medium-sized family saloon with plenty of luggage space; in both appearance and size it may be said to fit between the M.G. Magnette and the Riley Pathfinder.

Generally speaking, the V6-cylinder engine is smooth and makes no protest whatever when peaked in the intermediate gears, yet on occasion it does produce a slight noise and vibration of a kind peculiar to the design, and not felt in a straight Six. The gear ratios are all high, and as a result it is necessary to start in bottom gear and definitely desirable to drop down to this gear when brought almost to a standstill in traffic.

The two portraits of the Aurelia on this page—the upper one in a setting strangely suggestive of the car's native Italy but in fact taken beside the Thames—show the plain yet distinctive lines. The rear bumper wraps well round, continuing the line of the lower moulding and it provides the only side embellishment other than the wheel styling

Right: An unusually neat crackle-enamel-finished V6 engine compartment. The device on the extreme left is the central chassis lubrication system with separate plungers for front suspension and other chassis points. Pillarless saloons are rare today. The clear, wide opening of the two doors with their top and bottom latches, and also the ample upholstery are well shown here

Second gear is extremely lively for ordinary slow traffic work, while third feels no lower than the top gear of some English cars. The Aurelia does a speedometer 80 m.p.h. in third. Top is a fine, long-distance cruising gear but it provides little urge at under 35 m.p.h.; between 50 and 80 m.p.h. it pulls very hard and the maximum speed is a little over 90 m.p.h. The hydraulic brakes feel adequate for this performance. Driven in a normal manner with plenty of city traffic included, the fuel consumption worked out at about 22 m.p.g.

Michelin X tyres probably have quite an influence on one's impression of ride and suspension. On smooth roads the car glides like a luxury town chariot. Over cobbles, according to speed, it rumbles to a greater or lesser degree. If one runs down a line of cat's eyes, it feels as if the chassis were dragging across corrugated iron. On the other hand, if it is driven quite fast over deep-set gratings, tram-tracks and potholes, it rides them almost as well as a 2 c.v. Citroen—and this is high praise. Very large potholes, gullys and ridges are also taken well, but with considerable displacement of the body. This comfortable behaviour from a car which scarcely rolls at all on corners and remains glued on the road at high speed is quite remarkable.

Steering is light and more positive in action than it feels. A certain amount of the road vibration comes back to the driver's hands, and the self-centring action is insufficient to straighten the car up when accelerating out of a corner, unless the driver pulls the wheel back into neutral position. If an ordinary driver reaches the point of worrying about under- or over-steer, he is probably taking the corner too fast for a saloon car. There is no consciousness of either one with the Aurelia, but if provoked, the rear end will break away first (which for most people is as it should be).

The gear-shift lever is rigid and very precise in operation. Selection of the gears in the quadrant requires a little practice, because it must be accurate if the changes are to be made quickly and cleanly. The gears themselves engage extremely sweetly, and it is not possible to beat the synchromesh for the top three.

A combined trafficator and light lever on the right of the steering column is convenient to operate. Up and down movement gives winking direction lights in the same sense as the turn of the adjacent wheel rim; push in columnwards gives dipped or full head lights according to the position of the master light switch on the panel; pull up—a spring loaded position—gives a signalling flash of the head lamps.

General finish of the car inside—including under the bonnet—and out is good, if unusually plain. A heavy black gloss enamel is used for the "tin" facia, which is neatly styled and carries only the essential instruments. Some might consider additional dials desirable on this class of car; the total U.K. price is now £2,326 7s. The courtesy light works only from the driver's front door.

In spite of it being a pillarless saloon the doors close snugly and no rattles, draughts or air noise could be detected from the joints. The windows, when up, extend farther into their channel seals than do those of most other cars. One can thus expect draught- and dust-sealing to be good.

Both the wiper and heater are noisy and the heater—not surprisingly, perhaps, for a car from the warmer Italian climate—is of the added afterwards rather than built-in kind. There is very little rake on the front floor where the passenger's feet would normally rest. This fact, coupled with the rather short rearward travel of the bench front seat, means that all but the shortest passenger and driver must travel with ankles turned up more than is comfortable. Pedal travel is largely an in-and-out rather than an up-an-down movement. This is strange in a car in which pendant pedals would be more geometrically convenient to operate.

For a car of its quality, black rubber flooring and lower trimming is rather austere though obviously practical. Less practical on this particular car was the soft, fawn felt-cloth used for the seats. In spite of care over their design, the front seats do not support the passenger as well as they might. The quality of the interior fittings and chromium plate is high.

The back rest of the front seats can be adjusted for angle from vertical right down to horizontal, enabling occupants to lie full length in the car. Substantial folding centre arm-rests are provided both front and rear.

One appreciates the provision of a sensible hand throttle lever mounted midway on the steering column, together with the choke. The ability to select a suitable engine speed during the warming up period enables the choke to be dispensed with as soon as the engine is firing.

The lines are plain, sensible and something of an acquired taste; on the other hand, they do not offend anyone. There is a doubt about the snub nose and tail, and about the balance of wheel size and body shape which the deflated look of the Michelin X tyres does nothing to help. The bumpers are of good quality, substantial and sensibly well wrapped round at the rear. This is one of the few cars to retain fixed, draught-excluding panes across the top of each window.

Of several drivers who recently tried out the Aurelia, all enjoyed the experience and none found cause to criticize more than a minor detail or two. In view of the growing interest and influence of women drivers, it may be added that the car was found also to have feminine appeal, particularly in regard to steering.

M. A. S.

Few production saloon cars have a de Dion type rear suspension—often inaccurately described as semi-independent. Note that both clutch and gearbox assemblies and the rear brakes are all either integral with or grouped around the final drive and thus form part of the sprung weight of the car

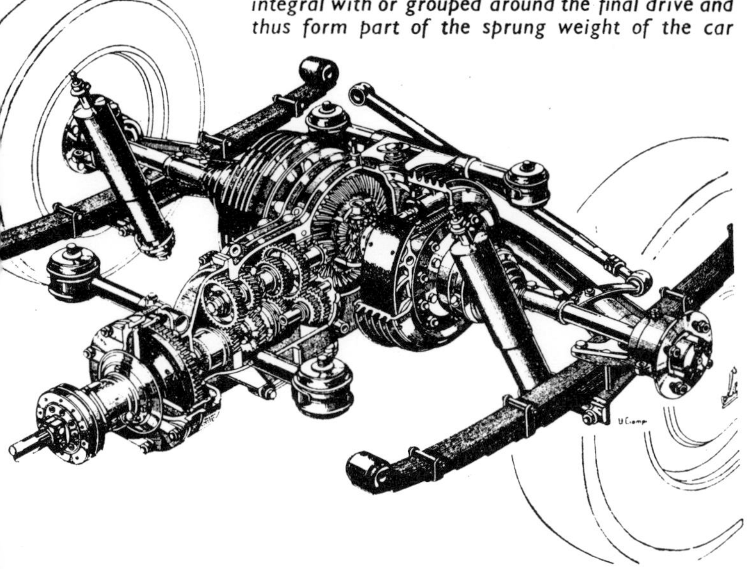

The Sport

1956

February 10th, 1956

Fangio, in the winning Lancia. Note the filler cap in the tail, filler cap in the side tank and exhaust stubs poking out through the rear end of the side tank

August 10th, 1956

AFTER a race that was noteworthy for its amazingly high casualty rate rather than excitement or tension, J. M. Fangio (Ferrari-Lancia) won the German Grand Prix at the Nurburgring last Sunday, taking the lead in the World Championship from Peter Collins. It was an exceedingly popular win, and demonstrates that, though one or two younger drivers at present can surpass him in one or two races, Fangio still remains the world's finest driver. Stirling Moss, in a slightly slower car, did his best to catch him, and on one occasion, it looked as if the Maserati might do so. However, on a signal from the pit to speed up, Fangio replied by setting up a new lap record for the Ring, at 87.74 m.p.h. (9min 41.6sec).

Syracuse Grand Prix
April 20th, 1956

With Villoresi's Maserati well behind, the final laps became an ordered procession for the Lancia-Ferraris of Fangio, Musso, and Collins

Belgian Grand Prix
June 8th, 1956

Champion of Belgium and second home in his country's Grand Prix, Paul Frère is here seen rounding the dead slow La Source hairpin in his Ferrari-Lancia

Argentine Grand Prix
December 21st, 1956

Six of the modified formula I Lancia-Ferraris have left for the Argentine. The four Solex twin-choke carburettors have been given a 20 degree inward cant, and the power output of the engines has been raised to between 290 and 295 b.h.p. Ferrari mechanics, Cassani (left) and Parenti (right) change plugs

Immaculately restored from what was once a rusting hulk, this 1st series Aprilia Berlina is owned by Peter Garnier

This 1955 Aurelia GT was still in regular use by its owner, Anthony Smallhorn, some 20 years and 360,000 miles after its initial construction, having been completely restored by Smallhorn. The specification is basically the same as the car tested by Autocar in November 1957 (see pages 113–116).

One of the last Flavias to bear the name, this 1971 Sedan is owned by Bill Dove. In the same year that it was made, the Flavia became the 2000, although the mechanical specification remained the same, power coming from a 1,991cc flat four engine driving the front wheels.

With crisp, classic lines and no protuberances to disturb the air stream, the Lancia Aurelia is remarkably free from wind noise at high speed

The Autocar ROAD TESTS 1659

Lancia Aurelia
Gran Turismo 2500

THE Lancia Aurelia *Gran Turismo* 2500 is of wide academic interest, not only to the sporting fraternity but also to all who can appreciate fine machinery and enterprising design, even when it may be priced beyond their grasp.

It is now more than six years since the G.T. coupé version of the Aurelia made its bow—at Turin in April, 1951. Since that time engine dimensions and power have been increased (1953) and an all-independent rear suspension replaced by a de Dion layout (1954), with the axle tube supported on conventional half-elliptic leaf springs and located laterally by a Panhard rod. *The Autocar's* previous Road Test of a G.T. Aurelia (conducted in Italy) was published in August of 1954, and was, therefore, of a 2½-litre car with de Dion axle—but at that time it was not available in the U.K.

Since then the peak engine power has been reduced slightly from 118 to 112 nett b.h.p., but a compensating gain in torque at low crankshaft speeds has improved tractability. Additionally, more thorough balancing of the crankshaft has brought about a higher degree of smoothness and refinement in running. The Aurelia is unique in the world, incidentally, in having its six cylinders arranged in two blocks of three, with an included angle of 60 deg.

It will be remembered that clutch, gear box and final drive on the Aurelia form a single unit situated beneath the rear seat cushion. A pinion and crown wheel set having 13 and 48 teeth respectively has recently replaced an 11 × 41 set, and the previous geared-up top has been abandoned in favour of a direct drive. The overall ratio remains virtually unchanged.

Though the Aurelia has been credited always with a splendid braking system, the current version now has an air-ducting scheme to cool the front ones and harder, non-fade linings. A handsome and comfortable light alloy three-spoke steering wheel with a wooden rim has replaced a two-spoke plastic-covered black one, and there are now hinged ventilating panels in the door windows.

An immediate impression on taking over the test car from the Lancia works at Alperton, near Wembley (the long-established British subsidiary of the Italian company) was of unexpected detailed quality and finish, particularly of the body and its trimmings; Lancia engineering quality under the bonnet and elsewhere about the working parts always has been quite exceptional. A close examination confirms the impression, but comfort, refinement, ease of maintenance and a long potential life are paid for in weight as well as money, and the Aurelia, with two up, a full fuel tank and a little baggage, weighs little short of 1½ tons—more, in fact, than in 1954.

Gran Turismo in the case of this car might well be interpreted "grand for touring," for its sporting characteristics are no more pronounced than its purely touring attributes. During initial acquaintance in crowded city traffic, the Lancia proved as smooth, quiet, tractable, light to steer and softly suspended as many a town carriage; on the car tested the effect was marred only by a clutch which refused to engage smoothly from rest, however carefully it was nursed. Although the makers rather curiously recommend take-offs in second speed, these tactics were even less welcome. The clutch also discourages quick upward changes by continuing to spin after the pedal has been released unless treated very gently; a full-throttle downward change also will result in clutch spin.

In view of the distance from the steering column to the rear-mounted gear box, it is scarcely surprising that the

The rear-mounted gear box allows a small transmission tunnel. Seat trim is in fine quality grey cloth. The light alloy wheel has polished wood grips

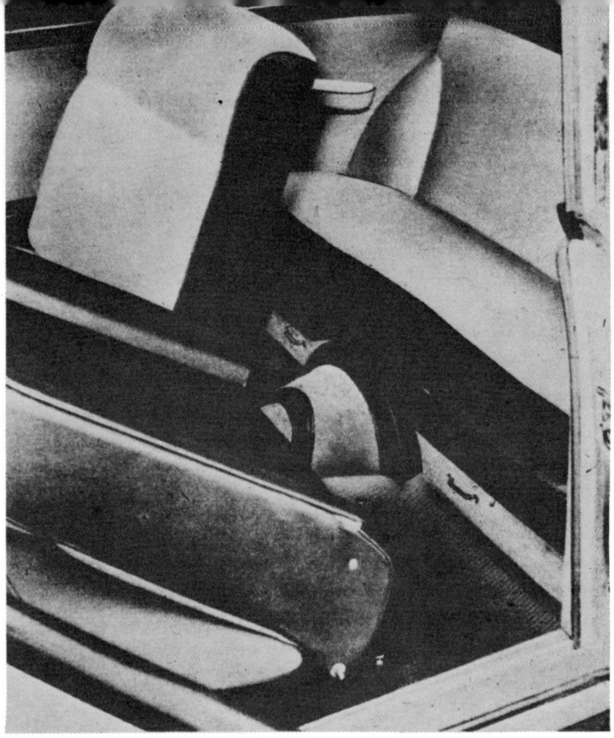

Left: Threaded stops control the angles of the front seat back rests. The front seats must be well forward to provide any leg room behind. There are strap fixtures to secure luggage on the rear seat cushion. Right: The front apron is studded with a battery of six lamps, all recessed into the bodywork. Despite a small frontal area the Gran Turismo can seat three abreast

Lancia Aurelia G.T. 2500 . . .

action of the lever is disappointing to those who remember previous Lancia gear-change mechanisms. It is above average in feel and precision for the type, but it requires considerable movement between the ratios, and quick changes do not come naturally. The convertible Aurelia has a central floor change, and it is understood that this variant may be fitted to the coupé at extra charge.

To give the Lancia an opportunity to show its true paces it was taken to the Continent and driven all-out along a high-speed *autoroute*. The mean maximum speed of 110 m.p.h. recorded requires one or two qualifications: first, the car had covered little over 3,000 miles, and although run in to the extent that it felt free, a vehicle of this class may need even 10,000 miles on the mileometer before it reaches peak form. Moreover, a moderate side wind was blowing. The Michelin X tyres were maintained at the normal recommended pressures of 24 to 25 lb sq in for these runs.

A mystery about the Lancia not wholly resolved is the makers' true limit for engine revolutions. A red line at 5,300 r.p.m. on the tachometer dial corresponds with advice in the instruction manual, yet Italian journals speak freely of 6,200 being attainable. Certainly the makers' advertised maximum speed for the car represents about 5,600 r.p.m. Although it was found that the engine remained relatively quiet and remarkably smooth if taken to 90 m.p.h. (about 6,200 r.p.m.) in third speed, the stop watch proved that this practice produced no reduction in time spent accelerating from 70 to 90 m.p.h., as compared with top. During acceleration tests the limit of 5,300 r.p.m. was observed.

Mean acceleration figures from rest through the gears are slightly inferior to those of the 1954 model (a difference amounting to only 2.7 sec up to 100 m.p.h.), yet some of the intermediate figures, particularly in top gear, show improvement due to the altered torque curve.

Figures in the 20 m.p.h. ranges reveal the Aurelia's even power delivery—in third, for instance, there is a difference of less than half a second between its times for 10-30, 20-40, 30-50 and 40-60 m.p.h. It will pull away smoothly from 14-15 m.p.h. in top, and there is never a trace of pinking on premium fuel. It will readily trundle up quite a steep gradient in top at a low speed without protest. The characteristic beat associated with engines having the vee layout is almost entirely absent, although when accelerating hard from low crankshaft revolutions there is a trace of unevenness in the intake note.

When the car is driven hard there is, in addition to some carburettor roar, a pronounced but not unpleasant whine emanating from the six-blade, cast aluminium radiator fan. The gear box, which has efficient synchromesh in second, third and top, is commendably quiet except in first and reverse gears; when the engine is ticking over at a standstill the constant mesh gears are faintly audible. The final drive in the car tried was silent.

Steering characteristics of the Lancia are first-class, with the reservation that directional stability at speed with a side wind is not all one might expect, the nose of the vehicle being over-sensitive to such influences; tail fins might upset the æsthetics of the Lancia profile, but could pay dividends in straight-line motoring. A wavy road surface, too, will bring about a curious rocking motion of the front, which can be felt at the wheel but never to a disconcerting degree. There was a complete absence—at any speed—of the shake of the wheel hitherto associated with Lancias. The mechanism is very light and sensitive, and the turning circle is usefully compact at 32ft.

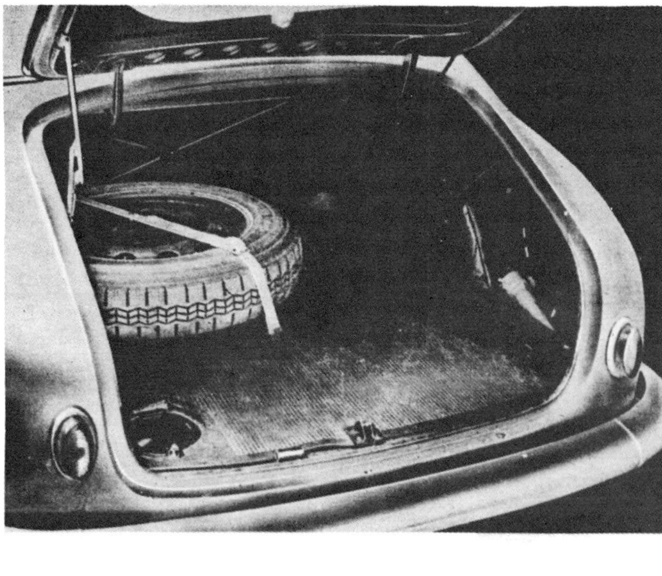

Luggage space is reduced by the spare wheel. The wheel arches and the deep wells behind them are thickly padded. Any overflow from the fuel filler, which is beneath a hinged flap on the floor, escapes to the road

Lancia Aurelia G.T. 2500 . . .

Often the other motorist's view of the Aurelia: the right-hand grip beside the number plate pivots to release the lid catch. Absence of bumper overriders causes anxiety in city parking

Disposition of its transmission mass at the rear has given the Lancia a clear weight bias at that end. Undoubtedly this has endowed it with its lightness and sensitivity of control, and contributed towards outstanding cornering abilities for both high-speed curves and more restricted radii. In fact, on a cross-country run the Lancia often can eat up the miles quicker than a potentially faster vehicle.

A curious effect peculiar to the Lancia sliding pillar type of independent front suspension is that, when cornering fast on an indifferent surface, powerful rebound damping apparently prevents the outer front wheel from dropping after one bump before it hits the next, and abnormal compression of the coil spring then results in some pounding.

The ride is much softer than expected, and the only harshness apparent is that of the Michelin X tyres fitted as initial equipment. On a wavy surface a little pitch is induced at times, but roll becomes apparent only with a quick double change of direction, as when taking a main road roundabout or the S-bends of a mountain pass at speed. First-class braking completes the Lancia's claims to exceptional roadworthiness. Although requiring relatively heavy pedal pressure, the brakes are very powerful, entirely predictable and virtually free from fade. On a wet surface heavy application may cause the rear wheels to lock before the front ones. The hand brake is efficient, but the pendant lever is awkwardly placed beneath the facia.

A remarkable absence of wind noise at speed is appreciated, and the body is commendably free from resonances due to either engine or road surface vibrations. Its simple shape makes it particularly easy to wash, and the mudguarding is efficient.

Above eye level the driver's view is limited by a shallow screen, but both front wings are visible over the low bonnet. The seat cushions and backrests give little lateral support during fast cornering, but a folding central armrest is fitted in the passenger's wide backrest. Both backrests are adjustable for rake by threaded stops; these cannot be reached while the car is moving. Trim in light grey cloth (rather easily marked) and blue leatherette looked attractive in the silver-grey car tested.

A comfortable driving position is spoilt by awkwardly grouped minor controls, of which the functions and relative positions take time to learn. Widely spaced pedals discourage heel-and-toe operation of brake and throttle, but the clutch and brake pedals protrude far from the toeboard. Provided that the seat can be moved well back, their angle is satisfactory at the point of operation. The throttle linkage geometry produces too wide an opening for initial movement of the pedal, and the unsupported right foot all too easily generates a transmission jerk which may continue until the throttle is released. The door window winders are too low-geared—quick-lift levers are needed—and the hinged ventilating panels have poor locking cams; the rear quarter windows are hinged on their leading edges. Only the driver's door can be locked from outside.

Two high-quality French Jaeger instruments confront the driver: A speedometer containing also gauges for oil pressure, fuel level and water temperature, plus indicator lamps for the flashing signals; and a tachometer dial, including a clock and indicator lights for choke, dynamo charge and side lamps. The dial bezels and other chromed items reflect in the screen in daytime. A multi-purpose signalling and dipping lever is mounted on the steering-column, supplementing a push-pull lighting switch on the facia. The head lamps give excellent spread for rapid driving on twisty roads, with a sufficient range to allow fast travel in a straight line, and the cut-off beams are fully adequate. There is no reversing lamp. Two penetrating yet harmonious horns are operated via a button in the steering wheel boss.

There are two flexible sun visors, and the driving mirror has a dipping reflector for night driving. The screen wipers sweep wide arcs, and their fulcrum points are off-set to give

Black crackle finish for wiring ducts and valve covers smartens the engine compartment (extreme left). A twin choke Weber carburettor feeds separate manifolds to each block. The grille must be detached to use the starting handle (left). There are thermostatically controlled radiator shutters

Lancia Aurelia G.T. 2500 . . .

the driver an especially comprehensive view. They are single-speed and irritatingly fast for city driving.

Standard equipment includes a Trico screen washer, a cigar lighter and two self-cleaning ashtrays. The effective Smiths heater and ventilation unit has a too noisy booster motor. A small locker in the facia is supplemented by long map pockets in the doors. A modest fuel consumption adds merit to the provision of a $16\frac{1}{2}$-gallon fuel tank, which includes a reserve controlled by a tap on the floor beneath the driver's legs.

Exceptionally invigorating to drive when in a hurry, the Lancia GT 2500 is yet surprisingly well behaved in the contrasting role of docile town carriage. In appearance it is classically stylish without need of ornament, and the general standard of finish, of both bodywork and mechanical components, is almost beyond criticism; without doubt it is one of the most desirable sporting cars of the decade.

LANCIA AURELIA GRAN TURISMO 2500 COUPÉ

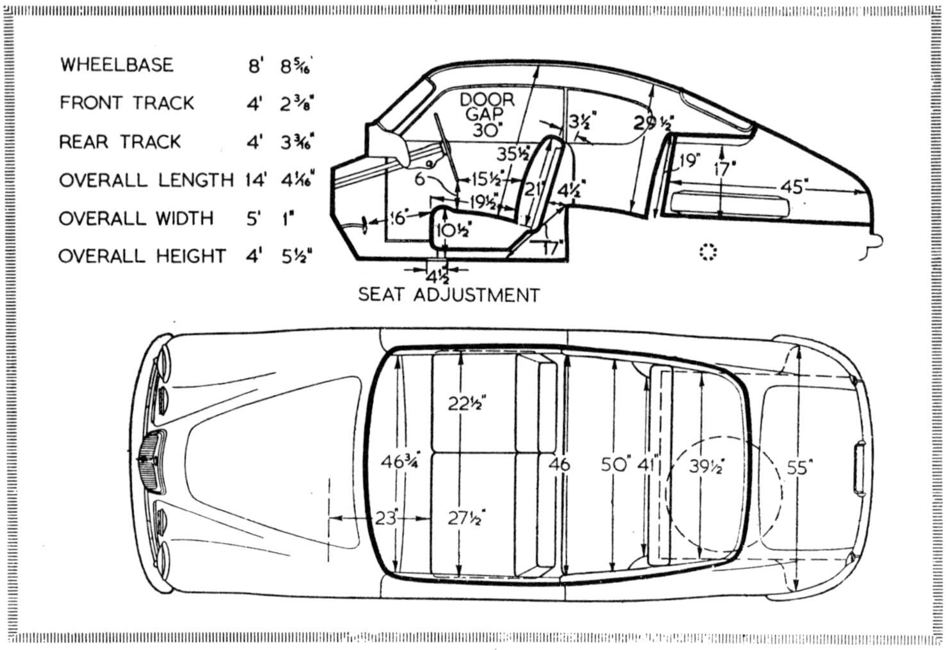

Measurements in these ¼in to 1ft scale body diagrams are taken with the driving seat in the central position of fore and aft adjustment and with the seat cushions uncompressed

DATA

PRICE (basic), with coupé body, **£2,230.** British purchase tax, **£1,116 7s.** Total (in Great Britain), **£3,346 7s.**

ENGINE: Capacity: 2,451 c.c. (141 cu in).
Number of cylinders: Vee-6.
Bore and stroke: 78 × 85.5 mm (3.07 × 3.36in).
Valve gear: o.h.v., pushrods.
Compression ratio: 8.4 to 1.
B.H.P.: 118 (gross) at 5,000 r.p.m. (B.H.P. per ton laden 83.0).
Torque: 126.5 lb ft at 3,500 r.p.m.
M.P.H. per 1,000 r.p.m. on top gear, 20.5.

WEIGHT: (with 5 gals fuel), $25\frac{7}{16}$ cwt (2,849 lb).
Weight distribution (per cent): F, 47.9; R, 52.1.
Laden as tested: $28\frac{7}{16}$ cwt (3,185 lb).
Lb per c.c. (laden): 1.3.

BRAKES: Type: Sabif.
Method of operation: hydraulic.
Drum dimensions: F, 11.8in diameter; 3.0in wide. R, 11.0in diameter; 2.8in wide.
Lining area: F, 83.6 sq in. R, 127.0 sq in (148.1 sq in per ton laden).

TYRES: 165—400 mm.
Pressures (lb per sq in): F, 23-25; R, 23-25 (normal).

TANK CAPACITY: 16.5 Imperial gallons.
Oil sump, 9 pints.
Cooling system, 16 pints.

TURNING CIRCLE: 32ft 9in (L and R).
Steering wheel turns (lock to lock): $3\frac{3}{4}$.

DIMENSIONS: Wheelbase: 8ft $8\frac{5}{16}$in.
Track: F, 4ft $2\frac{3}{8}$in; R, 4ft $3\frac{3}{16}$in.
Length (overall): 14ft $4\frac{1}{16}$in.
Height: 4ft $5\frac{1}{2}$in.
Width: 5ft 1in.
Ground clearance: 6in.

ELECTRICAL SYSTEM: 12-volt; 50 ampère-hour battery.
Head lights: Double dip; 45-40 watt bulbs.

SUSPENSION: Front, vertical sliding pillars with coil springs. Rear, de Dion axle with Panhard rod, swinging axle shafts, and semi-elliptic springs.

PERFORMANCE

ACCELERATION: from constant speeds.
Speed Range, Gear Ratios and Time in sec.

M.P.H.	**3.69 to 1**	**5.22 to 1**	**7.59 to 1**	**11.42 to 1**
10—30..	—	**7.2**	**4.9**	**3.7**
20—40..	**10.2**	**7.0**	**4.9**	—
30—50..	**10.2**	**7.1**	**5.2**	—
40—60..	**11.1**	**7.4**	—	—
50—70..	**11.5**	**8.5**	—	—
60—80..	**12.6**	**11.1**	—	—
70—90..	**15.9**	—	—	—

From rest through gears to:

M.P.H.	**sec.**
30	**4.9**
50	**10.0**
60	**14.0**
70	**18.4**
80	**24.4**
90	**33.7**
100	**47.4**

Standing quarter mile, 19.6sec.

SPEEDS ON GEARS:

Gear		M.P.H. (normal and max.)	K.P.H. (normal and max.)
Top	(mean)	**110**	**177.0**
	(best)	**113**	**181.8**
3rd		**62—82**	**99.8—132.0**
2nd		**42—56**	**67.6— 90.1**
1st		**28—37**	**45.1— 59.5**

TRACTIVE RESISTANCE: 24lb per ton at 10 M.P.H.

TRACTIVE EFFORT:

	Pull (lb per ton)	Equivalent Gradient
Top	191	1 in 11.7
Third	300	1 in 7.4
Second	436	1 in 5.0

BRAKES (in neutral at 30 m.p.h.):

Efficiency	Pedal Pressure (lb)
36 per cent	25
45 per cent	50
84 per cent	75
95 per cent	100

FUEL CONSUMPTION:
23.6 m.p.g. overall for 680 miles (12 litres per 100 km).
Approximate normal range 21-27 m.p.g. (13.4-10.5 litres per 100 km).
Fuel, Premium grade.

WEATHER: Dry, cross breeze.
Air temperature 60 deg F.
Acceleration figures are the means of several runs in opposite directions.
Tractive effort and resistance obtained by Tapley meter.

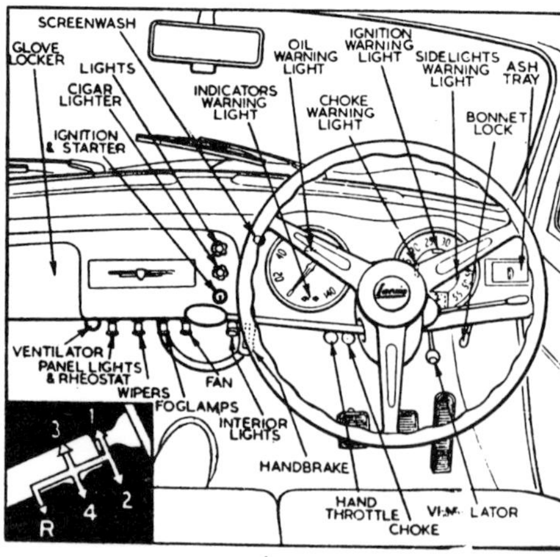

SPEEDOMETER CORRECTION: M.P.H.

Car speedometer:	10	20	30	40	50	60	70	80	90	100	110
True speed:	7	17	27	36.5	46	56	65.5	74.5	84	94	104

A crisp, neat appearance is in keeping with the character of the Flaminia. The rear bulwarks (for they are hardly fins) are very helpful for siting when reversing into a confined space

The Autocar ROAD TEST 1711

Lancia Flaminia

ITALIANS will tell you that the Flaminia is now their finest car; they omit more expensive Maseratis and Ferraris from the considerations because these they regard as competition models. The Flaminia is indeed a fine car technically, and in performance and appearance. Recently three new variants were announced, but the four-door saloon with body designed by Pinin Farina, which is the subject of this test, continues in full production. Flaminias are being made entirely in the Lancia factory at Turin at the rate of about 100 a month.

Only in special circumstances does *The Autocar* agree to test cars wholly abroad. The Flaminia is unlikely to be available in right-hand-drive form for some months to come; a L.H.D. example was, therefore, accepted in Italy, and tested over many kinds of roads, including *autostrade* and mountain passes. Right-hand-drive will be offered first on the new two-door short chassis Flaminias which have a floor gear lever.

A reminder of the unusual mechanical design of the Flaminia may be helpful. The engine is a 2½-litre, 60 deg vee-6 with push-rod operated valves and a Solex 2-choke downdraught carburettor. At 7.8 to 1 the compression ratio is relatively low; during the test no pinking was heard, although Continental premium petrol is usually of lower grade than that in the U.K. The engine differs in several respects—including the bore and stroke—from that of the Aurelia G.T.; in particular, it produces higher maximum torque at lower r.p.m. (141 lb ft at 3,000 r.p.m. compared with 126.5 lb ft at 3,500 r.p.m.).

In respect of front suspension the Flaminia breaks tradition by having wishbones in place of the sliding pillars of earlier models. Its directional stability at high speed benefits when compared with that of the Aurelia, for example.

At the rear, a de Dion axle supported on leaf springs is used, and in unit with the hypoid rear transmission are the gear box and clutch and two inboard drum brakes. Lancia refer to this as the propelling unit. Heavy mechanical components are thus divided evenly between the two ends of the car, and the transmission is sprung weight. This is, no doubt, responsible in part for the car's good traction and tenacity to the road. It is seldom possible to hear the transmission of the Flaminia.

This car was fitted with Michelin X tyres at 26 lb sq in front and 28 back—raised by 2lb all round above normal for the performance testing. The familiar characteristics were observed—outstanding tyre adhesion in all conditions, minimum of squeal, and thumping over serrations or studs in the road. Steering is commendably light, even at low speeds.

Without difficulty the Flaminia accommodates six people, for it is a big car, 15ft 11in long and weighing almost 32 cwt unladen. Its plain, artistic exterior makes it appear smaller but, when sitting inside, the driver gains a spacious as well as a bright impression of the car.

All but the very large will find a comfortable driving position by adjusting the seat on its rails and the seatback for angle. If there is a criticism, it would be that even with the seat fully back, the knees of a tall driver find hardly enough room under the steering-wheel rim when the feet are on the pedals. This is a little surprising because the wheel itself is set quite high and, in fact, the top of the rim would come into the field of vision of a short driver. For those who adopt the long arm position at the wheel the front seat needs to be on its back stop, in which setting the knee-room for rear seat passengers is marginal for comfort. The steering column is not adjustable for length.

We do not recall any car with a more pleasing column-mounted gear lever. If all could be as well engineered there would be less criticism of this position of lever on the majority of cars. It is more surprising on the Flaminia because the linkage has to be extended back to the gear box at the rear. Synchromesh is provided for the four forward speeds, the lever movements through the gate—with light spring loading down-column—are very short, and changes can be made as quickly and positively as with floor-mounted lever. The synchromesh proved to be unbeatable, even during extreme handling while obtaining acceleration figures.

First experience of the car was on the *autostrada* where its stability and ride-comfort quickly became apparent. It cruised effortlessly up to 90 m.p.h., reaching this speed quickly. On the rougher patches of road there was the minimum of pitching, and no road shocks were transmitted

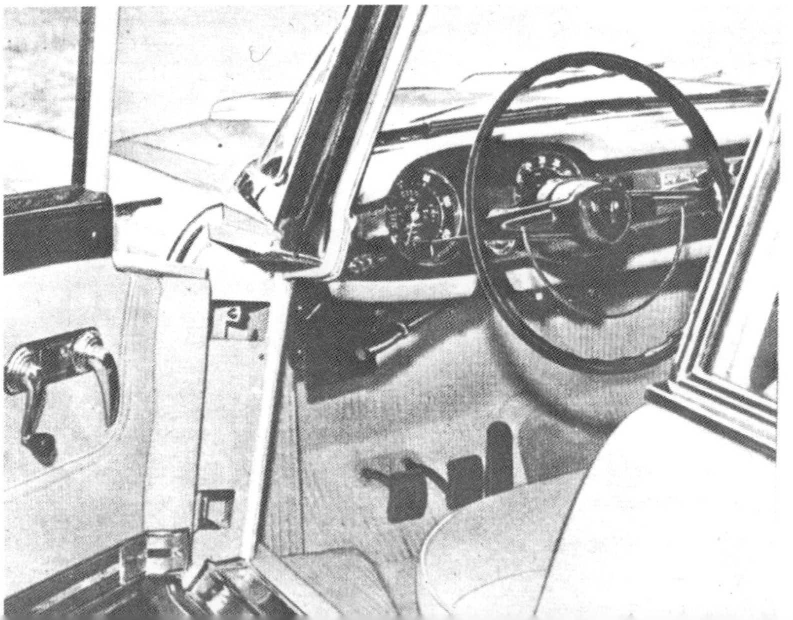

A modern, two-dial instrument layout is viewed through the wheel. The lower edge of the panel is padded and leather trimmed. Fitted rubber mats are used in the front only

Lancia Flaminia . . .

Wide doors with a reasonably high roofline give convenient access to front and rear seats. The rear quarter vents are vacuum operated

through the steering wheel. The silence and smoothness of the engine are apt to mislead as to the speed, so that the rapid rate of closing with other vehicles comes as a surprise at first. It would be an improvement if the engine cooling fan could be silenced; the whirring undertone it produces above 3,000 r.p.m. engine speed is the only disturbing sound when cruising at speed with windows closed.

When the car was driven fast through winding mountain roads, other qualities became apparent. Cornering is virtually roll-free, and the steering remains light right up to full lock. On cambered and rough-edged roads the car is unusually pleasant to control, because there is complete absence of free movement or spring in the steering linkage, and thus positive corrections can be made however small they may be. There is quite strong self-centring action, and this was welcome when taking successions of sharp or hairpin bends. In these conditions the light steering is appreciated, although a little less wheel-winding would be an advantage—there are 4½ turns from lock to lock. The lock itself is very good in both directions.

Conventional live axles are seen at their worst in climbing mountain passes; almost invariably wheel spin and some axle hop develops as a car so equipped pulls away from the steep part of a hairpin bend. The Flaminia's de Dion "rear end" apparently scores here; the wheels grip firmly and the car will come smoothly out of the corner at full power.

Because it is customary to comment on under- or oversteer characteristics, it is often assumed that all cars have one or the other. The Flaminia is neutral, exhibiting neither characteristic to a noticeable degree. It gives a better conception of its entirely orthodox handling to state that if the car is pulled round a corner excessively fast and with power on, the back end will slide first. Additionally, as with almost all cars, a corner is completed more satisfactorily with the engine pulling. Important, too, is the ability in an emergency to brake quite hard during cornering without throwing the car off its line.

Some kinds of regular cobbles cause rumbling in the car, but badly laid sets and potholes are taken very well indeed, whether slowly or quickly. Driven fast over surface irregularities of the rolling type, the car bottomed on the rear springs on two or three occasions, when carrying two passengers and luggage.

The precise nature of the gear change, already mentioned, is also an advantage both in the mountains and in traffic. The Flaminia has a 3.91 to 1 top gear, giving 21 m.p.h. per 1,000 r.p.m. It runs smoothly without snatching down to 18 m.p.h. in top, but a change down at about 25 m.p.h. is advisable, for there is practically no pull in top below that speed. Third gear ratio is 5.9 to 1, and the gap seems considerable; this ratio looks after most traffic requirements.

Drivers who use the full performance of the car would probably prefer a rather higher third and more than 68 m.p.h. at peak revs (5,200) in this gear. Both second and third gears are needed frequently for pick-up when driving fast. The engine is very free-revving, and it is easy to exceed the 5,200 limit in the intermediate gears. There is no additional noise, fuss or vibration to warn that 5,200 or even 5,500 has been reached.

If we may judge from this and previous Lancias tested, it seems that the makers favour a very gentle clutch. When attempting a rapid get-away from standstill, either clutch-slip or low initial engine speed must be accepted; acceleration figures are not appreciably affected either way. The car moves off quickly, and for all ordinary purposes the clutch is precise, light and smooth.

When the engine was hot there was a tendency to stall while idling in traffic. This responded to adjustment in part but not entirely. On the car tested, also, there was a moment of hesitation when the accelerator was depressed which made it difficult to obtain an entirely smooth pick-up from crawling speed or after a gear change. This could have been caused by need for a carburettor adjustment, by pedal linkage fault, or a combination of the two. The car was taken from ordinary works transport at the factory in Turin and had no special preparation for the test. It had already done 16,700 miles.

But for the advent of servo-assisted disc brakes, the Flaminia's four large drum brakes would have been described as very good; as it is, "entirely adequate" is a fair term. They pull the car up firmly with moderately heavy pedal pressure, and at no time did they fade. From high speed, braking produced some slight rumbling—felt through the pedal rather than heard. No definite attempt was made to fade them, and the weather during the test was mostly cool and wet, but it was noted that there was no deterioration after repeated applications down hill. Brake pedal travel increased in the course of the test, and towards the end it was sometimes necessary to pump the pedal once or twice to obtain normal pedal feel and travel. The hand

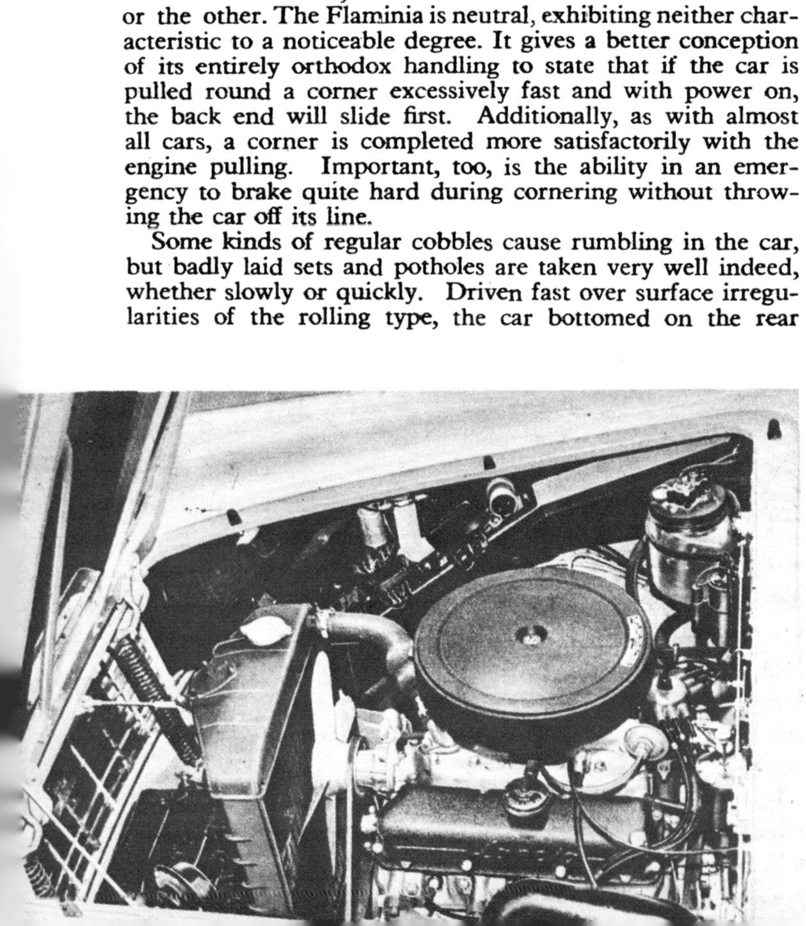

Left: A 60 deg vee-6 engine can be kept very short—note the space and accessibility. The battery cover is seen low down in front of the radiator. Below: The boot is large and neatly trimmed; its load line is low and wide. An exceptionally good toolkit is provided. Styled-in bumpers, though neat, are more easily damaged and transfer damage

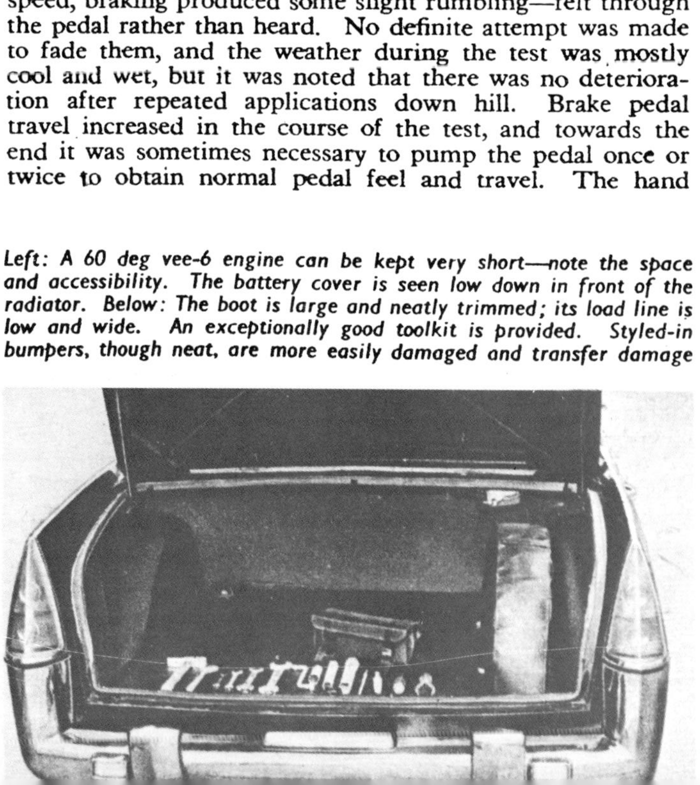

brake is operated by a sturdy transverse lever under the dash; as adjusted on the test car it was not very powerful.

For owners who have to watch fuel consumption, a figure of about 22 m.p.g. for ordinary driving would be representative; on long runs perhaps 24 m.p.g. might be achieved. Hard driving brings this down to about 19 m.p.g. The overall consumption figure for the test of 1,380 miles was 20.8 m.p.g.

Many pages could be written about the equipment of the Flaminia and about its ingenious fittings. The doors are large and of heavy construction; they shut, fit and seal very well. It is easy to enter any of them, and the deep windows and screen provide a good view for all.

Light grey cloth upholstery is used in the test car, and this effectively prevents slipping. Folding centre arm rests provide for two or three abreast seating, both front and rear seats being of bench type.

Roof trim is in light plastic material, and the doors are cloth-covered, with bright metal and black enamel mouldings. Leather is used for the coaming over the instrument panel, for the spongy visors and the outer arm rests in front (which also serve as door pulls). Leather is applied also as piping for the seats and the edges of the door pulls, and to cover the padded lower edge of the instrument panel.

Pale grey moulded and fitted rubber matting is fitted over the floor in front, neat and practical, but not to everyone's taste in a luxurious car. The rear passengers are provided with pile carpeting.

The instrument panel is of high gloss black enamel with a bright metal band across it; there were no irritating reflections in the screen at night. A radio is neatly styled into its centre. The driver's instruments are grouped in front of him and are easily seen through the wheel (which has only two horizontal spokes and a lower half horn ring). A small locker with key is provided in front of the passenger.

Lighting and other controls take the form of unlabelled, similar black knobs below and beside the radio. Some twist, others pull or even pull, twist and pull again. They look neat enough, but can be confusing for quick use.

Incorporated in the screen wiper knob is a press button for the washer. The button automatically starts both the blades and the spray, and stops them again. If the spray button is used when the wipers are already twist-switched on, it stops the blades after spraying the screen. Although the windscreen is well wrapped round, most of the area in front of the driver is wiped by offsetting the blade pivots to the driving side.

Four more buttons, three to the left and one to the right of the steering column, respectively apply manifold vacuum to open the rear extractor quarter-lights separately, close them both together, and operate the electric rear window wipers, of which there are two inside and two outside in pairs. The rear window occupies the full width of the body and is flat, but the small anti-dazzle rear view mirror does not take full advantage of it to give an adequate rear view. There is a shelf behind the rear seats, and a second radio speaker is mounted there. Two interior lights are provided, one on each side, and these have courtesy switches on the doors as well as an overriding switch on the panel. There is a cigar lighter, and ashtrays are fitted at front and rear.

A very neat lamp arrangement has been devised; two head and two large side lamps are built in. A dipper lever is mounted on the left of the steering column, which also allows semaphore use when moved up or down, but only when the side lamps are switched on. This lever, moved at right angles, operates self-cancelling turn indicators. In practice this is not entirely satisfactory, because it can result in one or other function occurring inadvertently. The side lights also contain the signalling blinkers and yellow fog bulbs, all of which work independently. The white blinkers show clearly through the yellow fog lights. Small additional amber signalling repeaters are mounted on the sides of the body.

Frontal appearance typical of Farina's current production designs. The bonnet is hinged in front. The subsidiary lamps each include side, fog and indicator bulbs

There can be few cars with a more effective hot and cold air system. Over 30 m.p.h., ram effect gives an increasing blast of air—cold or hot according to the position of a central under-panel water tap. Two pairs of additional levers control the delivery of the air to the front occupants' feet or to the four screen slits, or to both. The inner screen slits have hinged deflectors which enable the air to be delivered up and over the screen or, by turning them over, back to the passengers. With this arrangement the screen can be demisted and, we should imagine, defrosted in seconds—or the passengers roasted. In slow traffic, a silent booster fan can replace the ram air flow. The heater control levers are all out of sight and must be felt for beneath the panel, which is perhaps not the simplest arrangement. No attempt has been made to cover in their cables nor, in fact, any of the other wires and leads under the panel.

A very large boot is somewhat obstructed by the vertically mounted spare wheel, but few people would need more accommodation. An above-average tool kit is provided, but there is no starting handle or provision to use one. The fuel tank holds only $12\frac{1}{2}$ gallons, including $1\frac{3}{4}$ gallons in reserve, and thus gives a safe cruising range of no more than 230 miles. The reserve tap is on the floor in the front of the car; no reserve warning light is provided. There is a warning light to show that the choke lever is in cold starting position.

The exterior door handles, of the type with grip and separate thumb button, are neat and comfortable to use. Instead of the sharp edges on the inside of the grips which are found too often on cars these days, the Flaminia has a comfortable inlaid rubber pad. The driver's door carries the lock with key.

Under the front hinged bonnet (released by a two-stage catch beneath the facia) the short, compact engine, dominated by a quickly detachable, circular air filter, looks small, and the radiator block, with its thermostatically controlled shutters, sticks up like a tombstone in the spacious engine compartment. Easily reached ahead of the radiator

A slab-sided appearance is subtly and neatly avoided by shaping, and without recourse to strips or decoration. Twin wipers are fitted for the rear window. The wheel trims look attractive but are easily dented and make it difficult to apply airline or gauge

block and mounted, transversely, low down in the cold air stream is the 12-volt battery. There are two under-bonnet lights and alternative oil filters, one on each rocker cover, each with a breather pipe feeding into the air filter. The dip stick is easy to reach but, going in or out, it rubs No. 2 cylinder plug lead, to the detriment of the insulation. Everything beneath the bonnet is clean and accessible, and has an air of quality about it.

At present eight standard colour schemes are available, four being duotone and one metallic. Practically all the equipment is standard. Extra items involving additional cost are radio, leather upholstery, separate front seats and Saxomat two-pedal control.

The Flaminia saloon is a select model of international importance and appeal costing the equivalent of £1,650 in its native country. It combines in one car many of the requirements and desires of discerning motorists; accommodation for the whole family together with adequate luggage space within moderate exterior dimensions, the lively performance and impeccable handling for which Lancias are traditionally noted, tasteful Farina styling and a modest fuel demand.

LANCIA FLAMINIA

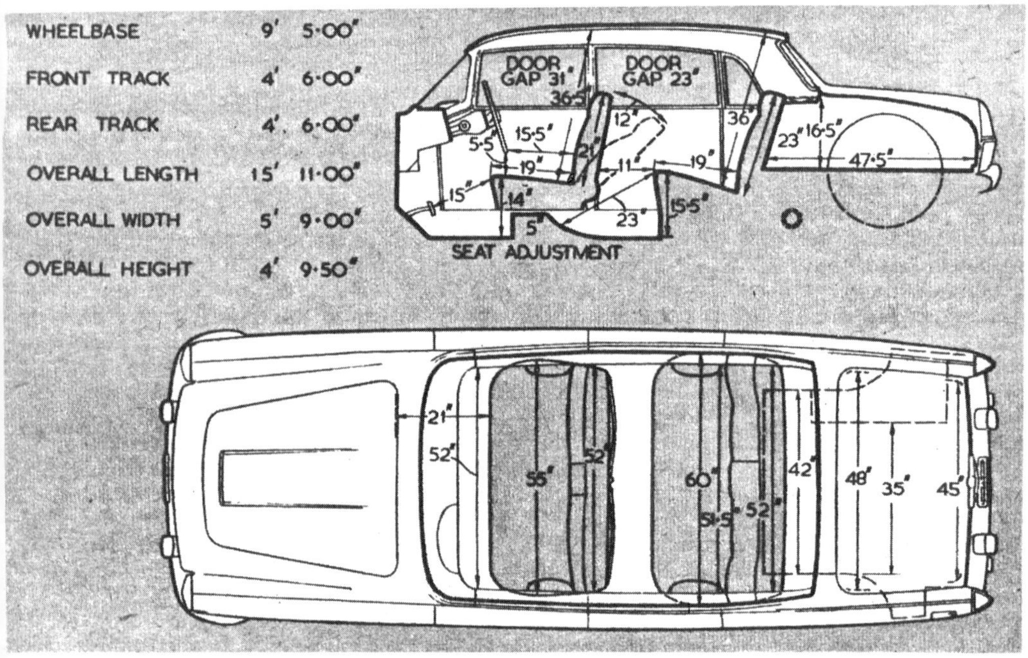

Scale ¼in to 1ft. Driving seat in central position. Cushions uncompressed.

PERFORMANCE

ACCELERATION:

Speed Range, Gear Ratios and Time in sec.

M.P.H.	3.91 to 1	5.91 to 1	8.60 to 1	12.94 to 1
10—30 ..	—	7.3	5.0	4.0
20—40 ..	11.3	7.0	4.8	—
30—50 ..	10.8	6.9	—	—
40—60 ..	11.3	7.7	—	—
50—70 ..	11.6	—	—	—
60—80 ..	13.9	—	—	—
70—90 ..	19.7	—	—	—

From rest through gears to:

M.P.H.	sec.
30	5.0
40	7.9
50	11.3
60	15.6
70	22.1
80	31.0
90	43.3

Standing quarter mile, 20.2 sec.

MAXIMUM SPEEDS ON GEARS:

Gear		M.P.H.	K.P.H.
Top ..	(mean)	102.3	164.6
	(best)	103	165.8
3rd	At 5,200 r.p.m.,	68	109.4
2nd	recommended	46	74.0
1st	limit ..	31	50.0

TRACTIVE EFFORT:

	Pull (lb per ton)	Equivalent Gradient
Top	207	1 in 10.8
Third	315	1 in 7.0
Second	467	1 in 4.7

BRAKES (at 30 m.p.h. in neutral):

Pedal load in lb	Retardation	Equivalent stopping distance in ft
25	0.09g	340
50	0.32g	94
75	0.63g	48
100	0.92g	33

FUEL CONSUMPTION:

M.P.G. at steady speeds

M.P.H.	Direct Top
30	38.2
40	35.5
50	32.6
60	29.6
70	26.4
80	22.2
90	19.1

Overall fuel consumption for 1,376 miles, 20.8 m.p.g. (13.6 litres per 100 km).

Approximate normal range, 19-24 m.p.g. (14.9-11.8 litres per 100 km).

TEST CONDITIONS: Weather: overcast, damp tarmacadam road surface, slight breeze. Air temperature, 62 deg. F.

Acceleration figures are the mean of several runs in opposite directions.

Tractive effort obtained by Tapley meter.

Model described in *The Autocar* of 27 April, 1956.

SPEEDOMETER CORRECTION: M.P.H.

Car speedometer:	20	30	40	50	60	70	80	90	100
True speed:	19	28	38	48	57	67	77	87	97

DATA

PRICE (basic), including heater, with saloon body, **£2,500 0s 0d.** British purchase tax, **£1,215 7s.**
Total (in Great Britain), **£3,715 7s.**

ENGINE: Capacity: 2,458 c.c. (150 cu in).
Number of cylinders: 6 in 60 deg. vee formation.
Bore and stroke: 80 × 81.5 mm (3.15 × 3.21 in).
Valve gear: o.h.v., pushrods and rockers, hemi-spherical chambers.
Compression ratio: 7.8 to 1.
B.H.P. 112 (gross), 100 (nett) at 4,800 r.p.m. (B.H.P. (nett) per ton laden 56.8).
Torque: 141 lb ft at 3,000 r.p.m.
M.P.H. per 1,000 r.p.m. in top gear, 21.

WEIGHT: (with 5 gals fuel), 32.1 cwt (3,610 lb).
Weight distribution (per cent): F, 48.7; R, 51.3.
Laden as tested: 35.1 cwt (3,946 lb).
Lb per c.c. (laden): 1.51.

BRAKES: Type: SABIF hydraulic.
Drum dimensions: F, 11.81in diameter; 2.75in wide. R, 11.0in diameter; 2.75in wide.
Lining area: 236 sq in (134 sq in per ton laden).

TYRES: 165–400mm Michelin X.
Pressures (lb sq in): F, 26; R, 28 (normal). F, 28; R, 30 (fast driving).

TANK CAPACITY: 12.5 Imperial gallons (includes 1.75 reserve).
Oil sump, 11 pints.
Cooling system, 18 pints (including heater).

STEERING: Turning circle:
Between kerbs, 38ft 4in L. 41ft 4in R.
Between walls, 39ft 7in L. 42ft 7in R.
Turns of steering wheel from lock to lock, 4¼.

DIMENSIONS: Wheelbase: 9ft 5in (287cm).
Track: F, and R, 4ft 6in (137cm).
Length (overall): 15ft 11in (485cm).
Width: 5ft 9in (175cm).
Height (unladen): 4ft 9.5in (146cm).
Ground clearance: 5.5in (14cm).

ELECTRICAL SYSTEM: 12-volt; 42 ampère-hour battery.
Head lights: Double dip; 45–40 watt bulbs.

SUSPENSION: Front, independent, wish-bones, coil springs and Sabif telescopic dampers. Anti-roll bar.
Rear, de Dion-type axle, half-elliptic leaf springs, Sabif telescopic dampers. Panhard rod.

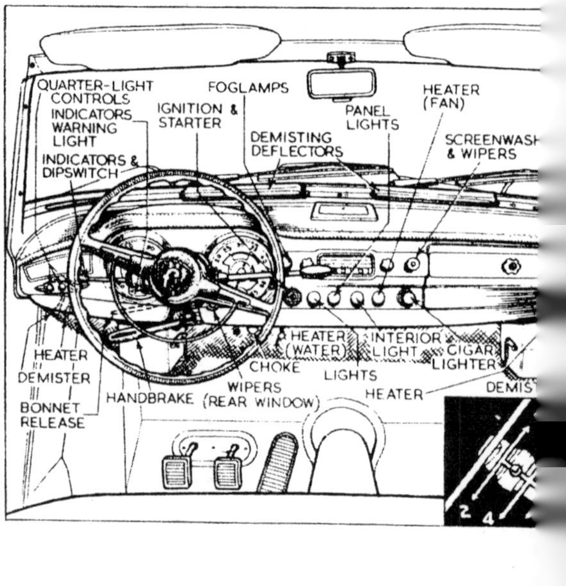

The Autocar ROAD TESTS 1783

Lancia Flaminia Coupé

Attracting interest and admiration wherever it goes, the Lancia Flaminia coupé by Pininfarina is simple in outline and free from ostentation

IN December of 1958 *The Autocar* published a road test of the Lancia Flaminia standard four-door saloon with left-hand drive, which was driven in Italy because none was then available in this country. Today one model in the Flaminia range is made with right-hand drive—the series production coupé by Pininfarina on the intermediate length chassis (9ft 0·7in. wheelbase). One of these was submitted for test by Lancia (England), Ltd. To put this type into proper perspective in relation to the rest of the Flaminia family, it seems appropriate to outline briefly its sister cars. In addition to the standard saloon on a 9ft 5in. base, there are three short-wheelbase (8ft 3·2in) two-seater Flaminias in series production by specialist coachbuilders —the G.T. coupé and convertible by Touring, and the Zagato Sport coupé.

All models other than the standard saloon are powered by the G.T. engine, which develops 119 b.h.p. at 5,100 r.p.m., as compared with just over 100 at 4,800. Compression ratio of the G.T. engine is 9·0 to 1, whereas the standard ratio is 7·9 to 1. In view of its rather formidable kerb weight (29·2 cwt, including 5 gallons of fuel), the Pininfarina car has the same transmission gearing as the standard saloon, whereas the lighter Touring and Zagato cars are higher geared overall, and have closer ratio gearboxes.

Since the unconventional (by touring car standards) design and layout of the Lancia give a powerful clue to its magnificent behaviour on the road, a few basic technicalities are worth noting by anyone unfamiliar with them. It has a lightweight 2·5-litre pushrod o.h.v. engine with six cylinders arranged in a 60deg vee; a divided propeller shaft takes the drive right back to a chassis-mounted transmission unit comprising clutch, four-speed fully synchronized gearbox, and hypoid bevel final drive with exposed half-shafts to the rear wheels. These are joined by a de Dion tube carried on half-elliptic springs, and unsprung weight is kept low by placing the Dunlop disc brakes inboard, adjacent to the final drive casing. Front suspension is conventional, by coil springs and wishbones of unequal lengths. By these means weight is distributed unusually evenly over the car's four wheels, with the slightly greater proportion over the rear, and very high standards of mechanical engineering support the Lancia design team.

Sitting at the wheel of the Flaminia for the first time, the driver needs to be briefed concerning the minor controls, since none has visual means of identification; they are quite quickly learned, but this lack of marking would at least hinder a thief. For cold starts there is a rich mixture lever, hidden beneath the middle of the facia; a red lamp in the instrument panel remains lit while this is in operation. To start the engine, the ignition key is turned clockwise, then pressed in to energize the starter motor.

Weather during the test period was mostly mild, but some mixture enrichment was needed for a mile or two after a cold start. Effective carburation of the test car's engine at low crankshaft speeds was not a strong point, whatever the engine temperature—this being governed, incidentally, by thermostatically controlled shutters on the radiator. The pick-up was sluggish and often hesitant up to about 2,500 r.p.m., and sometimes there would be a complete lack of response when the throttle was opened at 1,000-1,500 r.p.m.

These comments are emphasized by a direct comparison with acceleration figures for the standard saloon, of which the engine has a wider useful torque range, and develops its greatest power at a lower crankshaft speed. The coupé cannot match the saloon's top gear acceleration to about 75 m.p.h., but thereafter shows an appreciable improvement up to a maximum some 3 m.p.h. higher. When accelerating through the gears from a standstill, however, the coupé can out-perform the saloon by virtue of the higher speeds obtainable in the indirects, the recommended peak of the G.T. engine being 5,600 r.p.m. This can be reached in all forward gears, including top, and in the indirects a watchful eye must be kept on the rev counter to avoid over-speeding, since there are no indications from under the bonnet that the engine has approached valve bounce or is falling appreciably from peak power.

Throughout its range the engine runs smoothly, although

Deep and fully trimmed, the roomy luggage locker carries the spare wheel vertically in a well. The lid is spring-loaded, and self-supporting

Amber flashing signals behind each front wheel arch supplement those at front and rear. Bumpers and rubbing strips at wheel-centre height give all round protection for the body panels. Rather vulnerable against high kerbs are the bright metal rings fitted to the wheel rims

there are vibration tremors at 75-80 m.p.h. originating, perhaps, from the propeller shaft of which the centre bearing is carried in an extremely flexible rubber mounting.

Up to 90 m.p.h. the car cruises very easily and happily, but above this rate increasing mechanical fuss and wind roar discourage one from maintaining speeds nearer the maximum. The exhaust note remains agreeably restrained throughout, in keeping with the car's sporting—rather than sports—character.

It will be seen in the performance data that the fuel consumption rate falls only just below 20 m.p.g. when a constant 90 m.p.h. is maintained, and that better than 24 m.p.g. was recorded at 70 m.p.h. On an 80-mile run over give-and-take roads, during which 60 m.p.h. was not exceeded, a figure of 27·2 m.p.g. resulted. Thus the makers' claim of 21 m.p.g. as a representative figure seems well justified. As for oil, exactly a quart was required to top up the sump after over 1,000 miles of rigorous test-driving.

Having made the point that the Flaminia coupé is more than usually dependent on its gearbox, even when one is in no particular hurry, this can now be praised very highly for the ease and precision of the changes, the complete freedom from any sounds of gear engagement, however quickly the lever is moved, and the quiet running of all gears. The final drive could be heard faintly in the overrun. While the indirect ratios may be ideally suited to road conditions in the car's native Italy, sporting drivers in this country might prefer higher gearing for second and third. In first, about 1-in-4 is the steepest gradient on which a start can be made from rest with two up, a process made rather tricky by the fact that the parking brake, as on most disc-braked cars, cannot hold the car on such a slope.

Where this Lancia scores over almost all its rivals, at any price, is in its wonderful combination of the essentials to safe and enjoyable road travel—springing and road-holding, steering and brakes. Even by today's generally high standards it represents a pinnacle of development in suspension, the more remarkable when one considers the orthodox basic components.

Although firm enough to avoid any suggestion of sloppiness, the Flaminia gives a supremely stable and comfortable ride on average road surfaces, free from pitch and with roll strictly controlled during very fast cornering indeed. For these reasons it is an unusually restful vehicle over long journeys for driver and passengers, and practically no road noise is transmitted through the body structure.

Taken at increasing speeds over a specially laid section of concrete corrugations, the Lancia passed through the inevitable vibration periods and settled down to 60 m.p.h. and over with equanimity; an incidental fault below this speed was that the gear lever developed such violent fore-and-aft vibration as to overcome the selector springs and throw it into neutral—a point which the makers would need to rectify before marketing these cars in countries where washboard roads abound. The car was equally impressive over a section of Belgian pavé, over which it ran on a mostly level keel and with practically no float at over 50 m.p.h.

Dividends of the clever weight distribution are paid off handsomely through the steering gear; yet the front wheels still have to bear nearly 14½cwt, so that there must be supplementary reasons for the remarkably light control. Indeed, the Lancia provides an object lesson to those who now consider power assistance necessary or desirable for cars of this weight. On the move it requires remarkably little effort, and even at parking speeds is as easy to manœuvre as other cars weighing half a ton less.

When Lancia replaced the old sliding pillar suspension by coils and wishbones, they had to accept much wider turning circles, this car taking over 40ft between walls. Full lock to full lock requires 4¼ turns of the steering wheel; although the gearing is thus fairly low, surprisingly little movement of the wheel is called for when motoring fast along twisting roads. So precise and easy is control then that steering the Flaminia becomes almost instinctive, entailing practically no conscious mental or physical effort, so that one's attention may be focussed almost wholly on the other duties of a fast motorist. There is plenty of feel with little or no kick-back through the wheel, and the right degree of self-centring action.

After stepping out of more humdrum cars, it takes some courage to drive this one faster and faster round curves in search of the limit, for its cornering abilities are outstanding; ultimately the tail slides first, but not without warning, and the Lancia's quick responses to control make recovery straightforward.

Disc Brakes

To state that a car is fitted with Dunlop disc brakes is sufficient to reassure drivers who have experienced these; for the Lancia installation they are power-assisted by a Lockheed vacuum servo, and there are separate hydraulic systems for front and rear sets—hence the possibility of total failure is so unlikely as to be disregarded. During our tests the car would stop repeatedly from 30 m.p.h. on a dry surface in just over 30ft without wheel locking; it will be noted, incidentally, that moderately high pedal pressures are required at this speed, whereas from 50 m.p.h. a 0·90g stop (equivalent to about 33½ft from 30 m.p.h.) could be achieved with only 70lb pressure. This is quite normal behaviour for a disc brakes system, which achieves its peak efficiency from higher speeds. When braking hard on a wet, straight road the front wheels would occasionally lock up unexpectedly easily, so that some care had to be taken. One wonders, therefore, whether the rear brakes might be made to do a little more work in proportion, although it is noteworthy that already they have the larger swept area.

Opinions of the test staff were divided concerning the driving position, several finding the steering wheel set a little too high and intruding in their line of sight. Some would have preferred brake and clutch pedals to be set an inch or so higher in relation to the floor. These pedals are pivoted below their pads, and follow a more natural arc of movement than do most pendant arrangements. The organ-type throttle pedal is so placed that heel-and-toe downward changes while braking are possible. One appreciates the spacious floor area, obstructed only by a slender tunnel covering the propeller shaft.

Left. Squabs of the front seats are recessed to allow extra space for rear-seat passengers' knees, and contain large pockets. The back floor is trimmed with carpet, the front with moulded rubber. Right. Large windows make the interior light and airy. On the floor, just forward of the driving seat (not seen here) is a tap for a $1\frac{3}{4}$-gallon fuel reserve. Beneath the facia is a softly padded protection strip: the cowl above is not padded

In general, the finish of the Pininfarina body is good without being superlative, and with the exception of some indifferent detail work, including an excess of self-tapping screw heads. The tiny locker in the facia cannot hold a typical twin-lens reflex camera, and the lips of the door pockets are immediately beneath the armrests, so that they are made practically useless. A particularly practical and safe design of sun vizor was appreciated.

Attractive and luxurious to the eye, the front seats are frankly disappointing functionally, giving so little lateral support that one cannot reap full benefit from the car's exceptional cornering abilities. The cushions and squabs have raised side pads, but these are several inches too far apart to fit most people. Leather trim is now standardized in this country. The backrests are adjustable for angle over a limited range by screw-stops. An ingenious mechanism slides the cushion forward when the backrest is folded forward (to give easy access to the rear seat). A disadvantage of this design is that there is a tendency for the passenger to slide forward with the seat under heavy braking, unless the feet are planted firmly on the toeboard.

By recessing the forward backrests, adequate knee room has been provided for rear-seat travellers, who have more space and comfort than is usual in close-coupled saloons of this type. There is just enough head room for people of average size, and a folding central armrest is fitted. The rear side windows are hinged for ventilation, and have neat over-centre catches; when opened, they promote rather pronounced wind roar. Swivelling vents in the front door windows are limited to a 45deg opening. The winding windows lower flush into the doors; on the test car the handles were rather stiff to turn.

Minor Controls

At the extreme right of the facia is a pull-and-twist knob for side and head lamps, complemented by a two-way lever sprouting from the left of the steering column housing—a bit too far behind the wheel for true finger-tip control. This selects side lamps or dipped beams with the knob half out, main or dipped beams with it fully out. The same lever also works the self-cancelling direction signals; its movements should be better defined. For instance, at night the head lamp beams may be raised or dipped accidentally when the intention is merely to make a signal. No provision is made for signal-flashing the head lamps in daylight, nor is a reversing lamp supplied. Very full illumination is given by the Carello head lamps on both raised and dipped beams, and two fog lamps give an excellent short-range spread to the road sides. A half-ring in the lower sector of the steering wheel (where it does not obscure the instrument dials), with thumb extensions along the horizontal spokes, sounds two melodious, penetrating horns.

The two main instruments—large, easy to read and commendably accurate—are a speedometer, including trip distance recorder, and a tachometer reading to 5,700 r.p.m. An electric clock is included in this dial. Within the speedometer are an agreeably precise fuel level gauge, and three others to indicate oil pressure, water and oil temperatures. There is no ammeter. Small tumbler switches at each side of the steering column control the roof light and the fog lamps, the latter being in unit with the parking and signalling lamps, which keeps the frontal appearance of the car simple and uncluttered. To the left of the instruments is a pull-switch for the single-speed screen wiper motor, and beneath is a button for the suction-operated washer jets, that on the driver's side being placed on the wrong side of the wiper spindle so that it ejects mostly round the corner of the screen. The wipers are not wholly effective when the car is moving fast, and slightly longer blades to increase the swept area would be an improvement.

With temperature set by a tap beneath the facia, supplemented by a single-speed booster, distribution of hot or cold air is thereafter controlled individually by the driver and front passenger, above whose feet are rather clumsy-looking boxes with very stiff levers to proportion the supply between screen and car interior. Once the car has reached 30–40 m.p.h. these air streams become very powerful even without the booster which, incidentally, makes a subdued

Accessibility under the forward-hinged bonnet, lined for sound insulation, is excellent. Left of the shuttered radiator is an oil cooler, and the brake servo is in the immediate foreground. A transparent plastic bottle for brake fluid is seen beside the screenwash reservoir

Lancia Flaminia Coupé . . .

whistle which is somewhat reminiscent of a jet engine.

Twelve greasing points on the front suspension require attention every 2,000 miles, and the outer universals of the rear half shafts, easily reached by removing the wheel hub caps, should be lubricated at the same intervals.

Over many decades one has come to expect so much of a Lancia that one judges it inevitably by very high standards. Although it is now costly to buy in this country, protagonists of the marque recalling earlier days when, for instance, an Aprilia was priced for a short time at under £300, may console themselves with the knowledge that the current products remain fully worthy of their famous name badge. Representing the highest level in current Italian concept and workmanship, the Flaminia coupé has a strong and attractive character, underlined by impeccable road manners, which make it as rewarding to drive in this country as in its native land.

LANCIA FLAMINIA COUPÉ

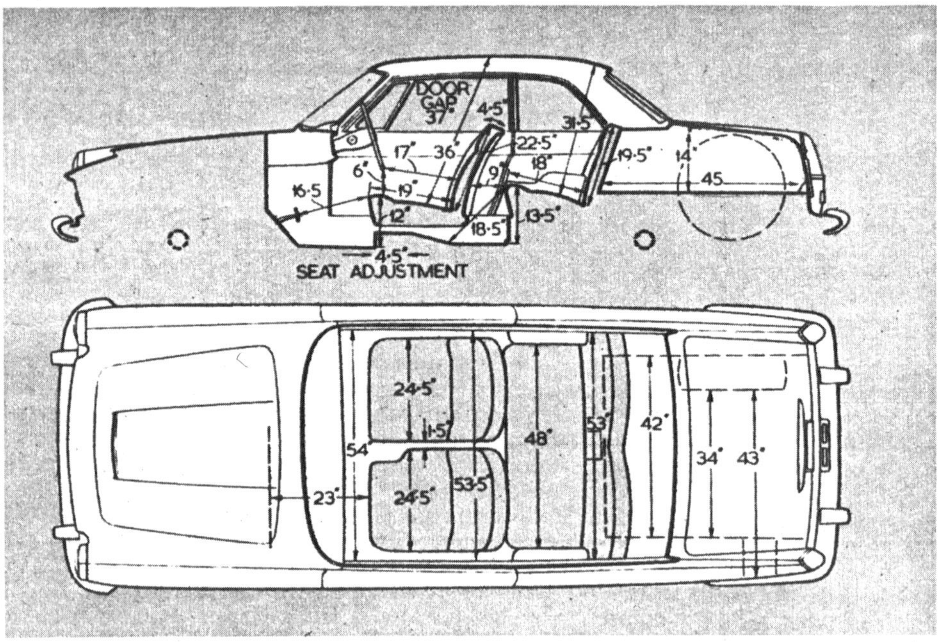

Scale ¼in. to 1ft. Driving seat in central position. Cushions uncompressed.

PERFORMANCE

ACCELERATION TIMES (mean):
Speed range, Gear Ratios and Time in Sec.

m.p.h.	3·92 to 1	5·92 to 1	8·62 to 1	12·98 to 1
10—30	—	—	5·0	3·7
20—40	12·0	7·1	4·8	—
30—50	11·3	6·9	5·3	—
40—60	11·9	7·0	—	—
50—70	12·0	8·6	—	—
60—80	13·6	—	—	—
70—90	17·3	—	—	—

From rest through gears to:

30 m.p.h. ..	4·4 sec.
40 „ ..	7·0 „
50 „ ..	10·1 „
60 „ ..	13·6 „
70 „ ..	18·7 „
80 „ ..	26·0 „
90 „ ..	36·0 „

Standing quarter mile 19·1 sec.

MAXIMUM SPEEDS ON GEARS:

Gear		m.p.h.	k.p.h.
Top ..	(mean)	105·5	170·0
	(best)	107	172·3
3rd ..	.. ..	73	117·5
2nd ..	.. ..	50	80·5
1st ..	.. ..	34	54·7

TRACTIVE EFFORT (by Tapley meter):

	Pull (lb per ton)	Equivalent gradient
Top	220	1 in 10·1
Third	345	1 in 6·4
Second ..	490	1 in 4·5

BRAKES (at 30 m.p.h. in neutral):

Pedal load in lb	Retardation	Equiv. stopping distance in ft
25	0·22g	137
50	0·47g	64
75	0·74g	41
100	0·84g	36
125	0·97g	31·1

FUEL CONSUMPTION (at steady speeds in top gear):

30 m.p.h.	35·1 m.p.g.
40 „	31·0 „
50 „	29·4 „
60 „	26·5 „
70 „	24·1 „
80 „	21·9 „
90 „	19·5 „

Overall fuel consumption for 1,052 miles, 20·1 m.p.g. (14·0 litres per 100 km.).

Approximate normal range 17-27 m.p.g. (16·6-10·5 litres per 100 km).

Fuel: Super premium grades.

TEST CONDITIONS: Weather: Occasional showers, mostly dry surfaces, 5 m.p.h. wind.

Air temperature, 68 deg. F.

STEERING: Turning circle.:
Between kerbs, L and R, 38ft 1in.
Between walls, L and R, 40ft 1in.
Turns of steering wheel from lock to lock, 4·25.

SPEEDOMETER CORRECTION: M.P.H.

Car speedometer:	10	20	30	40	50	60	70	80	90	100
True speed:	12	18	28	38	48	58	68	78	88	98

DATA

PRICE (basic), with two-door saloon body, **£2,730.**
British purchase tax, **£1,138 12s 6d.**
Total (in Great Britain), **£3,868 12s 6d** (Heater standard).
Extras: White wall tyres, **£28 1s 8d** (inc. P.T.).
Electrically-operated windows, electro-magnetic locks on front seat backs, rear window defroster, **£122 10s 10d** (inc. P.T.).
Woollen front carpets, **£36 16s 8d** (inc. P.T.).

ENGINE: Capacity, 2,458 c.c. (150 cu in).
Number of cylinders, 6, in vee formation.
Bore and stroke, 80·0 × 81·5 mm. (3·15 × 3·21 in).
Valve gear, overhead, pushrods.
Compression ratio, 9 to 1.
B.h.p. 119 (net) at 5,100 r.p.m. (b.h.p. per ton laden, 73·9).
Torque, 137 lb ft at 3,500 r.p.m.
M.p.h. per 1,000 r.p.m. in top gear, 18·7.

WEIGHT: (5 gals fuel), 29·2 cwt (3,266lb).
Weight distribution (per cent); F, 49·1; R, 50·9.
Laden as tested, 32·2 cwt (3,602lb).
Lb per c.c. (laden), 1·46.

BRAKES: Type, Dunlop disc.
Method of operation, hydraulic, with tandem master cylinder, Lockheed vacuum servo.
Disc diameter: F, 11·5 in; R, 12·0in.
Swept area: F, 200 sq in; R, 236 sq in. (271 sq. in per ton laden).

TYRES: 175–400. Michelin X.
Pressures (p.s.i): F, 26; R, 31 (All conditions)

TANK CAPACITY: 12·5 Imperial gallons, including 1·75 gallons reserve.
Oil sump, 11·75 pints.
Cooling system, 18 pints (including heater).

DIMENSIONS: Wheelbase, 9ft 0·7in.
Track: F and R, 4ft 6in.
Length (overall): 15ft 4·5in.
Width: 5ft 8·5in. Height: 4ft 7·9in.
Ground clearance: 4·0in.
Frontal area: 17·5 sq ft (approximately).

ELECTRICAL SYSTEM: 12-volt; 42 ampère-hour battery.
Head lamps: Double dip; 45–40 watt bulbs.

SUSPENSION: Front, independent, coil springs and wishbones, telescopic dampers, anti-roll bar.
Rear: de Dion-type axle, half-elliptic leaf springs, telescopic dampers, Panhard rod and anti-roll bar.

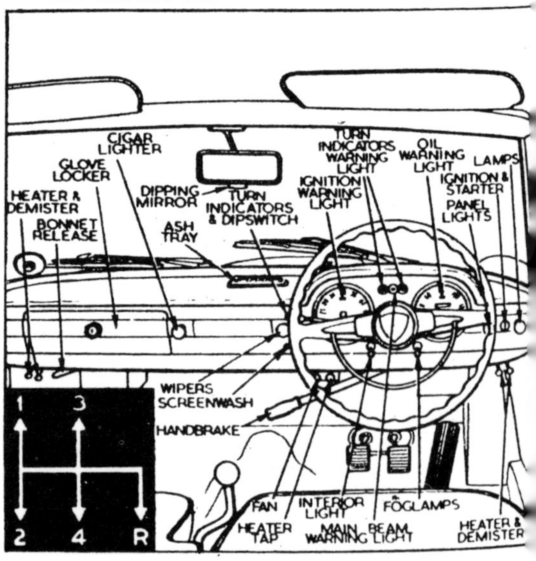

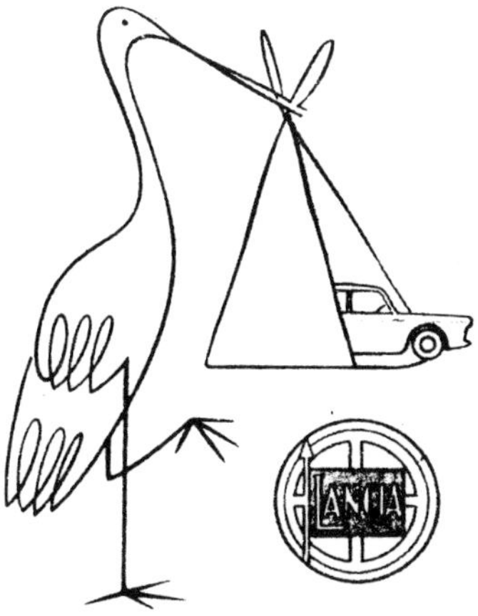

LANCIA FLAVIA

ITALY'S FIRST FRONT-WHEEL-DRIVE CAR: 1½-LITRE HORIZONTALLY OPPOSED FOUR CYLINDER ENGINE

EVER since the foundation of the Lancia company in 1908 by Vincenzo Lancia—originally a well-known racing driver and engineer with the F.I.A.T. company—they have enjoyed a reputation for sound engineering, and the courage to adopt an unorthodox approach to engineering matters if it were theoretically desirable. Cost often seemed a secondary consideration. Although some of this tradition might have departed when the company passed out of the hands of the Lancia family, this, in fact, has not occurred. It is not surprising, therefore, that with this background, Lancia are the first Italian company to go into production with a front-wheel-drive car, to be known as the Flavia. This title is in line with the policy of using names of highways into Rome for model designation; the roads themselves are named after Roman statesmen.

The Flavia has a flat-four, horizontally opposed, water-cooled 1½-litre engine mounted forward of the front wheels. From the clutch the drive passes through the hollow hypoid pinion of the final drive to a pair of single helical gears, mounted outside the gearbox portion of the transmission. All four gears, each having synchromesh of the baulk ring type, are thus indirect. The drive shafts, which have Rzeppa type constant velocity joints at each end, with ball-and-groove sliding splines, are supplied by Hardy Spicer Ltd. This is in line with established Lancia policy of obtaining the best equipment, irrespective of the country of origin. Other British components used are Vandervell bearings and bushings (which Lancia have fitted on all models since 1954), Dunlop disc brakes at front and rear, and a Hobourn-Eaton internal rotor oil pump.

Design of the Flavia is the work of Professor Fessia, who joined Lancia during the period that the Flaminia was under development, and was responsible for the substitution of wishbone suspension for the company's traditional sliding pillar type on that car. Professor Fessia was with Fiat pre-war, and designed the famous Topolino. He left them and produced the Cemsa-Caproni, a front-wheel-drive car with a 1,100 c.c. horizontally opposed, four-cylinder engine which appeared as a prototype in 1948. Its object was to utilize the surplus capacity of the Caproni aircraft factory during the post-war years, but the design did not proceed beyond the prototype stage. Returning to Fiat, he produced a similar layout for the Fiat 600, in parallel with Dr. Giacosa's rear engine design, which was ultimately adopted when the car went into production. It is a logical evolution that Professor Fessia should now propound and develop his ideas for the Flavia.

Right-hand-drive versions of the car will be available immediately production commences; this is expected to be in full swing by the end of the year. Prices were not available at the time of writing, but were to be announced at the opening of the Turin Show yesterday, and will be given in the report on that Show in next week's issue. It is expected that the price will be between 1,700,000 and 1,800,000 lire, equal to £1,000 to £1,060.

With a wheelbase of 8ft 8·33in. and a widest track of 4ft 3·2in., in conjunction with mounting of the engine forward of the front wheels, the Flavia is a very roomy car in the 1½-litre class. Three adults can sit abreast on the rear seat, which has a maximum width between trim

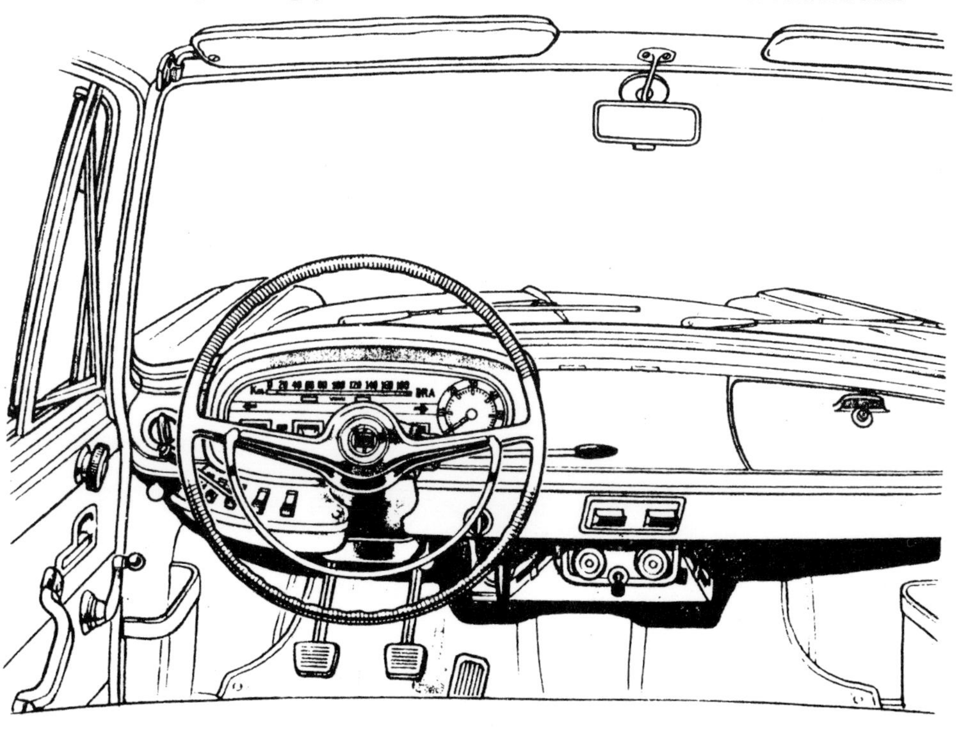

Control switches are mounted on an arcuate panel blending with the facia and steering column. Gear change lever is to the right and the turn indicator lever to the left; this layout will be interchanged on right-hand-drive cars

LANCIA FLAVIA . . .

At the rear there is an unusual "fold" in the body styling which seems out of balance with the main contour. Twin light clusters contain turn indicators, parking and stop and reversing lamps. Overriders have twin reflectors and there is a number plate lamp in the bumper

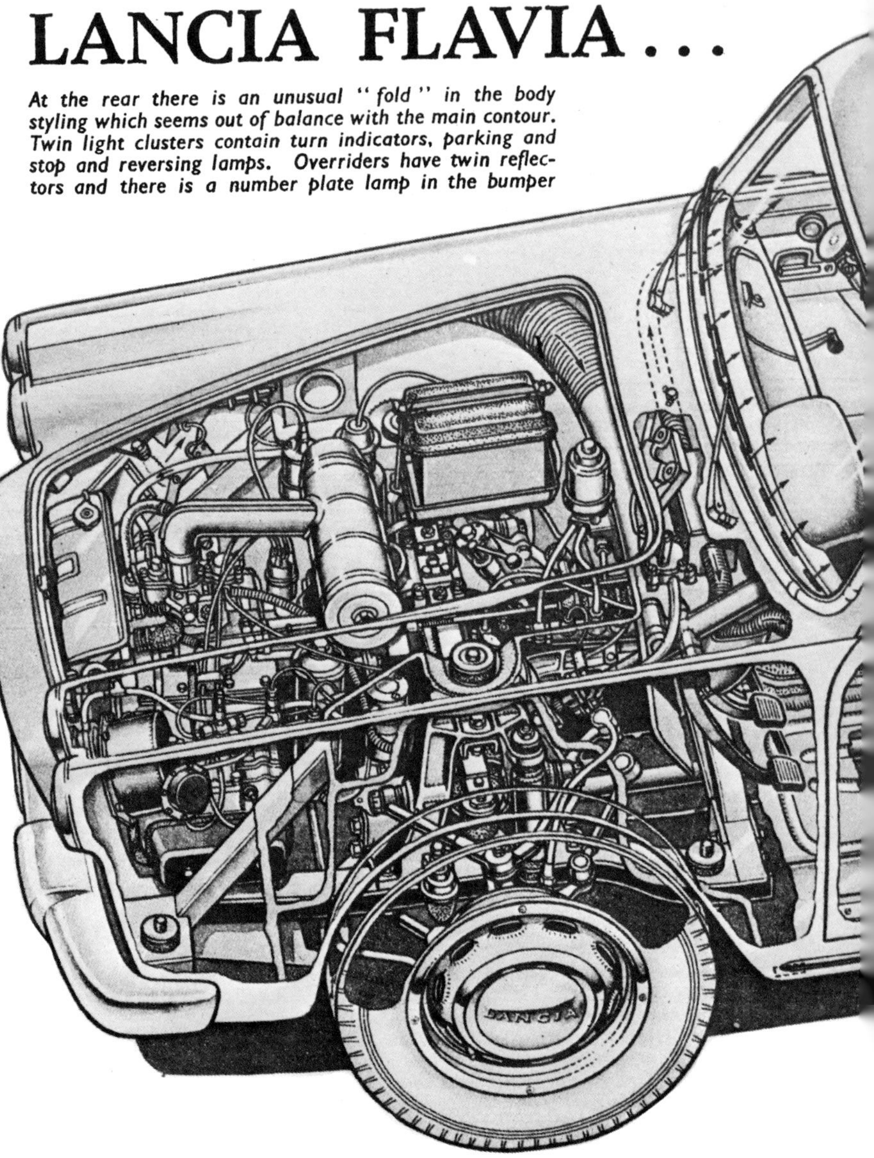

panels of 4ft 5in.; the corresponding width at the front is 1·25in. greater. With a vertical height of 2ft 10in. measured from the uncompressed seat cushion to the roof lining—an identical dimension front and rear—and with 6·5in. knee room for the rear passengers when the front seat is in its rearmost position, the car is commodious for its size.

Upholstery is carried out in cloth and Vinyl, over foam rubber cushions and squabs. Floors are covered with rubber mats front and rear. There is an armrest on each door but, rather surprisingly, not one of the folding type for the front or rear seats. Small parcel stowage is provided in the form of a lockable cubby hole on the facia and a container at each side adjacent to the toeboard for front passengers. Rear passengers have the use of an elastic map pocket in the front seat back, and a deep rear window parcel shelf.

Fully Equipped

Swivelling quarter ventilators are fitted to each front door; they are operated by a worm-and-nut mechanism having a circular operating knob so that they can be finely adjusted and secured in any desired position; this is also a useful thief-resisting provision. The facia is covered with imitation leather, underlaid with a shockproof foam material.

Set in a cowled panel in line with the steering wheel, instruments comprise a ribbon-type speedometer with trip and total distance recorders, and a circular rev-counter. Beneath the speedometer scale are rectangular instruments for fuel contents, water temperature and oil pressure, and an ammeter. There are, in addition, warning lights for excessive water temperature, fuel reserve, low oil pressure, headlamp main beam, parking lamps, and a combined one for parking brake and carburettor choke, which is hand operated.

Control switches are in an auxiliary arcuate panel on the lower edge of the facia, between the steering wheel and the driver's door. From left to right these switches, which are of the tilting touch-button type, are for electric screen washer, two-speed screen wiper and lamps. Next come the direction indicator lever, instrument panel light and parking light.

Dual headlamps, using 5·75in. diameter sealed beam units, are standard fittings. After bringing these into circuit by the main switch, changeover from main to dipped beam is obtained by a touch on the button on the end of the turn indicator lever. This operates a solenoid which selects each of the beams in sequence; the wiring is arranged so that the meeting beam is always obtained first when the headlamps are switched on.

In the centre of the steering wheel there is a press button for headlamp flashing, the horn being operated by a half-ring. Courtesy lights, operated when any of the four doors are opened, are located on the upper part of each door pillar. Desirable safety features are red marker lamps fitted to the rear edge of each front door, with automatic switching coupled to the courtesy lights. In addition, operated automatically as the respective lids are raised, there are two lights in the engine compartment and one in the luggage locker (which is very capacious, with the spare wheel mounted vertically on one side).

A comprehensive heating and ventilation system is part of the standard equipment. There is a fresh-air intake on the right front side of the car, with a butterfly regulator valve. A separate control is provided for the degree of heat and for distribution to either of the two outlets for general interior heating or for screen defrosting; there are 10 slots extending across the width of the screen at its base. This circuit includes two butterfly controls on each side of the facia, which can be used for defrosting the side windows. Air flow can be boosted, if required, by a single-speed fan.

The pressed-steel body hull follows normal practice for this integral type of construction. Beam strength is provided in two deep and wide sills at each side. They merge into the rear seat pan structure, shallow channel section floor tunnel which houses the exhaust pipe, and the scuttle assembly which in turn merges into the wing valances; from these a wheelbarrow box-section arm projects forward at each side. There is a removable front sub-frame attached at six rubber mountings; this unit can be detached and wheeled away complete

The sliding, full width front seat has an adjustable and fully tilting backrest, in the rear of which is a map pocket and central ashtray. Each door, with flush-fitting pull-out handles, has an armrest and a plastic combined door pull and grab handle

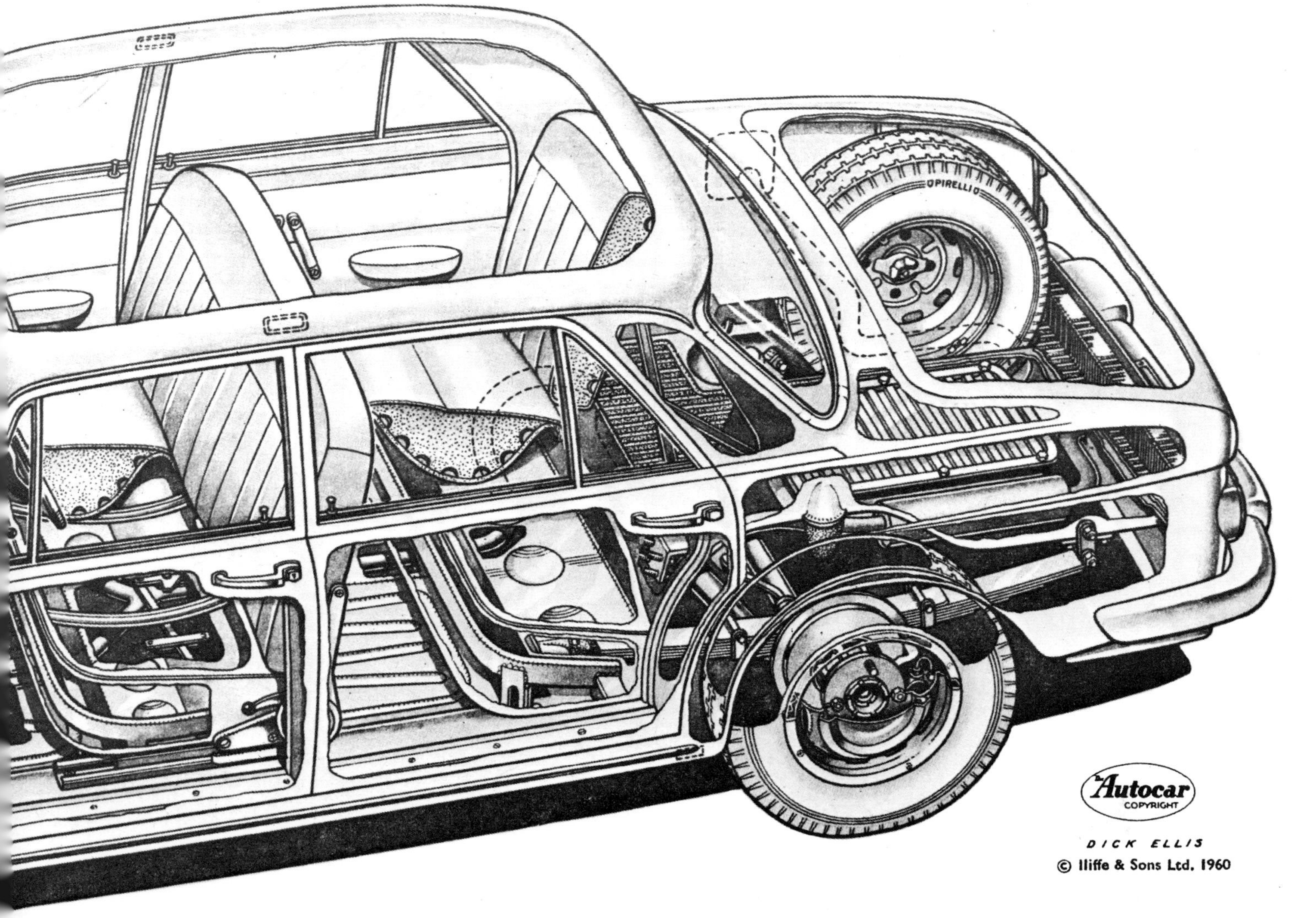

with the engine, transmission, suspension and steering linkages. Such a construction has the advantage of unit assembly during manufacture, and aids service at major overhauls.

The front sub-frame consists of two box-section side members joined front and rear by cross members of the same dimensions. Bolted to this welded subframe is a substantial aluminium casting at each side, to which the wishbones, steering box and idler lever are also attached. These castings are braced with three steel channel-section members across the upper and lower extremities. The upper one forms the saddle mounting for the transverse leaf spring, which at each outer end is attached to its upper wishbone by a substantial rubber bobbin. The use of a leaf spring is undoubtedly related to the front-wheel drive layout, for it is quite difficult to utilize coil springs and avoid the wheel drive-shafts without having an offset load on the wishbones or a high reaction point for the springs, if mounted above them.

Each wishbone has tubular arms, copper-brazed to forged steel ends. Rubber bushings are used at the inboard attachments to the aluminium casting and they are noticeable for their very wide spacing. Ball pivots, 1·5in. dia. spaced at 10·25in., are used top and bottom for the outer swivel joints. Each is sealed with a rubber gaiter and has a lubrication point. Typical of the attention to detail is the upper ball joint which, on the Flavia, takes the greatest load. It is in two halves, with a ball thrust race between them to lighten steering loads. A de Carbon telescopic damper is mounted to the rear of each lower wishbone.

Expense has been subordinated to ideal design in the construction of the Hardy Spicer front-wheel drive-shafts, which are often the Achilles heel of such a layout. A constant velocity Rzeppa-type joint of approximately 3·25in. dia. is used inboard and outboard. The outer case of the inner one is formed with six equally spaced semi-circular grooves, matching with similar ones in the surrounding pot joint. In each of these grooves five 0·375in. dia. balls are trapped in position. These accommodate endwise movement of the shaft arising from wheel movements, and virtually eliminate sliding friction. Each joint is gaitered and sealed with lubricant for life. An anti-roll bar, connected to the lower wishbones, passes beneath the side members of the sub-frame.

Steering is by a rear-mounted, three-piece track rod system, such that the steering box, which is of the worm and roller type, can be interchanged with the idler lever for either right- or left-hand drive. In the shaft between the box and the steering wheel there is a rubberized fabric coupling.

Several types of rear suspension, including independent, were tried on the prototype car before the choice settled on a tubular steel beam attached to a half-elliptic leaf spring at each side. It was considered by Professor Fessia that the best compromise of handling characteristics was obtained with this light beam. Coil springs and radius arms, in conjunction with the tubular beam, were considered, but the leaf spring arrangement made least intrusion into luggage space.

Dunlop disc brakes—of the same size as are used on the Mark II Jaguars—are fitted to all wheels. They are servo-assisted, with separate front and rear hydraulic circuits. This independence is achieved by the use of a tandem master cylinder, each half having its own circuit

Front-wheel-drive permits a clean under tray, with a minimum ground clearance of 5in. in the unladen condition. Wheels are 15in. diameter

LANCIA FLAVIA . . .

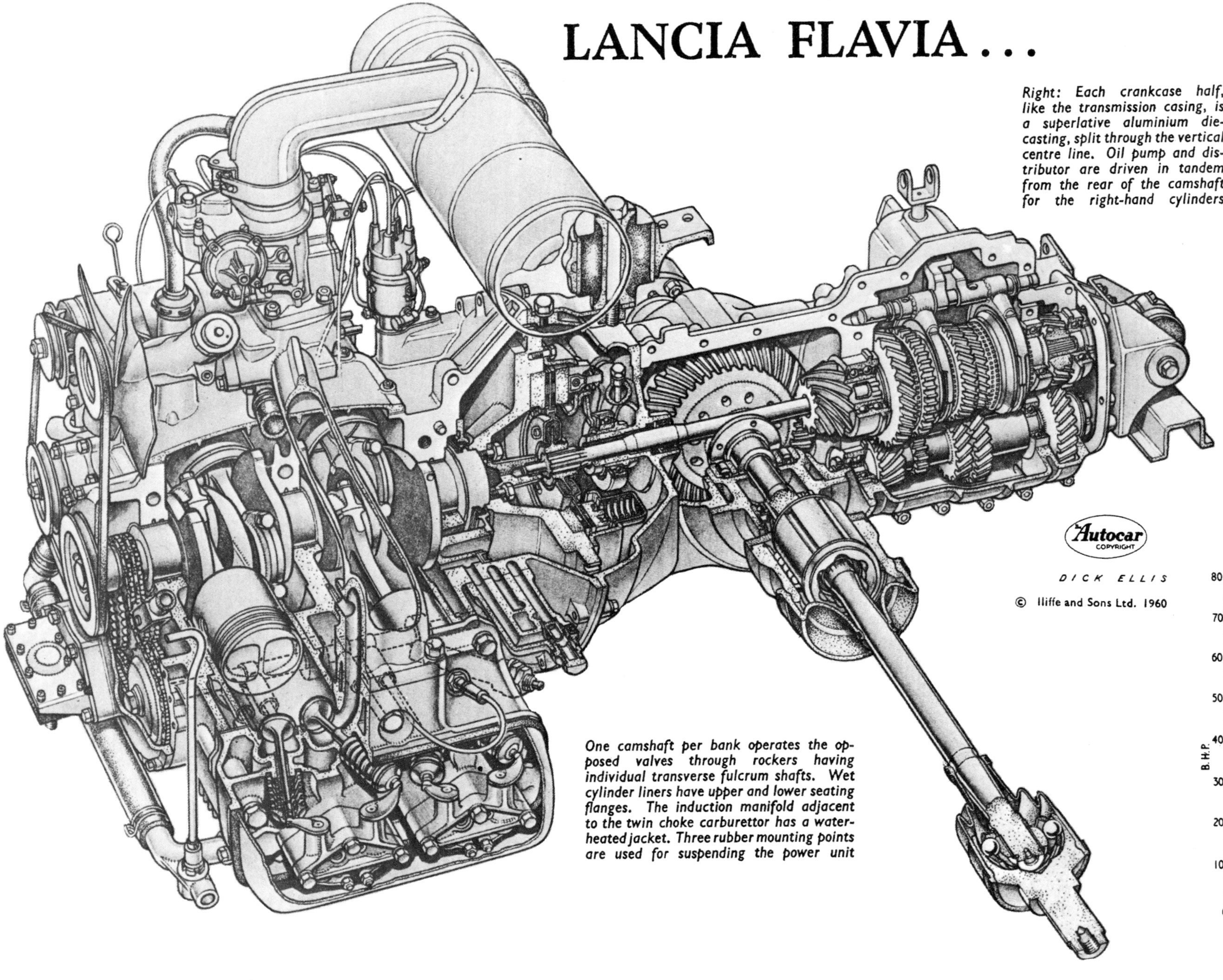

Right: Each crankcase half, like the transmission casing, is a superlative aluminium die-casting, split through the vertical centre line. Oil pump and distributor are driven in tandem from the rear of the camshaft for the right-hand cylinders

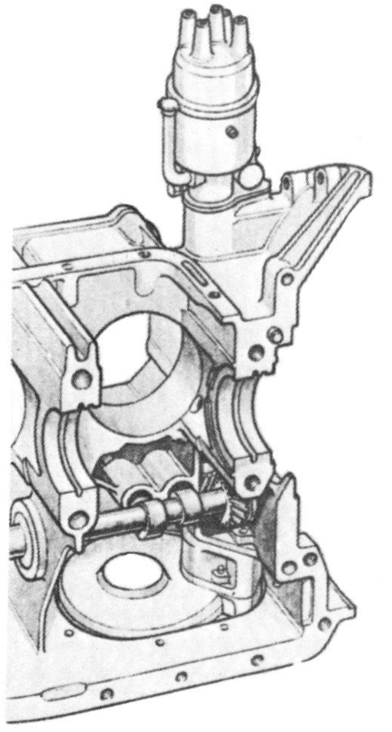

Below: Net power curves showing the relatively flat b.m.e.p. and corresponding torque characteristics. The dotted power curve is the minimum standard for production engines

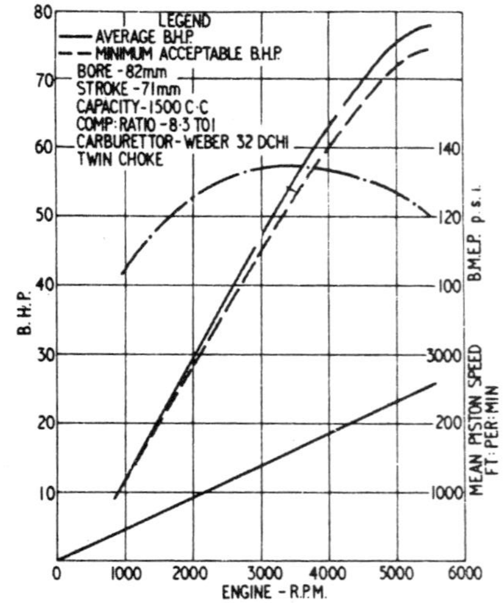

DICK ELLIS

One camshaft per bank operates the opposed valves through rockers having individual transverse fulcrum shafts. Wet cylinder liners have upper and lower seating flanges. The induction manifold adjacent to the twin choke carburettor has a water-heated jacket. Three rubber mounting points are used for suspending the power unit

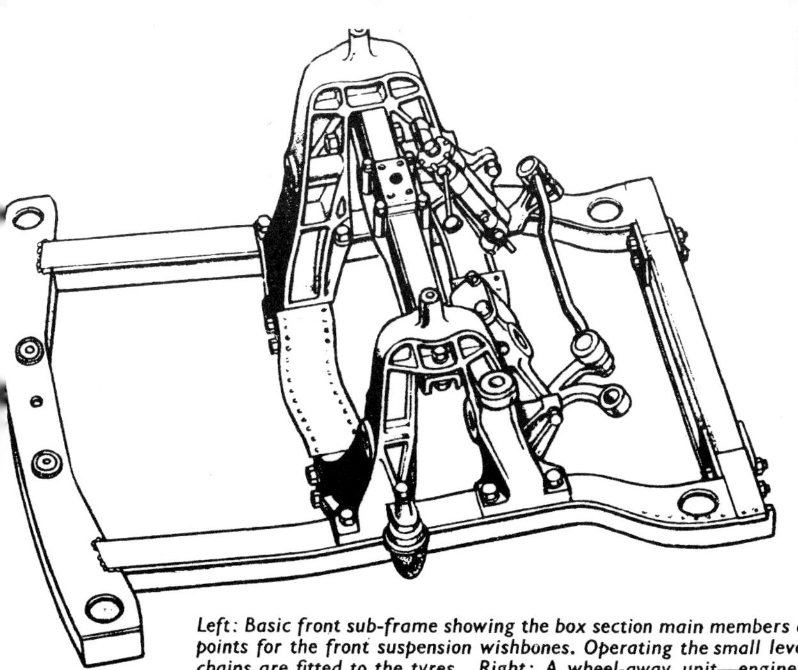

Left: Basic front sub-frame showing the box section main members and two aluminium castings bolted to it, which form the attachment points for the front suspension wishbones. Operating the small lever adjacent to the steering lever bearing restricts wheel lock when chains are fitted to the tyres. Right: A wheel-away unit—engine, transmission and suspension assembled on their sub-frame—is attached to the body hull by a rubber bobbin mounting at each corner and a similar one at the top of each aluminium casting

to the servo unit. Like the clutch, the brakes are operated by a pendant pedal; the throttle pedal is of organ type. Parking brakes with cable operation to the rear wheels are operated by a lever under the instrument panel.

There are many attractions in a horizontally opposed four-cylinder layout; there are also some shortcomings if the main advantages are exploited to the full. It is almost certainly more expensive than an in-line arrangement; if its virtue of compactness is applied, bearing sizes and crankweb thicknesses can be marginal. Lancia have avoided the snags, and accepted the greater cost.

Most horizontal cylinder layouts use a single camshaft in the plane of the crankshaft, but this calls for long pushrods with high reciprocating masses, and thus valve gear heavily stressed at high speeds. The Flavia uses two camshafts to overcome this defect, so that its maximum power at 78 b.h.p. net is produced at 5,200 r.p.m., and the engine is capable of revving up to 6,000 r.p.m. The two camshafts are driven by a duplex roller chain from the crankshaft, the chain incorporating a hydraulic tensioner. The pushrods have a duralumin tubular centre section to match the expansion rates of the aluminium crankcase and cylinder heads.

If the adjacent cylinders are spaced to use a minimum fire joint between the block and the head, crankshaft scantlings and bearings are of meagre proportions. In the Flavia the design seems to have been centred initially around the crankshaft and its bearings, for the cylinders are much wider than they need be for gasket width or water space between the cylinders. Another factor was undoubtedly the use of opposed valves in a hemispherical combustion chamber; they have an included angle of 39 degrees, which gives just sufficient clearance for the valve springs on the adjacent inlet valves, as seen on the cross-section drawing.

This opposed valve arrangement is made possible by the use of individual transverse fulcrum shafts, as first applied on the Aurelia. Individual inlet ports are uppermost on the cylinder head, the exhaust ports projecting downwards to separate flanges on the underside of each head. Valve head diameters are 38mm (1·496in.) for the inlet and 33mm (1·300in.) for the exhaust; these are large by current standards, indicative of good breathing over a wide speed range. The valves seat on cast-in iron inserts.

Crankshaft bearings are massive by any standards, the mains having a diameter of 2·375in., and widths of 1·06in., 0·93in. and 1·375in. for the front, intermediate and rear respectively. Like the mains, the big ends are Vandervell indium-infused lead-bronze type, with a diameter of 1·937in. and a width of 0·875in. Crankweb thicknesses adjacent to each main bearing are 0·5 in., the intermediate flying webs being 0·75in.

Bearing lubrication is from a Hobourn-Eaton internal rotor oil pump with a gauze pick-up filter, and a circuit through a full-flow filter before the oil is fed to a drilled gallery in the left crankcase half. Connecting rods have an angular serrated faced joint and 1in. dia., fully floating gudgeon pins. The German Mahle pistons, which have two compression rings and an oil control ring above the gudgeon pin, are noticeable for deep recesses in the crowns. These are not required for valve clearance at top dead centre, but are undoubtedly provided for increasing compression ratio at some future date.

The combined crankcase and cylinder block is split on its vertical centre line like the transmission casing. A great deal of thought has been put into these components, and they are produced as aluminium die-castings with open sides so that loose pieces in the internal cores are avoided throughout. The sump, with its cooling fins, is integral with each crankcase half, access to the oil pump

Cylinder block construction consists of two aluminium die-cast halves with wet cylinder liners. Camshafts and their tappets run direct in the aluminium casting. Individual transverse rocker shafts and pushrods—an arrangement first used on the Aurelia—provide for a neat layout of opposed valves in a hemispherical chamber

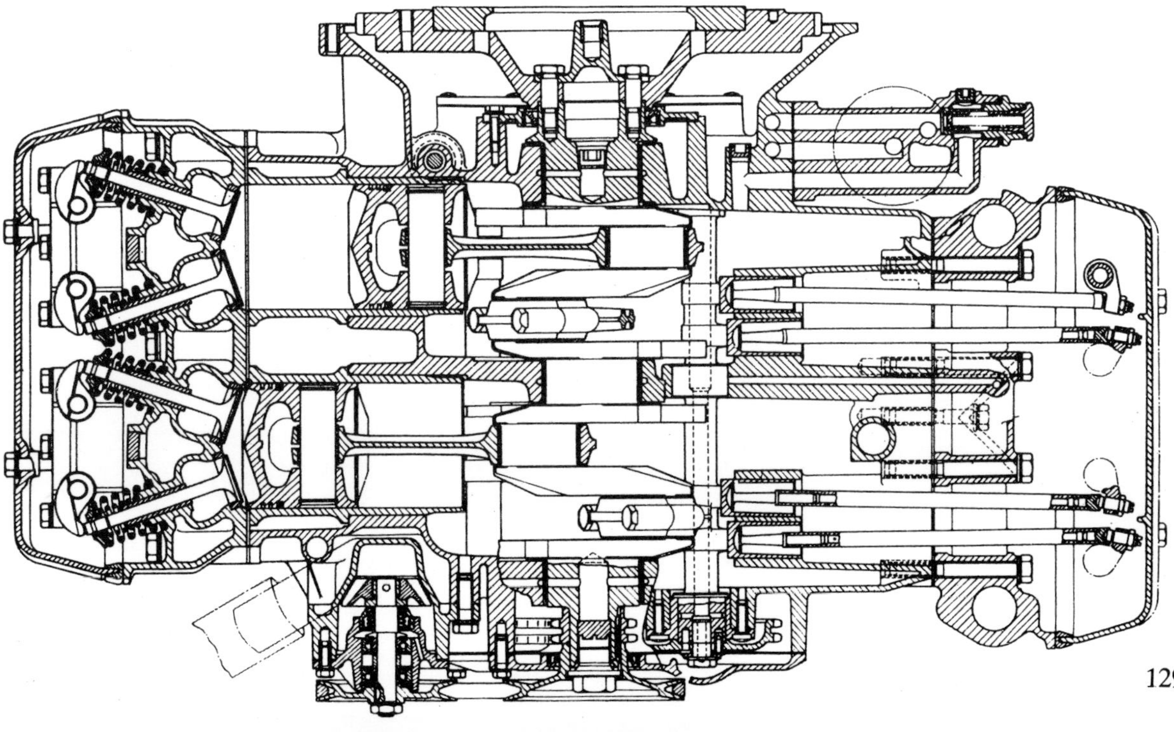

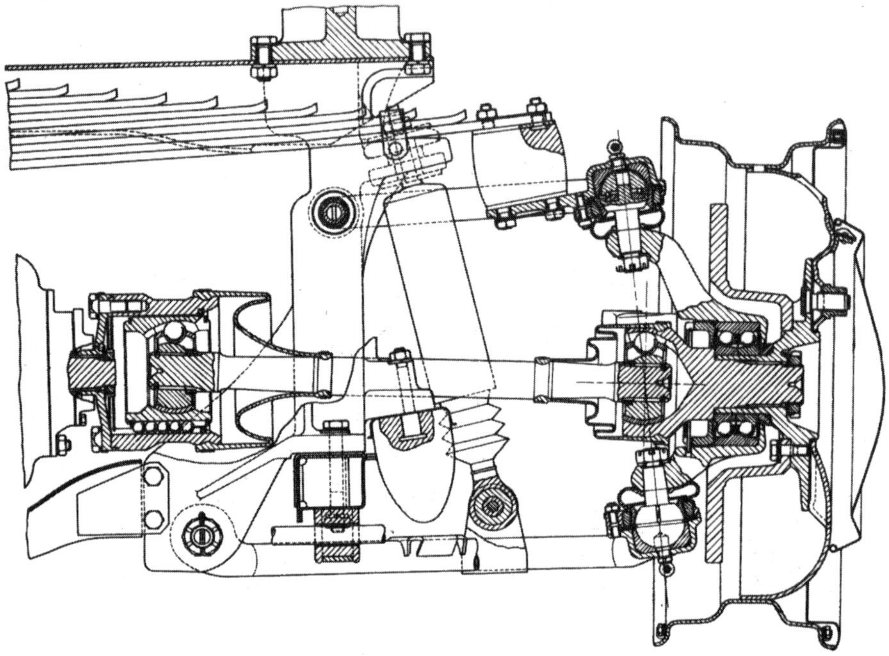

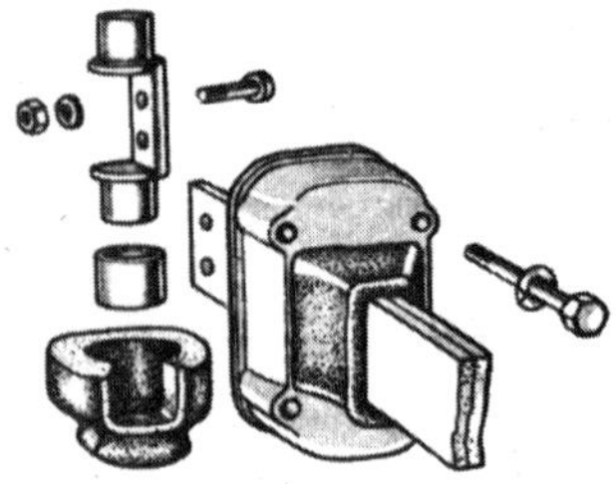

Above left: Rear suspension consists of a dead tubular beam axle suspended on a half-elliptic leaf spring at each side with forward-facing telescopic dampers and an anti-roll bar. Left: Rear spring shackle with its trunnion mounting and nylon bushes clamped in a rubber housing. Above: Front suspension consists of double wishbones with bdll pivots at each side, and an upper transverse leaf spring with a rubber cushion block at the outer attachment point to each upper wishbone. Changes in drive-shaft length are accommodated in sliding ball splines on the outside of the inner constant velocity joint

LANCIA FLAVIA . . .

and its pick-up filter being through a separate inspection cover. The halves are held together by set bolts on either side of each main bearing; Helicoil inserts are used in the female threads. There is, in addition, a series of bolts around the periphery of the joint face.

The wet cylinder liners are held in compression. The amount of nip is controlled solely by the depth of the recess in the casing and the distance between the two flanges on the liner; in other words, no shims are used. A rubber ring, fitting into the chamfer of the lower seating flange, forms the water seal. Between cylinder head, liner and crankcase there is a copper asbestos gasket with a machined concentric V-section groove in the liner top face and around the combustion chamber in the cylinder head. A single water pump, with split outlet to each cylinder bank, is belt-driven from the crank in a four-point drive which includes the dynamo (hinged for adjustment) and an aluminium cooling fan.

Carburation is either by a down-draught twin-choke Solex or a Weber instrument. The two chokes lead into a common water-jacketed hot spot, from which individual pipes merge into separate intake ports on each cylinder head.

From the Fichtel and Sachs clutch, which incorporates a patented Lancia cushion drive plate, the drive is taken through the hollow hypoid pinion shaft to a pair of helical gears at the rear of the main gearbox casing. All gears are in constant mesh with helical teeth, except for reverse; this is a separate train of straight spur gears placed between first and second. All forward ratios have synchromesh of baulk ring type; selection is by a column-mounted lever.

Road Impressions

During investigation into the technicalities of the Flavia, an early prototype was placed at our disposal for opinion and impressions, during which it was possible to cover some 50 miles in the hilly district around Turin. Throughout this short test there were five occupants, the three at the rear commenting favourably on the comfort of the seats and the amount of room. The front passengers would have preferred a central armrest or some slight curvature of the seat squab to provide support during severe cornering.

The driving position is excellent, with a well-raked wheel which does not intrude into the line of vision, and good all-round visibility. Pedal relationship to the seat is good and the pendant pedals are not difficult to operate—unlike many with this type of layout. Gear change lever movements are short and light, and the touch-button change-over switch for the dual headlamps is a clever innovation. Road noise has been well suppressed, and it was not possible to detect any body vibration or resonance when fully laden. Once one becomes familiar with the position of the controls on the switch panel, they are easy to find and operate.

Without previous knowledge that a front-wheel-drive layout had been utilized, it would be difficult to detect any characteristic revealing this feature. There is a degree of understeer, but no kick-back at the steering wheel or change in attitude in cornering on hard lock with the engine alternating between drive and overrun.

The smoothness and tractability of the engine are memorable. Several times the car was taken up to 5,500 r.p.m. in the gears and it remained unobtrusive. Lancia claim a maximum speed of 92 m.p.h. It would need quite a long run to achieve this figure and, with full load, the acceleration was not outstandingly lively, but for 1½-litre it is rather a heavy car at 24 cwt. It is, nevertheless, very refined in all that it does, and in its appointments.

SPECIFICATION

ENGINE

No. of cylinders ...	... 4 horizontally opposed water cooled
Bore and stroke ...	... 82 x 71 mm (3·23 x 2·79in.)
Displacement ...	... 1,500 c.c. (91.6 cu in.)
Valve position ...	... Overhead, pushrods and rockers
Compression ratio ...	... 8·3 to 1
Max. b.h.p. (net) ...	... 78 at 5,200 r.p.m.
Max. b.m.e.p. (net) ...	... 135 p.s.i. at 3,500 r.p.m.
Max. torque (net) ...	... 82 lb ft at 3,500 r.p.m.
Carburettor ...	... Twin choke Weber 32DCHI or Solex 32PAIA3
Fuel pump ...	... Bendix electric
Tank capacity ...	... 10·5 Imp. gallons (48 litres), including reserve
Sump capacity ...	... 11 pints (6·24 litres)
Oil filter ...	... Full flow
Cooling system ...	... Pressurized, pump, fan and thermostat
Battery ...	... 12 volt 40 amp. hr.

TRANSMISSION

Clutch ...	... Single dry plate, 7·87in. dia.
Gear box ...	... Four speeds; synchromesh on all forward ratios; steering column lever
Overall ratios	... Top 4·09; 3rd 6·71; 2nd 9·53; 1st 16·16; reverse 18·00 to 1
Final drive ...	... Hypoid bevel, ratio 4·09 to 1

CHASSIS

Brakes ...	... Dunlop disc, vacuum servo assistance
Disc dia. ...	... 11·0in., front and rear
Suspension: front ...	... Independent, double wishbones with transverse leaf spring and anti-roll bar
rear ...	... Dead axle, with half-elliptic leaf springs and anti-roll bar
Dampers ...	... de Carbon telescopic
Wheels ...	... Pressed steel (4·5in. wide rims)
Tyres size ...	... 6.50—15
Steering ...	... Worm and roller
Steering wheel ...	... Two-spoke, 15·5in. dia.
Turns, lock to lock ...	2·5

DIMENSIONS (Manufacturer's figures)

Wheelbase ...	... 8ft 8·33in. (265 cm)
Track: front ...	... 4ft 3·18in. (130 cm)
rear ...	... 4ft 2·39in. (128 cm)
Overall length ...	15ft 0·24in. (458 cm)
Overall width ...	5ft 3·23in. (161 cm)
Overall height ...	4ft 11·06in. (150 cm)
Ground clearance (laden) ...	... 5in. (13 cm)
Turning circle ...	36ft (11·0m)
Kerb weight ...	... 2,698 lb, 24 cwt (1,210 kg)

PERFORMANCE DATA

Top gear m.p.h. at 1,000 r.p.m.	18·1
Torque lb ft per cu in. engine capacity...	0·89
Brake surface area swept by linings	496 sq in total
Weight distribution (kerb weight)	F. 60 per cent R. 40 per cent

La Donna è Mobile

When she was good she was very, very good . . .

THAT'S the opening phrase of a song from Verdi's "Rigoletto" — you know, the one which goes "te-pom-pom-pom-POMtepom." Literally, I suppose it means the lady is on the move; well, so she is figuratively, too, for *mobile* is Italian for fickle. That's the way it was with Miss Lancia Flaminia Zagato 340516-TO. One moment she was mobile, English-style, and the next she was *mo-bi-le,* Italian-style.

It wasn't really fair to rush her all the way from Turin to Venice and back, because she still wasn't looking or feeling her best after the Liège-Rome-Liège a few weeks earlier. But she looked irresistible; although wearing no jewellery like bumpers and hub caps, in other respects she was better equipped than other ladies of the same breed—extra fuel tankage, three screen wipers and special rally equipment.

Sitting beneath that low Zagato roof with its double-bubble section, and behind those almost horizontal screen pillars, one felt just like a Maglioli or a Frescobaldi, an effect accentuated by the full-throttle roar of air rushing into six chokes of three Weber carburettors. We made fast progress eastwards, mostly along fine *autostrada*—Milan, Brescia, Verona, Vicenza, Padua. . . . It is quite exciting to watch a speedometer needle sweep round to 200, even when one has to multiply by five and divide by eight to reduce kilometres to the more modest English miles—and perhaps even then to take 125 m.p.h. with a pinch of salt.

Right to its maximum on these roads the Lancia ran true as an arrow; just the pressure of one finger against the steering-wheel rim was sufficient to hold it on course. Off the *autostrada* and hurried round tight curves, she had some of the feel of a rear-engined car, with a pronounced tail swing; we were too short of time to experiment with different fore-and-aft ratios of tyre pressure. Steering was wonderfully light and positive, and the Dunlop disc brakes perhaps the best in lightness, sensitivity and efficiency that we could remember. Although the Zagato Sport body is mounted on the shortest of three Flaminia wheelbases (8ft 3·16in.), the car rode remarkably softly for a sports model, yet maintained a level keel.

And so we went to Venice where, of course, the people all row about in old Lagondas. Next morning the weather was a bit overcast and dismal for the return journey, and Miss Flaminia was in one of her moods. When we drew up to pay our dues on entering the first stretch of *autostrada,* her heart suddenly stopped beating. The starter was dead, and the horn wouldn't blow to let us warn the escort car, which motored quickly away. . . . Then the electricity all came back again and we thought it was just a faulty ignition switch.

We rushed on to the end of that *autostrada,* and her heart stopped again. And the horn. And the starter. And the lights—everything. We checked battery connections, loose wires under the dash; took out the ignition switch, stripped it and put it together again. She fired and away we went. Perhaps it was connected with the dynamo cut-out, and she would stay lit if we didn't let the revs drop below 1,000 p.m. Then, passing through the next town, we blew the horn while travelling slowly and the engine stopped. Thereafter, pressing the horn button was taboo. Next, an investigation of the horn circuit, of all the fuses, of the ignition switch again.

Suddenly everything was live once more, and a fourth time she died, only to come to life again for no clear reason. Then, not far along the Milan-Turin *autostrada,* she cut at speed. Panic! . . . Nowhere to pull off, it was dark and now pelting with rain. It *could* be the main fuel supply run dry, so we hastily turned on the reserve tap; after dropping to a tantalizing 15 m.p.h. she suddenly picked

. . . but when she was bad she was horrid

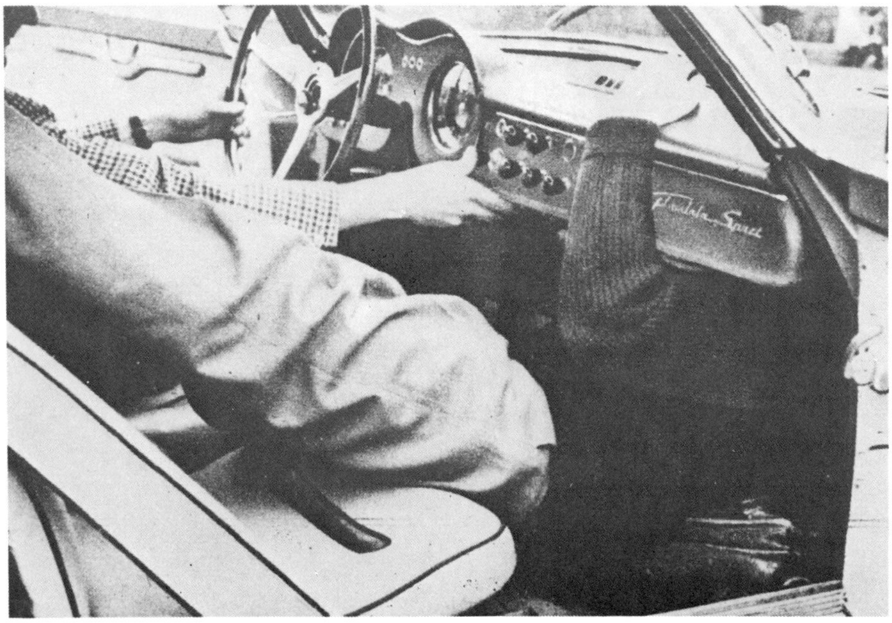

All right, try the blessed starter!

up again, so maybe it really *was* fuel this time. Turin was still too far away to risk reaching it on reserve, so after a time we flashed lamps at the escort and pulled in at the next petrol station, where they wouldn't allow engines to be kept running. This time no amount of artificial respiration would bring her to life again.

We rang Turin. Would they please send an ambulance to the Chivasso filling-station to carry her those last twelve or so miles home? Yes, they would. The last view of her was through the back window of our escort car—a low, black silhouette merging quickly into the sodden gloom, *sans* volts, *sans* amps, *sans* watts, *sans* almost anything.

Back home in England they said: "Drive any nice cars in Italy?" "Of course," we replied. "A super this and a smashing that, and a wizard Lancia Flaminia Zagato which had competed in the Liège-Rome-Liège." "Was it the red one which went out with *electrical* trouble right at the beginning, or the white one which . . . .?" "Well, yes," we said, "it was red. . . ."

R. B.

O.K., *he's right on our tail again . . .*

Damn, I thought it was too good to last . . You look at the fuses and I'll check the horn circuit . . . Not again?

LANCIA APPIA III

The windscreen of the Appia is fairly shallow and the pillars rather thick by current standards, but these are minor criticisms when related to the car's appealing characteristics and performance

IT is a matter for regret that, with the disappearance of many small firms, or their integration into larger organizations, much is being missed by the generation of post-war motorists. The number of cars which have that difficult-to-define yet undeniable distinction summarized as character, which endears them to their owners, is becoming increasingly rare. Few firms can rival Lancia in having produced a succession of models which are still regarded with reverence by many; such names as Lambda, Dilambda, Aprilia and Aurelia need only to be mentioned in motoring circles to rekindle nostalgic memories. The Appia III carries on this long tradition, for it can be stated at once that although it may not be fully in keeping with modern thought in respect of style, and vision from the driver's seat, it outclasses many of its more modern rivals by its road manners, particularly its ability to take rough surfaces in its stride, and a general feeling of tautness and mechanical refinement throughout its structure.

Since the Appia has several unusual features which have a bearing on its character, they must be noted as part of this assessment. The body hull is an integral structure, and the doors, with front and rear hinges respectively, close at the centre of the car without the use of a pillar. Thus, with each pair open there is unrestricted entry to the front or rear seats. This type of construction was popular in the late thirties, but when applied to flimsy coachbuilt bodies it was a failure. With an integral and, therefore, rigid body construction, with which Lancia have had long experience for it was used on the Lambda in 1923, it is perfectly satisfactory.

Front suspension is of the vertical-pillar type with enclosed coil springs and integral dampers, a development of the basic type used on all Lancias since the Lambda, until the advent of the Flaminia and Flavia. Rear suspension is orthodox, with a live axle mounted on half-elliptic leaf springs. Brakes are large for the car's kerb weight of 18·5 cwt, and the front drums are of aluminium with a cast-iron working surface.

The 1090 c.c. four-cylinder engine is noteworthy for its real compactness, although this virtue has not been fully exploited to make maximum use of passenger space within the wheelbase. Cylinders are set in narrow vee formation, the angle between them being 10 deg 14 min., and the unit has an overall length approximately equivalent to an in-line three-cylinder unit. This compactness permits the crankshaft to run on two main bearings without a trace of roughness. There are two chain-driven side camshafts to operate the opposed valves, in hemispherical chambers, through a system of pushrods and rockers.

On taking the wheel of the Appia one is impressed imme-

Left: The boot lid is self-supporting on a single stay which needs to be released against light spring pressure. The floor is rubber lined and its low level permits easy loading. Lighting is provided by number plate lamps. Right: Compactness is the outstanding feature of the vee-four-cylinder, two-bearing engine. There is a plunger on top of the brake fluid reservoir which, if pulled upwards, maintains a constant pressure in the hydraulic system and enables the brakes to be bled single handed. In the foreground is the oil tank and two plungers for automatic lubrication of suspension

diately by the quality of the controls and fittings; a good driving position is enhanced by the small two-spoke steering wheel (16 in. dia.). In line with the steering wheel are two circular dials in a common cowling. The outer one is the speedometer (9 m.p.h. optimistic at maximum speed on the test car), with total distance and trip recorders. The inner one has segments for the petrol-level indicator (with warning light to show approaching emptiness), water temperature and oil pressure.

Centrally mounted on the facia is a row of five pull-out controls with nice large plastic knobs. They have no visual means of functional identification, but from left to right they are windscreen sprayer control—which is pulled out and released for automatic operation—windscreen wiper, heater fan, instrument panel lamp with rheostat control, and headlamp and sidelamp master switch. At each side of the facia is a circular pull-out ashtray.

On the passenger's side is a locker in the facia (for extremely small gloves), but to augment stowage space there is a receptacle adjacent to the toeboard on each side and large pockets in all four doors. The starter switch is facia-mounted on the right of the steering column and is of the usual Continental pattern with a quarter-turn to bring the normal electrical services into circuit; a full half-turn switches on the ignition, and the end of the key is pressed to energise the starter.

For cold starts there is a pull-out rich-mixture lever tucked away under the facia to the left of the steering column. On the other side is a pull-out and turn-to-release handbrake lever which was light and rigid in action and held the car on a 1-in-4 gradient. Cold starts always required the use of the choke either at half or full setting, depending upon the temperature. With the car as received from the manufacturers, it was noticed during the early part of the test that the engine hesitated on pick-up and stalled frequently unless the choke was set at between a quarter and half open for the first two miles.

It was noted also, however, that the coolant temperature was below 160 deg. F. and in the green segment, which indicates the lower operating range. An investigation of the thermostatically operated radiator shutters, which are a standard fitting, showed that they were not fully closed when the engine was cold. An adjustment to the linkage put this matter right, after which there was no further difficulty with the carburation and, moreover, the heater became very effective indeed.

The engine gives a surprising performance for its size. It is never absolutely quiet, but there is no harshness or vibration throughout its range. Such refinement as it has is inherent, and is not dependent upon soft engine mountings or on noise suppression by a barrier of sound-deadening materials. Some of the noise originates from a not unpleasant air-intake roar. Throttle response is instantaneous, there are no flat spots throughout the range, and torque is developed progressively. The engine's eagerness encourages the driver to do things in step with it—making rapid gear changes for example.

This eagerness is reflected in the overall fuel consumption, which worked out at 32·6 m.p.g. for 1,098 miles. Driven in a more leisurely fashion, with the driver resisting the temptation to use high speeds in the intermediate gears continuously, 40 m.p.g. is not an impossible target. Premium fuel was used during the greater part of the test, including performance testing, but a 50-50 mixture of regular and premium does not result in pinking. One test run using regular grade only resulted in slight pinking at low speed and wide throttle openings, but even this could be avoided by suitable use of the throttle. Oil consumption was also economical, one pint being added to the sump at the end of the test.

Stainless steel is used for the bumpers, window surrounds and rubbing strips. The fuel tank, with its filler behind the lockable hinged flap, has a range in excess of 300 miles at economical cruising speeds

The mean maximum speed of 81·4 m.p.h., with a best one-way figure of 82 m.p.h., is very creditable. Normal cruising is in excess of 70 m.p.h., and from this speed up to the maximum the engine remains smooth, and gives the impression of being able to run continuously at such speeds.

Column gear changes, particularly those for use with a four-speed gearbox, have come in for much criticism, but if they had all been engineered as well as that of the Appia there would have been less clamour for a return to the floor-change. Movements of the rigid lever between gears and through the gate are light, short, and precise. The shape of the knob on the end of the lever is also very comfortable for the hand, and even reverse can be engaged quietly and smoothly. There was little gear noise on the indirect ratios, aided no doubt by mounting the three lower gears between the bearings in the main casing, with top separately mounted with a third bearing in the end cover. Synchromesh, unbeatable on snatch changes, is provided with the upper three ratios, which are properly spaced for the sporting character of the car; third gear is slightly higher than is the usual Lancia practice.

For performance testing, maximum speeds of 23 m.p.h., 40 m.p.h., and 61 m.p.h., which occurred at 6,000 r.p.m., were used in the indirect gears. This is higher than the maximum recommended by the manufacturers (5,200 r.p.m.) but still 400 to 500 r.p.m. below valve bounce.

Steering is lower-geared than one would expect in a car of this type, and certainly more so than in earlier Lancias or the Flaminia tested more recently. As a result, quite large movements of the steering wheel are required for

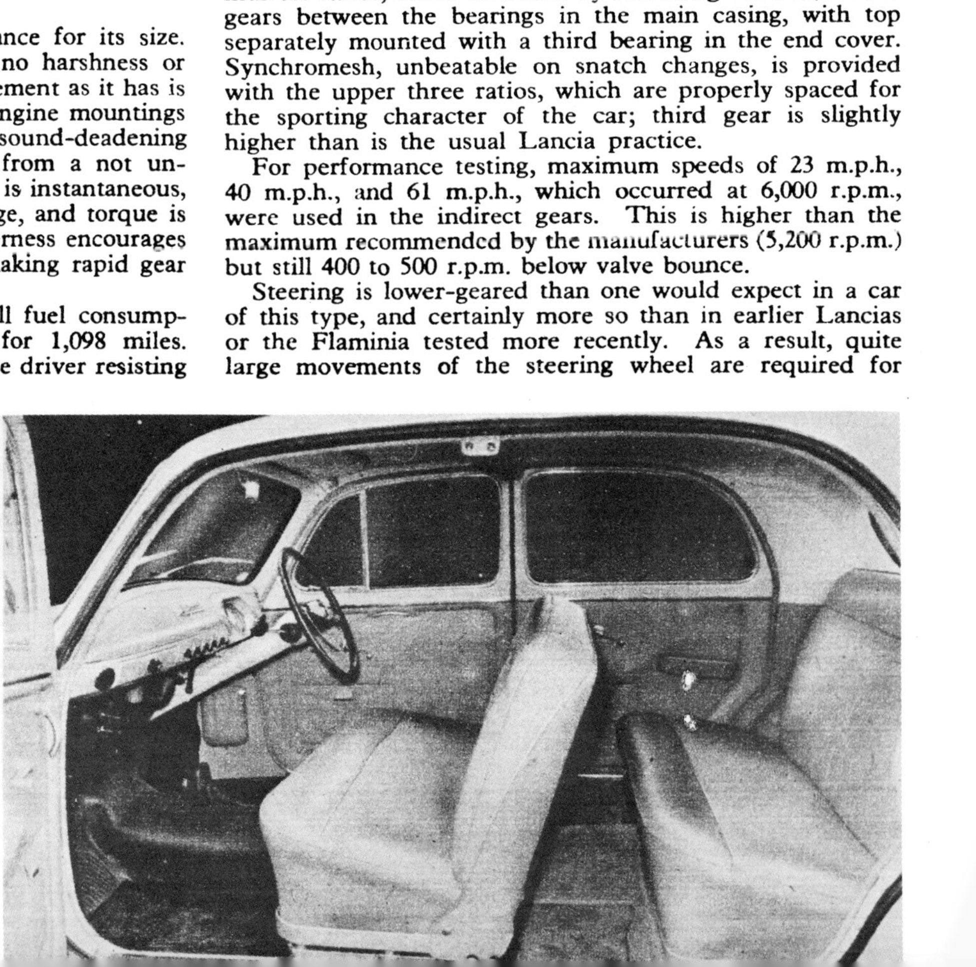

It might be thought that the doors had been removed to take this picture, such is the excellent entry to front and rear seats afforded by the pillarless type of construction. The front seat back is adjustable by thumb screws at each side; a fully reclinable type can be supplied at extra cost. Moulded ribbed rubber mats at the front and carpets at the rear are used for floor covering

LANCIA APPIA 111...

Body style is a blend of classic and modern lines. Amber turn indicators on the front wings augment the usual ones incorporated in the sidelamps

small corrections. There is little castor action, but the car maintained a natural straight line and was not affected by quite severe side winds. Initially, the impression was formed that the car had inherent understeering characteristics, but subsequent investigation proved that, in fact, it was neutral in this respect. This characteristic, together with that of low-geared steering, particularly around the straight ahead position, seems to emanate from an unusual construction of the steering drop arm. This is a two-piece affair, with some rubber cushioning between, and designed to reduce reaction at the steering wheel resulting from the use of the vertical pillar-type front suspension, in conjunction with a one-piece track rod. Rather surprisingly, there was no impression of excessive lost movement or springiness resulting from the use of this rubber in the steering. A disappointment was the poor turning circle, quite out of keeping with Lancia tradition. On right lock it required 37ft 10in. between kerbs on full lock, which is very surprising with the Appia type of front suspension, which theoretically should allow larger lock angles.

The Appia always can be placed and held on a chosen line with little effort, even in hard cornering, and there are negligible reactions at the steering wheel on rough surfaces. Initial roll is arrested quickly and there is no tyre squeal at all. Adhesion in the dry, with the driver only aboard or when fully laden, is very good. On slippery surfaces the rear wheels broke away sooner and more quickly than was expected, and partly because of the low-geared steering some energetic action was necessary to restore stability.

Ride comfort is extraordinarily good for such a small car. The suspension is not particularly soft, yet bumps are smoothed out very well. Even more impressive is the quietness over bad surfaces on which the ride and stability remain at a very high standard. In fact, the suspension seems to excel where the roads are worst. An undulating surface produced some pitch, but it was not pronounced. The front dampers are adjustable by means of a lever on top of each unit. Presumably the adjustment is connected with the oil viscosity, for the owner's handbook quotes summer and winter settings. Throughout most of the test they were used in the winter position as set by the manufacturer. Changing them to the other setting made the ride slightly harsh.

Brakes, as may be judged from their size, were very efficient and virtually fade free. They were progressive throughout the range and light in operation; as a special safety measure there are separate hydraulic circuits for the front and rear systems. The maximum stop achieved with driver and observer in the car was 0·82g with a pedal load of 80lb, which was just below the point where the rear wheels locked. Tyre adhesion and braking efficiency improved with the car fully laden, and the balance between the four wheels was always perfect up to the point of wheel locking.

Good Pedal Position

The driving position is such that the driver's legs are nearer to the vertical than in most modern cars, but this is one that is preferred by many people. As a result, the position of the feet relative to the bottom-pivoted clutch and brake pedals and organ-type throttle pedal, which has a short and progressive action, does not lead to fatigue. The clutch pedal has a light action, with short travel, and the drive is taken up very smoothly. The only occasion when excessive slip occurred was when taking off from a 1-in-3 incline, which needed full throttle. Front and rear seats, which were covered in wool cloth and plastic (leather trim can be supplied as an optional extra), were too firmly sprung for most tastes. Another criticism is that the front one provided no lateral support. Its backrest is adjustable by means of a thumbscrew at each side, and a near arm's-length driving attitude can be adopted without cramping rear passengers for leg room.

A tall driver notices the beetle-browed effect of the low screen top-rail particularly, but, on the credit side, the seating is rather high and the bonnet short, so that there is never difficulty in seeing the forward quarters for accurate placing. One advantage of the relatively small and slightly curved screen is that the wipers clear a large area of the glass.

It is difficult to imagine an easier car to enter than the Appia. All the doors are spring-loaded towards their closed positions. On releasing them off the retaining stay they slam shut automatically; but usually to the secondary safety catch, rarely to the primary one. Each has a window which winds down fully, the front ones having swivelling quarter vents. Door handles, window winders and fittings are made from attractively designed polished aluminium die castings.

Transmitted road noise was virtually non-existent, and at maximum speed wind noise did not interfere with normal conversation. The body structure is extremely rigid, the sealing is very effective and not a single rattle developed throughout the test. After the adjustment to the radiator shutters previously mentioned, the heating and ventilating system was very effective for front seat occupants, although less so for those in the rear, and demisting rapid when the total flow was directed to the screen.

Among the items of interest to the enthusiast—and par-

Up and down movement of the small lever on this side of the column changes the lamps from dipped to main beam or side to dipped, depending on the position of the facia master switch; a radial movement operates the self-cancelling turn indicators. On the other side of the column is one of the best four-speed gear-changes ever tested by The Autocar

ticularly the owner-driver—are bolt-on attachments inside the rims for wheel balancing. The electrical system uses negative earth and there is a socket for an inspection lamp under the facia. Mounted on the frame front cross member is a towing attachment. There is a comprehensive tool kit of good quality supplied in a proper bag, and a lifting jack of the vertical column type with winding handle; this is used at a central jacking point at each side. There is no starting handle, nor provision for one.

Maintenance requirements are very few. Under the bonnet there is an oil feed tank with two piston rods which need to be operated at intervals of approximately 2,000 miles to lubricate each front suspension unit. Every 2,000 miles the steering ball joints need greasing, and at intervals of 6,000 miles the pedal cross shaft requires similar attention.

For those who require a four-seater car of lively performance and excellent road manners, and to whom motoring means more than mere transportation, the Appia is a very desirable possession, although a relatively expensive one in this country. Although one cannot assess the endurance properties of a car in a thousand-mile test, one at least can form impressions in this respect. The Appia gives every indication of being an unfailing servant over a very long period. Confirmation of this is evident from a test undertaken three years ago by the Italian journal *Quattroruote* on a Series II Appia—the only difference from the Series III is the front end styling. This car completed 100 circuits of the tough Mille Miglia course non-stop, equivalent to 97,200 miles, at an average speed of 43·6 m.p.h.; the overall fuel consumption was 33·2 m.p.g. No major breakdowns occurred and when the car was examined after the test none of the main components needed replacement.

LANCIA APPIA III

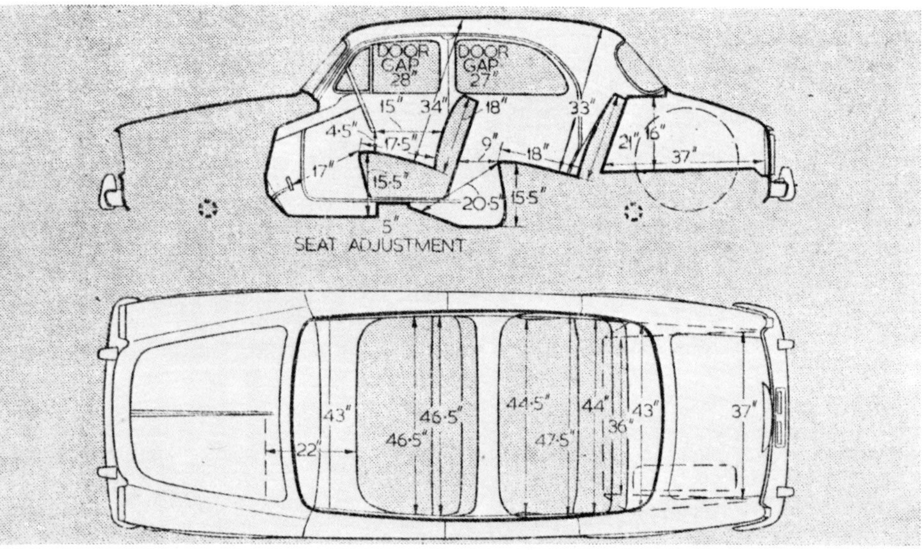

Scale ¼in. to 1ft. Driving seat in central position. Cushions uncompressed.

DATA

PRICE (basic), with four-door saloon body (including heater), **£1,120.**
British purchase tax, **£467 15s 10d.**
Total (in Great Britain), **£1,587 15s 10d.**
Extras (including purchase tax):
Leather trim **£151 11s 8d.**
Fully reclining front seat **£31 17s 6d.**

ENGINE: Capacity, 1,090 c.c. (66·5 cu in).
Number of cylinders, 4, in 10 deg 14 min vee.
Bore and stroke, 68 × 75 mm (2·68 x 2·95in).
Valve gear, overhead, pushrods and rockers from two camshafts.
Compression ratio, 7·8 to 1.
B.h.p. 48 (net) at 5,200 r.p.m. (b.h.p. per ton laden 45).
Torque, 63 lb ft at 3,000 r.p.m.
M.p.h. per 1,000 r.p.m. in top gear, 15·8.

WEIGHT: (with 5 gal fuel), 18·5 cwt (2,065 lb).
Weight distribution (per cent); F, 50; R, 50.
Laden as tested, 21·5 cwt (2400 lb).
Lb per c.c. (laden), 2·2.

BRAKES: Type, SABIF drum. F, 2LS in aluminium finned drums: R, L and T in cast iron drums.
Method of operation, hydraulic.
Drum dimensions: 9in diameter; 2in wide, front and rear.
Total swept area: 226 sq in (211 sq in per ton laden).

TYRES: 155—14in Michelin S.D.S.
Pressures (p.s.i.): F, 18·5; R, 21 (normal).

TANK CAPACITY: 8·5 Imperial gallons.
Oil sump, 6·6 pints.
Cooling system, 10 pints (including heater)

DIMENSIONS: Wheelbase, 8ft 2·81in.
Track: F, 3ft 10·38in; R, 3ft 10·5in.
Length (overall), 13ft 2·25in.
Width, 4ft. 10·25in.
Height, 4ft 8·88in.
Ground clearance, 4·25in.

ELECTRICAL SYSTEM: 12-volt; 40 ampère-hour battery.
Headlamps, 45–40 watt bulbs.

SUSPENSION: Front, vertical pillar type, enclosed coil springs and hydraulic dampers.
Rear, live axle, half-elliptic springs and hydraulic dampers.

PERFORMANCE

ACCELERATION TIMES (mean):

Speed range, m.p.h.	Gear Ratios and Time in Sec. 4·18 to 1	6·35 to 1	9·95 to 1	17·1 to 1
10—30	—	8·6	5·4	—
20—40	13·4	8·1	6·1	—
30—50	14·3	8·9	—	—
40—60	16·9	13·3	—	—
50—70	24·8	—	—	—

From rest through gears to:

30 m.p.h.	5·9 sec
40 ,,	9·6 ,,
50 ,,	15·2 ,,
60 ,,	23·7 ,,
70 ,,	38·9 ,,

Standing quarter mile 22·5 sec.

MAXIMUM SPEEDS ON GEARS:

Gear		m.p.h.	k.p.h.
Top ..	(mean)	81·4	131
	(best)	82·0	132
3rd	at 6000 r.p.m. (see text)	61	98
2nd		40	64
1st		23	37

TRACTIVE EFFORT (by Tapley meter):

	Pull (lb per ton)	Equivalent gradient
Top ..	165	1 in 13·5
Third	265	1 in 8·4
Second	420	1 in 5·2

BRAKES (at 30 m.p.h. in neutral):

Pedal load in lb	Retardation	Equiv. stopping distance in ft
25	0·15g	200
50	0·38g	80
75	0·70g	43
80	0·81g	37·3

FUEL CONSUMPTION (at steady speeds in top gear)

30 m.p.h.	44·4 m.p.g.
40 ,,	41·6 ,,
50 ,,	37·7 ,,
60 ,,	33·1 ,,
70 ,,	28·1 ,,

Overall fuel consumption for 1,098 miles, 32·6 m.p.g. (8·7 litres per 100 km).

Approximate normal range 30–42 m.p.g. (9·4–6·7 litres per 100 km.).

Fuel: Premium grade.

TEST CONDITIONS: Weather: Air temperature, 36 deg. F. 4 to 5 m.p.h. wind, damp tarmac surface.

STEERING: Turning circle:
Between kerbs, L, 34ft 11in; R, 37ft 10in.
Between walls, L, 36ft 1in; R, 39ft 0in.
Turns of steering wheel from lock to lock, 3·25.

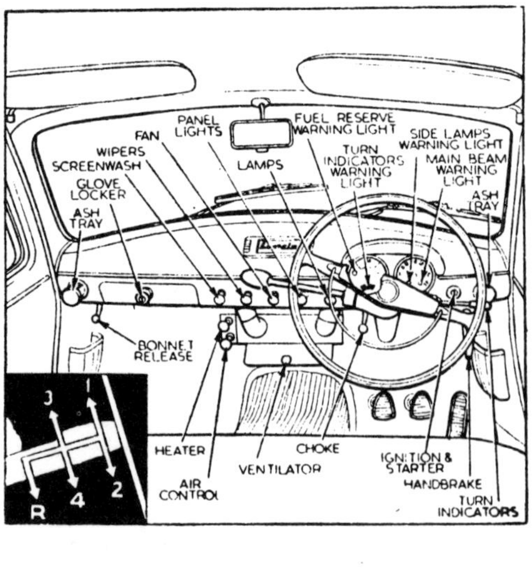

SPEEDOMETER CORRECTION: M.P.H.

Car speedometer ..	10	20	30	40	50	60	70	80	90
True speed ..	7	17	26	35	45	53	63	72	81

NEW MODEL

LANCIA FULVIA

How a 30-year cycle has brought back the boot and boxy look: Top to bottom—Augusta, Aprilia, Appia I, Appia III, and Fulvia

JUST three decades ago Lancia introduced their first small car, the 1,196 c.c. Augusta. It had a compact, narrow-angle vee-four engine with vertical overhead valves, independent front suspension by coil springs enclosed in so-called sliding pillars, a semi-integral frame and a four-door body with no centre pillars.

During the intervening 30 years it has been succeeded in time by the revolutionary 1,352 c.c. Aprilia (1936), the simpler 903 c.c. Ardea (1939) and the 1,090 c.c. Appia (1953). Although these have varied considerably in specification and appearance, all have carried forward certain fundamental features of the Augusta—the vee-four engine, rear-wheel drive, the traditional Lancia front suspension, pillarless body structure.

With Professor Fessia in control of Lancia design, and his front-drive 1,500 c.c. Flavia (introduced in 1960) an established success, it is no surprise that the new small car, to be presented at the Geneva Show next week, has front drive with a leaf-spring suspension. The pillarless body style had to go because it necessitates rear-hinged back doors, no longer legal for new cars in some countries. Yet one master link with Lancia tradition has been retained—indeed, strengthened. For the new Fulvia has a narrow-angle vee-four engine, of practically the same cylinder capacity as its predecessor, the Appia.

Proving that the choice of this form of engine was no half-hearted concession to tradition, it is a completely new short-stroke design bearing scarcely a detail similarity to the Appia unit. One practical result is a 21 per cent increase in power, from 48 to 58 net b.h.p.

In its other mechanical constituents and their layout the Fulvia follows the Flavia very closely indeed, quite a few parts being interchangeable. Thus, the engine and transmission unit, together with the front suspension and steering components, are carried in a separate subframe with six rubber-cushioned attachment points to the main structure. Dunlop disc brakes, without servo assistance, are fitted all round.

Although its contents are not identical, since the two cars have different gear spacings and final drive ratios, the transmission casing is common to both. In each case the front wheels are carried on long and short wishbones, and a transverse leaf spring is used in conjunction with de Carbon telescopic dampers. At the back is a "dead" axle beam carried on leaf springs, with a transverse Panhard rod (not found on the Flavia) to locate it laterally. Both cars also share the same wheel tracks, 4ft 3·2in. front and 4ft 2·4in. rear, representing a significant increase over the Appia's 3ft 10in. and 3ft. 10·5in. The Fulvia's wheelbase, at 8ft 2·4in., is an inch or so shorter than the Appia's, 6in. shorter than the Flavia's.

Thus the Fulvia body has virtually the same internal width as the Flavia and is a full five-seater. However, individual front seats are fitted, as six passengers would clearly overload such a small engine. These are probably the best front seats fitted to a Lancia for many years, having plenty of shape and resilience to hold one firmly but unobtrusively in place. The backrests have a lever adjustment for rake, and can be lowered right down to form a "wagon-lit." While the back seat looks a bit short fore-and-aft in the cushion, it is, in fact, comfortable and leaves adequate knee room.

As can be seen in the photographs the body designers have sacrificed nothing

Completely new 1,091 c.c. vee-four engine, inclined at 45 deg: front-wheel drive: disc brakes

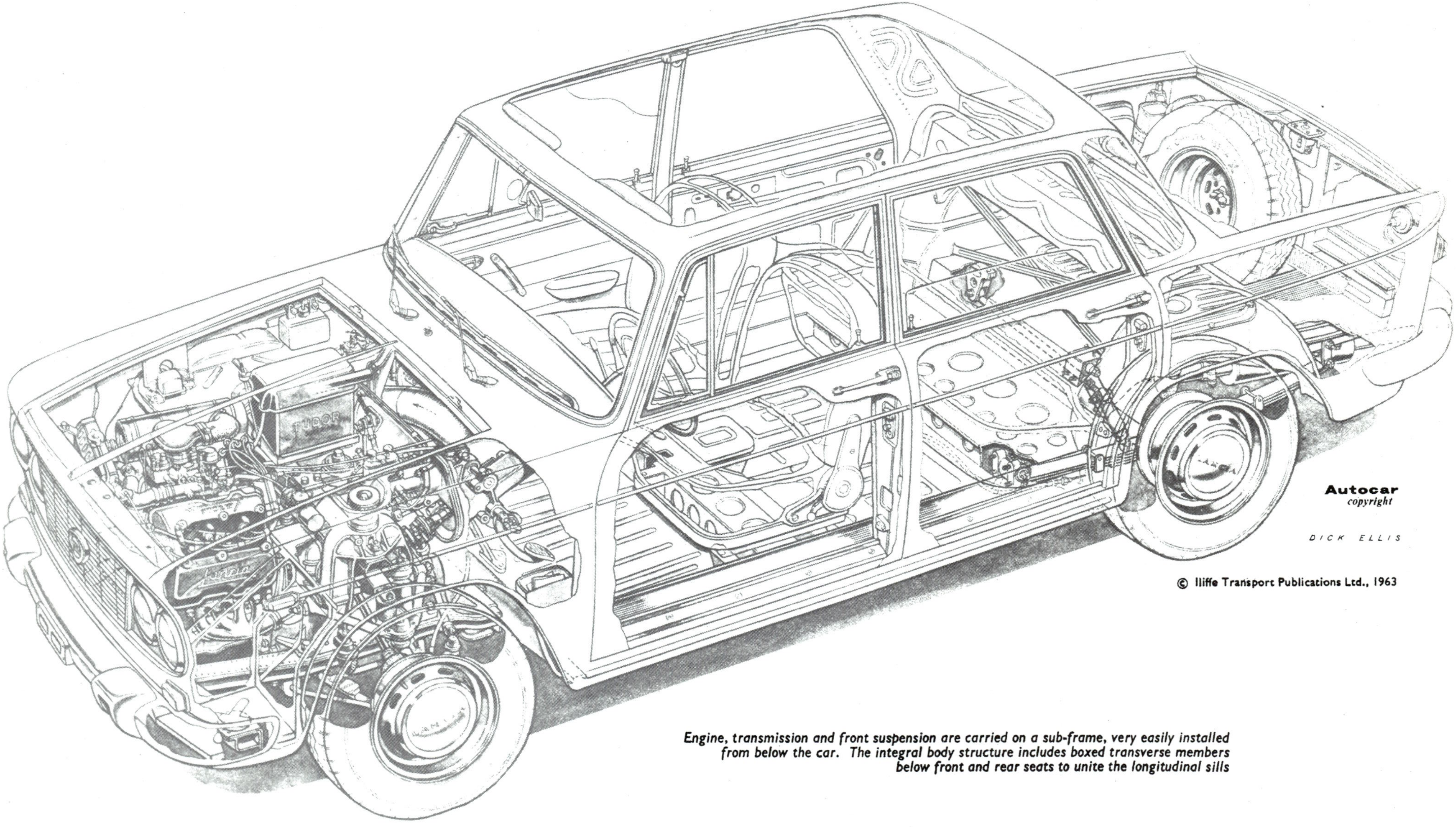

Autocar
copyright

DICK ELLIS

Engine, transmission and front suspension are carried on a sub-frame, very easily installed from below the car. The integral body structure includes boxed transverse members below front and rear seats to unite the longitudinal sills

LANCIA FULVIA . . .

in passenger space to aerodynamics, and there is plenty of headroom for all. Standard seat trim is in soft-coloured nap cloth of fine quality, and there is nothing jazzy about the interior. As the Fulvia, like its predecessors, must be the world's most costly "1100" in quantity production, one naturally expects this quiet good taste. Black rubber mats cover the flat and unobstructed floor, and the facia, free from sharp edges or corners, is neatly trimmed with matt black p.v.c. over a shock-absorbing backing.

It is interesting to observe the trend, among family saloons, back to windscreens with little rake or curvature.

Most of the facia is padded, and even the top rail above the screen. A rotating drum speedometer is novel, and there are tell-tales for the handbrake and choke

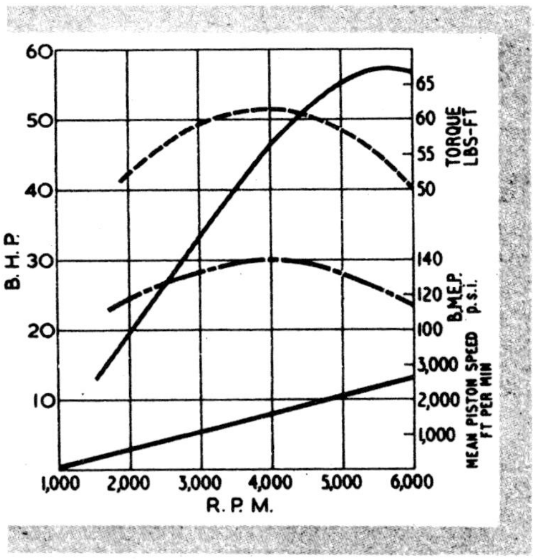

***Above:** Net power curves for the Fulvia vee-four. **Right:** Included angle between each pair of cylinders is 13 deg. The two cylinders nearest the exhaust side have long induction tracts in the head, the other two long exhaust tracts*

Compared with the steeply sloping double-curvature pattern with wrapped-round corners, it is less subject to optical distortions, allows larger door openings, reduces annoyance from sun dazzle, eases the task of the screenwipers—and costs less.

An old idea is revived for the speedometer, a large white drum with black calibrations, rotating on a vertical axis. To the left of this are three vertical slots containing gauges for fuel level, oil pressure and water temperature.

Behind a pleasing steering wheel, with knurled top surface and deep finger grips, are the gear lever (four speeds, all with synchromesh) and a smaller lever controlling the turn indicators and headlamp beams. In daytime, or when the sidelamps only are lit, the headlamps can be signal-flashed by pressing the steering-wheel boss, and there is a full horn ring.

Four piano-key switches in the middle of the facia control the side- and headlamps, instrument lighting, heater-fan and wipers. Two large handwheels with red and blue markings govern the fresh air intake and heating, and butterfly valves at each end of the facia can be set to demist the side windows.

Very large doors have substantial handles with press-button releases outside and neatly recessed triggers inside. Each front door has a red lamp in its trailing edge, automatically lit when the door is opened. There are two interior lamps, and others in the luggage boot and under the bonnet, incidentally.

As the "dead" rear axle beam is set well below wheel hub level, the luggage boot floor is low and flat, extending right to the back of the rear seat. An 8·5-gallon fuel tank is recessed in the floor behind the axle. Neat fibre panels retained by thumb-screws conceal the backs of the rear lamp clusters. Twin reversing lamps are included. The spare wheel, with plastic cover, sits vertically just behind the tail panel.

In the interests of structural stiffness the boot forms a rigid box up to waist level, with the disadvantage that luggage must be lifted up-and-over. The boot lid and bonnet, unusually robust by today's standards, are sound-insulated.

With its crisp, angular lines, the Fulvia invites a perhaps rather fanciful reflection to that first small Lancia of 1932, and the accompanying thumbnail sketches trace its ancestry from that point. The 17th-century Italian poet Vico had something to say about life's time cycles, and these things also occur in engineering.

For the engineer it is unquestionably the new power unit that must attract

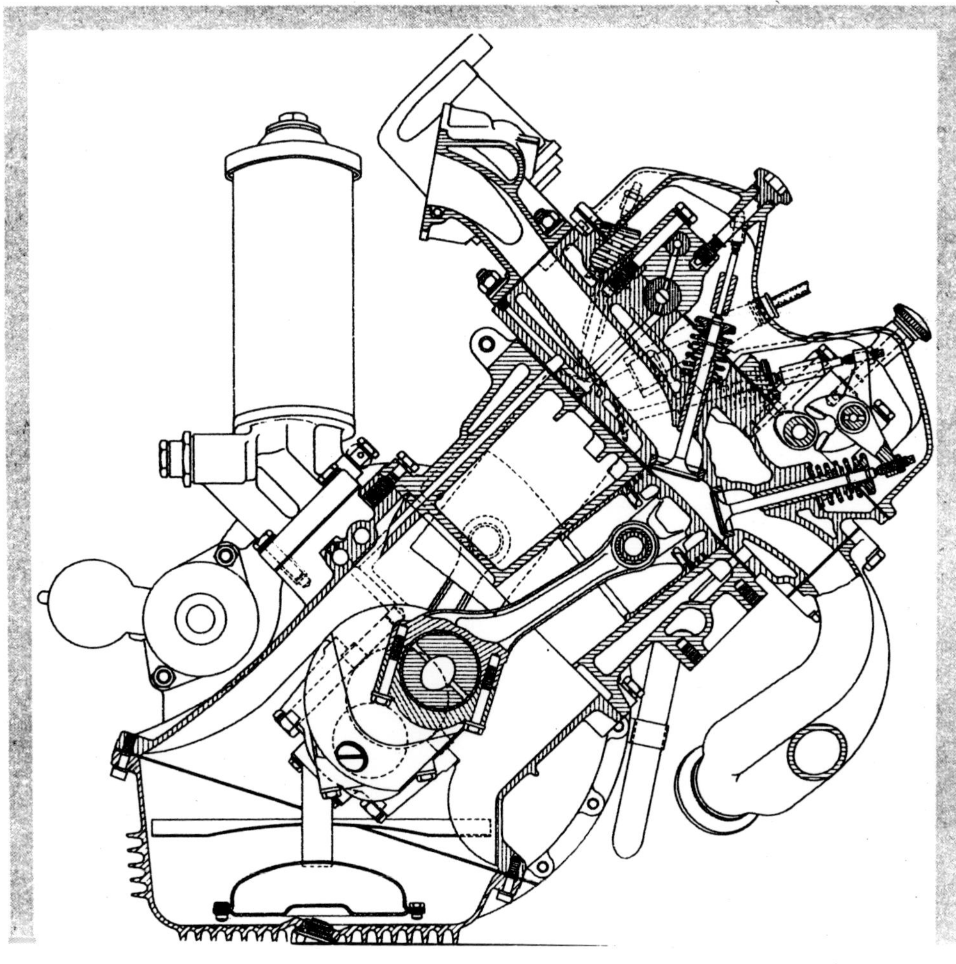

An aluminium head with hemispherical combustion chambers rests on a cast iron cylinder block. There are separate inlet and exhaust camshafts, chain-driven, which operate the valves through rockers and, in the case of the four nearest the centre, short tappets

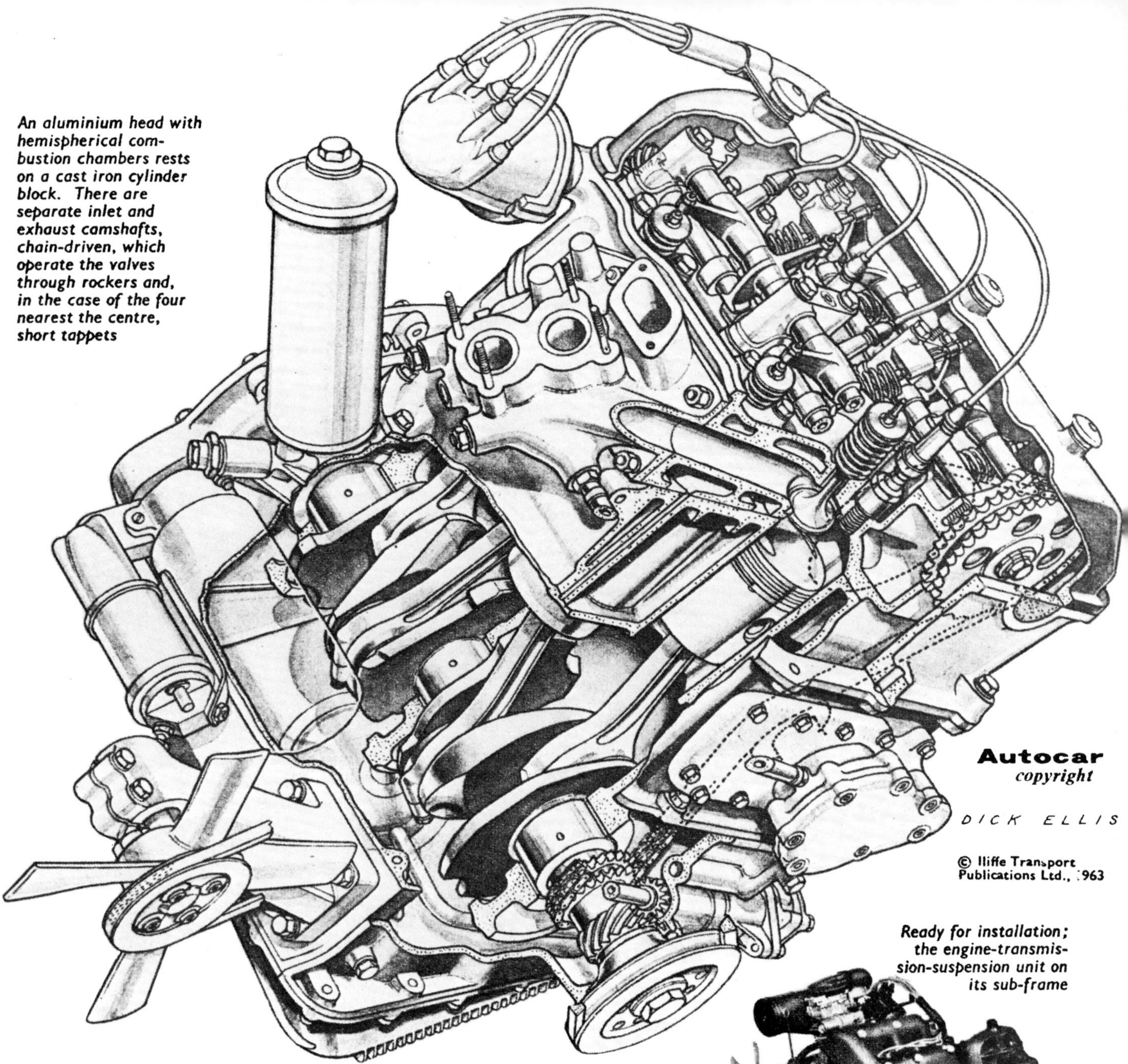

Ready for installation; the engine-transmission-suspension unit on its sub-frame

most of his attention since, as stated already, the rest of the car's working parts will be familiar to those who know the Flavia's constituents. While the Flavia's flat-four engine was clearly so designed that it could be increased substantially in cylinder capacity and power output, and it would have been illogical to adapt it to a smaller capacity, it may seem surprising that the advantages of the opposed layout, so ably demonstrated with that engine, should not have been applied to the Fulvia.

Although long traditions must have influenced the decision to carry on with the vee-four, other factors were probably its compactness, better overall accessibility for maintenance, and lower production costs. Yet Lancia have never allowed this last consideration to deter them from the complications of what may seem to them the best engineering solution; and the new engine is no exception to that dictum.

As well as being tilted across the frame at 45deg from the vertical, the engine is also inclined at 6deg downwards towards the rear of the longitudinal axis. Apart from this, the most significant changes from the Appia are that the crankshaft runs in three, instead of two main bearings; that the two camshafts are now overhead instead of in the crankcase, and that the bore is now greater than the stroke, the new figures being 72 × 67mm (1,091 c.c.) compared with 68 × 75mm (1,090 c.c.). Thus the engine speed range is greatly extended, and maximum power (58 b.h.p.) is now developed at 5,800 r.p.m.,

Wide doors are double-sealed, and the separate front seats have adjustable backrests. Anchorages for safety harness are built into the centre pillars

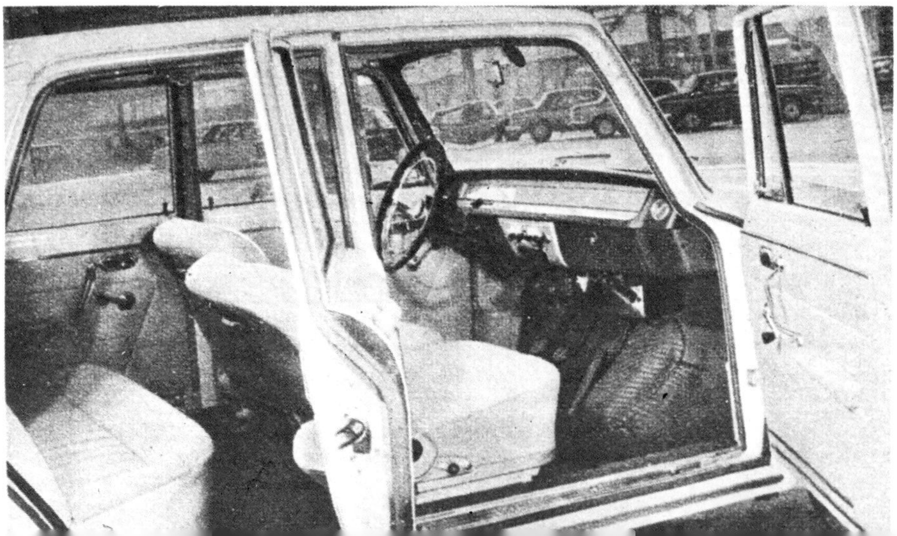

Boot lid and flat rear panel meet with a knife edge decorated with stainless steel. The bumpers, too, are stainless, and reflectors are inset in the overriders

LANCIA FULVIA ...

the previous peak of 48 b.h.p. (at 5,000 r.p.m.) being passed at 4,100 r.p.m.

Basic components of the unit comprise a crankcase composed of three bolted-together aluminium pressure die castings, sealed below by a die-cast sump in the same material; a remarkably compact and shallow cylinder block in cast iron without liners; and an eight-port head cast in aluminium and carrying opposed valves in hemispherical chambers. It is secured to the block by no fewer than 19 set-bolts.

Main journals of the shaft are all 55mm (2·17in.) dia., the big-ends 50mm (1·97in.). To provide equal firing impulses numbers 1 and 4 crankpins do not lie on the same plane as numbers 2 and 3, as they do for a conventional four-in-line engine, but are displaced at an included angle of—to be exact—24deg 32min 40sec. The Vandervell main and big-end bearing shells are faced with indium-infused lead bronze, and are lubricated by a Hobourn-Eaton internal rotor pump. Forged steel connecting rods have a centres-to-stroke ratio of 2·28; their serrated face joints are machined at 50deg to the rod centres, and the caps are secured by two 8mm dia. (0·315in.) set-bolts. The little-ends are bronze-bushed to carry 20mm (0·79in.) fully floating gudgeon pins, restrained by Seeger circlips.

Cast-in iron inserts control expansion of the solid skirt pistons, which are of German design and have three rings, all above the gudgeons. Top ring is chromium-plated, the centre ring is plain and the oil control ring slotted and chamfered. To provide adequate valve clearance crescent-shaped recesses are machined into the slightly domed piston crowns, which are angled to bring them parallel with the head face. Included angle between the valve stems is 60deg, their head dimensions being 34mm (1·34in.) for the inlets, 30mm (1·18in.) for the exhausts. They seat on cast-in iron inserts, and operate in bronze guides.

Overhead camshafts have conferred more benefits than just the reduction in weight of the valve gear's reciprocating parts; for one thing, there are no passages for tappets and pushrods intruding on water circulation in the cylinder block; for another, the ports in the head are no longer partly obstructed by pushrod tubes, and are consequently less tortuous than those of the Appia. This is the fourth major reshuffle of valve gear for the small Lancia engine since the original Augusta.

Each camshaft being confined to either inlet or exhaust valves, their relative timing can be altered. Whereas the rockers act directly on the four valves nearest to the sides of the head (exhausts for the left pair of cylinders, inlets for the right), the other four have short, needle-like tappets running in guides integrated with the light alloy rocker-shaft housings, which also cap the camshaft bearings. There are three of these to each shaft, which runs direct in the rear two, whereas the one nearest the camshaft sprocket has a large diameter bronze sleeve.

Fulvia and Appia cylinder blocks compared: the Fulvia is less compact, cylinder spacings being greater due to the addition of a centre main bearing. The space at the front accommodates the camshaft chain

A Marelli ignition distributor is driven by a skew gear on the tail-end of the inlet camshaft. The duplex camshaft chain, joined by a spring link, also drives the water pump; it is kept in tension by a hydraulically damped shoe, 3·3in. long and faced with bonded rubber, said to be much quieter than the Appia's jockey sprocket. Fine setting of valve timing is achieved by having unequal numbers of holes drilled in the sprocket and the camshaft flange to which it is attached, and inserting a dowel pin in those that line up nearest to the appropriate setting. The valve gear cover is shaped to give direct access to the sparking-plugs.

A twin-choke Solex downdraught carburettor (of which the second choke is controlled progressively by manifold depression) is attached to a water-heated manifold with separate ducts to each of the four inlet ports in the head. A small pressurized radiator is offset to the right behind the front grille, and assisted by a four-bladed fan to cast aluminium. The engine-transmission unit is attached to the sub-frame at four rather oddly disposed points: two side-by-side in series at the left front of the engine, one above the final drive housing, and one at the right rear of the gearbox.

From the clutch, a primary shaft passes through the hollow pinion of the hypoid drive to a pair of helical gears in the back end of the gearbox casing. Single helical gears with baulk-ring synchromesh carry the drive forward again. Front-wheel drive shafts by Hardy-Spicer have Rzeppa-type constant velocity universals at each end, the inner ones encased in telescopic pot-joints of the ball-and-groove pattern.

Appia production at the end of its run has reached 45 cars daily; by the end of this year daily production of the Fulvia at the new Chivasso factory—not yet completed—should reach 100, and that figure may be doubled by the end of 1964. At the time of writing the price had not been fixed, and it was not known when right-hand drive versions would be available in this country.

Specification

ENGINE

No. of cylinders...	4 in 13 deg Vee, water cooled
Bore	72mm (2.83in.)
Stroke	67mm (2.64in.)
Displacement ...	1,091 c.c. (66.6 cu. in.)
Valve position and operation	Overhead, opposed valves. Twin overhead camshafts and rockers
Compression ratio	7.8 to 1
Max. b.h.p. (net)	58 at 5,800 r.p.m.
Max. b.m.e.p. (net)	140 p.s.i. at 4,000 r.p.m.
Max torque (net)	62lb ft at 4,000 r.p.m.
Carburettor ...	Solex downdraught C32 PAIA/8 double choke
Fuel pump ...	Mechanical
Tank capacity ...	8.4 Imp. gallons (38 litres)
Sump capacity ...	6 pints (3.5 litres)
Oil filter ...	Fram full-flow
Cooling system ...	Pressurized, pump, fan and thermostat
Battery	12 volt, 42 amp. hr.

TRANSMISSION

Clutch	Single dry plate, 7.87in. dia.
Gearbox ...	Four speeds, all-synchromesh; steering column lever
Overall gear ratios	Top 4.78; 3rd 7.35; 2nd 12.15; 1st 20.58; reverse 22.93
Final drive ...	Hypoid bevel, ratio 4.78 to 1

CHASSIS

Brakes	Dunlop disc, separate hydraulic systems front and rear, no servo
Disc dia.	10.4in. front and rear
Suspension: front	Independent, double wishbones with transverse leaf spring and anti-roll bar
Suspension: rear	Dead axle, with half-elliptic leaf springs and Panhard rod
Dampers ...	de Carbon telescopic
Wheels ...	Pressed steel disc, 4.5in. rims
Tyre size ...	155—14
Steering ...	Worm and roller
Steering wheel ...	Two-spoke, 15in. dia.

DIMENSIONS

Wheelbase ...	8ft 2.4in. (248cm)
Track: front ...	4ft 3.2in. (130cm)
Track: rear ...	4ft 2.4in. (128cm)
Overall length ...	13ft 7in. (414cm)
Overall width ...	5ft 1.2in. (155cm)
Overall height (unladen)	4ft 7in. (140cm)
Ground clearance (laden)	5in. (12cm)
Turning circle ...	34ft (10.5m)
Kerb weight ...	2,200lb, 19.6 cwt (998kg)

PERFORMANCE DATA

Top gear m.p.h. per 1,000 r.p.m. ...	14.7
Torque lb. ft. per cu. in. engine capacity	1.05
Brake surface swept by linings...	410 sq in.
Weight distribution	F, 53 per cent R, 47 per cent

'64 Models

Larger-Engined Lancias

THE FLAVIA 1·8 AND FLAMINIA 2·8

SIGNIFICANT mechanical revision of the flat-four, front-wheel-drive Lancia Flavia and the vee-6 Flaminia came into effect yesterday. Both models have larger engines and new gear ratios to suit; but in the case of the Flavia the new 1·8-litre car supplements the 1·5, which continues in production virtually without change.

Dealing first with the new-type Flavia, its cylinder capacity has been raised from 1,500 to 1,800 c.c. by an increase in both bore and stroke. The dimensions are 88×74mm (3·46×2·91in.) in place of 82×71mm (3·23×2·79in.), and the net power is up to 92 b.h.p. for all versions of this car, the compression ratio being 9·0 to 1. By comparison the 1·5-litre saloon's engine develops 78 b.h.p., and hitherto there has been a 90 b.h.p. variant for the sporting coupé and convertible. Claimed top speeds are 100 m.p.h. for the 1·8 saloon and 107 m.p.h. for the others, which have higher final drive gearing.

A steering lock is now featured on the Flavia

Flavia body styling is unchanged

Whereas maximum power is still delivered at 5,200 r.p.m. (as on the standard 1·5-litre engine), the point of maximum torque—now up from 82 to 105 lb. ft.—has been lowered from 3,500 to 3,000 r.p.m. Widespread criticism of the 1·5 saloon's low indirect gear ratios, and especially of the very wide spacing between top and third, has obviously reached a sympathetic ear in Turin's via Vincenzo Lancia, for all the indirects have been raised appreciably. In fact, they are higher than those of the superseded 1·5-litre coupé and convertible. Final drive gearing of the saloon is unchanged at 4·1 to 1, but for the other types it is henceforth 3·9 to 1.

Overall ratios are now as follows, with the previous figures in brackets:—

	Saloon	Coupé and Convertible
Top	4·10 (4·10)	3·91 (4·10)
3rd	5·70 (6·71)	5·42 (5·82)
2nd	8·08 (9·53)	7·68 (8·94)
1st	13·65 (16·16)	12·99 (15·13)

These changes should add greatly to the Flavia's versatility off *autostrade* and motorways, and will be especially welcomed by potential buyers in this country. A new mechanical feature is that a cooler is now incorporated in the engine lubrication system, the unit being mounted vertically beside the water radiator. The body designs are unchanged except that the four-door saloon now has a folding armrest to divide the back seat, and a steering lock is incorporated.

In the case of the Flaminia 2·8 the engine capacity is up from 2,458 to 2,775 c.c., the bore having been opened up from 80 to 85mm while the stroke remains unchanged at 81·5mm. In inches, the new bore and stroke measurements are 3·35×3·21.

The new net power outputs, with superseded figures in brackets, are: long-wheelbase four-door saloon, 129 b.h.p. at 5,000 r.p.m. (110 at 5,200); medium wheelbase coupé, 140 b.h.p. at 5,400 r.p.m. (127 at 5,600); short wheelbase convertible, G.T. and G.T.L., 150 b.h.p. at 5,600 r.p.m. (140 at 5,600). In each case the compression ratio is standardized at 9·0 to 1. Claimed maximum speeds for the three types are 106, 112 and 118-120 m.p.h. respectively. These are only fractionally faster than the superseded 2·5-litre cars could manage, but the gains in engine torque, together with revised gear ratios, are of much greater practical importance.

Maximum torque figures for the three stages of engine tune are now: 169lb. ft. at 2,500 r.p.m. (was 139 at 3,000); 163 at 3,000 (was 135 at 3,500); and 165 at 3,500 (was 150 at 3,600). Whereas the standard saloon's final drive ratio is practically unchanged at 3·92 to 1, the medium-wheelbase coupé has been raised from that figure to 3·77, and the other three from 3·62 to 3·54.

New overall gear ratios, with the former figures bracketed, are:—

	Saloon	Coupé	Convertible, G.T. and G.T.L.
Top	3·92 (3·91)	3·77 (3·91)	3·54 (3·62)
3rd	5·57 (5·91)	5·35 (5·91)	4·53 (5·10)
2nd	8·03 (8·60)	7·73 (8·60)	6·58 (7·52)
1st	12·11 (12·94)	11·65 (12·94)	10·94 (11·80)

There are no changes to the Flaminia coachwork, and at the moment of writing there is no news of any changes to the little vee-four Fulvia introduced at Geneva last spring.

Prices in this country of the Flavia 1·8 and Flaminia 2·8 have not yet been fixed. The Flavia 1·5 saloon remains unchanged at £1,456 (£1,760 including purchase tax), but the Fulvia price has been substantially reduced from £1,195 (£1,445 with tax) to £1,149 (£1,389 with tax).

Lancia Flavia Coupé 1,800 c.c.

ONE-MAKE enthusiasts have a tendency to be blind, and to see no wrong in the beast they worship. Their eulogies can be boring to the uninitiated, who become sceptical in defence, and judge the car when they see one with unaccustomed severity. To withstand such a stringent ordeal the car not only must be good, but pleasing in the little things as much as the big ones; and to say that the Lancia Flavia coupé offers few disappointments is tantamount to praise of a very high order.

Well over two years have elapsed since we last tested a Flavia (10 November, 1961) so it will help to run over briefly the interesting mechanical specification. Motive power stems from a flat four-cylinder engine ahead of the front wheels and driving them through a four-speed, all-synchromesh gearbox. Front suspension consists of double wishbones and a transverse leaf spring, while at the back there is a lightweight beam axle located transversely by a Panhard rod and sprung with conventional half-elliptic leaf springs. Anti-roll bars are fitted fore and aft, and there are de Carbon telescopic dampers all round.

In our previous test of the saloon version with 1,500 c.c. engine we commented that the car "would benefit greatly from an increase in engine capacity and hence torque," so it was in a way satisfying when the 1·8-litre power unit came on the scene last September—as an option on the saloon and standard on the coupé and convertible. Until then these more sporting variations had been fitted with a tuned version of the 1·5-litre engine with separate twin-choke Solex carburettors for each cylinder bank, developing 90 b.h.p. at 5,800 r.p.m. The larger engine has reverted to a single progressive-choke Solex mounted centrally with long induction pipes, so that although the peak power is only marginally increased to 92 b.h.p. at 5,200 r.p.m., the peak of the torque curve (if one can pin-point it, so flat

PRICES	£	s	d
Pininfarina Coupé	2,066	0	0
Purchase tax	430	19	7
Total (in G.B.)	2,496	19	7

How the Lancia Flavia Coupé compares:

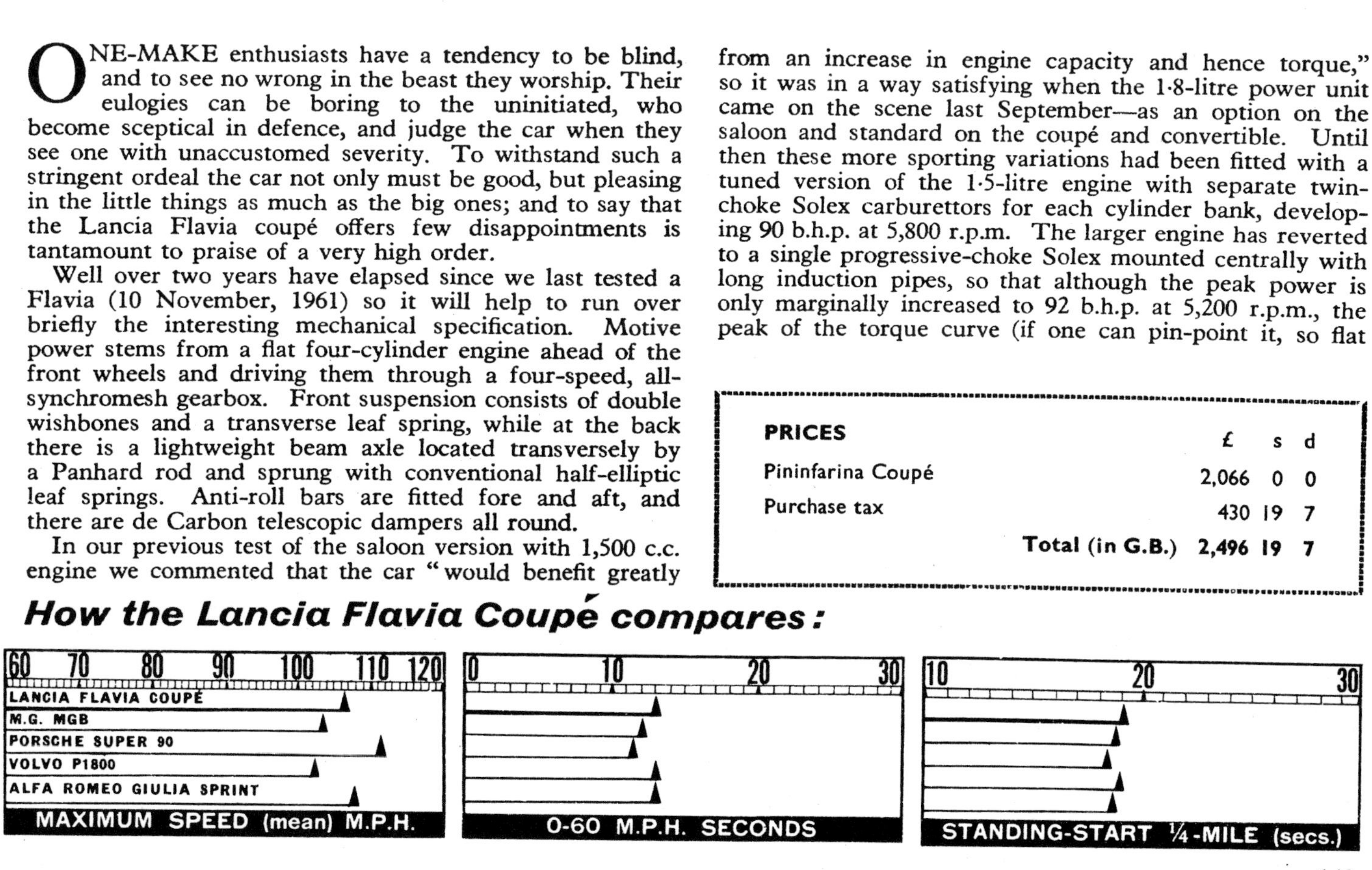

Make • LANCIA Type • Flavia Coupé (1,800 c.c.)

(Front engine, front-wheel drive)

Manufacturer: Lancia & C., via Vincenzo Lancia 27, Turin, Italy
U.K. Importers: Lancia (England) Ltd., Ealing Road, Alperton, Wembley, Middlesex

Test Conditions

Weather.........Dry and cloudy with 5 m.p.h. wind
Temperature.....................4 deg. C. (40 deg. F.)
Barometer..29·5in. Hg.
Dry concrete and tarmac surfaces

Weight

Kerb weight (with oil, water and half-full fuel tank) 22·3 cwt (2,494lb-1,131kg)
Front-rear distribution, per cent F. 61·5; R. 38·5
Laden as tested...........25·5 cwt (2,830lb-1,329kg)

Turning Circles

Between kerbs............L. 34ft 5in.; R, 33ft 7in.
Between walls............L, 36ft 11in.; R, 36ft 1in.
Turns of steering wheel lock to lock .... 4·6

FUEL AND OIL CONSUMPTION

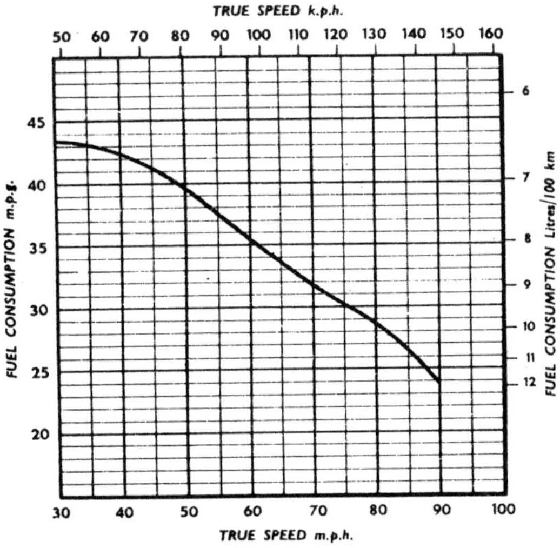

FUEL................................ Premium grade (95–97 octane RM)

Test Distance.......................1,043 miles

Overall Consumption...........22·9 m.p.g. (12·3 litres/100 km.)

Estimated Consumption (DIN) 28·6 m.p.g. (9·9 litres/100 km.)

OIL: S.A.E. 20W......Consumption negligible

HILL CLIMBING AT STEADY SPEEDS

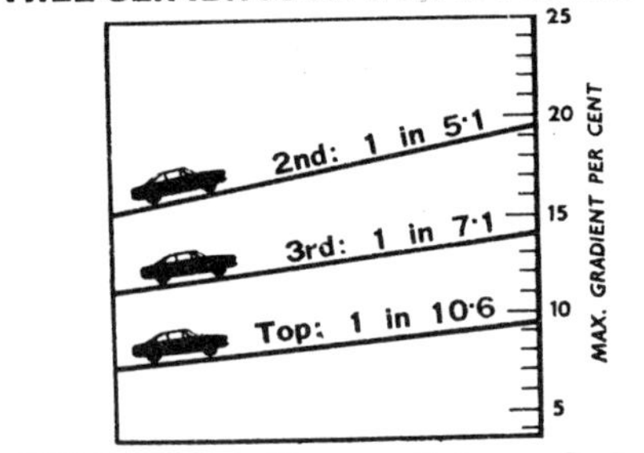

GEAR	Top	3rd	2nd
PULL (lb per ton)	210	310	430
Speed Range (m.p.h.)	50–60	38–42	28–31

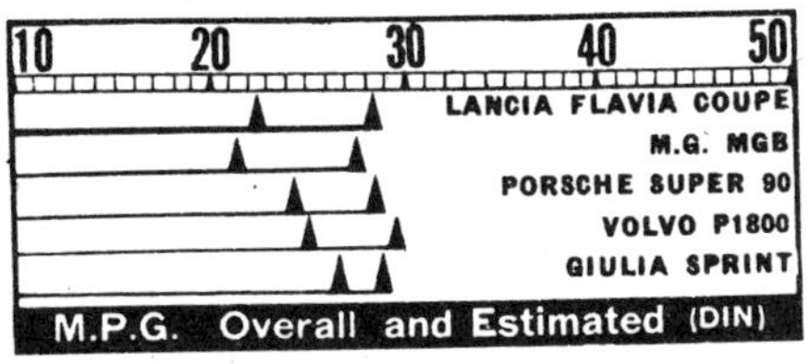

MAXIMUM SPEEDS AND ACCELERATION TIMES

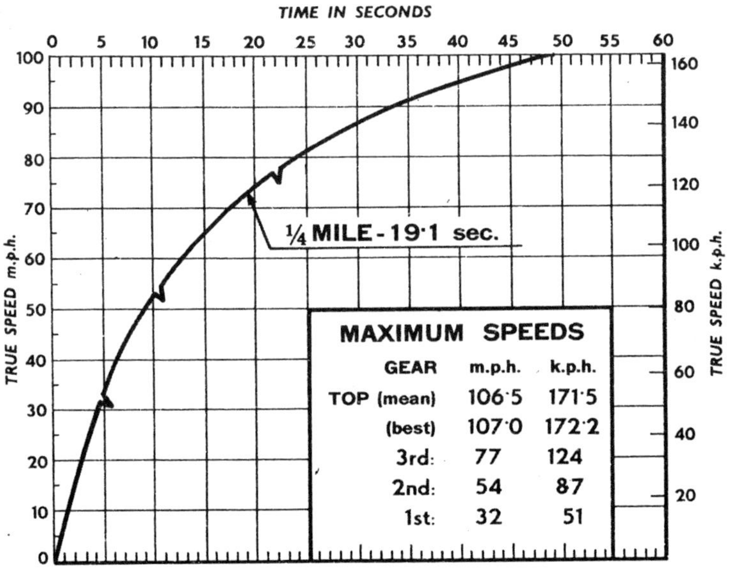

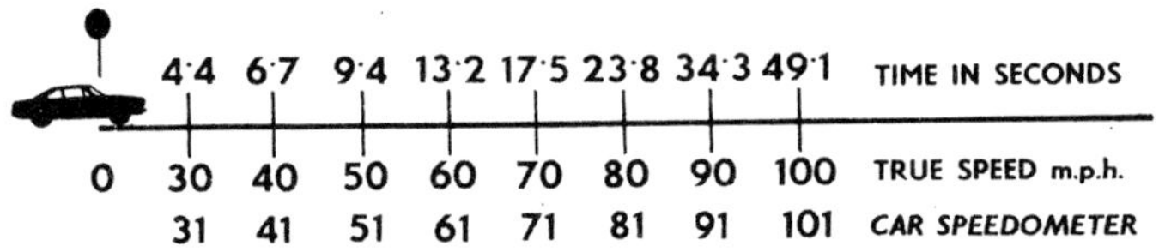

Speed range, gear ratios and time in seconds

m.p.h.	Top (3·91)	3rd (5·42)	2nd (7·68)	1st (12·99)
10—30	—	7·3	5·0	3·4
20—40	10·2	7·3	5·2	—
30—50	10·6	7·0	5·2	—
40—60	10·4	7·3	—	—
50—70	11·9	8·0	—	—
60—80	13·5	—	—	—
70—90	17·0	—	—	—
80—100	23·8	—	—	—

BRAKES	Pedal Load	Retardation	Equiv. distance
(from 30 m.p.h. in neutral)	25lb	0·42g	72ft
	50lb	0·80g	38ft
	75lb	0·97g	31·0ft
	Handbrake	0·30g	100ft

CLUTCH Pedal load and travel—45lb and 5in.

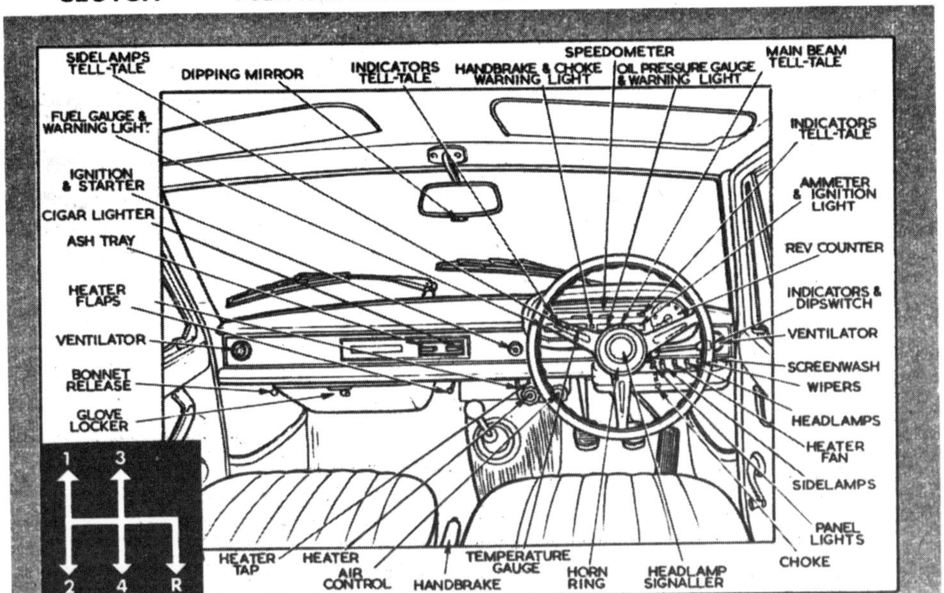

Left: Mahogany rimmed steering wheel almost matches the mock wood facia panel which has swivelling vents at each extremity. The gear lever is robust and very businesslike in appearance. There are pockets each side of the foot wells. Right: On releasing the catches each side the seat backs spring forward to make it easier to climb into the back. Unless the front seats are right forward knee-room is restricted

Lancia Flavia Coupé . . .

is the shape) comes 500 r.p.m. lower at 3,000 and its value is greatly improved from 85 to 108 lb. ft.

Another point of criticism has always been the low indirect gear ratios, particularly in the saloon, which seemed to be out of character with the car. With the extra torque of the larger engine it has been possible to raise these on all models, and on the coupé and convertible to fit a higher final drive ratio as well, to take full advantage of the lower drag shape of the body. This results in the very even spacing of 32, 54, and 77 m.p.h. that we recorded as the maxima in the indirect gears. These road speeds correspond to the manufacturer's recommended engine limit of 5,650 r.p.m. which is denoted by a tiny red blob on the rev. counter. As the scale extends to 6,500 r.p.m. and there is no emphatic warning in the handbook, we tried going beyond this limit to about 6,000 r.p.m. during our performance measurements. The engine remained perfectly smooth with no signs of distress at all, and there were some slight gains in the acceleration times from a standing start, but later in the day a rocker arm fractured (due to a material fault) so perhaps owners would be advised not to exceed the suggested limit.

One of the most remarkable things about the Lancia was the consistent way in which it reproduced its performance even in opposite directions. Not only did each run often produce an identical time, but reference to the table for 20 m.p.h. speed ranges in individual ratios shows that the torque curve must indeed be flat, so close are the figures in each gear.

Even in top gear the same was true. On four runs in opposite directions the rev. counter went straight to the red mark (106·5 m.p.h.) and stayed there for mile after mile. The ribbon-type speedometer proved very misleading at all times, for it suffered from a combination of over-damping and friction that made it extremely slow to react. Sometimes it took as long as two or three minutes to reach the steady speed we were holding.

Because the pull is so uniform, one gets no great impression of power when accelerating, yet from rest to 100 m.p.h. in 49·1 sec is decidedly brisk. When on the road, the engine always responds sweetly and without fuss except for one major fault—fan noise. Part of the cooling system is controlled by shutters in front of the radiator block which open automatically when the engine temperature rises. During our December weather not only did the shutters never open, but the temperature gauge never moved off its bottom stop; the noise of the air trying to suck its way past the obstructive shutters was very irritating and gave the impression at high revs that the engine was being flogged. A high-temperature thermostat, or better still a thermostatically controlled fan would be very desirable.

With some 61·5 per cent of the weight on the front, and the drive at that end, one might expect the Lancia to feel rather different from a conventional rear-drive car. This is not the case at all, and very few drivers would be able to detect anything unusual in the handling. With the throttle open through a corner there is slight understeer which gives excellent stability once the car has been set up for the corner. Lifting off half way round causes the nose to dive in a little, but this seems to check itself once the transition is over. At the standard tyre pressures of 27 p.s.i. back and front we found this tendency to swing rather alarming, especially on downhill bends, and felt much happier with an extra 3 p.s.i. in the back.

During fast cornering there is very noticeable body lean,

Much deeper than it looks here, the boot is amply large enough to carry all the luggage four people would take away on holiday. A plastic tool case is lashed down behind the spare wheel

Pininfarina's close-coupled coupé looks particularly pretty on the Lancia chassis. The test car was very well finished in a subtle dark (but not traditional) Lancia blue

but all the wheels stay firmly on the ground and the Michelin X tyres howl a protest only when the road surface is particularly polished. With far the greater proportion of the weight over the wheels doing the driving it is very hard to provoke wheelspin, even in the wet.

On rough surfaces the ride of the Flavia is quite outstanding, and all the more impressive because it is so quiet. Some harshness from the braced-tread tyres can sometimes be felt as a thumping, but most of the time one is continually surprised at the way irregularities and badly repaired road works can be stormed across without a murmur and hardly a tremor. Compared with the saloon we tested before, the coupé even falls a little short in this respect and it may be that the suspension has been stiffened slightly in the interests of cornering power.

As with all front-wheel-drive cars, the directional stability is unimpaired by the violent lurching on a *pavé* surface. There were no rattles anywhere and the whole car felt taut and firm even at 50 m.p.h. Closely spaced undulations could be taken as fast, but not quite with the same abandon, as in the saloon, probably on account of the 6·7in. shorter wheelbase.

With 11in. dia. Dunlop discs on all four wheels, and a vacuum-servo to lighten the pedal loads, the brakes were well able to cope with all the demands we made on them. There was never any hint of fade—in fact they became more sensitive the hotter they were. We took our measurements with them in this warm state and reached an ultimate figure of 0·97g at only 75 lb load when all four wheels were just on the point of locking together. The handbrake did not have enough bite to lock the back wheels, however hard the driver pulled, but nevertheless it produced 0·3g retardation. It also held the car firmly on 1-in-3 facing up or down.

Getting away again on a 1-in-4 produced some clutch slip and smells of hot linings, but there was no permanent damage, and once it had cooled down again all the former efficiency was restored. There was just enough grip to spin the wheels momentarily during a sprint getaway, but ultra-fast gear changes caused a brief period of clutch slip before the drive took up fully.

A particularly enjoyable feature of the Flavia is the really superb driving position. One sits fairly high with a commanding view over the bonnet and square-topped wings, and the relationship between the wood-rimmed steering wheel and the pedals is so arranged that one can settle into the classical arms-stretched posture very naturally. The backrests can be adjusted for rake, and they are all well rounded to hold one in place during fast cornering.

Tall drivers found the headroom rather restricted, but this could be overcome by leaning back at a greater angle. From the bulkhead between the seats a truly massive gear lever protrudes and works in a more or less vertical "gate", heavily spring-loaded towards third and top. There is very powerful synchromesh on all the ratios, but this makes first gear selection on the move quite stiff unless one double-declutches to reduce the drag. The clutch and brake pedals have hard synthetic rubber pads that produced slip with certain types of shoe soles.

To the right of the driver is a small shelf containing four piano-key switches for the accessories. There is no identification and in the dark this system can be very

The flat-four engine is hardly visible beneath all the accessories. There is a rubber cover on the battery, and a block of 12 (no less) fuses alongside. An automatic inspection lamp comes on with the ignition switch when the bonnet is up

confusing; it would be better if they were grouped in two pairs. The choke is tucked away under the dashboard and switches on a bright red light when in use. This same light comes on with the handbrake.

Standard Italian practice is to fit a warning lamp to show when the sidelamps are lit, and this gives a dull green light. In addition to the gauges there are tell-tale lamps to attract the driver's attention when there is low oil pressure or lack of dynamo charge. When three gallons are left in the 10·5-gallon tank, enough for about 75 miles, the fuel warning lamp starts to flash on left-hand corners, and it glows continuously after another gallon has been consumed.

The headlamp switch works through a relay so that the dipped pair of outer lamps only can be turned on first. Main beams of all four lamps are then selected with the button on the tip of the indicator lever. These give a tremendous blaze of light, which makes the dipped cut-off seem all the more abrupt. Dipped beams can be flashed at any time with the outer ring of the steering wheel boss. The inner button sounds strident FIAMM air horns.

Temperature control for the heater is on the air-mixing system so that it is instantly adjustable by means of a small handwheel. For summer use the hot water supply can be turned off separately, and there are individual trap doors to direct the air supply to either driver or passenger.

Although the coupé is close-coupled, strictly speaking, with only two-plus-two accommodation, the back seats are not unduly cramped, and with the front ones slid well forward there is adequate leg-room. The sloping roof line does not restrict headroom as much as one has come to expect from this styling, probably because the seat cushions are near the floor.

The standard upholstery material is cloth, which has a very luxurious feel and look about it, and which we know from our experience with much older Lancias wears very well indeed. Being light coloured on the test car, it tended to show grubby marks a bit, but cleaning with spirit was no problem. Leather upholstery is a very expensive extra (£111) and a hard one to justify.

In front of the passenger there is a large drawer with its own lock, and the two keys (one for this and the boot, and the other for the doors and ignition) have black and white plastic handles to identify them. The interior door handles are particularly well designed to operate as a natural part of the action of swinging the door open, and on the passenger's door there is a stout grab handle. Only the front quarterlights are clumsy to manipulate, but this can be forgiven as they create no wind roar or draught even at maximum speed.

We called the Flavia saloon a "car for the connoisseur" when we summed it up two years ago. This is even more true of the Flavia coupé, for its price is heavily inflated by duty and tax. Nonetheless, it is a very desirable car that would be a continual source of pleasure and satisfaction to its owner. The Pininfarina styling of the coupé is elegant from any angle, and the standards of construction and finish live up to the looks, even under the closest scrutiny. There are many cars for the individualist, but few like the Flavia that immediately class him as a knowledgeable enthusiast who appreciates the finer points of motoring enough to invest in a thoroughbred of engineering.

Specification: Lancia Flavia Coupé

PERFORMANCE DATA

Top gear m.p.h. per 1,000 r.p.m. ...	18·9
Mean piston speed at max. power ...	2,520 ft/min.
Engine revs. at mean max. speed...	5,640 r.p.m.
B.h.p. per ton laden	72·0

Scale; 0·3in. to 1ft. Cushions uncompressed.

ENGINE

Cylinders	4, horizontally opposed
Bore	88mm (3·46in.)
Stroke	74mm (2·91in.)
Displacement ...	1,800 c.c. (110 cu. in.)
Valve gear ...	Overhead, pushrods and rockers
Compression ratio	9-to-1
Carburettor ...	Solex progressive choke
Fuel pump ...	Bendix electric
Oil filter	Fram full flow
Max. power ...	92 b.h.p. (net) at 5,200 r.p.m.
Max. torque ...	108 lb. ft. at 3,000 r.p.m.

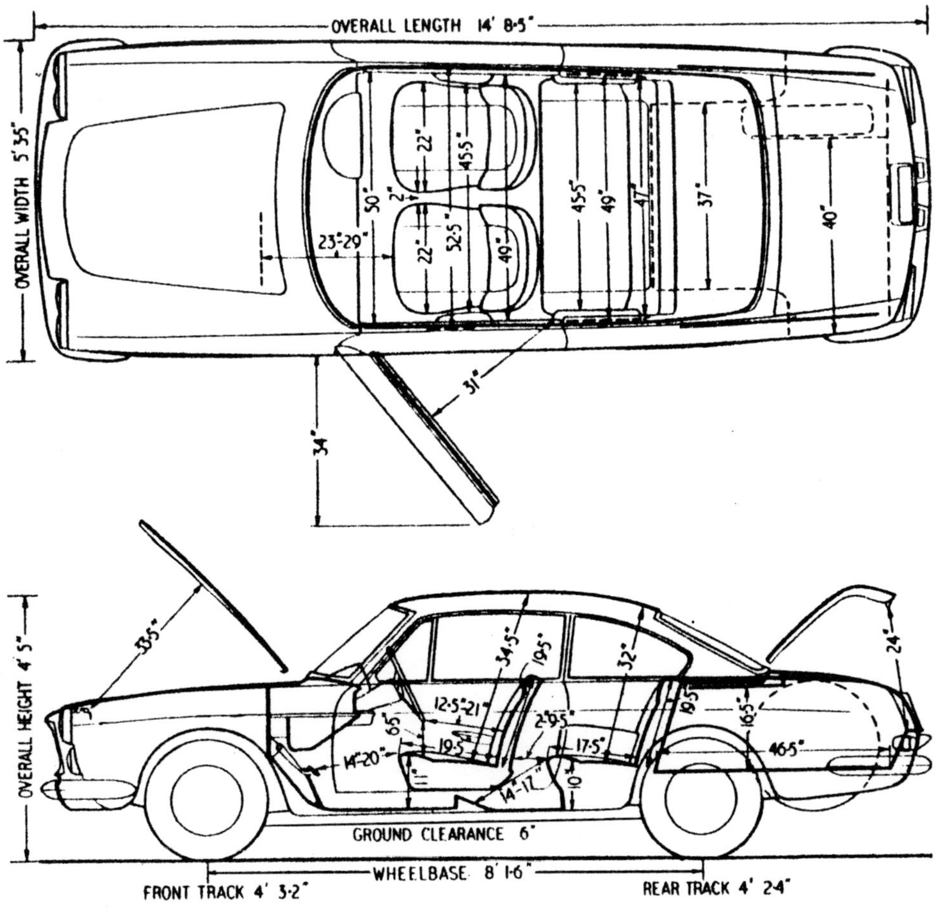

TRANSMISSION

Clutch	Fichtel and Sachs s.d.p., 8·0in. dia.
Gearbox	Four-speed, all-synchromesh
Overall ratios ...	Top 3·91, third 5·42, second 7·68, first 12·99, Reverse 14·48
Final drive ...	Hypoid bevel, 3·91 to 1

CHASSIS

Construction ...	Integral with steel body

SUSPENSION

Front	Doublé wishbones, transverse leaf spring, de Carbon telescopic dampers, anti-roll bar
Rear	Beam axle, half-elliptic leaf springs, de Carbon telescopic dampers, anti-roll bar
Steering	Gemmer worm and roller. Wheel dia. 15·9in.

BRAKES

Type	Dunlop disc front and rear with Lancia vacuum-servo
Dimensions ...	F, and R, 11in. dia. discs
Swept area ...	F, and R, 232 sq. in. Total: 464 sq. in. (364 sq. in. per ton laden)

WHEELS

Type	Pressed steel, four studs, 4·5in. wide rim
Tyres	165-15in. Michelin X or Pirelli Cinturato with tubes

EQUIPMENT

Battery	12-volt 42-amp. hr.
Headlamps ...	Carello dual system—45-40 watt
Reversing lamps ...	Two
Electric fuses ...	12
Screen wipers ...	Single speed, self-parking
Screen washer ...	Standard, vacuum operated
Interior heater ...	Standard, fresh-air type
Safety belts ...	Extra, anchorages provided
Interior trim ...	Cloth, p.v.c. headlining
Floor covering ...	Moulded rubber
Starting handle ...	No provision
Jack	Scissor type
Jacking points ...	Two each side
Other bodies ...	Saloon and convertible

MAINTENANCE

Fuel tank	10·5 Imp. gallons (no reserve)
Cooling system ...	14 pints (including heater)
Engine sump ...	10 pints SAE 20W. Change oil every 2,000 miles; Change filter element every 4,000 miles
Gearbox and final drive	4 pints SAE 90. Change oil every 6,000 miles
Grease	11 points every 2,000 miles
Tyre pressures ...	F and R, 27 p.s.i. (normal driving); F, 27; R, 30 p.s.i. (fast driving). See text

LANCIA – A High-Performance Fulvia

Unlike the standard sedan, the Fulvia 2C has no bumper overriders

TO coincide with the opening of the Turin Show tomorrow, the famous and universally respected house of Lancia introduce a supplementary version of the 1,091 c.c. vee-4 Fulvia. To be known as the type 2C, it has the same four-door saloon body as the standard model introduced at Geneva in 1963 but a considerably greater power output, as well as certain other technical modifications.

By raising the compression ratio to 9·0 from 7·8 to 1 and fitting two twin-choke Weber carburettors on a new intake manifold, power output is raised from 60 to 71 b.h.p. net at 6,000 r.p.m. Maximum torque is given as 68lb ft at 4,300 r.p.m., compared with 62 at 4,000. Fuel consumption in normal use is said to average around 34 m.p.g. A full-flow oil filter has been added. To complement the more sporting character of this model, and the engine's ability to rev faster, the indirect gear ratios have been closed up appreciably. Maximum speeds in the three indirects are given as 24, 43 and 67 m.p.h. respectively, and a top speed exceeding 90 m.p.h. is claimed. The factory's figures for acceleration include zero to 50 m.p.h. in 10·6sec and to 60 in just under 17.

Higher-geared steering and modified mountings for the sub-frame carrying engine, transmission, suspension and steering are said to have improved the car's handling, and extra braking power for reduced pedal loads results from a new friction material for the Dunlop disc pads, together with a revised double master cylinder. It has been Lancia practice for some time past to have independent hydraulic circuits for front and rear brakes on all their models.

Better insulation of the body from the noise and feel of the engine is claimed to result from the latest sub-frame mountings. Also contributing to greater passenger comfort are larger ducts for the heating and ventilation system, assisted by a more powerful fan, and the fore-and-aft length of the rear seat cushion has been extended. A rev counter with a quadrant dial supplements the standard instruments. Particularly neat and practical is the 2C's switch panel under the facia, which is hinged to swing down and expose the comprehensive fuse box.

External differences are limited to the 2C monogram on the rear panel and the discarding of bumper overriders. It is not yet known when this very intriguing newcomer will be produced with right-hand drive for the British market.

The little, narrow-angle vee-four engine, has individual camshafts for inlet and exhaust valves, and twin carburettors

Below left: Checking electrical fuses or switchgear is easy

Below right: A fuller cushion gives back-seat passengers a better ride. Front seats are the reclining type

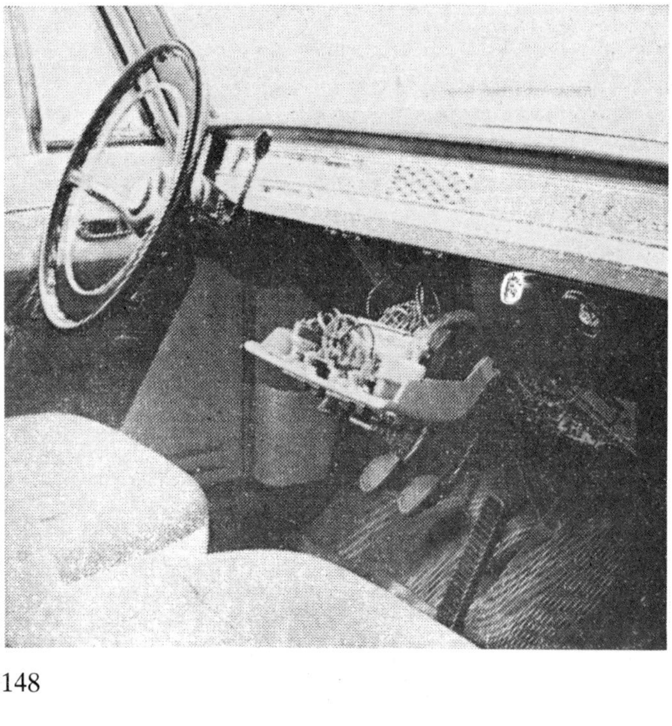

Lancia Flavia Zagato Sport 1,800 c.c.

BY including in their standard catalogue ranges a few individualistic creations by the specialist coachbuilders, the major car manufacturers of Italy broaden their own commercial scope while lending support to an important local industry. Being made in relatively small numbers, these are inevitably rather more expensive than the standard lines.

Zagato is still a quite small family business with a factory near Milan, backed by a long tradition of never-to-be-forgotten designs for sports cars. Their open "spider" 2-seaters for Alfa Romeo in the 30's were absolute classics. Lancia provide special short-wheelbase variations of their vee-6 Flaminia and flat-4 Flavia to carry the coachbuilt bodies, and in the case of the streamlined Zagato coupés tune the engines above their regular outputs.

Beauty being in the eye of the beholder, and the Zagato style for the Flavia being aggressively off-beat and controversial, it certainly does not please all the people all the time. Yet most of us liked the look of the car better and better as we grew accustomed to it, and as a provocative eye-catcher it would be hard to rival. While the æsthetics of a body have no real part in a road test, its functional efficiency certainly has. The special merits of this one lie, first, in its aerodynamic form and tidy detail on the exterior, enabling it to penetrate the air at the car's maximum speed (110-115 m.p.h., depending on conditions) with scarcely a whisper of turbulence; and, secondly, in a novel and remarkably effective system of ventilation.

But one must complain of a very restricted view of what goes on behind the car. The concave rear window is shallow, amplifies reflections, and is poorly served by the internal mirror. A dark, non-reflective trim for the shelf behind the back seat would help. Moreover, the blind rear quarters supporting the roof are wide; although external mirrors above the wings are provided, the driver's view in the one nearest him is distorted by the curved screen. Nowadays one is the more aware of restricted vision of this sort because the average standard has become so high. The view forward and to the sides is excellent.

Hinged along its top, the back window can be opened

PRICES	£	s	d
Zagato Sport coupé	2,263	0	0
Purchase tax	473	0	5
TOTAL (in G.B.)	2,736	0	5

How the Lancia Flavia Zagato Sport compares:

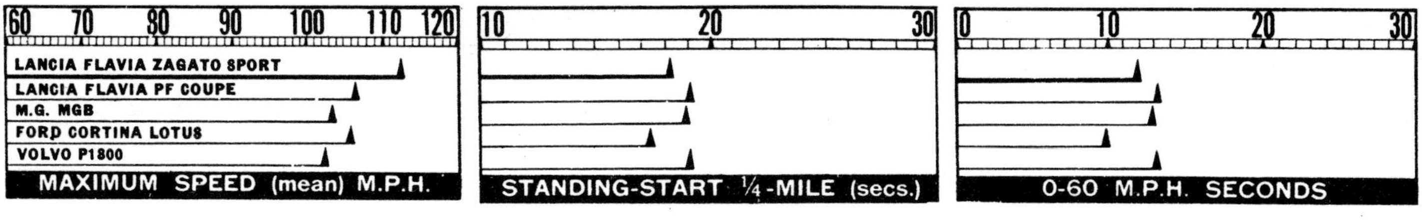

Make · LANCIA Type · Flavia Zagato Sport

(Front engine, front-wheel drive)

Manufacturer: Lancia & C., Via Vincenzo Lancia 27, Turin, Italy.
U.K. Concessionaires: Lancia Concessionaires Ltd., 16 Albemarle Street, London, W.1.

Test Conditions

Weather .... Fine, with nil wind
Temperature .... 5 deg. C. (41 deg. F.)
Barometer .... 29·44in. Hg.
Dry concrete and tarmac surfaces.

Weight

Kerb weight (with oil, water and half-full fuel tank) 20·6cwt (2,310lb-1,050kg)
Front-rear distribution, per cent F. 63; R. 37
Laden as tested .... 23·6cwt (2,646lb-1,205kg)

Turning Circles

Between kerbs .... L. 40ft 2in.; R. 37ft 1in.
Between walls .... L. 42ft 3in.; R. 39ft 3in.
Turns of steering wheel lock to lock .... 3·8

FUEL CONSUMPTION

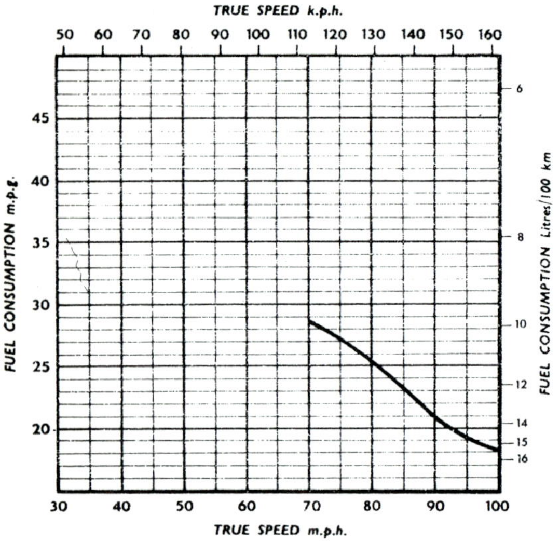

At Steady Speeds in Top

30 m.p.h. ....
40 ,, ...
50 ,, ...
60 ,, ...

Due to suspected inconsistencies in our fuel meter readings, the lower speed figures will be published in a later issue.

70 ,, ... 28·5 m.p.g.
80 ,, ... 25·3 ,,
90 ,, ... 21·7 ,,
100 ,, ... 18·0 ,,

Test Distance .... 1,013 miles

Overall .... 20·5 m.p.g. (13·8 litres/100 km.)

Estimated (DIN) .... 28·5 m.p.g. (9·9 litres/100 km.)

Normal range .... 18-24 m.p.g. (15·7-11·8 litres/100 km.)

Grade .... Premium (96–98 octane RM)

OIL CONSUMPTION (SAE 10W30) 2,700 m.p.g.

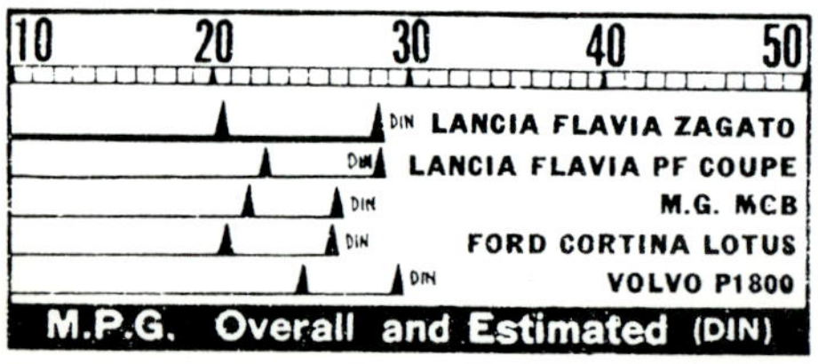

MAXIMUM SPEEDS AND ACCELERATION MEAN TIMES

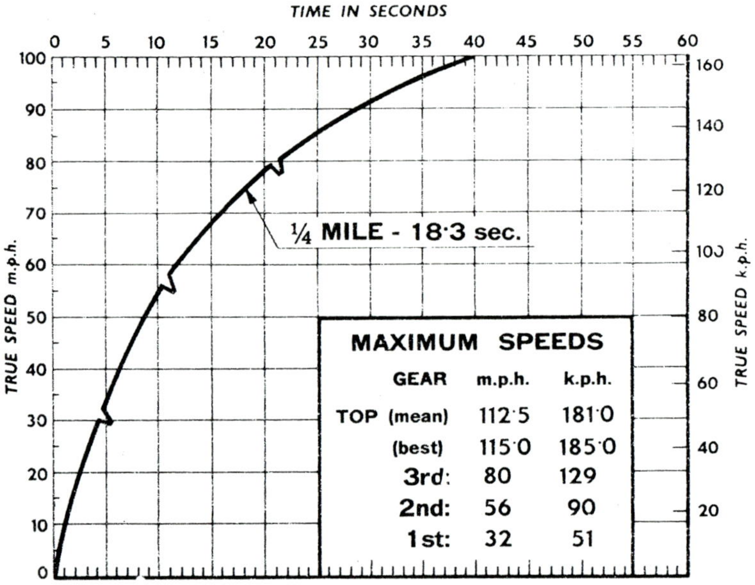

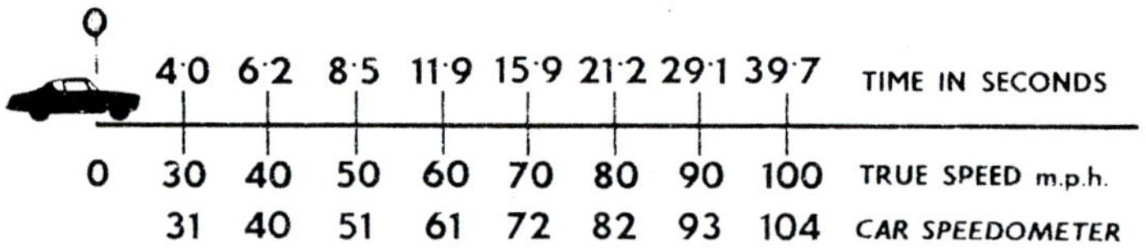

Speed range, gear ratios and time in seconds

m.p.h.	Top (3·82)	Third (5·3)	Second (7·12)	First (12·7)
10—30	—	—	—	3·3
20—40	—	7·2	4·7	—
30—50	10·7	6·2	4·8	—
40—60	9·9	6·6	—	—
50—70	10·1	7·5	—	—
60—80	11·5	9·6	—	—
70—90	14·2	—	—	—
80—100	18·5	—	—	—

BRAKES	Pedal load	Retardation	Equiv. distance
(from 30 m.p.h. in neutral)	25lb	0·25g	120ft
	50lb	0·60g	50ft
	75lb	0·75g	40ft
	85lb	0·84g	36ft
	160lb	0·91g	33·1ft
	Hand brake	0·29g	104ft

CLUTCH Pedal load and travel—40lb and 5·5in.

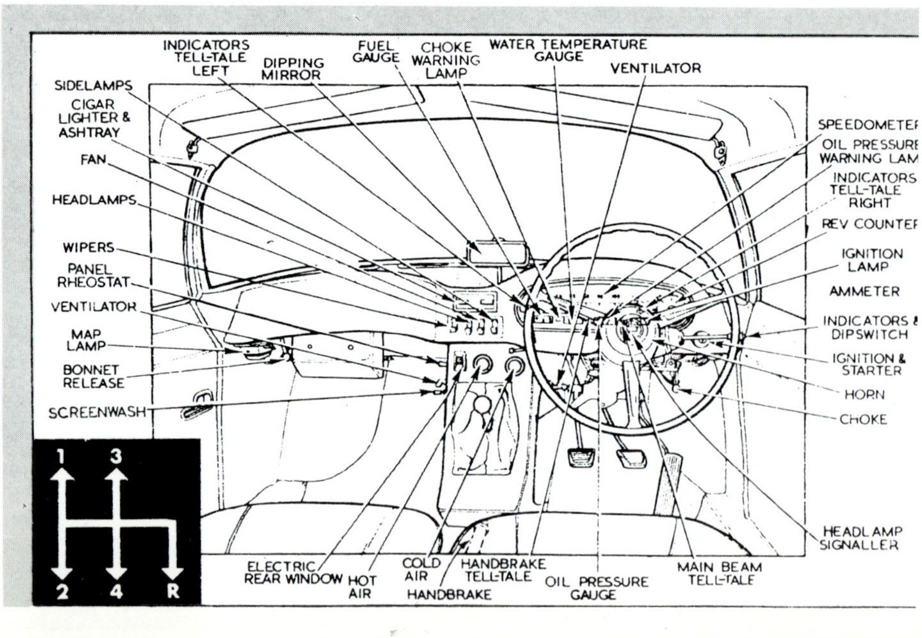

Left: Trimmed in pale plastic, the front seats have adjustable backrests and deep cushions. Door windows are unframed. The wood-rimmed steering-wheel is set rather high, and the central gear lever's arc of movement is nearly vertical.

Right: In the back is a simple but reasonably practical seat, although there is barely enough room for heads and legs

Lancia Flavia Zagato Sport . . .

two or three inches at the base, an electric motor with two-way switch within the driver's reach enabling him to adjust it while the car is moving. This aperture being in a low-pressure area, one has only to open the forward fresh air intake, directing the air current to pass through or miss the heater as required, for a consistent and unobtrusive flow to be induced. So long as the side windows are kept shut, the car's interior is maintained at a very even temperature without draught, wind road, or "mugginess," and without needing the booster fan except in crawling traffic; non-smokers in particular appreciate the manner in which tobacco fumes are carried away. Provided that the front ventilator is even partially open, the flow continues; shutting it while the back window is open immediately brings cold draughts down one's neck.

Whereas the other Flavia models (standard saloon, Pininfarina coupé and Vignale convertible) share a common engine type with single, twin-choke carburettor, the Zagato Sport version has two compound carburettors with an individual choke for each cylinder; its net output of 100 b.h.p. at 5,200 r.p.m. is 8 b.h.p. higher, and its 120 lb. ft. maximum torque compares very favourably with the single-carburettor type's 108.

Slightly higher final drive gearing (3·82 to 1, in place of 3·91) complements the extra power, light weight and low drag of the body. Unfortunately our test car arrived with only 850 miles behind it, and although the figure had reached 1,450 before performance figures were taken, Lancies need much more than this before they "free."

Nevertheless their claim of 112-113 m.p.h. top speed was reached and supported by excellent acceleration figures. Inevitably one compares the Zagato Sport with the heavier, less powerful Pininfarina coupé we tested last winter (17 January 1964); mean top speed for that car was 106·5 m.p.h. The Zagato covered the standing-start quarter-mile in 18·3sec (PF coupé 19·1) and reached 60 m.p.h. from rest in 11·9sec (13·2) 80 m.p.h. in 21·1sec (23·8) and 100 m.p.h. in 39·7 (49·1). In the indirect gears we restricted ourselves to the manufacturer's rather conservative maxima of 32, 56 and 80 m.p.h. respectively, all of which are below the recommended limit of 5,800 r.p.m. But to reach a true 115 m.p.h. in top took the revs rather higher, to about 5,900 r.p.m. in theory, although the rev counter showed about 6,200 r.p.m. Perhaps this exaggeration is a deliberate safety valve.

With a choke to each cylinder and air cleaners that do not silence much, there is a rather insistent induction "beat" when the car is accelerated hard, sounding very like a familiar sports coupé with air-cooled flat-four engine at the back. Recalling the exceptional quietness and refinement of the standard Flavia saloon, it comes as a surprise to find this one so noisy under the bonnet—but, of course, some sporting drivers prefer it that way. On the overrun back-pressure in the exhaust produces an intermittent, gravelly resonance, but with the throttles just cracked open to maintain a moderate speed the car wafts along extremely quietly. Incidentally, the Lancia's running gear is unusually free from restraining frictions, for when brought to a stop on the slightest "invisible" slope it will often start rolling.

On cold mornings the engine starts easily, sounds a bit rattly until warmed to proper running clearances, but pulls away strongly almost at once. It is docile and tractable down to low crankshaft speeds, and the transmission allows it to do this without jerking and snatching. There are no vibration periods right up to maximum revs, nor sympathetic resonances in the body roof or floor. Moreover, on motorways it rolls along extraordinarily easily and quietly for mile after mile at 105-110 m.p.h. with no real fuss or apparent strain. A refined instrument, the gearbox is very quiet-running and has unbeatable synchromesh for all forward speeds. The lever moves easily, is lightly spring-loaded across a narrow gate, and a pleasure to use. Its arc of

In the ample boot tools are stored behind a panel on the left, the spare wheel with plastic cover on the right. Powerful reversing lamps are included in the rear lamp groups

Side windows that extend into the roof panel, and a concave rear window hinged for ventilation, give the Zagato body individuality—if a bit bizarre

travel is near-vertical, which soon seems natural enough.

While the parking brake could not quite hold the car pointing either way on our 1-in-3 test hill, there was sufficient power and clutch "bite" to take it away from here forwards or backwards. The clutch, which functions smoothly and progressively, also stood up well to the usual energetic acceleration testing.

If our test car was typical, as we understand, the balance of braking between front and rear wheels needs urgent attention. As it is, the back wheels lock and slide far too easily, whereupon the car's directional stability is usually lost, even when the roads are dry.

While taking brake test figures, about 0·8*g* was the limit before the rear wheels locked; doubling pressure on the pedal (at 160lb) to get the best possible *g* figure still did not lock the front ones. With four people on board, putting more weight on the back wheels, one can do much better of course. Rumour has it that competition drivers halve the pad area in contact with the rear wheel discs to correct the balance. Apart from this the brakes are all one would wish—powerful, progressive, and with no fade problem.

Our drivers found the front-wheel-drive Flavia Sport exceptionally sensitive to tyre pressures, and were unhappy with it on the recommended 28·5 p.s.i. all round. After trying various combinations, we sided with a private owner who recommended 27 p.s.i. in the front ones, 30 p.s.i. in the back. While the car's cornering power is obviously very high indeed, one has to "live" with it for a time to gain full confidence and get the best out of it safely. Fast drivers, accustomed to the fine directional control and stabilizing effects that power applied to the rear wheels can give them, inevitably have to learn a new technique for this one, remembering for instance that it is not so easy to recover if one steps beyond the limit of front-tyre adhesion. The plus qualities of Michelin X covers are well enough known, but their final breakaway is rather rapid. They are also harsh when the car is moving slowly, thumping hard over cat's eyes and minor blemishes in the road surface, but roll very quietly at higher speeds, when the car's directional stability is sure and relaxed.

Front-wheel drive plays no tricks with Flavia's steering mechanism as such, for it does not tug or jerk on sharp lock, nor become particularly heavy at low speeds. Although the gearing is fairly low with nearly four turns of the wheel lock-to-lock (for wide turning circles that would make Vincenzo Lancia turn in his grave), the response is quicker than this might suggest. Self-centring action, weak when the car is moving slowly, becomes quite adequate at normal touring speeds. The steering-wheel is placed rather high and offset considerably to the right. With the driving seat well back it is a bit remote. Its wooden rim looks well, gives a sure grip and never feels icy cold.

Virtually roll-free cornering and a quite soft and comfortable ride, with damping that is positive without being suggestive, result from the Flavia suspension arrangement, which has a transverse leaf and double wishbones at the front, a lightweight "dead" axle on half-elliptic springs behind, and anti-roll bars at each end. Over certain indifferent surfaces the seat springs seem to get into phase with the road springs, and become somewhat bouncy, but generally are comfortable and give good, well-defined support. The car rode very well over the special *pavé* and washboard surfaces with no chronic body creaks or rattles and the structure gives an impression of great strength.

A good pedal layout allows heel-and-toe operation of accelerator and brake, and leaves plenty of space for the left foot beside the clutch, the pendant levers for this and the brakes being long and moving through logical arcs. The centre boss of the steering-wheel flashes the headlamp dipped beams, an arrangement less useful at night than in daylight, as one cannot signal except when driving on side-lamps only. Around the boss is a small annular ring for sounding powerful twin air horns.

A row of four identical black and white rocking switches control screenwipers, headlamp low beams, heater fan and parking lamps—in that order. They have no means of identification, and it is all too easy to lose the headlamps, for instance, when intending to switch off the wipers. One separate lighting switch remote from the rest would be a safer arrangement. Main or low beams are selected by pressing a repeater button in the end of the indicator stalk, a familiar Lancia feature and perhaps the best arrangement of all. While four main beams give a splendid range and spread of illumination, the two dipped ones are restricted by British standards, putting one at a disadvantage on busy roads.

Inside the body there are lamps beneath each extremity of the facia panel, and beneath the bonnet are two festoon bulbs. Single-speed wipers begin to lift from 80 m.p.h. upwards, and the press-button for the vacuum-operated

Two oval air filters indicate where the carburettors are—and hence the horizontally opposed cylinders below them. Other items in this view include the radiator shutters, and dual-circuit brake master cylinders beside their vacuum servo

sprays is somewhat remote, to the left of the substantial structure beneath the facia from which the gearlever sprouts. Beside it is a rheostat switch for the instrument panel lamps, which are not strong enough. A ribbon-type speedometer, although giving fairly accurate readings while the car was accelerating, was sluggish and inaccurate while speed was dropping. Beneath it are gauges for fuel contents (with low-level warning lamp), water temperature, oil pressure and dynamo charge. Despite the thermostatically controlled radiator shutters, we never saw the thermometer needle move far from the low-temperature end of the scale. Details of the heating and ventilation arrangements include rotary handwheels for temperature control and for regulating fresh-air intake but to direct full blast to the screen one must close small flaps either side of the centre structure—remote and difficult to find in a hurry, and crude by today's standards. One cannot have cool air coming up while warm air is being fed downwards. However, as we commented earlier, the overall efficiency of the system is extremely high. One would welcome more stowage space for travelling odds and ends inside the car, there being no glove locker in the facia, but merely small and inadequate pockets in the doors.

Like all current Lancias, the Zagato coupé has automatic red lamps in the door trailing edges. Trim of this car was in a pale plastic which quickly became grubby, but was easily cleaned off with a damp leather. Above the waistline the interior, including padded roof trim and all paintwork, was in black, which looked well and practical. There is nothing fancy or decorative about the neatly finished interior.

While headroom in the front is adequate except for the very tall, in the back there is none to spare, hinged sun visors for the curved side windows getting in the way unless dropped down. The passenger compartment as a whole is free from dangerous projections, and the door catches are recessed; there is ample resilient padding below the facia and built-in attachments for safety harness are provided.

A surprisingly roomy luggage boot houses the spare wheel vertically beneath a plastic cover. The two keys provided—one for the ignition and doors, the other for boot and fuel filler flap—have blue and white plastic grips respectively for easy identification. Exterior paint finish is excellent, while its smooth shape and low build make it easy to wash.

Under the bonnet one finds plenty of evidence of typical Lancia engineering detail, and all the accessories are obviously good quality products. Twelve fuses protect the electrical circuits, and are housed in a convenient box below the dash on the passenger's side.

At £2,736 (including P.T.) the Zagato Sport is beyond the pockets of many who would appreciate its strong character and special qualities. For that money, of course, one could buy cars that are faster, quieter, roomier, more luxurious—what you will. However, the world has not yet run out of wealthy connoisseurs with an appreciative eye for the highly individualistic products for which the Lancia factory has long been renowned.

Specification: Lancia Flavia Zagato Sport

PERFORMANCE DATA

Top gear m.p.h. per 1,000 r.p.m.	19·5
Mean piston speed at max. power	2,520 ft/min.
Engine revs. at mean max. speed	5,800 r.p.m.
B.h.p. per ton laden	84·8

ENGINE

Cylinders	4, horizontally opposed
Cooling system	Water: pump, fan and thermostat, automatic radiator shutters
Bore	88mm (3·46in.)
Stroke	74mm (2·91in.)
Displacement	1,800 c.c. (109·8 cu. in.)
Valve gear	Overhead, pushrods and rockers, two camshafts
Compression ratio	9·0-to-1
Carburettors	Two Solex twin-choke C32PAIA8
Fuel pump	Bendix electric
Oil filter	Fram full-flow, renewable element
Max. power	100 b.h.p. (net) at 5,200 r.p.m.
Max. torque	120 lb. ft. (net) at 3,000 r.p.m.

▼ *Scale: 0·3in. to 1ft. Cushions uncompressed.*

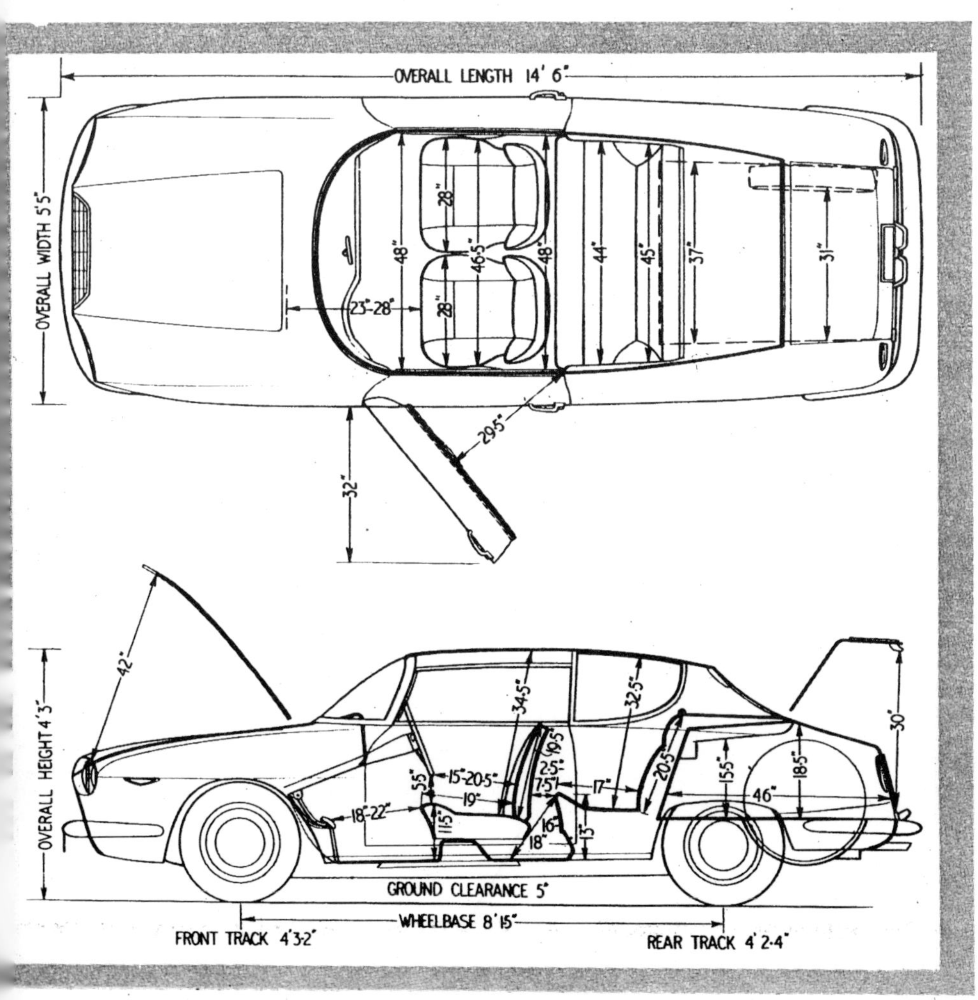

TRANSMISSION

Clutch	Fichtel and Sachs s.d.p., 8 in. dia.
Gearbox	Four-speed, all-synchromesh
Gear ratios	Top 1·0, Third 1·39, Second 1·86, First 3·33, Reverse 3·71
Final drive	Hypoid bevel, 3·82-to-1

CHASSIS

Construction	Integral, with aluminium body panels on steel frame

SUSPENSION

Front	Double wishbones, transverse leaf spring, de Carbon telescopic dampers, anti-roll bar
Rear	Beam axle, half-elliptic leaf springs, de Carbon telescopic dampers, anti-roll bar
Steering	Gemmer-France, worm and roller
Turns	Lock-to-lock 3·8. Wheel dia. 16in.

BRAKES

Make and Type	Dunlop discs F and R, with Lancia vacuum servo. Independent circuits F and R
Dimensions	F and R 11in. dia.
Total swept area	496 sq. in. (421 sq. in. per ton laden)

WHEELS

Type	Pressed steel with perforated discs, four studs. 4·5in. wide rim
Tyres	165—15in. Michelin X with tubes

EQUIPMENT

Battery	12-volt 42-amp. hr.
Generator	Marelli 62F 300W
Headlamps	Carello dual system, 40-45 watt
Reversing lamps	Two, standard
Electric fuses	12
Screen wipers	Single-speed self-parking
Screen washer	Trico suction, standard
Interior heater	Fresh air, standard
Safety belts	Extra, anchorages provided
Interior trim	P.v.c. seats, cloth headlining
Floor covering	Carpet
Starting handle	No provision
Jack	Scissors type
Jacking points	Two each side in body sills

MAINTENANCE

Fuel tank	10·5 Imp. gallons (48 litres) (with low-level warning lamp)
Cooling system	14 pints (7·8 litres) (including heater)
Engine sump	12 pints (7·1 litres) SAE 10W30. Change oil every 2,500 miles. Change filter element every 5,000 miles
Gearbox and Final Drive	4·5 pints SAE EP 90. Change oil every 7,500 miles
Grease	11 points every 2,500 miles
Tyre pressures	F 27, R 30 p.s.i. (all conditions)

SOMEHOW that rusty, dishevelled old forefront poking through the rain-sodden shrubbery seemed to be taking a last, despairing look for someone to rescue it from its plight before decay and corrosion could swallow it completely. A broken lance—*Lancia* in Italian—a connoisseur's piece bearing the tattered remains of a once-magnificent convertible from the proud house of Pininfarina, *circa* 1938.

Michael Scott and I were on the look-out for spares for our Lancia Asturas, and here was the very thing. However beautiful once, it was clearly beyond restoration—or was it? When towed into the light of day, the long, supremely elegant form still caught one's breath. We could not bear to dismantle it, and for months it lay dormant in Michael's garage.

At one of the Continental shows I handed a photograph of it to Signor Pininfarina the elder: "If your friend would care to put the mechanical parts in working order and drive this car to my factory," he said, "I shall make the body like new for him for no charge." This, then, was to be a modern fairy tale—the sort of happy chance that most of us can only dream about.

More months passed while the engine and chassis received a thorough overhaul, and eventually the day came when the old Astura, now sound in wind and limb but

A FATHERLY

1 From nose to tail the old Lancia's tapered form, with lamps to match, is a paragon of the panel beater's art. The four-piece vee-screen divides to fold flat

2 As it was found, the old splendour sadly faded

3 Seat trim in soft brown leather includes plaited backrests and folding centre armrests, and new curved glasses had to be moulded for the side windows

shabby as a tramp, could set off on the long haul south to Turin.

At the factory the foreman of the experimental body shop, to be entrusted with this formidable task, came out to survey the worst; his face fell a mile: "But this is impossible!" he pleaded. "Nevertheless," said Dott. Giorgio Colombo, Signor Pininfarina's right-hand-man, "it is our President's wish that this car should be made like new." Somewhat embarrassed, the owner retreated with a silent prayer that they would not decide, after all, that the old car had passed the point of no return. From time to time I brought him encouraging messages from Dott. Colombo, and even from the President's own lips, when we met at functions.

Eighteen months passed before he received a telegram summoning him to Turin to take delivery. He tore down with his friend John Bowman in a Type 57C Bugatti, certain that so renowned a firm would have made a good job of it, yet half-anxious that they might have had to improvise here and there. Signor Pininfarina was there in person to hand the car over. It was to all intents and purposes new, not a restoration job. Not a detail had been overlooked, no pains or expense spared to reproduce the original in exactitude. Henceforth the old Astura will be preserved as a tribute to a master craftsman's past achievements, and to his present generosity. **R. B.**

INTEREST

HOW PININFARINA TOOK PITY ON AN OLD COACHBUILDING MASTERPIECE AND DIRECTED ITS RENAISSANCE

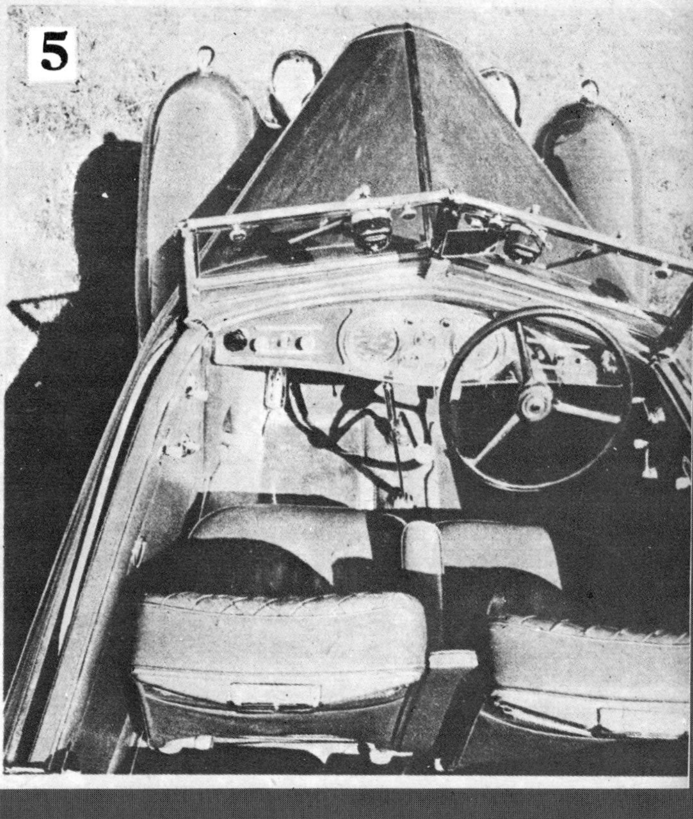

The power-operated hood is now flawlessly smooth and tastefully lined inside, while the beetle-shaped tail carries a supplementary luggage rack **4**

On the seat backs ashtrays are set in inlaid wood, and beneath them are plaited leather hand-holds **5**

Enormously long, in the fashion of the late '30s, the bonnet covers a compact narrow-angle vee-8 of just under 3 litres. Even the wheel discs are new, specially made to the original pattern **6**

PHOTOGRAPHY: MICHAEL COOPER

Autocar

ROAD TEST

NUMBER 2105

Lancia Fulvia Coupé 1,216 c.c.

AT A GLANCE: Exclusive Italian coupé with front-wheel-drive and vee-4 engine. 80 b.h.p. engine gives 100 m.p.h. performance. Superb, light steering and excellent road-holding with no f.w.d. effects. Large, powerful disc brakes fade-free and light. Practical rather than luxurious interior; heater disappointing. Precision car, unique in the market.

MANUFACTURER

Lancia & Cie, Via Vincenzo Lancia 27, Turin, Italy.

BRITISH CONCESSIONAIRES

Lancia (England) Ltd., Lancia Works, Ealing Rd., Alperton, Middlesex.

PRICES

Basic	£1,211 0s 0d
Purchase Tax	£279 4s 10d
Total (in G.B.)	£1,490 4s 10d

PERFORMANCE SUMMARY

Mean maximum speed	100 m.p.h
Standing start ¼-mile	20·0 sec
0-60 m.p.h.	15·8 sec
30-70 m.p.h. (through gears)	16·3 sec
Overall fuel consumption	28·3 m.p.g.
Miles per tankful	240

SMALL Lancias are still a rare sight on British roads; there are two versions of the Fulvia imported at the moment plus four types of the slightly larger Flavia, all with front wheel drive. The Fulvia saloon has similar chunky lines to the Flavia, but in true Lancia tradition its engine is a narrow-angle vee-4, canted over at 45deg to the left in the car and having an overhead camshaft for each set of valves. The engine is mounted ahead of the front wheels, which are driven through the same robust gearbox as is used on the 1,800 c.c. Flavia.

The coupé version of the Fulvia is 6in. shorter than the saloon and is built on a 5in. shorter wheelbase. It weighs 1½cwt less, but at 18·6cwt unladen is no stripling; the cylinder bore of the coupé engine is 4mm larger, giving a capacity of 1,216 c.c. instead of 1,091 c.c. Power output is 80 b.h.p. net at 6,000 r.p.m. (9 more than the saloon) and peak torque comes high in the rev range at 4,000 r.p.m.

Despite this high specific output and sporting engine characteristics, the coupé is as docile a little town-carriage as one could wish for; yet when the driver wants to hurry it sings up to peak revs with remarkable smoothness and a surprising turn of speed for such a small machine. Two twin-choke Solex carburettors are fitted, and the best technique when starting from cold is to use full rich mixture and leave the accelerator alone. Usually the engine fires at once and idles with a loud hiss from the strangled induction. Almost immediately the choke lever can be pushed fully back, and it is not normally needed again throughout the day's use of the car. According to the gauge on our car, the oil pressure exceeds 70 p.s.i. (top calibration) at all normal running speeds.

Suddenly opening the throttles from really low engine speeds causes a gulp and splutter, but at all other times pick-up is smooth and free from hesitation. To about 4,000 r.p.m. there is not a great deal of punch, but by 4,500 r.p.m. the engine is beginning to give of its best and from then on, to the red warning marked between 6,000 and 6,200 r.p.m., the slight exhaust and cam-shaft noise rises in a smooth hum. We found it paid during acceleration tests to go slightly beyond this limit to 6,500 r.p.m.

A typically "soft" Lancia clutch restricts full-throttle standing starts, and our acceleration figures would

Autocar Road Test 2105

MAKE: **LANCIA**

TYPE: **Fulvia Coupé**

WEIGHT

Kerb weight (with oil, water and half-full fuel tank): 18·6 cwt (2,073lb-940kg)
Front-rear distribution, per cent F, 63·9; R, 36·1
Laden as tested .. 21·6 cwt (2,409lb-1,092kg)

TURNING CIRCLES

Between kerbs .. L, 36ft 5in.; R, 34ft 5in.
Between walls .. L, 38ft 3in.; R, 36ft 3in.
Steering wheel turns lock to lock .. .. 4·2

PERFORMANCE DATA

Top gear m.p.h. per 1,000 r.p.m. .. .. 16·2
Mean piston speed at max. power .. 2,635ft/min
Engine revs at mean max. speed 6,170 r.p.m.
B.h.p. per ton laden .. .. 74·1

OIL CONSUMPTION

SAE 10W/40 .. .. .. 500 miles per pint

FUEL CONSUMPTION

At constant speeds

30 m.p.h.	58·0 m.p.g.	70 m.p.h.	36·1 m.p.g.
40 ,,	56·4 ,,	80 ,,	32·8 ,,
50 ,,	47·6 ,,	90 ,,	27·8 ,,
60 ,,	41·7 ,,		

Overall m.p.g. .. 28·3 (10·0 litres/100km)
Normal range m.p.g. 26-35 (10·9-8·1 litres/100km)
Test distance (corrected) .. 1,502 miles
Estimated (DIN) m.p.g. 32·8 (8·6 litres/100km)
Grade .. .. Super Premium (99·4-101·7 RM)

TEST CONDITIONS

Weather .. .. Dry with 0-5 m.p.h. wind
Temperature .. .. 14 deg. C. (58 deg. F)
Barometer .. .. .. 29·5in. Hg.
Surfaces .. .. Dry concrete and tarmac

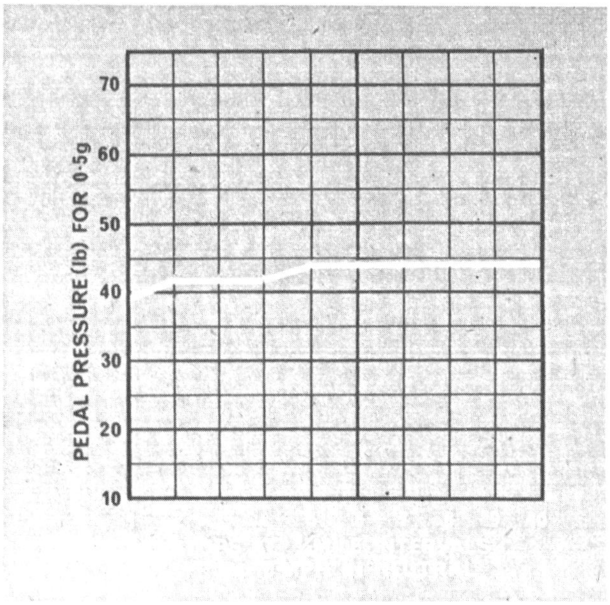

Speed range, gear ratios and time in seconds

m.p.h.	Top (3·9)	Third (5·5)	Second (8·5)	First (14·3)
10—30	—	9·9	5·9	3·8
20—40	14·7	8·7	4·6	—
30—50	14·8	8·7	4·5	—
40—60	15·3	9·3	—	—
50—70	17·7	10·0	—	—
60—80	21·2	—	—	—
70—90	28·9	—	—	—

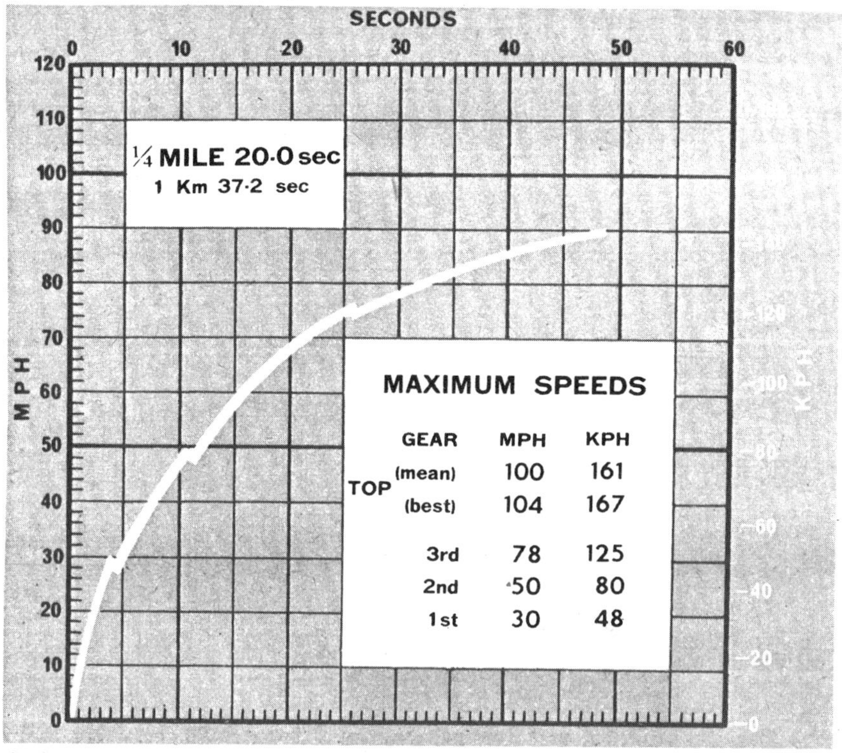

4·7	7·8	10·7	15·8	21·0	31·3	48·8					TIME IN SECONDS
30	40	50	60	70	80	90	100	110	120		TRUE SPEED MPH
31	42	52	62	73	84	95	106				INDICATED MPH

BRAKES	**Pedal load**	**Retardation**	**Equiv. distance**
(from 30 m.p.h.	25lb	0·26g	116ft
in neutral)	50lb	0·56g	54ft
	75lb	0·82g	37ft
	85lb	0·90g	33·5ft
Handbrake		0·34g	89ft

CLUTCH Pedal load and travel—40lb and 6in.

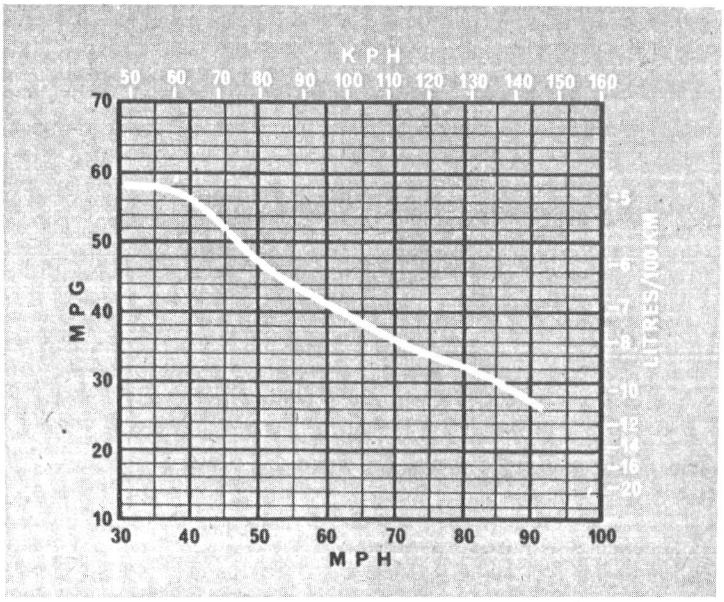

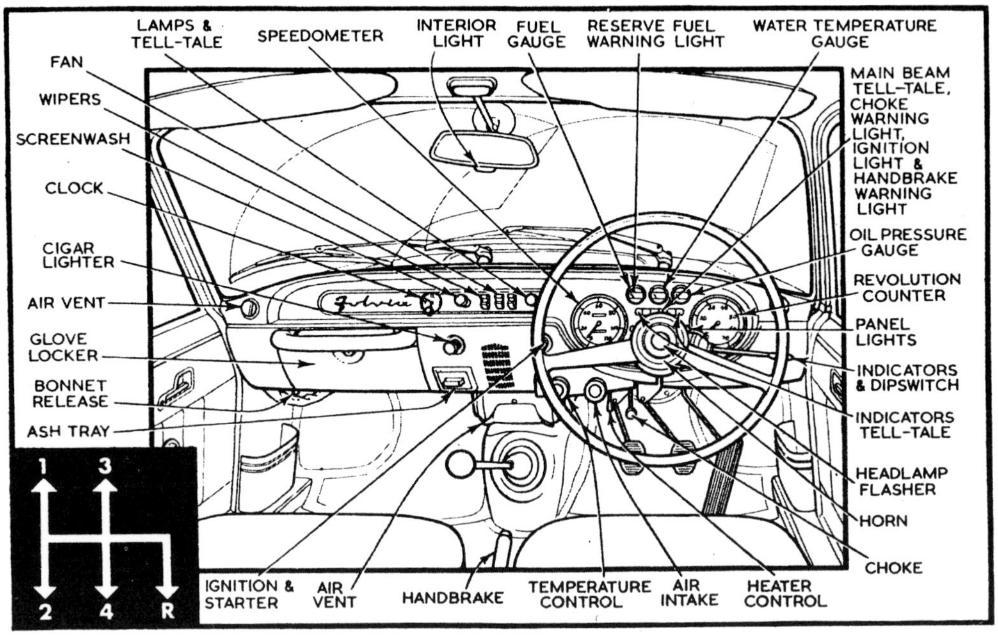

certainly be improved with more positive "bite." During sprint getaways the clutch continues to slip up to 20 m.p.h., and full-throttle gear changes also cause some delay. On the road this behaviour is barely noticed, and the smooth take-up is a characteristic to be preferred on a touring car. Despite the difficulties of balancing a vee-4 engine, the power unit of the Fulvia is completely free from vibration periods and one has no qualms over using all the rev range regularly for maximum performance.

Although there is a rather wide gap between 2nd and 3rd gears, the long, rigid gear lever sprouting out of the bulkhead directly behind the gearbox makes changing very positive. Movements up and down between the gears are long, but the gate is narrow, with spring loading towards top and third. Occasionally we had difficulty in selecting first at rest, but a second dab on the clutch would always settle any difficulty. Even though the gearbox and final drive are near the floorboards, and all gears are indirect, there is no noticeable transmission noise.

Fuel consumption

Fuel consumption figures recorded at steady speeds were excellent, with a surprising 58 m.p.g. at 30 m.p.h. Even at 70 m.p.h., 36·1 m.p.g. was measured, giving an estimated (DIN) overall consumption of nearly 33 m.p.g. The actual measured overall figure was rather less, yet still a creditable 28·3 and a mixture of commuting trips and journeys in no particular hurry returned better than 30 m.p.g. The compression ratio is 9 to 1, but the concessionaires urged us to use super premium fuel, which rather offset the otherwise excellent economy of this 100 m.p.h. car.

The whole of the Lancia range has been developed around radial-ply tyres, and the Fulvia was shod with Michelin X. All aspects of the road behaviour reached a very high standard indeed and it was extremely difficult to fault the Fulvia in this respect. Most testers could not detect any front-wheel-drive effects at all, and there is no change in attitude between power-on and power-off in the middle of a corner.

Perhaps the really outstanding feature of the car is its ultra-light and positive steering. From lock to lock, 4·2 turns are needed on a 35ft turning circle, but there is no impression of low gearing and the little car always follows the chosen line perfectly and with fine, quick response.

Somehow Lancia have practically eliminated the characteristic front-wheel-drive understeer and the cornering of the Fulvia is as near neutral as makes no difference. At high cornering speeds there is some roll, but the tyres seem to stay firmly stuck to the road, regardless.

Like other Lancias, the Fulvia has an excellent main road ride, gliding smoothly and quietly over minor bumps, ridges and waves. On the

Accessibility of plugs, battery, distributor and carburettors is good; the camshaft covers are finished in black crackle enamel

Left: The straightforward cockpit arrangement with its elegant woodrim steering wheel, handsome dashboard and the hefty-looking but precise gearlever. Right: The reclining front seats are very comfortable but accommodation behind is strictly "occasional"

Lancia Fulvia Coupé . . .

M.I.R.A. *pavé* track the car felt impressively solid, although not outstanding in its ability to absorb the considerable disturbances, and above 45 m.p.h. some correction was needed to keep the nose pointing straight. Corrugations were completely smoothed out at about 60 m.p.h., but the long-pitch waves caused the front suspension to bottom at only 40 m.p.h. The shorter-wheelbase of the coupé loses something to the saloon on this test.

Brakes

The Fulvia is generously equipped with Dunlop disc brakes on all four wheels with the pads rubbing no less than 380 sq. in. of disc for every laden ton. Such stopping power is probably unrivalled by any other production car and naturally the brakes were impeccable. With servo assistance, pedal pressures were light, progressive and always reassuring. There was negligible fade during our severe testing, and throughout our 1,500-mile test there was no loss of efficiency at any time.

Surprisingly for a car with rear discs and 64 per cent of its weight on the front wheels, the handbrake recorded 0·34g when used on its own from 30 m.p.h. It only just held the laden car on a 1-in-3 test hill and a restart was not possible because of clutch slip.

The position behind the wheel is typically "arm-stretch-Italian," but there is ample fore and aft seat adjustment for all shapes and sizes of driver and the backrest can be set at different angles as well. There are twin ventilation slits in each backrest, and a quick-release catch for tipping it forward without losing the setting of the backrest angle.

Really the Fulvia coupé is little more than a 2+2, for the back seat is small with restricted headroom. When tall people move their front seats back, the rear legroom practically disappears, so for family motoring it is a matter of compromising on the space available.

Many British buyers might expect leather seats and a carpeted floor for close to £1,500, but the coupé has pvc seats and moulded rubber mats. There is, however, no compromise in the instruments provided. Let into a French-polished wooden panel are a large circular speedometer and rev counter with fuel level, oil pressure and temperature gauges between them. A red warning lamp is built into the fuel gauge to warn when the level is getting low. In the Italian fashion, the steering wheel boss incorporates a centre button to flash the lamps, ringed by another one to sound the strident horns. As is cus-

Tools are neatly stowed inside the spare wheel

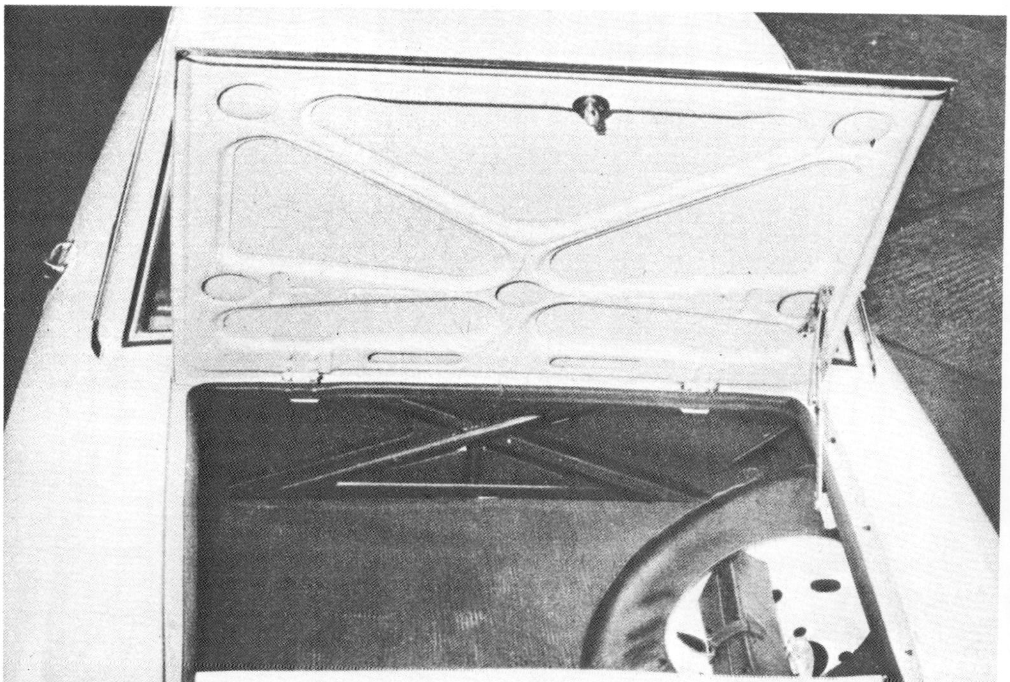

Clean lines of the Fulvia Coupé attract much attention everywhere

TOTAL PRICE	
	£1,490
	Discontinued
	£1,553
	£1,016
	£1,001

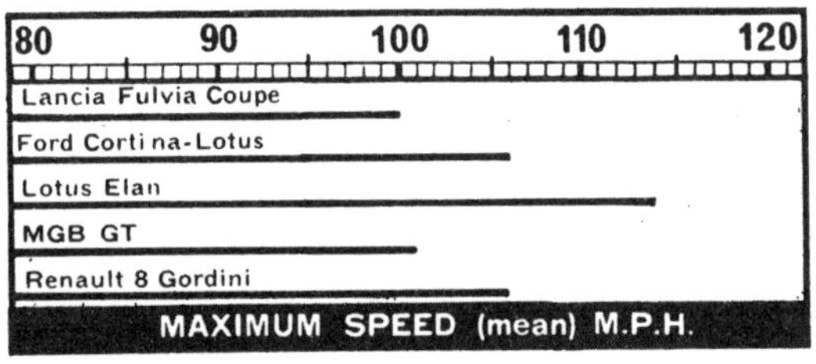

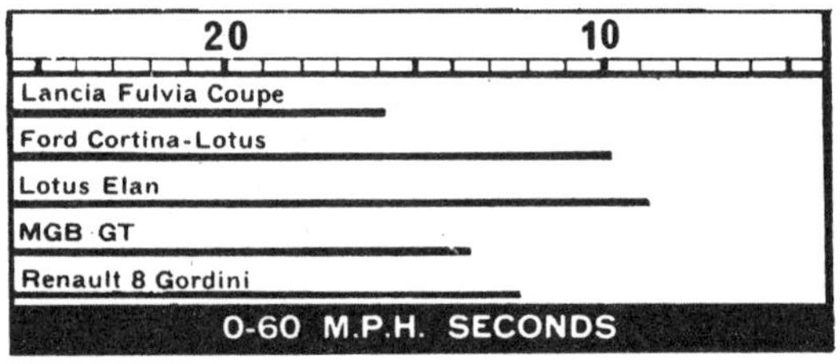

HOW THE LANCIA FULVIA COUPÉ COMPARES:

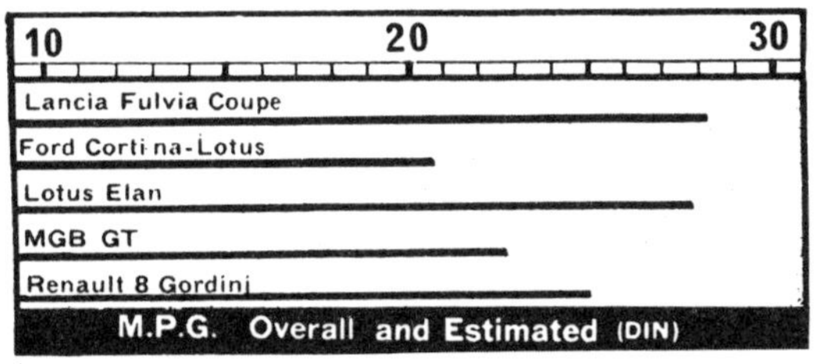

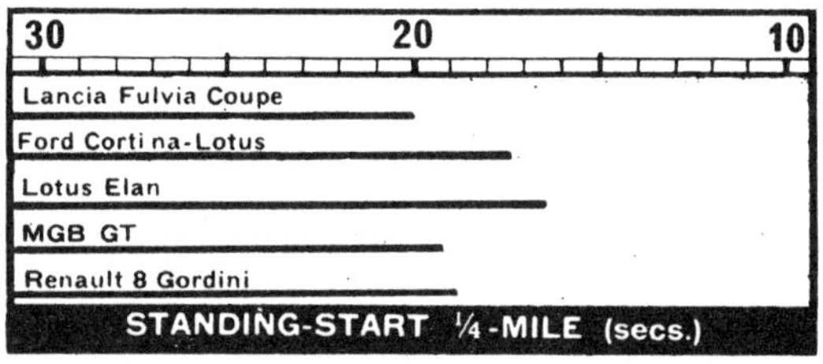

tomary on the Continent, only dipped beams can be flashed.

Headlamp dipping and the indicators are controlled by a single stalk on the steering column. Two unlabelled rocker switches in the centre of the panel operate single-speed wipers and the heater fan which is extremely noisy but vigorous. A third is a spare in case an accessory such as a fog lamp is fitted later.

Ventilation and heating on the Fulvia are disappointing. Two round handwheels below the facia control the air flow and temperature, while a separate lever regulates the rate of hot water circulation in the matrix. However, there never seemed to be enough air of any sort, even when the rear quarterlights were opened as extractors. Window misting was difficult to prevent in heavy rain, and the blower seemed to be needed all the time. Tiny cool-air nozzles at each end of the facia never produced any noticeable breeze.

Baggage Space

There is not much space to store oddments in the Lancia. Only a small glove locker can hide valuables, and there are a couple of open boxes alongside the foot wells on each side of the car. The boot is large for such a small car and its floor is covered with rubber matting. The spare wheel is shielded to protect delicate luggage.

Another traditional Lancia feature is a red warning lamp let into the trailing edge of each door; these switch on automatically as a warning at the kerbside as soon as a door is opened. There are automatic inspection lamps under the bonnet and in the boot; these work only in conjunction with the master lighting switch. Twin Siem headlamps have a sharp cut-off when dipped, but a really long range and wide spread on full beams.

Lancia build their cars to run well and to be easy to maintain. Under the bonnet the layout is delightfully clean and accessible; there are a lot of shiny aluminium castings and all parts needing attention are at the top and easy to reach. The four plugs are in the top of the cylinder head, while the carburettors dominate the middle of the bonnet opening. The distributor is above and behind the carburettors and the long flexible dipstick is between the carburettors and the offset radiator. The battery is well placed alongside the engine, but the oil filter is rather tucked away. All the electric fuses and control boxes are grouped together in a tray under the facia which can be slid out on to one's lap for attention. When we decided to adjust the clutch free play early in the test, we were surprised and pleased to find the release lever could be reached from above the engine and did not even need a spanner; literally a 2min. job.

For a long time there have been pleas for a quality car that is not large, and this little Lancia more than fills the bill. One has only to open the bonnet to see where the money goes, and many aspects of the car's character can be likened to a precision watch. The exclusive styling attracts a lot of attention and the practical package size make the Fulvia an efficient car for threading through traffic or tucking into a parking space. Away from the towns, its true breeding begins to show and the coupé becomes a fast touring car with few rivals. ■

SPECIFICATION: LANCIA FULVIA COUPE, FRONT ENGINE, FRONT-WHEEL DRIVE

ENGINE

Cylinders	4, narrow-vee
Cooling system	Water, pump, fan and thermostat
Bore	76mm (2·99in.)
Stroke	67mm (2·64in.)
Displacement	1,216 c.c. (74·2 cu. in.)
Valve gear	Overhead camshaft, needle tappets, rockers
Compression ratio	9·0-to-1
Carburettors	Two twin-choke Solex C32PHH
Fuel pump	Fispa mechanical
Oil filter	Carello, full flow, renewable element
Max. power	80 b.h.p. (net) at 6,000 r.p.m.
Max. torque	76·6 lb ft (net) at 4,000 r.p.m.

TRANSMISSION

Clutch	Fichtel & Sachs, single-dry-plate
Gearbox	4-speed, all-synchromesh
Gear ratios	Top 1·00, Third 1·42, Second 2·18, First 3·69, Reverse 4·11
Final drive	Hypoid bevel, 3·91

CHASSIS and BODY

Construction	Integral, with all-steel body

SUSPENSION

Front	Independent, wishbones, transverse leaf spring, anti-roll bar, telescopic dampers
Rear	Dead axle, half-elliptic leaf springs, Panhard rod, anti-roll bar, telescopic dampers

STEERING

Type	Worm and roller. Wheel dia. 14 in.

BRAKES

Make and type	Dunlop, disc front and rear
Servo	Lancia
Dimensions	F, 10·15in. dia. discs; R, 10·5in. dia. discs
Swept area	F, 205 sq. in.; R, 205 sq. in. Total 410 sq. in. (380 sq. in. per ton laden)

WHEELS

Type	Pressed steel disc, 4·5in. wide rim
Tyres	Michelin X tubed. Size 145—14in.

EQUIPMENT

Battery	12-volt 42-amp. hr.
Generator	Bosch, 360-watt
Headlamps	Siem 45/40-watt
Reversing lamp	Standard
Electric fuses	10
Screen wipers	Single speed, self-parking
Screen washer	Standard, manual plunger
Interior heater	Standard, fresh air
Safety belts	Extra, anchorages built in
Interior trim	Pvc seats, pvc headlining
Floor covering	Rubber mats
Starting handle	No provision
Jack	Scissor type
Jacking points	4, under body sills
Other bodies	Zagato Coupé

MAINTENANCE

Fuel tank	8·5 Imp. gallons (no reserve) (38 litres)
Cooling system	11·2 pints (including heater) (6·3 litres)
Engine sump	7 pints (4 litres) SAE 10W-30. Change oil every 4,300 miles. Change filter element every 4,300 miles
Gearbox and Final drive	4·5 pints SAE EP-90. Change oil every 8,600 miles
Grease	6 points every 2,000 miles, 5 points every 4,000 miles
Tyre pressures	F, 26; R, 26 p.s.i. (normal driving)

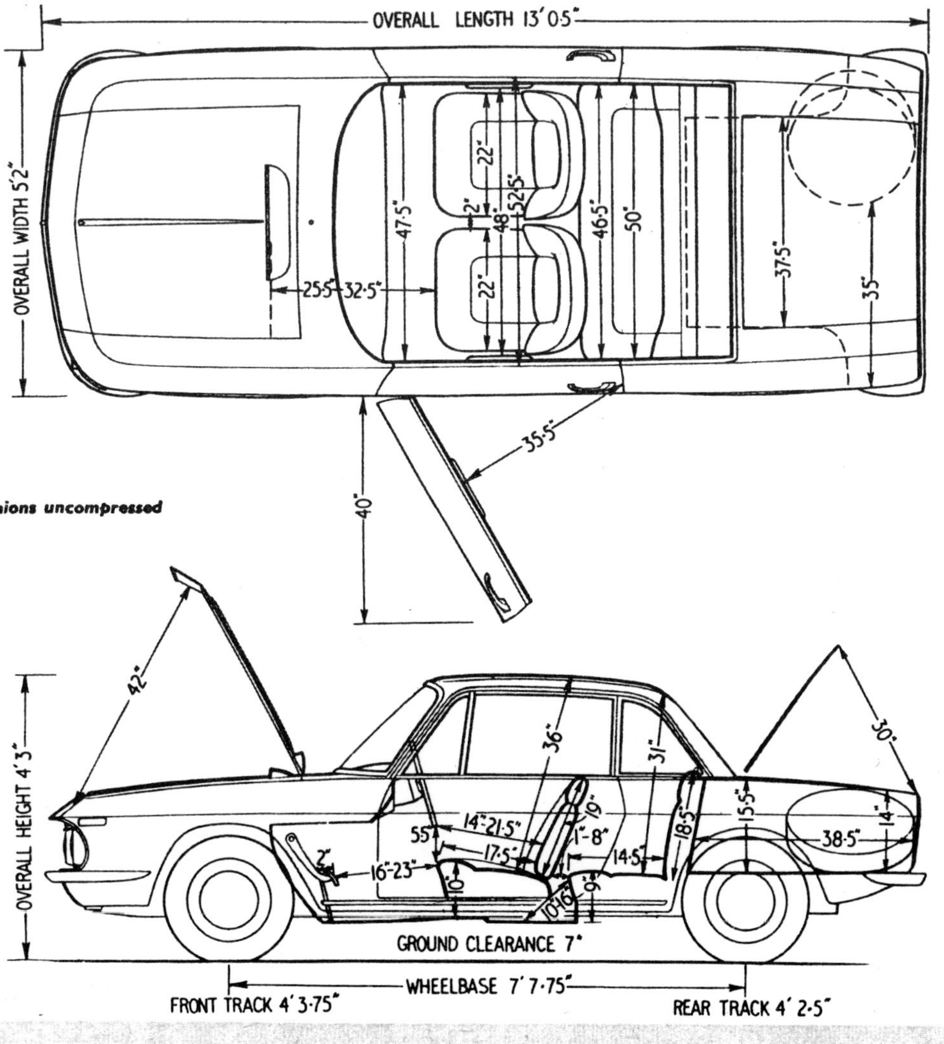

Scale: 0·3in to 1ft. Cushions uncompressed

FLEETER FULVIAS

Squat, bulbous even, but purposeful in every line, the latest Lancia Fulvia 1·3 Sport takes a short rest during our tests. It is capable of over 110 m.p.h.

BIGGER ENGINES, MORE POWER—ROAD IMPRESSIONS

NOW that there are six different Fulvias, the engine-body-chassis combinations are becoming confusing; the model's history should be explained. The original five-seater Fulvia saloon, announced in March 1963, had a 58 b.h.p. 1,091 c.c. narrow-angle vee-4 engine, and a single twin-choke Solex carburettor. It was certainly no raving beauty, and—since it weighed over a ton—no ball of fire either.

The Italians demanded more power, so in October 1964, the Fulvia 2C appeared, having two twin-choke Weber carburettors, a 9·0 compression ratio (instead of 7·8), and 71 b.h.p. at 6,000 r.p.m. Five months later, the Fulvia coupé was released, and for the first time the engine size was increased, from 1,091 to 1,216 c.c. The new engine has a bore 4mm bigger, with dimensions of 76×67mm; 80 b.h.p. were produced at 6,000 r.p.m. Though the suspension and general layout was not changed, the coupé had a 15cm (5·9in) shorter wheelbase, and weighed only 18·6cwt; its body was all-steel and a central gearchange was standard. To make the coupé even more competitive the coupé HF appeared in January 1966, and a further tuned engine producing 90 b.h.p. This car was several hundred pounds lighter than the steel-bodied version and has had a very successful competition career. Meantime, Zagato had produced an individually styled 2-seater coupé body which was adopted by the factory and called the Fulvia Sport.

The single carburettor saloon and the original 1,216 c.c. HF and Zagatos have all been dropped, and four new variants added to the line. The saloon now has the 1,216 c.c. coupé engine (80 b.h.p.) and optional central gearchange; it is renamed the "GT" saloon. All the other Fulvias have an even bigger engine, which at 1,298 c.c. is up to the limit of the 1,300 c.c. class. Because there is no space to bore out much further, the stroke has been lengthened as well, and the revised dimensions are 77×69·7mm. Both the coupé (now called the Rallye 1·3) and the Sport (called the Sport 1·3) have 87 b.h.p. at 6,000 r.p.m., while the lightweight competition HF has 101 b.h.p. at 6,000 r.p.m. The HF's 14 b.h.p. increase is gained by using a 10·5 to 1 compression ratio, different camshafts and a hand-worked cylinder head. The Zagato coupé is high geared (top, 3·54), and the other coupés have a 3·7 ratio. The GT saloon has a 4·3 axle ratio to give better acceleration with that heavy body. An important improvement to the Rallye 1·3 is that it has been lightened by 77lb with light-alloy doors, bonnet and boot lid.

Driving impressions—Zagato first

"Come to the factory by about 10 a.m.," Lancia had said in their invitation, "so that you can choose a car and make your own way to Cervinia." Since our destination was a ski-resort high in the Alps 80 miles north of Turin, with snow and ice on site and a really sporting approach road up the valley from the Aosta highway, my thoughts immediately turned to the stark but purposeful HF Rallye coupé. But too late—when I arrived the HFs had already been booked. I settled for a sleek little Zagato Sport 1·3 instead.

Since I had previously been impressed by our Road Test Fulvia coupé (11 November 1966) I was quite prepared to note the excellence and refinement of the beautifully finished Zagato body. Mechanically it is identical with the 1·3 Rallye coupé, except for the higher final drive ratio. The facia layout and driving position are the same, but the falling

FLEETER FULVIAS

roof line dictates no rear seats. Instead there is a long carpeted luggage space, loaded through a rear window/boot lid like the MGB GT or the Triumph GT6. The extra refinement that I had forgotten became obvious when my passenger pressed what he thought was an electrically winding window switch; with a subdued but expensive whine that boot lid opened by a couple of inches! This fitting, of course, is on the other Zagato Lancias, being intended to improve ventilation.

My passenger, being new to Fulvias, was entranced by the Zagato, and swopped seats with me at the earliest possible moment. Only the low-geared rack and pinion steering gear takes the edge off perfection for me; a more direct rack is being built, and will be homologated as a competition option in the near future. Nevertheless, the little car seems to go *exactly* where it is steered, holding the road impeccably and riding silently and level. Any sort of cruising speed up to 100 m.p.h. is effortless and quiet, and we recorded a timed maximum of 112 m.p.h. on the Ivrea autostrada, which corresponds to 6,000 r.p.m. (ideal gearing too). Acceleration, even with the second-string 87 b.h.p. engine, was brisk indeed, and our standing kilometre in 32·8sec equals other exotic cars like the Alfa Giulia Sprint GTV, and makes such cars as the TR4A and the MGB GT look slow by comparison. In this form, the Zagato Sport must be the fastest 1·3-litre car in quantity production.

Once off the Ivrea autostrada, pressing on uphill to the 6,500ft heights of Cervinia, the perfectly balanced handling began to show through. Front-wheel-drive, Michelin X tyres and a typically straight-arm Italian driving position combined to make me superbly comfortable and extremely confident at all times.

The Fulvia HF rally car

During lunch in Cervinia, where we met Ove Andersson, Sandro Munari and John Davenport of the Lancia rally team, mechanics were putting studded tyres on all the test cars, and there was the prospect of trying the cars on a closed snow-covered track during the afternoon. For the particularly adventurous, there would be descents of the same track riding "shot-gun" with Ove Andersson in an authentic HF rally car which had just creaked back from the difficult Rallye de Fiore.

I was first to experience Andersson's particular genius in his rally car, though I have watched him—with amazement and admiration—several times on the major international rallies. Every effort of mine became completely insignificant after I had hung-on and studied him. Fully spiked rallying tyres give impressive grip on packed snow, but Ove's cornering method is to tweak the car many degrees out of line, fighting centrifugal force with front-wheel drive and 100+ b.h.p., left-foot-braking his way into many of the corners and twirling the steering wheel all the time like a well-drilled octopus. "Were you trying hard?" I asked when we reached the bottom of the hill. "Not really," replied Andersson, "later I have to drive motoring writers who have never seen a rally before; they might die of fright if I went any quicker!"

After that, I completely stopped trying to impress myself in the new cars, but took out a 1·3 Rallye coupé HF (on studded tyres) just the same. With a power/weight ratio of about 130 b.h.p./ton compared with the steel-bodied car's 95 b.h.p./ton, and our 1,216 c.c. Road Test car's 88 b.h.p./ton, the HF is much faster through the gears. In the effort to keep weight right down, the trim is more spartan, the seats smaller but figure-hugging, and the sound-deadening more or less non-existent. Naturally there is a lot more noise, and one can hear every valve being opened and closed, but the Fulvia HF is assembled so carefully that the noises are as pleasing as those emitted by an excellent Swiss watch. I had no chance to test Lancia's performance claims, especially as the car had studded tyres fitted, but the HF should be quicker than a 1275S Mini-Cooper, at least in over-the-counter condition. In competition, the 1,216 c.c. Fulvia HF was rarely as fleet as a "works" Cooper S, so the extra 82 c.c. will be welcomed. Since the Fulvia is still young in its development, while B.M.C. have been campaigning the Cooper S for over three years, 1967 could be very exciting for HF Squadra Corse.

Somehow I never found time to drive the latest 1·2 GT saloon, but returned to Turin in the normal-bodied Fulvia 1·3 Rallye coupé. The Fulvia front-wheel-drive power pack is very free-running and economical at steady speeds (a fact discovered when the petrol gauge registered "Empty" in the mountains at 5.30 a.m. in the morning!), but a 90 m.p.h. cruising speed is smooth and quiet. The sumptuous seats have adjustable, ventilated backrests, and only the rubber-matted floor is less luxurious than a British buyer with £1,500 would expect.

All the Fulvias have benefited from their larger engines, which have made them that much easier to drive comfortably, and increased their creditable performance still further. When we discussed our Road Test coupé last year we agreed that its specification was unique; the latest improvements separate it from "the common herd" even further. Such quality has to be paid for, especially in this country, but I—for one—am quite convinced that the Fulvia coupés are worth every penny.

Graham Robson

Left: Only the new badges reveal that the Fulvia saloon now has a bigger engine and more power. The 1,216 c.c. engine previously fitted to the coupé is standard; the coupés behind the saloon now have the 1,298 c.c. engine. Right: Cesare Fiorio's own Pininfarina Flavia coupé almost became part of the scenery during our stay

NEW FLAVIA TASTED

TWO weeks ago Lancia of Turin announced completely re-styled versions of the Flavia saloon, and let us try them on the hill roads of the Portofino peninsula (Italian Riviera). Mechanically there are no radical changes; three types are offered, the Flavia (with 1·5-litre engine), the Flavia 1·8 (1·8-litre engine) and the Flavia 1·8 "iniezione" (1·8-litre fuel injection engine) —the Pininfarina Coupé, the Vignale Convertible and the Zagato Sport, all younger designs, continue unchanged.

Description

The original Lancia Flavia, Italy's first front-wheel-drive car, appeared at the end of 1960. A somewhat square body hid a 1·5-litre flat-4 o.h.v. engine mounted with the gearbox and final drive unit in front of the wheels on a hefty, box section steel sub-frame. A transverse half-elliptic leaf spring was carried above the transmission on two large aluminium castings for the wishbone front suspension. At the rear, two more leaf springs located a tubular "dead" beam axle; an anti-roll bar was added. Brakes were large, 11in. dia. discs all round, with two separate hydraulic circuits and vacuum servo assistance.

It was not a light car at 23·3 cwt, and we did feel that more power would be an improvement. So, apparently, did the makers, for in 1963 the 1·8-litre engine was offered as an option. Two years later fuel injection was made a further option on the 1·8. At present the 1·5-litre gives 80 b.h.p. (net) at 5,600 r.p.m., the carburettor 1·8-litre 92 b.h.p. at 5,200 r.p.m. and

Instrument layout is simple and clear, the panel of switches being sunk within deep safety padding. The floor is flat and rubber covered

The injection 1·8 litre engine uncovered. Note the alternator (right) and new plastic-bladed fan

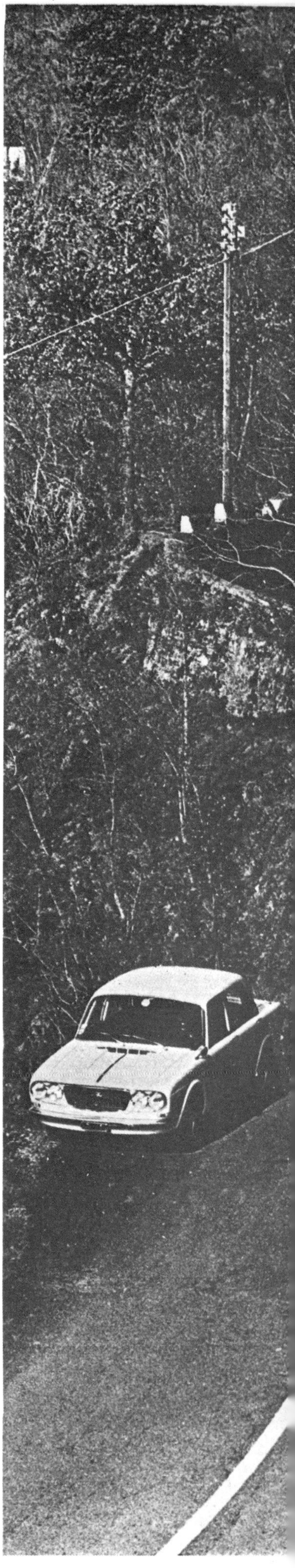

One of the best views of the Flavia is from above. Only when cornered hard does it roll appreciably

the injection 1·8-litre 102 b.h.p. at 5,200 r.p.m.

On the new Flavias the only changes to the engine are modifications to the crankcase castings to take an alternator in place of a d.c. generator (all models) and ZF power-assisted steering (optional), an electro-mechanical plastic-bladed fan (1·8 models only), a larger radiator, a more accessible position for the dip-stick and different engine-gearbox to sub-frame mounts.

Larger Fuel Tank

A larger petrol tank (12 instead of 10·5 gallons) and a fuel return feed for the carburettor from a mechanical instead of an electric pump are the fuel system changes. A different clutch centre plate has a torsional damper permitting increased movement under load. To improve further the Flavia's already excellent low road-noise level, the transverse front leaf spring has been widened (also for longer life) and its anti-vibration mounting altered. Wider wheels (5in. instead of 4·5in.) are used for the same tyres as before—Michelin X, Pirelli Cinturato or Ceat 165-15 —though Michelin XAS are optional.

More even distribution of braking has been achieved by reducing the size of the rear caliper cylinders, and the umbrella handbrake has a better pawl push button to guard against accidental release.

Body Changes

The big change is in the styling of the body. Still essentially (and fashionably) square in shape, it has had its previously sharp corners rounded, giving a more slender look which should please most buyers. The bluff aspect of the original front, with its high-placed twin headlamps, has been softened, headlamps being mounted lower within a chromium line which encloses the familiar grille. The deep-windowed appearance of the saloon itself is still there, providing excellent visibility yet still in proportion. A waist line breaks up any slab-sided effect and there is an appreciable overhang of the tail and the roomy boot.

Laminated glass replaces toughened for the windscreen and a heated rear window is available as an extra. Air for the new heating and ventilation system enters via a conventional scuttle intake instead of from a wheel arch; a small round louvre on each side of the rear seat foot wells supplies air for the back. The two-speed centrifugal blower has been made quieter.

A full set of instruments is set in a handsome wood-trimmed panel recessed inside a padded lip. All Flavias now have a Bloster steering lock and a new steering wheel with its rim ribbed between the spokes to give grip. Normally a steering column gearchange is fitted but a central one is optional on the two 1·8s. The alternator provides a maximum charging current of 33 amp and the windscreen wipers are two-speed with thin-framed blades designed to stay on the glass at high speeds. Inner headlamps are iodine vapour main-beam only, the outer lamps having similar bulbs for low beam and separate off-set tungsten bulbs for parking lamps; these last are controlled by the ignition switch. Fuses are reached from inside the cockpit.

Driving Impressions

Given first an ordinary Flavia (1·5) we followed the "Prova Lancia" signs which marked the suggested test route. The road wiggled continuously from Santa Margherita Ligure most of the way to Rapallo, climbing and winding round uncounted corners. We found the beginning of the *autostrada* and started looking for a straight and level bit. The two carriageways plunged into tunnels through the coastal hills and out again, flying high above the valleys on great slender viaducts —scenically magnificent. Later I asked Ing. Fiorio (head of Lancia's publicity department) where it was possible to do some maximum speed runs on a level road. Smiling, he said that he thought the tunnels were level. As the 1·8-litre car is capable of about 100 m.p.h. I felt that general driving impressions were more important than figures this time.

From the driving seat of the Flavia one is conscious of the uprightness of both car and driving position. Although reclining seats are fitted, for a tall driver like me (I am just 6ft) the seat was best when adjusted right back with the squab fairly upright; my arms were then reasonably extended and my legs just—but only just—right for the pedals. The car is one of those pleasantly open-feeling saloons in which, thanks to the high screen, a slightly drooping nose and generous windows, the view is excellent; you quickly feel in charge.

On the move it impresses immediately with its quietness. Driven normally there is little engine noise and none from the transmission. The elaborate driving unit sub-frame design all begins to make much more sense when you listen for road noise; the low level which has been achieved is remarkable.

Still driving quietly, the other truly astonishing feature of the engine in all three forms is its flexibility. The clearly marked tachometer read 1,000 r.p.m. at tickover but leaving the car in top gear I braked it down to 600 r.p.m.—about 10 m.p.h. on the 1·8—and then started accelerating away again. It did so smoothly with only the slightest tremor at first. Power delivery is even all the way to maximum r.p.m. (5,600 r.p.m.) and there is really nothing to choose between the carburettor and injection 1·8-litre cars on this score.

While the standard Flavia (with the 1·5-litre engine) is not a startling performer, both the "milleotto" (carburettor 1·8) and "iniezione" (injection 1·8) engines are very satisfying when pressed. There is plenty of power for overtaking and hill-climbing, when, of course it pays to use the gears. Calculated maximum speeds in 1st, 2nd, 3rd and top at 5,600 r.p.m. for each model are respectively (in m.p.h.) 25, 43, 67 and 94 (1·5); 30, 52, 74 and 101 (1·8 carburettor); 32, 53, 76 and 103 (1·8 injection).

Although a steering column gearchange and bench seat are standard equipment, the majority of cars imported into the U.K. will have the optional floor change and separate seats. Having a very narrow movement across the gate for such a long lever, this works well. The all-synchromesh engagement could sometimes be beaten when changing gears very quickly.

Steering is accurate and only heavy when parking or slightly so when accelerating round a bend. There is virtually no lost motion and because the car has a reasuringly flat, almost roll-free, ride at touring cornering speeds, one is encouraged to be more adventurous. I found that the Flavia had very high cornering power on both Michelin X and XAS tyres. Only its bulk and the fact that the seats, though comfortable, did not locate the driver well limited one's exuberance.

Good Brakes

Finally, such a car must be well braked; all Flavias undoubtedly are. Pedal pressures are light and the pedal itself is in the right place relative to the accelerator for easy heel-and-toe working. The car pulls up square, locking all four wheels if crash-stopped; I experienced no fade during some rapid zig-zag descents.

All in all, the Lancia Flavia, in its 1·8-litre forms, is a very refined car, big enough for five people to travel in comfort with appreciable performance and great safety. I thoroughly enjoyed it.

Michael Scarlett.

Lancia Flavia Injection 1,800 cc

AT A GLANCE: Expensive Italian front wheel drive flat-four fuel injection engined saloon with new more rounded body. Very smooth quiet engine lacks punch at low speed. Deceptive performance is faster than it feels. Excellent ride. Fade-free brakes. Good road-holding.

MANUFACTURER
Lancia & Cie, Via Vincenzo Lancia 27, Turin, Italy.

British Concessionaires
Lancia (England) Ltd., Lancia Works, Ealing Road, Alperton, Middlesex.

PRICES

Basic	£1,544 0s 0d
Purchase Tax	£355 11s 0d
Seat belts (pair, approx.)	£10 0s 0d
Total (in G.B.)	£1,909 11s 0d

PERFORMANCE SUMMARY

Mean maximum speed	103 m.p.h.
Standing-start $\frac{1}{4}$-mile	19.7 sec
0–60 m.p.h.	15.0 sec
30-70 m.p.h. (through gears)	15.6 sec
Fuel consumption	28 m.p.g.
Miles per tankful	336

THE Lancia Flavia appeared in 1960 as Italy's first front-wheel drive car, a 1.5-litre flat-4 engine propelling a very bluff and square-looking body. We tested the car in 1961 and thought a lot of it, except it felt under-powered. Two years later the first 1.8-litre engine appeared and two years after that, Kugelfischer fuel injection was offered, giving a further boost to the car's performance. In the spring of this year Lancia announced a new Flavia (described in *Autocar* of 11 May) with a more attractive body but little change mechanically.

The engine and gearbox are mounted ahead of the wheels on a substantial sub-frame. The suspension uses leaf springs, one transversely mounted at the front and working on wishbone-located wheels and two at the back conventionally placed to bear a tubular dead-beam axle with anti-roll bar and Panhard rod.

Still one gets the impression that the acceleration is rather leisurely, although this is not borne out when measured against a stopwatch. Power output is a claimed 102 bhp at 5,200 rpm (10 more than the £150-cheaper carburettor 1800) but the nature of the performance makes it appear slower than in fact it is. Low-speed torque is not strong, even though the engine will pull from as low as 1,000 rpm in top. There is an extraordinarily smooth and refined "feel" about the way the engine runs, partly due to its quietness. Apart from the fuel pump, which can be heard whining at idling, and the injector pump (which clatters somewhat) there is no mechanical noise. A great improvement over previous Lancias is the lack of fan noise, because the thermostatically controlled radiator shutters which never seemed to open have been abandoned in favour of an electro-mechanical fan clutch.

The Flavia is a very restful car to cruise fast and the high gearing gives only 3,700 rpm at 70 mph in top. Speeds of 33, 56, and 79 mph in the gears at 5,800 rpm are possible.

Fuel consumption worked out at 25.3 mpg overall, and on one or two clear runs we managed 28.

Starting is easy and quick from cold, an automatic rich mixture device being set by flooring the accelerator once. A red light on the dashboard glows while this device is working and also if the handbrake is left on. A yellow light tells if the fuel feed pressure is not high enough. Once warm the idling settles to about 800 rpm although it was sometimes erratic when hot, stalling occasionally. The clutch is very smooth but lacks bite, so much so that we could only just restart on a 1-in-4 slope. During deliberately rapid gearchanging for our acceleration runs through the gears, the clutch spun very easily and lost the car a few tenths of a second.

The gearchange is a stout lever sprouting at 45 deg from the lower bulkhead; it is light to use but has a clumsy and long movement vertically. Synchromesh is adequate for unhurried changes but grunts if one rushes it. The

Autocar road test Number 2155 Make: Lancia Type: Flavia Injection 1,800 c.c.

TEST CONDITIONS
Weather: Cloudy dry. Wind: 10-15 m.p.h.
Temperature: 19 deg C (65 deg F)
Barometer: 29.6in. Hg.
Humidity: 50 per cent
Surfaces: Dry concrete and asphalt

WEIGHT
Kerb weight 24.0 cwt (2,687lb-1,220kg)
(with oil, water and half-full fuel tank)
Distribution, per cent F, 62; R, 38
Laden as tested: 27.3 cwt (3,059lb-1,389kg)

Test distance 1,150 miles. Figures taken at 1,200 miles by our own staff at the Motor Industry Research Association proving ground at Nuneaton.

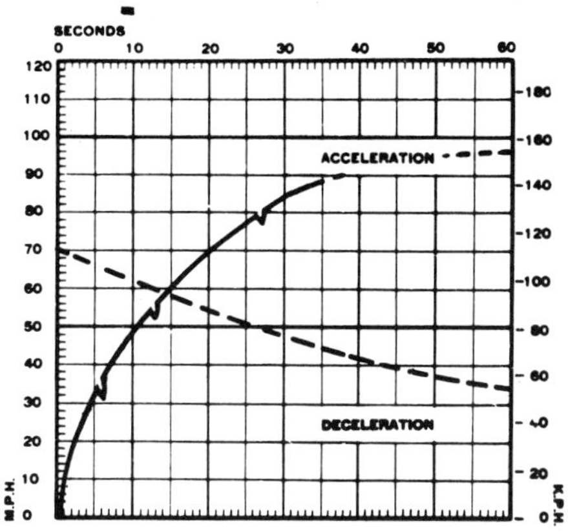

MAXIMUM SPEEDS

Gear	m.p.h.	k.p.h.	r.p.m.
Top (mean)	103	166	5,450
(best)	105	169	5,600
3rd	79	127	5,800
2nd	56	90	5,800
1st	33	53	5,800

Standing ¼-mile 19.7 sec 69 m.p.h.

Standing Kilometre 36.3 sec 86 m.p.h.

FUEL CONSUMPTION

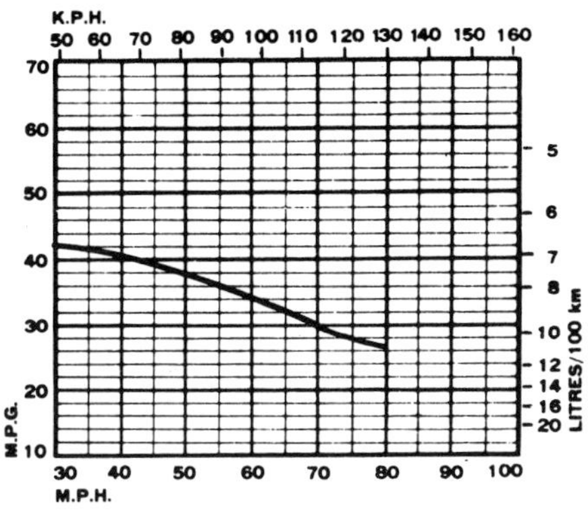

TIME IN SECONDS	4.8	7.5	10.5	15.0	20.4	29.1	42.7	
TRUE SPEED M.P.H.	30	40	50	60	70	80	90	100
INDICATED SPEED	34	44	54	65	75	85	95	106

Mileage recorder 0.9 per cent over-reading

(At constant speeds—m.p.g.)

30 m.p.h.	41.7
40	39.8
50	37.7
60	33.4
70	30.1
80	27.0

Speed range, gear ratios and time in seconds

m.p.h.	Top (3.91)	3rd (5.42)	2nd (7.68)	1st (13.02)
10-30	—	8.7	6.1	3.9
20-40	12.1	7.8	5.3	—
30-50	11.8	7.8	5.5	—
40-60	10.6	7.9	—	—
50-70	13.2	8.7	—	—
60-80	18.0	14.6	—	—
70-90	22.9	—	—	—

Typical m.p.g. 28 (10.1 litres/100km)
Calculated (DIN) m.p.g. 27.4 (10.3 litres/100km)
Overall m.p.g. 25.3 (11.2 litres/100km)
Grade of fuel, Premium, 4-star (min. 97RM)

OIL CONSUMPTION
Miles per pint (SAE 10W/40) 1,150

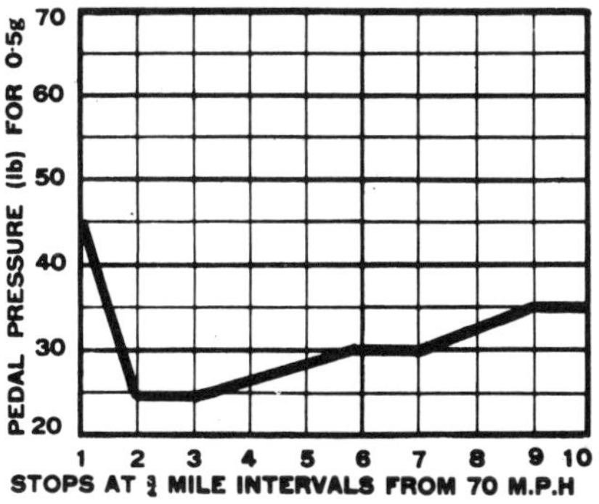

BRAKES (from 30 m.p.h. in neutral)

Load	g	Distance
25lb	0.16	188ft
50lb	0.32	94ft
75lb	0.75	40ft
100lb	0.95	31.7ft
Handbrake	**0.25**	**120ft**

Max. Gradient 1 in 5
Clutch pedal 35 lb and 5.5in.

TURNING CIRCLES
Between kerbs L, 38ft 11in.; R, 36ft 0in.
Between walls L, 41ft 0in.; R, 38ft 5in.
Steering wheel turns, lock to lock 4.5

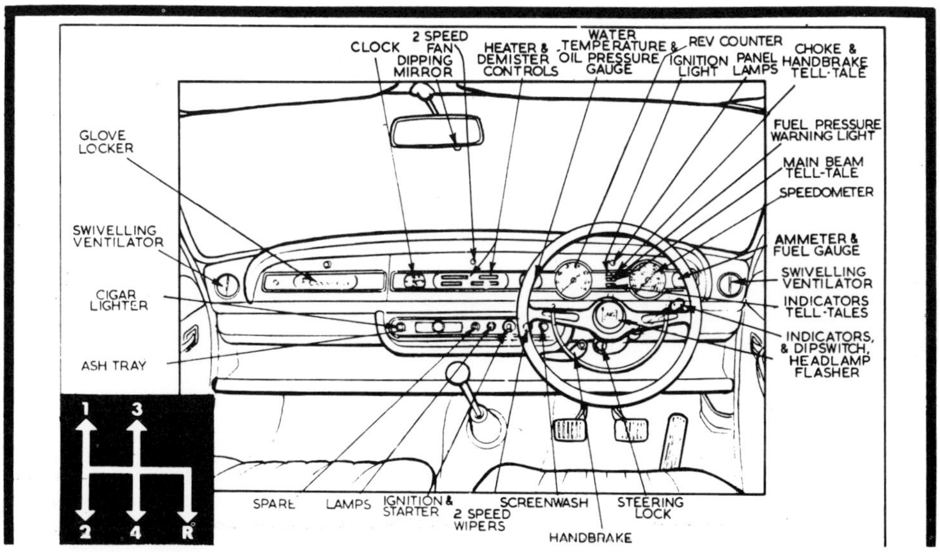

HOW THE CAR COMPARES

MAXIMUM SPEED (mean) M.P.H.

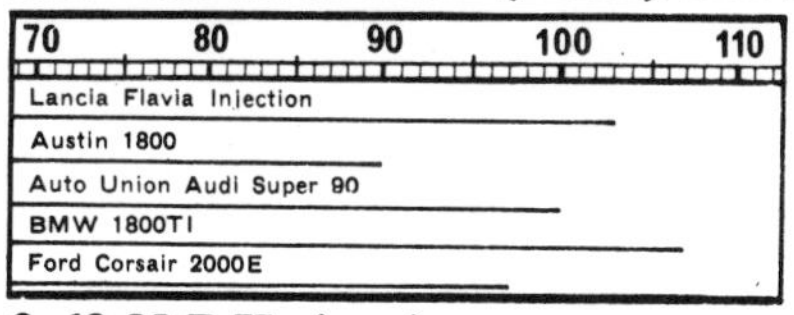

0-60 M.P.H. (sec.)

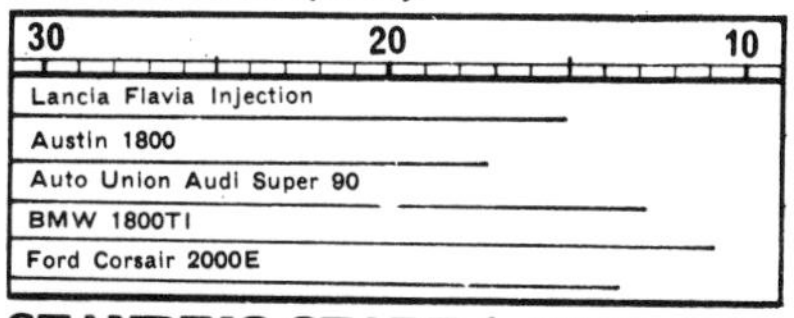

STANDING START ¼-MILE (sec)

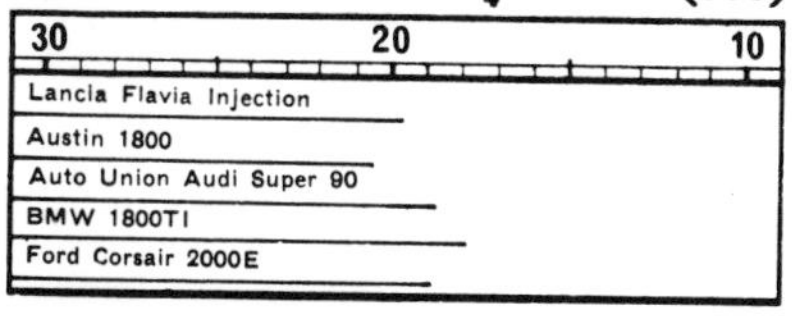

M.P.G. OVERALL

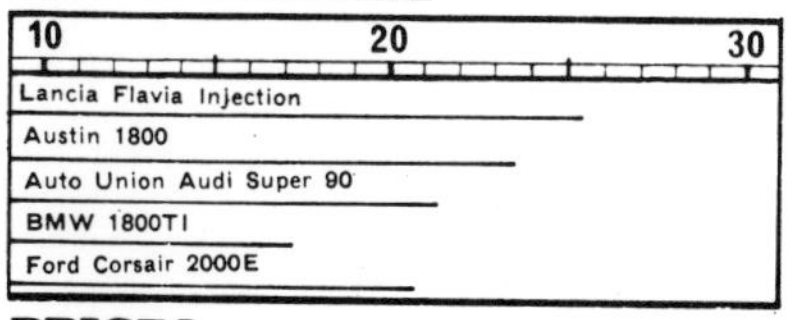

PRICES

Lancia Flavia Injection	£1,909
Austin 1800	£924
Auto Union Audi Super 90	£1,194
BMW 1800TI	£1,498
Ford Corsair 2000E	£1,008

accelerator pedal had a sticky movement on the test car and the pendant brake and clutch pedals are poorly angled relative to the driver's feet. There is a damper in the injection system which prevents snap shutting of the throttle; if the engine is revved with the gearbox in neutral, it takes about 5 sec for the revs to die down. This disguises the tail-out effects of lifting the throttle foot during cornering, and seriously reduces engine braking.

On the whole the Flavia's suspension gives a very comfortable ride, its springs having a very soft rate. Sometimes the suspension is caught out by acute dips, and the car can bottom on its exhaust pipes at the front as it did at about 40 mph on the long wave pitching surface at MIRA, unlike the original Flavia which crossed those same waves without any disturbance at an incredible 75 mph. There is some bump-thump and road noise transmitted from the radial-ply Michelin XAS tyres, but most of the time they grip very well indeed.

The steering, though fairly low geared with 4.5 turns from lock to lock, is still hard work to operate when parking at very low speeds. There is some slight play in the straight-ahead position which one does not notice on the move. Turning circles are rather large—especially on left lock.

Brakes are very good, being light to work, progressive, free from any squeal and virtually free from fade. They are also well balanced but we could not better 0.95g on dry tarmac. The handbrake would only manage 0.25g on its own and would not hold on the 1-in-4 hill.

One feels a little remote in the driving seat from the handsome dashboard, but the upright position gives a clear and commanding view. The steering wheel is at a comfortable angle, but the ribbed parts of its rim can irritate rather than help when spinning it through one's hand to straighten the car. There is a half horn ring to work the excellent and very powerful Fiamm air horns, whilst what looks like a horn button in the centre of the wheel is actually the headlamp flasher. The column has a Bloster steering lock separate from the ignition.

Stowage space inside is quite adequate with a long parcel shelf under the facia, open pockets down by one's feet and a lockable cubby-hole in front of the passenger. Judging by the difference between room for back seat passengers' knees and the length of the boot, design priorities have remained a little confused. The pvc material used for the seats and trim panels gave off an unpleasant sickly rubber smell during the test period, but from previous experience of other Continental cars with this complaint, it usually wears off after a ▶

The Flavia follows a common trend amongst 1,800 c.c. cars with its long tail and thrust forward look

A bewildering jumble of machinery, pipes and wires at first, but in fact not too difficult to service. The white bomb-shaped object on top is part of the Kugelfischer fuel injection

The boot floor is rubber covered and the selection of tools provided is more comprehensive than on most other cars

Flexible pockets are provided in the seat backs but with tall occupants in the front and back they are filled at the expense of knee room. Dashboard layout is clear and uncluttered except for the switches which are unlabelled

Lancia Flavia Injection

little use. The seats did not "breathe" satisfactorily and in humid weather one began to sweat.

Unless a window is wound open a little, ventilation is not very good, and it takes a careful study to understand the complicated heater controls. There are four adjustments possible, for distribution, temperature, air intake and water flow plus a two-speed fan which runs quieter than most. It is not possible to have cool air playing on one's face with warm air on the feet.

The Flavia is advanced in having iodine vapour lamps for its main beam and these produce a very good driving light. Unfortunately the contrast between the brilliance of these and the sharp cut-off and low intensity of the dipped beams makes fast night driving against oncoming traffic difficult. In the rare event of electrical trouble, one has the reassuring knowledge that there are 11 fuses to protect the wiring, and that the complete fuse tray and switches can be withdrawn to be serviced inside the car, an excellent piece of Lancia forethought.

Unlike the original Flavia it is now quite easy to get at the usual items needing regular attention. The dipstick is still a little awkward because of pipes and wires in the way but it is no longer necessary to remove plates in the wheel arches to remove a sparking plug.

Summing up our impressions of the 1800 Flavia with fuel injection is not easy. It is undoubtedly a very refined car in which one may travel far and fast without fuss. There are a number of points about it which show how much careful thought has gone into its making. Whether it is worth paying £150 extra to have the fuel injection and its 10 extra bhp is not so certain. ■

SPECIFICATION: LANCIA FLAVIA INJECTION (FRONT ENGINE FRONT WHEEL DRIVE)

ENGINE

Cylinders	4, horizontally opposed
Cooling system	Water, pump, electro-mechanical fan and thermostat
Bore	88mm (3.46in.)
Stroke	74mm (2.91in.)
Displacement	1,800 c.c. (109.8 cu.in.)
Valve gear	Overhead, pushrods and rockers, two camshafts
Compression ratio	9-to-1: Min. octane rating: 97RM
Induction	Kugelfischer port-type fuel injection
Fuel pump	Electric
Oil filter	Full flow, renewable element
Max. power	102 bhp (net) at 5,200 rpm
Max. torque	112.7 lb.ft. (net) at 3,500 rpm

TRANSMISSION

Clutch	Fichtel and Sachs single dry plate with integral torsional damper
Gearbox	4-speed, all synchromesh, in unit with final drive
Gear ratios	Top 1.0 Third 1.39 Second 1.97 First 3.33 Reverse 3.71
Final drive	Hypoid bevel, 3.91-to-1

CHASSIS and BODY

Construction	Integral, with steel body, subframes for suspension

SUSPENSION

Front	Independent, transverse half elliptic leaf springs, wishbones, anti-roll bar, telescopic dampers
Rear	Dead beam axle, half elliptic leaf springs, Panhard rod, anti-roll bar, telescopic dampers

STEERING

Type	Worm and roller
Wheel dia.	16

BRAKES

Make and type	ATE disc front and rear, separate hydraulic circuits front and rear
Servo	Vacuum
Dimensions	F, 11.02in. dia. R, 11.02in. dia.
Swept area	F, 248 sq. in R, 248 sq. in. Total 496 sq. in. (363 sq. in/ton laden)

WHEELS

Type	Pressed steel disc, 4-stud fixing 5in. wide rim.
Tyres—make	Michelin
—type	XAS, radial-ply tubed
—size	165—15Xmm

EQUIPMENT

Battery	12-volt 42-amp.hr.
Alternator	SEV Motorola 42 amp
Headlamps	Four headlamps system, sealed filament outer, iodine vapour main beam inner 110/220-watt (total)
Reversing lamp	Standard
Electric fuses	11
Screen wipers	2-speed, self-parking
Screen washer	Standard, vacuum
Interior heater	Standard, water valve type
Heated backlight	Extra
Safety belts	Extra, anchorages built in
Interior trim	PVC seats, PVC headlining
Floor covering	Moulded rubber mats
Starting handle	No provision
Jack	Screw scissors
Jacking points	2 per side, under sills
Windscreen	Laminated
Underbody protection	Bitumastic on all surfaces exposed to road

MAINTENANCE

Fuel tank	12 Imp. gallons (no reserve) (55 litres)
Cooling system	12.8 pints (including heater) (7.5 litres)
Engine sump	12 pints (6.8 litres) SAE 20w/40 Change oil every 4,300 miles; Change filter element every 4,300 miles;
Gearbox and final drive	4.4 pints SAE 90; Change oil every 8,600 miles
Grease	11 points every 4,300 miles
Tyre pressures	F, 26; R, 26 p.s.i. (normal driving) F, 28; R, 28 p.s.i. (fast driving) F, 28; R, 28 p.s.i. (full load)

PERFORMANCE DATA

Top gear m.p.h. per 1,000 r.p.m.	18.8
Mean piston speed at max. power	2,520 ft./min.
Bhp per ton laden	74.7

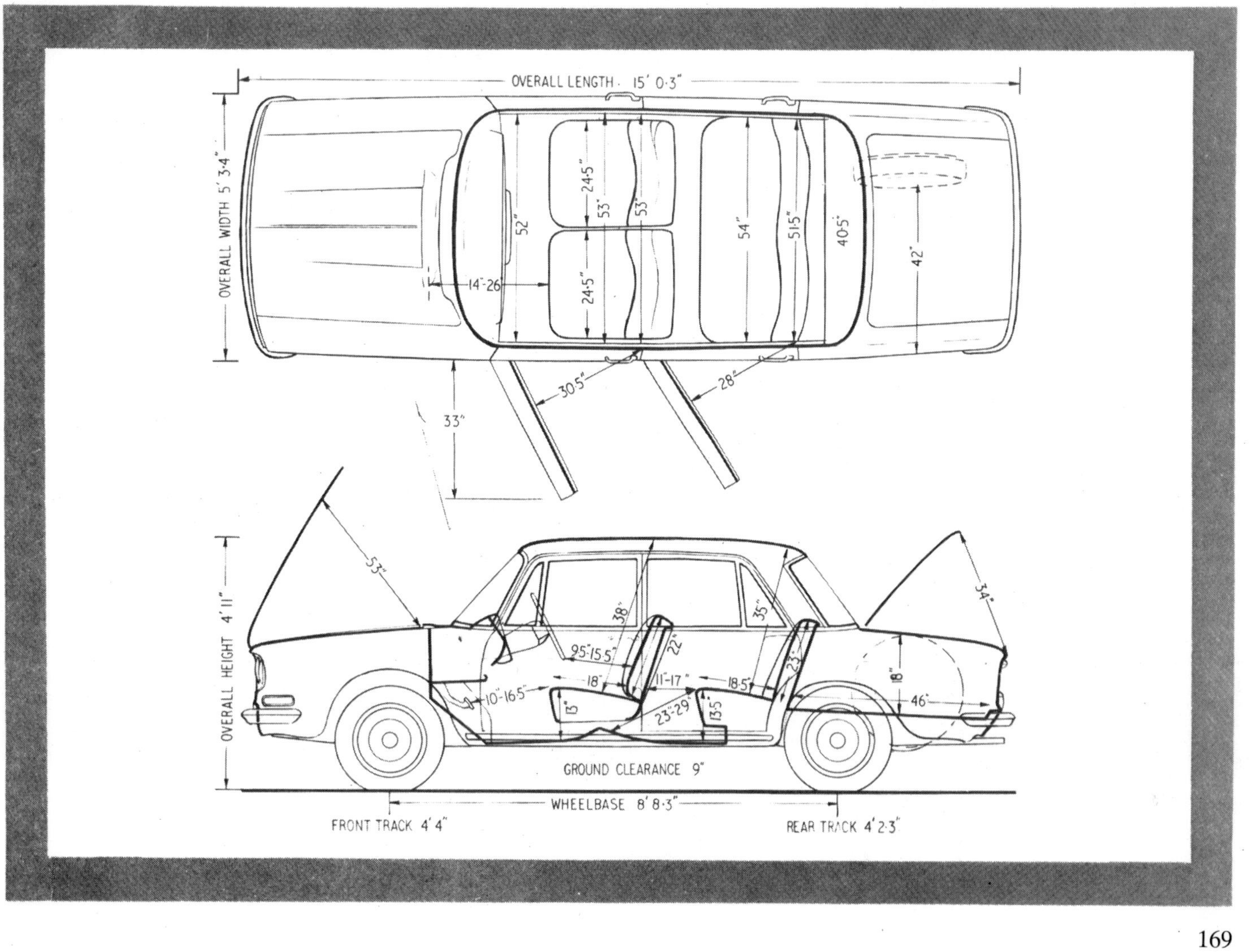

With its tall "greenhouse" and very distinctive lines, the Fulvia Rallye is immediately noticeable: The indicators at the front are mounted on the edge of the wings, clearly visible from front and sides

BRIEF TEST

LANCIA FULVIA RALLYE 1,298 c.c.

WHY buy an Omega wristwatch, when a Timex will do? Why live in Mayfair instead of Putney; and why choose a Lancia Fulvia instead of a Triumph? Lots of people will give you good answers to all these questions, from quality comparisons to that individual streak which stops us all being stereotyped. Probably the extra cost can be accounted for, but it doesn't matter if it can't; that's not the point. What it all boils down to basically is pride of possession, and you will not find one Lancia owner who is not proud of his machine and hates to see it dirty.

On paper at least, the specification for the Fulvia Rallye may not look too exciting: this is no Lamborghini. It is a compact little coupé—with 1,298 c.c. engine driving the front wheels (like the BMC Mini-Cooper S and Triumph 1300). Performance is brisk without being in any way remarkable. It is extremely economical. Steering, ride and handling, those dynamic qualities which mean so much to one's enjoyment of a car, on the other hand are truly exceptional. Anyone who gets as far in the buying sequence as a test drive is hardly likely to turn back, once he has sampled the responsiveness and suppleness of this car on any kind of surface.

It was in November, 1966, that we published our test of the Fulvia coupé, then with 1,216 c.c. engine. Performance was disappointing, although it reached 100 mph mean maximum and accelerated from rest to 60 mph in 15.8sec. With the extra 82 c.c. (derived from a bore and stroke change) comes 7 bhp more, just over 7 lb. ft. more torque, both of which play their part in making the Rallye 1.3 a good deal quicker.

During several flat-out laps of the MIRA banked track, the speed eventually built up to a mean of 107 mph and there should be some more still after a long straight run on a motorway. Claimed top speed is only 104 mph, and although it is rare for Lancia claims to be anything but spot-on, our test car had the advantage of 6,000 miles behind it, which is unusual for a Press demonstrator.

From rest the Rallye was nearly 2sec quicker to 60 mph (13.9) and over 6sec quicker to 80 mph (now 24.7 instead of 31.3sec). There has been no gearing change, so the maxima in the lower ratios were identical with the earlier car; the red mark on the rev counter starts at 6,200 rpm, and they mean it, even though the scale goes on to 7,500.

It seems out of character to get into this quality car costing over £1,600 and find moulded rubber mats on the floor and rather smelly plastic upholstery. This practical approach is typical of the Italians; but we would want it changed to something more in keeping with the quality of the car—like carpets, and leather (or, better still, cloth) to sit on. Materials apart, the seats are exceedingly comfortable, with soft padding and a good wrap-round shape; backrests recline, and the keen driver can settle back at armstretch feeling like one of those spectacular works *pilotes* who put up such a good show in HF coupés on rallies.

There is wood rim to the two-spoke steering wheel, which matches a mahogany instrument panel. All the dials are set inside the upper arc of the wheel, flanked by large speedometer and rev counter, with supplementary gauges in between. Switches are across in the middle of the car and you need to learn their functions because nothing is labelled. The heater has two handwheels for air and temperature regulation plus a lever for distribution. The choke is down under the facia together with another heater lever which shuts off the hot water flow altogether. All this seems very complicated at first acquaintance, but it is logical and easy to work once the functions are understood.

The engine starts easily without choke, after the usual turn on the key followed by a push to work the solenoid. With a pair of twin-choke horizontal Solex carburettors it has a deep induction throb and a zippy response to the accelerator. From under the front comes a sweet mechanical zing of camshaft chains and tappets.

Peak torque comes in at 4,500 and peak power at 6,000 rpm, so the engine needs to

The narrow-angle vee-4 engine is angled to the left, with the two twin-choke Weber carburettors filling the gap on the right

be revved to give its best. It is smooth all the way up, but gets a bit noisy at the top end. The clutch is light, and typically "soft" with a delayed take-up initially. A great solid bar of a gear lever pokes out from a hump in the floor; it is strongly spring-loaded towards the top and third gear plane.

Steering is absolutely precise without any stickiness and with very little kick-back. Yet it is light and so responsive that the Lancia can be positioned to extremely fine limits when cornering fast. Stability at speed is superb. Without knowing first, it would be hard to detect that this is a front-drive car. None of the usual understeer and throttle sensitive attitude changes seem to occur at all, and there is just neutral (and immediate) response the whole time.

The other excellent Lancia feature is ride, and the Fulvia keeps level and jolt-free the whole time, no matter what the wheels are running over. Aside from everything else, there is at least a £1,600 ride, and we know of no other car of this weight and with similar dimensions which comes near the standard.

Under the bonnet accessibility is easy, although there looks to be lots of cables, pipes and wiring. The boot has a rubber floor mat and the spare wheel takes up too much of the available space. Behind the front seats is a rather upright bench with good width, reasonable headroom, but barely any legroom at all. Children only would be the rule here.

Summing it up, the Rallye 1.3 is something of a mis-nomer, because this is no instant rally car. It is an expensive, exclusive and extremely comfortable coupé. It is built like a watch, to last and never to miss a beat. That sort of engineering costs money, but repays for itself in time. □

Rear seat space is for children only, with little legroom or lateral support. At the front, the flat floor provides plenty of space, and the pedals are well spaced

PERFORMANCE DATA

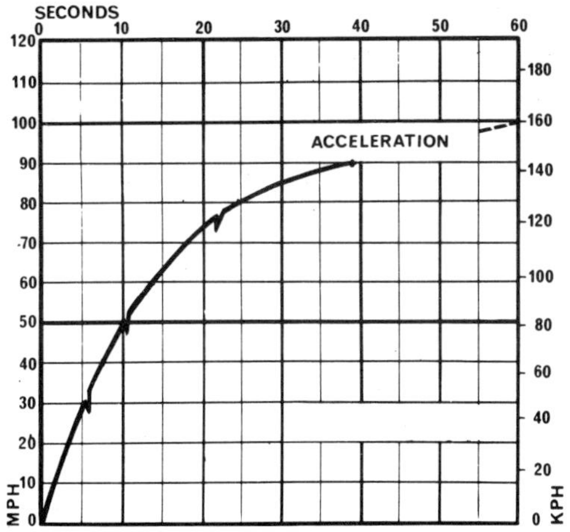

MAXIMUM SPEEDS

Gear	mph	kph	rpm
Top (mean)	107	173	6,000
(best)	110	178	6,150
3rd	78	126	6,150
2nd	51	82	6,150
1st	30	48	6,150

Standing $\frac{1}{4}$-mile 19.9 sec 73 mph
Standing Kilometre 36.4 sec 89 mph

TIME IN SECONDS	5.1	7.6	10.0	13.9	18.2	24.7	39.2
0							
TRUE SPEED MPH	30	40	50	60	70	80	90
INDICATED SPEED MPH	35	45	55	65	75	85	95

SPEED RANGE, GEAR RATIOS AND TIME IN SECONDS

mph	Top	3rd	2nd	1st
10-30	—	9.4	5.5	3.5
20-40	—	8.0	4.6	—
30-50	12.9	7.4	4.8	—
40-60	12.1	7.7	—	—
50-70	14.0	8.2	—	—
60-80	17.4	10.3	—	—
70-90	21.3	—	—	—

FUEL CONSUMPTION

Overall mpg 30.3 (9.3 litres/100km)

Autotest

LANCIA FULVIA COUPE 1.6 HF (1,584 c.c.)

AT-A-GLANCE: This year's RAC Rally winner in civilised, retail-selling form. Excellent performance, highly responsive handling, but not easy to drive smoothly or quietly; very expensive in Great Britain.

MANUFACTURER
Lancia S.p.A., Via Vincenzo, Lancia 27, Turin, Italy

UK CONCESSIONAIRES
Lancia (England) Ltd., Ealing Road, Alperton, Wembley, Middlesex

PRICES

Basic	£1,933	0s	0d
Purchase Tax	£592	18s	7d
Total (in G.B.)	£2,525	18s	7d
PRICE AS TESTED	£2,525	18s	7d

PERFORMANCE SUMMARY

Mean maximum speed	106 mph
Standing start ¼-mile	17.6 sec
0-60 mph	9.9 sec
30-70 mph through gears	10.7 sec
Typical fuel consumption	24 mpg
Miles per tankful	200

WHEN Lancia began rallying the little Fulvia Coupé a few years ago, it rapidly became evident that a lot of development would be needed before they stood a serious chance of winning the rougher, faster events. At that time the car was simply not strong enough, and lacked not only power, but torque as well in relation to its weight.

That the strength problem has been solved should be evident from the way the Fulvias now last through major rallies. At the same time, the power and torque deficit has been made up by taking the easy way out, and fitting a larger engine. For some time the new 1,584 c.c. unit was strictly a works special; but it has now been made available in a suitably modified version of the coupé body, and can be bought by any Briton with £2,500 to spend.

The larger engine capacity has been achieved by both boring and stroking the existing 1.3 litre unit. The highly original configuration—a very narrow-angle vee with two overhead camshafts, one operating the inlet and the other the exhaust valves—is retained. The HF engine can be identified readily by the blue and yellow finish applied to the block and head. Compared with the 1.3S Coupé which was the last Fulvia to pass through our hands, the HF has a higher compression ratio (10.5 instead of 9.5, necessitating the use of five-star petrol), larger twin-choke Solex carburettors, and wider camshaft profiles.

The overall result is a 25 per cent increase in net power, developed at slightly higher rpm,

Above: Fulvia HF interior shows few signs of the car's adaptation to semi-competition status. The only real give-away is the bigger gearbox bulge and shorter, more upright gear lever, when compared with the Fulvia 1300S. The oil temperature gauge (hidden behind the left-hand rim of the steering wheel), replaces the clock fitted in other versions

Above: Under the bonnet, only the blue-and-yellow tappet cover announces that the engine is of the high-performance HF variety. The carburettors are very like those used on the 1300S, but are rather bigger. Accessibility to most points is good; the oil filler is an exception

Left and below: The alloy doors, bonnet and boot lid blend beautifully with the rest of the body, which is still of steel. Note the larger pair of inner headlamps and the glassfibre flares added to the wheel arches to cover the larger tyres

and even more important, a 31 per cent increase in torque. This is taken through the same 8 in. dia. clutch—which seems to stand up to the extra load remarkably well—and into a five-speed gearbox. Compared with the four-speed box in the 1.3, top and bottom gears remain the same (top being direct-drive), and the three intermediates are spread out in the gap previously covered by only two. The result is a set of fairly close ratios, although when driven for ultimate performance there still seems to be something of a gap between third and fourth. Lancia reckon on a rev limit of 6,500 for the HF, compared with 6,200 for the smaller-engined cars, but the tachometer in our test car had its red line set at 7,000 rpm. Final drive ratio on the HF is identical, at 3.7, but the overall gearing is slightly affected by the use of fat Michelin XAS tyres on 13in. rims instead of the 145-14in. covers used on the 1.3S.

Most of the other changes are concerned with getting rid of excess weight. The doors, bonnet and boot lid of the HF are of light alloy instead of steel. Glassfibre fillets extend the wheel arches to cover the wide tyres. The brake servo is deleted; rally drivers prefer it that way. The neat little bench back seat is banished in favour of a stark (though still upholstered) shelf, and the front seats are semi-skeletal structures shaped to locate their occupants very firmly—only the one on the passenger side hinges forward to permit access to the back. The result of all this is a very useful saving of a hundredweight or so, without by any means gutting the car in full-blooded competition style. Aside from the changes already mentioned, the only noticeable points inside are that the gear lever is a stubby, vertical little thing stirring a remote-control linkage, in place of the traditional direct-acting pole emerging from under the dashboard; and an oil temperature gauge replaces the clock in front of the passenger.

Superb headlamps

An interesting recognition point outside is that the inner (main beam) pair of 5¾in. light units have been replaced by 7in. ones. In fact the whole lighting system has been rearranged, each of the four headlamps containing a single H1 tungsten-halogen bulb. The outer pair operates alone to provide dipped beam, and all four come on together to provide one of the most effective long-range main beams we have ever come across.

Our test car was delivered with relatively few miles on the clock, and we concentrated first on adding as many as possible before the performance testing session at MIRA. First impressions were that the gearchange was very notchy indeed, and the engine stiff and lumpy. As time went on, it became obvious that the car was loosening up and becoming smoother. Even though we delayed taking performance figures for as long as we could, it seems likely that were we to try again when the car had double the mileage behind it, we should do even better.

Even at that early stage, the car showed itself to have something of a Jekyll and Hyde character. It would cruise very sweetly and quite quietly at 4,000rpm—which is a true 75mph; raise it to 5,000 and the noise level increased greatly. Most of the noise was mechanical, with significant contributions from the exhaust, and the tyres, on some surfaces.

Our acceleration figures show that the Fulvia in this form is no mean performer. Despite the difficulty of getting it smartly off the line—all that happens is that the wheels spin like mad and the torque drags the nose over to the right—it still gets to 60mph in under 10sec, as fast as an Escort Twin Cam (which is 1cwt lighter).

ACCELERATION

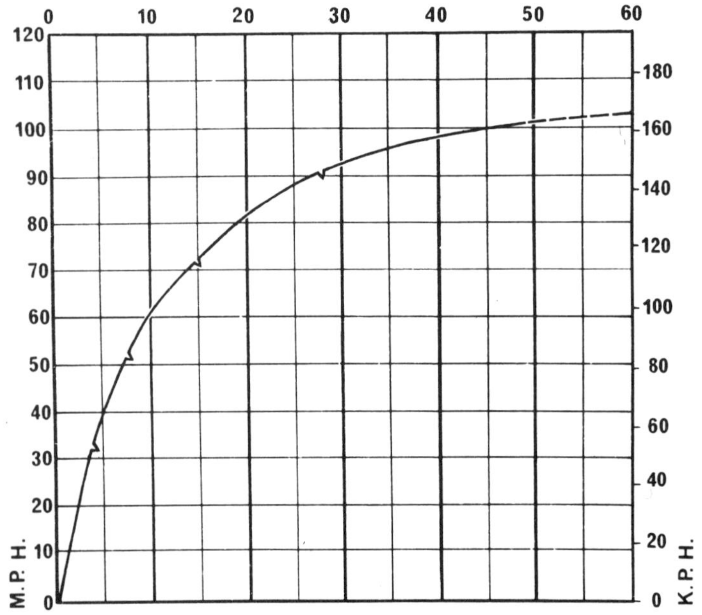

SPEED MPH TRUE / INDICATED	TIME IN SECS
30 / 33	3.5
40 / 43	5.2
50 / 52	7.5
60 / 62	9.9
70 / 73	14.2
80 / 83	19.1
90 / 94	27.3
100 / 105	46.0

SPEED RANGE, GEAR RATIOS AND TIME IN SECONDS

mph	Top (3.70)	4th (4.84)	3rd (6.40)	2nd (9.21)	1st (13.65)
10-30	—	—	—	3.7	2.4
20-40	—	—	5.2	3.1	—
30-50	10.2	7.2	4.6	3.8	—
40-60	10.1	6.5	5.0	—	—
50-70	10.4	7.3	6.9	—	—
60-80	11.4	8.6	—	—	—
70-90	14.6	13.6	—	—	—

Standing ¼-mile
17.6 sec 78 mph
Standing kilometre
32.7 sec 94 mph
Test distance
1,610 miles
Mileage recorder
3.7 per cent
over-reading

PERFORMANCE

MAXIMUM SPEEDS

Gear	mph	kph	rpm
Top (mean)	106	171	5,700
(best)	109	176	5,860
4th	103	166	6,600
3rd	70	113	6,600
2nd	50	80	6,600
1st	33	53	6,000

BRAKES

(from 70 mph in neutral)
Pedal load for 0.5g stops in lb

1	40	6	50-45
2	40	7	50-45
3	45-40	8	50
4	45	9	50-45
5	50-45	10	50-45

RESPONSE (from 30 mph in neutral)

Load	g	Distance
20lb	0.17	160ft
40lb	0.47	64ft
60lb	0.70	43ft
80lb	0.89	34ft
90lb	0.94	32.0ft
Handbrake	0.28	

Max. Gradient 1 in 3

CLUTCH

Pedal 40lb and 4in.

MOTORWAY CRUISING

Indicated speed at 70 mph	73 mph
Engine (rpm at 70 mph)	3,760 rpm
(mean piston speed)	1,850 ft/min
Fuel (mpg at 70 mph)	27.0 mpg
Passing (50-70 mph)	10.4 sec

COMPARISONS

MAXIMUM SPEED MPH

Alfa Romeo 1750 GTV	(£2,300)	116
Ford Escort Twin Cam	(£1,242)	113
BMW 2002	(£1,747)	107
Lancia Fulvia 1.6 HF	**(£2,526)**	**106**
Lancia Fulvia 1.3S	(£1,745)	106

0-60 MPH, SEC

Lancia Fulvia 1.6 HF	**9.9**
Ford Escort Twin Cam	9.9
BMW 2002	10.6
Alfa Romeo 1750 GTV	11.2
Lancia Fulvia 1.3S	12.7

STANDING ¼-MILE, SEC

Ford Escort Twin Cam	17.2
BMW 2002	17.4
Lancia Fulvia 1.6 HF	**17.6**
Alfa Romeo 1750 GTV	18.0
Lancia Fulvia 1.3S	18.7

OVERALL MPG

Lancia Fulvia 1.3S	28.2
BMW 2002	25.5
Alfa Romeo 1750 GTV	23.9
Lancia Fulvia 1.6 HF	**22.9**
Ford Escort Twin Cam	21.5

GEARING (with 175—13in. tyres)

Top	18.6 mph per 1,000 rpm
4th	15.6 mph per 1,000 rpm
3rd	10.7 mph per 1,000 rpm
2nd	7.5 mph per 1,000 rpm
1st	5.0 mph per 1,000 rpm

TEST CONDITIONS:
Weather: Cloudy. Wind: 3-6 mph. Temperature: 8 deg. C. (47 deg. F). Barometer 29.7 in. hg. Humidity: 65 per cent. Surfaces: dry concrete and asphalt.

WEIGHT:
Kerb weight 17.7 cwt (1,977lb—896kg) (with oil, water and half full fuel tank). Distribution, per cent F, 66.6; R. 33.4. Laden as tested: 21.8cwt (2,432 lb—1,101kg).

TURNING CIRCLES:
Between kerbs L, 37ft 5in; R, 36ft 4in. Between walls L, 38ft 10in; R, 37ft 8in. Steering wheel turns, lock to lock 4.2.

Figures taken at 3,200 miles by our own staff at the Motor Industry Research Association proving ground at Nuneaton and on the Continent.

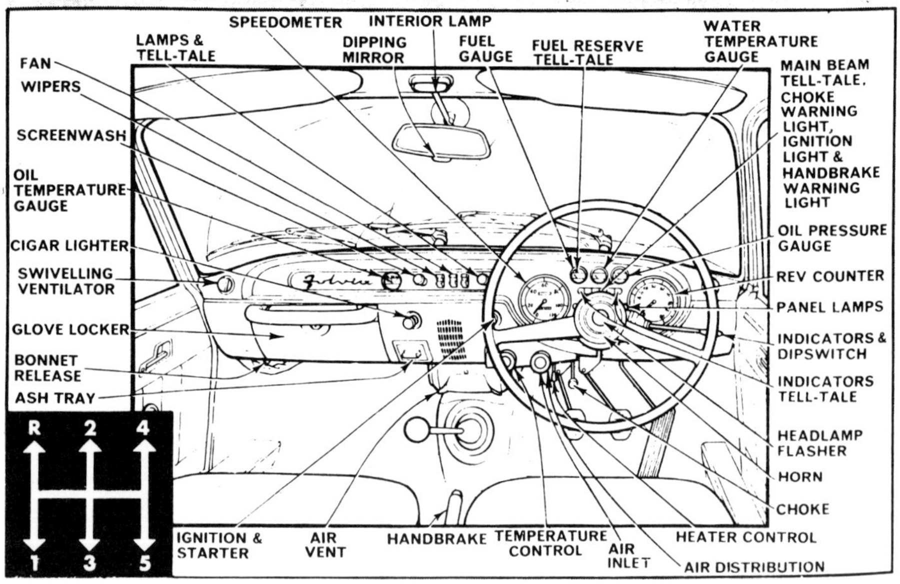

CONSUMPTION

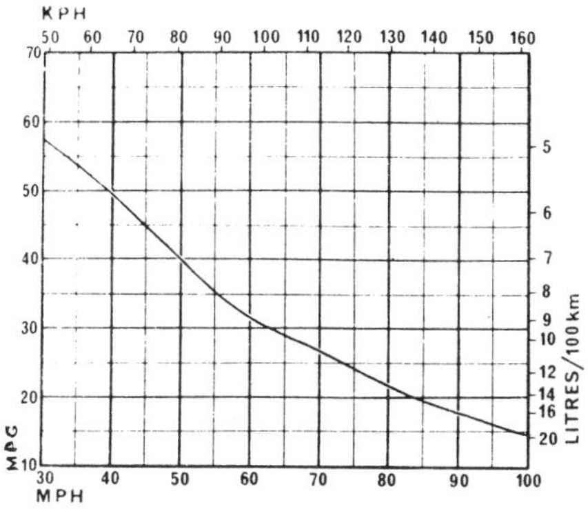

FUEL

At constant speeds—mpg)

30 mph	57.1
40 mph	49.4
50 mph	40.0
60 mph	31.3
70 mph	27.0
80 mph	21.7
90 mph	17.9
00 mph	14.8

Typical mpg 24 (11.8 litres/100km)
Calculated (DIN) mpg 24.6 (11.5 litres/100km)
Overall mpg 22.9 (12.4 litres/100km)
Grade of fuel . . . . Super Premium, 5-star (min. 100 RM)

OIL

Consumption (SAE 20W/50) . . . negligible

SPECIFICATION

FRONT ENGINE, FRONT-WHEEL DRIVE

ENGINE

Cylinders	4, in 13 deg. vee
Main bearings	3
Cooling system	Water; pump, fan and thermostat
Bore	82.0mm (3.22 in.)
Stroke	75.0mm (2.95 in.)
Displacement	1,584 c.c. (96.7 cu.in.)
Valve gear	Overhead camshafts, needle tappets, rockers
Compression ratio	10.5-to-1. Min. octane rating: 100 RM
Carburettors	Two Solex C42DDHF
Fuel pump	Fispa mechanical
Oil filter	Fram full-flow, replaceable element
Max. power	115 bhp (net) at 6,200 rpm
Max. torque	112 lb.ft. (net) at 4,500 rpm

TRANSMISSION

Clutch	Fichtel & Sachs, 7.9 in. dia.
Gearbox	Five-speed all-synchromesh
Gear ratios	Top 1.0 Fourth 1.31 Third 1.73 Second 2.49 First 3.69 Reverse 4.11
Final drive	Hypoid bevel, ratio 3.7 to 1

CHASSIS and BODY

Construction	Integral, with steel body (alloy doors, bonnet and boot lid)

SUSPENSION

Front	Independent, double wishbones, transverse leaf spring, telescopic dampers, anti-roll bar
Rear	Dead axle, semi-elliptic leaf springs, Panhard rod, telescopic dampers, anti-roll bar

STEERING

Type	Worm and roller
Wheel dia.	15.5 in.

BRAKES

Make and type	Girling discs front and rear
Dimensions	F 10.5 in. dia. R 10.5 in. dia.
Swept area	F 205 sq.in., R 205 sq.in. Total 410 sq.in. (376 sq.in./ton laden)

WHEELS

Type	Cast light alloy, 6.0 in. wide rim
Tyres—make	Michelin
—type	XAS radial ply tubed
—size	175-13 in.

EQUIPMENT

Battery	12 volt 42 Ah
Alternator	Bosch 33 amp a.c.
Headlamps	Carello tungsten-halogen, 110/220 watt (total)
Reversing lamp	Standard
Electric fuses	10
Screen wipers	Single-speed, self-parking
Screen washer	Standard, manual
Interior heater	Standard, water valve type
Heated backlight	Not available
Safety belts	Standard
Interior trim	Cirrus seats, PVC headlining
Floor covering	Carpet
Jack	Screw pillar
Jacking points	Two each side under body
Windscreen	Laminated
Underbody protection	Bitumastic overall

MAINTENANCE

Fuel tank	8.5 Imp. gallons (38 litres)
Cooling system	12 pints (including heater)
Engine sump	9 pints (5.8 litres) SAE 20W/50. Change oil every 4,300 miles. Change filter element every 4,300 miles
Gearbox and final drive	4.5 pints SAE 90EP. Change oil every 8,600 miles
Grease	11 points every 4,300 miles
Tyre pressures	F 21; R 21 psi (all conditions)
Max. payload	704 lb (320kg)

PERFORMANCE DATA

Top gear mph per 1,000 rpm	18.6
Mean piston speed at max. power	3,050 ft./min.
Bhp per ton laden	106

STANDARD GARAGE 16ft x 8ft 6in.

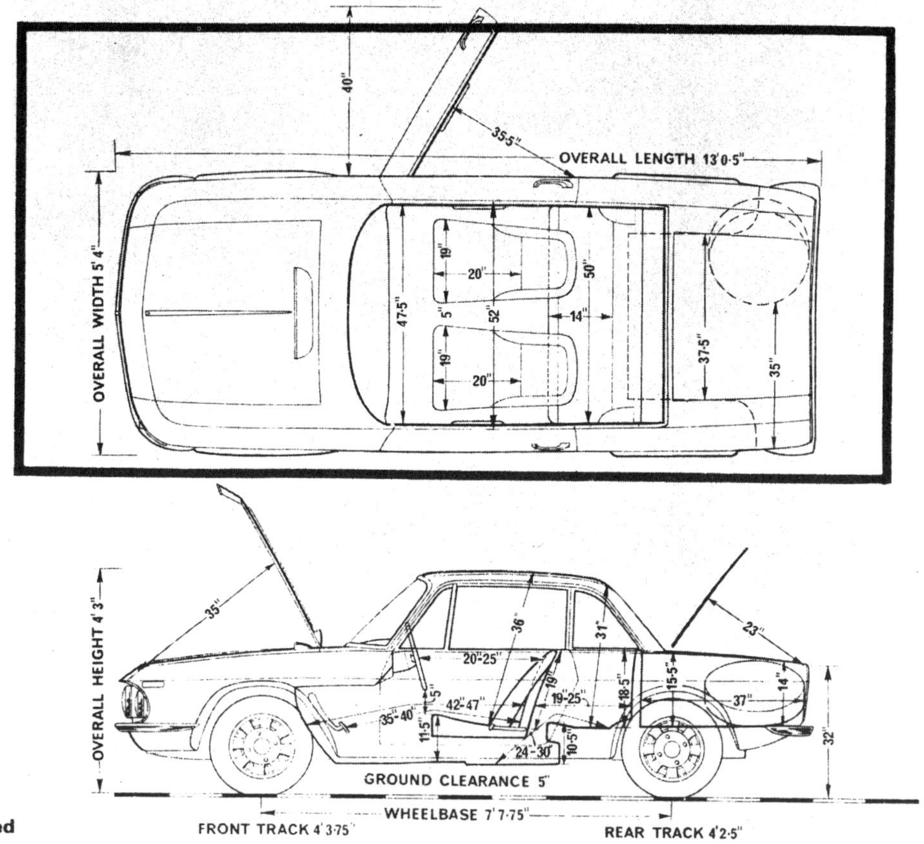

SCALE 0.3in. to 1ft
Cushions uncompressed

Left: There is a fair amount of ground clearance, and we never succeeded in bottoming the car even on really rough going

Below: The wide-rimmed spare wheel with its fat Michelin XAS takes up a good deal of room in the boot, but there is still space for a fair amount of luggage

AUTOTEST LANCIA FULVIA . . .

Any attempt to use lower revs for the start simply resulted in "dropping off the cam", with an accompanying fit of the shudders and the loss of a second or so in the time. We found that the best way of getting started was to let the clutch in quite suddenly at 4,500rpm, more or less at the peak torque figure.

It could hardly be said that this is the most flexible of units. When taking our acceleration figures in the gears, we found it impossible to pull away from 20mph in fourth gear, let alone top, and 30mph had to suffice. Clearly the gearbox has to be used very freely if the car is to perform satisfactorily. Fortunately, it is a very pleasant one to use. Reverse gear is left and forwards, opposite first; the other four gears are arranged in a conventional H-pattern. This works well, because first is so low that one tends to use it as a sort of ultimate weapon; a little judicious slipping of the clutch enables smooth starts to be made in second, even on marked uphill gradients. Gear changes require a fair amount of effort, but only over a very short distance. Synchromesh is very effective on the upper four gears but strictly nominal when changing down to first—double-declutching is essential here.

Top-end performance is, according to our figures, a little disappointing. The maximum speed of 106mph is no higher a mean than we achieved with the 1.3S earlier this year. It could be, however, that the test car was a little off-song following its rapid running-in, and that the stiffness which was still evident was having its greatest effect at high revs. Certainly, a similar but well loosened-up specimen which we were able to try briefly in Italy earlier this year had no difficulty in reaching and holding 115mph.

The tightness (and the high compression) shows also when starting. On cold mornings, the starter motor had trouble turning the engine, although the battery was in a perfectly good state of health. Once warm, starting was never a problem—which is more than can be said for some engines delivering over 70 (net) bhp per litre.

In the mid-range, from 4,000 to 6,000 rpm, the engine behaved very well indeed, giving excellent overtaking performance. Again, however, one noticed the sharp increase in noise level as 5,000rpm was approached.

If performance is one of the important aspects of a car intended for off-the-shelf rallying, then handling is the other. The Fulvia's steering is in fact quite low-geared, with over four turns of the wheel between extremes of a far from good lock. On the road, one is rarely aware of it, because in normal circumstances the understeer is very gentle. When the car is driven really hard, however, it certainly cannot be said (as it can of the smaller-engined Fulvias) that the driver is hardly aware of the fact that it is the front wheels which are driven.

It is possible to enter a corner extremely fast, feel the understeer build up as you haul the car on to line, and then back off; the transition to oversteer is far from violent, but it takes a noticeable steering wheel movement to hold the outward movement of the tail and maintain course. An alternative, and quite practicable, approach, is to keep a lot of power on and drag the nose round by sheer traction. In either case the steering remains remarkably light considering the size of the tyres, but response feels rather twitchy. In many ways, in fact, the Fulvia HF feels very like its rival the Escort Twin Cam, which is likewise over-tyred to an extent which makes the handling very delicately balanced; it takes a driver of above-average skill to drive either car really fast without falling off the edge either nose- or tail-first.

The Michelin tyres feel like a very fair compromise for most road conditions, although for serious competition use they would have to be replaced by something more specifically tuned to the surface to be tackled. When we tried the test car on a very soft surface, the nose-heaviness finally took charge and the understeer became really excessive, to be countered only by frequent lifting-off and judicious tweaks on the handbrake. In these conditions, a set of really deep-treaded cross-country tyres are the only answer.

The big disc brakes are well up to their job. It proved possible to pull the car up very quickly in a straight line on almost any sort of surface (which again says much for the tyres), although care was needed when braking in mid-corner. Brake response felt a little odd, with a slow initial build-up of retardation but a considerable improvement after the first 30-40 lb of pedal effort had been applied. The system survived our fade test with no sign of misbehaviour, and the handbrake was light and effective.

The HF feels as though it has a considerably stiffer ride than the ordinary Fulvia Coupés, but it remains smooth and pleasant on good surfaces. On rougher roads it starts to react a good deal more sharply, and on very bad surfaces the suspension starts to run out of travel, especially at the front, with a consequent deterioration in handling. Overall, it seems to exhibit the same sort of split personality which is evident in its performance; quiet and smooth when driven gently in civilized surroundings, sharp and noisy at high speed on minor roads.

The seats initially strike one as being very good indeed. It is possible to set up a good driving position for a wide range of sizes (the seats are mounted on sloping runners so that they drop as they move rearwards). The steering wheel is close to vertical, and the pedals—still standard Fulvia—are well spaced. Headroom is rather limited, but there is enough room in the back for a third person to sit in reasonable comfort.

After a few hours of continuous driving, the seats start to feel less satisfactory. To some extent this is because their shape prevents one from shifting position to avoid constant pressure on the same points; but it would certainly help if the cushion was better shaped to prevent an inexorable tendency to slide forwards. The seat brackrest angles are not adjustable, but are well chosen.

The main instruments are very clear and well placed, although the fuel gauge tended to waver, and its built-in warning light started to flash a long time before the fuel was down to panic level. For all that, the 8.5 gallon tank gives an effective range of little over 200 miles unless the car is driven gently. One notable and praiseworthy point was that once the car was warmed up, the water temperature settled at 160deg.F., and the oil temperature at 90degC., and neither varied thereafter regardless of how the car was driven.

Minor shortcomings

Minor controls have never been well laid out in the small Lancias, and the HF is no exception. The wipers are only single-speed, which hardly seems adequate for the sort of conditions the car might have to put up with, and the washer knob is pulled out against a spring, spraying the screen as it returns to its original position. The heater controls—two levers and two small handwheels—are confusing in operation, and it seems difficult to strike a happy medium between too much heat and too little. There is no face-level ventilation.

When trying to assess the Fulvia 1.6HF, one has to remember that it costs roughly £800, or 50 per cent, more than the very civilized, and quite rapid, 1.3S version. The extra money buys a good deal more performance and a five-speed gearbox—despite which, the car is undoubtedly less tractable and more difficult to drive smoothly. The body modifications have obviously been made with the idea of providing at least the basis for a highly competitive rally car. Whether many people in this country will look at it this way when they can have an Escort Twin Cam at half the price is rather doubtful, even though its RAC Rally win emphasizes its superiority in really slippery conditions. On the other hand, the Lancia retains most of the characteristics which endear the smaller-engined vdrsions to buyers; it represents a very different approach from the average run of British-made high performance saloons, and is undoubtedly enormous fun to drive—without ever leaving the driver with the uncomfortable feeling that really enthusiastic driving may lead to mechanical disaster. □

All the Winners:

RAC Rally

Lancia Fulvia 1.6 HF

By Jeffrey Daniels and Michael Scarlett

WE laid hands on Harry Källstrom's Lancia Fulvia less than a week after it had won the RAC Rally, and in that time nothing whatever had been done to it; it was ours for the day, just as it had finished. Even bodily it was in good condition, considering. The right front wing had been mildly clobbered, and so had the right-hand door (the car is left-hand drive). Mechanically, there were no worries at all. Harry had been working to an 8,000rpm rev limit in the rally, but we were asked to constrain ourselves to more like 7,000. With this one instruction, we were cast loose on to the North Circular.

At first acquaintance, the car was abominably noisy. It took only a few minutes, however, to discover that there was a 'quiet zone' around 3,000rpm, which could be used to waffle the car through suburban shopping centres without causing offence. With the gearing fitted, this corresponded to 30mph in fourth gear and 40mph in fifth.

The gearchange was a lot looser and lighter than on our Road Test Fulvia 1.6HF, and the gearbox was still functioning perfectly after its hammering; a tribute both to Lancia engineering and to Harry Källstrom's driving. The brakes felt even heavier than they were on the Road Test car—and they were heavy enough, in all conscience—but it was possible to get used to the pedal loads in time, and then to appreciate the fine control of braking effort which the system allowed.

The homologated weight of the Lancia is just under 15½ cwt, but this is with an empty tank, and we were running with the 90-litre (20-gallon) tank full, adding another 160 lb to the official figure. Compared with the production-standard car, Källstrom's is near enough 200 lb lighter, but there is little indication of where the weight has been saved, especially when one considers the massive undershield which protects both engine and transmission. The big fuel tank (twice the standard size) is an L-shaped container built around the single spare wheel in the boot.

In contrast to the gimmicky, cluttered interiors beloved of some would-be rallyists, the Lancia's 'office' was virtually standard. An ammeter had been added in the centre, and the inevitable Halda Twinmaster in front of Mr. Haggbom's seat on the right. Needless to say, the Halda was spot-on; it was also shielded to stop any stray light from distracting the driver. Other than this, it all looked reassuringly like our Road Test car. The only other differences were on the floor on the passenger's side, where a footrest had been added, and a wheelbrace and hammer clamped to the floor.

Above: Apart from absence of air cleaners, the under-bonnet appearance is pretty standard; which is more than can be said for the boot, with its massive non-standard fuel tank. Right: The sturdy little Lancia ploughs through anything, until it comes to the stage where the sump guard takes over as a sledge; even then, progress is rapid and stability good. The wide Dunlop SP44s provide excellent grip and control even in these conditions. Below: The Fulvia's 'office' is virtually standard, with absolutely nothing in the way of gimmicks or superflous equipment—just the vital Halda in front of the navigator

Performance

A little delicately, not wishing to break our valuable mount, we took some standing-start acceleration figures. Clearly, the car is very low-geared—our calculations suggest something like a 5.1 final drive instead of the standard 3.7—but we thought it safe to use 7,500rpm to get figures, giving speeds in the five gears of 27, 41, 58, 77 and 101mph.

Our starts tended to confirm what we found with the Road Test car, that varying the start technique changes the amount of wheelspin, but has little effect on the 0-30mph time which remains obstinately at about 3.5 sec. After that, times to 60mph are hampered by the fact that two more gearchanges intervene (one having already gone before 30mph). Thereafter the works car simply scampers away, with its lower gearing and higher power. It is getting on for 2sec faster to 70mph, 3sec to 80, 6sec to 90 and 16sec to 100. In terms of distance, the quarter-mile comes up nearly a second quicker (and 4mph faster), and the kilometre 1.6 sec faster. As the car passes the kilometre, its speedometer shows the kilometric equivalent of 101mph—plus its steady 3 per cent optimism—and the tachometer reaches 7,500rpm. The car is clearly very willing to do more.

Considering that standing-start performance is not a prime requisite for a rally car, and that we were loth to strain our mechanical sympathy too far, the figures look very convincing. Perhaps of more consequence is the way the gear ratios fall so that the useful rev ranges in third and fourth correspond very nicely to the most useful speed ranges for the tighter forest sections and the more open ones.

Although the performance is delivered very noisily for the most part, there is no sense of any sudden increase of noise or power at any particular engine speed; simply a gradual build-up which starts in earnest from about 3,500rpm. The car can be trickled along gently at speeds well below this, and the engine will idle, though rather lumpily, at 1,100rpm.

Handling

We described the standard car as twitchy and delicately balanced. The works car is the same, only rather more so. On a main road with gentle bends it is very easy to over-control until you get the hang of relaxing and letting the car more or less drive itself. The steering is incredibly light, taut and precise, with no road surface shocks being passed to the driver even though the tyres are massive, knobbly Dunlop Weathermasters. One is still vaguely conscious of under- and oversteer. The former hardly matters on the road because the response is so good; the car never gets into a situation where so much lock is required that understeer could threaten to limit cornering ability. There is a good deal more in the way of oversteer, however, particularly if power is reduced or the brakes applied in mid-corner. It does seem that the car has deliberately been set up just on the oversteering side of neutral.

On rough and slippery tracks, the car really comes into its own. The big Dunlops are very

good at providing a combination of radial-ply handling together with excellent traction. The lag in the response of the radial-ply sidewalls hardly matters (it is barely noticeable in any case) because all steering in these conditions is basically a matter of pointing the car by hanging the tail out in the appropriate direction. This is easily achieved by a double flick of the wheel, one to start the tail moving and the other to stop it; the technique comes so naturally in the Fulvia that virtually any competent driver would find himself doing it, even if he lacked any previous rough-road experience.

Of the standard car, we commented both that a change of tyres would be needed for best performance on unmade roads—and certainly the Weathermasters make an enormous difference—and that the front suspension seemed to run out of travel over really rough surfaces, badly affecting the handling when it did so.

Although the ride hardly seems any stiffer than in the production car, this just doesn't happen in the works car. To some extent it could be that very sharp bumps, which would normally push the suspension to the upper limit of its travel, are stopped short by coming up against the sled-shaped undershield. Certainly one is conscious of this massive piece of metal earning its living from time to time, even though a sensibly chosen line round most corners will avoid contact.

What is outstanding is the way the car can be hurled along rough tracks, still under control and preserving its crew from all but the worst effects of the surface. One begins to appreciate how it is possible for someone as good as Källstrom to drive so fast for so long and still end up fresh.

The other thing which gradually came to impress us was the conviction that this car was a lot closer to the production version than some. The near-standard interior was probably the factor which started us thinking along these lines. After that, everything started to fall into place. The engine had been meticulously prepared, to be sure, but it still felt much the same as the 1.6HF; it just revved higher. The handling certainly felt the same in most circumstances. For once, one was really left with the feeling that a competent mechanic could take the standard car and turn it into something quite like Harry Källstrom's, without having to do a complete rebuilding job from the ground up.

That in itself is praiseworthy; even more so is the way in which this RAC Rally winner was prepared to give of its best without missing a beat, despite being given to us in exactly the condition in which it finished the rally.

J.R.D.

PERFORMANCE CHECK

Maximum speeds

Gear	mph R/T	mph Works	kph R/T	kph Works	rpm R/T	rpm Works
Top (mean	106	101	171	163	5,700	7,500
(best)	109	101	176	163	5,860	7,500
4th	103	77	166	124	6,600	7,500
3rd	70	58	113	93	6,600	7,500
2nd	50	41	80	66	6,600	7,500
1st	33	27	53	43	6,600	7,500

Standing ¼-mile
R/T: 17.6 sec 78 mph
Works:
16.7 sec 82 mph

Standing kilometre
R/T: 32.7 sec 94 mph
Works:
31.1 sec 101 mph

Acceleration

Time in seconds								
R/T:	**3.5**	**5.2**	**7.5**	**9.9**	**14.2**	**19.1**	**27.3**	**46.0**
Works:	**3.5**	**5.2**	**7.2**	**9.6**	**12.6**	**16.2**	**21.0**	**29.7**
True speed mph	30	40	50	60	70	80	90	100

Available in both left and right drive versions, the new Lancia is a replacement for the Flavia 1,500 and 1,800 cc versions which have now been running for eight years. Pininfarina styling carries traditional Lancia lines, while at the same time introducing a four-seater Gran Turisimo image.

NEW LANCIA FLAVIA COUPE

2-litre version of flat-four engine: Restyled Pininfarina body

LANCIA will be giving the first public showing of their new front-wheel-drive Flavia Coupe 2000, at the Geneva Motor Show, opening on 13 March.

The four seater, Pininfarina designed body is powered by a new 1991c.c. flat-four engine, being a development of the now eight-year-old 1,500 and 1,800c.c. models which it will replace. Its capacity now gives Lancia a model in what has become known as the "European Class".

The new 2-litre engine produces 30 per cent more power—131 bhp at 5,400 rpm—than the previous model, achieved by increasing bore and stroke to 89mm and 80mm respectively and so lifting the bore-stroke ratio to nearly "square" at 0.89. Maximum torque is also increased to 132 lb.ft. Otherwise the engine is traditional Flavia with flat-four layout and three bearing crankshaft, further weight saving being made with aluminium alloy cylinder head, block and crankcase castings. The four-speed all-synchromesh gearbox gives maximum speeds of 31 mph, 62 mph and 89 mph in the indirect ratios and a claimed top speed of 115 mph.

First introduced in 1961 on the forerunners of the current front-wheel-drive layout Fulvia and Flavia series, the complete engine, clutch, gearbox and transmission as well as the steering assembly and front suspension, are mounted on a removable chassis subframe, with drive to the front wheels being transmitted through double constant-velocity joints.

Power-assisted steering is available for both left and right hand drive models, the mechanical worm and roller layout having 3½ turns lock to lock.

Servo-assisted disc brakes are fitted to all wheels with independent front and rear hydraulic circuits of Lancia's own design. In addition, a pressure limiting valve operates on the rear circuit to reduce the risk of back end lock-up under heavy braking.

The body is the result of collaboration between Lancia and Pininfarina to produce an elegant contemporary design, while maintaining basic traditional lines. To match the streamlined body, the nose of the new Lancia is low, with a forward opening bonnet which carries the air intake for the heater and ventilating systems. At the back, the design has resulted in a particularly large boot of 15.9 cu.ft. capacity, which also houses the spare wheel. Slim window pillars all round reduce potential blind spots: a laminated safety glass windscreen is fitted and the rear window is electrically heated to prevent fogging or icing. Electrically operated side windows are available.

Adequately padded seats are adjustable in the front for both length and rake, and all the essential controls can be operated without removing either hand from the steering wheel. The lockable glove compartment also houses all circuit fuses.

The front-wheel drive and Gran Turisimo rear styling contribute towards a particularly large boot with 15.9 cu ft available for luggage. Additional height and length in the passenger compartment makes more room for the rear seats.

Forward opening doors incorporate red "Door Open" warning lamps in the trailing edges which operate in conjunction with the courtesy lamps. Upholstery is available in cloth, vinyl or leather and the headlining is of elastic vinyl strips longitudinally mounted on expanded resin. The front seats are adjustable for reach and rake.

Special care has been taken over control layout so that horn, indicators, driving lamps, flasher, two speed wipers and electric screen washers can be operated without removing either hand from the steering wheel. The ignition switch is situated on the steering column and is combined with a steering lock.

The instrument panel is finished in matt shock absorbing material and instruments are located so as to avoid reflections. The facia has dark grey oxidised-aluminium fittings and houses the speedometer, tachometer, fuel-gauge (with reserve warning light) as well as separate engine temperature and oil pressure gauges. A lockable glove compartment with magnetic catches, also houses all circuit fuses in a compact panel.

A central console below the glove compartment contains the ventilation and heating controls and air extractors are fitted to the base of the rear window pillars. Further cold air ventilation is available from swivelling air vents, positioned at each end of the facia panel.

At a kerb weight of 2,623 lb (1,190 kg) the "2000" is 14ft 10¾in. long, 5ft 3¼in. wide and has an overall height when laden of 4ft 4¼in. □

AUTOTEST

LANCIA FULVIA SEDAN (1,298 c.c.)

AT-A-GLANCE: Refined front-wheel-drive 1300 four-door saloon from long-established Italian manufacturer. Good performance despite high weight. Safe handling, low geared steering. Comfortable and quiet. Expensive.

MANUFACTURER
Lancia S.p.A., Via Vincenzo Lancia 27, Turin, Italy.

UK CONCESSIONAIRES
Lancia (England) Ltd., Ealing Road, Alperton, Wembley, Middlesex.

PRICES

Basic	£1,070 0s 0d
Purchase Tax	£329 4s 9d
Seat belts (approx.)	£14 0s 0d
Total (in GB)	£1,413 4s 9d
EXTRAS (inc PT)	
Heated rear window*	£26 2s 3d
Metallic paint	£50 0s 0d
PRICE AS TESTED	£1,439 7s 0d

* Fitted to test car

PERFORMANCE SUMMARY

Mean maximum speed	96 mph
Standing start ¼-mile	19.7 sec
0-60 mph	15.6 sec
30-70 through gears	15.9 sec
Typical fuel consumption	30 mpg
Miles per tankful	280

LANCIA'S current Fulvia Sedan ("Berlina" in its native Italy) is the result of a "rationalization" of the previous range of three Fulvia saloons, which had grown from the original design of 1963. From the time of last year's Turin Show—which was also when details of Fiat's take-over of Lancia were announced—there ceased to be any 1,091 or 1,231 c.c. versions. Only the 1,298 c.c. unit from the Fulvia Berlina GTE remained, being put into a similar body of slightly bigger wheelbase and overall length.

Although the somewhat upright appearance does not suggest the unconventional, design of the Fulvia is anything but ordinary. The engine is a narrow angle vee 4 (13deg) with staggered cylinders, 77 x 69.7mm bore and stroke, three main bearings and one overhead camshaft per bank operating valves through rockers; one camshaft works all the inlet valves, the other all the exhausts. Running on 97RM-octane fuel this gives a claimed 87 bhp (DIN) at 6,000 rpm, with maximum torque of 84 lb. ft. at the relatively high speed of 4,500 rpm.

Drive to the front wheels is via a clutch shaft which passes through the hollow final drive pinion to a pair of helical gears at the back of the four-speed all-synchromesh gearbox. The Hardy Spicer drive shafts have Rzeppa-type constant velocity joints at both ends; suspension "plunge" is accommodated by telescopic ball-and-groove pot joints. A hefty sub-frame embodying stout cast members carries engine, transmission and front suspension, the latter consisting of a top leaf spring, double wishbones, an anti-roll bar and telescopic dampers. Steering is by worm and roller, and braking on discs all round with vacuum servo assistance. At the rear there is a simple dead axle located by longitudinal leaf springs and a Panhard rod.

All Lancias are full of little idiosyncrasies, of them excellent. First to strike anyone new to the marque are the plastic-handled keys, each of a sensibly small size, one in black for the ignition switch and steering lock and front doors, the other in white for glove locker, boot and fuel filler lids. Both door-lock and door-opening actions have a smooth "quality" air to them, and entry is easy because of the generous headroom. Having inserted and turned the key, you must push it to start, which in the good summer weather of the test period was never difficult. There is a not unpleasant whine to the engine which responds eagerly once warm; its generally quite low noise level is helped by an electric fan, only just audible when running at tickover in a heavy traffic jam.

Performance despite weight

The engine must be revved to get the best out of it and does very well indeed, considering that it has appreciably over a ton of kerb weight to pull; the Fulvia is a good hundredweight heavier than its nearest direct competitor, the Alfa Romeo Giulia 1300TI, and nearly a third as heavy again as the MG 1300 MkII. Therefore it is not surprising that it is not the fastest 1300 on the market. Nevertheless, performance is very satisfactory mainly because of its refinement. From a standing start in gusty conditions 50 mph comes up in 10.8sec, 60 in 15.6sec, the ¼-mile in 19.7sec and 80 in 32.9sec; given better weather these figures could certainly be improved slightly. The same applies to the 96 mph mean maximum speed obtained round the MIRA banking; the manufacturer's claimed 100 mph would be reached with less wind—as it was, we saw 102 on the downwind straight, corresponding to a shade over peak power rpm. Maximum allowed engine speed is 6,200 rpm, and it pays to take it up to 6,000 for best acceleration. Driven more gently, at not more than 5,000 rpm, the Fulvia impresses with its quietness and smoothness. It will cruise happily at an easy 80 mph on long journeys, which is when it is at its best, low wind and road noise helping considerably. Gear ratios are very much Italian mountain ones, with an unusually low 1st which is a little tiresome in towns, and correspondingly "short" 2nd and 3rd; top gear, at 16.8 mpg per 1,000 mph is just right.

Unlike the corresponding Fulvia coupé's, the gearlever is now a relatively short vertical affair, with a pleasantly large ball knob. Its action is delightful, being precise and quick, helped by good synchromesh. Heel and toe changes are very easy, as befits the refined but sporting nature of the engine. The only serious criticism one can make of the controls is of the movement of the throttle, which it is difficult to open smoothly. To make comfortable and jerk-free progress through stop-start traffic one must throw out the clutch more often than should be necessary, which is additionally tiring because of higher-than-average pedal effort. There is also too much intitial slop in the clutch pedal, though this is automatically forgotten after a while.

With a pair of twin-choke Solex carburettors—which you can at first sight easily mistake for Webers—and the high specific output, fuel consumption is very much a function of the heaviness of the driver's right foot. With reasonable restraint 30mpg should be obtained by owners, though taking the willing noises made by the engine at their word by driving harder must be paid for to the tune of down to 25 mpg.

With nearly 62 per cent of the car's weight on the front wheels, stability in a straight line is understandably excellent. Correspondingly, the final characteristic of the Fulvia Sedan's handling is understeer, though you have to corner pretty fast before this becomes pronounced. There is little roll, virtually no lift-off front-wheel-drive tuck-in effect, but an undue amount of tyre squeal from the Michelin ZX tyres. Roadholding is excellent. The steering, though adequately precise in action and light when on the move, has too much slop about the straight-ahead, is too low-geared (4.3 turns) and has a quite limited lock for the size of car (37ft 8in. mean). Although closely related, the Sedan cannot be flung about like the Fulvia coupés. It does, however, have excellent self-centring, which is all too rare with many contemporary cars, and one's hands are well insulated against feeling any road shocks. Ride is a nice combination of firmness with comfort on British roads.

Response to brake pedal pressure varies in a sensible way. Average sorts of stop need less than average effort by the driver, but pedal loads go up a little in proportion for really rapid stops; the best figure obtained, a creditable better-than-1g, occurred with front wheels on the point of locking. Fade performance is very good indeed. The handbrake works directly on the rear discs, yet performs reasonably. It holds the car pointing up a 1-in-3 slope, but not pointing down, when the locked back wheels slip. Restarting up the 1-in-3

Restraint almost to the point of inconspicuousness, plus much that is practical characterize the exterior of the little Fulvia

Right: Impressive and unusual engine room. The engine is all angles—a 13deg vee-4 inclined at 45deg from the vertical and 6deg downwards Far right: The roomy boot and its counter-balanced lid

two-up was only feasible by using the spinning front wheels as a sort of clutch.

The Fulvia impresses both driver and front passenger as very comfortable immediately they get in as well as after a long journey. The fully reclining seats hold and support one well in all directions. Tall drivers would welcome slightly more leg adjustment and a slightly higher steering wheel; one knee tends to foul it when lifting from accelerator to brake, but in the main the driving position is good, with all controls within reasonable reach. One of the little details that has a perhaps disproportionately large effect on one's impressions of a car's quality is the action of the various switches; all perform very pleasingly on the Fulvia. The two-speed wipers and the electric windscreen-washer are switched on from a steering-column stalk, always at one's fingertips. On the opposite side of the column there are the lighting control stalk and indicator lever, again well placed.

This latest Fulvia has a redesigned dashboard which is on the whole an improvement on its predecessors. Four round dials carry all the essential instruments a properly equipped car should have. In the outer smaller dials are an ammeter and fuel gauge and water temperature and oil pressure, and in the larger inner ones an 0–120 mph speedometer and 0–7,000 rpm revcounter, which in spite of the handbook's assurance that maximum revs are 6,200, is red-lined at 6,000. In the centre is a battery of warning lights for headlamp high beam, sidelamps on, alternator not charging, handbrake and choke left on, and winkers going. The choke might otherwise be easy to forget as it is mounted under the facia. Two unidentified knobs control instrument lighting and trip zero, and there is a clock in front of the passenger.

Visibility is generally very good. Window areas are generous except around the slightly heavy three-quarter rear panel, and an undeniable advantage of the chunkily proportioned body is that all four corners are easily seen when manoeuvring. Smokers will be glad of the front quarter-lights, especially as there is no righthand ashtray for the driver. Stowage space is reasonable in front, thanks to the two little side "buckets" down by one's feet, and the locking glove compartment in front of the passenger. Installing a radio need not deny you any of the limited space in the centre ahead of the gearlever as there is provision for a receiver in the facia. A welcome touch is the placing of the 11-strong fuse panel inside the cockpit, behind a removable panel under the heater controls.

These last look a little complicated at first and are only somewhat vaguely identified. The heater is an air-blending type, blending being controlled by the central lever. The upper one determines whether or not hot water is admitted to the heater matrix and the lower one whether the outer air-intake flap is open. side-window demisting is allowed for by the two little vents at each end of the dash. Through-flow of air seems to depend largely on whether one has at least a quarter-light open.

Rear room is just adequate for larger adults as far as their legs are concerned, though again there is plenty of headroom. Little support can be derived from the vestigial armrests on the doors. In spite of a vertically mounted spare wheel (which has a neat cover) boot-space is sensible, as is the fitting of a rubber mat to its floor; you must, however, lift your luggage over the high back sill. The bootlid has an effective pneumatic jack to hold it open when necessary.

Open the bonnet and you are presented with the handsome-looking sight of the black-crackle-finished engine and its impressive carburettor equipment. Plugs, distributor, coil, and all filling points are easily accessible and the delightful, expensively produced handbook with its slightly old-fashioned typescript (and not always perfect English) gives the owner-driver enough help to perform most regular servicing himself.

With iodine-vapour bulbs for both high and low beam on the four-lamp system, lighting is good, with a typically sharp Continental cut-off. A half-hornring operates the effective not-very-Italian toned horns.

With little change worth mentioning out of £1,400 if you buy a Fulvia Sedan, it is a very expensive car for its capacity in Great Britain. It offers no performance advantage over its main competitors, but is their equal in comfort and—in most instances—their peer in refinement, not to mention individuality. □

Above: The clean front with its rubber-tipped bumper (there is another one behind)

Left: Good door openings and headroom make entry and exit reasonably easy. One of the small details which please about the Fulvia is the way the doors shut

ACCELERATION

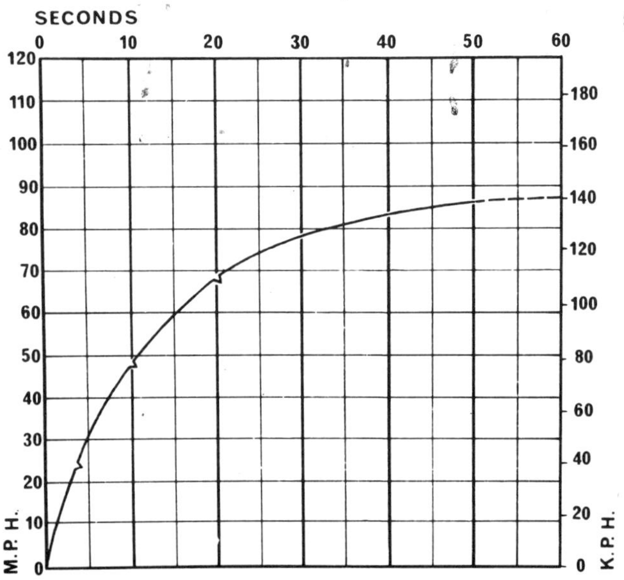

SPEED MPH TRUE	INDICATED	TIME IN SECS
30	32	4.8
40	42	7.3
50	52	10.8
60	63	15.6
70	74	20.7
80	85	32.9
90	96	

SPEED RANGE, GEAR RATIOS AND TIME IN SECONDS

mph	Top (4.10)	3rd (5.82)	2nd (8.94)	1st (15.99)
10-30	—	10.2	6.1	—
20-40	14.6	8.5	5.2	—
30-50	13.9	9.2	—	—
40-60	15.4	9.6	—	—
50-70	19.0	—	—	—
60-80	24.6	—	—	—

Standing ¼-mile
19.7 sec 68 mph
Standing kilometre
36.9 sec 82 mph
Test distance
1,290 miles
Mileage recorder
4.3 per cent
over-reading

PERFORMANCE

MAXIMUM SPEEDS

Gear	mph	kph	rpm
Top (mean)	96	154	5,720
(best)	102	164	6,070
3rd	73	117	6,200
2nd	48	77	6,200
1st	27	43	6,200

BRAKES

(from 70 mph in neutral)
Pedal load for 0.5g stops in lb

1	30—25	6	30—25
2	30—25	7	30—25
3	30—25	8	30—25
4	30—20	9	30—25
5	30—25	10	30—25

RESPONSE (from 30 mph in neutral)

Load	g	Distance
20lb	0.27	111ft
40lb	0.56	54ft
60lb	0.74	41ft
80lb	0.84	36ft
100lb	1.03	29ft
120lb	1.06	28.4ft
Handbrake	0.30	100ft

Max. Gradient 1 in 4 (see text)

CLUTCH

Pedal 35lb and 5½in.

MOTORWAY CRUISING

Indicated speed at 70 mph	74 mph
Engine (rpm at 70 mph)	4,170 rpm
(mean piston speed)	1,905ft/min.
Fuel (mpg at 70 mph)	29.4 mpg
Passing (50-70 mph)	19.0 sec

COMPARISONS

MAXIMUM SPEED MPH

Renault 16TS	(£1,235)	102
Alfa Romeo Giulia 1300TI	(£1,299)	97
MG 1300 Mk II	(£931)	97
Lancia Fulvia Sedan	**(£1,399)**	**96**
Fiat 124 Special	(£1,025)	96

0-60 MPH, SEC

Renault 16TS	12.4
Fiat 124 Special	12.8
MG 1300 Mk II	14.1
Alfa Romeo Giulia 1300TI	15.3
Lancia Fulvia Sedan	**15.6**

STANDING ¼-MILE, SEC

Renault 16TS	18.8
Fiat 124 Special	19.0
MG 1300 Mk II	19.6
Lancia Fulvia Sedan	**19.7**
Alfa Romeo Giulia 1300TI	19.8

OVERALL MPG

MG 1300 Mk II	26.8
Lancia Fulvia Sedan	**24.1**
Renault 16TS	23.3
Fiat 124 Special	22.6
Alfa Romeo Giulia 1300TI	21.3

GEARING (with 155-14in. tyres)

Top	16.8 mph per 1,000 rpm
3rd	11.8 mph per 1,000 rpm
2nd	7.7 mph per 1,000 rpm
1st	4.3 mph per 1,000 rpm

TEST CONDITIONS:
Weather: Cloudy. Wind: 8-14 mph. Temperature: 20 deg. C. (68 deg. F.). Barometer: 29.6 in. hg. Humidity: 40 per cent. Surfaces: dry concrete and asphalt.

WEIGHT:
Kerb weight 21.1 cwt (2,360lb—1,070kg) (with oil, water and half-full fuel tank). Distribution, per cent F, 61.8; R, 38.2. Laden as tested: 25.1 cwt (2,810lb—1,274kg).

TURNING CIRCLES:
Between kerbs L, 37ft 10in.; R, 37ft 7in. Between walls L, 40ft 8in.; R, 40ft 1in. steering wheel turns, lock to lock 4.3

Figures taken at 5,000 miles by our own staff at the Motor Industry Research Association proving ground at Nuneaton.

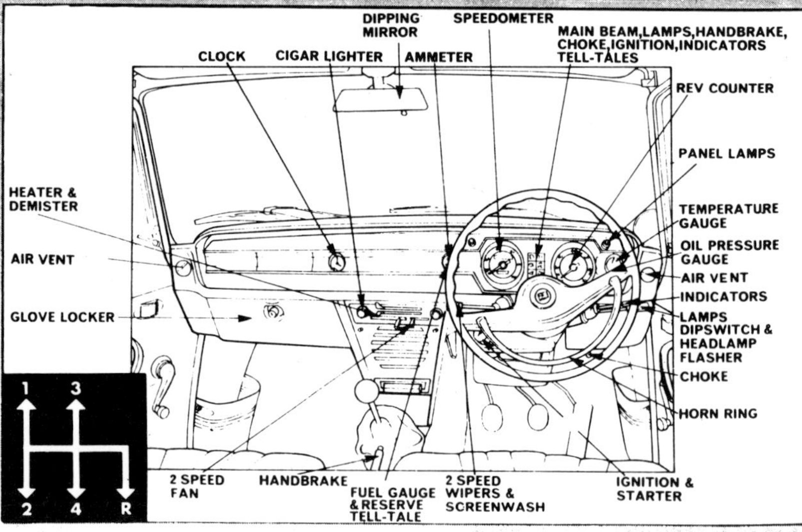

CONSUMPTION

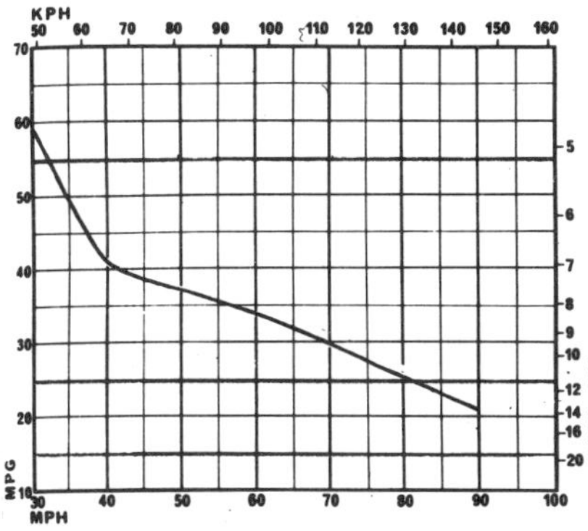

FUEL

(At constant speeds—mpg)

30 mph	58.8
40 mph	41.6
50 mph	37.0
60 mph	33.5
70 mph	29.4
80 mph	25.7
90 mph	21.1

Typical mpg 30 (9.4 litres/100km)
Calculated (DIN) mpg 26.8 (10.6 litres/100km)
Overall mpg 24.1 (11.7 litres/100km)
Grade of fuel. Premium, 4-star (min. 97 RM)

OIL

Miles per pint (SAE 10W/40) 1,500

SPECIFICATION FRONT ENGINE, FRONT-WHEEL DRIVE

ENGINE

Cylinders	4, in 13 deg vee
Main bearings	3
Cooling system	Water, pump, fan and thermostat
Bore	77.0mm (3.03in.)
Stroke	69.7mm (2.74in.)
Displacement	1,298 c.c. (79.2 cu.in.)
Valve gear	Single overhead camshaft per bank, rockers
Compression ratio	9.0-1. Min. octane rating: 97 RM
Carburettors	2 Solex C35 PHH
Fuel pump	Fispa mechanical
Oil filter	Carello/Fram full flow, replaceable element
Max. power	87 bhp (DIN) at 6,000 rpm
Max. torque	84 lb.ft (DIN) at 4,500 rpm

TRANSMISSION

Clutch	Fichtel and Sachs diaphragm-spring
Gearbox	4-speed, all-synchromesh
Gear ratios	Top 1.0 Third 1.42 Second 2.18 First 3.90 Reverse 4.11
Final drive	Gleason hypoid bevel, ratio 4.1-to-1

CHASSIS and BODY

Construction	Integral, with steel body

SUSPENSION

Front	Independent; double wishbones, transverse leaf spring, telescopic dampers, anti-roll bar
Rear	Dead axle, half-elliptic leaf springs, Panhard rod, telescopic dampers

STEERING

Type	Worm and roller
Wheel dia.	15.5in.

BRAKES

Make and type	Dunlop discs front and rear
Servo	Bonaldi vacuum
Dimensions	F 10.5in. dia. R 10.5 in. dia.
Swept area	F 205 sq.in., R 205 sq.in. Total 410 sq.in. (328 sq.in./ton laden)

WHEELS

Type	Pressed steel disc, 4-stud fixing, 4.5in. wide rim
Tyres—make	Michelin
—type	ZX radial ply tubed
—size	155-14in.

EQUIPMENT

Battery	12 Volt 45 Ah
Alternator	Bosch 28 amp a.c.
Headlamps	Carello tungsten-halogen, 110/220 watt (total)
Reversing lamp	Standard
Electric fuses	11
Screen wipers	2-speed
Screen washer	Standard, electric
Interior heater	Standard, water-valve type
Heated backlight	Extra
Safety belts	Extra, front and rear mounting points standard
Interior trim	Pvc seats and headlining
Floor covering	Carpet
Jack	Screw scissor type
Jacking points	2 each side under body
Windscreen	Laminated
Underbody protection	Bitumastic overall

MAINTENANCE

Fuel tank	9.3 Imp. gallons (42 litres)
Cooling system	11 pints (including heater)
Engine sump	7.5 pints (4.3 litres) SAE 10W40. Change oil every 4,000 miles. Change filter element every 4,000 miles.
Gearbox and final drive	4.5 pints SAE 90EP. Change oil every 8,000 miles
Grease	11 points every 4,000 miles
Tyre pressures	F 24; R 24 psi (all conditions)
Max. payload	890 lb (400 kg)

PERFORMANCE DATA

Top gear mph per 1,000 rpm	16.8
Mean piston speed at max. power	2,740 ft/min
Bhp per ton laden	69.7 (DIN)

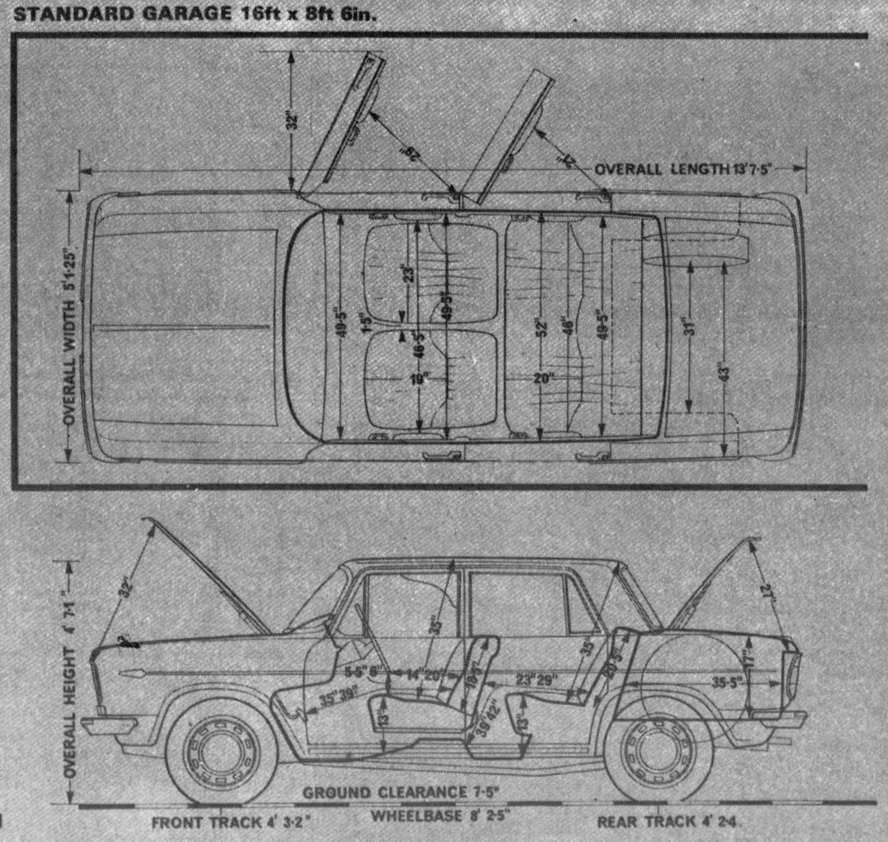

SCALE 0.3in. to 1ft
Cushions uncompressed

Right: Most expensive model in the range is the Pininfarina styled Flavia coupé. Right centre: A black finished facia distinguishes the Flavia coupé from the saloon. The Philips cassette player is extra. Far right: Flavia coupé engine compartment with front hinged bonnet

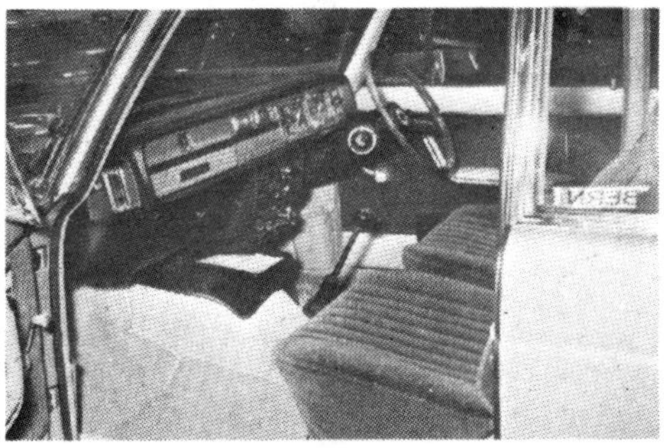

Right: The 2000 sedan is easily distinguished from the Flavia coupé by the different frontal treatment. Right centre: A wood-finished facia with square instruments and cloth seats are features of the 2000 sedan. Far right: 2000 sedan engine compartment

Right: Fulvia Rallye HF Lusso. Right centre: Interior of the Lusso. Note the head restraints and the wrap-round bucket seats. Far right: The 1,584 c.c. vee-4 engine fits neatly under the Lusso's bonnet

Right: Zagato styling for the Fulvia Sport S2 turns it into a fastback. Right centre: Instrumentation on the Sport S2 is fairly similar to the S2 coupé but the seats are different. Far right: A forward-opening bonnet is a feature of the Sport S2

Right: Fulvia coupé S2 with 1.3-litre engine. Right centre: Specification of the coupé S2 includes reclining front seats, a five-speed gearbox and full instrumentation. Far right: Angled vee-4 twin carburettor engine under the bonnet of the Fulvia coupé S2

Right: Cheapest model in the range is the Fulvia sedan: Right centre: In the Fulvia sedan most of the facia is finished in black. Far right: Attention to detail on the sedan includes a telescopic damper for the bonnet lid

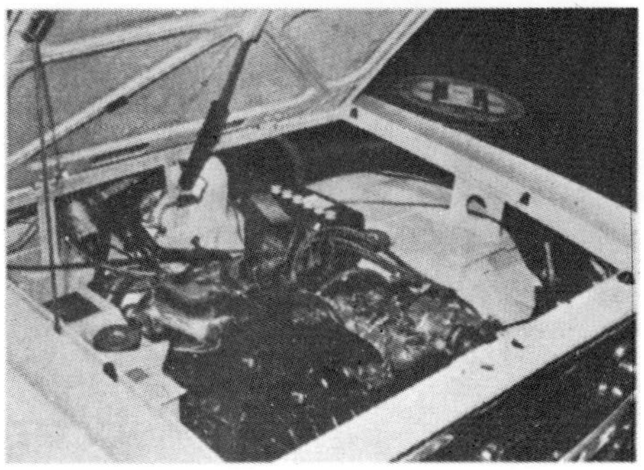

THE CURRENT LANCIA RANGE

FOUR Fulvia models and a 2000 saloon (or sedan as Lancia call it) and coupé make up the range of Lancias currently available in the UK. Basic model is the 1,298 c.c. vee-4 engined Fulvia four-door sedan which, like all current models in the range, features front-wheel drive. Variations on this are the three Fulvia coupés — the Rallye S2, Sport S2 with Zagato coachwork, and the recently introduced Rallye HF Lusso which has considerably more power from its 1,584 c.c. 115 bhp engine. Both the 2000 sedan and Flavia coupé 2000 use horizontally opposed four-cylinder engines, the coupé having coachwork by Pininfarina.

Specifications and prices

FULVIA SEDAN

Engine: V4-cyl, 77 x 69.7mm (3.03 x 2.74in), 1,298 cc (79.2 cu. in.); C.R. 9.0 to 1; twin ohc; 2 Solex carbs, 87 bhp (DIN) at 6,000 rpm, max torque 84 lb. ft. (11.6 mkg) at 4,500 rpm.

Transmission: Front engine, front drive. Manual: 4.1, 5.26, 7.36, 11.06, 17,07, rev 17.38. Top gear mph/1000 rpm 16.8.

Suspension: ifs, transverse leaf spring, wishbones, anti-roll bar. Rear, dead axle, half elliptic leaf springs, anti-roll bar. Steering, worm and roller.

Brakes: Dunlop (servo), 10.5in. front discs, 10.5in. rear discs.

Dimensions: Wheelbase, 8ft. 2.5in. (250cm); front track 4ft. 3.2in. (130cm), rear track 4ft. 2.4in. (128cm). Overall length 13ft. 7.5in. (416cm), width 5ft. 1.2in. (155cm), height 4ft. 7.1in. (140cm), ground clearance 4.7in. (12cm). Turning circle 35ft. (10.7m). Unladen weight 2,360 lb (1,070kg).

Service: Tyres 155-14in.; 4.5in. rims; F 24psi (1.69kg/cm^2) R 24psi (1.69kg/cm^2). Capacities: Fuel 9.2gal (42 litres); coolant 12 pints (6.3 litres); oil 8 pints (4.5 litres). Major maintenance interval 4,300 miles (7,000km.). Max payload 860 lb (390kg.).

Price including Purchase Tax £1,370.63.

FULVIA COUPE RALLYE S2: Specification as for Fulvia Sedan except for:

92 bhp (DIN) at 6,200 rpm, max torque 95 lb.ft. (13.1 mkg) at 4,500 rpm.

Gear ratios, 3.91, 5.02, 7.01, 10.54, 16.27, rev 16.55. Top gear mph/1000 rpm 17.1. Wheelbase 7ft. 7.7in. (233cm); overall length 13ft. 0.5in. (397cm); height, 4ft. 3.2in. (130cm). Unladen weight 2,050 lb (930kg.).

Tyres 165-14in. F 26psi (1.83kg./cm^2). R 26psi (1.83kg./cm^2); max payload 688 lb (309kg.). Oil 8.7 pints (5 litres).

Price including Purchase Tax £1,791.88.

FULVIA SPORT S2: Specification as for Coupé Rallye S2 except for:

Overall length 13ft. 5in. (409cm); width 5ft. 1.8in. (157cm), height 3ft. 11.2in. (120cm). Unladen weight 2,061 lb (935kg.); max payload 516 lb (234kg.).

Price including Purchase Tax £2,155.63.

FULVIA COUPE RALLYE HF LUSSO

Engine: V4-cyl, 82 x 75mm (3.22 x 2.95in.), 1,584 cc (96.7 cu.in.); C.R. 10.5 to 1; twin ohc; 2 Solex carbs, 115 bhp (DIN) at 6,200 rpm; max torque 112 lb.ft. (15.5 mkg) at 4,500 rpm.

Transmission: Front engine, front drive. Manual: 3.70, 4.84, 6.40, 9.21, 13.65, rev 15.20. Top gear mph/1,000 rpm 18.6.

Suspension: ifs, wishbones, transverse leaf spring, anti-roll bar. Rear, dead axle, half-elliptic leaf springs, anti-roll bar. Steering, worm and roller.

Brakes: Girling (servo); 10.5in. front discs, 10.5in. rear discs.

Dimensions: Wheelbase, 7ft. 7.7in. (233cm); front track 4ft. 3.2in. (130cm), rear track 4ft. 2.4in. (128cm). Overall length, 13ft. 0.5in. (397cm), width 5ft. 4in. (162cm), height 4ft. 3.2in. (130cm), ground clearance 5in. (12.5cm). Turning circle 36ft. 10in. (11.2m). Unladen weight 1,977 lb (896kg.).

Service: Tyres 175-13in.; 6.0in. rims; F 21psi (1.48kg./cm^2) R 21 psi (1.48kg./cm^2). Capacities: Fuel 8.5gal (38 litres); coolant 12 pints (6.8 litres); oil 9 pints (5.8 litres). Major maintenance interval 4,300 miles (7,000km.). Max payload 704 lb (320kg.).

Price including Purchase Tax £2,321.88.

2000 SEDAN

Engine: 4-cyl, 89 x 80mm (3.5 x 3.15in.), 1,990 cc (121.5 cu.in.); C.R.9.2 to 1; ohv; Solex carb, 115 bhp (DIN) at 5,500 rpm; max torque 123 lb. ft. (17 mkg) at 3,500 rpm.

Transmission: Front engine, front drive. Manual: 3.91, 5.73, 8.86, 14.80, rev 17.18. Top gear mph/1,000 rpm 19.2.

Suspension: ifs, transverse leaf spring, wishbone, anti-roll bar. Rear, dead axle, half elliptic leaf springs, anti-roll bar. Steering, worm and roller (power-assisted).

Brakes: Dunlop (servo), 11.1in. front discs, 11.1in. rear discs.

Dimensions: Wheelbase, 8ft. 8.3in. (265cm); front track 4ft. 3.9in. (132cm), rear track 4ft. 2.4in. (128cm). Overall length, 15ft. 2in. (462cm), width 5ft. 3.25in. (161cm), height 4ft. 9.5in. (146cm), ground clearance 4.7in. (12cm). Turning circle 36ft. 0in. (11.0m). Unladen weight 2,716 lb (1,235kg.).

Service: Tyres 175-14in.; 4.5in. rims; F 26psi (1.83kg/cm^2). R 26psi (1.83kg/cm^2). Capacities: Fuel 12gal (55 litres); coolant 14.1 pints (8 litres); oil 12.7 pints (7.2 litres). Major maintenance interval 4,300 miles (7,000km.). Max payload 1,032 lb (469kg.).

Price including Purchase Tax £2,153.13.

FLAVIA COUPE 2000

Engine: 4-cyl, 89 x 80mm (3.5 x 3.15in.), 1,990 cc (121.5 cu.in.); C.R. 9.2 to 1. ohv; Solex carb, 115 bhp (DIN) at 5,500 rpm; max torque 123 lb. ft. (17 mkg) at 3,500 rpm.

Transmission: Front engine, front drive. Manual: 3.73, 5.46, 8.46, 14.1, rev 16.4. Top gear mph/1,000 rpm 19.75.

Suspension: ifs, transverse leaf spring, wishbones, anti-roll bar. Rear, dead axle, half-elliptic leap springs, anti-roll bar, Panhard rod. Steering, worm and roller (power-assisted).

Brakes: Dunlop (servo), 11.1in. front discs, 11.1in. rear discs.

Dimensions: Wheelbase, 8ft. 1.5in. (248cm); front track 4ft. 4in. (132cm), rear track 4ft. 4in. (132cm). Overall length, 14ft. 10.7in. (454cm), width 5ft. 3.25in. (160cm), height 4ft. 4.5in. (133cm), ground clearance 4.7in. (12cm). Turning circle 36ft. 0in. (11.0m). Unladen weight 2,618 lb (1,190kg.).

Service: Tyres 165-15in.; 5.5in. rims; F 28psi (1.97kg./cm^2) R 28psi (1.97kg./cm^2). Capacities: Fuel 12gal (55 litres); coolant 13 pints (7.5 litres); oil 15.5 pints (8.8 litres). Major maintenance interval 4,300 miles (7,000km.). Max payload 688 lb (312kg.).

Price including Purchase Tax £2,635.63.

Optional Extras (inc. P.T.)

Metallic paint £71.88.

Electrically heated rear window (Fulvia) £25.00.

Power assisted steering (Flavia Coupe) £116.25.

AUTO TEST

LANCIA FULVIA SEDAN

Five-speeds for an Italian gentleman

AT-A-GLANCE:
New five-speed gearbox improves performance of Lancia's unique little 1,300 c.c. front-wheel drive saloon. Very stable, fair radi, pretty refined. Expensive.

IT is only just over a year ago that we tested the Fiat-rationalized Lancia Fulvia Sedan (*Autocar* 17 September 1970), then available for the first time only with the largest of its three engine options, the 1,298 c.c. version. Since then that unusual thing, a rationalization upwards, has been made, in the adoption of a modified version of the five-speed gearbox first used on the rally-winning 1.6 HF Fulvia coupé, providing the main reason for once more trying this idiosyncratic Italian quality small car.

As far as the actual "gate" of the gearchange is concerned, Lancia have perhaps deliberately not followed the pattern set by their rivals Alfa Romeo. Reverse, which on the four-speed original versions was "bottom right" is now approximately opposite first, "top left". We say "approximately" because on the test car it took some of us a little while to select reverse as it was necessary to allow the lever to move a little to the right of the expected full-left position before it would go into reverse. First is bottom-left; second top-middle and so on, in the usual H. The pleasingly ball-knobbed short lever is spring-loaded into the centre, and must be moved vertically to get past the reverse safety lock.

The action is generally very pleasant, and the ratios progressively arranged to give gradually closing rev drops as one goes up the box. We were surprised to find the synchromesh between 2nd and 3rd not quite up to its job, but on the other gears it proved unbeatable. First is a real Italian mountain gear, extremely low at only just over 4 mph per 1,000 rpm, (and slightly lower than the previous four-speed first), which with a top speed of 26 mph makes it somewhat absurd in ordinary driving. But its effect is noticeable on the getaway; over $\frac{1}{5}$sec was chopped off the 0-30 mph time. One is grateful for it in very slow speed traffic, when the now not so heavy clutch can be allowed fully home with the car crawling at very low speed.

There are no changes reported on the still highly unusual narrow angle vee-4 engine with its staggered cylinders, over-square proportions, three main bearings and one overhead camshaft per bank working, through rockers, in one case all the inlet valves and in the other all the exhausts. It produces its maximum power, a claimed 85 bhp (DIN) at the relatively high speed of 6,000 rpm, with correspondingly high-set maximum torque, 83 lb. ft. at 4,500 rpm. In actual performance it feels like the high-revving, rather fussy unit that those figures suggest. Having to propel 21 cwt and such an uncompromisingly blunt body through the air, the engine and all five gears have to be made full use of if one is in any kind of hurry. It is, however, pretty smooth and very willing to rev, making a not unpleasant and fairly subdued yowl on full song.

Overall gearing is unchanged, at 16.8 mph per 1,000 rpm, and there is no change in maximum speed. As on the last occasion when we tested the Fulvia Sedan, somewhat high winds prevented the car giving its absolute best, but nevertheless there was a surprising improvement in through-the-gears standing-start times, as follows (four-speed times in brackets): From rest to 50 mph in 9.7sec (10.8), to 60 in 13.9 (15.6), to the mile in 19.1sec (19.7) and to 80 in 29.5 (32.9). In the

Right: Photographed by the side of MIRA's variously graded test hill, the steepest slope of which the car will climb from standstill with spinning front wheels, a telephoto lens makes the Fulvia Sedan even chunkier in appearance than it in fact is. Apart from slightly ponderous rear quarter panels, deep windows afford good all-round visibility. Below: Rear seats are shaped to suit two passengers only, who find adequate room for themselves in all directions. The oddly quilted appearance of the door upholstery is given by the protective plastic covering, which an owner normally removes. Perhaps a reflection on the enthusiastic tendencies of the Lancia's native drivers in winding country, grab handles (not visible here) are provided over all passenger doors. The door armrests contain small ashtrays, but, somewhat surprisingly, there is no central rear armrest

Above: Amongst the many excellent examples of detail design, one of the best is the fitting of automatically switched warning lamps on the front doors. A typically unusual Lancia feature are the curved-edge glass gussets fixed in the top rear corners of the front doors, intended to cut down draughts with open windows

Right: The extremely unusual engine and its accommodation, somewhat confined, with its two twin-choke Solex carburettors. Accessibility to routine items needing attention isn't too difficult. The power unit, a 13deg vee-4, is mounted at 45deg to the vertical and 6deg downwards

Extreme right: Roomy boot with a sensible rubber floor and protected insides; the sill is high. Note another sensible feature, the rubber faced bumper

Below: Chaste interior devoid of clashing vulgarities; the seats give good overall support. The boxy body has about the same overhang front and rear

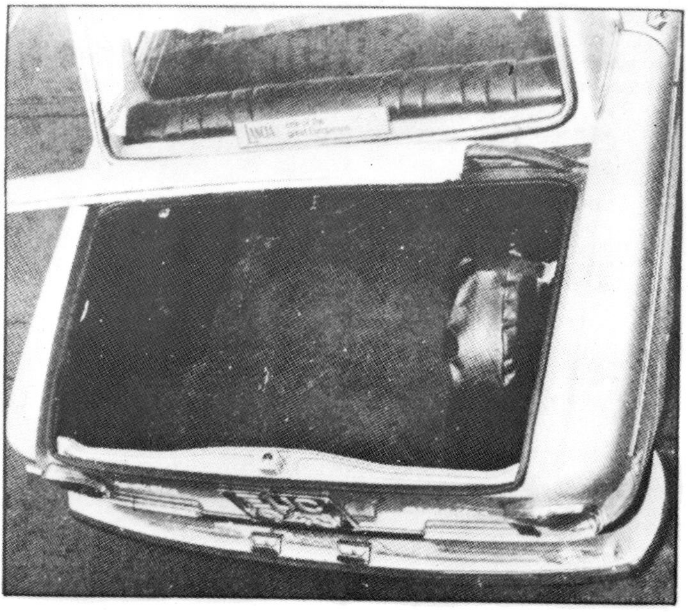

comparison figures this improves the Lancia's position *vis-à-vis* its competitors to a worthwhile extent.

As usual with relatively highly developed small engines in large-ish bodies, fuel consumption depends very much on the greed of the driver. Used to the full, it is understandable that the additional gear and the fact that one can more nearly stay on peak power all the time must reduce the car's economy, as shown in the overall consumption figures. The five-speed Fulvia's 22.4 mpg must be compared with the four-speed's 24.1, but driven quietly there should be no reason why one cannot equal the earlier car's good fuel figures similarly conducted. A frugal man should see up to 30 mpg without difficulty. Oil consumption is light, at 1,500 miles per pint, and the power unit keeps nicely clean.

Ride and handling

One's first impression at the wheel is of how rubbery and, to a degree, sloppy the steering is, but immediately you start driving the car you learn that this is misleading. It steers on the whole quite well, with excellent self-centring, but it cannot be flung about like its very different sporting brother, the Fulvia coupé. One can take a line through a bend in a pleasingly precise way and, thanks to the car's surprisingly low degree of understeer, hold that line consistently. On a smooth road, straight stability is of a very high order, and so is side-wind stability. On a bumpy or uneven road, there is a tendency for the car to bump-steer very slightly, which can be felt in the steering wheel, though not to any sort of uncomfortable extent. It rolls little and has no pronounced front-wheel-drive characteristics like excess

LANCIA FULVIA SEDAN (1,298c.c.)

ACCELERATION

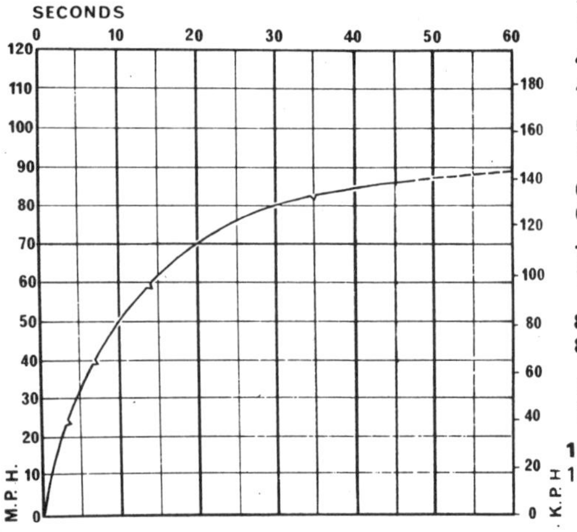

SPEED MPH TRUE	INDICATED	TIME IN SECS
30	30	4.2
40	41	7.0
50	51	9.7
60	62	13.9
70	73	20.1
80	84	29.5
90	95	
100	105	

GEAR RATIOS AND TIME IN SEC

mph	Top (4.10)	4th (5.27)	3rd (7.35)
10-30	—	—	7.1
20-40	14.8	10.0	6.2
30-50	14.2	9.7	6.2
40-60	16.1	10.1	—
50-70	19.7	11.7	—
60-80	23.8	16.5	—

Standing ¼-mile
19.1 sec 69 mph
Standing Kilometre
36.0 sec 83 mph
Test distance
674 miles
Mileage recorder
3.2 per cent over-reading

PERFORMANCE

MAXIMUM SPEEDS

Gear	mph	kph	rpm
Top (mean)	96	155	5,700
(best)	102	164	6,050
4th	84	135	6,400
3rd	60	97	6,400
2nd	40	64	6,400
1st	26	42	6,400

BRAKES

FADE
(from 70 mph in neutral)
Pedal load for 0.5g stops in lb

1	27-30	6	30-38
2	30	7	30-38
3	30-35	8	30-38
4	30-35	9	30-38
5	30-35	10	30-38

RESPONSE
(from 30 mph in neutral)

Load	g	Distance
20lb	0.34	89ft
40lb	0.75	40ft
60lb	0.90	33.4ft
Handbrake	0.23	131ft
Max. Gradient	1 in 3	

CLUTCH

Pedal 30lb and 6.0in.

COMPARISONS

MAXIMUM SPEED MPH

Renault 16TS	(£1,301)	102
Alfa Romeo Giulia 1300TI	(£1,299)	97
MG 1300 Mk II	(£931)	97
Lancia Fulvia Sedan	**(£1,371)**	**97**
Fiat 124 Special	(£1,101)	96

0-60 MPH, SEC

Renault 16TS	12.4
Fiat 124 Special	12.8
Lancia Fulvia Sedan	**13.9**
MG 1300 Mk II	14.1
Alfa Romeo Giulia 1300TI	15.3

STANDING ¼-MILE, SEC

Renault 16TS	18.8
Fiat 124 Special	19.0
Lancia Fulvia Sedan	**19.1**
MG 1300 Mk II	19.6
Alfa Romeo Giulia 1300TI	19.8

OVERALL MPG

MG 1300 Mk II	26.8
Renault 16TS	23.3
Fiat 124 Special	22.6
Lancia Fulvia Sedan	**22.4**
Alfa Romeo 1300TI	21.3

GEARING

(with 155-SR14 in. tyres)

Top	16.8 mph per 1,000 rpm
4th	13.08 mph per 1,000 rpm
3rd	9.37 mph per 1,000 rpm
2nd	6.22 mph per 1,000 rpm
1st	4.04 mph per 1,000 rpm

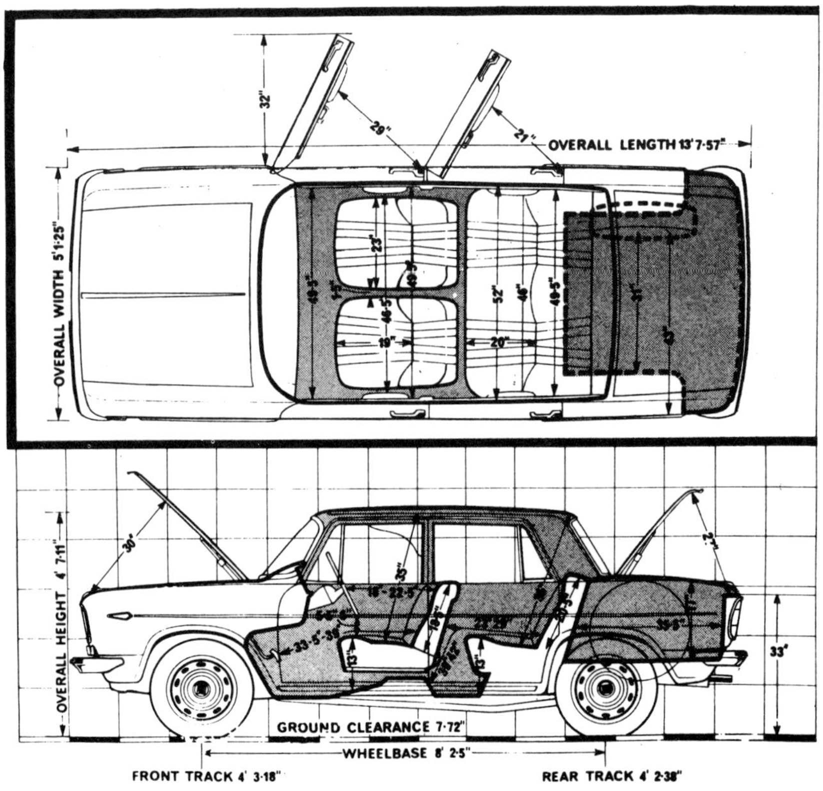

STANDARD GARAGE 16ft x 8ft 6in.

CONSUMPTION

FUEL
(At constant speed—mpg)

30 mph	35.0
40 mph	35.4
50 mph	34.3
60 mph	30.7
70 mph	27.0
80 mph	22.8
90 mph	18.0

Typical mpg . . . 29 (9.7 litres/100km)
Calculated (DIN) mpg 24.6 (11.5 litres/100km)
Overall mpg . . 22.4 (12.6 litres/100km)
Grade of fuel Premium, 4-star (min. 97 RM)

OIL
Consumption (SAE 10W/40) . . . 1,500

TEST CONDITIONS:
Weather: Dry, gusty Wind: 10-15 mph.
Temperature: 9 deg.C. (48 deg. F.)
Barometer: 29.90 in. hg. Humidity: 58 per cent.
Surfaces: Dry concrete and asphalt.

WEIGHT:
Kerb Weight 21.1 cwt (2,360 lb-1,070 kg) (with oil, water and half full fuel tank) Distribution, per cent F, 61.8; R, 38.2 Laden as tested: 25.1 cwt (2,810 lb-1,27- kg).

TURNING CIRCLES:
Between kerbs L, 37 ft 10 in.; R, 37 ft 7 in
Between walls L, 40 ft 8 in.; R, 40 ft 1 in
Steering wheel turns, lock to lock 4.3
Figures taken at 6,000 miles by our own staff at the Motor Industry Research Association proving ground at Nuneaton

SPECIFICATION

FRONT ENGINE, FRONT-WHEEL DRIVE

NGINE	
:ylinders	4, in 13deg vee
Main bearings	3
:ooling system	Water; pump, electric fan and thermostat
ore	77.0mm (3.03in.)
troke	69.7mm (2.74in.)
)isplacement	1,298 c.c. (79.2 cu.in.)
'alve gear	Single overhead camshaft per bank, rockers
'ompression ratio	9.0-to-1 Min. octane rating: 96RM
arburettor(s)	Two Solex C35 PHH 18
uel pump	Fispa mechanical
il filter	Carello/Fram full flow, renewable element
1ax. power	85 bhp (DIN) at 6,000 rpm
1ax. torque	83 lb.ft (DIN) at 4,500 rpm
RANSMISSION	
lutch	Fichtel and Sachs diaphragm spring, single dry plate
earbox	5-speed, all-synchromesh
ear ratios	Top 1.0 Fourth 1.284 Third 1.793 Second 2.698 First 4.159 Reverse 4.239
nal drive	Gleason hypoid bevel, 4.1-to-1
HASSIS and BODY	
onstruction	Integral, with steel body
USPENSION	
ont	Independent, transverse leaf spring, double wishbones, telescopic dampers, anti-roll bar
ar	Dead axle, half-elliptic leaf springs, Panhard rod, telescopic dampers
TEERING	
pe	Worm and roller
heel dia.	15.5 in.
RAKES	
ake and type	Girling discs front and rear
rvo	Bonaldi vacuum
mensions	F 10.2 in. dia. R 10.88 in. dia.
ept area	F 220 sq. in. R 200 sq. in. Total 420 sq. in. (335 sq. in./ton laden)
HEELS	
e	Pressed steel disc, 4-stud fixing 4.5 in. wide rim
es—make	Michelin
—type	ZX radial ply tubed
—size	155SR14-in.
UIPMENT	
tery	12 Volt 45 Ah.
ernator	Bosch 28 amp a.c.
adlamps	Carello tungsten-halogen, 110/220-watt (total)
ersing lamp	Standard
ctric fuses	11
een wipers	Two-speed
een washer	Standard electric
rior heater	Standard water-valve
ated backlight	Extra
ety belts	Extra, anchorages built in
rior trim	Pvc seats, pvc headlining
or covering	Carpet
k	Screw scissors
king points	2 each side, under body
dscreen	Laminated
erbody otection	Bitumastic overall
INTENANCE	
tank	9.3 Imp. gallons (42 litres) (no reserve)
ling system	11 pints (including heater)
ine	7.5 pints (4.3 litres) SAE 10W40. Change oil every 4,000 miles. Change filter element every 4,000 miles.
rbox and nal drive	4.5 pints SAE 90EP, change oil every 8,000 miles
ase	8 points every 4,000 miles.
pressures	F 27; R 24 psi (normal driving) (all conditions).
. payload	890 lb (400 kg)
RFORMANCE DATA	
gear mph per 1,000 rpm	16.8
n piston speed at max. power	2,740 ft/min.
per ton laden	67 8

AUTOTEST LANCIA FULVIA SEDAN . . .

Every possible major control is grouped around the steering column on stalks, which makes the car easier to drive. A full set of the right instruments is provided, including an ammeter (always preferable to a battery voltmeter) and an excellent clock (far left) with full sweep second hand. The "grained" sections of the steering wheel spokes now operate the horns (instead of the previous half horn ring) and are too easily worked accidentally. All controls, however minor, work with delightful precision

front-end "tuck-in" when one decelerates. Roadholding in both wet or dry conditions on the Michelin ZX tyres is very good indeed; ultimately pressed to its remarkably high limits, the Fulvia simply runs wide, as one would expect. On the debit side the steering is rather too low-geared (4.3 turns lock to lock), and has too restricted a lock (37ft 8in. average) for the size of car.

The car rides on the whole well, with a pleasant combination of firm damping and adequate softness; it is above all quietly suspended, with subdued bump-thump and hardly any detectable road-roar.

The performance of the servo-assisted all-disc brakes caused us to suspect that pad material of a softer grade has been substituted since our previous test. On that occasion we found that rather too much pedal pressure (120lb) was needed for maximum retardation, but that a clear 1g was obtained. On this latest car, maximum braking came up at only 60lb, but was limited to 0.9g by seemingly premature front-wheel locking. Fade resistance during our standard test proved adequate, but some experimental hard driving, perhaps more nearly typical of what some native Lancia drivers will demand up in the hills, did produce some fade accompanied by subdued pad rumble. This need not worry the majority of drivers. The handbrake coped with 1-in-3, this time just not allowing the car to slip down with locked back wheels when facing forwards; restarting up the same slope, as usual, was best achieved by spinning the front wheels, in order to avoid fading the clutch linings.

Tasteful interior

Perhaps the only noticeable change inside the car — noticeable because it makes itself heard too easily — is the substitution of spoke-switch operation of the fine horns for the previous half horn ring. The trouble with such an arrangement is that in the Lancia's case the operating parts of the switch are extended too far out towards the rim, with the result that even when one has got used to the car, one still tends to hoot at people at all sorts of unintended, not to say occasionally embarrassing, times. Convenience of all controls is otherwise very good except for the somewhat inaccessible rich mixture knob.

A stalk looks after the superb iodine-vapour headlamps, which give a magnificent amount of light when you want it, and have a good cut-off at other times. British drivers might prefer the lamp flashing switch to work on main beam instead of dipped. Heater controls are poorly identified for anyone strange to the car, but work tolerably well once you are familiar with them; there appears to be adequate extraction, and one welcomes the provision of side-window de-misting. An air-blending temperature control would be an improvement on the present water-valve one, though it works better than most.

Seats give good general support, have beautifully smooth and easily moved slides with about 2in. too little rearward movement to them for tall drivers. If that movement was obtainable, the same drivers would then find that they were too far from the wheel. Heel and toe changes are very easy with the excellent pedal arrangement. So many small details of interior design are pleasing on the Lancia, such as the differently coloured plastic handled keys, the retracting boot lock, the way the doors shut and all controls move.

Such subtle satisfactions are probably part of the reason why this expensive, average-fast 1300 saloon sells in Britain. It has a quietly quality air to it that distinguishes it from the rest. □

MANUFACTURER:
Lancia S.pA., Via Vincenzo Lancia 27, Turin, Italy.

UK CONCESSIONAIRES:
Lancia (England) Ltd., Ealing Road, Alperton, Wembley, Middlesex.

PRICES

Basic	£1,095.00
Purchase Tax	£275.63
Seat belts (approx.)	£15.00
Total (inc. P.T.)	£1,385.63

EXTRAS (inc. P.T.)

Metallic paint	£71.88
*Heated rear window	£25.00

*Fitted to test car

PRICE AS TESTED	£1,410.63

BETA
a new start for Lancia

By J. R. Daniels, B.Sc.

Latest Lancia shows Fiat influence in several important areas. Engine is twin-cam Fiat 132 unit, but transverse-mounted for front-drive application; MacPherson struts and disc brakes all round. Produced in 1400, 1600 and 1800 versions; replaces Fulvia saloon, but coupé continues

THREE years ago, Fiat bought out Lancia for a strictly nominal price, and in the process inherited considerable debts and a load of trouble. The existing Lancia models, worthy though they were of the firm's long and splendid tradition, had been in production for some time, and no new models were in the pipeline to replace them. Production was poorly organised and much of the equipment was archaic — as were some of the methods.

Fiat's answer was to conduct a holding operation by up-dating the two production cars, the Fulvia and Flavia, turning the latter into the 2000 with its new body, five-speed gearbox, fuel injection and revised braking system. In the meantime they set about rejuvenating the Lancia factories, concentrating mainly on the newest, at Chivasso to the east of Turin. Finally, they went to work to produce the new model which was so badly needed, and which has emerged now in the form of the Lancia Beta.

The very choice of name is symbolic, for the Beta of 1909 was Lancia's first true production car, and launched the firm's tradition of advanced engineering. The new Beta is a different kind of starting point — the first car in which Fiat's production and structural expertise is joined with Lancia's advanced thinking.

Although the Lancia design team started with a clean sheet of paper as far as the chassis was concerned, they were committed to using the Fiat twin-cam engine in its various sizes. Fiat were already developing this unit for their forthcoming 132, with the result that it was available in 1400, 1600 and 1800 form. Lancia elected to offer all three engine sizes in the Beta, so covering a much wider section of the market without suffering multiplied production costs.

While the engine is the familiar Fiat unit with its belt-driven twin overhead camshafts, the manner of its installation is Lancia's own. With such a strong tradition of front wheel drive they would contemplate no other layout for the Beta, and the engine was therefore installed transversely, just ahead of the front axle line and inclined towards the rear at an angle of 20 degrees. Lancia have tuned it only by changing the camshaft profiles, and their timing actually involves less overlap (13-45-49-9 compared with 12-53-52-13 for the Fiat 132). The compression ratio remains the same, at 8.9 to 1. Although their installed power is higher, with the 1800 engine producing 110bhp (DIN) in the Beta compared with 105bhp in the Fiat 132, Lancia's main aim was to alter the shape of the power curve to suit the ratios in their five-speed gearbox.

Viewed from the driver's seat, the engine sits well to the right of the car's centre line, and the drive is carried in a straight line through a conventional diaphragm-spring clutch to the gearbox mainshaft. The gearbox itself is a two-shaft, all-indirect, five-speed design; a spur reduction gear takes the drive from the inboard end of the output shaft to the final drive. The drive shafts are of unequal length and diameter, and have constant-velocity joints at both ends; the inboard joints accommodate any driveshaft plunge.

The two-shaft gearbox layout was chosen to keep the length of the unit to a minimum, for although the engine is not particularly long, space is still at a premium if the turning circle is not to be restricted. The gear ratios are the same for all three engine sizes but the final drive ratios are different; 4.46 to one for the 1400, 4.21 to one for the 1600, and 4.07 to one for the 1800. Even when taken in conjunction with the 0.92 top gear ratio and the 14in. wheels, this gives fairly low overall gearing; the 1800 pulls 18.2mph per 1,000rpm in top gear.

The gear ratios are much closer than in the older Lancia gearboxes, with first a good deal higher. Lancia claim maxima of 31, 48, 71, 94 and 109mph for the 1800, the speeds in the intermediate gears representing the engine's safe limit of 6,400rpm. The maximum speed in top corresponds almost exactly with the power peak of 6,000rpm, and the smaller-engined versions sacrifice very little in the way of high-speed performance. Lancia claim 106mph for the 1600, and 102mph for the 1400.

The whole engine and transmission assembly is mounted on a front sub-frame. Two of the mounting points are close to the centre of the car, one holding the final drive casing and the other supporting the gearbox/clutch bell housing. The third, pillar-type support holds the front (or, from the driver's viewpoint, the right hand side) of the engine in the region of the camshaft drive. The subframe in its turn is mounted to the body shell at four symmetrically-disposed points, two on either side of the car centre line. Twin exhaust pipes pass through the subframe before reaching a junction beneath the body, while the gearchange linkage is taken to an idler lever mounted on the subframe, from which a further linkage operates the gear selectors. The clutch is cable-operated.

All-independent suspension

Previously, Lancia have used dead axles at the rear of their front-drive designs, in the interests of cost and simplicity. The Beta, however, uses independent rear suspension because its designers felt it was the only way to achieve the desired standard of ride without sacrificing handling in any way. Clearly Fiat theory and practice played a part in this decision, for the Beta has MacPherson struts all round, like the Fiat 128 and 130. In detail, though, Lancia's answers are new.

The front suspension is largely conventional, and remarkable for its geometrical simplicity. When viewed from the side, the McPherson strut is mounted upright, with no offset of the lower swivel pin and therefore no castor angle. The struts are, however, canted inwards some 5deg, and there is a small amount of lateral offset, although the extended steering axis passes well within the

Above: Boot is a regular rectangular shape and low sill makes for easy loading; fuel tank is situa[ted] beneath floor. De luxe models have carpeted b[oot] Right: Standard of interior equipment is high, wi[th] full range of instruments and (in the de luxe versi[on]) cut-pile carpet and velvet seats

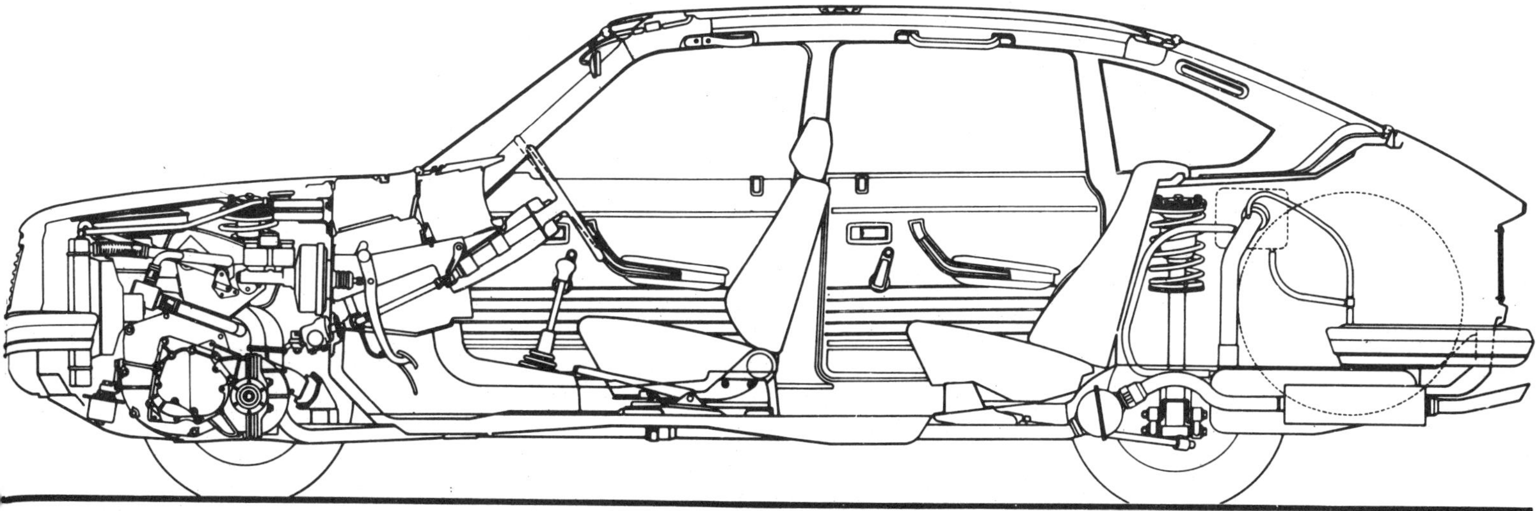

area of the tyre contact patch. The axis of the damper does not coincide with the steering axis, with the result that the coil spring is not concentric with the damper. An anti-roll bar, rubber-mounted on the sub-frame, plays no part in locating the wheels.

The MacPherson struts at the rear are simpler in design, with concentric spring/damper units. Twin transverse tubular arms locate each wheel against sideways movement; these arms are very long — almost half the wheelbase — and ensure that camber changes are kept to a minimum. They also effectively form a very narrow wishbone, but fore-and-aft location is actually taken care of by the rear anti-roll bar, whose ends sweep back to form drag links. There is no rear sub-frame as such, and rubber insulation is built into the mounting points of the lower arms and the anti-roll bar. Remarkably little sound insulation appears to have been incorporated into the main struts, however.

The use of MacPherson struts all round, with front and rear anti-roll bars, is a layout of which Fiat have a good deal of experience. The widely separated mounting points make for a light and efficient structure, while the roll centres are high and so, therefore, is the roll axis, allowing the suspension to be kept relatively soft without the car laying over on its beam ends when cornered quickly. The desired handling characteristics can then be set up by adjusting the stiffness of the two anti-roll bars.

Rack and pinion steering is used in the Beta, with the rack mounted on the engine compartment bulkhead so that all the main mechanical components protect the steering in the event of a collision. The steering arms embody rubber insulation at their inboard ends, so cutting off another path by which road noise could enter the body. A

Left: Engine compartment looks rather crowded, due in part to width of twin-cam cylinder head. Diagonal struts look like design afterthoughts to stop front-hinged bonnet moving backwards in a collision Above: Front view of engine, transmission and lower front suspension assembled on front subframe

Above: Six-light styling (from Lancia's own studio) is reminiscent of Citroen GS and Alfasud, though the shovel nose might almost have been borrowed from Toyota Left: Direct front view shows four halogen headlamps, wide tyres on 14in. wheels and relatively low mounting of front subframe Below: Rear quarter view emphasises fastback shape and slim pillars, which promise good visibility

BETA 1800LX

double-jointed steering column is used, and the wheel itself is adjustable for rake; the claimed turning circle is a moderate 35ft, and there are four turns of the wheel from lock to lock.

In contrast with Fiat's 132, which is in many ways a car of similar size, Lancia retain 14in. wheels for the Beta, trading ground clearance and stability for the small sacrifice in internal room taken up by the wheel arches. The wheels have 5.5in. wide rims and are shod with low-profile 175/70 radial-ply tyres, except for the 1400 version which has 155-14in. tyres on 5in. rims.

Another point in favour of larger wheels is that larger disc brakes can then be accommodated without running into problems. The Beta uses 10in. discs all round, operated by a "superduplex" hydraulic system: in effect, the front wheels have two independent sets of brake calipers, but the rear wheels only one. A brake circuit failure therefore leaves the driver at least with front wheel braking — which means, in a front wheel drive car, that relatively little is lost.

Medium-sized but roomy

One can compare the Beta with both the Fulvia saloon which it effectively replaces, and with the Fiat 132, a conventional car of much the same size and using the same basic engine. It is at once apparent that the Beta offers much more room than the Fulvia. Something is gained in useful length, with a 1.5 in. increase in wheelbase to add to the space saved by the transverse mounting of the engine. The Beta's longer nose, which is largely responsible for the fact that the new car is five inches longer than the Fulvia, is not wasted space, of course, but contains the radiator and electric fan mounted ahead of the engine and transmission.

Perhaps more important, the Beta is five inches wider than the Fulvia, which should add greatly to the impression of space. The narrowness of the older car was one of the things which betrayed its age, though it was not necessarily a bad thing in itself.

The most significant thing of all is that although the Beta is a rather bigger car with a bigger engine, it weighs very little more than the Fulvia. The basic Beta 1400 has a kerb weight only 28lb greater than that of the Fulvia Sedan, despite its ability to meet all immediately foreseen safety requirements. Since the weight of a car reflects in some degree what it costs to build, the influence of Fiat's structural expertise has clearly been used to good effect in allowing the Beta to be produced more profitably.

Compared with the Fiat 132, the Beta is marginally smaller but slightly heavier. In part, this reflects the Lancia's very high standard of equipment; it is notable also that the Beta has a higher rated payload than the 132.

The styling of the Beta body with its six-light fastback shape was carried out by Lancia's own styling department. Its shape follows a growing European trend, typified by the Citroen GS and the Alfasud — like the Beta, both advanced front-wheel-drive cars. Lancia claim to have paid careful attention to aerodynamics, but they do not quote a drag coefficient and the claimed maximum speed suggests little improvement in this respect over the three-box shape of the Fiat 132.

Thanks to the front wheel drive, there is plenty of space at the back of the car for a large boot with a usefully regular shape. it is not quite as large as in some of the Beta's competitors, for the 11-gallon fuel tank is housed beneath the floor and the spare wheel is mounted upright on the right hand side. The MacPherson strut housings also intrude. Although the Beta's shape clearly lends itself to a five-door treatment, there is less demand for such a car as one moves up the market. The Beta's boot lid consists of the whole rear panel aft of the rear window, opening to leave a low sill and easy access. To make a five-door version would call for considerable redesign, for there is a stressed diaphragm aft of the back seat.

As one would expect in a Lancia, the standard of equipment is very high. Speedometer, rev counter, fuel, water temperature and oil pressure gauges are fitted, together with a clock and no fewer than twelve warning lights. Minor controls follow the now well-established Lancia pattern, with three column-mounted stalk switches. A very comprehensive air-blending heating and ventilation is built in, with four face-level inlets in the facia and a separate warm air delivery to the back seats. Stale air is extracted via slots on either side of the rear window, and the window itself is electrically heated.

Production under way

As we have said, the Beta comes in 1400, 1600 and 1800 versions, with either standard trim or (for the 1600 and 1800) a de luxe package including such items as velvet seats, cut-pile carpet, intermittent wipers, a tinted windscreen and a number of features aimed at improving the appearance without cluttering the styling — Lancia were anxious to avoid an over-abundance of chrome. Options include a sunroof, electric windows, light alloy wheels, air conditioning and alternative upholstery materials. Automatic transmission is not yet offered, but is apparently on the way.

Beta production is centred on the big modern plant at Chivasso, where 350 cars a day are currently produced, with 600 a day as the ultimate aim. The first cars will be for the Italian market, with the most important export markets — among which Lancia include Britain — being served from next spring. There is as yet no indication of the price that will be asked, but the clear aim is to produce the Beta in larger numbers at a lower price than hitherto has been the case with Lancia models. The economy will be one of scale and more efficient methods; there will be no slackening of traditional Lancia standards. Output in 1972 is expected to amount to 50,000 cars compared with 33,000 in 1969, and a profit is not expected until 1975, when the production target is 100,000 cars. Fiat can only be congratulated on continuing to support Lancia's resuscitation despite their own current difficulties (the Fiat group will make a considerable loss this year because of further labour problems and the general Italian economic situation). It is even more of a relief to see that their answer does not take the form of badge-engineered Fiats. If the Lancia Beta lives up to its paper promise — as yet, journalists have yet to drive it — it should make a major contribution to the firm's recovery, and their major problem may well be an inability to produce enough cars. □

SPECIFICATION

FRONT ENGINE, FRONT-WHEEL DRIVE

ENGINE

Cylinders	4, in line, transversely mounted
Main bearings	5
Cooling system	Water, pump, electric fan and thermostat
Bore	84.00mm (3.31in.)
Stroke	79.2mm (3.12in.)
Displacement	1,756 c.c. (107.1 cu.in.)
Valve gear	Twin overhead camshafts, direct-acting toothed belt drive
Compression ratio	8.9-to-1 Min. octane rating: 97RM
Carburettor(s) no., make and type	Weber 34DMTR or Solex C34 CIC
Fuel pump	Fispa mechanical
Oil filter	Full flow, replaceable cartridge type
Max. power	110 bhp (DIN) at 6,000 rpm
Max. torque	106 lb.ft. (DIN) at 3,000 rpm

TRANSMISSION

Clutch	Diaphragm - spring, cable - operated, 8.5in. dia.
Gearbox	Five-speed, all-synchromesh
Gear ratios	Top 0.92
	Fourth 1.15
	Third 1.52
	Second 2.24
	First 3.50
	Reverse 3.07
Final drive	Helical spur, ratio 4.07-to-1

CHASSIS and BODY

Construction	Integral, with steel body

SUSPENSION

Front	Independent; Macpherson struts, lower wishbones, coil springs, telescopic dampers, anti-roll bar
Rear	Independent; MacPherson struts, twin lower transverse links, coil springs, telescopic dampers, anti-roll bar

STEERING

Type	Rack and pinion
Wheel dia.	15.4 in.

BRAKES

Type	Disc front and rear
Servo	Vacuum
Dimensions	F 9.9 in. dia. R 9.9 in. dia.
Swept area	F 223 sq. in., R 223 sq. in. Total 446 sq. in. (298 sq. in./ton laden)

WHEELS

Type	Pressed steel disc, 5-bolt fixing, 5.5 in. wide rim
Tyres—make	Michelin or Pirelli
Tyres—type	radial ply tubeless
Tyres—size	175/70-14 in.

EQUIPMENT

Battery	12 Volt 45 Ah
Alternator	62 amp a.c.
Headlamps	Carello halogen four-lamp system, 220/110 watt (total)
Reversing lamp	Standard
Electric fuses	10
Screen wipers	Two-speed plus intermittent
Screen washer	Standard, electric
Interior heater	Standard, air blending type
Heated backlight	Standard
Safety belts	Extra, mounting points standard
Interior trim	Velvet seats, pvc headlining
Floor covering	Carpet
Jacking points	2 each side, under body sills
Windscreen	Toughened
Underbody protection	Phosphor treatment prior to painting

MAINTENANCE

Fuel tank	11.2 Imp. gallons (51 litres)
Cooling system	15 pints (including heater)
Engine sump	8 pints (4.5 litres) SAE 10W/40. Change oil every 6,000 miles. Change filter element every 6,000 miles
Gearbox and final drive	8 pints SAE 80EP. Change oil every 12,000 miles
Grease	No points
Tyre pressures	F 24; R 24 psi (normal driving)
	F 27; R 27 psi (fast driving)
	F 27; R 27 psi (full load)
Max. payload	940 lb (425 kg)

DIMENSIONS

Wheelbase	8ft 4in. (254cm)
Track: front	4ft 7½in. (141cm)
Track: rear	4ft 6¾in. (139cm)
Overall length	14ft 1in. (429cm)
Overall width	5ft 6½in. (169cm)
Overall height (unladen)	4ft 7in. (140cm)
Turning circle	34ft 0in. (10.5m)
Kerb weight	2,420 lb (1,095kg)

PERFORMANCE DATA

Top gear mph per 1,000 rpm	18.2
Mean piston speed at max. power	3,120 ft/min.
Bhp per ton laden	73.3 (DIN)

YYO 208T

FULVIA HF COUPÉ

When first introduced as a production car in 1963, the Fulvia was a small but relatively heavy front-drive saloon with a 1,091 c.c. motor producing less than 60 bhp—hardly an obvious candidate for international motor sport honours. Nevertheless, it was quickly and successfully developed for competition and established the Lancia name in world-class rallying throughout the late 1960s. The first success came in 1965, when Leo Cella won the Italian Rallye dei Fiori, while the same combination finished fifth on the 1966 Monte Carlo. That event also saw the competition debut of the Fulvia Coupé, which used the same 1,091 c.c. motor but which was smaller, lighter and much more nimble. Cella gave the Coupé its first win on the 1966 Rallye dei Fiori and a similar car, driven by Ove Andersson, very nearly won that year's RAC Rally, mechanical failure forcing him back to seventh.

In 1967, the larger 1,298 c.c. power unit arrived with over 100 bhp, roughly the same output as the rival Mini Coopers, although the Lancias were still far heavier. The team tried to overcome the inferior power-to-weight ratio by using a very low final drive ratio allowing a top speed of only 80 mph; and to overcome this, team manager Cesare Fiorio tried all sorts of technical tricks, including an eight speed gearbox (the normal four speed box allied to a two-speed box, which was talked through scrutineering on the grounds that it was a 'mechanical overdrive'). The works drivers were much relieved when a normal, five-speed gearbox was homologated at the end of 1967. That year saw Andersson finish second on the Monte Carlo and Acropolis rallies, and he won the Spanish. Lancia's new driver, Sandro Munari, whose arrival in the team was doubly important because he was an Italian, won the Tour de Corse, on which he was so fast that he almost became the first man ever to finish without road penalties. Fulvias were also used for occasional races, taking class wins on the Targa Florio and the Nurburgring 1,000 Kms.

The following year was not as successful, with the Porsche team proving invincible on most rallies, although Hannu Mikkola did take a Fulvia into second place on the Austrian Alpine and Pat Moss took second on the San Remo.

In 1969, a 1,584 c.c. engine (still V4) was introduced and power went up to 130 bhp, which restored the Fulvia's competitive edge, albeit at the expense of driver comfort—with ever more powerful limited slip differentials required to minimise the wheelspin, it was becoming hard work to drive at any speed. As the new engine was not homologated, Harry Kallstrom drove the 1600HF in the prototype section of the Monte Carlo Rally, which he duly won (although not winning the overall event), and after homologation he took outright victory on the Italian Flowers Rally, with Fulvias also taking second and third. Kallstrom went on to win the San Remo, the Spanish and the RAC Rally, thereby clinching the European Rally Championship. Munari, meanwhile, dominated the Italian Rally Championship.

The Fulvia continued to be raced in 1969, tackling a number of events with its roof cut off—best results were sixth at Mugello and ninth on the Targa Florio.

With the Fulvia going so well, Fiorio widened the team's horizons in 1970, and the car was entered on such events as the Safari and the Portuguese Rally, where Lampinen and Munari scored a convincing one-two ahead of Porsche. The year was completed by Kallstrom's second win on the RAC.

Despite power outputs as high as 160 bhp, by 1971 the Fulvia was becoming out-classed, particularly by the rear-engined Alpine-Renault and the powerful Ford Escort RS1600, but Kallstrom took third on the Swedish, Ballastrieri and Barbasio managed second and third on the San Remo and Lampinen was third on the Acropolis. The team clearly needed a new competition machine and, with no obvious alternatives on the production line, they wanted a purpose-built replacement. But Lancia were in financial trouble and the climate was far from ripe for the considerable investment that such a programme would involve.

Then, in January 1972, just as the Fulvia was about to be phased out from both production and competition, Sandro Munari won the Monte Carlo Rally with Fulvias also placing fourth and sixth. Production of the Fulvia was extended, although only of the Coupé, and a special commemorative 1.3-litre version named the Monte Carlo was sold in limited quantities on the home market. The Monte win also convinced the company's management that they could afford to risk the building of the Stratos and plans to build the necessary 400 for international homologation were approved.

The Stratos, of course, heralded the end of the Fulvia as the factory's official rally car, but the last full year proved to be triumphant. After Munari's Monte win, Lampinen won the very rough Morocco Rally and was second on the Acropolis; and Ballestrieri, Barbasio and Bosetti scored a one-two-six on Lancia's home event, the San Remo, clinching the World Rally Championship for the marque.

For both 1973 and 1974, the Fulvia had to share the spotlight with the Stratos, but Munari used it on many of the events which helped him to victory in the 1973 European Championship and he drove a Fulvia to third on the 1974 Safari, one of the very last events on which a factory-entered Fulvia 1600HF Coupé was seen.

Throughout its competition career, one of the most impressive features of the rallying Fulvia Coupé was how close to standard it remained: the interior of this 1969 factory car (*opposite left*) remains almost identical to that of a road car, complete with carpets and a wood-faced dashboard. Only the steering wheel, seats and Halda Twinmaster are different. The vee-4 engine (*opposite right*) was never as highly tuned as those used by many rivals: the most powerful road-going Fulvias produced around 125bhp, while the rallying versions rarely exceeded 160bhp.

The Fulvia 1600HF Coupé on the 1970 Monte Carlo Rally (*above*) is significant mainly for its driver, Daniele Audetto, who went on to take over as Competitions Manager at Lancia after Fiorio.

Fulvia Coupé S3

By late 1974, with production of the Beta range in full swing, the only version of the Fulvia still available in Britain was the Series Three 1.3-litre Coupé shown here. The car weighed well over one ton and the vee-4 engine produced no more than 80 bhp, so that the standard five-speed gearbox was essential if a driver was to make full use of the excellent handling. Performance fell well short of the old 1.6HF, of course, and the S3 was noticeable low-geared to provide decent acceleration, limiting the top speed to only 104 mph when *Autocar* tested it. Nevertheless, it was an outstanding cross-country car and found much favour with enthusiasts at a price of just over £2,000.

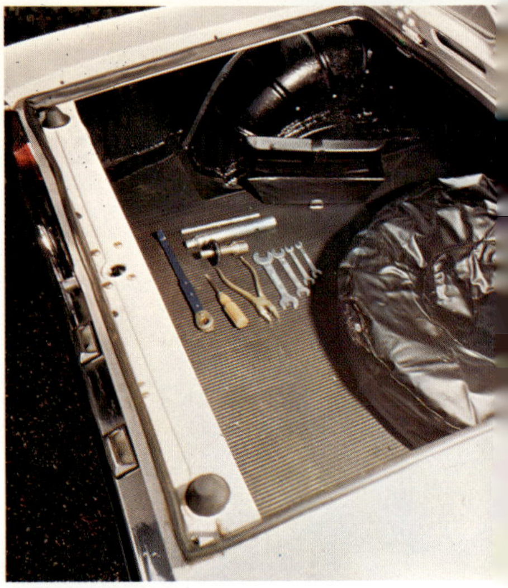

THE SPORT 1972

One of the most significant results in the history of Lancia's long involvement in motor sport was that achieved on the 1972 Monte Carlo Rally, when Sandro Munari and Mauro Mannucci (*below*) beat off the assembled might of Renault-Alpine, Porsche and Datsun to win the event in a Fulvia 1600HF. That result enabled Competitions Manager Cesare Fiorio to obtain the backing for the Stratos project. Fulvias went on to win such varied events as the Morocco and the San Remo, although Simo Lampinen and John Davenport (*bottom*) were unable to repeat Lancia's 1969/70 wins on the RAC Rally of Great Britain. The Marlboro sponsorship had been acquired mid-season.

AUTO TEST

LANCIA 2000 FIVE-SPEED INJECTION SEDAN

Italian refinement

AT-A-GLANCE:
Latest version of this most refined Italian marque's 2-litre sedan, with five-speed gearbox and fuel injection. Excellent performance, superb power steering, road-holding, handling and brakes. Rather heavy fuel consumption. Very good controls, generally good ride, quiet and unobtrusive.

ITALY is one of the homes of good motor cars — with the difference that virtually all good Italian cars are fun to drive. Lancia are a little different from the other Italian makers (we are told that Fiat, who nowadays have an interest in Lancia, are wisely determined to keep them so). Thanks latterly to the rallying successes of the delightful Fulvia coupés, Lancia maintain a fine competition record. But they are also unusual amongst their car-making countrymen in providing some externally conservative saloons combining good performance with unusual refinement.

If, for the benefit of Britons familiar only with the traditional character of British marques, one sought to liken the fuel-injection Lancia 2000 sedan to any other car, one could say that it is a sort of Italian Wolseley — hastily adding that "Italian" is here a synonym for "appreciably faster" and "zestful". Also, we say "externally conservative" because under that somewhat staid outside there is hidden the highly individual Lancia power train and suspension. The 1,991 c.c. engine is a horizontally opposed 4-cylinder with two camshafts working overhead valves through pushrods and rockers. With Bosch electronically controlled fuel injection, it develops a claimed 125 bhp (DIN) at 5,800 rpm, with 127 lb ft maximum torque at 3,700 rpm. The five-speed gearbox is in unit with the hypoid final drive, which works the front wheels through constant-velocity jointed drive shafts. Independent front suspension uses a transverse leaf spring and double wishbones, with an anti-roll bar; along with the power unit it is mounted in a strong sub-frame with hefty cast-aluminium side members. Steering is by ZF power-assisted recirculating ball — one of the very best systems we have so far encountered. At the back, Lancia use the logical system for a front-wheel-drive car, a lightweight tubular dead axle to keep the wheels parallel at all times, located by half-elliptic leaf springs and a Panhard rod, with an anti-roll bar.

Performance

We had completed a full Road Test (unpublished) in this country on the earlier four-speed carburettor 2000 when Lancia announced to the press that this earlier model was to be superseded. The opportunity was therefore offered of testing the new car in Italy — hence the left-hand-drive model illustrated. The comparison was most interesting.

Typical of mountain-bred Italian cars, 2nd gear is lowered slightly, along with other changes; gear speeds at the allowed maximum engine speed of 6,250 rpm from 1st to 4th work out thus (with the four-speed figures in brackets) — 31 (32), 48 (54), 72 (83), and 100 mph. Although the claimed difference in engine output is only 10 bhp, the injection car achieved a very creditable 115 mph mean on autostrada in light airs, compared with 105 mph mean at MIRA in a 10-15 mph wind for the carburettor one. With the same lack of wind and given a straight level road, the four-speed car would however have done better, as MIRA's banking takes quite a bit of speed off at around 105.

In acceleration from a standing start the margin was similarly clear. 30 mph came up in only 3.3 sec (4.1), 40 in 5.5 (6.1), 50 in 7.8 (8.6), 60 in 10.4 (12.2), 70 in 14.6 (16.1), the quarter-mile in 17.9 (18.2), 80 in 19.6 (22.2), 90 in 25.8 (31.5) and the kilometre in 33.0 (33.7). The fuel injection car then carries on to record 36.4 sec for 0 to 100 mph, which the carburettor car would not achieve within MIRA's horizontal-mile straights, even with a flying start.

As our comparison tables show, the latest version is more than a match for several other cars in its class; the only price paid for propelling such a relatively heavy car (24.2cwt unladen) so quickly is in fuel consumption, which is on the heavy side. Steady speed fuel consumption figures were not available from the makers (our equipment is unfortunately not compatible with high pressure fuel-injection), but we would guess that only with very gentle driving will any owner do better than 25 mpg. During the actual taking of performance figures, the car returned 18.2 mpg; overall, including a mixture of heavy Turin traffic driving and a good proportion of main road and mountain running we achieved 20.1 mpg. Accordingly the 12-gallon tank is a little on the small side for the fast long-distance high-speed cruising at which the car excels.

The engine is most pleasingly smooth, with only a very slight high frequency vibration at the top end felt through the gearlever. Cold starting in spring weather was very good indeed. One of its most extraordinary attributes is its willingness to tolerate and pull from very low speeds. In one queue of cars up a slight incline, we found ourselves crawling along without a suggestion of distress at only 700 rpm. There is no obvious "step" in the power curve; the delivery is progressive throughout the range, though it obviously is at its best from 3,000 to 6,000 rpm. We found it better to change gear during the performance runs at 6,000 rpm and not go on to the maximum.

An interesting difference between the carburettor and fuel injection cars is in engine noise; the former was very quiet at all times, whilst a slight clatter was audible on the latter, we suspect from the metering unit. Borletti air conditioning fitted to the test car (but not normally to be offered here) allowed some engine noise into the interior. A non-air-conditioned injection 2000 we tried was noticeably quieter. In both cases, one is only aware of how much the engine is working when one revs it really hard, which is not normally necessary; a slight and not unpleasant amount of valve-gear noise is the main source, plus some intake noise.

Interior insulation is obviously pretty good, as it is only when one stands at the roadside whilst the car is accelerated that one is aware of the noticeable amount of flat-out exhaust noise. A subdued whistle accompanies small changes of throttle opening at low speeds, and an equally subdued rattle from the transmission is heard on tickover; it disappears on de-clutching. Slightly more general noise is audible in the back, but the level is still low.

The gearchange, with its ideally shaped large-ball knob, has a five-speed gate spring-loaded Alfa-style into the middle 2nd-3rd plane, with the difference that reverse is opposite 1st instead of top. Apart from some occasional baulking when selecting gear from rest, it works well, being free of any imprecision and having good synchromesh. If anything it needs a little more accuracy of movement than an Alfa one, and is not the easiest of examples to change really quickly across the gate; normally no driver need worry about this — we only noticed it during the standing-start acceleration runs.

The square lines of the Lancia are almost dateless. It has hardly changed since it was introduced in 1961, except to become more powerful slightly crisper in styling. Below: Upholstery is in nylon velour and the seats are as comfortable as they look to sit in

Wind noise is kept well below average even at the Lancia's natural cruising gait of around 100 mph, whilst bump-thump is a little better than average.

On the previous car we were very struck by the exceptionally low rolling resistance — one found the car rolling forward or backward on the very slightest of slopes, on which almost any other car would stay still. The fuel injection model was exactly the same, saying a lot for the care which obviously goes into Lancia assembly.

Handling, ride and brakes

The last Flavia we tested (19 October 1967) was the 1.8-litre fuel-injection car with non-assisted worm-and-roller steering which required $4\frac{1}{2}$ turns from lock to lock. On all the current 2000s (*not* called Flavia, since such a large amount of detail re-design has gone into them) Lancia wisely took the opportunity to step up the ratio when the adoption of power steering gave them the chance. Only 3.3 turns are now needed, although the turning circle is still surprisingly large, at $38\frac{1}{4}$ft mean diameter.

If we begin by saying that one or two drivers who tried the 2000 did not at first realize that

LANCIA 2000

ACCELERATION

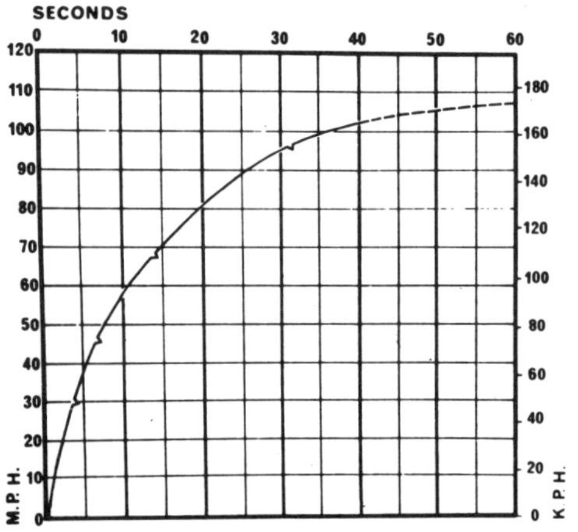

SPEED MPH TRUE	INDICATED	TIME IN SECS
30	31	3.3
40	41	5.5
50	52	7.8
60	63	10.4
70	73	14.6
80	84	19.6
90	94	25.8
100	104	36.4
110	114	

GEAR RATIOS AND TIME IN SEC

mph	Top (3.91)	4th (4.67)	3rd (6.52)
10-30	—	12.6	6.8
20-40	11.2	9.5	5.7
30-50	10.6	9.5	5.5
40-60	10.8	9.3	5.7
50-70	11.6	9.5	6.9
60-80	12.5	10.9	—
70-90	14.8	14.0	—
80-100	21.9	—	—

Standing ¼-mile
17.9 sec 75 mph
Standing Kilometre
33.0 sec 97 mph
Test distance
442 miles
Mileage recorder
1 per cent over-reading

PERFORMANCE

MAXIMUM SPEEDS

Gear	mph	kph	rpm
Top (mean)	115	185	6,030
(best)	116	187	6,100
4th	100	161	6,250
3rd	72	115	6,250
2nd	48	77	6,250
1st	31	50	6,250

BRAKES

FADE
(from 70 mph in neutral)
Pedal load for 0.5g stops in lb

1	25-15	6	25-30
2	25	7	30-35
3	25	8	30-35
4	25	9	30-35
5	25-30	10	30-35

RESPONSE (from 30 mph in neutral)

Load	g	Distance
20lb	0.40	75ft
30lb	0.77	39ft
40lb	0.92	33ft
50lb	1.05	28.7ft
Handbrake	0.26	116ft

Max. Gradient 1 in 5

CLUTCH

Pedal 30lb and 6in.

COMPARISONS

MAXIMUM SPEED MPH

Lancia 2000 inj.	**(£2,399)**	**115**
Ford Cortina 2000GXL	(£1,361)	105
Rover 2000TC	(£1,884)	105
Austin 2200	(£1,364)	104
Vauxhall Victor 2300SL	(£1,299)	96

0-60 MPH, SEC

Lancia 2000 inj.	**10.4**
Ford Cortina 2000GXL	10.7
Rover 2000TC	12.2
Austin 2200	12.4
Vauxhall Victor 2300SL	12.4

STANDING ¼-MILE, SEC

Lancia 2000 inj.	**17.9**
Ford Cortina 2000GXL	18.1
Vauxhall Victor 2300SL	18.2
Rover 2000TC	18.5
Austin 2200	18.7

OVERALL MPG

Ford Cortina 2000GXL	25.1
Rover 2000TC	22.4
Austin 2200	22.3
Vauxhall Victor 2300SL	21.6
Lancia 2000 inj.	**20.1**

GEARING

(with 175-14 in. tyres)

Top	19.07 mph per 1,000 rpm
4th	15.97 mph per 1,000 rpm
3rd	11.43 mph per 1,000 rpm
2nd	7.63 mph per 1,000 rpm
1st	4.96 mph per 1,000 rpm

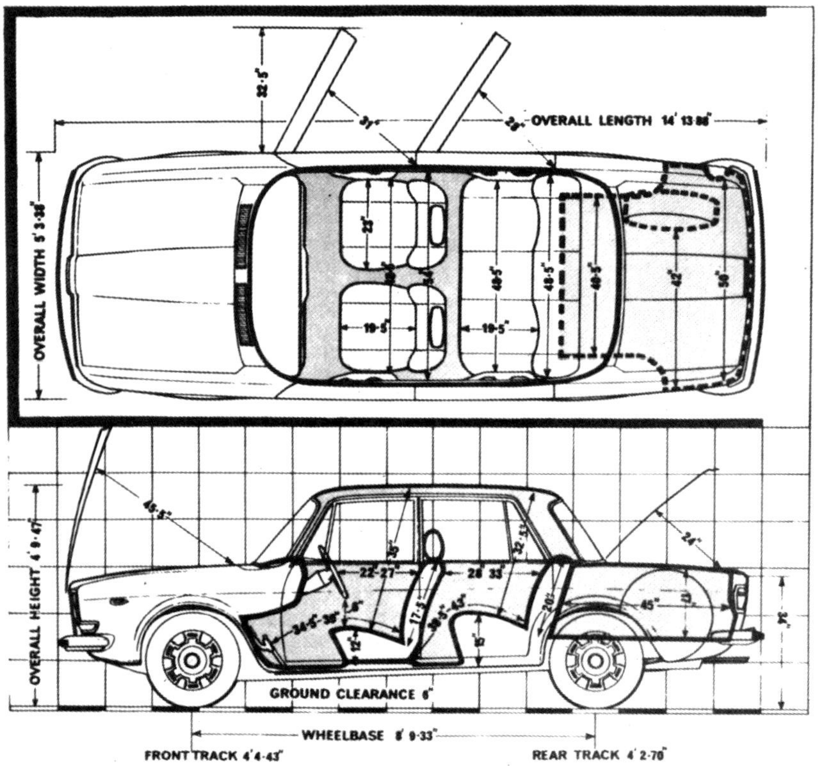

STANDARD GARAGE 16ft x 8ft 6in.

CONSUMPTION

FUEL

Bosch fuel injection fitted to the Lancia 2000 is not compatible with our steady speed fuel consumption test equipment; no figures available from manufacturer.

Typical mpg . . 23 (12.3 litres/100km)
Overall mpg . . 20.1 (14.1 litres/100km)
Grade of fuel Premium, 4-star (min. 98 RM)

OIL

Consumption (SAE 20W/50) 1,200 miles/pint

TEST CONDITIONS

Weather: Fine, sunny. Wind: 5-8 mph.
Temperature: 13 deg. C. (55 deg. F).
Barometer: 29.0 in. hg. Humidity: 60 per cent
Surfaces: Dry concrete and asphalt.

WEIGHT:

Kerb Weight 24.2 cwt (2,715 lb-1,232 kg). (with oil, water and half full fuel tank). Distribution, per cent F, 63.7; R, 36.3. Laden as tested: 28 cwt (3,135 lb-1,422kg).

TURNING CIRCLES:

Between kerbs L, 38 ft 3 in.; R, 38 ft 4½ in.
Between walls L, 40 ft 1 in.; R, 40 ft 7 in.
Steering wheel turns, lock to lock 3.3.
Figures taken at 3,800 miles by our own staff in northern Italy.

SPECIFICATION
FRONT ENGINE, FRONT-WHEEL DRIVE

ENGINE

Cylinders	4, horizontally opposed
Main bearings	3
Cooling system	Water; pump, thermostatically de-clutched fan, and thermostat
Bore	89mm (3.50in.)
Stroke	80mm (3.14in.)
Displacement	1,991 c.c. (121.5 cu.in.)
Valve gear	Overhead, pushrods and rockers, two camshafts
Compression ratio	9.2-to-1 Min. octane rating: 98RM
Induction	Bosch electronic fuel injection
Fuel pump	Electric
Oil filter	Full flow, renewable element
Max. power	125 bhp (DIN) at 5,800 rpm
Max. torque	127 lb. ft (DIN) at 3,700 rpm

TRANSMISSION

Clutch	Single dry plate diaphragm spring
Gearbox	5-speed, all-synchromesh, in unit with final drive
Gear ratios	Top 1.0
	Fourth 1.19
	Third 1.67
	Second 2.50
	First 3.85
	Reverse 3.98
Final drive	Hypoid bevel, 3.9-to-1

CHASSIS and BODY

Construction	Integral, with steel body, sub-frames for suspension

SUSPENSION

Front	Independent, transverse half-elliptic leaf spring, wishbones, anti-roll bar, telescopic dampers
Rear	Dead beam axle, half-elliptic leaf springs, Panhard rod, anti-roll bar, hydraulic dampers

STEERING

Type	ZF power-assisted recirculating ball
Wheel dia.	14.8in.

BRAKES

Make and type	Girling disc front and rear, dual hydraulic circuit with load-controlled rear pressure valve
Servo	Girling vacuum
Dimensions	F $10\frac{1}{3}$in. dia.
	R $10\frac{3}{4}$in. dia.
Swept area	F 208 sq. in., R 186 sq. in.
	Total 394 sq. in. (281 sq. in./ton laden)

WHEELS

Type	Pressed steel disc, 5in. wide rim
Tyres—make	Michelin
—type	XAS radial ply tubed
—size	175-14in.

EQUIPMENT

Battery	12 Volt 45 Ah.
Alternator	SEV Motorola $62\frac{1}{2}$ amp a.c.
Headlamps	Four headlamp system, iodine vapour sealed beam 220 watt (total)
Reversing lamp	Standard
Electric fuses	10
Screen wipers	Two-speed
Screen washer	Standard, electric
Interior heater	Standard, water-valve type
Heated backlight	Standard
Safety belts	Standard
Interior trim	Nylon velvet seats, plastic headlining
Floor covering	Carpet
Jack	Screw scissors
Jacking points	Five, centre of front sub-frame and under sills front and rear
Windscreen	Laminated
Underbody protection	Bitumen based coating

MAINTENANCE

Fuel tank	12.1 Imp. gallons (55 litres) no reserve
Cooling system	14 pints (including heater)
Engine sump	12.6 pints (7.2 litres) SAE 20W/50 Change oil every 4,400 miles. Change filter element every 4,400 miles.
Gearbox and final drive	8 pints SAE GZ90. No change needed
Grease	8 points every 4,400 miles.
Tyre pressures (XAS)	F 24; R 24 psi (normal driving)
	F 27; R 27 psi (fast driving)
	F 27; R 27 psi (full load)
Max. payload	880 lb (400 kg)

PERFORMANCE DATA

Top gear mph per 1,000 rpm	19.07
Mean piston speed at max. power	2,930 ft/min.
Bhp per ton laden	89.5

AUTOTEST LANCIA 2000 FIVE-SPEED INJECTION SEDAN . . .

the steering was power-assisted, but simply thought it an accurate, beautifully weighted, feel-transmitting normal set-up, some idea may be gained of how very good the steering is. The only comparable power-steering we know are those systems on the NSU Ro 80 and (though much lighter) the one on the Jaguar XJ6. There is enough help given when manoeuvring, but never too much. One feels what the front wheels are doing, but is not jarred by bumps. The steering wheel is not too big and has a well-shaped rim; our only criticism of it in passing is that especially on first acquaintance it is far too easy to let off the magnificent Fiamm horns unintentionally — because the spoke-located horn switch arms are carried out too near the rim.

Straight stability is very good, though not quite as absolute as it is on some trailing-arm rear-suspended competitors, notably the Citroens and the British Leyland 1800; the Panhard rod is probably at the root of this. But the Lancia's cornering power and behaviour is right in the top of the class; we rate it one of the best-handling large front-wheel-drive cars made. In spite of nearly 64 per cent of its unladen weight on the front wheels, the understeer you would expect is kept remarkably low. In fact, *in extremis* there is a tendency sometimes for the tail to break away nicely, although the normally low roll angle has by then risen to a degree that would alarm most owners. In a search foiled by cloud for suitable backgrounds for photography we drove up to Cervinia; on the twisting ascent, but more particularly on the descent through any safe series of open-S-bends, the 2000 was a delight, hanging on magnificently and going exactly where one pointed it with only the occasional squeak of the inside rear-wheel locking momentarily under braking and the slight lack of sideways location in the seat betraying the speed. The 2000 is not the Lancia that is rallied so successfully, but one sensed the family likeness clearly enough.

Ride is generally pretty good, the majority of bumps being ironed out well, though some seem to catch it out. The brakes work very well indeed, the inside rear-locking mentioned above only occurring harmlessly enough when provoked most unfairly on braking late into corners. Without being at all abrupt, the pedal needs very little effort or driver's skill to pull the car up all-square with the front tyres beginning to lock, recording over 1g in the process for only 50lb effort. Fade resistance is good too, though some slight rumble is encountered on hard use, but the handbrake which employs a drum-within-the-rear-disc arrangement will only hold on 1-in-4.

Multitude of good details

There is little one can criticize about the driving position or controls (except for the horn arrangement already voiced). The seats, upholstered in luxurious-feeling nylon velvet which we all liked, recline if needed until their backs rest on the rear seat cushions; when normally used they are comfortable and, so far as the 6ft driver is concerned, have just enough rearward adjustment.

One sits quite high in the car, so that it seems a little low-eyebrowed; one virtue of the very squared-up shape is that one can easily see both ends, important when manoeuvring with such a relatively long tail. Lancia have for some time made an excellent point of putting all controls that matter within fingertip reach of the driver's hands even though he keeps them on the steering wheel. Even the lighting master switch is on one of the stalks, all of which work with delightful precision. British drivers would probably prefer main-beam headlamp flashing; both test cars flashed the dipped beam which, being well-directed does not give sufficient range on some occasions. The lamps themselves, iodine-vapour on both main and

Power steering unit (bottom left of picture) and its pipes make the under-bonnet look more crowded that it really is. Some items on the flat-four engine are difficult to get at

AUTOTEST LANCIA 2000 FIVE-SPEED INJECTION SEDAN . . .

dip, are very good indeed, and well up to the car's performance; one is not plunged into relative tungsten-filament darkness when one dips, which is the unpleasant case with some other Continental four-lamp systems.

Pedals are well arranged for heel-and-toe changes but as usual on some other originally left-hand-drive cars you have to place the unused clutch foot under the clutch pedal on rhd models as there is too little room to the left. On the other hand it is nice to find a left-hand-drive manufacturer who takes the trouble to provide true right-hand-drive wiper arcs, although there is still a rather large uncleared area on the far right of the windscreen. An excellent big door mirror is standard, close to the eye so that it gives a good field of view. Visibility generally is good, unless one has allowed that rather pre-war provision, the back-window curtains, to become untidy on each side.

In one notable respect this is a most unusual Italian car. Its ventilation works very well indeed, so that one is surprised to find that large swivelling quarter lights, typical of Italian saloons, are still retained. There seems little need for them (smokers, who are not provided as usual with a right-hand ashtray will be grateful for them) as the through-flow of cold air (even on non-air-conditioned models) is excellent, although we wished that the facia outlets could be directed fully at the driver's face instead of only halfway. The heater works tolerably well.

Above: The 2000 always has a slight nose-down attitude unless the rear seats are occupied

Left: There is enough kneeroom in the rear for most adults, even with the front seats right back

Below left: The mahogany facia contains a full set of instruments, only a clock being absent. Switches for the electric windows are in the centre under the cold air vents

Below: The boot has a high sill, but a big square lid. The tool kit is comprehensive and well thought out

In the back there is just enough kneeroom for long-legged passengers when the front seats are set right back. Headroom is generous, a rare-enough attribute nowadays. Electric windows, which are standard on the fuel injection 2000, have individual switches in the back, but move a little slowly.

Typical of the Lancia, indeed of any Lancia, is the instrumentation, which tells all the discerning driver normally needs to know, yet is carried out with style and taste. The same sort of buyer will delight in the thoughtful details once more found, such as the way the boot-lock release winds itself in when locked, making forcing more difficult. And the provision of a comprehensive tool roll, including a wheel-nut socket fitted with a large-diameter plastic collar to make spinning the nut off easier. And the most sensibly small-sized keys (most welcome nowadays) which need not ruin or clutter pockets, and which consist of one black-handled one for the ignition and steering lock and the other, white-handled and thus easily identified for all outside locks; and knurled dashboard-securing screws which have no screwdriver slots to be ruined by carelessness if an instrument lighting bulb is changed.

In conversation with the importers before the announcement of this model's arrival in this country, we were asked to guess the price. The Lancia is not a cheap car in its native land, and we did not expect much change out of £2,700 by the time it got here. It was a pleasant surprise to learn that it is in fact £300 cheaper than we supposed. Lancias have not been cheap here, but compared with the accelerating price of competitors with the same distinction and quality, £2,398.90 is by no means as expensive nowadays as it used to be. The 2000 sedan achieves much of what it sets out to do. Some will not find it the prettiest of designs — it does not attract undue attention — but it is that rare thing today, a car completely devoid of any tasteless vulgarity. □

MANUFACTURER:
Lancia & Cie, Via Vincenzo Lancia 27, Turin, Italy.

UK CONCESSIONAIRES:
Lancia (England) Ltd., Lancia Works, Ealing Road, Alperton, Middlesex.

PRICES	
Basic	£1,984.00
Purchase Tax	£414.90
Total,(in G.B.)	£2,398.90
EXTRAS (inc. P.T.)	
Metallic paint	£96.67
PRICE AS TESTED	£2,398.90

THE SPORT 1973/1974

Lancia used three different models during this period: the Fulvia Coupé was phased out during 1973, one of its last major works-entered appearances being on the RAC Rally (*left*)—this is the car of Ballestrieri/Maiga. By the same time in 1974, the Beta Coupé (*centre*) had been tried on several events—this is Simo Lampinen/Solve Andreasson on the RAC—but the problems involved in persuading a 200 bhp front-drive car to handle were proving too great. The solution to every rally problem, as it turned out, was the all-conquering Stratos, which in 1974 won the San Remo, the Rideau Lakes (*bottom*), the Giro D'Italia and the Tour de Corse to clinch the World Championship for Lancia.

AUTO TEST

Lancia Beta 1800

Old name revived for brand-new design

AT-A-GLANCE: Luxuriously appointed and very spacious. Performance and economy good, but engine noisy when working hard. Ride and road-noise better than average, but handling something of an acquired taste. Braking efficiency unusually dependent on temperature. Solidly built and nicely finished.

BETA, THE SECOND letter of the Greek alphabet, has a special place in Lancia history. This was the name chosen by Vincenzo Lancia for his first production car, introduced in 1909. Sixty-three years later, in October 1972, the name was revived for another new model — one heralding the start of a new era in the company's fortunes. Not only did the Beta's introduction signify radical changes in Lancia's design, manufacturing and marketing policies, but it was their first all-new design since becoming part of the Fiat empire.

Although firmly established in Italy and elsewhere in Europe, the Beta has only recently become available in right-hand-drive form. Exceptionally spacious and very well-appointed, it comes in 1400, 1600 and 1800 forms — all based on the same four-door bodyshell. A stylish coupé was added to the range at this year's Frankfurt Show, but what is essentially a small-volume variant need not concern us here.

Remembering Fiat's involvement, it is no surprise that a certain amount of design rationalization has taken place. This is largely confined to the power units, all of which derived from Fiat twin-cam designs of equivalent size (actual displacements being 1,438 c.c., 1,592 c.c. and 1,756 c.c).

In almost all other respects, the Beta displays considerable design originality. Unlike Fiat twin-cam applications, the engine is mounted transversely with its cylinder axes inclined rearwards at 20 deg. A conventional diaphragm-spring clutch transmits the drive to the cluster gear of the all-indirect, five-speed gearbox (the cluster being concentric with the engine crankshaft). At the output end of the gearbox mainshaft is a final-drive unit of helical-spur gear design; this incorporates a conventional bevel-gear differential. Gearbox and final-drive share the same SAE 90 lubricant. A particular advantage of the layout is that the engine forms a separate unit which may be unbolted and withdrawn from the transmission in the usual way. Another good point is the absence of a separate transfer-gear train, with its attendant risk of noise problems.

Fiat influence is evident in the choice of MacPherson-strut suspension for all four wheels. At the front, pressed-steel wishbones serve as track-control arms, rubber bushes at their inner ends providing a measure of fore-and-aft compliance. A different set-up is used at the rear, parallel pairs of transverse arms (two of fixed length, the other two adjustable) providing means of setting the toe-in. The diagonal ends of an anti-roll bar effect fore-and-aft triangulation, a measure of compliance again being incorporated. Coil springs, supplemented by progressive-action snubbers, are used at both front and rear.

Another departure from traditional Lancia practice is the adoption of rack-and-pinion steering gear, this being mounted on the engine-bay bulkhead. Somewhat unusual is the use of resilient rubber bushes at the inner ends of the two trackrods, these being sited close to the rack centre.

Disc brakes, with floating-type calipers, are used for all four wheels. A direct-acting servo and a duplex master cylinder operate two separate hydraulic systems; one actuates the front brakes only, whereas the other actuates both front and rear units. Other good points are the provision of a pressure-regulating valve in the line to the rear and of a lamp to warn of excessive wear in the front pads.

Performance

Having had appetites whetted by the model's advanced specification, prospective buyers will be keen to learn how it behaves on the road. With a few minor reservations, they will not be disappointed.

Under ideal conditions, speeds of 109 mph were achieved in two opposite directions. Representing a shade under 6,000 rpm in top (fifth) gear, this is precisely the figure claimed by the factory.

It is significant that maximum speed is coincident with the peak of the power curve; it is also the point at which the tachometer's striped "precautionary" band begins. Whilst such gearing is ideal from the all-out performance viewpoint, it does rob the car of the ability to cruise unobtrusively at wide throttle openings. Anything more than 95 mph on the clock (a genuine 93 mph, equivalent to around 5,000 rpm) involves considerable fuss.

In contrast to conditions existing at the time of the maximum speed runs, heavy rain persisted for the remainder of our MIRA test session. Nevertheless, the Beta acquitted itself exceedingly well. Any attempt at full-power getaways resulted in furious wheelspin; indeed, loss of traction resulted also from snatched changes into second. Eventually, it was found that the best results were achieved using little more than a fast tickover for the actual step-off — a technique which was rewarded by the creditable 0-30 mph time of 3.7 sec. Changing up at 6,400 rpm (the start of the "solid" red sector on the dead-accurate tachometer), 60 mph came up in 10.7 sec and the quarter-mile post in 17.9 sec (equivalent to 77 mph). Despite the poor conditions, the Beta forged strongly ahead to reach 90 mph in 27.2 sec and the kilometre post in 33.1 sec (equivalent to 95 mph). Whilst these results fall a little short of Lancia's claims (e.g. 0-60 mph in 10.2 sec, standing quarter-mile in 17.3 sec, standing kilometre in 32.0 sec), there is little doubt that the discrepancies are largely attributable to the inclement weather.

With five well-chosen ratios available, the driver of a Beta is assured of a gear to suit all needs. Nevertheless, the engine is pleasantly flexible, enabling the car to be driven quite lazily if so desired. Reflecting the model's relatively low overall gearing, acceleration in top (fifth) is brisk enough for most motorway and main-road requirements. As an example, each 20 mph increment between 20 and 70 mph occupies comfortably less than 11 sec. A change into fourth renders the car distinctly lively, 30-70 mph occupying only 15 sec.

Economy poses no problems. Despite being driven brutally hard the test car averaged 24.3 mpg whilst in our hands. Observations made during brief spells of more moderate driving, together with steady-speed figures recorded at MIRA, suggested that 26 mpg should easily be attained by the majority of owners. With a tank capacity of 11.4 gal, this gives a range well in excess of 250 miles. No measurable quantity of oil was consumed over the 1,100-mile test period.

What really matters is how the Beta fares against its immediate rivals. Particularly revealing are comparisons between it and the somewhat higher geared Fiat 132 Special 1800 — a car of very similar power and weight. The Beta has the advantage in terms of top speed; it might well be deduced that this is simply a function of its lower gearing, but its superior economy suggests that shape may also be a significant factor. This theory is borne out by comparison of the upper range acceleration, 80-100 mph times being 22.1 and 26.3 sec for the Beta and Fiat respectively. True, the Fiat returned marginally better 0-60 mph and standing-quarter times, but these were achieved in bone-dry conditions.

Engine and transmission

Use of full choke results in immediate starting from cold. Rather disturbing is the attendant bearing knock — a trait which disappears in a second or two, as soon as build-up of oil pressure takes place.

Almost immediately, the choke may be returned to the half-way position — a setting which provides acceptable driveway flexibility without undue richness. Not until the car has been driven half-a-mile or so can the choke be completely dispensed with.

Top: Some idea of the Beta's sure-footedness is given by this view of the car cornering on a flooded track
Centre, left: Although lacking the elegance of some earlier Lancia designs, the Beta has a clean and efficient appearance
Centre, right: The abnormally high rear window gives rise to problems when reversing in awkward spaces. Note the depth of the boot lid, and the useful protective strip on the face of the bumper
Bottom, left: Despite the crowded underbonnet appearance, accessibility is generally good
Bottom, right: Sumptuously upholstered and trimmed, the seats are very comfortable. Headrests are provided but were not fitted at the time this shot was taken

PMG 11 L

PMG 11 L

PMG
11 L

Lancia Beta 1800

Reflecting Fiat influence, a hand throttle is standard equipment. We found this to have a very insensitive action. Moreover, the behaviour of the cold starting device was such that there was never any need to use the hand throttle.

Warm-up is comparatively slow, there being little output from the heater for three miles or so. Nevertheless, carburation gives no cause for complaint apart from a flat-spot just as the second stage comes into play. Even when the engine is thoroughly warm, this hesitation persists to some extent.

Although the engine idles quietly enough, the general level of mechanical noise is higher than expected in a car of this class. Certainly, the unit sounds exceedingly busy at anything over 5,000 rpm —. this despite having the benefit of an electric cooling fan.

In contrast, the transmission is quiet apart from mild whine under drive (as distinct from overrun) conditions and a tendency for the change-lever to rattle above an indicated 90 mph in fifth.

Lancia quote the engine's octane requirement as 96 RM — just above the minimum standard for British 3-star "economy" petrols. Despite being run on premium (4-star) grades, it occasionally suffered bouts of running on and would pink quite appreciably if made to pull hard at very low revs (below 1,500 rpm).

A cable-cum-rod mechanism is used to actuate the diaphragm-spring clutch, the system having the benefit of an assist spring to minimize pedal effort. The action is delightfully sweet and peak pedal load is a modest 29lb.

Take-up characteristics are good, yet the clutch has ample bite. Restarts presented no problems when reversing up MIRA's 1-in-3 test hill, but the model was defeated by lack of wheelgrip in the forward direction (in wet conditions); forward restarts were feasible on the 1-in-4 gradient.

A glance at the engine bay reveals that a comparatively intricate linkage connects the gearbox with the floor-mounted lever. Even so, the change quality is good. True, it hasn't quite the crisp precision of the better conventional linkages, but its quick and certain action allows the driver to make the most of the car's considerable performance. Incidentally, the lever is spring-loaded towards the centre (third-fourth) plane; reverse is opposite fifth and is protected by a spring-loaded guard (lever depressed to clear).

Ride and handling

Inevitably, the concentration of mechanical components at the front has resulted in considerable nose-heaviness. No less than 59 per cent of the kerb weight is over the driving wheels — a situation which is conducive to heavy steering. To allay this problem, Lancia have settled for fairly low gearing, no fewer than 4.1 turns of the wheel being required between average locks (a mean of 36ft 5in. between kerbs). Even so, considerable effort is called for when parking and when tackling bends at speed. On the credit side, the model is reassuringly stable no matter what the road conditions.

The Beta's balance and general behaviour are greatly dependent on the amount of power being used. Even in the dry, fierce getaways result in considerable wheelspin; not only this, but the car squats appreciably and displays a tendency to veer to the right.

Under most driving conditions, the Beta's steering self-centres quite vigorously. In general the harder the model is cornered, the more evident is this trait. Less predictable is its behaviour on tight right-hand bends — here application of power causes total loss of self-centring action. Adding to the problem is the fact that lift-off results in a sudden and violent return to straight-ahead.

Such a blow-by-blow account might give the impression that the Beta scores badly in terms of handling. This is by no means the case; once the driver has adjusted to the model's peculiarities, it is found that most impressive averages are achieved over give-and-take routes.

Of equal importance are the model's riding qualities. All who travelled in it were immediately impressed by its air of comfort and well-being. Much of this stems from the low level of road-generated noise, but the ride itself plays no small part. If overall impressions are cast aside, one realizes that stiff damper settings make for appreciable firmness at lowish speeds. However, factors such as the aforementioned freedom from road noise, the way the suspension irons out the roughest of roads and the sumptuous comfort afforded by the cloth-trimmed seats will render the Beta an attractive proposition for a great many people.

Noise

The only aspect not already covered is that of wind noise. Up to 80 mph or thereabouts, there is little to worry about. Beyond this, one is aware of a certain amount of disturbance from the vicinity of the right-hand centre pillar — possibly an isolated case of faulty sealing. We also discovered the importance of ensuring that the face-level vents are truly closed when not in use; failure to observe this precaution gives rise to an objectionable high-pitched whistle.

Brakes

Normal road use prompts one to think that the brakes are rather too sensitive, the pedal efforts required for check purposes being quite exceptionally low.

Our response checks at MIRA showed a somewhat different picture. Allowing a full 3 minutes between each application, an effort of no less than 200lb (representing full-scale deflection on the pressometer) was reached before sliding took place. At this juncture, the deceleration was 0.84 g — the best achieved under the atrocious conditions.

Prompted by the results obtained during the fade test (more of which anon), some random rechecks were made with the brakes thoroughly hot (immediately after concluding the fade test). This time, a deceleration of 0.84 g (again the optimum value) called for an effort of only 60 lb.

Up to the half-way point, the fade test showed a progressive decrease in pedal effort. Thereafter initial efforts remained substantially constant, but some increase was called for during the course of each stop.

Such characteristics are fine for those who drive briskly and are aware of the braking-behaviour pattern. However, it is conceivable that some drivers could be caught napping.

Below: Although plain in appearance, the facia has a good complement of instruments and warning lamps. Note the built-in provision for loudspeakers in the doors
Below right: The car is notable for the generosity of its foot- and leg-room. Note "belt-and-braces" sealing of doors. The window cannot be wound below this point

Tested cold, the handbrake achieved a peak deceleration of 0.26 g — this without wheel locking. It proved equal to the task of holding the car when facing up the 1-in-3 hill, but lack of wheelgrip prevented a repeat performance in the opposite direction.

Fittings and furniture

One cannot fail to be impressed by the Beta 1800's comprehensive equipment and luxurious trim. Starting with the large and comfortable front seats, these are trimmed in their entirety (sides and backs included) in nylon cloth. The material used for the centre panels of the actual seating surfaces is transversely ribbed to provide a most pleasing effect. Adjustable headrests are standard, as are elasticated pockets on the seat backs. Geared rake adjustment is provided but, even with headrest removed, the backrests cannot be lowered level with the rear seat cushion.

The rear seat is of a similar standard and is equipped with a folding centre arm-rest. Unusually, provision is made for installing three safety belts for the rear passengers (the belts themselves being extra-cost options).

On the test model, the obligatory front safety belts (also extras) were of the inertia-reel pattern. Made by Bero, these are designed for one-handed buckling. Our only complaint concerns a certain reluctance on the part of the reel to retract the driver's belt when not required.

Continuing with the furnishings, a luxurious cut-pile carpet covers the floor. Door panels are largely trimmed in the brushed-nylon material used for the seats, but feature hard-wearing vinyl cappings at both top and bottom. All four doors have substantial, if somewhat firm armrests-cum-pulls.

Grained and perforated pvc of tasteful appearance is used for the headlining. Supplementing the tinted area at the top of the laminated windscreen are a pair of padded visors. That on the passenger's side features a vanity mirror, while the driver's one incorporates a document pocket. Both can be swung to the sides if desired, but their large size renders them something of a visibility hazard when used in this way. Above each passenger door is a grab handle, those at the rear being equipped with sliding coat hooks.

There are courtesy switches for all four doors; those at the front activate a lamp which is situated just above the dippable rear-view mirror, while those at the rear activate an equivalent lamp in the rear compartment. Both these lamps can be operated independently of the doors and of each other simply by depressing their lenses (once for "on", once again for "off"). A good point is the provision of a safety marker lamp (coloured red) in the edge of each door, these being activated by the courtesy switches. Less pleasing is the absence of child-proof devices for the rear locks.

Two keys are provided — one for the ignition-cum-steering lock, the other for the doors, glove box, boot and fuel-filler flap. Good points are the recessing of the private-lock buttons into the doors (locked position) and the way in which the boot lid button retracts when locked. Mildly irritating is the inability to slam-lock the front doors.

Despite the facia's clean appearance, there is abundance of instruments and warning lamps. Dominating the panel are a speedometer and matching tachometer — both circular instruments with rather coarse markings. Between them are rectangular temperature and oil pressure gauges, a similarly styled fuel gauge lives to the left of the speedometer, with a clock beyond that. A battery of strategically placed warning lamps monitor oil pressure, coolant temperature, charging system, front-pad wear, brake-fluid level, choke position, handbrake position (automatically flashes when brake is applied) and fuel level (illuminated when contents are down to 1 gal or less). Likewise, there are tell-tales for the direction indicators, sidelights, main beams, and heated rear window (the latter being a standard fitment on all Betas). A single inclined lens over the whole of the panel eliminates reflection problems. The rather ineffective instrument lighting features rheostat control. A minor criticism concerns the siting of the fuel gauge, which is obscured by the rim of the steering wheel.

The steering column is adjustable for rake and carries three control stalks. On the left is that for windscreen washing and wiping: pulling it towards the wheel activates the washer pump: moving it down (counter-clockwise) provides intermittent and low-speed wiping facilities. A separate tumbler switch is provided for increasing the operating speed.

The upper (shorter) of the two stalks on the right looks after the direction indicators. The other controls the lights; essentially, the knob on the end serves to operate the main lighting switch whilst the stalk itself is used for dipping and flashing.

Living with the Beta 1800

Lancia have taken advantage of the compactness of the engine/transmission unit to provide better-than-average legroom. Doors are large and open quite wide; this and the shallowness of the sills make the Beta an easy car to enter and leave. Another good point concerns the shallowness of the centre tunnel in the rear compartment.

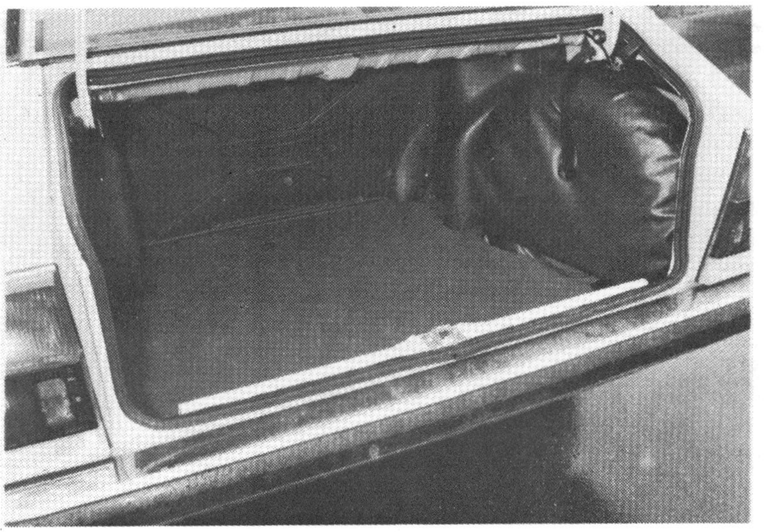

Boot is enormous and is beautifully trimmed. Most will appreciate shallowness of sill

Despite the provision of generous column-rake and seat adjustment, some people find that the driving position not to their taste. it seems that the problem concerns the positioning of the pedals in relation to the steering wheel and gearchange lever. In fairness, it must be said that there are others who find no cause for complaint.

All who drove the car complained of poor visibility towards the rear. This is something which is evident more when reversing than when driving in normal traffic.

In contrast, forward visibility is good. Helping in this connection is a first-class wiper pattern — an example of the trouble taken over the right-hand-drive adaption. Even at maximum speed, the wire-framed blades suffered no lift problems.

In addition to featuring air-blending control, the heater is equipped with an inter-connected water valve. As well as the usual footwell and screen outlets, the Beta installation has adjustable shin-level ones at both front and rear. There is a face-level vent at each end of the facia, but these are totally dependent on ram effect. Vents flanking the rear window take care of extraction.

Although slow to get going from cold, the heater provides ample output. Moreover, it responds quite quickly tm changes of setting. Less pleasing is the way its output fluctuates with changes of speed — a condition aggravated by the absence of boost for the face-level vents. Incidentally, the fan is pleasantly unobtrusive on the lower of its settings and acceptably so in its higher one.

There is reasonable provision for the stowage of odds and ends within the car. On the left of the facia is a lmckable glovebox with automatic lighting. Rigid pockets are affixed to the cowl sides. At the rear of the console is a shallow well, big enough for a packet of cigarettes or the like. The rear shelf forms a usefully deep well. Finally, there are the afocementioned elasticated pockets on the backs of the seats.

In relation to the car's overall size, the boot is truly vast. Moreover, it has a most useful shape and is tastefully trimmed (good quality looped-pile carpet on the floor, accurately moulded fibreboard panels elsewhere). It features automatic lighting and has an exceptionally shallow sill (a point which appeals to a great many people).

The spare wheel, with its elasticated cover, lives alongside the right-hand quarter panel. A stout rubber strap holds it securely in place. Behind is strapped the robust screw-pillar jack. Two jacking points are provided — one on each sill.

In a polystyrene tray at the left-hand rear corner of the boot floor lives a useful toolkit. Typically Fiat in design, it comprises a purpose-made box containing a good assortment of tools. Particularly neat is the provision of a telescopic handle for the wheel nut wrench.

The forward opening bonnet is partially counterbalanced, the torsion bars doubling as an automatic prop. Again, automatic lighting is a standard feature.

In general, accessibility is good. The engine dip stick is fairly easily reached, as is that for the transmission. Very accessible are the oil-filler cap, distributor, battery, brake-fluid reservoirs, washer bottle, coolant header tank and alternator ("fan" belt) adjustment. Using the right spanner, plug renewal is easy enough. Carburettor access presents no problems, especially with the air cleaner removed. Less easy are the fuel pump (positioned close beneath the intake manifold) and the disposable-type oil filter (located just above the subframe).

Four Cibie halogen headlamps are used,

LANCIA BETA 1800 (1,756 c.c.)

ACCELERATION

SPEED MPH TRUE / INDICATED	TIME IN SECS
30 / 29	3.7
40 / 40	5.6
50 / 50	7.8
60 / 61	10.7
70 / 71	14.3
80 / 82	19.5
90 / 92	27.2
100 / 103	41.6

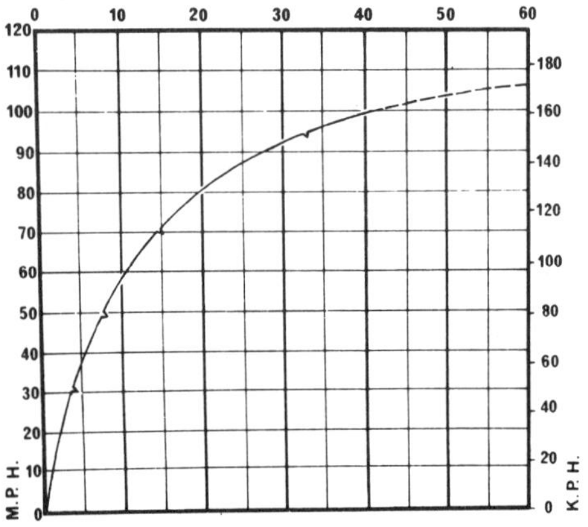

GEAR RATIOS AND TIME IN SEC

mph	Top (3.77)	4th (4.69)	3rd (6.20)
10-30	—	8.5	5.6
20-40	10.4	7.5	5.1
30-50	10.0	6.9	5.0
40-60	10.3	7.3	5.2
50-70	10.8	8.1	6.3
60-80	12.2	9.3	—
70-90	15.7	12.1	—
80-100	24.4	—	—

Standing ¼-mile
17.9 sec 77 mph
Standing Kilometre
33.1 sec 95 mph
Test distance 1,100 miles
Mileage recorder
3.7 per cent over-reading

PERFORMANCE

MAXIMUM SPEEDS

Gear	mph	kph	rpm
Top (mean)	109	175	5,990
(best)	109	175	5,990
4th	94	151	6,400
3rd	71	114	6,400
2nd	49	79	6,400
1st	31	50	6,400

BRAKES

FADE
(from 70 mph in neutral)
Pedal load for 0.5g stops in lb

1	50-38	6	16
2	35-30	7	15-20
3	20	8	15-20
4	20	9	15-20
5	18	10	15-20

RESPONSE
(from 30 mph in neutral)

	Load	g	Distance
Brakes Cold	20 lb.	0.35	86
	40 lb.	0.52	58
	80 lb.	0.64	47
	120 lb.	0.72	42
	160 lb.	0.78	39
	200 lb.	0.84	36
Brakes Hot	40 lb.	0.76	40
	60 lb.	0.84	36
Handbrake		0.26	116
Max. Gradient		1 in 4 (see text)	

CLUTCH

Pedal 29 lb. and 6.4 in.

COMPARISONS

MAXIMUM SPEED MPH

Lancia Beta 1800	**(£1,989)**	**109**
Audi 100LS	(£2,227*)	106
Fiat 132 Special 1800	(£1,697)	104
Wolseley Six	(£1,720)	104
Saab 99L CM4	(£1,874)	101

*Subject to surcharge

0-60 MPH, SEC

Fiat 132 Special 1800	10.6
Lancia Beta 1800	**10.7**
Audi 100LS	11.9
Saab 99L CM4	12.0
Wolseley Six	13.1

STANDING ¼-MILE, SEC

Fiat 132 Special 1800	17.8
Lancia Beta 1800	**17.9**
Saab 99L CM4	18.5
Audi 100LS	18.7
Wolseley Six	18.7

OVERALL MPG

Saab 99L CM4	25.8
Lancia Beta 1800	**24.3**
Audi 100LS	23.7
Fiat 132 Special 1800	23.2
Wolseley Six	22.3

GEARING

(with 175/70-14in. tyres)

Top	18.2 mph per 1,000rpm
4th	14.7 mph per 1,000rpm
3rd	11.1 mph per 1,000rpm
2nd	7.6 mph per 1,000rpm
1st	4.9 mph per 1,000rpm

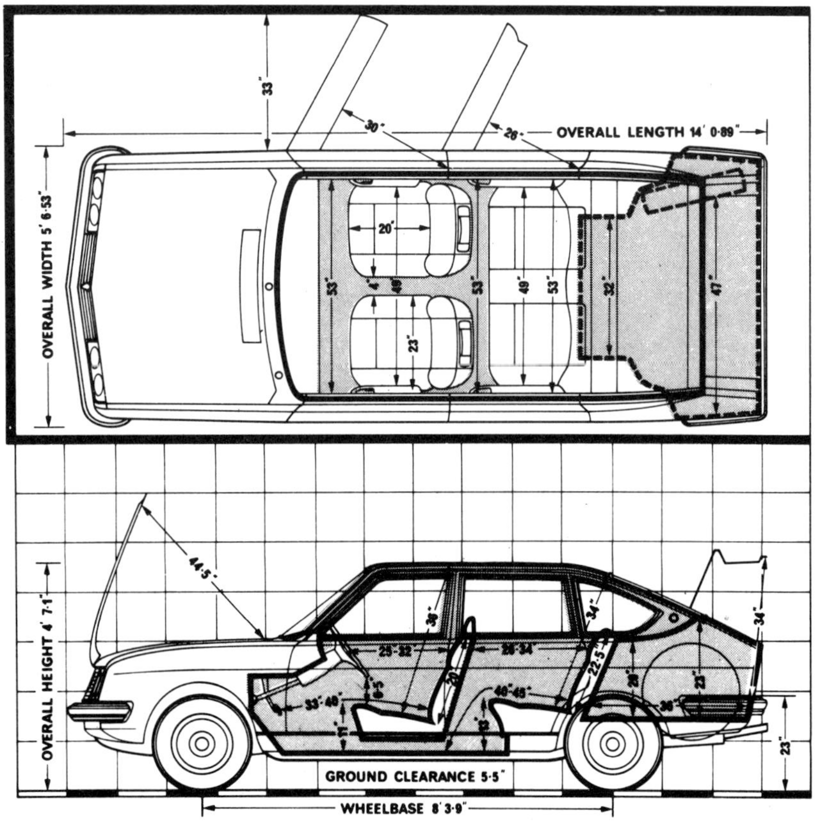

STANDARD GARAGE 16ft x 8ft 6in.

CONSUMPTION

FUEL
(At constant speed — mpg)

30 mph	47.2
40 mph	42.5
50 mph	38.0
60 mph	33.7
70 mph	29.6
80 mph	25.6
90 mph	21.6
100 mph	17.7

Typical mpg . . 26 (10.9 litres/109km)
Calculated (DIN) mpg 26.9 (10.5litres/100km)
Overall mpg . . 24.3 (11.6 litres/100km)
Grade of fuel Premium, 4-star (min. 97 RM)

OIL
Consumption (SAE 10W-50) Negligible.

TEST CONDITIONS:
Weather: Heavy rain Wind: 6-10 mph.
Temperature: 13 deg. C. (56 deg. F).
Barometer: 29.5in.hg. Humidity: 90percent.
Surfaces: Wet concrete and asphalt.

WEIGHT:
Kerb Weight 21.6 cwt (2,421lb-1,099kg).
(with oil, water and half full fuel tank).
Distribution, per cent F, 59; R, 41.
Laden as tested: 25.2 cwt (2,820lb-1,280kg).

TURNING CIRCLES:
Between kerbs L, 35 ft 5 in.; R, 37 ft 0 in.
Between walls L, 37 ft 5 in.; R, 39 ft 0 in.
Steering wheel turns, lock to lock 4.1.
Figures taken at 4,800 miles by our own staff at the Motor Industry Research Association proving ground at Nuneaton.

SPECIFICATION

FRONT ENGINE, FRONT-WHEEL DRIVE

ENGINE

Cylinders	4 in line transversely, canted at 20 deg towards rear
Main bearings	5
Cooling system	Water, pump, thermostat, electrically-driven fan
Bore	84 mm (3.31 in.)
Stroke	79.2 mm (3.12 in.)
Displacement	1 756 c.c. (107.1 cu.in.)
Valve gear	Twin overhead-camshaft; toothed-belt drive
Compression ratio	8.9-to-1. Mln. octane rating: 96RM
Carburettor	Weber 34 DMTR 21 compound twin-choke (Solex C34 CIC-1 alternative fitment)
Fuel pump	Mechanical
Oil filter	Disposable canister
Max. power	110 bhp (DIN) at 6,000 rpm
Max. torque	106 lb. ft. (DIN) at 3,000 rpm

TRANSMISSION

Clutch	Single dry plate, diaphragm spring, mechanically activated
Type	
Gearbox	Five-speed, all-synchromesh
Gear ratios	Top 0.925
	Fourth 1.152
	Third 1.522
	Second 2.235
	First 3.5
	Reverse 3.071
Final drive	Helical spur, 4.071-to-1

CHASSIS and BODY

Construction	Integral steel; bolt-on front wings and lower front panel; detachable front sub-frame

SUSPENSION

Front	Independent; MacPherson-type struts, coil springs, pressed wishbone-type lower arms, anti-roll bar.
Rear	Independent; MacPherson-type struts, coil springs, tubular lower arms (adjustable), anti-roll bar.

STEERING

Type	Rack-and-pinion
Wheel dia	15.3 in.

BRAKES

Make and type	Discs front and rear; dual-line hydraulics, both activating fronts; pressure-regulator in line to rear
Dimensions	F 9.9 in. dia
	R 9.9 in dia.
Swept area	F 192 sq. in., R 170 sq. in.
	Total 362 sq. in. (286 sq. in./ton laden)
Servo	Direct acting

WHEELS

Type	Pressed-steel, four-bolt fixing 5.5in. wide rim
Tyres-Make	Michelin
type	ZX radial ply tubed
size	175/70-14in.

EQUIPMENT

Battery	12 Volt 45 Ah
Alternator	750 watt
Headlamps	4 Cibie 220/110 watt (total)
Reversing lamp	Standard
Electric fuses	12
Screen wipers	Two-speed, plus intermittent wipe facility
Screen washer	Standard, electric
Interior heater	Standard, air-blending plus water-valve
Heated backlight	Standard
Safety belts	Extra
Interior trim	Nylon-cloth seats, pvc headlining
Floor covering	Cut-pile moquette carpet
Jack	Geared screw-pillar
Jacking points	One at centre of each sill
Windscreen	Laminated; tinted zone at top
Underbody protection	Electro-phoretic treatment prior to painting; underbody sealant applied after painting

MAINTENANCE

Fuel tank	11.4 Imp. gallons (52 litres)
Cooling system	14.6 pints (inc. heater)
Engine sump	8.8 pints (5 litres) SAE 10/50. Change oil every 3,100 miles
Gearbox and final drive	3.2 pints. SAE 90. Change every 18,600 miles
Grease	No points
Valve clearance	Inlet 0.0165 in. (cold)
	Exhaust 0.0188 in. (cold)
Contact breaker	0.015/0.017 in. gap
Ignition timing	10 deg. BTDC (Static)
Spark plug	Type: Champion N6Y. Gap 0.020/0.024 in.
Tyre pressures	F24; R 24 psi (normal driving)
	F27; R27 psi (high speed and/or full load)
Max. payload	930 lb. (425 kg)

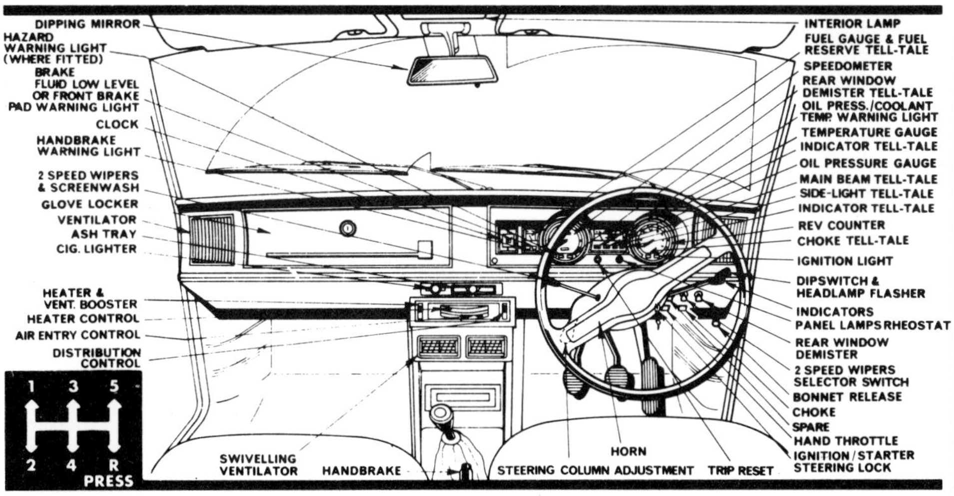

Service Interval	3,100 miles	6,200 miles	12,400 miles
Time Allowed (hours)	1.00	5.00	7.00
Cost @ £3.30 per hour	£3.30	£16.50	£23.10
Oil Change	£1.67	£1.67	£1.67
Oil Filter	—	£2.66	£2.66
Air Filter		£1.37	£1.37
Contact breaker points	—	—	£0.95
Sparking plugs	—	—	£1.32
Total Cost:	£4.97	£22.20	£31.07

Routine Replacements:	Time hr min	Labour	Spares	Total
Brake Pads	1 36	£5.28	£20.25	£25.53
Exhaust System	0 48	£2.64	£28.00	£30.64
Clutch (complete unit)	3 00	£9.90	£40.00	£49.90
Dampers — Front (pair)	0 30	£1.65	£18.70	£20.35
Dampers — Rear (pair)	1 06	£3.63	£17.80	£21.43
Replace Drive Shaft	0 42	£2.31	£58.00	£60.31
Replace Alternator	0 24	£1.32	£86.00	£87.32
Replace Starter	036	£1.98	£67.00	£68.98

the outer two providing dipped beams and all four operating in the main-beam position. Unusual is the provision of automatic levelling devices for the outer lamps. Operating on hydrostatic principles, the system features a pair of rams actuated by two displacers, one each linked to the front and rear suspensions. The system works well, although its rapid response tends to accentuate the suspension movement which occurs on rough roads. Concerning the lamps themselves, these provide an excellent spread of intensely white light.

Considerable care has gone into the layout of the electrical system. Beneath a snap-on plastic cover on the engine bulkhead is a fusebox, together with a group of three relays. There are 10 fuses in the box itself and another alongside it. The cooling fan motor has its own fuse, mounted alongside the unit itself.

By no means all of the Beta's fitments have been mentioned. For example, not only is there provision on the facia for a radio or tape player, but the layout caters for the installation of four speakers (one at the bottom of each front door, plus a further two beneath the rear window). The wiring is already in place, as is a co-axial cable for a radio aerial.

Built-in tow hooks are provided at both ends, that at the rear serving as a platform for use of a garage jack. It also provides an attachment point for a tailor-made towing bar (an extra-cost option) which picks up also on the fuel-tank mounts.

The standard of construction and finish is excellent. Seldom have we seen a mass-produced car with such narrow and regular margins. Paintwork is good and there is little brightware to suffer corrosion. In any event, much of what there is is in stainless steel. A good example is the substantial bumpers, with their protective rubber facings. Indeed, our only criticism under this heading concerns the possible inadequacy of the door checks; that at the left-hand rear of the test model had failed to prevent the panel contacting the edge of the adjacent door.

Conclusions

Without doubt, the Beta's appeal lies in its spaciousness, its comfort and the quality of its construction and finish. Good performance is allied to commendable economy, but the engine is somewhat noisy mechanically. Not everybody will like its handling and braking characteristics. Overall, however, the model represents excellent value for money.

MANUFACTURER:
Lancia & C., Via Vincenzo Lancia 27, Casella Postale 430, Torino.

UK CONCESSIONAIRES:
Lancia (England) Limited, Ealing Road, Alperton, Middlesex.

PRICES

Basic	£1,669.00
Car Tax	£139.08
VAT	£180.80
Total (in GB)	**£1,988.88**
Seat Belts (inertia reel)	£16.94
Licence	£25.00
Delivery charge (London)	£20.00
Number plates	£5.00
Total on the Road (exc. insurance)	**£2,055.82**
Insurance	Group 6
EXTRAS (inc. PT)	
Metallic paint	£100.00
TOTAL AS TESTED ON THE ROAD	**£2,055.82**

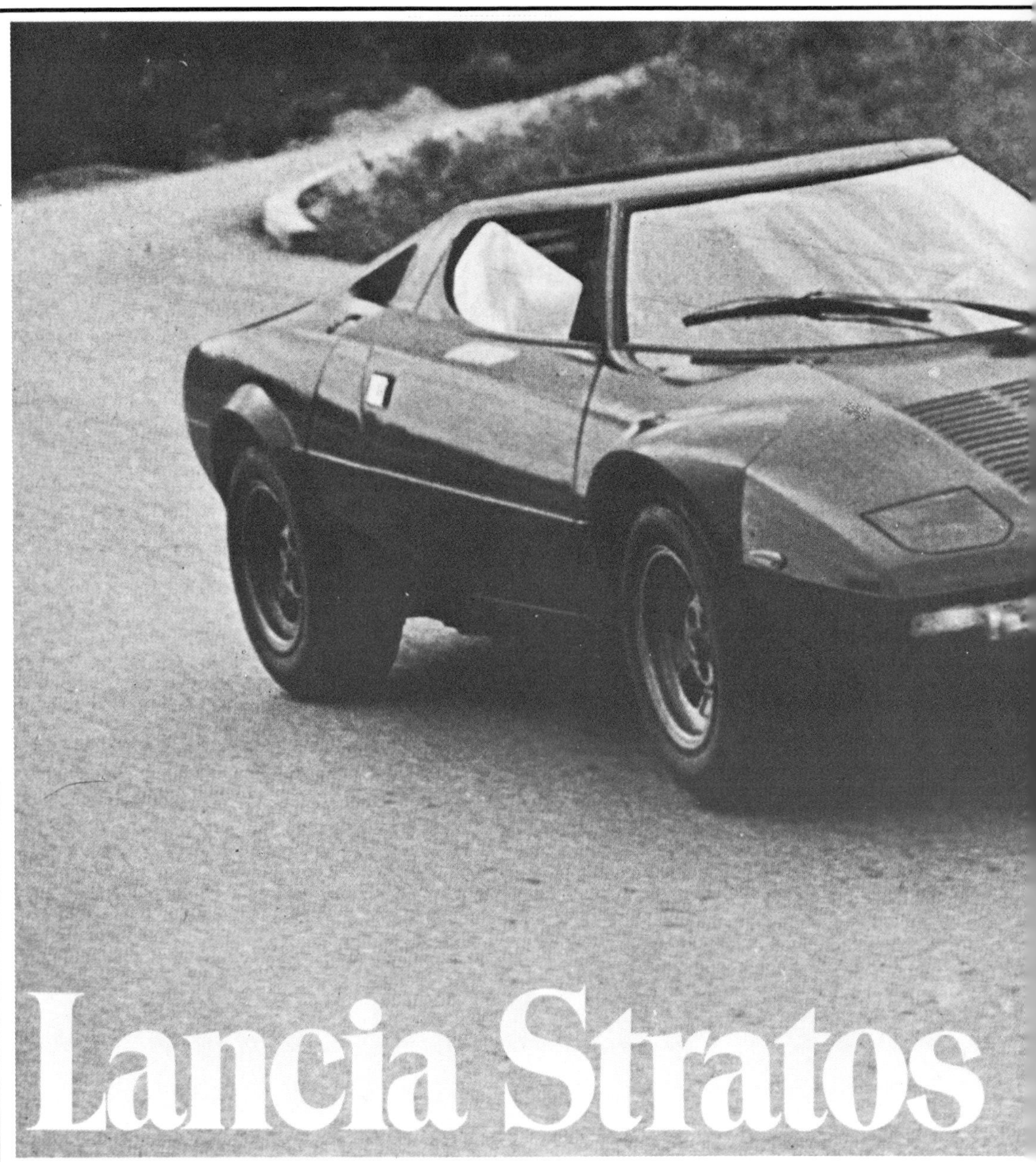

Lancia Stratos

Designed for rallying, it represents a new concept of a sports car

Technical description by **Andrew Shanks**
Driving impressions by **Ray Hutton**

YOU HAVE to go a long way back in time to find the origins of the Lancia Stratos, in fact as far back as the days when Fiat were not involved in Lancia, and to the time when Bertone produced a design exercise that just happened to be powered by a Lancia 1600 engine.

The first futuristic Stratos appeared at the Turin Motor Show in 1970 and was strikingly unusual, having a very reclining driving position and top opening door. This design exercise did, however, show the feasibility of using a Lancia 1600 engine and transaxle in the rear of the car in a mid-engine configuration.

By the following Turin Show, the design had evolved into the more familiar shape of the current rally car, and the project had advanced to the point where prototypes were running on the road.

Below: How it started. The original Stratos was a Bertone show car with a top-opening door and Fulvia power train

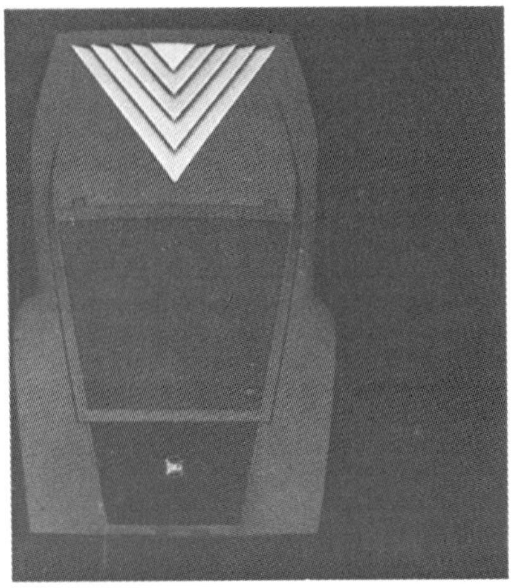

This model had become designated Lancia Stratos HF, and there were enthusiastic noises that the car would have its competition debut in 1972. In fact, the debut was not too encouraging for in the Tour de Corse, it retired with fuel injection and suspension troubles, but it redeemed itself somewhat by leading the Costa del Sol Rally until the very last stage. This prototype adopted the Ferrari 2.4-litre V6 Dino engine and five-speed gearbox which have been retained since, despite rumours of a less sophisticated Fiat unit.

During 1973, development of the car has continued and the previous reliability gremlin has been laid. In the Targa Florio, Munari and Andruet finished a splendid second, and might have even challenged for the lead had they not been delayed by a broken seat. But the high spot of the year was the car's victory in the Tour de France with Munari and Mannucci at the wheel.

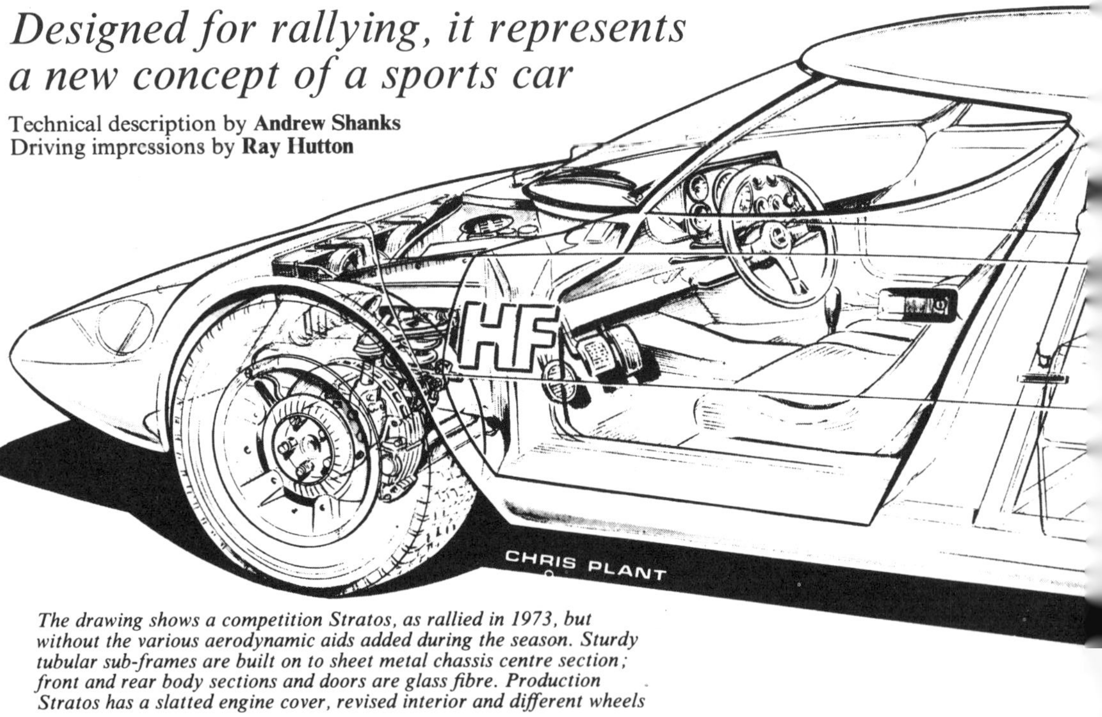

The drawing shows a competition Stratos, as rallied in 1973, but without the various aerodynamic aids added during the season. Sturdy tubular sub-frames are built on to sheet metal chassis centre section; front and rear body sections and doors are glass fibre. Production Stratos has a slatted engine cover, revised interior and different wheels

For 1974, it is proposed to enter the Stratos in all-tarmac rallies like those entered to date, some GT races (including Le Mans)—and some rough road events.

Now, after a period of uncertainty, the Stratos has gone into limited series production. It is intended to produce the first 500 by July in order that the car can qualify as an FIA Appendix J Group 4 Special Grand Touring car. The bodies are now in production at Bertone's works, assembly is carried out at the Lancia factory, also in Turin, and the first Stratos was due to be delivered to a customer a few days ago. The Stratos sells for about the same price as the Ferrari Dino in Italy: around £5,000 before taxes.

Comparison of the Stratos' dimensions with those of the Dino show just how small the Lancia is; at 12ft 2in., it is 19in. shorter than the Dino though its overall width of 5ft 8in. is about the same. Its very squat stance can be gauged by realizing that the track is slightly wider than the Dino's while the wheelbase is 6in. shorter, at 7ft 2in.

Technical Description

The most obvious feature of the Lancia Stratos is the immense strength of the steel monocoque construction. Chief Engineer Gian-Paulo Dallara claims that torsional rigidity is in the order of 77 lb. ft. per degree and certainly the dimensions of the relevant base unit and bulkheads would confirm this.

The construction is based on two wide longerons joined at both ends by full-width hoops. That at the front supports the doors and screen surround and forms the scuttle. Projecting forward of this hoop are flanged-welded large square tube extensions which provide the top suspension mounting points, and beyond these, the mountings for the radiator.

At the rear the frame is similarly robust. Extending upward from the longerons are two fabricated square tubes linked transversely at head height by a further tube. At the upper corners of the square that is formed are the ends of the square tubular roll-over bar which follows the contours of the roof section at the rear.

Extending rearwards from the peripheral rear bulkhead are further large section tubular chassis frames which support the rear suspension bottom mounting points and, from a pair of vertical extensions, also support the coil spring/damper units in a turret mounting. The two side-members are braced by a square transverse tube on which the rear engine mountings are carried on rubber bushes. The tops of the rear suspension mounting points are joined to the bulkhead by further longitudinal members which are again braced transversely at their rear end by a square tube member. The effect of the chassis tubing is to form a complete three-dimensional frame of great strength onto which such items as the rear cover locating brackets, exhaust system, etc, are hung. The rear chassis tubes project back from a some 12 in. inboard of the outer edges of the longerons at the bottom, and at the top, run inwards at an angle to the narrower rearmost bulkhead. Thus space is left at the sides for fuel tankage, immediately behind the engine bulkhead; the two tanks total 19 gal capacity in the production Stratos.

The rear suspension follows racing car practice in that a reversed bottom wishbone is employed for location of the bottom of the hub, with a long forward facing radius rod running from the bottom of the hub to a mount-

Above: The colour photographs show the production Stratos, which differs in several details from the competition version illustrated in the cutaway drawing. Rounded body sides dictate an unusually central seating position but space inside is adequate. Revised tail treatment provides luggage compartment above exhaust silencer in production cars, while steeply curved windscreen is swept by a single wiper in definitive version

Lancia Stratos...

ing on the rear bulkhead tubing. Top location of the hub is provided by the long coil spring/damper unit. This arrangement is similar in appearance to the Lotus Elan set-up, except that the bottom wishbone/link can be adjusted for toe-in as well as camber. On the competition cars, the rear hubs are steel fabrications welded to a substantial clamp on their top into which the cylindrical end of the damper is fitted and retained by a pair of hefty pinch-bolts.

The ride-height can be adjusted simply by elevating or lowering the base plate of the coil spring which screws up and down a threaded portion of the damper; another piece of racing car practice. The short, solid drive shafts have Birfield-Rzeppa constant-velocity joints at both ends, the inboard one being of the sliding type.

The front suspension is very orthodox, a fact dictated by the use of Fiat 124 front hubs. The wide fabricated bottom link is curved downwards to allow a sufficiently low mounting point for the coil spring/damper unit to provide the desirable spring length and travel. Again, ride-height is is adjustable in a similar fashion to the rear. Bottom location and castor change facility for the front suspension is provided by an adjustable forward-facing radius rod.

There are adjustable anti-roll bars at both ends of the car, that at the rear bearing on the outer end of the bottom wishbone from a leading transverse pivot position mounted on the underside of the top rear transverse chassis tube. At the front of the car, the anti-roll bar is mounted in a trailing position, bearing again on the bottom link.

Steering is by rack-and-pinion and is much lower geared on the production version than the rally cars: $3\frac{1}{4}$ turns from lock to lock instead of approximately two turns.

Ventilated disc brakes are used front and rear, and both sets are mounted outboard. A dual braking circuit is used with tandem master cylinders but there is no provision for adjustment of the balance between front and rear, although a pressure-limiting valve for the rear circuit has been tried in testing and discarded. Porsche 917-type drilled discs were tried on Andruet's Stratos on the Tour d'Italia.

The wheels are in cast magnesium-alloy by Campagnolo and have a 5-spoke design, allowing generous brake-cooling slots. Production cars will have $7\frac{1}{2}$ in. wide rims of 14 in. diameter but widths of up to 9 in. at the front and 12 in. at the rear have been tried for racing and rallying.

The power-unit is the familiar 2.4-litre V6 Ferrari Dino engine. It is mounted transversely far enough back from the cockpit bulkhead to allow a reasonable run for the fabricated exhaust pipes for the right-hand (furthest forward) half of the vee. This set of exhausts curve towards the offside of the car before turning through 90 degrees to exit at the rear on the nearside. The exhausts for the rearmost back of cylinders curve towards the rear on the nearside.

On the Tour d'Italia, the car used by Andruet was using an experimental four-valves per cylinder head design, with Lucas fuel injection, and this may be offered as a competition option for the production car. Racing versions will also use a Borg and Beck diaphragm spring racing clutch mounted on the left hand side of the engine, drive from which is taken downwards by three helical spur gears to the gearbox input shaft. This transfer gear train is contained in its own alloy cover which can be unbolted from the engine and gearbox side. By altering the relative size of the idler gear and engine output/gearbox input gears it is possible to charge the overall gearing simply, without resort to a change of final drive ratio. The transfer gear case can be changed in less than 15 min and at the moment, there are three choices of ratio. Those of the five-speed Dino gearbox will be the same as for the Ferrari production cars, but the option of a close-ratio set (and also the choice of transfer gear ratio sets) will be available for competition-minded customers.

A steel skin clothes the chassis frame at the centre section incorporating the scuttle, inner wheel arches at the front, the roof, and the side sills. Doors, weighing only 6 kg each, are glass fibre with perspex windows. The windows are lowered by a simple pivot from their trailing edge and secured with wing-nut clamps. It is proposed to offer proper glass windows to any customer who wants them. The front and rear body sections are also glass fibre and open away from the centre of the car. The rear section is released by two levers on the left hand door jamb and the front by two Dzus-type fasteners. The top of the front section is heavily louvred to aid extraction of air from the front-mounted radiator, which itself incorporates a pair of electric fans to pull air through the radiator if necessary.

Integral with the rear cover immediately behind the engine and gearbox, is a surprisingly generous —if warm—luggage compartment with its own lockable lid. Incorporated into the wings of the front cover are "pop-up" halogen headlights, very similar in appearance to those on the Lotus Elan.

Inside the car, the two corduroy-covered bucket seats are adjustable for reach, and ahead of the driver is a full display of round instruments. On the rally versions there are two water temperature gauges which indicate water temperature at both the engine and the radiator, so that the driver can be assured of adequate water circulation. Engine oil is cooled by an ingenious heat exchanger system utilizing cooled water returning from the radiator.

A full technical description of the Ferrari Dino was published in *Autocar* of 8 March 1973. It is apposite to recap on the basic details of the engine and transmission:

The capacity of the six-cylinder unit is 2,418 c.c. and each cylinder has a bore and stroke of 92.5 mm and 60 mm respectively. The two banks of cylinders are arranged at a 65 deg angle, and the block in itself is shell-moulded in cast iron. The two light alloy cylinder heads each have chain-driven twin overhead camshafts which run directly in the head. The production engine has two valves per cylinder inclined at an angle of 47 deg to each other, and three twin choke DCNF Weber carburettors.

In standard form this engine produces 190 bhp (net) at 7,000 rpm (195 bhp is claimed for the Ferrari installation) and 160 lb. ft. at 4,500 rpm.

The transmission, including the five-speed gearbox is made up of three castings, the main one of which is integral with the engine sump, but divided so that engine and gears run in their own oil. The gearbox casing also houses the final drive and ZF self-locking differential. **ADS**

Rally car of the Marlboro-sponsored Lancia works team. Later cars had rear spoilers, a front air dam, flared wheel arches and a little aerofoil wing at the back of the roof. An engine "air box" intake was also tried

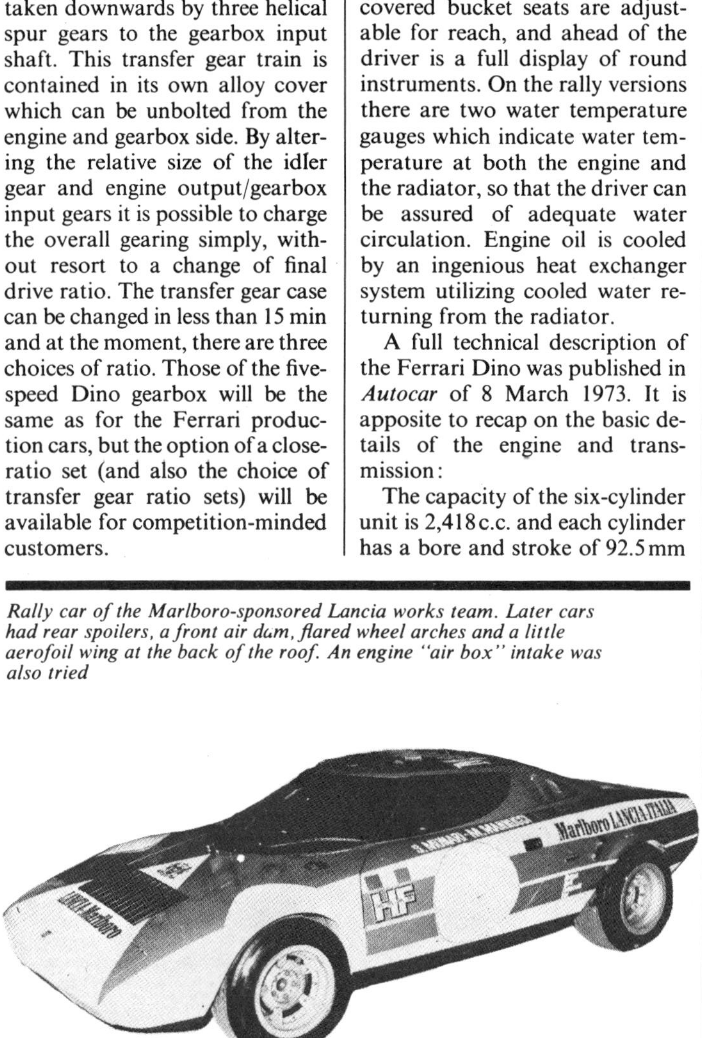

Stratos experience

Just sitting there it looks incredibly exciting. A rich red wedge, tiny but slightly tubby, with a deep windscreen so curved it reminds one of a racing driver's integral crash helmet. That is appropriate, for the Stratos is a car designed specifically for competition. We are used to seeing racing prototypes of course, but this Lancia is probably unique—though it will be raced, it was designed from the ground up as a rally car. You can argue that the same comment applies to the Alpine-Renault, the Ford GT70, or the Chrysler France CG-MC, but the Alpine really owes its development, rather than its origins, to rallying and the Ford and the Simca have not progressed beyond the prototype stage.

The Stratos in front of us was the "last prototype" before the design for the production run was finalized. As such it differed in only a few details from the car that up to 500 lucky customers will be able to use for their rallying—or simply drive on the road for fun. That's the point about rallying in its broadest sense; a good rally car needs to have many of the attributes of a good road car which is never used in competition. It needs to be habitable—and it needs to start easily, run untemperamentally and have reasonable flexibility. The Stratos has all these things. It's a purpose-built rally car, but Lancia's competitions chief Cesare Fiorio says that he likes to think of it as "a new concept of a sports car".

From the moment I slipped into the long, close-fitting bucket seat it felt right; more like putting the car on than getting into it. This feeling of "oneness" was reinforced by the reassuring way that the flared tops of the wheel arches indicated clearly the position of the front wheels, seemingly only inches away. Visibility to the front and front quarters through the deep screen could not be better; never before have I felt that I could place an enclosed-wheel car so exactly where I wanted. At the sides the curved doors rise up to one's shoulders, and effective side visibility ceases about half way along the doors, leaving a sizeable rear quarter blind spot. It is not too much better through the little heavily-slatted rear window—or rather air intake cover since the window itself is vertical—just behind your right ear. I'm sorry, but my Stratos is going to have to have side mirrors.

Seat adjusted—there is quite a lot of fore and aft flexibility—I surveyed the row of clear instruments, and turned the key. A single pump on the throttle and the splendid mechanical buzz of the Ferrari engine builds up behind. A final check on pedal movements, ease the gearlever down towards the seat and into first, and out on to the open road.

The revs rise cleanly—after all, this has a standard Dino unit—and about 5,000 rpm seems to be a good compromise change point between startlingly eager acceleration and caution on blind mountain roads. The five-speed gearbox is satisfying to use but takes a little learning; unlike the Dino it has no gate. In practice the engine is so flexible that third and fourth are all that are needed on give-and-take roads.

First impressions are of leech-like roadholding, and even as one's confidence builds up it is no less impressive. Within my modest personal limits the handling characteristics were as near-neutral as one could hope to get. This, light and moderately geared steering, and the excellent forward visibility, give the Stratos tremendous precision of line; one can aim to "brush" a wall for an ideal line knowing that you will be within an inch or so, and gauge a tight gap within centimetres. There's no body roll of course and the only movement is the personal one under the cornering forces generated. As I held on during a "demonstration" run with Lancia works driver Amilcare Ballestrieri he explained that he had suggested bigger section rear tyres than the 205/70VR-14 Pirelli Cinturato CN36 fitted all round at present. He said that this was to reduce the oversteer, applying a heavy right foot and touch of opposite lock out of a tight hairpin to illustrate his point.

It is worth pointing out that is one of the very few production cars to be offered with fully adjustable suspension in the racing car sense, so a knowledgeable owner will be able to set it up in the way that best suits his driving style and the conditions of an event. Among the many homologated options to be offered will be the wider wheels fitted to the Marlboro-sponsored works cars and the higher-geared steering that they use.

Also optional will be the various wings, spoilers and things that the rally cars sprouted over the course of last season. Their growth does not so much indicate that Bertone paid more attention to style than function as emphasize the great variety of events that rallying now encompasses. In Tour de France trim the Stratos had a rear spoiler, a front air dam and a little wing on the roof. Ballestrieri told me that he regarded the air dam as important for events where speeds towards the 140 mph maximum might be involved. Fiorio is very anxious that the standard specification should leave Bertone's clean lines uncluttered; one suspects that he wishes to avoid the arguments with motor sport's rule-makers that BMW have encountered with their 3.0 CSL "Batmobile".

Above: Neat, uncluttered interior; view forward through deep windscreen is superb

Left: Bulging body sides allow stowage space for crash helmets in door bins

Below, left: Plastic windows pivot from the rear, are secured by wing-nut in slide within

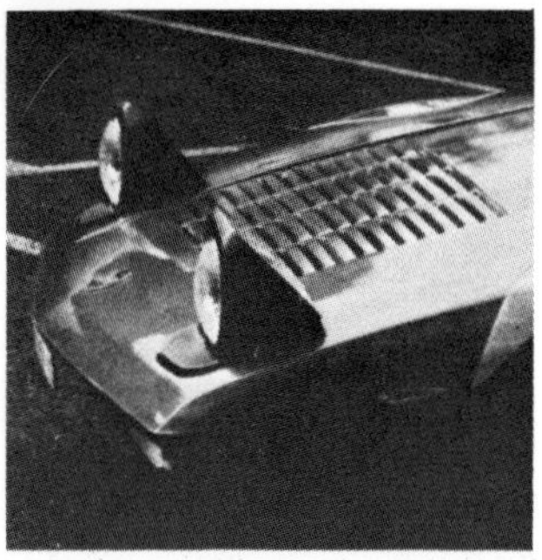

Below, right: Halogen headlamps pop-up electrically. Small rectangular spot lamps are fitted alongside radiator grille

It may have been built as a competition car but the Stratos doesn't seem like a detuned racer. Though that glorious engine note is much in evidence, there is no uncomfortable vibration, very little wind noise and surprisingly few creaks and rattles from the suspension considering that it uses a good number of Rose-type ball joints.

I was not as happy with the brakes, which compared to the other controls had a heavy and dead feeling. Put to the test, they work well—suggesting that this car at least was using a very hard competition pad material.

Although they do not normally work in glass fibre for production models (and I gather would much rather have used aluminium alloy), Bertone have made a good job of the body mouldings and their integration with the metal centre section. The floor of the cockpit is also a one-piece glass fibre moulding, thinly carpeted in a delicate shade of orange, while the curved facia and other trim is covered in black suedette. With such a big windscreen (remarkably free of distortion) an anti-glare interior is of particular importance. The screen's shape allows a single long windscreen wiper.

One of the most intriguing features of the interior is the bins within the doors which bulge out behind one's elbows to accommodate a crash helmet. This was very much part of the design, for mid-engined cars can present real problems in stowing helmets and the other paraphernalia that a rally crew need. The Stratos bins are big enough to take a coat too, and there is a narrow but symmetrical luggage boot in the tail section. This is what I mean by rally cars having to have the same characteristics as good road cars. The Stratos is one of the most practical mid-engined sports cars I have encountered, having a much better interior layout than, for example, a Lotus Europa or a Lamborghini Miura.

As a rally car it has already proved its worth, but it comes as something of a surprise to discover that, despite its weight-saving bodywork and the absence of any unnecessary trim ("not even an ashtray", Fiorio points out), the Stratos carries a weight disadvantage. It weighs about 840 kg (16.5 cwt) which is nearly 200 kg higher than the homologated weight of an Alpine-Renault and 50 kg more than a rally prepared Fulvia HF coupé. Fiorio blames the weight of the Ferrari engine for this. Then he reminds you of the 300 bhp 24-valve engine. And the 350 bhp turbocharged one . . . **RH**

CARS UP-TO-DATE

Lancia Beta Coupé

— *GT style for post-Fiat saloon*

FIRST SHOWN as a pre-production design at the Frankfurt Show last year the Lancia Beta Coupé is now available on the Continent—as from 2 March. No date has yet been given for the introduction of right-hand drive cars in the UK. As with the saloons, the four-cylinder in-line twin-cam engine is front-mounted across the car, driving the front wheels. It comes in 1600 and 1800 c.c. forms, as distinct from the saloon's 1400, 1600 and 1800 c.c., and the principal differences between the two versions are as follows (figures in brackets apply to the saloon version):

1600 c.c.: Max. power output 108 bhp DIN (100) at 6,000 rpm; max torque, 99·77 lb. ft. DIN (94·7) at 4,500 rpm (3,000). Compression ratio, 9·8 to 1 (8·9). Manufacturer's performance comparisons: Top speed 111·8 mph (105·6); standing 400 metres (approx. ¼ mile) 16·5sec (17·7); standing kilometre, 31·5 sec (33·0); 0–100 kph (62·5 mph) in 10·2sec (11·4).

1800 c.c.: Max. power output 120 bhp DIN (110) at 6,200 rpm; max. torque 110·6 lb. ft. DIN (106·3) at 4,500 rpm (3,000). Compression ratio 9·8 to 1 (8·9). Manufacturer's performance comparisons: Top speed, 118·1 mph (108·7); standing 400 metres (approx. ¼ mile) 16sec (17·2); standing kilometre, 30·5sec (31·8); 0–100 kph (62·5 mph) 9·5sec (10·5).

No prices have yet been announced for the car in the UK, though it is expected that it will cost between 16 and 20 per cent more than the equivalent saloon version. In appearance, the Beta Coupé is quite different from the saloon, with restyled radiator grille and new body pressings, though both cars have the same distinctive high-tailed appearance and sharp cut-off at the rear. The styling gives the coupé a particularly commodious boot; a good feature. The car is very well appointed indeed, and the interior styling has the same feeling of modern originality as the saloon's, though again, it is in no way a revamp. The instrument layout, though extremely comprehensive, is needlessly complicated and takes some time to get used to. In contrast with the saloon's large, chair-like front seats, the Coupé's are small, with unusually low back-rests, relying on the adjustable head restraints to give the required height. On the pre-production 1800 we drove recently, they were too lightly built, both the driver's and the passenger's back-rests breaking away at the pivot points. Since the exciting new Lancia Stratos was robbed of a clear-cut win in last year's Targa Florio by three pit stops with a broken seat, the company must be aware of this shortcoming! Passenger space, as might be expected in a sporting coupé, is very limited at the back and is unsuited for more than one person on a long journey.

On the road the car is as impressive as its specification suggests, and the manufacturers' claimed top speed of 118 mph for the 1800 seems reasonable, in view of the two-direction maximum of 109 we achieved with the 1800 saloon (*Autocar*, 1 November 1973). The ride is stiff and taut over small bumps, and it smooths out the larger ones while clinging firmly to the road. There is very little roll on corners; and, again, all four wheels remain firmly on the road even through the endless *lacets* in the Alpes Maritimes where the Coupé was tested. Steering is low-geared (four turns lock-to-lock), the ratio being selected to help offset the heaviness in manoeuvring caused by the nose-heavy weight distribution. Self-centring is strong, the wheel spinning back through one's hands as required—and it is strongest from left-lock. In fact, under full power it almost disappears from right-lock, though the driver very soon gets accustomed to these slight peculiarities.

Circumstances did not allow us to check wind noise at high speeds, though there is virtually none up to around 80 mph, and road noise is very low indeed. Braking is very impressive and almost excessively sensitive, the pedal effort to check the speed being surprisingly low; and never, during repeated use of the brakes on fast descents of the Col du Tende and Col de Braus, was there any sign of fade or even deterioration.

The Coupé's appeal lies very much in its individuality and its comprehensive specification, coupled with an exciting performance, surprisingly low flexibility and great safety in handling and braking—once the driver has learned about them in the space of half-an-hour or so. And, if the 1800 saloon is anything to go by, all this is achieved with good fuel economy. The manufacturer's claimed DIN consumption figures are 30·1 and 29·9 mpg for the 1600 and 1800 respectively. □

Above: Lancia's Beta Coupé is very different from the saloon, although it retains the rather high tail line

Left: The interior is well but rather garishly equipped

AutoTEST

Lancia Beta 1600 Coupé

1,592 c.c.

Stylish addition to successful Lancia Beta range. Smooth Fiat-based engine gives good performance for its size. Excellent handling and taut ride. Good brakes. High standard of finish throughout and acceptable seating for four. Reasonable economy. Good value for money

Elegant from any angle, the Beta Coupé belies its considerable interior space in a frontal view

WHEN CONSIDERING a new car from Lancia, first thoughts are inevitably centred on whether the car simply maintains the high reputation of the marque or whether it enhances it. In the case of the Beta Coupé there is no doubt that Lancia's reputation for good-looking cars that feel right is most definitely enhanced and this new model will take its place among the many cars that have built up the company's reputation over the years.

Basis of the Beta Coupé is the saloon of the same name that was announced in October 1972 and which revived the name of the company's very first production car, introduced 63 years earlier. Like the saloon, the Beta Coupé carries its transversely-mounted Fiat engine on a separate subframe with the twin-overhead camshaft engine canted backwards 20 deg.

In Italy, both 1,592 and 1,756 c.c. equivalent versions to the saloon range are marketed, but for the moment at least, only the smaller of these two is available here. As fitted to the Beta Coupé, this engine develops 108 bhp (DIN) at 6,000 rpm and 100 lb. ft. (DIN) of torque at a realistic 4,500 rpm. The engine transmits its drive via a conventional diaphragm spring clutch that is positioned alongside the engine, to the cluster gear for the 5-speed all-indirect gearbox. The final drive unit (which shares its oil with the gearbox) is of helical-spur gear design incorporating a bevel-gear differential and the whole forms a compact unit from which the engine can be removed in the normal way and withdrawn entirely separately.

Like the Beta saloon, the Coupé has independent suspension front and rear by MacPherson struts, with lower wishbones at the front and twin transverse links at the rear. Adjustment for toe-in is provided on the rear suspension as the rearmost of the two links is adjustable for length. A measure of fore and aft compliance is assured at both front and rear by the use of rubber bushes at the inner ends of the track control media and the plentiful use of Silentblocs and rubber pads ensures that the effects of road shocks are not transmitted to the main body structure. Following the lead set by its saloon stablemate, the Beta Coupé has rack-and-pinion steering which is mounted safely out of harm's way on the engine bulkhead.

The braking system is identical to that of the Beta saloon, having floating caliper disc brakes front and rear and incorporating twin circuits. The system is unusual in that the direct-acting servo and duplex master cylinder operate one circuit for the front brakes and a second circuit that operates both the rear brakes and also one of the two pistons

Lancia Beta 1600 Coupé

with which each front brake caliper is fitted. Thus in the event of a failure of the circuit that exclusively operates the front brakes, full braking is still available from the "mixed" circuit. A further safety feature is that the brake pads operated by the pistons rather than the floating portion of the caliper are fitted with wear limit indicators that operate a warning lamp on the facia. The rear braking circuit is fitted with a load-sensitive limiter to avoid premature locking when the car is lightly laden. The handbrake operates mechanically on the rear brake pistons and has an automatic adjustment for wear.

Performance

Acceleration from rest reveals the problems of weight transfer associated with a fwd design, for although 62 per cent of the weight is over the front wheels, it proved difficult to control the amount of wheelspin when getting off the mark. Thus the time of 3·3 sec taken to reach 30 mph is not especially good with a

Comparisons

MAXIMUM SPEED MPH

Lancia Beta 1600 Coupé	**(£2,450)**	**113**
Fiat 124 Coupé 1800	(£2,475)	107
Audi 80GT	(£2,459)	106
Sunbeam Rapier H120	(£2,633)	105
Volkswagen Scirocco TS	(£2,198)	104

0–60 MPH, SEC

Audi 80GT	9·5
Lancia Beta 1600 Coupé	**10·4**
Fiat 124 Coupé 1800	10·5
Sunbeam Rapier H120	11·1
Volkswagen Scirocco TS	11·1

STANDING ¼-MILE, SEC

Audi 80GT	17·2
Lancia Beta 1600 Coupé	**17·3**
Fiat 124 Coupé 1800	17·4
Sunbeam Rapier H120	17·7
Volkswagen Scirocco TS	18·3

OVERALL MPG

Audi 80GT	29
Volkswagen Scirocco TS	28
Lancia Beta 1600 Coupé	**24**
Fiat 124 Coupé 1800	24
Sunbeam Rapier H120	22

Performance

ACCELERATION

True speed mph	Time in Secs	Car Speedo mph
30	3·3	33
40	5·4	43
50	7·4	53
60	10·4	63
70	14·0	74
80	18·6	85
90	25·2	95
100	37·6	106

Standing ¼-mile
17·3sec 87 mph

Standing kilometre
32·9sec 96 mph

Mileage recorder: accurate

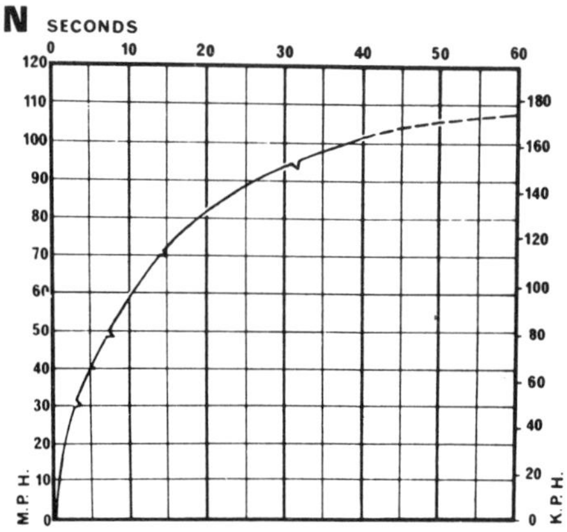

GEAR RATIOS AND TIME IN SEC

mph	Top (2·84)	4th (3·54)	3rd (4·67)
10–30	—	—	6·5
20–40	—	8·2	6·0
30–50	10·6	8·0	5·6
40–60	10·9	7·9	5·7
50–70	11·9	8·2	6·7
60–80	13·1	9·0	—
70–90	15·5	15·5	—
80–100	20·3	—	—

GEARING

(with 175/70HR14in. tyres)

Top	18·3 mph per 1,000 rpm
4th	14·7 mph per 1,000 rpm
3rd	11·1 mph per 1,000 rpm
2nd	7·6 mph per 1,000 rpm
1st	4·9 mph per 1,000 rpm

MAXIMUM SPEEDS

Gear	mph	kph	rpm
5th (mean)	113	182	6,200
(best)	113	182	6,200
4th	94	151	6,400
3rd	71	114	6,400
2nd	48	78	6,400
1st	31	50	6,400

BRAKES

FADE (from 70 mph in neutral)
Pedal load for 0·5g stops in lb

1	35	6	40
2	35	7	40
3	35–40	8	40
4	40	9	40
5	40	10	40

RESPONSE (from 30 mph in neutral)

Load	g	Distance
20lb	0·38	79ft
40lb	0·54	56ft
60lb	0·80	38ft
80lb	0·90	33ft
100lb	1·05	29ft
Handbrake	0·38	79ft
Max Gradient	1 in 3	

CLUTCH

Pedal 24lb and 5·8in.

Consumption

FUEL

(At constant speed – mpg)

30 mph	40·1
40 mph	40·7
50 mph	38·2
60 mph	35·0
70 mph	31·1
80 mph	27·0
90 mph	23·2
100 mph	19·6

Typical mpg 26 (10·9 litres/100km)
Calculated (DIN) mpg 28·3 (10·0 litres/100km)
Overall mpg 24·0 (11·8 litres/100km)
Grade of fuel Premium, 4-star (min 97RM)

OIL

Consumption (SAE 10W–50) Negligible

TEST CONDITIONS:
Weather: Fine
Wind: 0–5 mph
Temperature: 15 deg C (60 deg F)
Barometer: 29in. Hg
Humidity: 60 per cent
Surface: Dry concrete and asphalt
Test distance: 1,340 miles

Figures taken by our own staff on the Continent

Dimensions

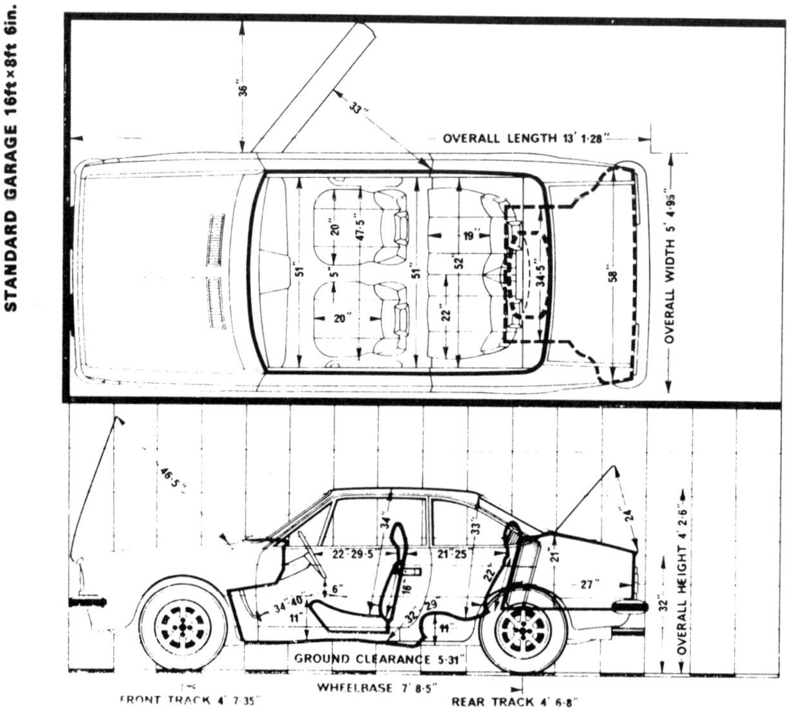

TURNING CIRCLES:
Between kerbs
L, 32ft 2in.; R, 33ft 9in.
Between walls
L, 34ft 4in.; R, 35ft 11in.
Steering wheel turns, 3·7 lock to lock

WEIGHT:
Kerb Weight 19·9cwt (2,226lb–1,010kg) (with oil, water and half full fuel tank)
Distribution, per cent F, 62; R, 38
Laden as tested: 23·5cwt (2,632lb–1,195kg)

corresponding effect on the time taken to reach higher speeds. However, a time of 10·4sec to reach 60 mph is well up with the class competitors. It should be mentioned that the car failed to match Lancia's claims for it of 31·5sec for a standing kilometre, a fact that might be due to the very low mileage of the test car.

Reflecting the higher (numerically lower) final drive ratio, the Coupé did not prove markedly more flexible than the 1,756 c.c. Beta saloon tested in *Autocar* of 1 November 1973, e.g. it took longer for each 20 mph increment up to 70 mph in 5th gear than the saloon but did manage 70 to 90 mph in two-tenths of a second less. In correct fashion, the ratios close up as each higher gear is taken and it is true to say that there is "a gear for every occasion".

Like its saloon brother, the Beta Coupé proved relatively economical during its time with us, returning an overall fuel consumption of 24 mpg despite being used hard on twisting and demanding mountain roads in France. It proved possible to return figures in the high 20s when full performance was not used and thus a typical figure of 26 mpg is suggested. With a tank capacity of 11·2 gallons, a safe range of over 250 miles is available and a warning light on the facia gives accurate warning when the last two gallons in the tank have been reached.

Specification

Lancia Beta 1600 Coupé

FRONT ENGINE, FRONT-WHEEL DRIVE

ENGINE

Cylinders	4, in-line, canted 20deg towards rear
Main bearings	5
Cooling system	Water; pump, thermostat, electric fan
Bore	80mm (3·15in.)
Stroke	79·2mm (3·12in.)
Displacement	1,592 c.c. (97·2 cu. in.)
Valve gear	Twin overhead camshaft; toothed belt drive
Compression ratio	9·8 to 1. Min octane rating: 97RM
Carburettors	Twin choke downdraught (Weber 84 DMTR21 or Solex C34 CIC–1)
Fuel pump	Mechanical
Oil filter	Disposable canister
Max power	108 bhp (DIN) at 6,000 rpm
Max torque	100 lb. ft. (DIN) at 4,500 rpm

TRANSMISSION

Clutch	Single dry plate, diaphragm spring, cable operation
Type	
Gearbox	Five speed, all-synchromesh
Gear ratios	Top 0·925
	Fourth 1·152
	Third 1·522
	Second 2·235
	First 3·5
	Reverse 3·071
Final drive	Helical spur gear, 4·071 to 1
Mph at 1,000 rpm in top gear	18·3

CHASSIS and BODY

Construction	Integral steel; bolt-on wings and lower front panel, detachable front sub-frame

SUSPENSION

Front	Independent; MacPherson-type struts, coil springs, anti-roll bar, pressed steel lower wishbone
Rear	Independent; MacPherson-type struts, coil springs, twin lower transverse links, anti-roll bar acting as longitudinal reaction arm

STEERING

Type	Rack and pinion
Wheel dia	15½in.

BRAKES

Make and type	Discs front and rear; dual-line hydraulics, both activating fronts, load-sensitive pressure regulator in rear circuit
Servo	Vacuum
Dimensions	F, 9·9in. dia R, 9·9in. dia
Swept area	F, 192 sq. in., R, 170 sq. in. Total 362 sq. in. (308 sq. in./ton laden)

WHEELS

Type	Pressed steel disc, 4-stud fixing 5½in. wide rim
Tyres – make	Pirelli
– type	Radial ply tubed
– size	175/70HR14in.

EQUIPMENT

Battery	12 volt 45 Ah.
Alternator	63 amp a.c.
Headlamps	4 Cibié 220/110 watt (total)
Reversing lamp	Standard
Electric fuses	12
Screen wipers	Two-speed, plus intermittent wipe facility
Screen washer	Standard, electric
Interior heater	Standard, air-blending plus water valve
Heated backlight	Standard
Safety belts	Extra
Interior trim	Nylon-cloth seats, pvc headlining
Floor covering	Cut-pile moquette carpet
Jack	Geared screw-pillar
Jacking points	One each side, at sill centre
Windscreen	Laminated; tinted zone at top
Underbody protection	Electrophoretic treatment prior to painting; underbody sealant applied after painting

MAINTENANCE

Fuel tank	11·2 Imp gallons (51 litres)
Cooling system	14½ pints (inc heater)
Engine sump	8¾ pints (5 litres) SAE 10/50. Change oil every 3,100 miles. Change filter every 6,200 miles
Gearbox and Final Drive	3·2 pints. SAE 90. Change every 18,600 miles
Grease	No points
Valve clearance	Inlet 0·0165in. (cold) Exhaust 0·0188in. (cold)
Contact breaker	0·015/0·017in. gap
Ignition timing	10deg BTDC (static)
Spark plug	Type: Champion N6Y Gap 0·020/0·024in.
Tyre pressures	F, 24; R, 24 psi (normal driving) F, 32; R, 32 psi (high speed) F, 28; R, 28 psi (full load)
Max payload	705lb (320kg)

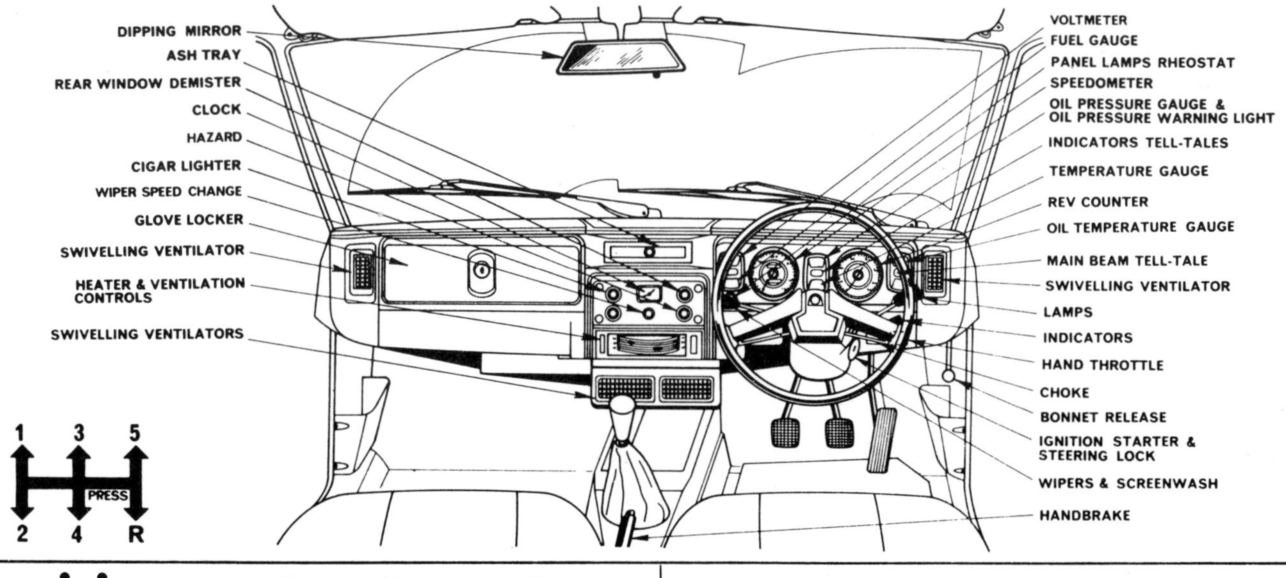

Servicing

	3,100 miles	6,200 miles	12,400 miles
Time Allowed (hours)	1·00	5·00	7·00
Cost at £4.30 per hour	£4.30	£21.50	£30.10
Engine oil	£2.33	£2.33	£2.33
Gearbox oil	£—	£—	£—
Oil Filter	£—	£3.39	£3.39
Air Filter	£—	£—	£—
Contact Breaker Points	£—	£2.38	£2.38
Sparking Plugs	£—	£—	£1.44
Fuel Filter	£—	£—	£—
Total Cost:	£6.63	£29.60	£39.64

Routine Replacements:	Time hours	Labour	Spares	TOTAL
Brake Pads – Front (2 wheels)	0·6	£2.58	£6.74	£9.32
Brake Pads – Rear (2 wheels)	0·6	£2.58	£11.12	£13.70
Exhaust System	0·8	£3.44	£66.53	£69.97
Clutch (centre+driven plate)	4·2	£18.06	£39.80	£57.86
Dampers – Front (pair)	1·3	£6.59	£46.72	£53.31
Dampers – Rear (pair)	1·8	£7.74	£44.92	£52.66
Replace Drive Shaft	0·7	£3.01	£11.13	£14.14
Replace Alternator (exchange)	0·5	£2.15	£37.40	£39.55
Replace Starter (exchange)	0·7	£3.01	£39.96	£42.97

Lancia Beta 1600 Coupé

Brakes

As well as being technically impressive on paper, the brakes proved above reproach in use. Normal check braking of 0·4g required only 20lb pressure and the response improved progressively as pedal pressure was increased. Optimum retardation of 1·05g required 100lb pedal pressure which could be applied without difficulty as the position of the pedal and the angle of attack on it are good. Our normal fade test revealed no tendency for the brakes to lose their efficiency and after only three applications to warm up, the brakes required a consistent 40lb pedal pressure to give 0·5g for the remaining seven stops. As the car was tested in France, the unusual opportunity to test the brakes in Alpine conditions was taken and even after repeated hard applications, no tendency to fade was evident. Unlike earlier Lancias – the Fulvia Coupé in particular – the handbrake proved most effective, holding the car easily on a 1-in-3 slope in either direction and proving capable of providing 0·38g retardation on its own – or sufficient to stop the car from 30 mph in 79ft.

Ride and handling

With so much weight over the driven wheels, the force needed to turn the wheels is inevitably high. For this reason, a low ratio has been chosen for the steering and 3·7 turns are needed from lock-to-lock for a mean turning circle between kerbs of 33ft. Despite the low ratio, the effort needed is high at parking speeds and when cornering hard at speed. However, under most conditions, the steering is acceptably precise and the car can be placed most accurately on the road being helped in this by minimum overhangs front and rear.

For a car whose wheelbase is only 7ft 9in. the ride is good over all surfaces with no tendency to pitch. A relatively wide track enables fairly soft suspension to be used without loss of roll stiffness, although some roll is evident. From the occupants' point of view, this is undoubtedly helped by the careful choice of seat springing which ensures a comfortable shock-free ride.

Like most high performance fwd cars, the Lancia Beta Coupé exhibits strong self-centring when accelerating hard. Thus when leaving all but the most gentle of corners under full power, a firm grip must be kept on the wheel and conscious correction must be made for the amount of pull to the right that is also evident.

Although the car understeers, it does so to a lesser extent than the heavy front end weight bias might lead one to expect. The amount of grip at the front of the car is impressive and it can be hustled along at very high speed on both dry and wet roads. The typical fwd trait of tucking in if the throttle is released is limited, and indeed can be used to great advantage when the driver is trying especially hard – particularly on a strange road. In this context, the braking stability is good and even if the brakes are still applied on the entry to a corner, there is no tendency for the rear end to run wide.

A strong contributor to the feeling of comfort when on a journey is the low level of noise from any source. With the exception of a slight rasp from the exhaust at 2,250 rpm, the engine noise is well subdued.

Furniture and fittings

The Beta Coupé is available on the UK market with either pvc or cloth upholstery to choice, but in either case the design of the seats is the same. Those in the front are curiously shaped with what appears to be overly short

Left: Although of rather exaggerated shape, the seats provide good lateral support and are comfortable. The seat backs tip well forward to allow rear seat access

Centre left: There is a full complement of instruments immediately ahead of the driver and all controls are within convenient reach

Top right: Rear seats are comfortable if lacking in head room for occupants of above average height. Head restraints are standard front and rear. The rear compartment has a separate courtesy light seen between the seat backs

Below: Tail treatment is the least happy aspect with a high base to the rear window to allow adequate boot space. The alloy wheels are standard on UK market cars but optional on our Italian test car

Centre right: The boot's regular shape and considerable depth gives good accommodation for a car in this class. The tools stow in the bottom right hand corner of the space

Bottom right: The rearward cant of the twin-cam Fiat engine can be clearly seen. Although untidy in appearance, the underbonnet layout allows good access to routine service items

backrests. In practice these give the desired support at shoulder level but little support in the small of the back.

The driver is confronted with a full set of clearly-marked instruments that are well lit at night. The facia panel itself is none too neat with an incongruous wood veneer behind the centrally positioned switches. However, all controls are within easy reach of the driver, even when strapped in. The heater controls are positioned centrally and operate a most effective combination air blending and water valve heater which allows the proper distribution of warmed air up to waist level and cool air at head level. As well as the cold air that can be directed through the heater ducts, there is a separate fresh air system that has its own facia level vents but this uses ram air only and cannot be boosted with the fan.

There is plenty of useful stowage space inside the car; as well as a lockable glove-box, there are bins in each footwell side and a large tray at the front end of the central console.

A heated rear window is standard as is a useful pocket torch which can be recharged from the car's battery by plugging into a socket beneath the facia.

Living with the Lancia Beta Coupé

Full choke is needed to get the engine started whenever it is cold, but this can be returned to a mid position almost immediately, and can be dispensed with in the first mile.

The action of the gear-change is positive but not particularly light in weight. The gate is H-shaped with 5th gear to the right and forward with reverse opposite. There is a nice feel to the stubby lever and even with the seats in their rearmost position, all the gear positions are within reach. The change is spring-loaded quite heavily towards the 3rd/4th gear plane.

The diaphragm spring clutch is operated by a cable-cum-rod mechanism which with the help of an assist spring gives light and positive action. Takeup is sweet yet there is ample bite and this is a car that is easy to drive from the outset.

There is more than ample adjustment of the seats in a rearward direction for drivers of average height and there is also adjustment of the steering column rake. The driving position is distinctly Italian and a splayed knee position is necessary to clear the soft-rimmed steering wheel. It is also necessary to adopt such a position when sitting in the back of the car since legroom is marginal in the back for tall people. Also marginal in the back is the amount of headroom and it is necessary for anyone of taller-than-average height to slouch down in the seat to get comfortable.

Visibility in all directions is good with thin pillars front and rear. Right-hand-drive cars have the proper wiper layout and the wipers themselves clear the screen well, leaving no blind spots. Looking forwards, the square bonnet is all in view but it is a stretch to see the extent of the tail from the driver's seat. At night, the four-headlamp system gives impressive illumination on either full or dipped beam but the Beta Coupé lacks the self-levelling system of the saloon version.

Among the pleasant surprises for an Italian car is the efficiency of the heater. In addition to providing heated air at foot level, two adjustable grilles in the centre of the facia allow heated air to be directed at waist level and the volume of air that can be felt through these vents is high.

In contrast to the boot of the Fulvia Coupé, that of the Beta is large enough to take a full set of golf clubs. The shape is regular with only the spare wheel in its position at the back of the boot to restrict the available space.

Access beneath the front-hinged bonnet is good to the items that require regular checking. To remove the dipstick, it is easiest to first remove the capillary tube that enables the sump contents to be checked on a gauge on the facia. With the tube removed, the dipstick can be withdrawn easily.

Attention to the electrics is excellent with a clearly marked fusebox on the engine bulkhead containing 10 fuses with another fuse alongside; the thermostatically-controlled cooling fan has a 16amp fuse of its own and the fan was only heard to operate once during the test after a prolonged period of town running.

Conclusions

Even though the price of the Beta Coupé has recently gone up, the standard of finish and the generous specification mark it out as outstanding value at this time. There are so many delightful touches in the design of the car that it is even beyond the scope of an *Autocar* Road Test to mention them all. Clearly, Lancia engineers are heaving a great sigh of relief now that they are not quite so restricted by lack of resource as they were before Fiat stepped in. They can now introduce all those touches into the design that make the car a "Lancia" and not just "another" motor car.

Truly a car in the Lancia tradition. □

MANUFACTURER:
Lancia Co., Via Vincenzo Lancia 27, Casella Postale 430, Torino, Italy
UK CONCESSIONAIRES:
Lancia (England) Ltd., Ealing Road, Alperton, Middlesex

PRICES	
Basic	£2,094.00
Special Car Tax	£174.50
VAT	£181.48
Total (in GB)	**£2,449.98**
Seat Belts	£21.60
Licence	£25.00
Delivery charge (London)	£20.00
Number plates	£7.41
Total on the Road (exc insurance)	**£2,523.99**

EXTRAS (inc VAT)	
Metallic Paint	£105.30
PVC upholstery	f.o.c.
* Inertia reel seat belts	£29.70
* *Fitted to test car*	
Insurance	Group 6
TOTAL AS TESTED ON THE ROAD	**£2,553.69**

Built on the Beta saloon dimensions (same wheelbase, track and overall length), the Beta HPE is 3½in. lower and has the same width as the shorter wheelbase Beta Coupé. Its weight is quoted as 20·9cwt, 1cwt more than the Coupé

High Performance Estate

Driving impressions of the Lancia Beta HPE

by Michael Scarlett

"HPE" does indeed, so we are told, stand for High Performance Estate, even in this recently introduced Lancia's native Italy. Lancia seem oddly addicted to what is presumably a modish use of foreign suffices – remember the Fulvia HF (Hi Fi)? "High performance" estate is perhaps a little strong for the Beta HPE; GPE would be more accurate (good performance), since whilst it is a true 100 mph car and does look more of a sports coupé than a station wagon, it isn't *very* fast.

The one we drove during a too-brief encounter near Turin recently was a 1600 c.c. model; there is an 1800 too. Like other Fiat units, the twin-ohc over-square engine is not very quiet, but the noise it makes is not at all unpleasant. It is a willing unit, eager to please, accepting low speed demands passively but preferring to be revved. The red line is at 6,400 rpm; the crisp sound of the engine never seems too obtrusive even at top speed. Maximum power is quoted at

Front end is inherited from the handsome Coupé rather than the shovel-fronted saloon

Luggage space is quite good. Back seat folds forward in halves, once the cushions have been removed

100 bhp (DIN) at 6,000 rpm, with 95 lb. ft. peak torque at 3,000 rpm, the same as in the saloon.

The gearchange isn't bad by front-wheel-drive standards – a bit clonk-y perhaps, though not as much so as some. Thanks to the excellent Alfa-style centre-biased five-speed gate, finding the right gear is never difficult. A curious, near-grotesque fitting is the gearlever gaiter, which is so large that no stem is visible, the gaiter reaching to the knob, which is large and conical, not the preferable large ball found on some other Lancias. Pedals allow easy heel-and-toe changes, and minor controls are very convenient. We liked the instrumentation, which is comprehensive as on other Betas, with the bonus of an oil level indicator like the Beta Coupé.

The roads of the Po plain are generally flat, smooth and straight, which made judgement of ride and handling difficult. What bumps there were the HPE dealt with comfortably enough. Road noise is limited to slightly below-average bump-thump, and wind noise proved to be well-subdued on the car we tried. The behaviour of the HPE on straights and on bends is what you'd expect – excellently stable in a straight line (we had no serious side winds to affect the car's course) and progressively understeering on curves. There were no opportunities to experience ultimate cornering limits.

Seats in front give good sideways support; driving position is typically Italian. Facia is identical to the Beta Coupé

Most people will agree that the HPE is a good-looking car. Our only objection to its otherwise neat appearance are the size of the rear quarter panels – they get in the way of view at awkward junctions – and the rather fussy treatment of those quarters outside, which continue the Venetian blind lines found in the back window.

Lifting the nicely counterbalanced tailgate reveals a useful luggage platform, which can be extended either fully or half width by folding forward each half of the seat back. There is then quite a lot of load space, although inevitably one pays for the elegant rake of the back in height, and for the suspension layout in the very intrusive big boxes housing the spring units. The seats are very comfortable and easy to adjust exactly as one wants; a simple lever allows one to release the front seat backs for rear entry. The seats offer unusually good sideways location, cupping one very well.

All being well, the Lancia Beta HPE should be seen here at the Motor Show. At around £400 more than the Beta 1800ES, it should be about £3,050, appreciably cheaper than the Reliant Scimitar GTE (£3,563 at the moment), and a good bit more than a Ford Capri II 1600 GT (£2,202 now). We must wait for a Road Test to judge finally how it compares. Initial impressions are that it will have a quite wide appeal, especially for the person who wants a stylish but practical car, with some dash and distinction to it. **MS**

THE SPORT 1975

After winning the World Rally Championship in 1974, Lancia set out to repeat the achievement in 1975. Munari won the Monte Carlo Rally, new driver Bjorn Waldegaard won the Swedish and the same pair finished second and third on the Safari, emphasising the versatility of the Stratos. On the Acropolis, Waldegaard was fastest on almost every stage, only to retire near the finish with dust in the distributor; the conditions can be judged by this shot of Raffaele Pinto on the same event. Munari won the team's home event, the San Remo, however, and so clinched Lancia's second title.

Mike Parkes, the Englishman who worked for Ferrari as a driver and then race engineer for many years, went to Lancia to develop two projects: the Stratos and the Beta Coupé rallying programme. Success with the Beta proved elusive, however, as the team tried to persuade it to handle with up to 200 bhp going through the front wheels. Bigger wheels and power steering (to cope with the limited slip differential) were among the experiments tried. This is Mauro Pregliasco on the San Remo.

Practically mid-engined?

Lancia's Beta Monte Carlo studied; is it the most nearly sensible mid-engined coupé available? It will be on sale here in January, on show at Earls Court

by Michael Scarlett

Résumé
LANCIA were taken over by Fiat in October 1969; the first car to appear as a new Lancia design after the takeover was the Lancia Beta, a revival of an old Lancia name (it was first used by them in 1909), continuing Lancia's latterday tradition of building front-wheel-drive cars (since the original Flavia of 1960) but using the Fiat 1·4, 1·6 or 1·8-litre, belt-driven, twin ohc engine arranged transversely. The Beta Monte Carlo began life as the Abarth Fiat X1/20, seen first at Turin in 1974. It appeared in the Lancia production form at Geneva in March this year; we described a brief drive in it in *Autocar* of 14 June. *Autocar* artist Dick Ellis later visited Lancia and Pininfarina to see how the car is built (it is the first with bodywork styled *and* made by Pininfarina as opposed to that famous coachbuilder adding his ideas to someone else's vehicle), and to prepare our exclusive cutaway drawing. It will be shown on Pininfarina's stand at Earls Court. Lancia plan to sell it here in January; a full Road Test will appear in our issue of 1 November.

Lancia's answer

A racing-car style north-south engine working through a Porsche-type transaxle takes up a lot of length, in spite of the compact layout of the transmission. The VW-Porsche 914 contrived to offer a comparable amount of boot in the back because its flat-four (or flat-six) engine was low enough to allow a useful tray on top whilst preserving a more nearly ideal weight distribution (47/53 for the 914, 43·3/56·7 for the sadly now extinct 914-6). If you haven't got a boxer in your repertoire, a transverse upright engine with gearbox and final drive arranged around it is short, and therefore a great help for a mid-engined two-seater. Lancia's Beta saloon uses such a unit, except that the engine does not stand upright, but inclined 20 deg rearwards – a further help as it makes room between itself and the firewall for the downdraught twin-choke Weber carburettor and distributor – or rather allows the firewall to be closer to the back axle line.

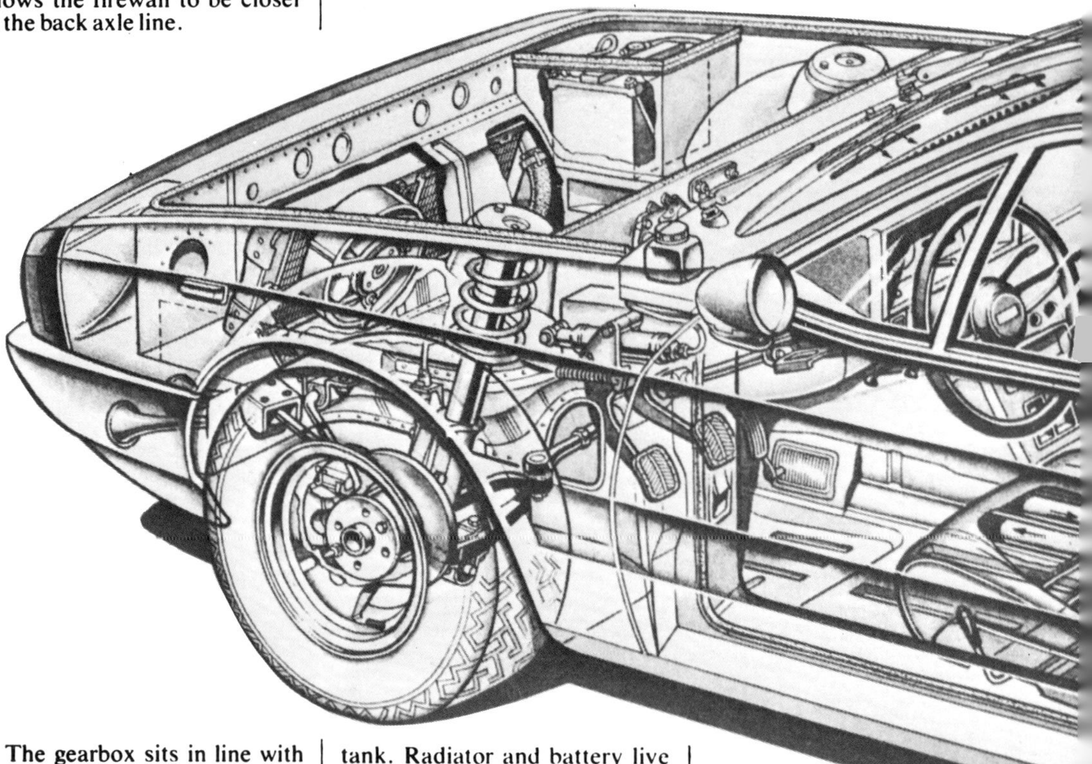

The gearbox sits in line with the flywheel-clutch centre, as in a conventional car, but naturally as close as possible. The driven shaft sits below and behind, so that the helical final drive can be placed aft, near the clutch, but not central, making the drive shafts longer on the right hand (engine) side. The disadvantage is that the closeness of the drive unit to the axle line dictates slightly rear-heaviness (41·3/58·7 comparing interestingly with its similarly laid-out ancestor the Fiat X1/9's 41·3/58·7 *one-up*). In addition, a further space-saving at the front is achieved by nesting the spare wheel in the open space behind the engine on the gearbox side. There is no pretence at providing any boot in the back; what space remains is left vacant except for the water header tank. Radiator and battery live at the front, partly to redress the weight balance and partly because there's plenty of cooling air up that end; hot air from the radiator and electric fan is ducted away downwards to exhaust under the car, more for the sake of keeping it out of the front boot than for aerodynamics. Theoretically, to keep the polar moment down, it would have been better to have put the battery more centrally and to use mid-mounted side radiators, but no doubt it was argued that the difficulty and complication for such a small improvement wasn't worth it.

Another good reason for the relatively open space behind the engine and beside the spare is underbonnet temperature. The wheel rests partly on a half-floor across the back, which shields it from the heavily radiating bulk of a lengthily serpentine exhaust system and large transverse silencer; from the twin end of the manifold, two pipes duck down under the silencer, then bend across into a common end bolted to a single pipe turning up through 180 deg to feed another 180 deg pipe at one end of the silencer. Add a bellmouth and you would have a new variety of brass instrument for the tuba family. There are louvres in the

skirt underneath the bumper to help air flow past the exhaust; there are others above, behind the spare wheel space, and in the side-hinged engine cover. Unusually, in order to lead ambient-temperature air unwarmed by the radiator to the front side of the engine and gearbox, there is a 11¾ × 2¾in. intake in the middle of the nose under the bumper trunked back down the centre tunnel. It would be interesting to know whether this was in the designer's mind from the start, or whether early development proved it necessary.

A further advantage of a transverse engine and transmission is that you don't have to semi-circumnavigate the engine with the gearchange. From the bottom of the gearlever (but on top of and separate from the cold air trunking, which is a separate part), a pushrod carries twist (across gate) and fore-and-aft (into gear) movements down the tunnel to a vertical shaft with a bell crank at each end. Through an upward extension of the pushrod a ball-jointed rod works another bell crank on the gearbox top moving the selector shaft up and down, whilst the top bellcrank on the vertical shaft moves the lever which turns the selector via another higher pushrod; it sounds more complicated than it is. The fact that actual gear

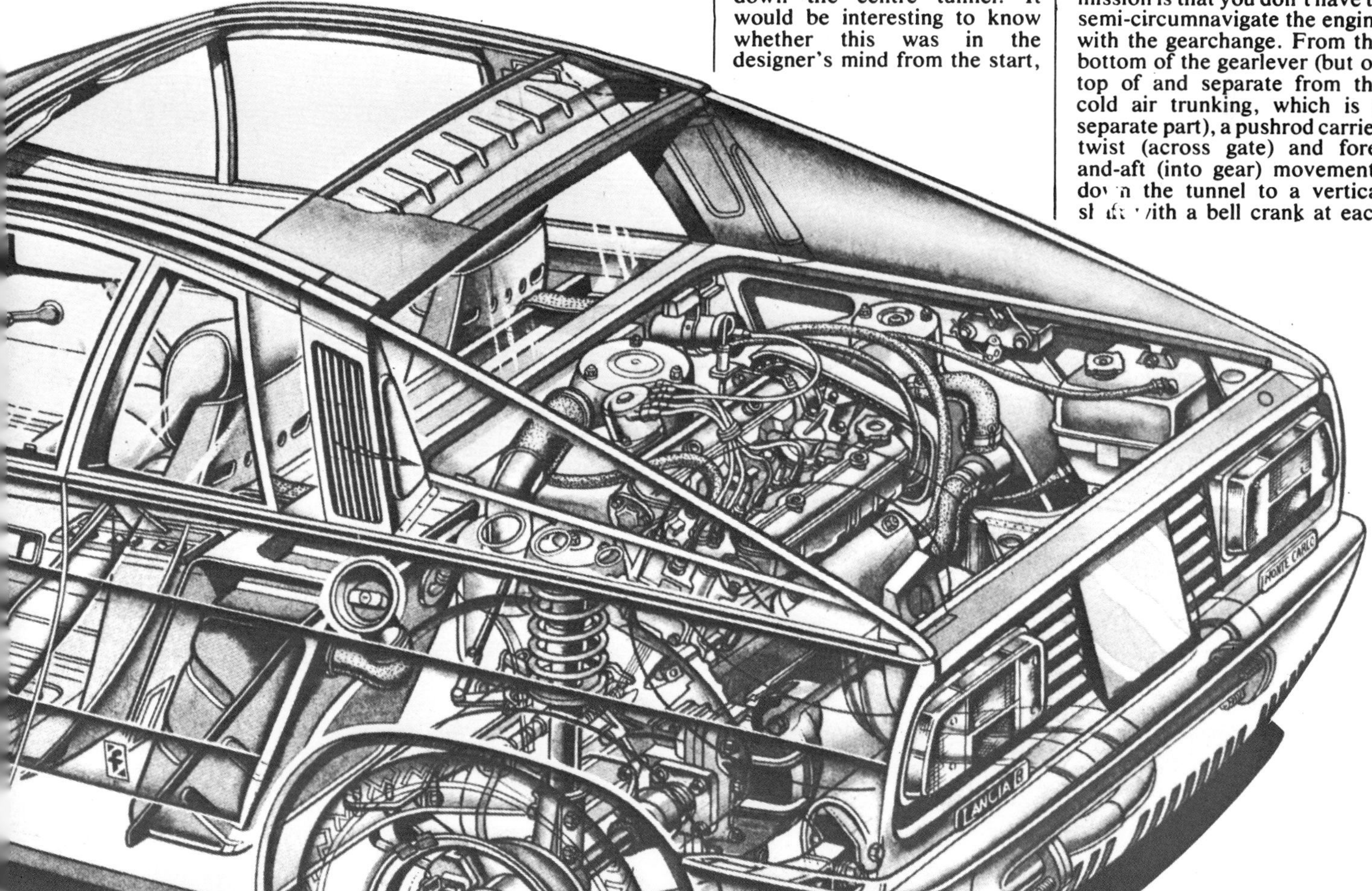

MacPherson strut suspension front and rear and very wide based bottom rear wishbone are immediately apparent in Dick Ellis' cutaway drawing. The serpentine meanderings of the exhaust system is apparent too. The engine cover is side-hinged to permit good access to the front (right hand) side of the Fiat-based d.o.h.c. engine

selection depends on the torsional stiffness of the quite lengthy vertical shaft, which appears to be only a small-diameter tube with one end squashed could explain why, on the driving-impressions car, we found that it was necessary to push the gearlever right to the ends of its movement to ensure a proper change. The principal looks sound. Clutch operation is made easy by hydraulics.

Drive and gearing

The engine itself is of course an enlarged, longer-stroke version of the Fiat 132 engine, 84 × 90mm, 1,995 c.c. instead of 84 × 79·2mm, 1,756 c.c. It has a cast-iron five-bearing block, an aluminium alloy head with valve inserts, and inclined valves worked by separate inlet and exhaust camshafts driven by toothed belt. Air is taken via the cleaner from the presumably cooler atmosphere between firewall and gearbox. Fuel from the 13-gal tank mounted upright behind the driver's seat is pumped electrically round a circulating system via carburettor back to the tank, to avoid vapour lock in hot weather. Claimed power output is 120 bhp (DIN) at 6,000 rpm, with maximum torque of 121½ lb. ft. at 3,500 rpm, and a red line on the revcounter at 6,200 rpm. On the 185/70HR–13in. tyres used (at both ends) and with the 3·714 final drive geared up to 3·436-to-1 in top gear, overall gearing works out at 19·5 mph per 1,000 rpm. Apart from first, which is lower, and the final drive which is higher, the all-indirect gear ratios are those of the Beta saloon, returning claimed top speeds of 28, 50, 75, 96 and around 117 mph, which makes it correctly geared in top.

Body-chassis

The Monte Carlo is a unitary construction body, in numerous mild steel pressings welded together. Partly because of its declared target, North America, and partly for sensible-enough reasons of safety, both design and the finished weight (just over a ton at the kerb) suggest that it is a strong car. The basic floor pressing is strengthened longitudinally by the centre tunnel in the cockpit area and what are effectively side box members which, with continuations formed by the boot sides, boxed lower down, run from bumper to bumper. It would look as if progressive collapse of the nose in a bad crash is aimed for in the usual way, by using the gradually increasing section strength as the nose tapers upwards to the scuttle. Both scuttle and firewall are ribbed and kinked to form stiff cross-frames near-vertically, whilst the anti-lozenging effects of the boot and cockpit floors are repeated behind the engine gap by the half-floor carrying the spare wheel. Some extra beam

Practically mid-engined?

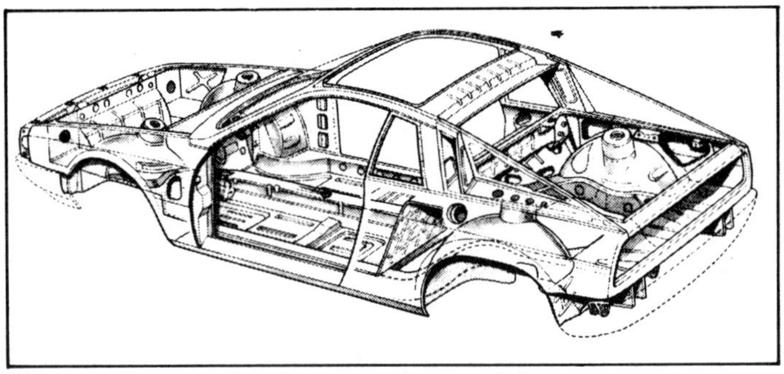

The great strength of the hoop over the rear of the passenger compartment is apparent here. Some 4,600 spot or arc welds are needed to piece together the 270 panels that make up the complete body shell

strength must be provided by the roof structure, and suspension spring loads are spread from the spring-damper strut turrets into the naturally strong wheel arch pressings. The roof with more importantly its side frames, is an arch; there is no flat top section. This, added to the obviously great strength of what is in effect a stoutly pillared, sturdy bridge over the back window suggests that the Monte Carlo is exceptionally strong in the roll-over case. The tapering folded gussets which continue the line of the roof to the tail add further strength, though one suspects that they are not needed structurally; adding as they do to the bulk of the roll bar pillars, over-the-shoulder vision is accordingly poor. It is claimed that aerodynamic efficiency and cross wind stability are both improved by these fins. Cabin air outlets are placed in the side pillars. The doors hide strong, internally braced, channel box members to resist intrusion in a side-on crash.

Bumpers are skinned plastic mouldings, and so is the protective band round the tip of the nose. Sills are sprayed in black resin, partly in an effort to give slenderness to what is really a rather stubby profile overall, and, more usefully, to protect them from scrapes and rust. A most pleasing feature of the Monte Carlo is Pininfarina's insistence on a minimum of brightwork. The windscreen, blue tinted above "to protect passengers from sun beams" (as the Pininfarina description puts it), is glued flush to the body, by a patented process, as are the other fixed glasses. Another Pininfarina patent protects the very clever folding fabric sun roof of the Spider version; the fabric folds very neatly into the roll bar bridge, and when unfolded draws out its finishing strip with it.

Inside the cockpit one finds straightaway one most refreshing improvement on other mid-engined two-seaters. There is a quite useful shelf behind the seats, formed by the horizontal fold of the firewall over the tank space. The short near-upright back screen is sheltered under the roll bar, and, as opposed to the more graceful long glass tapering to the tail, has several valuable advantages. Glass is amongst the heaviest materials used in any car, and anything which needs less of it is a weight-saver. The short upright glass is easier to see through – vision is normal to it instead of very oblique which means optical inefficiency – and it won't act as an engine noise reflector.

Cockpit layout is straightforward and sensible, as one has come to expect from Fiat-Lancia. Those delightfully simple stalks control all important minor functions, except the air horns, which are worked from the best and most quickly found place, the middle of the steering wheel. Instruments are limited to a trip speedometer, revcounter, oil pressure, water temperature and fuel gauges, plus a central clock. All other warnings are given by warning lamps, with danger indicators all on the same side of the console. Doors are unusual in having large horizontal pads, like stub wings almost, continuing the line of the top of the dash. As in other mid-engined cars, the moulded plastic seat backs cannot be rake-adjusted.

Suspension, brakes and steering

Fiat MacPherson-strut-type suspension is used at both ends, fully independent if one discounts the anti-roll bars. The latter work only as anti-roll

Three 2-litre mid-engined coupés compared

	Wheelbase in.	Track f/r	Ov. Length in.	Width in.	Height in.	Kerb Weight lb	Bhp/ton laden
Lancia Beta Monte Carlo	90·6	55·6/57·3	150·1	66·8	46·6	2,290	99·9
VW Porsche 914/6	96·5	52·9/54·5	156·9	65·0	48·4	2,112	98·1
Lotus Esprit 700	96·0	59·5	165·0	73·0	43·5	2,105	144·7

bars, and not as part of the suspension. Interestingly, at the front there is no sub frame; both the short forged track control arm (to use Ford parlance) and tubular trailing tie rod pivot in flexible bushes directly from the side "members" of the body. At the back, there is only one form of separate cross member carrying the pivots for the front ends of the wide-based channel and box-tube bottom wishbones; the rear ends pivot again directly on to the brackets on the body. To hold the wheel straight steering-wise, there is a steering-arm-like forging reaching back from the hub carrier and held via a ball joint by a lateral tubular member single-bolted to the rear leg of the wishbone. This is adjustable for toe-in. The rear struts are leaned inwards to give noticeable negative camber, of which there is some at the front end too. This type of suspension has the advantages of taking up little body space, and having notable mechanical simplicity and cheapness, and the small disadvantages that, with MacPherson geometry at both ends, track changes over uneven ground produce slight steering effects, and that effective camber depends on roll angle, and is not counteracted as it is by a good double wishbone set-up.

Steering, rack and pinion of course, lies behind the front wheel line, with a two-jointed safety column. The brakes use the same size discs at each end, with vacuum-servo-assisted split hydraulic circuits, all by Girling. The disc size is 8·94in. dia., roughly 1in. smaller than on the Beta saloon, presumably because of the use of 13in. wheels instead of the saloon's 14in. ones. Tyres are carried on 5½J rims; the wheels are cast light alloy, designed by Pininfarina.

Summary

The Lancia Beta Monte Carlo makes an interesting comparison with the superseded VW Porsche 914/6 and the new Lotus Esprit, announced (and fully described in *Autocar*) last week. As the table shows, it is the shortest of the three, the heaviest, and similar in power-to-weight ratio to the 914/6. It isn't as generous in luggage space as the Porsche, but certainly a little better than all in interior space. There would seem to be little to choose between all three in crash safety, although it is certain that the Lancia would not be the weakest. It *looks* like the most practical in access, space, mechanicals and, arguably, in minor repair. Certainly it is one of the most sensible designs we have seen so far in this field; it will be interesting to hear the conclusions of our Road Test team. □

AUTOTEST

Lancia Beta Monte Carlo

Recently on view at Earls Court, the Monte Carlo is amongst the most practical of mid-engined designs. Two-litre Beta engine gives 120 mph performance and reasonable economy but with the penalty of a high noise level. Well finished and sensibly engineered

IT IS always interesting to follow the fortunes of practical design exercises from the styling studios of Pininfarina, and none have been more interesting to keep tabs on than the Fiat X1/20 – Abarth "030"/X1/20 which eventually became the Lancia Beta Monte Carlo. First clues that Pininfarina was working on a mid-engined sports car arose through the sighting of a red and matt black novelty around Turin at the end of 1972. Not too dissimilar from the Bertone-designed Fiat X1/9, in ignorance the prototype was immediately labelled X1/20 as it was thought that the power unit was a 2-litre version of the Fiat/Lancia dohc 1,800 c.c. engine current in the Beta/124 Coupé of the time. The car did not look all that much like a Lancia or a Fiat and since it ran on Ferrari-like wheels, the project stayed shrouded in mystery.

Persistent rumours abounded, however, that Fiat intended to replace the ageing 124 Spider with a mid-engined car, but the rumours took little account of the fact that the 124 was being given 5-mph bumpers

Stubby but purposeful in shape, the Monte Carlo will be easy to spot when it first appears here in the new year

The threequarter rear aspect shows the panelled-in rear quarters that lead to poor visibility in traffic or when manoeuvring. In general, detail finish of exterior trim is neat and practical

and full emission equipment to continue its successful sales run in North America. The plot was thickened considerably by the appearance in 1974 of a device based obviously on the original Pininfarina prototype but styled "Abarth-Pininfarina "030" in deference to Abarth who did the competition development and Fiat whose 3-litre V6 engine from the 130 range was used. With a claimed 285 bhp on tap, this car proved very fast and in fact had some competition success during 1974. But we were no closer to seeing a production car out of all this, whether from Fiat or Lancia.

It is, in fact, fair to assume that while the "030" diverted attention, the decision had been made to go ahead with the production of the Monte Carlo and that the intervening period between 1974 and the Geneva Show this year was taken up with the finalizing of the design and the installation of the necessary production facilities to allow the car to be produced entirely by Pininfarina, with the exception of the mechanical details which were to be furnished by Lancia. Thus it was that out of all the mystery and intrigue, the Lancia Beta Monte Carlo was unveiled as a Lancia model at this year's Geneva Show.

The car was fully described in *Autocar* of 11 October 1975 but a few of its significant details will help to indicate what sort of a machine it is – strictly a two-seater, although it makes good use of the space behind the seats for the stowage of on-journey paraphernalia. Under the "bonnet" is a deep boot of regular shape which provides generous luggage space for a sports car. At the other end, a big side-hinged engine cover swings clear to reveal the 2-litre Lancia Beta engine transversely mounted with the front of the engine on the right, and the inline clutch and 5-speed gearbox on the left as viewed from the back of the car. The suspension also follows Beta principles having MacPherson struts at both ends, and stout anti-roll bars front and rear to allow fairly soft springs.

Visually, attention is immediately drawn to the long nose and the panelled-in extensions to the cockpit sides, which are the least practical aspect of the design. The presence of the radiator in the front of the car is less well disguised than in some other designs (notably the new Lotus Esprit) but the purposeful appearance is attractive, to most eyes at least. Considerable use is made of matt-black sections to attempt a visual "stretch" of the design which is markedly dumpy in shape when seen as a separate body unit, without running gear and before painting.

Above: Space inside the cockpit is generous. The facia top might benefit from a lip, at its rear edge to allow it to be used for maps etc. A neat, but superfluous detail is that the padded facia rail is continued onto the door

Below: The engine is distantly located at the front of the engine bay but is accessible enough, especially after removal of the spare wheel

Performance

Sturdy, safety-conscious construction results in a kerb weight of 20·4cwt and as tested with two staff members and their equipment aboard, the Monte Carlo weighed 23·4cwt. Thus with 120 bhp (DIN) to propel it, the performance is rapid without being outstanding. In view of its faster cruising speed potential, the Monte Carlo's gearing is higher than that of the Lancia Beta saloon or coupé through the use of a higher final drive ratio (3·71 compared with 4·07 for the Beta 1800 saloon or 3·93 to 1 for the Beta Coupé) but the gearbox internal ratios are unchanged except for bottom gear which is 7 per cent lower. The end result is that top gear gives 19·5 mph/1,000 rpm, resulting in near-ideal overall gearing: the top speed of 119 mph is only 100 rpm over the engine's power peak at 6,000 rpm. The rev counter is marked with a cautionary yellow section from 5,800 to 6,300 rpm, and a red section from 6,300 to 8,000 rpm. Taking 6,200 rpm as the maker's recommended maximum revs, the speeds in the lower gears are 30, 50, 74 and 94 mph, which is excellent spacing except that second gear could well be a little higher. Acceleration through the gears is only average for a car of such weight; from rest to 60 mph takes only just under 10sec, while 100 mph comes up in 30·5sec – similar performance to the Triumph Dolomite Sprint but comfortably quicker than the Beta Coupé.

There is no noticeable step in performance delivery and in fact, the acceleration in each gear shows a fairly flat torque curve. It proved possible, for instance, to pull third gear comfortably from as low as 10 mph and even in 5th gear, the acceleration from 20 to 40 mph was by no means slow.

Despite the weight, our overall fuel consumption emerged as

Lancia Beta Monte Carlo

Maximum speeds

Gear	mph	kph	rpm
Top (mean)	119	192	6,100
(best)	120	193	6,150
4th	94	151	6,200
3rd	74	119	6,200
2nd	50	80	6,200
1st	30	48	6,200

Acceleration

True mph	Time secs	Speedo mph
30	**3·0**	29
40	**5·0**	40
50	**7·0**	50
60	**9·8**	62
70	**12·8**	72
80	**16·9**	82
90	**21·8**	93
100	**30·5**	103
110	**41·0**	113

Standing ¼-mile: 16·0sec 77 mph
Standing kilometre: 30·2sec 99 mph

mph	Top	4th	3rd
10–30	—	—	5·4
20–40	10·2	7·1	4·8
30–50	9·0	6·5	4·7
40–60	8·4	6·2	4·9
50–70	8·9	6·9	5·4
60–80	9·8	7·4	—
70–90	11·1	8·6	—
80–100	14·8	—	—
90–110	19·2	—	—

Consumption

Fuel

Overall mpg ..25·2 (11·2 litres/100km)
Calculated (DIN) mpg
29·0 (9·7 litres/100km)

Constant speed:

mph	mpg
30	41·4
40	44·4
50	44·4
60	36·6
70	31·9
80	30·3
90	27·0
100	22·2

Autocar formula:
Hard driving, difficult conditions
22·7 mpg
Average driving, average conditions
27·7 mpg
Gentle driving, easy conditions
32·8 mpg

Grade of fuel: Premium, 4-star (97RM)
Mileage recorder: Accurate

Oil

Consumption (SAE 10W/50)
Negligible

Regular Service

Not yet available from makers

Brakes

Fade *(from 30 mph in neutral)*
Pedal load for 0·5g stops in lb

	start/end			start/end	
1	40	35	6	45	45
2	35	40	7	45	45
3	40	50	8	50	50
4	40	50	9	50	50
5	45	55	10	50	40

Response *(from 30 mph in neutral)*

Load	g	Distance
20lb	0·18	150ft
40lb	0·40	75ft
60lb	0·70	43ft
70lb	0·90	33·4ft
75lb	0·95	31·7ft
Handbrake	0·30	100ft

Max. gradient 1 in 3

Clutch

Pedal 37lb and 6½in.

Test Conditions

Wind: 0–5 mph
Temperature: 27 deg C (81 deg F)
Barometer: 29·6in. Hg
Humidity: 60 per cent
Surface: Dry asphalt and concrete
Test distance: 460 miles

Figures taken at 7,700 miles by our own staff on the Continent.

Parts Costs

Not yet available from makers

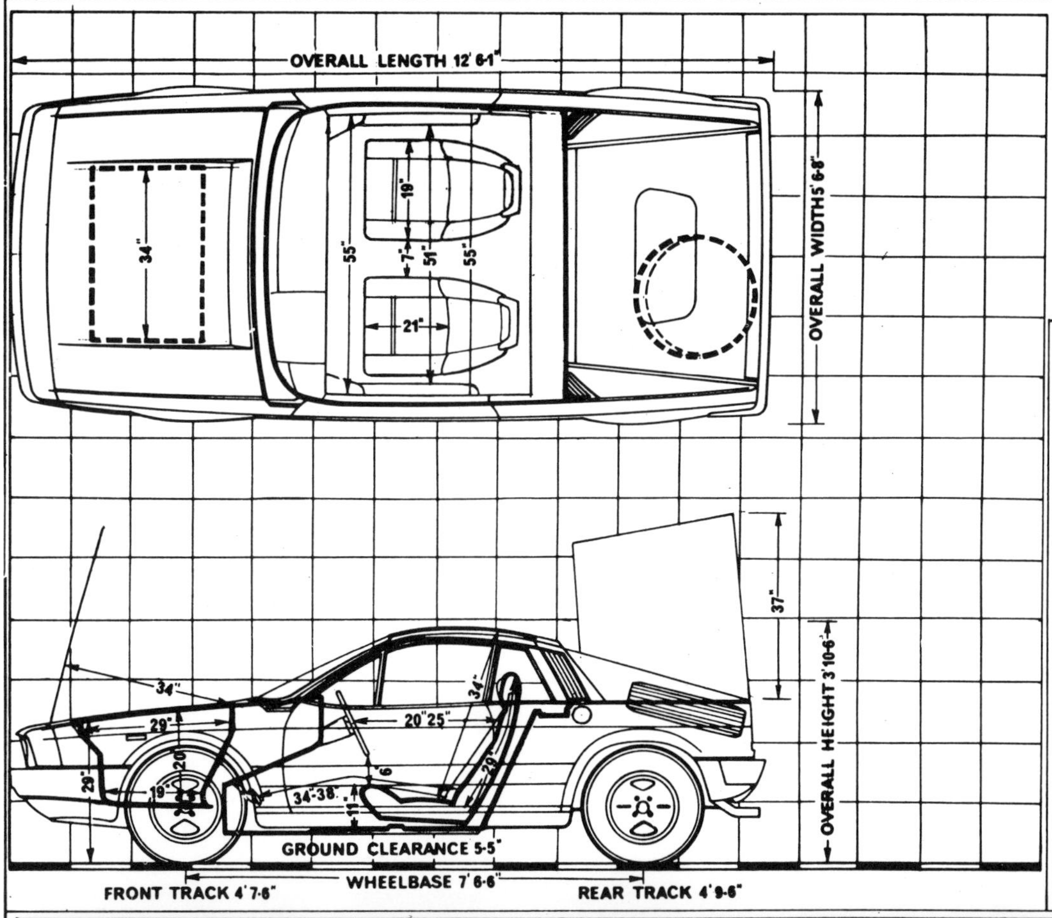

Weight

Kerb, 20·4cwt/2,290lb/1,040kg
(Distribution F/R, 41/59)
As tested, 23·4cwt/2,620lb/1,190kg

Boot Capacity: 7·2 cu. ft.

Turning Circles:
Between kerbs
L, 34ft 6in.; R, 34ft 9in.
Between walls
L, 36ft 0in.; R, 36ft 3in.
Turns, lock to lock 3½

Test Scoreboard

Average of scoring
by *Autocar* Road Test team

Ratings: 6 *Excellent*
5 *Good*
4 *Better than average*
3 *Worse than average*
2 *Poor*
1 *Bad*

PERFORMANCE	4·33
STEERING AND HANDLING	4·00
BRAKES	3·80
COMFORT IN FRONT	3·33
COMFORT IN BACK	—
DRIVER'S AIDS *(instruments, lights, wipers, visibility etc.)*	3·86
CONTROLS	3·63
NOISE	3·50
STOWAGE	3·33
ROUTINE SERVICE *(instruments, lights, wipers, visibility etc.)*	4·50
EASE OF DRIVING	3·82
OVERALL RATING	**3·84**

Comparisons

Car	Price £	max mph	0–60 sec	overall mpg	capacity c.c.	power bhp	wheelbase in.	length in.	width in.	kerb weight	fuel gall	tyre size
Lancia Monte Carlo	**N/A**	**119**	**9·8**	**25·2**	**1,995**	**120**	**91**	**150**	**67**	**20·4**	**13**	**185/70HR 13**
Lotus Esprit	5,844	138*	6·8*	N/A	1,973	156	96	165	73	18·0	15	195/205/70VR 13
TVR 3000M	3,256	121	7·7	21·4	2,994	142	90	158	64	20·0	12	185/70HR 14
MGB GT V8	3,227	124	8·6	23·0	3,528	137	91	155	60	21·3	12	175HR 14
Triumph TR7	N/A	N/A	N/A	N/A	1,998	100†	85	153	66	20·0	12	175/70SR 13

*Manufacturer's claim (one-up) †approximated

Specification

ENGINE	
Cylinders	4, in-line
Main bearings	5
Cooling	Water
Fan	Electric
Bore, mm (in.)	84 (3·31)
Stroke, mm (in.)	90 (3·54)
Capacity, c.c. (in.^{3})	1,995 (123)
Valve gear	Dohc
Camshaft drive	Toothed belt
Compression ratio	8·9 to 1
Octane rating	97RM
Carburettor	D/d 2-choke Weber
Max power	120 bhp (DIN) at 6,000 rpm
Max torque	121 lb. ft. at 3,500 rpm
TRANSMISSION	
Clutch	Sdp, diaphragm spring, hydraulic

Gear	Ratio	mph/1,000 rpm
Top	0·925	19·5
4th	1·152	15·7
3rd	1·522	11·9
2nd	2·235	8·1
1st	3·750	4·8

Final drive gear	Helical spur gear
Ratio	3·71 to 1
SUSPENSION	
Front – location	MacPherson strut, lower arm, torque reaction rod
springs	Coil
dampers	Coaxial telescopic
anti-roll bar	Yes
Rear – location	MacPherson strut, bottom wishbone
springs	Coil
dampers	Coaxial telescopic
anti-roll bar	Yes
STEERING	
Type	Rack and pinion
Power assistance	None
Wheel diameter	14in.
BRAKES	
Front	8·9in. dia. disc
Rear	8·9in. dia. disc
Servo	Yes
WHEELS	
Type	Aluminium alloy disc
Rim width	5½in. J
Tyres – make	Pirelli
– type	CN36
– size	185/70HR 13
EQUIPMENT	
Battery	12V 45Ah
Alternator	38 amp
Headlamps	80/80
Reversing lamp	Standard
Hazard warning	Extra
Electric fuses	16
Screen wipers	2-speed and intermittent
Screen washer	Electric
Interior heater	Air blending
Interior trim	Pvc seats, pvc headlining
Floor covering	Carpet
Jack	Screw parallelogram
Jacking points	2 each side
Windscreen	Laminated
Underbody protection	Electrophoretic pre-treatment
MAINTENANCE	
Fuel tank	13 Imp. gallons (59 litres)
Cooling system	25 pints (inc. heater)
Engine sump	9 pints SAE 10W/90
Gearbox and final drive	3 pints SAE 85W/90
Grease	No points
Valve clearance	Inlet 0·018in. (cold); Exhaust 0·024in. (cold)
Contact breaker	0·016in. gap
Ignition timing	10 deg BTDC (static) 28 deg BTDC (stroboscopic)
Spark plug – type	Bosch W200 30 or Champion N7Y
gap	0·025in.
Tyre pressures	F 24; R 27 psi (normal driving)
Max payload	460lb (210kg)

The speed and rev counters are self evident and to their right can be seen the three supplementary instruments that indicate oil pressure, water temperature and fuel tank contents. The primary lamp control is to the left of the instrument binnacle, all other major control coming via the three finger tip stalks that are easy to use. The heater and ventilation controls can be seen behind the gear lever

a very reasonable 25·2 mpg. As usual with twin-choke carburettor arrangements with an accelerator pump, the overall consumption does not appear to be borne out by the suggested DIN figure of 29·0 mpg. The reason for this is that the DIN figure is calculated from a steady speed running figure, so that the effect of the accelerator pump is not taken into account. We would suggest that the average driver will return figures between 25 and 30 mpg, and thus the 13-gal fuel tank gives a safe range of comfortably over 300 miles.

Ride, handling and roadholding

Long bottom location of the suspension front and rear promises generous wheel travel with minimal change in camber at either end. Thus the ride is comfortable over most surfaces whether laden or light. As previously mentioned, soft springs are permissible because the front and rear anti-roll bars are quite stiff. The Monte Carlo corners with little roll and its handling is scarcely affected by differences in road surface. However, camber changes and undulations do lead to limited self-steering effects from both ends and indeed on some surfaces, a distinct weaving motion is set up. However, the accurate steering allows such motions to be easily controlled and there is in any case sufficient self-aligning effect in the front suspension to allow the car to run safely "hands off" up to its maximum speed. In the particularly calm weather with which we were blessed during the test period, there was no opportunity to see whether the Monte Carlo was affected by cross-winds but previous experience of mid-engined designs suggests that this would not be a problem. Incidentally, the filling-in of the rear quarter areas with panels stretching to the tail is claimed to improve cross-wind performance presumably through moving the centre of pressure rearwards.

Ultimate roadholding is high with good grip from the Pirelli tyres with which the test car was equipped. The heaviness of the steering suggests understeer but when the degree of castor of the front suspension is also taken into account, it is obvious that some of this heaviness is inherent, borne out by the effort needed at parking speeds. This is disappointing in view of the rearward weight distribution, but the tyre section (185/70HR 13) is wide for the weight if not character of the car. As cornering speeds increase, the weight of the steering does not markedly alter and it is possible to feel that the car is understeering more. It takes a very determined effort at lowish speeds to reduce the understeer by the application of power. If the driver is forced to lift off the accelerator in mid-corner, there is a gentle tightening of the line which can be used to advantage, especially on unfamiliar roads.

A joy of the handling is the amount of traction that the rearward weight bias confers and at no time was there any sign that the inside rear wheel was lifting, however hard the driver accelerated out of even sharp corners.

Brakes

The four-wheel disc system proved well up to the performance, revealing complete resistance to fade once the discs were thoroughly warm. The brakes gave off a smell of hot linings after the fifth of the ten consecutive stops that constitute the fade test but their efficiency was unimpaired. Peak efficiency under response checks was reached at a reasonable 75lb pedal pressure, beyond which the front wheels locked with a loss of stopping power. It was noticeable that this figure of 0·95g was repeatable with 10lb less pedal pressure when the brakes were warm, suggesting that the rear brakes need to be well warmed through before the best braking is available on the road.

Noise

Perhaps the most disappointing feature of the car is the continuously high level of engine noise, emphasized by the generally low level from other sources. Clearly, this problem is well known to the designers as they have taken all the familiar steps to prevent any "ringing" reverberations from the structure close to the engine. For instance, the engine firewall is heavily ribbed and the exhaust system is taken into a separate chamber before being turned left and right to enter and leave the big silencer – but noise there is.

With the ingenious folding roof stowed away, there is some drumming which can be relieved by slightly opening the side windows, but with the penalty of some draughts if this is done.

Lancia Beta Monte Carlo

Fittings and furniture
Although the seat design looks familiar enough, they are in fact moulded in polyurethane and have no springing medium at all. They are comfortable and hold the occupants well but in the hot weather of the test period, they did not "breathe" at all well and after only half an hour, driver and passenger are left with wringing wet shirts. Some of the cars at the factory of Pininfarina had seats with fabric coverings which might be better and if they are, let us hope that they will be specified for UK market cars. Although the seats cannot be reclined, the driving position is good for drivers of widely different heights despite the fact that only fore-and-aft adjustment is provided with no means of altering the length of the steering column.

Ahead of the driver is a full array of instruments contained in a rectangular binnacle. The rev counter and speedometer are proper circular dials but with rather vague markings, and the supplementary instruments are in a vertical row towards the centre of the car, with a row of warning lights alongside. Controls are the familiar Fiat-inspired fingertip stalks with the lights and indicators on the left and the windscreen wiper/washer control on the right. The first movement of the latter stalk produces an intermittent wipe of fixed frequency and moving the lever further produces a sustained wipe whose speed can be altered between fast and slow.

At the front of the central tunnel, and falling nicely to hand is the gearlever which has a familiar H-pattern for the lower four gears with 5th gear out to the right and forward with reverse gear below it. The handbrake is centrally mounted behind the gearlever.

The controls for the heating and ventilation system are placed rather awkwardly behind the gear lever. Those on the driver's side control volume and temperature while the passenger has control of distribution and the three-speed boost fan.

The pedal layout is excellent with a cunningly contrived shape to the accelerator pedal that permits comfortable heel-and-toe operation.

Living with the Lancia Beta Monte Carlo
Starting when hot or cold is without problems, an automatic choke coping well when the engine is cold. The clutch is by no means light in weight but the action helps to disguise its heaviness. Not so easy to disguise is the need for full movement of the pedal through its considerable travel of 6½in. all of which is needed to fully free the clutch when engaging reverse gear, and 1st gear when the car is at rest.

The boot space is carpeted and regular in its shape. The space is shared with the battery, the windscreen washer bottle (out of sight behind the cover on the far wing top) and the reservoirs for the twin circuit braking system and the hydraulic clutch

The view out forwards over the wide flat bonnet is commanding, and the front corners are in view. Although the screen pillars are thick, the driver sits far enough back for them not to obscure his view. Not so happy is the three-quarter rear visibility which is seriously limited by the quarter panels. A mirror is fitted on the driver's door, but one is needed on the passenger's door also to help in traffic situations.

Visibility at night or in rain is good, with a carefully controlled beam pattern for the rectangular headlamps and a full sweep for the wipers that leaves no serious unwiped areas.

On-journey stowage is frequently a poor feature of mid-engined designs and the Monte Carlo misses the chance to be good in this respect. Although there is a useful shelf the full width of the car behind the seats, the only other stowage space is in the drop-down glove locker and a diminutive oddments tray atop the central tunnel – a case here for door pockets at least.

The test car was fitted with static seat belts that were comfortable to wear and whose top mountings were neatly hidden behind the trimming for the engine bulkhead.

The heating and ventilating system coped well with the warm muggy weather of the test period, with plenty of fresh air supply through the three facia-top vents through which the supply can be boosted by the rather noisy fan. The heater worked well and proved capable of supplying warm air before the engine had reached working temperature despite the need for no less than 25 pints of water to be warmed through – a typical feature of designs with the radiator at the opposite end of the car to the engine.

The release for the bonnet is hidden away beneath the facia on the left-hand side, and when pulled allows the bonnet panel to be hinged forward and self-supported by a neat Fiat-type spring-loaded catch. In the bonnet area are the battery and the reservoir for the windscreen washer; the remainder of the area is available for luggage. The whole of the space is carpeted and a surprising amount of luggage can be stowed. Compared with its competitors, the Lancia has appreciably more room in the boot than the Porsche 911 and a similar amount to the new Lotus Esprit with which it begs the closest comparison.

The situation is not quite so happy at the other end of the car for, while engine access is good for a mid-engined design, it is poor by absolute standards. Main reason for this is that the engine is set some way inboard of the tail panel and thus it is a stretch to reach everything. However, all items needing routine attention are brought to the top of the space and the only really serious problem is presented by the carburettor in its position on the cabin side of the engine. The spare wheel is conveniently stowed on the left-hand side of the engine bay and is retained by rubber straps, allowing it to be removed easily and quickly. With the spare tyre out of the way, access to the clutch and gearbox is excellent.

The final "living with" item well worth discussing is the highly effective "targa roof". This is made of sturdy plastic material and its stowage in the rollover bar is particularly neat. Once released by turning the catch in the underside of the centre of the roll bar, the rear section of the roof can be pivoted forward to allow the front edge to be released from a channel on the top of the windscreen surround. The whole roof can then be rolled up, stowed in a space in the top of the roll bar and covered by the closing of the roof rear section. Although the opening and closing operation must be done from outside the car, it is the neatest system for the opening of the whole roof section that we have so far seen and it only takes half-a-minute or so to carry out. Although it was thought that the folding roof would be a standard feature of the Monte Carlo, it was noticeable that both fixed and opening roof versions were going down the production line and it is thought that the folding roof will be an optional extra on UK market cars.

In conclusion
While other mid-engined designs may possess some features that are better than equivalent ones on the Beta Monte Carlo, none are quite as practical *in toto*. There is a justified feeling of space inside the car, a good boot and engine access that is as good as any yet provided on a car of the type.

The chunky looks will not please everybody but there is no denying the amount of attention that the car attracts.

The design is eminently practical, the performance is respectable and the potential economy high.

No indications of British price are yet available but it is fair to assume that the car will come close to the Lotus Esprit over which it has the considerable advantage of a fuller dealership coverage. Two years ago, one would not have thought that two such cars were destined to come on the market and it will be most interesting to see how the public accepts these outstanding examples of what has now become "the sports car of today".

MANUFACTURER
Lancia Co., Via Vincenzo Lancia 27, Turin, Italy

UK CONCESSIONAIRES
Lancia (England) Limited, Ealing Road, Alperton, Wembley, Middlesex

Price as yet unannounced

Testing the Champion

Lancia Stratos given the works

MOST OUTSTANDING rally cars reach their zenith through a long and drawn out process of steady development. Porsche, Alpine, Ford Escort and even the Mini Cooper "S" were not instantly successful in the way that the Stratos was when it first entered competitions. Although the competition were going through bad patches when the Stratos first appeared, in the past two years they have all been competitive again; yet the Stratos won Lancia the World Rally Championship in only its second full year of competition.

It is not even true to say that the Stratos was designed as a competition car, for the first Bertone styling exercise used Lancia Fulvia running gear and transmission details. The Italians are fervent racing and rally enthusiasts and quickly saw the potential of the mid-engined design as a logical successor to the Fulvia; work was put in hand using the full potential of the Fiat empire. Hey presto, one Ferrari Dino-engined Stratos with a Dino gearbox cunningly engineered into a position underneath the engine with a splendidly accessible set of drop gears to allow very quick ratio changes. Development of the definitive Stratos as a race and rally competitor was in the capable hands of Mike Parkes and Ing. Gian-Paulo Dallara (of Lamborghini Miura fame) and in its first season of competition in 1973, won the Tour de France and challenged for the lead of the last proper Targa Florio before being delayed by a broken seat mounting. Then in 1974, the Stratos carried off the prestigious World Rally Championship and looks likely to repeat the win this year provided it does well enough in the Corsican Rally and our own RAC Rally.

To help them this year, the third team car will be the Chequered Flag Stratos which has been campaigned this year by Cahal Curley and Per-Inge Walfridsson. Any semblance of reliability, let alone success, has been denied this British team but following a complete rebuild to current specification at Lancia's headquarters at Milan, the team hope for the success that the car's considerable speed has suggested should be theirs. But it has been a trying year for "the Flag".

When the decision was made at the end of 1974 for Chequered Flag to re-enter motor sport through rallying, the choice of car was not immediate. The most competitive car for British rallies was obviously a Ford but this would have had no tie up with Chequered Flag's retail car dealership. Might not something from Lanciá tie in with their Lancia dealership? Imagine the scene when a Stratos was suggested, all eyes lighting up and sounds like cash registers tinkling in everyone's ears. But you have to hand it to Graham Warner, "the Flag's" indefatigable managing director who once he had been bitten by the idea devoted all his time and energy to bringing this exciting car into the British rally scene. The car that Warner eventually purchased was the ex-Pinto Monte Carlo car that crashed early on in the rally when both Pinto and Andruet ignored the advice of their "ice note" crew and crashed on the same patch of black ice.

The car was rebuilt in Milan and opened its British campaign with the Circuit of Ireland after only a minimum of testing. This had revealed that the Italian principle of narrow front wheels and wide rear ones gave the car strong understeer switching suddenly to oversteer, characteristics not designed to encourage Cahal Curley to drive the car as quickly as he might his Porsche. So in time for the Circuit, a set of Minilite wheels, 8in. wide at the front and 10in. wide at the rear were settled on and this combination gave much more predictable handling. But then on only the third stage of the Circuit, a piston broke — Chequered Flag's disappointing first season of rallying had started.

Since then, a finish has eluded both Curley and Walfridsson and only Tony Pond, driving deliberately within himself and the car, has managed a finish and third place in the Castrol 75 Aberystwyth Rally.

Driving the Stratos

What's it like to drive a car like the Stratos? The simple answer is that it is exhilaration and frustration at the same time. Exhilarating because the car responds so accurately to whatever input the driver gives, be that acceleration, braking or cornering. Frustrating in that the limits of adhesion are so high that only on a closed private area can the newcomer to the car even begin to explore the outer limits of roadholding. For on the open road, the limits of visibility and possibilities of other cars around mean that the speeds attainable hardly allow such things as under or oversteer to be enjoyed and it would be right to say that the Stratos just "steers". When you get it onto a surface with plenty of room, it then becomes possible to explore the car's character.

You might expect with all that weight on the rear wheels that they would be so glued to the road that the front of the car would just have to run wide. Certainly, there is a build up of steering effort to indicate that this is happening but such is the adhesion of the Pirelli hand-cut wet weather tyres that the front of the car just goes on gripping. As the cornering speeds are built up, the steering weight begins to diminish and the car begins to feel more balanced. When this has happened, the next stage is down to the driver for applying more power can be used to tighten or relax the line round any corner and the control is very high. The limited slip differential (35 per cent difference is allowed between one

Testing the Champion

wheel and the other) helps greatly in ensuring that the power distribution between the rear wheels is even enough to ensure that even sudden bursts of acceleration cannot make the tail step too suddenly out of line. But as ever with mid- or rear-engined cars, the thing to avoid is a mid-corner lift from the accelerator. Trying this just in the interests of science resulted in the quickest 180 deg. spin ever and once it had started, there was just no way of catching it. Thus in a rallying sense, it would seem to be more sensible to be "slow in, fast out" but in saying that, I completely ignore the talents of Per-Inge Walfridsson. Having been schooled on Volvos in Sweden, Per knows that the inertia of a car as heavy as the Volvo is not easy to control. It requires that the car be continuously unsettled in order to make quick changes of direction without straight-on understeering adventures off the road. This technique requires continuous left foot braking and the ability to let the car pendulum controllably into corners or curves. Such techniques applied to a car like the Stratos with its low polar moment of inertia would threaten disaster but it is a tribute to the Swede's extraordinary skill that not only does he get away with it but he is capable of setting fastest times against anybody in the car. Thus this year's RAC Rally will be certain to produce a battle royal at the front of the field between leading works Stratos driver Bjorn Waldegard and little Per. Graham Warner has consistently tried throughout the year to slow down the mercurial Walfridsson but to do so is to deny a lifetime of high speed tip-toeing that this diminutive Swede has enjoyed and we must hope that the recent complete rebuild that the Chequered Flag car has undergone in Milan will have given the car the reliability that can match Per's exuberant style.

How fast is it?

To begin with, this is very dependent on gearing. On the day that we had with the car at MIRA, it was fitted with the one of the six alternative gear sets that allows a top speed of about 120 mph (we dare not check precisely because the rev counter was over reading by an unknown amount). Suffice it to say that with this gearing, the Stratos gave acceleration figures that are startling to say the least. From rest to 100 mph occupied only 14·5sec despite a rather tardy time to 60 mph of "only" 5·8sec. The reason for some disappointment over the latter time is that the car is very difficult indeed to get off the line. Very wide rear tyres with high grip and a high first gear are not ingredients for a quick getaway and I was grateful for the rain that began to fall at the end of the day which made wheelspin starts a possibility. With tyres that might allow some wheelspin on dry tarmac, the car would undoubtedly have gone more quickly still. Soon after the test, the car went back to Italy where it was found that the engine was giving only 195 bhp compared with the 250 bhp which it is supposed to give and we hope to repeat our figures in the near future to see just how quickly the car should have been in A1 fettle.

The Stratos in the RAC Rally

This year, no fewer than three Stratoses will be competing in the RAC Rally, the Chequered Flag car being effectively the third works car. "The Flag" will be servicing the car themselves, however, with help from the works if necessary. Should trouble befall Waldegard's and Munari's cars you can bet that the full weight of the works support organization will be given to the black and white car of Walfridsson. If they should win, it would more than repay Chequered Flag for their season-long faith in a car that many have thought too fragile to do well in Britain's concentrated and hard rally world. **ADS**

Very full instrumentation is a feature. For the RAC Rally, the car is being fitted with a new facia. Careful air cleaning (but not silencing) is given by the double gauze filters over the intakes for the Weber carburettors. Other mods include improved oil cooling

Above: As the Stratos is mid-engined the space in the nose houses a transversely-mounted brake servo and the radiator which is cooled by twin electric fans. Left: Moody, squat, wide and very, very quick. Even with a down-on-power engine, the rally-equipped Stratos gave acceleration equal to the Porsche 3-litre Turbo

Acceleration

True mph	Time sec
30	2·8
40	3·7
50	4·7
60	5·8
70	7·5
80	9·8
90	11·7
100	14·5
120	24·3

¼-mile: 14·2sec 99 mph
Kilo: 25·8sec 122 mph

Top of the Lancia gamut

Driving (and looking at) the Lancia Gamma

By Michael Scarlett

LANCIA'S big front-wheel-drive 2½-litre Gamma saloon is an interesting, encouraging and in some respects mildly perplexing phenomenon. It is technically interesting — seemingly the largest flat-four in motor car use. It is politically encouraging — Lancia are not after all condemned to being a badge-engineered Fiat. And the protracted way it has and is being launched is curious. Widely predicted before, it appeared at this year's Geneva Show, and the Technical Editor described it in pretty full detail in our issue of 13 March. Last month Lancia invited journalists from all over Europe to come and try the car, presenting some further details. It goes on sale in Italy shortly, will be seen at Earls Court, but not sold here until the early part of next year.

LANCIA are understandably proud of the Gamma. Pininfarina has endowed it with a wind-tunnel tested body of, to most eyes, pleasing shape and what is claimed to be a good drag coefficient — 0.37, which is exceptional for saloons. Citroen's equally shapely CX is claimed by the same authorities to return around 0.33. As we suspected at the time of the launch, a two-box shape was chosen in the interests of low aerodynamic drag rather than any other reason; a hatchback was avoided because, say Pininfarina, of the inconvenience to rear passengers when luggage is being loaded — draughts and so on. (Our immediate reaction to that was that rear passengers should not be sitting inside when there is luggage to be loaded, but that does not always apply of course).

Although the body does not have any wedge pretensions, or the exaggeratedly high back of some other cars today, Pininfarina say that they were worried about the driver being able to see the rear when parking — and so one finds what must be the quite expensive-to-make provision of an extra strip of vertical glass in the back of the car below the raked back window and another piece hidden behind the slats of the tail itself. You do, I suppose, see a little more, though not much; the point seems to be that you have a better idea where the back proper is. Rear quarter panels are notable, but because they are relatively far back, do not obscure the view too much.

Lancia themselves claim that they went for the flat-four rather than the vee-six or vee-four they also considered (or a flat-six which they didn't mention) because it was more compact and lower. They were after a shorter big car, and are pleased with the fact that they are only beaten for shortness in their comparison table by the Renault 30. Their comparison does not include Leyland's Princess, which has the same wheelbase (105in.) as both the Gamma and the 30, the same if not better interior space, and is 2½in. shorter than the Renault. They also claim to have aimed for "economical service", which seems a little hard to reconcile with the extra complexity and well-known awkwardness of getting at a flat engine. An additional claim is to have kept power down slightly (140 bhp DIN at a modest 5,400 rpm) in order to ensure that 95 per cent of the peak torque — 154 lb. ft. at 3,000 rpm — is available as far down the scale as 2,000 rpm. If that is the case, one is puzzled why in these days of expensive fuel, Lancia did not make the five-speed gearbox a "four-speed" with a genuinely over-geared fifth. As it is, they have gone in for conventional five-speed with the car's 121 mph top speed achieved in fifth, which at 20.2 mph per 1,000 rpm is distinctly under-geared; this speed corresponds to 6,000 rpm. At the same maximum engine speed, maxima in the other gears are 33, 55, 79 and 101 – the ratios begin with a wide rev drop (down to 3,600 rpm from 1st when changing to 2nd), closing progressively up the scale (to 4,200, 4,700 and 5,000 rpm from 6,000 rpm).

The die-cast light alloy engine is lighter than other units of its capacity — 298lb — and the claimed overall kerb weight of the car is among the less heavy ones in its class — 2,910 lb or 26 cwt. Not surprisingly, although we could not check this properly at the time, Lancia's performance figures are healthy-sounding — 0-100 kph (62 mph) in 10 sec and the standing ¼-mile and kilometre in around 16.5 and 31.2 sec respectively.

Driving Impressions

It is most pleasing to be able to say that although there are traces of his existence in the Gamma, the Italian Standard Ape has not been allowed to dictate the driving position entirely; a most unusual state of affairs in a Lancia. They haven't provided a telescopically adjustable column which is a pity, but the steering wheel can be raked up and down, and it isn't too far from the driver who is a little longer in the leg. There is adequate legroom for once, too — and, as one would hope from a front-wheel-drive car of this wheelbase, there is enough legroom behind as well.

On the left-hand-drive model, fifth is rather remote, otherwise the gearchange is reasonably placed. We were surprised by one detail here. One associates Lancias with exaggerated gearchange gaiters, but the Gamma has none. Its absence is made more noticeable by the gearlever whose visible part ends in a ball socket on the floor. The top ball is visible too, and on the demonstration car was obviously a bit greasy, which might have worried a long-skirted woman. We were told this was the unwanted work of over-zealous mechanics who had greased the ball when they should not.

The change is a littly clonky, like several other remote control ones attached to the floor (Citroen especially) and not as precise as it ought to be, seeing how easily direct the transmission layout allows the linkage to be. There is a slight whine in the gears but not much. Other controls are nicely arranged — the usual stalks, except that the lights one has a French-style twist-end to switch on.

The horns, excellent Fiamm air ones, are worked from the steering wheel. Pedals favour those with smaller feet, who have none of the difficulty with heel-and-toe work found by the large-footed.

Considering that this aims at being the most prestigious Lancia since the Flaminia, the refinement of the engine on two cars driven was disappointing, though may be an Italian would not find it so. The quite obtrusive harsh noise of the

Above: The four-door saloon does not have a hatchback provision, although the appearance would indicate this

Left: Pininfarina's front-end treatment of the coupé, although with a fuller-width grille is similar to that of the saloon. The rear is more conventional than the saloon, with a noticeable absence of brightwork

engine when accelerating well is typically Latin and, to the enthusiast, quite satisfying — but it cannot be called quiet, except by someone used to the Citroen CX. More disappointing on "my" two cars was the vibration from the power unit — though, in view of the size of those big pistons (102 mm dia. with a 76 mm stroke) and despite the trouble Lancia have obviously gone to (little hydraulic dampers each side of the engine, and four extensive rubber mountings plus some additional stays) this was not really surprising. You can feel it inside the car, confirming your suspicion when you touch the gearchange, or more so, its base. It isn't the sort of thing you expect in this class though to be fair, a colleague who drove another car reported it free of the problem.

There *is*, however, a good spread of power, to a fairly un-Latin degree; you can potter the Gamma down to 800 rpm and pull away again reasonably. A smoother, more progressive throttle would help; it is not easy to drive smoothly on and off the accelerator. It is fun to rev it too, the nose rising appreciably under acceleration. The Gamma certainly goes enthusiastically and rewardingly, much more so than previous larger Lancias, which is a welcome improvement.

Where it impresses greatly is in its roadholding, steering and brakes. It grips the road very well indeed for a car of its type, and does not understeer too severely. Although we did not experience it on cars we drove, a colleague whose judgement I trust said that "his" car would throw its tail out ultimately if really provoked, which is a front-wheel drive safety factor in an emergency. Suspension, by the way, is all-independent coil-spring, MacPherson struts in front with a separate anti-roll bar, and strut-type at the back with long, twin lateral tubular links (adjustable for toe-in) and a forward anti-roll bar acting as a semi-trailing link, rubber resolving the compliance quarrel. Just occasionally one does feel a slight and brief wander on uneven surfaces, though it won't matter to most people; straight stability is basically excellent.

The steering is power-assisted rack and pinion and you hardly realise it is assisted. Americans might find it a little too heavy, but to us it is exactly the right weight, and it keeps the feel of a manual system — you can feel irregularities quite clearly without the steering kicking back unpleasantly. It is accurate and quite well geared — not so low geared as other Lancias, we suspect — and encourages one to take advantage of the delightfully low-roll cornering. On the sort of excitingly winding mountain roads behind the Liguarian coast line, the Gamma is fun. Our only reservations here were about the small initial difficulty of placing the car on nearside corners — the far borders of the car are not easily found — you tend to drive wide at first.

The other factor that helped here was the excellent brakes, which put up with a hard-driven, long and winding descent well, softening a little towards the end but recovering quickly. The ride is a trifle pitchy at times, though basically well damped to the point of knobbliness on poorer surfaces, but comfortable enough in general. Road noise is only a little better than average, but wind noise was on the whole well controlled.

The Gamma is a car of detail. The more you look at it, the more you find. Like the ingenious low beam headlamp levelling system (but why only low beam?) — first found on the Beta saloon; the

All the instruments (except the clock) and switches are located under a hooded binnacle; note the shaped grip on the gear lever

The flat-four 2.5-litre engine is buried beneath the air cleaner and ancilliary equipment. The dipped beam headlamp levelling unit is on the far wing

Gamma impressions

excellent ventilation system with vacuum-assisted air-blending heater controls, the temperature one of which moves itself automatically to full hot when the defrost control is switched; the night-time illumination of these controls — the depressed button glows red; the neat way the visors are recessed into the roof-lining; and lots more.

All windows are moved electrically, at a tolerable speed – you can wind two simultaneously, but none wind fully into the doors, so that chauffeur's lounging is not encouraged.

The not too pleasingly styled gauges mostly make no attempt to be anything better than mere indicators rather than measurers, but otherwise interior design is good, refined and unpretentious. A reasonably low waist gives a pleasant impression of airiness.

Overall, very much a Lancia in mostly worthwhile ways. And it is very warming to see this idiosyncratic and ancient Italian manufacturer being encouraged to maintain its individuality – the Gamma is a highly individual motor car. □

The four-door Lancia Gamma saloon, with handsome fastback styling compared with the elegant Pininfarina-styled two-door coupe. Mechanically, the cars are identical, with the flat-4 2.5-litre engine driving the front wheels

Lancia Beta 1300 and 2000

Top and bottom models of the Lancia Beta saloon range in comparison. Excellent engines and transmission. Good brakes and ride; but too much understeer, and steering response slow. Comfortable, refined and very well-equipped cars.

LANCIA launched their new Beta family saloon at the Turin Show in 1972; it was offered with engine options of 1,438, 1,592 and 1,756 c.c. Widening of this rather narrow choice of engine sizes came this year at the Brussels Show, and the middle range model — the 1600 — is now spanned by a smaller 1300 engine (actual capacity 1,295 c.c.) and a 2000 with capacity of 1,995. For many buyers the 1600 may prove a natural choice, but for this test we have taken the two extremes and run them in side by side comparison tests to see in particular whether the improved economy of the smaller engine compensates for its reduced performance.

With all three engines, the specification of the Beta is much the same. The engine itself is the familiar Fiat-based twin overhead camshaft four-cylinder unit with toothed belt drive for the camshafts. The engine is mounted transversely, with the gearbox in line and final drive behind, to the front wheels. The 1300 and 1600 have the same stroke, with different bore diameters, while the 1600 and 2000 have the same bore but different stroke.

The 2000 is distinguished by bright horizontal slats across the radiator grille, and the round headlamps are covered by a one-piece glass each side

Matt black radiator grille and no covers in front of the headlamps identify the 1300; but all Betas have halogen headlamps. Automatic headlamp adjustment for load is standard on 1600 and 2000, optional for 1300

In both the 1300 and 2000 versions tried, the engine is a delightful unit, giving smooth torque at low revs and an even spread of power right through to the 6,000 rpm limit. It is a very responsive engine and does not suffer from any vibration periods or today's all too common tendency to flat spots.

Starting is always immediate when hot, and reasonably prompt from cold — the 2000 proved the better engine in this respect having a very well-arranged automatic choke. The 1300 has a manual choke control and sometimes needs a few turns on the starter before it will respond, even with the choke pulled out. Both engines warm up quickly, and on the 2000 the automatic choke cuts out unobtrusively but only after at least a mile of running from cold. A peculiarity of Italian cars is the standard fitting of a hand throttle control, and this is present even on the 2000, whose inter-related fast idle control renders such a fitting not really necessary.

Performance of the 1300 is very fair for this size of car and engine, and when we were taking the standing start acceleration figures it went off from the line very well indeed, with a shriek of wheelspin, reaching 60 mph in 13.8 sec and covering the quarter-mile in 19.6 sec. Even by today's standards, an under-20 sec standing quarter time is creditable for a 1300. Above 80mph, however, it is rather up against the power requirements of the Beta's fairly large — albeit aerodynamic — body, and there was no hope of reaching 100 mph in the face of the rather brisk adverse wind on test day.

In these conditions, the 1300 returned a creditable top speed of 96mph, with a best of 102mph when the wind was behind it. The 2000 returned a top speed of 110mph as the mean of the MIRA banked circuit, and a best one-way of 114mph.

With the 2000, the times achieved are in a different class altogether, with the standing quarter-mile covered in 17.5 sec, and 100 mph reached from rest in the same time — 33.8 sec — that the 1300 takes to get up to just over 80mph. We found we had to practice once or twice to find just the right engine speed to engage the clutch, since anything much over 2,000 rpm simply provoked excessive front wheelspin and gave rather slower times.

The clutch operating load is on the heavy side, but not excessively so, and it takes up smoothly. It has plenty of bite, to the extent that an "ouch" of wheelspin is heard again when making a full power change up to second gear. It proved just possible, with some feeding in of the clutch, to restart on the 1-in-3 test hill with the 2000, but this produced a strong smell of burnt clutch facings and was not attempted with the 1300.

Transmission

All Betas have a five-speed gearbox, which is appreciated as much with the smaller engine as with the larger. The ratios in the gearbox are the same for all three models, but different final drive gears are used — 4.46-to-1 for the 1300, and 3.785 for the 2000. The gearchange is floor-mounted and well placed for the easy drop down of the driver's left hand from the wheel. Movement of the lever is definite enough but rather notchy. The synchromesh sometimes baulks the movement into one or other gear, especially when changing up into second or fifth, and the rather strong spring loading towards the third-fourth plane of movement means that the lever has to be held firmly over to the right for the change up to fifth, otherwise an inadvertent change back to third is made.

Particularly with the 2000, fifth gear is reasonably high-geared, giving relaxed and effortless cruising at up to 90mph. At higher speeds than this one becomes aware of appreciably more mechanical noise, but one could still call 100mph a cruising speed for the 2000. With the Beta 1300 the engine begins to sound rather busy at about 80mph, rpm at this speed being 4,800 instead of 4,100 with the 2000.

Our testers generally disliked the over-stylised gear lever knob, with its sharp edges and uncomfortable feel; a larger round knob for the gear lever would be a big improvement.

Ride, Handling and Steering

Suspension is independent all round on the Beta, using MacPherson struts both front and rear. There are also anti-roll bars at each end, and roll when cornering is well controlled. The handling is considerably affected by the amount of power applied, strong acceleration tending to accentuate the mild basic understeer. The cornering angle is much reduced as the driver lifts his foot, which gives an in-built safety factor for the unwary, especially since the transition takes place without any undue abruptness.

On wet roads the very light tail end of the car tends to slide out first, but correction is prompt on reducing the throttle or steering into the skid. Front wheelspin is much too prominent in the wet, especially with the 2000 whose ample power makes it rather difficult to make a smart getaway on a slippery surface.

Although a rack and pinion system is used, the Beta's steering is not its best feature. It is appreciably affected by front wheel pull and changes in steering feel according to how much power is applied. Also, because so much of the weight is carried on and ahead of the front wheels, steering response is slow. Quite large movements of the wheel have to be made for small deflections, and the Beta could be said to have a poor "swervability" factor. Although the 1300 is half a hundredweight lighter at the front than the 2000, its steering was liked less than with the more powerful car, since it seemed to have too little self-centring action on tight corners. The steering of both cars is decidedly heavy when manoeuvring so, although fairly low-geared, they could not reasonably be given higher-geared steering. Turning circles are good, so is the directional stability and the accuracy of the steering at high speed.

Ride comfort has always been a good feature of Lancias, and in the Beta the suspension is firm and very effectively damped. It copes particularly well with large bumps or undulations but seems to be upset by lesser ones at low speeds, producing sharp vertical jogging movements over irregularities. Road roar is well insulated. There is no trace of pitching, and the ride is certainly not of the kind to provoke sickness in any passengers who are prone to it.

Engine compartments are also largely the same. The dipstick is reached on the right hand side, near the air filter. All components, including battery, distributor and — after removing the air filter — the carburettor, are easily reached

Brakes

Servo-assisted brakes, with the same 9.9in. dia discs front and rear, feature on both cars, and the weight difference of the two engines is too small to have any noticeable affect on braking response. The Beta gives very reassuring braking from high speed and is not unduly prone to skid when braking hard in the wet. The response builds up in steady progression with extra load on the pedal, and fade in repeated hard use is minimal.

Lancia Beta 1300 and 2000

Specification

NOTE: Except where individual data given, figures apply to both

ENGINE

	Front; front drive
Cylinders	4, in line, transversely, inclined rearwards at at 20 deg
Main bearings	5
Cooling	Water
Fan	Electric
Bore, mm (in.)	**1300:** 76 (2.99); **2000:** 84 (3.31)
Stroke, mm (in.)	**1300:** 71.5 (2.81); **2000:** 90 (3.54)
Capacity, cc (in3)	**1300:** 1,297 (79.14); **2000:** 1,995 (122)
Valve gear	dohc
Camshaft drive	Toothed belt
Compression ratio	8.9-to-1
Octane rating	98 RM
Carburettor	**1300:** Weber 32DMTR or Solex C32 CIC 3 **2000:** Weber 34DATR or Solex C34 TCIC/1
Max power bhp (DIN)	**1300:** 82 at 6,200 rpm; **2000:** 119 at 5,500 rpm
Max torque lb/ft (DIN)	**1300:** 79.56 at 3,300 rpm; **2000:** 127.44 at 2,800 rpm

TRANSMISSION

Type	Manual, five-speed, all-synchromesh
Clutch	Single plate, diaphragm spring

Gear	Ratio	mph/1000 rpm 1300	2000
Top	0.93	16.5	19.1
4th	1.15	13.2	15.3
3rd	1.52	10.0	11.6
2nd	2.24	6.8	7.9
1st	3.5	4.4	5.0

Final drive gear:	Helical spur
Ratio:	**1300:** 4.46-to-1; **2000:** 3.785-to-1

SUSPENSION

Front — location	Independent MacPherson struts
springs	Coil
dampers	Telescopic
anti-roll bar	Yes
Rear — location	Independent MacPherson struts
springs	Coil
dampers	Telescopic
anti-roll bar	Yes

STEERING

Type	Rack and pinion
Power assistance	NA
Wheel diameter	15.25 in.

BRAKES

Front	9.9 in. dia disc
Rear	9.9 in. dia disc
Servo	Vacuum

WHEELS

Type	Pressed steel
Rim width	5J
Tyres — make	Michelin (on test cars)
— type	ZX
— size	155-14in.(1300) 175/70SR-14 (2000)

EQUIPMENT

Battery	12 volt 45 Ah
Alternator	750 watt
Headlamps	4 x 5¼ in. round halogen units
Reversing lamp	Standard
Hazard warning	Standard
Electric fuses	10
Screen wipers	2-speed (plus intermittent on 2000)
Screen washer	Electric
Interior heater	Water valve
Interior trim	Cloth seats, TVE headlining
Floor covering	Carpet
Jack	Screw pillar, winding handle
Jacking points	One each side under front door
Windscreen	Laminated
Underbody protection	Electro-phoretic treatment prior to painting; sealant after painting

MAINTENANCE

Fuel tank	11.4 Imp galls (52 litres)
Cooling system	15 pints (inc heater)
Engine sump	8 pints SAE 10W/50
Gearbox and final drive	4.5 pints SAE 50
Grease	No points
Valve clearance	Inlet 0.016 in. (cold) Exhaust 0.018 in. (cold)
Contact breaker	0.015 in. gap
Ignition timing	10 deg. BTDC (static)
Spark plug — type	Champion N7Y
— gap	0.020 in.
Tyre pressures	F 24; R 24 psi (normal driving)
Max payload	992 lb (450 kg)

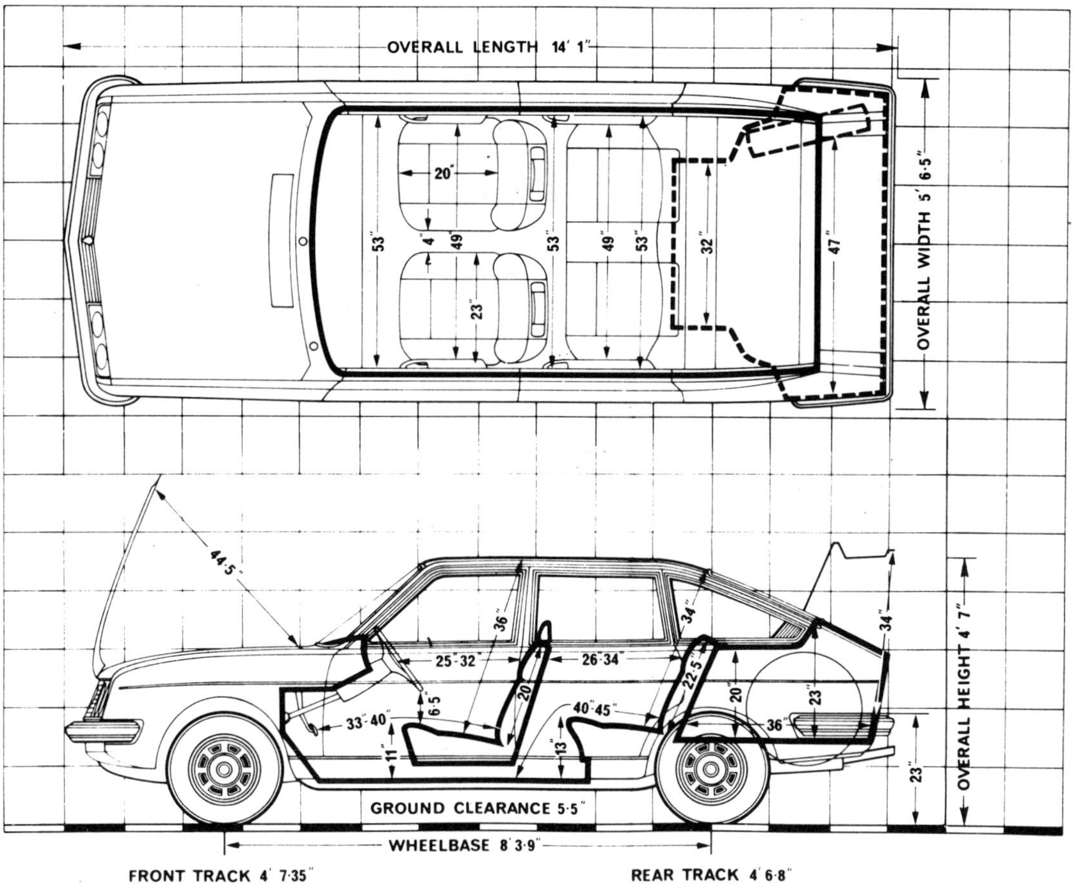

Set between the seats, slightly too low for large drivers, the handbrake gives good leverage and holds securely on the 1-in-3 test hill when pointing up the gradient. However, it is worth knowing that on a steep hill when parked pointing downwards, the forward weight transfer can allow the Beta to slide slowly downwards, dragging its locked rear wheels behind it.

A warning tell-tale on the facia flashes intermittently as a warning if the handbrake is set when the ignition is on, and beside it is a combined tell-tale for fluid level and front pad wear. The disc brakes are of swinging caliper type, and the two circuits for the hydraulic system duplicate the front brakes. One system works all brakes, and the other works the fronts alone; failure of either lights the fluid tell-tale and leaves at least the front brakes fully operative. The pressure limiting valve in the line to the rear brakes is load sensitive, allowing extra effort at the rear wheels when a full load is carried.

Fuel consumption

An important consideration in making the choice between these two cars is that of fuel consumption, and there is a natural presumption that the car with the smaller engine will always use less fuel. This is borne out to some extent by the overall consumption figures for the full test, which returned at 29.6 mpg for the 1300, and 24.0 mpg for the 2000. The saving of over 5 mpg is well worth having, and although 24 mpg is quite a good figure for a hard-driven 2000, there is much to be said for the formula which gives the same carrying capacity and still quite good performance for an overall figure of nearly 30 mpg.

It could be argued that if the 2000 is driven at the same speeds as the 1300, its much less stressed engine would give as good economy. Put another way, the 1300 used less fuel, it could be said, because it wasn't able to go as fast. To put this to the test, we ran both cars in convoy, each taking it in turn to be

Maximum speeds

Gear	1300 mph	1300 kph	1300 rpm	2000 mph	2000 kph	2000 rpm
Top (mean)	96	155	5,800	110	177	5,750
(best)	102	164	6,200	114	184	5,950
4th	80	129	6,000	92	148	6,000
3rd	60	97	6,000	70	113	6,000
2nd	41	66	6,000	47	76	6,000
1st	26	42	6,000	31	50	6,000

Acceleration

True mph	1300 Time secs	2000 Time secs	1300 Speedo mph	2000 Speedo mph
30	**3.8**	**3.3**	30	30
40	**6.6**	**5.1**	41	40
50	**9.8**	**7.0**	51	50
60	**13.8**	**10.1**	62	60
70	**19.6**	**13.3**	72	70
80	**28.2**	**17.5**	82	80
90	—	**23.4**	93	90
100	—	**33.8**	103	100
110	—	—	—	110

Standing ¼-mile:
19.6 sec, 70 mph (1300);
17.5 sec, 80 mph (2000)

Standing kilometre:
36.6 sec, 84 mph (1300);
31.9 sec, 98 mph (2000)

mph	Top 1300	Top 2000	4th 1300	4th 2000	3rd 1300	3rd 2000	2nd 1300	2nd 2000
10-30	14.5	—	12.0	7.6	7.4	5.6	4.6	3.4
20-40	13.7	9.5	9.5	6.8	6.6	4.7	4.6	3.1
30-50	14.2	9.1	8.9	6.2	6.8	4.5	—	3.6
40-60	16.8	8.5	10.2	6.4	7.4	4.9	—	—
50-70	22.3	9.0	11.6	7.1	—	5.8	—	—
60-80	27.2	11.1	14.2	8.2	—	—	—	—
70-90	—	13.8	—	9.8	—	—	—	—
80-100	—	18.5	—	—	—	—	—	—

Brakes

Fade *(from 70 mph in neutral)*
Pedal load for 0.5g stops in lb

1	35	6	40
2	35	7	40
3	35-40	8	40
4	40	9	40
5	40	10	40

Response *(from 30 mph in neutral)*

Load	g	Distance
20lb	0.38	79ft
40lb	0.54	56ft
60lb	0.80	38ft
80lb	0.90	33ft
100lb	1.05	29ft
Handbrake	0.38	79ft
Max gradient	1 in 3	

Clutch

Pedal 24lb and 6in.

Weight

1300
Kerb, 21.1 cwt/2360 lb
(Distribution F/R, 59.6-40.4)
As tested, 24.6 cwt/2.755 lb/1250 kg.

2000
Kerb, 21.8 cwt/2,440 lb.
(Distribution F/R 60.2/39.8)
As tested, 25.4 cwt/2,840 lb/1290 kg.

Boot capacity: 17.6 cu ft.

Turning circles: (both)
Between kerbs
L, 35ft 5in; R, 37ft 0in.
Between walls
L, 37ft 5in; R, 39ft 0in.
Turns, lock to lock 4.1.

Consumption

Fuel

Overall mpg:

1300	2000
29.6	**24.0**
(9.54 litres/100km)	(11.8 litres/100km)

Calculated (DIN) mpg

27.4	26.0
(10.3 litres/100km)	(10.9 litres/100km)

Constant speed: mph	1300 mpg	2000 mpg
30	51.3	52.6
40	48.0	45.5
50	42.4	38.8
60	35.5	32.4
70	30.1	28.6
80	25.8	23.8
90	20.3	19.8
100	—	17.6

Autocar formula
Hard driving, difficult conditions
26.6 mpg (1300); 21.6 mpg (2000)
Average driving, average conditions
32.6 mpg (1300); 26.4 mpg (2000)
Gentle driving, easy conditions
38.5 mpg (1300); 31.2 mpg (2000)

Grade of fuel: (both) Premium, 4-star (98 RM).

Mileage recorder: 4.5 per cent (1300) and 4 per cent (2000) over-reading.

Oil

Consumption (SAE 10W/50), negligible (both).

Test Conditions

Wind: 10-20 mph
Temperature: 20 deg C (68 deg F)
Barometer: 29.9 in. Hg
Humidity: 44 per cent.
Surface: dry asphalt and concrete
Test distance 1,444 miles (1300); 671 miles (2000) 4,800 miles (1300) and 5,300 miles (2000)

Figures taken at 4,800 miles (1300) and 5,300 miles (2000) by our own staff at the Motor Industry Research Association proving ground at Nuneaton.

Regular Service

Change (Interval)	6,000	12,000	18,000
Engine oil	Yes	Yes	Yes
Oil filter	Yes	Yes	Yes
Gearbox oil	Yes	Yes	Yes
Spark plugs	Yes	Yes	Yes
Air cleaner	Yes	Yes	Yes
C/breaker	Yes	Yes	Yes
Total cost	**£2.15**	**£30.10**	**£23.65**

(Assuming labour at £4.30/hour)

Parts Cost

(including VAT)

Brake pads (2 wheels) — front	£8.14
Brake pads (2 wheels) — rear	£7.43
Silencer, complete system	£90.14
Tyre — each (typical advertised)	£16.58 (£22.14 for 2000)
Windscreen	£88.21
Headlamp unit	£37.80
Front wing	£39.92
Rear bumper	£49.64

Warranty Period
Six months/unlimited mileage

Test Scorecard

(Average of scoring by *Autocar* Road Test team)

Ratings: *6 Excellent*
5 Good
4 Better than average
3 Worse than average
2 Poor
1 Bad

	1300	2000
PERFORMANCE	4.50	5.33
STEERING AND HANDLING	3.58	3.58
BRAKES	4.00	4.00
COMFORT IN FRONT	4.17	4.17
COMFORT IN BACK	3.57	3.57
DRIVER'S AIDS *(instruments, lights, wipers, visibility etc.)*	3.75	3.75
CONTROLS	3.88	4.00
NOISE	4.17	4.33
STOWAGE	3.67	3.67
ROUTINE SERVICE *(under-bonnet access: dipstick etc.)*	4.30	4.30
EASE OF DRIVING	4.00	4.05
OVERALL RATING	**3.96**	**4.05**

Comparisons

	Price £	max mph	0-60 sec	overall mpg	capacity c.c.	power bhp	wheel-base in.	length in.	width in.	kerb weight lb	fuel gal	tyre size
LANCIA BETA 2000	**2,985**	**110**	**10.1**	**24.0**	**1,995**	**119**	**100**	**169**	**66.5**	**21.8**	**11.4**	**175/70SR14**
BMW 320	4,149	108	10.2	21.2	1,991	109	101	171.4	63.4	20.4	11.4	165SR13
Princess 2200HLS(A)	3,905	98	14.2	21.8	2,227	110	105	175.4	68.1	24.2	16.0	185/70SR13
Triumph Dolomite 1850HL	2,962	100	11.8	27.7	1,854	91	96.8	161	62.5	18.9	12.5	155SR13
Vauxhall Cavalier GL Coupé	3,161	106	11.2	23.7	1,897	89	99	175	65	20.2	11.0	185/70RS13
Volkswagen Scirocco	3,140	103	10.3	27.6	1,588	85	94.5	152.5	64	16.1	10.0	175/70 13
LANCIA BETA 1300	**2,492**	**96**	**13.8**	**29.6**	**1,297**	**82**	**100**	**169**	**66.5**	**21.8**	**11.4**	**175/70SR14**
Alfasud SE	1,998	92	15.1	27.4	1,186	63	97	153.2	62.5	16.9	11.0	165/70 13
Citroen GS Pallas	2,499	94	15.9	28.6	1,220	60	100.5	162.5	63	17.2	9.5	145 15
Fiat 128S	1,933	90	13.9	32.6	1,290	60.5	96.5	151	62.5	16.1	8.3	145SR13
Ford Escort 1300 Ghia	2,475	93	13.5	29.3	1,297	70	94.5	156.5	60.5	17.2	9.0	155 13

in the lead, each handled by two drivers in turn. A representative route was chosen which included sections of motorways, ordinary road with a lot of overtaking, traffic running and some gentle cruising.

In these conditions, the gap narrowed considerably. The 1300 improved its consumption from the 29.6 mpg overall for the test, to 32.7 mpg. The 2000, however, improved from its overall of 24.0 mpg to 30.3 mpg on the test course. These results bear out to some extent the theory that when the two cars are driven at the same speeds and using the same amount of performance, there is not a great deal of difference in the amount of fuel they consume. The 1300 has to be driven that much harder to keep up. In theory, you could buy the 2000, drive it as quietly as you would have done had you purchased the 1300, and make the appropriate fuel savings; but just *try* holding it back!

All these fuel consumption figures, incidentally, are based on actual distances after correction for a rather naughty optimism of 4 and 4½ per cent in the two mileometers, although the speedometers were practically accurate, as mentioned in the equipment section. Neither car showed any significant drop in oil level during the test.

Fuel tank capacity is 11.4 gal, but the gauge is rather vague and discourages one from using more than about 10 gal without refuelling, so the working range is about 250 miles for the 2000, and 300 for the 1300.

Fittings and equipment

One has to delve and contrast to find significant differences between these two versions of the Beta, other than the over-riding one of engine size. In fact, some external distinction is given by the elimination of the one-piece lens over each pair of round headlamps on the 1300. On both cars, the lamps give good range of light but have a rather abrupt short-fall cut-off on dipped beam, making it a little difficult to be sure that the nearside

Model identity is given by a badge on the boot lid. Bumpers are rubber-faced and wrap well round the corners.

lane is clear of obstructions when driving in the face of oncoming traffic. Adjustment might have helped. When the **sidelamps** are turned on, a green courtesy wash of lighting shines down on to the floor. Instrument lighting is barely adequate, though one can read the mileage and trip digits; intensity is adjusted by a small rheostat button above the steering column. Even with the quite bright roof light on, the steering column lock on right hand drive cars is completely obscured and it is not easy to locate the keyhole.

The lights are controlled by a double action lever on the right of the column — rotated to switch on first side, then **headlamps**, while vertical movement of the lever gives choice of main or dipped beam when the headlamps are on, and dipped or side when sidelamps are on. Pulled towards the wheel, it flashes headlamps. The nearer lever above the lighting control is for the indicators, and it is a change for a Continental car to have this control on the right.

Windscreen wipers are worked by a three-position lever on the left of the column. In the central position they give intermittent wiper action, and the lever is raised to work electrically-operated screenwashers. These were poorly sited on both cars, their jets tending to hit the screen near the top of the wiper arc. As the wind action is always to move the water up the screen on the Beta, it is almost impossible to wet the entire wiper arcs without reducing speed so that the water can run down the glass.

The seats are well-shaped giving good lateral support by well-rounded backrests, while the cushions extend forward under the thighs. Headrests are fitted to both cars but they are readily removable for all-round visibility. A wide and padded folding centre armrest is fitted in the rear seat. There is barely adequate rearward seat adjustment, and a rotary hand wheel on the outer edge of each front seat gives infinitely variable backrest adjustment, down to full recline. Rear seat legroom is generous, and a small bleed from the heater is carried to the rear compartment, where it is fed through separately adjustable vanes in small paired outlets.

Heating and ventilation generally work well, though it takes a while to fathom how to regulate the system, since the triangular pointers suggest that the levers should work in the opposite direction from what is actually the case. In hot weather a good supply of cool air can be obtained from the adjustable vanes in the centre of **the console and, although the much-maligned water valve type of** temperature control is used, the provision of a combined air blending regulator makes it possible to obtain gentle warmth when required. Separate vents at each side of the facia are speed sensitive, and again one has to master the elaboration of their three separate thumb wheel controls. The control of air to the central console vents is regulated by the lower of the two sliding lever controls. The two-speed booster is rather noisy even on its slower setting, but there is good ram effect above about

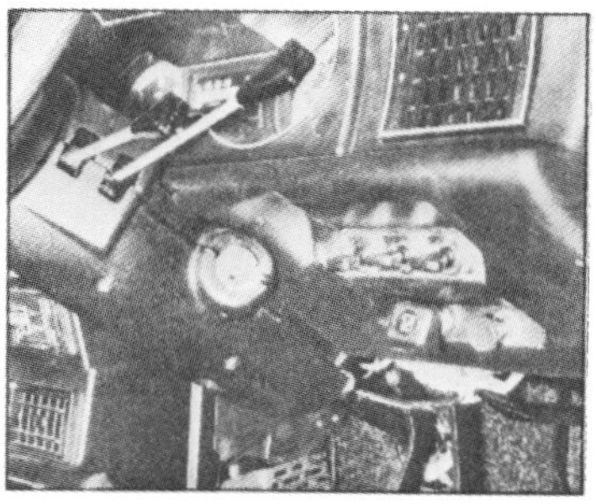

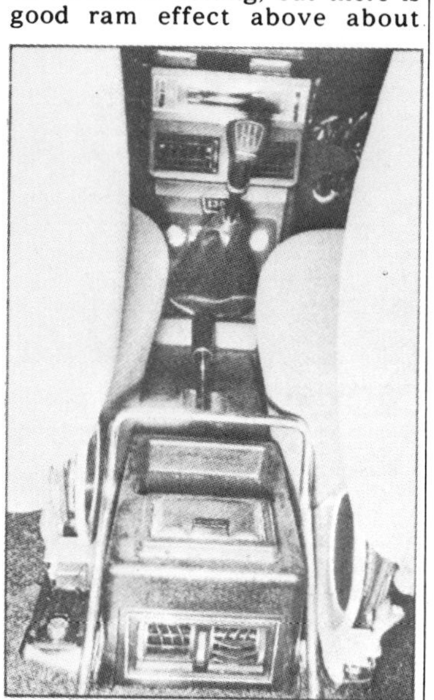

Above left: Even with automatic choke, the 2000 has a hand throttle. Beside it is the illuminated switch for optional *rear fog lamp. Switches on the panel above these are for the heated rear window, wipers fast speed, and a spare. Heater outlets to the rear compartment (above) have an on-off control and adjustable vanes. Instruments (left) are coolant thermometer and oil pressure gauge between the speedometer and rev counter, and fuel gauge on the left. Extreme left of the instrument recess is a clock. Controls for lights and indicators are on column-mounted stalks. The steering wheel has a lever release for vertical adjustment, and the centre bar of the wheel sounds the horns. Central knob beneath the radio is for the hazard flashers*

30mph, so it can largely be confined to traffic running. One cannot give much credit to the styling of the instruments, particularly for the use of red pointers on a black ground for the speedometer and rev counter. However, the accuracy of the 2000's speedometer was excellent right through the speed range. That of the 1300 exaggerated progressively to a still very acceptable 3mph flatter at 100mph. Minor instruments are a gauge for the 11½-gallon fuel tank, oil pressure gauge, coolant thermometer and a very accurate quartz clock.

A separate lockable release knob beneath the facia has to be turned to release the locker lid, which is then pulled down as a separate movement. There are oddments bins on the front kick trim each side, pockets for maps in the backs of the front seats, and a small note flap on the back of the driver's sun visor.

It is surprising that no childproof catches are provided for the rear doors. As a poor substitute, the sill locks when pushed down do isolate the interior handles as well as locking the outside ones. The boot can be left unlocked when required for convenience. When locked up — using the same key as that for the doors — its release button neatly retracts so that it cannot be forced. A useful light in the boot comes on with the side lamps, when the lid is open. The luggage compartment extends well forward and is reasonably deep. The spare wheel is stowed vertically at the right, and there is an unusually generous toolkit on the left, under the mat.

Extra refinements of the 2000 over the 1300 include such details as provision of a blue shaded portion at the top of the windscreen on the dearer model, and fitting of a switch to the right of the facia which gives choice of slow or fast speed wiper action in addition to an intermittent wipe function. However, the speed of wiping varied little with this. The 1300 has two-speed wipers, but no intermittent action. The 1600 and 2000 also have automatic headlamp adjustment of the dipped beams to compensate for changes in load and ride height.

At extra cost of some £370, the 2000 is available in ES form, which includes a sliding roof, electrically-operated windows, and light alloy wheels. A heated rear window is standard on all.

Where they fit in

Very nearly £500 separates the 1300 price from that of the 2000. With this considerable difference we can well sympathise with anyone who finds himself pondering on the possibility of buying the cheaper model. The best advice can only be that if one can run to the extra, the more powerful engine is very well worth having. But perhaps — as is often the case — the compromise solution is the best, in this instance the car we have not yet tested in saloon form: the Beta 1600. □

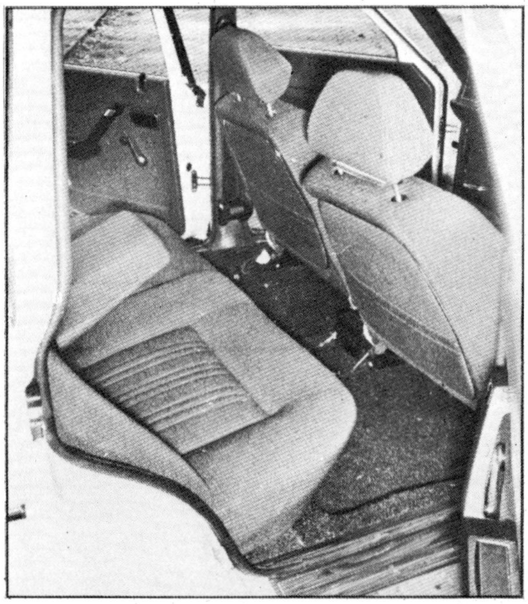

Above and right: Seats are pleated on the 2000. All models have a rear seat centre armrest, and front seat headrests (readily removable)

Below and right: In the 1300, the front seats have transverse pleating. Vertical adjustment for the steering wheel features even on this cheapest model

Left: The facia cubby is lockable and has a strange opening mechanism which drops the lid down vertically so it cannot serve as a tray for cups. Below: The boot can be left unlocked, and has its own interior light

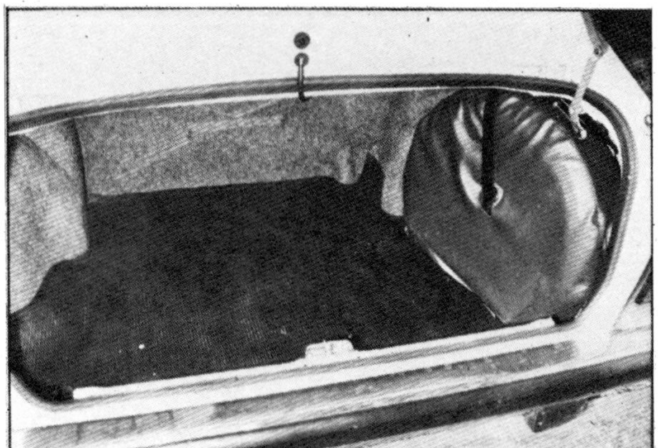

MANUFACTURER:
Lancia & C., Via Vincenzo Lancia 27, Casella Postale 430, Turin, Italy

UK CONCESSIONAIRES:
Lancia (England) Ltd, Ealing Road, Alperton, Middlesex HA0 1HE

PRICES	**1300**	**2000**
Basic	£2,130.00	£2,551.00
Special Car Tax	£177.50	£212.58
VAT	£184.60	£221.09
Total (in GB)	**£2,492.10**	**£2,984.67**
Seat Belts	**£33.00**	£33.00
Licence	**£40.00**	£40.00
Delivery charge (London)	**£35.00**	£35.00
Number plates	**£7.50**	£7.50
Total on the Road (exc insurance)	**£2,607.60**	**£3,100.17**
Insurance	Group V	VII
EXTRAS (inc VAT)		
*Metallic paint	£140.40	£140.40
*Light alloy wheels, sliding roof and electrically-operated windows (2000ES)	— —	£368.55
*Not on test cars		
TOTAL AS TESTED ON THE ROAD	**£2,607.60**	**£3,100.17**

Lancia Stratos: the end in sight

THE SENSATIONAL-looking car above is a works Lancia Stratos done up in Group 5, turbocharged, racing trim. It won't be seen internationally in 1977. With a win in the Tour of Italy, and several fiery dnfs behind it, the Group 5 Stratos racing programme is to be shorn, together with Lancia's two-car rallying effort. Next year, Cesare Fiorio announced in Turin last week, Lancia will concentrate on winning the new FIA rally drivers' cup for their man Sandro Munari — and that means they won't officially be contesting the World Rally Championship for Makes The FIA Cup takes in World Championship, European Championship and International-status events in an unduly complicated system that is designed to establish rallying's best all-round driver. In fact, it will give Lancia something new at which to aim (the Stratos has won the past three Rally Championship for Makes, and the Fulvia a fourth title in 1972). And, reflecting the "corporate decision" that today is very much a part of the Fiat-Lancia-Ferrari combine, it gives Fiat a fair crack at the World Championship with their Abarth 131.

Debonair Sandro Munari (left) and his regular co driver Silvio Maiga. After winning the unofficial FIA drivers' cup for the past two years, Munari will be trying for the official version in 1977

The works Stratos will still be seen in key international events, understand that. Three cars (two shod with Michelins, one with Pirellis!) will be seen on the Monte, three on the Safari and two on the San Remo. Sponsorship will continue to come from Alitalia; Olio Fiat will replace Agip; and Munari will compete in the Tours of Italy and France. With "Lele" Pinto, Bernard Darniche and Simo Lampinen on the driving strength, the effort is by no means low-key. But with Bjorn Waldegaard now signed for Ford, and with the Group 5 racers now standing as shapes at which to gape, the inference is also that Lancia are cutting back.

Not so. At least, that was the *feeling* at last week's press conference. "No army shows its weapons before battle," replied Gianfranco Sguazzini, Lancia managing director, to the query about long-term plans. But it is towards these plans, clearly, that the balance of the 1977 budget is being channelled. The Stratos has been with us, first as a Bertone styling special, and latterly as the ultimate rally car, for nearly five years, and so Lancia thoughts are turning towards its replacement. We understand this to be a Monte-Carlo-based chassis, powered by the 3-litre V8 from the Ferrari 308GTB. Technical director Mike Parkes says nothing, but this was the word from Italy last week. At its least exotic, the new car will be a Monte-Carlo fitted with Stratos mechanicals.

For 1977, though, there is still much to achieve. The 2.4-litre V6 Stratos has yet to be fully developed for fuel injection, and Safari-inspired longer-travel suspension, debuted by Munari on the 1976 RAC Rally, has yet to be given the acid test. Munari, too, spoke of personal goals. He very much wants to win the Safari, not because he considers it particularly challenging from a performance standpoint, but because it is an event "where it is important to do a good job, as a team." One can hardly imagine him being over-enthusiastic about the FIA cup, however. The FIA have awarded him a drivers' award for the past two years — as a token gesture!

The question of pursuing a drivers', rather than a manufacturers', series also non-plussed the Lancia heirarchy, and it was easy to see why. In Sandro Munari, they have the perfect driver. As an Italian sportsman, his reputation is up there with Adriano Panatta's; his rallying ability is unquestioned; and he is what the Lancia PR men describe as "very normal. He is married, he is quiet, he doesn't get worked up." He is, indeed, untypically Latin, and very much in the Lancia image.

At present, Munari's stature is at its highest. On the brink of his 12th season with Lancia, he has driven both racing and rallying cars, firmly opted in favour of the latter, and gone on to specialize on tarmac events. The RAC, which he led in 1974, and the Safari still elude him, for example. As a racing driver Munari showed immense promise, particularly as he was an Italian racing at a time when Arturo Merzario was their brightest hope. He was offered a works Ferrari drive for the 1972 Targo Florio, he accepted, and, with Merzario, he won. That year, he went on to finish fourth in the same car at the Osterreichring, but this was the race when he decided to concentrate on rallying. "I was competitive," he says in Ustinov English, "and I was able to put in regular legs (laps). But after three or four legs I began to lose concentration. The only thing was the speed. I liked the speed, but when i'd learned the Osterreichring I started to get bored. I couldn't concentrate for a race distance." Rallying, he says, is appealing because it has variety. Now, he thinks, he is at his peak. He feels he has proved himself as quick as Waldegaard, if not quicker. He says he is as much at home on snow and ice as he is on gravel and tarmac, and, business-wise, he is proud of his 1977 contract. "Before, Alitalia said that the driver must be *their* driver. This time I did a deal with Parmalat (a large Italian dairy firm) *before* I signed for Lancia-Alitalia!" He says the Stratos is a much easier car to drive than, say, the Fulvia. He doesn't left-foot brake, and he doesn't use the handbrake. He does, however, swiftly engage low gears without the use of the clutch. "This is one of the Stratos' best features."

Munari isn't fond of the no-pace-notes rallies. "Always," he says, "the local drivers have an advantage. If the roads can really remain secret, as they sometimes do on the RAC, then OK. But on most events it is a joke. I love the Thousand Lakes. It was the rally I made my name in. But today it is impossible for someone like me to know the roads as well as a Scandinavian. Simo Lampinen tells me he knows what is ahead before nearly every corner!"

In Britain, much was made of this year's San Remo Rally, which provided a Lancia clean sweep . . . and victory for Munari's team-mate, Bjorn Waldegaard. Shortly afterwards, Waldegaard signed for Ford, and the assumption was that Lancia were annoyed that Munari had been beaten in Italy. Munari says he was disappointed to lose, but not with Waldegaard. Fiorio did an excellent job in ensuring the two drivers were virtually equal as they went into the last stage, and then gave them a free hand. The quickest man over the last stage would win the event. Waldegaard won by seconds.

His subsequent departure from Lancia raised eyebrows in Britain, but not, it seems, in Italy. Fiorio says he had already told his drivers that only one Stratos would be entered on the RAC if the Championship was clinched in Corsica. It was, and so he, Fiorio, arranged for Waldegaard to drive for Fiat. Then came Ford with their offer, and Bjorn left. "But I wouldn't be surprised," said Fiorio, "to see Bjorn back in a Lancia in 1978."

By then, the Monte-Carlo should have arrived, perhaps under a new name. Meanwhile, the Stratos has reached a production run of over 700, and is still being ordered to the tune of 10 units a month.

THE SPORT 1977 Continued

As mentioned on the previous page, Sandro Munari's target for 1977 was the FIA Driver's Cup, the first official world title for a rally driver (as opposed to a manufacturer). In this he succeeded admirably, his victories including another win on the Monte Carlo (*above*). One of the very few events on which complete success eluded the Stratos was the East African Safari, on which it always proved the fastest car only to suffer from annoyingly minor problems which cheated it of victory—on more than one occasion the mid-mounted engine's propensity for ingesting dust of mud thrown up by the front wheels proved its downfall. At least one local driver was usually drafted into the team on Lancia's Safari expeditions: (*right*) Robin Ulyate is seen crossing a typically crude bridge in Kenya. By this time, the factory were willing and able to support a number of private teams who wished to rally Stratos' in their own countries: by far the most successful example of this was the machine rallied by Chardonnet, the French Lancia importers (*below*) for whom Bernard Darniche achieved innumerable wins and took the European Rally Championship in both 1976 and 1977.

Lancia Beta HPE 2000

Lancia's contender in the expanding sports-estate market. Impressive specification and the usual high standard of finish. Lively handling and performance somewhat spoiled by heavy, low geared steering and high noise levels. Versatile accommodation but poor driving position

CARS HAVE always been compromises of sorts. Estate cars are rarely used to their full volume or payload capacity; yet how many times have we seen saloons with bits of wood sticking out of the windows, or the boot lid flapping in the air and the handles of a lawnmower protruding incongruously upward?

With the varied requirements of car owners, it has been inevitable that car designers should seek ways to build better compromise cars. In Lancia's case, their answer in the 2-litre medium class is the Beta HPE — the "High Performance Estate".

The HPE has the same chassis base unit as the Beta saloon thus sharing the same wheelbase, track and layout of mechanical components. Clothing the chassis base is a more compact, three-door, coupé body giving a saving of ½in. in length (ahead of the front wheels), 3½in. height and 2¼in. width. The compactness is magnified by the pronounced inward rake of all four sides of the superstructure, and by having only one door on each flank of the body.

The result is a roomy cabin for a coupé with adequate head, shoulder and legroom for four adults and the ability to carry a third adult in the rear without too much discomfort. This latter facility has been cleverly devised by shaping the rear seat in such a way that the two outside passengers sit facing slightly inwards to gain valuable extra width at shoulder level.

Considered as an estate car, the HPE offers several ways in which the rear compartment may be used. The backs of the rear seat may be folded forward individually or together. When the car is to be used to transport larger items, the rear seat cushion is tipped forward, the seat back folds down and a closing board tips forward to protect the backs of the front seats. In this configuration, the length of flat floor is 4ft. 6in. with greater length higher up, as the closing panel is inclined forward beyond the vertical.

Specification

Thus far, we have considered the "Estate" portion of HPE, what of the "High Performance" part? The HPE 2000 uses a 2-litre development of the Fiat/Lancia dohc in-line, four-cylinder engine. This unit started at 1.6 litres but by an increase first in bore and now in stroke, it has arrived at its present capacity of 1,995 c.c. Running on a compression ratio of 8.9-to-1, this compact unit develops 119 bhp (DIN) at 5,500 rpm and (the main object of the stroking from 1.8 litres) a healthy maximum torque of 128lb. ft. at a conservative 2,800 rpm. Apart from the desire to grow up to the important fiscal limit, the object of going to 2 litres from the previous 1.8 litres is to be able to use higher final drive ratios without loss of performance. Such a move has the double virtue of quieter high speed cruising and higher potential economy.

Above: With the rear seat tipped forward and the backrests filling the gap, the full potential of the HPE can be seen. The tall suspension covers do tend to take up some useful room

Below left: The front seats are not quite as comfortable as they would appear, but the wheel rake device gives infinite adjustment. The trim is in cloth, with pvc side panels

Below right: By angling the rear seats slightly, elbow room can be improved when two passengers are being carried

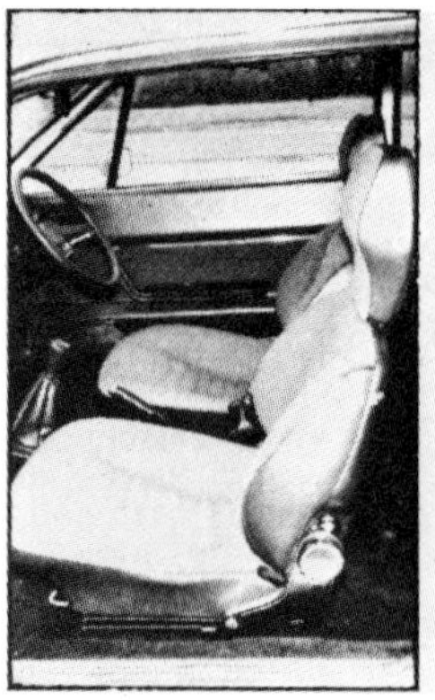

In the HPE installation, the engine leans back, driving to the five-speed, all indirect gearbox via an 8½in. dia. cable-operated clutch. The engine / transmission package is set transversely in the chassis with the engine's induction face at the front, and the gearbox set on the nearside of the car. Drive through the gearbox is "out and back" permitting the final drive to be positioned behind and towards the centre of the car. However, the drive shafts are of unequal length, a potential problem that Lancia get round by mounting a drive shaft bearing on the back (exhaust) face of the engine so that the articulated portion of each drive shaft is the same length.

Suspension components are shared with all the Beta range; MacPherson strut suspension front and rear with coil springs. At the front location is by a substantial, wide-based bottom wishbone and there is an anti-roll bar that has no location responsibility. However, at the rear, the anti-roll bar doubles as a reaction arm to look after longitudinal movements of the rear wheels, with a pair of lateral links controlling vertical suspension movement. Despite the considerable frontward bias of the weight distribution, the rack and pinion steering is unassisted for UK market cars (power steering is optional in Italy).

The section of the market at which the HPE is aimed seems to gain a new participant almost every week. Few manufacturers now consider that they can ignore the high-performance, high specification, three-door hatchback sector and there is a wealth of competition for the HPE. Most obvious competitor is another Italian, the Alfa Romeo Alfetta GTV 2000, whose price is within £138 of the HPE (£5,020 and £4,882 respectively), while among British cars, the Reliant Scimitar GTE (£5,480) and Ford Capri 3000S (£3,509) show how many different-priced vehicles can offer reasonable four-seat comfort and a versatile layout.

Performance and economy

Though 119 bhp (DIN) is a high specific output for a 2-litre engine, the HPE is no lightweight at 21 cwt kerb weight. Thus performance is quick rather than startling, as the performance table reveals. At 112 mph, the maximum speed is less than its rivals who all approach 120 mph, but the clue to the HPE's character is given by the fact that the maximum speed equates to an engine speed of only 5,700 rpm, only 200 rpm over the power peak. Considering that the engine happily runs to 7,000 rpm in the intermediate gears, this shows Lancia's desire to get overall gearing high enough to allow relaxed high speed cruising.

In terms of acceleration, 0 to 60 mph in 10.6 sec shows the Lancia lagging behind both the Ford Capri (9 sec) and the Alfa Romeo Alfetta GTV (8.9 sec) though in absolute terms, the Lancia's performance is quick enough. The concentration on low speed torque is revealed best by the acceleration in each gear. In third gear, for instance, each 20 mph increment from 10 to 70 mph occupies between 5 and 6 sec, emphasizing the praiseworthy flexibility. Fourth gear is just capable of taking the HPE over 100 mph and yet, with the minimum of fuss, will pull from as low as 10 mph. Not surprisingly, the high fifth gear was unhappy to pull from much under 20 mph.

The gear ratios are equally rather than ideally spaced; the ratio of second gear especially but of third too, might well be higher to make better use of the power available and perhaps provide better economy at the same time. Any shortcomings in the spacing of the gears are made up for by the engine's flexibility.

First gear is good for 33 mph, yet permits a restart (with a great flurry of wheelspin) on a 1-in-3 slope — nor was any difficulty experienced in restarting on the same slope in reverse, whose ratio is markedly higher than that of first.

In view of the *raison d'être* for the 2-litre engine, it was disappointing that the hoped-for economy was not apparent. Overall consumption for the period during which the HPE was with us was a disappointing 20.3 mpg. An indication that the consumption might be as poor as this was given by a DIN figure of 20.9 mpg and the fact that, at 80 mph, the HPE is only giving 21 mpg. Even when driven with sensible restraint, the best figure achieved fell short of 25 mpg. One has to say that owners must expect between 20 and 27 mpg at the very best.

Roadholding (handling and ride)

A number of factors in the specification explain the exceptionally good road behaviour found in the HPE. Independent suspension, generous wheel travel, well-controlled damping and 175/70-14 tyres all play their part in inspiring confidence.

Nose-heavy weight distribution and strong front-end roll resistance ensure that the HPE understeers, and that the understeer builds up with cornering speed until the limit is set by reaching full lock with the inside rear wheel very lightly laden indeed. However, it is quite possible to counter the understeer either by releasing the accelerator in mid-corner to take advantage of the well-controlled lift-off tuck-in

Lancia Beta HPE 2000

effect, or to "chuck" the car into its corners, catching the consequent roll oversteer with power. With increasing confidence and the realization that the initial roll oversteer when entering a corner is only transitory, the HPE can be driven with enthusiasm to give more than respectable cross-country average speeds.

Since power steering is not available in this country, we get the low-geared steering necessary to give acceptable steering effort at parking speeds. Nearly four turns of the big steering wheel are needed for a disappointing turning circle of a mean 36ft 8in. between kerbs. When negotiating narrow twisting streets and alleyways, much twirling of the wheel is necessary and this is probably the aspect of the car that will most disappoint the enthusiastic driver.

Though the response from the 70-series tyres is good enough, a lot of lock is needed even for fast sweeps on open roads. However, the rack and pinion steering gives excellent feel without transmitting road shocks and, at high speed in crosswind conditions, little movement of the wheel is needed to hold a straight course. Natural stability is good and camber and surface changes do not upset the chosen path at all.

The ride under both laden and unladen conditions is particularly good, progressive damping and the suspension's long travel keeping it away from the bump stops under all but the most demanding of conditions. There is no tendency to float over crests and the long wheelbase in relation to the overall length eliminates any pitching. Typically Italian, the ride is taut without any nervousness and it is at home on practically any surface.

Those familiar with front-drive behaviour on wet roads may be tempted to indulge in the practice of dabbing the brakes to cut down understeer. Do this with caution. Though there is a pressure limiting valve in the rear brake circuit, it operates on a load-sensing principle and thus, since there is a lack of anti-dive in the front suspension, enough forward weight transfer when the brakes are applied can lead to locked rear wheels. The consequent transfer into oversteer is very fast and needs catching very quickly.

Brakes

The HPE has the same dual-circuit arrangement as other models in the Beta range. In this system, one of each front caliper pistons is linked to the rear braking circuit while the other piston has a circuit of its own with the other front wheel. Thus, in both circuits, there is braking on the front wheels, so, in the event of either circuit failing, braking performance is relatively little affected.

Strong servo action gives light but not very progressive braking which is out of character with the HPE's sporting nature. A mere 10lb pedal pressure gives 0.35g braking and it is difficult to come to a halt at town speeds without standing the car on its nose. For the same reason, it is almost impossible to heel-and-toe well. Once through the initial retardation, if greater braking is required, the lack of progression shows; doubling the brake effort fails to double the retardation. Just as we found with the original Beta 1800 saloon, once past a certain pedal pressure (50lb), the increase in retardation is very slow and it was necessary to double this pressure to reach the best retardation with cold brakes — 0.92g. No further increase in retardation was possible because of locked front wheels.

The brake fade test reveals the same unhappy tale with very light initial pressure needing to be increased to hold the same rate of retardation. However, it must be said that once the brakes were thoroughly warmed through they showed no tendency to fade and in fact, when the response check was repeated with the brakes hot, a better optimum retardation of 0.95g was given by 90lb pedal pressure.

The handbrake, however, gave a good result, retardation of no less than 0.40g being given by the handbrake on its own. It also held the HPE facing up a 1-in-3 slope.

Noise

In 2-litre form, the Fiat/Lancia double ohc engine neither sounds nor feels as refined as it does in 1600 and 1800 forms. There is a high level of objectionable exhaust noise at all speeds and under acceleration, a harsh induction noise adds to the commotion. Only when cruising on part throttle at speed is the noise left behind. In respect of road and wind noise, the HPE is notably quiet, only the (standard) offside wing mirror being guilty of any discernible noisy turbulence.

Main instruments are rev counter (right) and speedometer (left) with total and trip mileage recorders. Smaller instruments are for fuel tank contents, oil pressure, sump level (with push button) and water and oil temperatures. Pull switches around clock are for heated rear window, hazard warning, rear wash/wipe, and cigarette lighter. Electric window lifts flank the ashtray. Steering column levers are for wipers, driving lamps, and indicators. Horns operate from steering wheel spokes. Note map bin on right-hand panel

Specification

ENGINE	Front, front drive
Cylinders	In-line, 4-cylinder transverse
Main bearings	5
Cooling	Water
Fan	Electric
Bore, mm (in.)	84 (3.31)
Stroke, mm (in.)	90 (3.54)
Capacity, c.c. (in³)	1,995 (122.5)
Valve gear	Dohc
Camshaft drive	Toothed belt
Compression ratio	8.9-to-1
Octane rating	97 RM
Carburettor	Single twin-choke Weber C34
Max power	119 bhp (DIN) at 5,500 rpm
Max torque	128lb. ft. at 2,800 rpm
TRANSMISSION	
Type	
Gear Ratio	mph/1000rpm
Top 0.925	19.6
4th 1.152	15.8
3rd 1.522	11.9
2nd 2.235	8.1
1st 3.500	5.2
Final drive gear	Helical spur
Ratio	3.785-to-1
SUSPENSION	
Front — location	MacPherson strut, lower wishbone
—spring dampers	Coil
—anti-roll bar	Yes
Rear — location	MacPherson strut, twin links
—spring dampers	Coil
—anti-roll bar	Yes
STEERING	
Type	Rack and pinion
Power assistance	No
Wheel diameter	15 in.
BRAKES	
Front	9.9in. dia. disc
Rear	9.9in. dia. disc
Servo	Yes, vacuum type
WHEELS	
Type	Aluminimum alloy
Rim width	5½in.
Tyres — make	Various
— type	Radial ply, tubed
— size	175/70 HR 14
EQUIPMENT	
Battery	12 volt 45 Ah
Alternator	42 amp
Headlamps	Halogen 110/220
Reversing lamp	Standard
Hazard warning	Standard
Electric fuses	13
Screen wipers	Two-speed plus intermittent
Screen washer	Electric
Interior heater	Water valve
Interior trim	Cloth seats, pvc headlining
Floor covering	Moquette carpet
Jack	Screw pillar
Jacking points	One each side beneath sill
Windscreen	Laminated
Underbody protection	Electrophoretic prior to painting, sealant after
MAINTENACE	
Fuel tank	11.4 Imp. gal (52 litres)
Cooling system	13 pints (inc. heater)
Engine sump	8 pints SAE 10W/50
Gearbox/final drive	4 pints SAE 90
Grease	1 point
Valve clearance	Inlet 0.016in (cold) Exhaust 0.018in (cold)
Contact breaker	0.015in. gap
Ignition timing	10 deg BTDC (static) 10 deg BTDC (stroboscopic at 800 rpm)
Spark plug — type	Champion N7Y, Bosch W200 T30
— gap	0.023in
Tyre pressures	F 24: R 24 psi (normal driving)
Max payload	990lb (450kg)

Maximum Speeds

Gear	mph	kph	rpm
Top (mean)	116	187	5,925
(best)	116	187	5,925
4th	101	162	6,400
3rd	76	123	6,400
2nd	52	83	6,400
1st	33	53	6,400

Acceleration

True mph	Time (sec)	Speedo mph
30	**3.4**	33
40	**5.5**	44
50	**7.5**	55
60	**10.6**	66
70	**14.0**	76
80	**19.4**	87
90	**26.0**	98
100	**37.8**	109

Standing ¼-mile:
17.7sec, 77mph
kilometre:
32.8sec, 97mph

mph	Top	4th	3rd	2nd
10-30	—	8.8	6.4	3.7
20-40	10.5	7.5	5.3	3.5
30-50	9.3	6.7	5.1	3.8
40-60	9.0	6.7	5.4	—
50-70	10.1	6.6	6.2	—
60-80	12.2	8.7	—	—
70-90	15.5	9.7	—	—
80-100	23.5	18.2	—	—

Consumption

Fuel
Overall mpg: 20.3
(13.9 litres/100km)
Calculated (DIN) mpg: 21.3
(13.3 litres/100km)

Constant speed:

mph	mpg
30	39
40	36
50	33
60	26
70	23
80	21
90*	18
100	16

Autocar formula
Hard driving, difficult conditions
18 mpg
Average driving, average conditions
22 mpg
Gentle driving, easy conditions
26 mpg
Grade of fuel: Premium, 4-star (97 RM)
Mileage recorder:
4 per cent overreading

Oil
Consumption (SAE 10W/50) negligible

Regular Service

Change	Interval (miles) 6,000	12,000	18,000
Engine oil	Yes	Yes	Yes
Oil filter	Yes	Yes	Yes
Gearbox oil	No	No	Yes
Spark plugs	Yes	Yes	Yes
Air cleaner	Yes	Yes	Yes
C/breaker	Yes	Yes	Yes
Total cost	**28.65**	**29.75**	**33.00**

(Assuming labour at £5.50/hour)

Brakes

Fade *(from 70 mph in neutral)*
Pedal load for 0.5g stops in lb

	start/end		start/end
1	15/12	6	12/25
2	12/18	7	12/25
3	12/18	8	15/25
4	12/20	9	15/25
5	12/20	10	15/25

Response *(from 30mph in neutral)*

Load	g	Distance
10lb	0.35	86.0 ft
30lb	0.77	39.0 ft
50lb	0.86	35.0 ft
70lb	0.90	33.4 ft
90lb	0.92	32.8 ft
Handbrake	0.40	75.0 ft

Max gradient 1-in-4

Clutch

Pedal: 35lb and 6in.

Test Conditions

Wind: 10-15 mph
Temperature: 8 deg C (46 deg F)
Barometer: 29.4 in. Hg
Humidity: 80 per cent
Surface: damp asphalt and concrete
Test distance: 820 miles

Figures taken at 11,250 miles by our own staff at the Motor Industry Research Association proving ground at Nuneaton.

Parts Cost

(including VAT)

Brake pads (2 wheels) — front	£10.34
— rear	£7.80
Silencers	£77.11
Tyre — each (typical advertised)	£33.48
Windscreen (laminated)	£52.59
Headlamp unit	£32.92
Front wing	£78.41
Rear bumper	£45.49

Warranty Period
6 months/unlimited mileage

Weight

Kerb, 21.4 cwt/2400lb/1088kg
(Distribution F/R, 59.8/40.2)
As tested, 23.9 cwt/2680lb/1215kg

Boot capacity: 10/42 cu ft.

Turning circles:
Between kerbs L, 35ft 8in; R, 37ft 8in.
Between walls L, 36ft 2in; R, 38ft 2in
Turns, lock to lock: 3.8

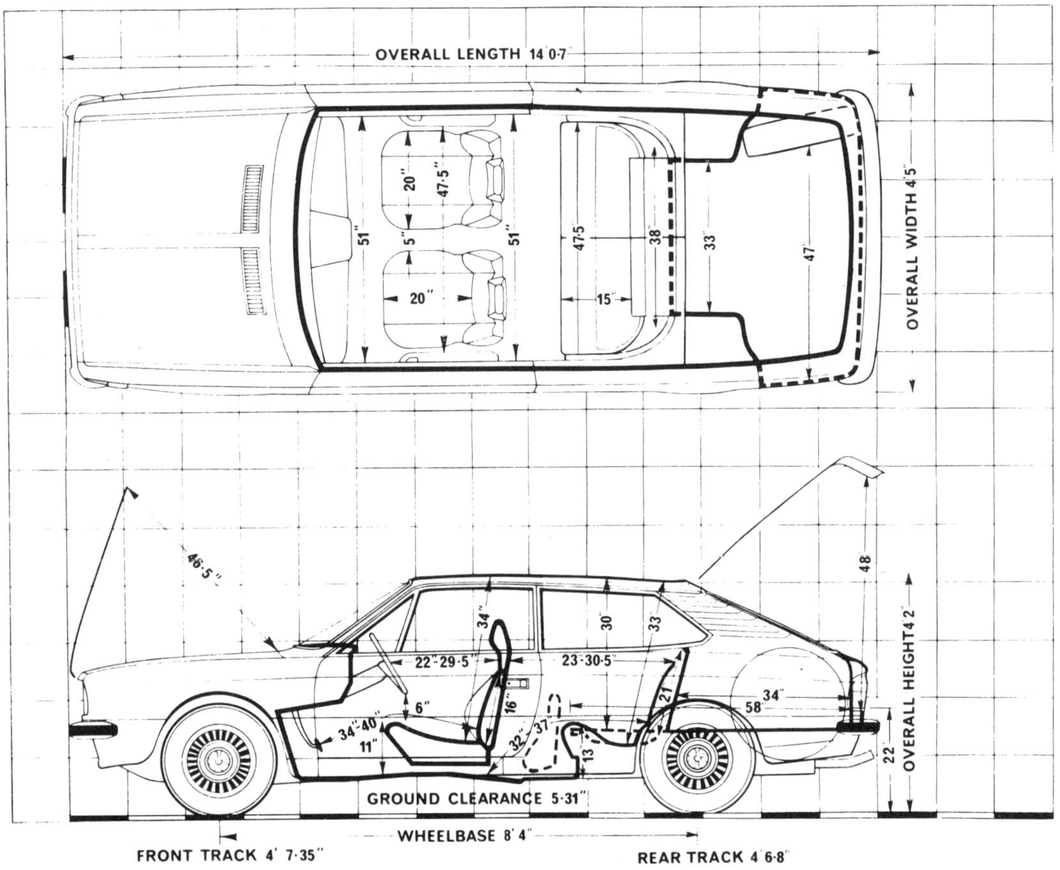

Test Scorecard

(Average of scoring by *Autocar* Road Test team)

Ratings: *6 Excellent*
5 Good
4 Above average
3 Below average
2 Poor
1 Bad

PERFORMANCE	3.33
STEERING AND HANDLING	4.33
BRAKES	3.60
COMFORT IN FRONT	4.50
COMFORT IN BACK	3.29
DRIVERS AIDS *(instruments, lights, wipers, visibility etc)*	4.13
CONTROLS	3.50
NOISE	3.50
STOWAGE	5.67
ROUTINE SERVICE *(under-bonnet access, dipstick etc)*	4.30
EASE OF DRIVING	3.36
OVERALL RATING	**4.01**

Comparisons

	Price (£)	Max mph	0-60 (sec)	Overall mpg	Capacity (c.c.)	Power (bhp)	Wheelbase (in.)	Length (in.)	Width (in.)	Kerb weight (cwt)	Fuel (gal)	Tyre size
Lancia Beta HPE 2000	**4,882**	**116**	**10.6**	**20.3**	**1,995**	**119**	**99.5**	**168.8**	**64.75**	**21.4**	**11.4**	**175/70-14**
Alfa Romeo Alfetta GTV	5,020	120	9.2	21.1	1,962	122	95.0	165.0	65.0	21.6	11.9	185/70-14
Ford Capri 3000 S	3,509	117	9.0	23.1	2,994	138	101.0	171.0	67.0	23.0	12.7	185/70-13
Reliant Scimitar GTE	5,480	118	9.4	21.1	2,994	135	103.8	174.5	67.3	24.8	20.0	185-14
BMW 320i	5,349	113	9.6	25.0	1,977	125	101.0	171.5	63.5	20.7	11.4	185/70-13

Air extraction from the cabin is rather lazy and the opening rear quarterlights are needed for good extraction, especially with four people in the car. A certain amount of wind noise results when these windows are opened.

Fittings and equipment

With the exception of the low production volume Beta Monte Carlo, the HPE 2000 is the most expensive version of the Beta range available in the UK. As befits such a position, the car has a wealth of standard equipment. A steel sunroof, electric window lifts, a rear window wiper and aluminium alloy wheels are all included in the price; so is the cost of inertia reel seat belts and of delivery. The general level of equipment and the finish of the body and trim are to a very high standard.

The interior treatment is a mixture of restrained traditionalism and modern plastic technology. The facia is a one-piece plastic moulding with a rather incongruous wood panel in its centre on which auxiliary switches are mounted. The carpets are a close-cropped velour material that is not yielding to the touch yet engenders a feeling of warmth inside the car.

Velour is also used for the wearing surfaces of the seats, pvc being used for the sides and backs. Both front seats are adjustable for rake and both have built-in head restraints adjustable for height. The several arrangements for the folding of the rear seats have already been covered, but one should add that the wearing surfaces are all properly protected against the kind of damage an estate car may suffer.

Covering the rear window is a slatted sun blind that does not hinder rear vision and may be removed if so desired. To cover luggage in the rear of the car, there is a roll-out blind which may be attached either to the backs of the rear seats, or to the top of the glass surround completely obscuring the window.

Lancia Beta HPE 2000

Above: Under the bonnet, the layout is rather cramped, with the radiator offset to the left. The wiper motor is in the heater plenum chamber
Right: Luggage can be concealed by this big roller blind which rises and unfurls with the tailgate
Below: The locking handle of the sunroof drops down to form a pull; when folded it lies flat on the headlining
Below right: The multi-spoked aluminium alloy wheels are standard equipment on the HPE

Living with the Lancia Beta HPE 2000

An automatic choke looks after mixture enrichment when starting from cold and the HPE starts readily enough. It is, however, very reluctant to run cleanly until well warmed through, and suffers hesitation and misfiring for the first two miles or so. Once warmed up, the engine pulls cleanly and copious warm air is available through the heater system, into which the outside pair of facia vents are also linked.

Though the seats look as though they will be comfortable, in fact few of our testers could find an entirely satisfactory seating position. The front seat backs lack support at shoulder level and at the base of the spine, and one is conscious of excess pressure from the exaggerated lumbar support. Only with the seat back raked well back does the cushion give reasonable support.

The seating position is typically Italian, with the pedals too close to the steering wheel for the comfort of tall people. The steering column may be adjusted for rake and this helps somewhat, but one is always conscious of driving with the knees well bent and splayed round the steering wheel rim. The layout of the pedals is good, with space to the left for the clutch foot, and a downward extension of the accelerator to enable it and the brake to be operated together.

The lightness of the brakes has already been referred to and this contrasts with the moderately heavy action of the clutch and accelerator. Clutch take-up is progressive and positive and, in this respect, the HPE is an easy car to drive on first acquaintance. Visibility is good forwards and to the sides, and only in merging conditions do the rear quarter panels obstruct.

Opening rear windows, a sunroof and four facia fresh air vents ensure that plenty of air can enter into the HPE in hot weather. The sunroof has a simple release lever which may be used to lock the sliding panel in any intermediate position between fully open and closed.

There is a pleasantly airy feel inside the HPE which results from the deep windscreen, and considerable tumblehome of the side windows. The windscreen wipers are arranged properly for right-hand drive and clear the screen well; there is the refinement of fast and slow operation for both intermittent and continuous wiping speeds. At night, the four headlamp system gives disappointing results on dipped beam but a good spread of light in the distance on main beam.

The HPE does not share the clever self-levelling arrangement for the headlamps found on saloon versions of the Beta. The headlamps are, however, easily adjustable by knurled knobs under the bonnet.

Generally, access to items requiring routine maintenance is good, but service items such as the oil filter are tucked low down in the bay. The HPE has a good arrangement for jacking in that only one point is required to lift the whole of one side, and the spare wheel may be removed from its position on one side of the luggage area without all the luggage being disturbed.

Where it fits in

Two versions of the HPE are available, the 2000 version as tested and a similar, lower specification model with the 1.6-litre version of the same engine. All the items of equipment that are found on the 2000 but not on the 1600 are available as options on the latter car.

Currently, there is a price difference of some £450 between the two cars and, considering the value of such items as the sliding roof and electric windows, the extra appears to be justified for the faster and more flexible 2000 version.

In conclusion

The specification of the HPE is impressive and the compromise in function that its design promises is very appealing. In one car exists a four-seater saloon, three-seater long load carrier or two-seater estate car, and such versatility has great attraction.

In terms of performance, the HPE has several strong rivals, and its lack of mechanical refinement is disappointing. So is the low-geared steering and a seating position which does not suit all drivers. On the credit side, there is the secure handling, excellent ride and general air of high quality, which bear out the prestige which the Lancia name has always enjoyed in Britain. □

MANUFACTURER:
Lancia S.p.A.
Casella Postale n.430
10100 Torino, Centro
Italy
UK CONCESSIONAIRES:
Lancia (England) Ltd
Ealing Road
Alperton
Middlesex HA0 1HE

PRICES	
Basic	£4,173.00
Special Car Tax	£347.75
VAT	£361.66
Total (in GB)	**£4,882.41**
Seat belts	No charge
Licence	£50.00
Delivery	No charge
Number plates	£10.80
Total on the Road (exc insurance)	**£4,943.21**
Insurance	Group 7
TOTAL AS TESTED ON THE ROAD	**£4,943.21**

Late but welcome

IT HAS TAKEN a long time to get here. Lancia showed the Monte Carlo, the mid-engined out-and-out sports car of the Beta range, at the Earls Court Motor Show in 1975. *Autocar*'s testers went out to Italy to assess the car that autumn and we reported that right-hand-drive cars would become available "early in 1976". Lancia dealers have been fending off enquiries for the car ever since. But from this week supplies of the Monte Carlo, in both Spider and Coupé form, start coming in to Lancia's British dealers.

The Coupé and Spider versions — they differ only in the roof centre panel which, in the Spider, is made of plastic material and can be rolled back into the roll bar — are identically priced at £5,927.

Whether the price is high or low depends on what you see as the Monte Carlo's rivals. It is certainly considerably more expensive than the Triumph TR7 which has comparable performance for only £3,335, but we tend to regard it as an alternative to rather more exotic offerings like the Lotus Esprit (£8,219) and the Porsche 924 (£6,999).

Technically the Monte Carlo is best regarded as a grown-up version of the much-praised Fiat X1/9. It started out as just that, with design and construction by Pininfarina, rather than Bertone as on the smaller car. As such it is a thoroughly modern sports car, mid-engined with adequate room for two adults and good luggage – if poor oddments – accommodation. There is a lot of the Ferrari Dino and its supercar cousins in its interior feel and style, but the Monte Carlo has avoided the exotic design compromises of flip-up headlamps and poor vision.

The Monte Carlo has changed little since our *Autotest* of a left-hand-drive model in 1975. Copies of the full test are available from our Readers' Service Department (see page 80 for details) but what follows here is a summary of the car's main features and our test team's findings. And to see how well the Monte Carlo shapes up against one of its more expensive rivals we have compared it *Wheel to Wheel* with the front-engined Porsche 924 starting on page 37.

Front to back

The basis of the Monte Carlo is a very strong floor pan braced torsionally by a complete roll hoop extending from the engine bulkhead to form the rear section of the roof panel. The engine accommodated in the rear of this tough body/chassis is the 2-litre version of the Fiat-derived, twin-camshaft engine used in all the top models of the Beta range, including the HPE which is the subject of this week's *Autotest* (page 20). In its Lancia application, the Monte Carlo is the only car in which this engine drives the rear wheels.

The front suspension uses MacPherson struts with a single bottom link and forward-facing tie rod, and there is an anti-roll bar. At the rear of the car, MacPherson struts are again used with a single, wide-based, bottom wishbone and anti-roll bar. As in its smaller brother, the Fiat X1/9, rear end steering is avoided by a radius arm that attaches to an extension at the rear of the hub carrier.

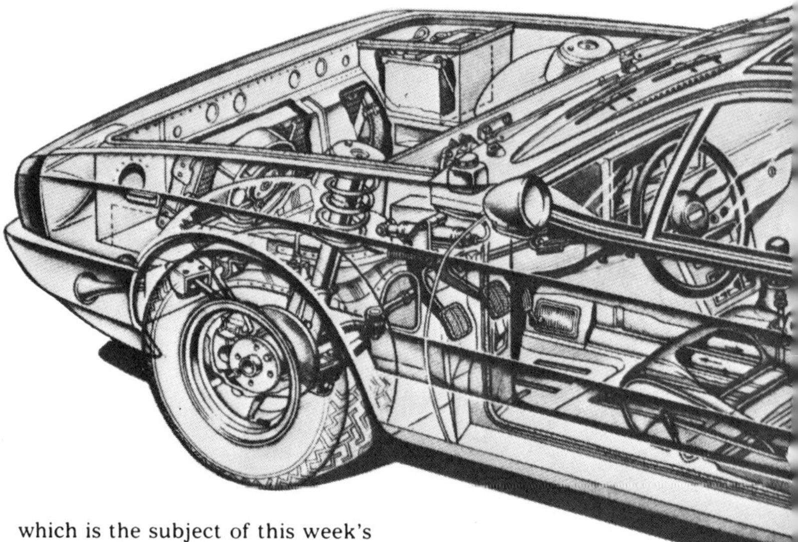

Cutaway drawing shows the all-round McPherson strut suspension, the front mounted radiator and battery, located there to improve the slightly tail-heavy balance, and the convolutions of the exhaust system. This lhd car also shows the ingenious folding fabric sunroof of the Spider version. All fixed glass panels are bonded straight to the bodywork so brightwork is kept to a minimum

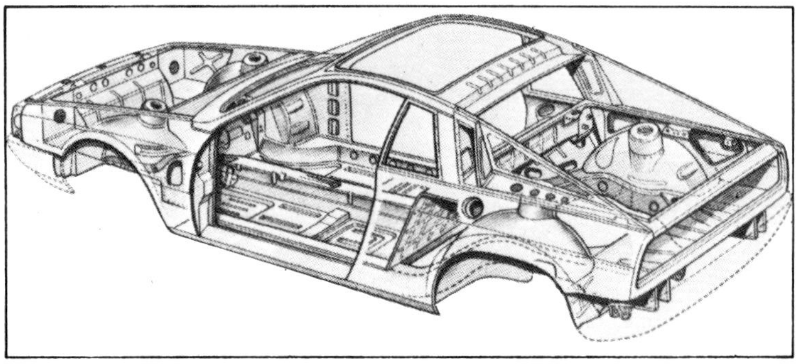

Basis of the Lancia Monte Carlo is its very strong floor braced by the hefty hoop at the engine bulkhead

Lancia's mid-engined Monte Carlo comes to Britain

By Andrew Shanks

Steering is rack and pinion, an easy installation being possible with no mechanical components at the front of the car. Disc brakes of equal size are used for all four wheels, and a vacuum servo helps to keep pedal pressures down.

The cockpit layout is straightforward and eminently sensible. Behind the two-spoke, padded steering wheel are the traditional Fiat (rather than Lancia) stalks which operate indicators, wipers/washers, and the lights though, again in Fiat style, there is a facia-mounted master switch for the lights.

The polyurethane foam-based seats have generous rearward adjustment, the driver's having an optional backrest angle adjuster. Clearly visible through the steering wheel are rather stylized instruments with horizontal scales for the minor gauges. Controls for the heater, the ashtray, cigarette lighter, and the standard clock are all contained in a central console whose base provides a surround for the gearlever and handbrake.

A kerb weight of 20.4 cwt, which went up to 23.4 cwt with two testers and their gear, meant that performance with 120 bhp (DIN) was rapid without being outstanding. Taking 6,200 rpm as the maker's recommended maximum revs, speeds in the intermediate gears work out at 30, 50, 74, and 94 mph, the only discernable gap being that between 2nd and 3rd gears, the former being a little low. Maximum speed of a mean 119 mph is reached at 6,100 rpm, indicating good overall gearing as maximum power is given at 6,000 rpm.

Acceleration through the gears saw 60 mph come up in 9.8 sec, 80 mph in 16.9 sec, and 100 mph in 30.5 sec while the standing kilometre took 30.2 sec. Acceleration in each gear did not reveal any noticeable "holes" in the torque curve. Overall fuel consumption on test was 25.2 mpg.

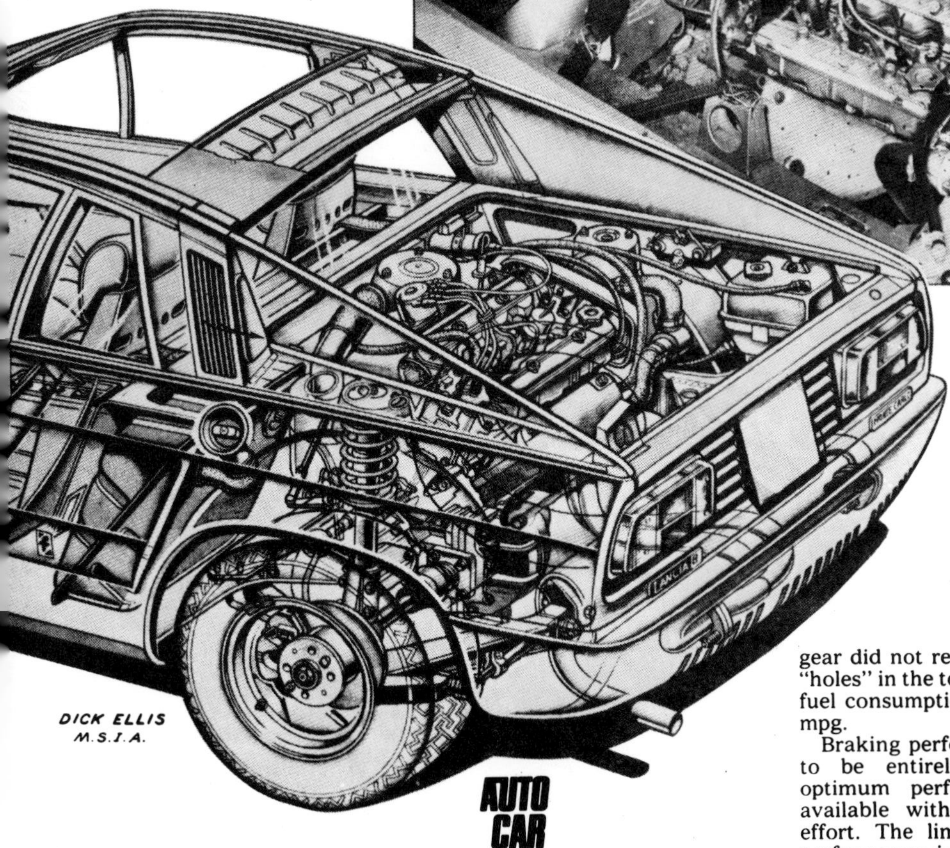

The 2-litre, Fiat-based engine sits at 20 deg back from the vertical, and virtually over the rear wheels. But the final drive is aft so it remains theoretically mid-engined, with a 41.3/58.7 weight distribution. Side hinging engine covers permit better than expected access to the engine bay

Braking performance was found to be entirely adequate, with optimum performance of 0.95g available with just 75 lb pedal effort. The limitation of braking performance is governed by front wheel locking, and this same characteristic needs to be guarded against when braking for downhill corners. Our test results revealed no tendency for the brakes to fade when worked very hard.

Though limited in space for very tall drivers, most testers found that the Monte Carlo was very comfortable for long journeys though the plastic material of the upholstery did not breathe well. The cars available in the UK have the option of cloth seat trim and we would certainly recommend owners to specify this.

Visibility came in for some criticism in our test and this has been considerably eased in the latest cars. When tested, the extensions to the rear quarter pillars were panelled in and gave rise to a lack of visibility in merging conditions. All cars for sale in the UK have glass in these panels which helps the rear three quarter view a great deal.

Our *Autotest* concluded that the Monte Carlo is, overall, the most practical answer to the problems of producing a mid-engined sports car, and this is an opinion which our two-car test reiterates. □

Specification

Engine: Four-cyl. 84 x 90 mm (3.31 x 3.54 in.), 1,995 c.c. (123 cu. in.); CR 8.9 to 1; D/d 2-choke Weber carbs, 120 bhp (DIN) at 6,000 rpm; max torque 121 lb. ft. at 3,500 rpm.

Transmission: mid mounted, transverse engine, rear-drive. Manual overall ratios 3.43, 4.27, 5.65, 8.29, 13.91. Top gear mph/1,000 rpm 19.5.

Suspension: ifs, MacPherson strut, lower arm, torque reaction strut, anti-roll bar. Rear, independent MacPherson strut, bottom wishbone, anti-roll bar. Steering, rack and pinion.

Brakes: Discs all round, servo, 8.9 in. front discs, 8.9 in. rear discs.

Dimensions: Wheelbase, 7 ft 7 in. (231 cm); front track 4 ft 8 in. (142 cm), rear track 4 ft 10 in. (147 cm). Overall length, 12 ft 6 in. (381 cm), width 6 ft 8 in. (203 cm), height 3 ft 11 in. (119 cm). Turning circle 36 ft 3 in. (11.1 m). Unladen weight 2,290 lb (1,040 kg). Max payload 460 lb (210 kg).

Others: Tyres 185/70HR 13 in.; 5½J rims. Fuel 13 gal (59 litres).

Comparisons	Price (£)	Max mph	0-60 (sec)	Overall mpg	Capacity (c.c.)	Power (bhp)	Wheelbase (in.)	Length (in.)	Width (in.)	Kerb weight (cwt)	Fuel (gal)	Tyre size
Lancia Monte Carlo	**5,927**	**119**	**9.8**	**25.2**	**1,995**	**120**	**91.0**	**150.0**	**67.0**	**20.4**	**13.0**	**185/70HR13**
Porsche 924	6,999	126	9.7	27.8	1,984	125	92.8	164.3	65.3	20.6	13.5	185/70HR14
Lotus Esprit	8,219	124	8.4	23.3	1,973	160	96.0	165.0	73.0	20.3	15.0	205/60, 205/70HR13
Alfa Romeo Alfetta GTV	5,020	118	8.9	23.5	1,962	122	94.5	165.8	65.5	21.7	12.0	185/70HR14
TVR Taimar*	5,383	121	7.7	21.4	2,994	142	90.0	158.0	64.0	20.0	12.0	185/70HR14
Triumph TR7	3,335	109	9.1	26.4	1,998	105	85.0	160.0	60.0	19.0	12.0	175/70HR13
Datsun 260Z 2+2	6,501	120	9.9	23.9	2,565	150	102.5	174.0	65.0	23.5	13.3	195/70HR14

**Figures for TVR 3000M*

The Lancia Beta range — from left the Berlina saloon, the HPE, the coupé, the Spider and the mid-engined Monte Carlo

Lancia Beta

ANYONE looking through the secondhand market for a medium-sized front-wheel-drive car now has a large, perhaps confusing, choice. Apart from British stalwarts like the Maxis and Allegros, he could buy VW Passats, Renault 12s, 14s and 16s, Chrysler Alpines, and several Japanese designs. The Italian contender is the Lancia Beta.

Betas have been on sale in Britain for nearly five years, and in that time a complex choice of engines, body shells and trim packs has been on offer. By any previous Lancia standards the Beta is a best-seller, and there is a good supply of most types on the secondhand market.

What is a Lancia Beta?

All Betas with the exception of the Monte Carlo share the same basic ''chassis'', with transversely-positioned twin overhead camshaft engines, five-speed manual gearboxes, front-wheel-drive, four-wheel independent suspension, and up-to-the-minute styling. There is a great deal of commonisation of mechanical parts from model to model, and most of the gearing differences are accounted for by final-drive changes.

The Monte Carlo is an oddity, and will not be considered in detail in this feature.

It uses the Beta's front-drive power pack to drive the *rear* wheels, and is mid-engined.

Depending on the model, and on the year in which it was built, a Beta may have an engine as small as 1,297 c.c. (82 bhp), or as large as 1,995 c.c. (119 bhp).

Beta bodies

The basic body is that of the four-door saloon, with a wedge-style nose, and a fast-back incorporating a separate boot. Built on conventional pressed-steel welded-construction principles, the saloons have a wheelbase of 8ft. 4in. On this basic ''building block'', other versions are built.

The Beta Coupé is sleek and stylish, still an almost-four-seater, with conventional two-door accommodation and a separate boot. It uses the basic Beta saloon floor-pan, but has a 7ft. 8.5in. wheelbase (7.5in. shorter than the saloon). Mechanically there are few differences.

The Beta Spider is mechanically like the Coupé, and is built on its short wheelbase and shares much of the same body panelling. It is unique in its passenger cabin which has a removable Targa-type roof panel, and a removable back window, while there is a reinforced roll hoop between the two. Although other panels may look the same, there are important differences. The bodies are partially completed by Zagato, the Italian coachbuilders.

The HPE is the most interesting amalgam. It is built on the saloon car's 8ft. 4in. wheelbase, and uses the Coupé's nose, bonnet and front wing panel, along with the windscreen and front door sheet metal. Above and behind the front doors, however, there is yet another bodyshell variant, which is in effect an estate car.

The Beta Monte Carlo Coupé/Spider has a completely different mid-engined pressed-steel structure, constructed by Pininfarina.

Beta power packs

All Betas, including the Monte Carlo, share the same basic power pack. Looking from the front of the car, on the left (i.e. on the right side of the car) is the transversely-mounted twin-cam four-cylinder engine, while on the right is the all-indirect two-shaft five-speed manual gearbox (where all forward gears have synchromesh). Behind the transmission is a spur-gear final drive, from which unequal-length drive shafts go to the driven wheels. On later models (effectively, on all Series 2 cars, and on Series 1 cars from chassis nos 14414 (1800 saloons) and 16334 (1600 saloons) there was a three-piece drive shaft system with equal length outer drive shafts.

All cars share the same internal gearbox ratios, in which fifth is geared up, with a ratio of 0.92-to-1. Axle ratios vary from 4.47-to-1 (1.3 saloons) to 3.78-to-1 (2.0 saloons and Coupés).

The engine situation is rather complex. Originally there were three choices — of 1,438 c.c. (80 x 71.5mm bore and stroke), 1,592 c.c. (80 x 79.2mm) and 1,756 c.c. (84 x 79.2mm). This range was too restrictive for customer choice, and in August 1975 (in Britain) a 1,297 c.c. engine (76 x 71.5mm) replaced the 1,438 c.c. unit.

Just prior to the announcement of the Series 2 range of cars (March 1976) the last batch of Series 1 cars were delivered with a 1,995 c.c. engine (84 x 90mm), which effectively replaced the 1,756 c.c. unit (although there was a short overlap).

Finally, at the time of introduction of the Series 2 cars, a different type of ''1600'' became available. The new engine was of 1,585 c.c. (84 x 71.5mm), compared with 1,592 c.c. (80 x 79.2mm), and was nothing more than a rationalisation of available cylinder bores and strokes.

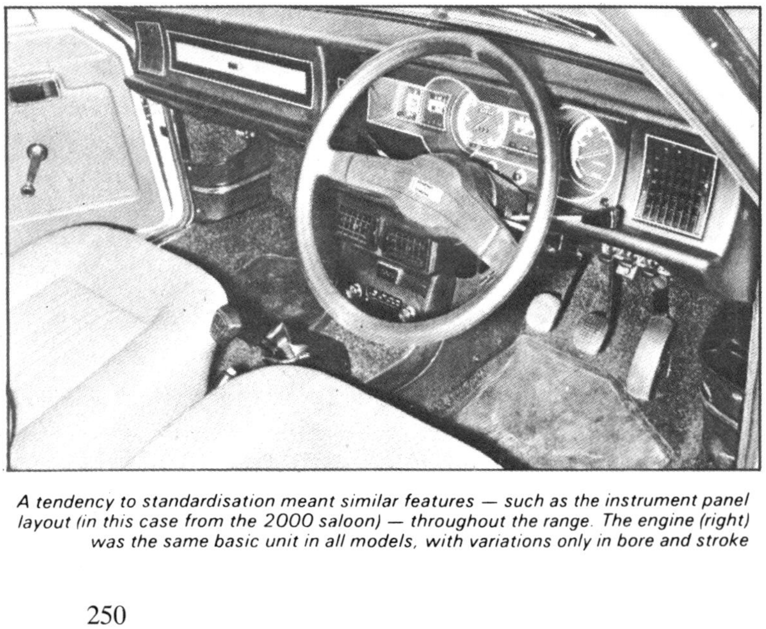

A tendency to standardisation meant similar features — such as the instrument panel layout (in this case from the 2000 saloon) — throughout the range. The engine (right) was the same basic unit in all models, with variations only in bore and stroke

The basic range was announced in November 1972, and went on sale in Britain in July 1973. Power outputs for the 1400, 1600 and 1800 engines were 90, 100 and 110 bhp, with axle ratios of 4.47, 4.21 and 4.07. All cars, basically, were the same, and shared the same basic equipment and fittings.

After nearly a year the 1800ES saloon was announced, which was mechanically like the normal 1800, but had extra trim, fittings and equipment.

In the meantime the Coupé/Spider models had been announced in Italy, and from September 1974 the Coupé 1600 (with 108 bhp and a 4.07 final drive ratio) came to Britain.

In the spring of 1976, there were two important developments. First, just before a more significant change to bodies and the model line-up, the 1,995 c.c. cars (Coupé/Spider/HPE) arrived.

March 1976 saw a very important change. Without looking noticeably different, all the cars became Series 2. Mechanically the main change was to the 1600 engine, which became the more oversquare (and therefore higher-revving) 1,585 c.c. unit. This, along with the standardisation of 1300 and 2000 units, produced power output alternatives of 80 bhp, 100 bhp and 119 bhp, and at this point the 1600 Coupé's power premium was withdrawn.

Styling/equipment changes on the special-bodied Series 2 cars were minimal. On the saloons, the restyling touches included a more vertical stance to the rear window (no longer in the same flush profiles as the tail's sheet metal itself), the screen was larger, and the side and rear quarter windows were all larger due to the door sheet metal being cropped lower than before. In the nose, the headlamps were now behind a single glass panel, while new grilles and modified wheels added to recognition points.

It is worth noting, however, that although power-assisted steering was made available on left-hand-drive cars, it has never been available on the British market (it is impossible to incorporate in right-hand-drive cars). It is also worth noting that although AP automatic transmission was announced, none have so far been delivered anywhere in the world.

Since then, the engine/bodyshell choice has steadily been widened. All three engines are now on offer for saloons and Coupés, with the 1600/2000 choice on Spiders and HPEs. All cars continue in successful full-scale production.

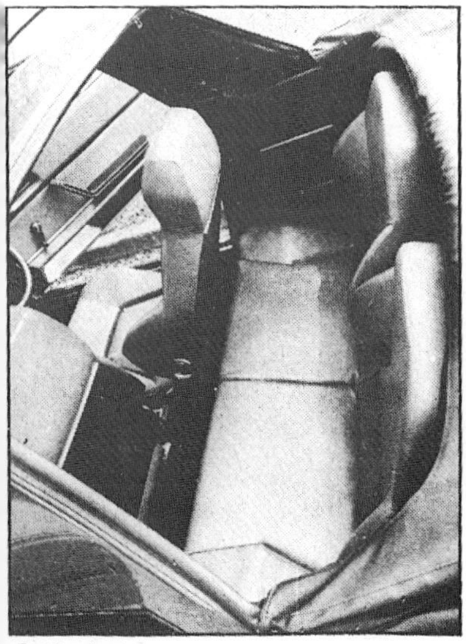

Spider had removable rear panel exposing back seats to the open air

What to look for

The first advice a customer needs is "What engine is available in which body?", and this is best dealt with by reference to our special chart. Basically, too, the largest choice matured with the introduction of Series 2 cars in spring 1976, though the last of the special-bodied Series 1 cars also benefitted.

It is best to consider engine/transmission combinations as a "black box" system — in other words to think that they are all the same, but produce different results. There is no space to go into detail here, but it is worth comparing — for instance — the effect of 1300 or 2000 packs in the same car, as tested in *Autocar* 25 September 1976. The 1300 runs at 16.5 mph/1,000 rpm in fifth, has a 96 mph top speed, and averages

Spares prices

	1300	1400	1600	1800	2000
Engine assembly — bare (exchange)	£486.00	£486.00	£486.00	£486.00	£486.00
Short engine — (exchange)	£199.80	£199.80	£199.80	£199.80	£199.80
Gearbox — (exchange)	£426.60	£426.60	£426.60	£426.60	£426.60
Clutch pressure plate — (new)	£23.28	£23.28	£23.28	£31.10	£31.10
Clutch driven plate — (new)	£20.61	£20.61	£20.61	£20.22	£20.22
Brake pads — front (set, new)	£7.45	£7.45	£7.45	£7.45	£7.45
Brake pads — rear (set, new)	£7.13	£7.13	£7.13	£7.13	£7.13
Suspension strut inserts — front (pair) (Saloons/HPEs only)	£54.17	£54.17	£54.17	£54.17	£54.17
Suspension strut inserts — front (pair) (Coupé/Spider only)	£45.36	N.A.	£45.36	N.A.	£45.36
Suspension strut inserts — rear (pair) (saloons/HPEs only)	£39.23	£39.23	£39.23	£39.23	£39.23
Suspension strut inserts — rear (pair) (Coupé/Spider only)	£50.80	N.A.	£50.80	N.A.	£50.80
Radiator assembly — (new)	£49.68	£49.68	£49.68	£49.68	£49.68
Alternator — (exchange)	£32.40	£32.40	£32.40	£32.40	£32.40
Starter motor — (exchange)	£37.80	£37.80	£37.80	£37.80	£37.80
Front wing panel — saloons only	£32.92	£32.92	£32.92	£32.92	£32.92
Front wing panel — other bodies	£38.49	N.A.	£38.49	N.A.	£38.49
Bumper — front (new) — saloons	£44.32	£44.32	£44.32	£44.32	£44.32
Bumper — front (new) — other bodies	£47.82	N.A.	£47.82	N.A.	£47.82
Bumper — rear (new) — saloons	£53.65	£53.65	£53.65	£53.65	£53.65
Bumper — rear (new) — other bodies	£52.49	N.A.	£52.49	N.A.	£52.49
Windscreen — laminated — saloons	£38.49	£38.49	£42.03	£44.26	£42.03
Windscreen — laminated — other bodies	£41.39	N.A.	£48.69	N.A.	£48.69
Exhaust system complete — saloon/HPE	£82.77	£75.00	£78.84	£75.00	£82.30
Exhaust system complete — other bodies	£75.21	N.A.	£75.60	N.A.	£79.06

All the above prices include VAT at 8 per cent.

Approximate selling prices

Price Range	Saloons					Coupés			HPEs	
	1300	1400	1600	1800	2000	1300	1600	2000	1600	2000
£1350-£1450		1974								
£1600-£1700			1974	1974						
£1700-£1800		1975								
£1800-£1900				1974*						
£1950-£2050	1976		1975	1975						
£2300-£2400			1976	1975*			1975			
£2450-£2550	1977			1976						
£2800-£2900			1977	1976*			1976			
£3100-£3200					1977	1977		1976		
£3350-£3500					1977*		1977		1976	
£3700-£3800										1976
£3900-£4050								1977	1977	
£4350-£4500										1977

Notes: Beta Spider is effectively a Beta Coupé with removable roof and back panels. It sells for between £400 and £700 more than the equivalent Coupé, depending on engine size and model year.

Monte Carlos are very rare — a 1977 model may sell for around £5,000.

*Denotes the ES version, which is mechanically identical but with a much higher level of trim and equipment.

There is no automatic transmission option. All Betas have a five-speed manual gearbox.

Performance Comparison

	Beta 1300 saloon	Beta 1800 saloon	Beta 2000 saloon	Beta 1600 Coupé	Beta 2000 HPE	Beta Monte Carlo
Road tested in *Autocar* of	25 Sep 1976	1 Nov 1973	25 Sep 1976	22 Feb 1975	23 Apr 1977	1 Nov 1975
Mean maximum speed (mph)	96	109	110	113	116	119
Acceleration (sec)						
0-30mph	3.8	3.7	3.3	3.3	3.4	3.0
0-40	6.6	5.6	5.1	5.4	5.5	5.0
0-50	9.8	7.8	7.0	7.4	7.5	7.0
0-60	13.6	10.7	10.1	10.4	10.6	9.8
0-70	19.6	14.3	13.3	14.0	14.0	12.8
0-80	28.2	19.5	17.5	18.6	19.4	16.9
0-90	—	27.2	23.4	25.2	26.0	21.8
0-100	—	41.6	33.8	37.6	37.8	30.5
0-110	—	—	—	—	—	41.0
Standing ¼-mile (sec)	19.6	17.9	17.5	17.3	17.7	16.0
Overall mpg	29.6	24.3	24.0	24.0	20.3	25.2
Typical mpg	33	26	26	26	22	28
Dimensions:						
Length Sln + HPE 14ft 1in., Coupé 13ft 1in., M.C. 12ft 6in.						
Width Sln +M.C. 5ft. 6.5in., Coupé + HPE 5ft. 5in.						
Height Sln 4ft 7in., Coupé + HPE 4ft. 2in., M.C. 3ft. 10.6in.						
Unladen weight (cwt)	21.1	21.6	21.8	19.9	21.4	20.4

29.6 mpg; the 2000 runs at 19.1 mph/1,000rpm, has a 110 mph top speed, and averages 24 mpg. Roughly speaking the 1600 performs mid-way between these extremes. It is up to the customer (in conjunction with a look at secondhand values) to decide which he needs. In fact the 1300 is surprisingly economical, as it is usually the case that an under-engined car is *less* economical, not more economical, than the larger-engined alternative.

The saloons, of course, are thoroughly practical four-door machines, but we should stress that in spite of their shapes they are *not* five-door hatchbacks. As a load-carrier, the HPE is a very smart and stylish hatchback, with all the dash of a Coupé and all the load-swallowing ability of an estate car. The Coupé is a perfectly usable four-seater if your passengers will accept more restricted rear leg room, while the Spider is a less practical but more versatile version of this.

Some cars, frankly, we do not consider very desirable — like the 1300/1400 versions of saloons and Coupés. Bigger-engined cars can do everything as well, if not better, are often as economical, are higher geared, and provide better all-round motoring. Similarly we feel that although a 1600 gives smooth motoring, there is no substitute for the lusty torque of a 2000 if you are the sort of driver who needs to go far and fast.

Some variants sold in Italy and elsewhere were not sold here, so do not expect to find an 1800 Coupé, or any Mk I HPEs (though the HPE was so listed for a few weeks).

The engines, although based on the Fiat 132 design, have been developed well away from the Fiat concept, and now have many different components. While things like gaskets and basic piston/connecting rod details are interchangeable, other major castings, and the camshafts themselves, are widely different. It is possible, a seasoned Lancia dealer, Patrick Batten of Millar Bros, Kenilworth, informs us, to tell a Fiat part from a special Lancia part by its basic part number.

Series 2 engines have automatic chokes, and different sizes have different clutches. The engines live long, and the twin-cam valve gear is easily adjusted. The clearance adjustment is specifically designed for easy change, and an enthusiastic owner could tackle it himself. A life of 80,000 miles is easily possible. Early units were oil leakers (from head/block joint), a malady now cured, and some are oil burners. The fabled Coupé low oil pressure malady is due more to faulty gauges than to the engine, and the quirk is only recognised at low rpm. The units are normally quite rattly even when in good health, but you should change the cogged belt drive to the camshafts at 30,000-mile intervals, and for efficient operation the valve clearances must be right. 2000s seem to be susceptible to incorrect oil levels — too much and they tend to suck it up and regurgitate the stuff through the carburettor system. An oil pressure relief valve problem is known, caused by dirt sticking under the valve. Rectification is cheaper than the symptoms would suggest, for only a good clean is usually needed. "Cold morning knock" and oil pump squealing are both prevalent, but neither is harmful. Most Series 2 engines appear to have carburettor flat spots, which are due to the ECE anti-emission tuning.

Regarding transmissions, a clutch change is a 4½-5-hour job, which is less than might be feared after looking into the engine bay. Gearboxes tend to be notchy especially 1st and 2nd engagement, and very especially when cold. It is 2nd gear syncromesh which disappears first — a good sign of general wear. Early cars were somewhat rattly in this region — a problem which appears to have been cleared up with improved quality in production.

Drive shafts are bomb-proof provided that the rubber "boots" covering universal joints are in good order. It is worth noting that what Lancia dealers call "three-piece" drive shafts are now fitted, which effectively means that the longer drive shaft is now split with a mid-length steady bearing, so that the articulation of both shafts at the wheel end is optimized. These latter shafts are much better to get, and keep, in balance.

In regard to suspension, wheel bearings seem to wear rapidly (they begin to rumble), and this may be a result of bad initial lubrication. Front ball joints last for 30-40,000 miles, but tyres may last even longer than this. Pads are good for more than 25,000 miles, but the sliding calipers must be kept well-lubricated (they may stick otherwise) and the height-sensitive valve to the rear brake lines must be in correct setting and adjustment.

Look for the most trouble in minor electrical problems, and (in the case of the HPE) for major trouble with the electrical winding windows. This has been so bad that the standard fitting has now been deleted to an option, and most cars are no longer so equipped. There appears to be a great deal of poor quality in the electrical fittings in general (earth return contacts regularly give trouble) and many cars, for instance, seem to have an unhealthy appetite for expensive halogen headlamp bulbs. There have been starter motor problems, but the alternators appear to have a good record.

That was the bad news. The good news is that there are about 120 Lancia dealers who are well-equipped with spares. The parts availability situation is very good (the models are still in full production, of course), and the VOR system (in which the British Rail Red Star service plays a part) works well. Lancia like dealer mechanics to have completed special Beta service courses, and most have. Since May 1976 the cars have carried a 12-month-plus-unlimited mileage guarantee scheme, which is transferable to the second owner. □

Milestones and chassis identification

		Series	Chassis No.
Saloons:			
July 1973. Beta range introduced to Britain (announced in Italy in November 1972), with f.w.d. and fastback styling. Available with three engine sizes — 1,438 c.c., 1,592 c.c., 1,756 c.c. Opening series as follows	Beta 1400	828AB2	—
	Beta 1600	828ABO	—
	Beta 1800	828AB1	—
May 1974. 1800ES version introduced, mechanically as 1800, but with extra trim fittings, and equipment. Series		828AB1	
August 1975. Beta 1400 discontinued, replaced by Beta 1300, with 1,297 c.c. engine. New series	Beta 1300	828BB3	—
March 1976. Original series cars discontinued. Replaced, effectively from May 1976, by revised SII cars, in 1,297, 1,585, 1,995 c.c. guise. Changes limited to revised engine line-up, more window glass, revised trim and decoration. From	Beta 1300	828CB3	2463
	Beta 1600	828CBO	2757
	Beta 2000	828CB1	1667
	Beta 2000ES	828CB1	3598
Final 1800/1800ES number			21706
Coupé/Spider/HPE models:			
September 1974. Coupé 1600 introduced to GB (announced in Italy March 1974). As saloon, but with short wheelbase and special two-door body. New series	1600	828ACO	—
July 1975. Spider model introduced, mechanically as for Coupé, with different top and open-air arrangements	1600	828ASO	—
February 1976. 2000 versions first imported, along with new HPE 2000 model. HPE on normal wheelbase, with Coupé nose, but three-door shell		828AF1	—
March/April 1976. All Coupés, spiders and HPEs become SII, and 1600 version of HPE also available. 1600 engine now 1,585 c.c. instead of 1,592 c.c. Series	Coupé 1600	828BCO	1104
	Coupé 2000	828BC1	2341
	Spider 1600	828BSO	1004
	Spider 2000	828BS1	1145
	HPE 1600	828BFO	1358
	HPE 2000	828BF1	2070
May 1977. Introduction of Beta 1300 Coupé, structurally as other Coupés, but with 1300 saloon-type engine and transmission. Opening chassis number	Coupé 1300	828BC3	3889
Monte Carlo:			
April 1977. Mid-engine Monte Carlo Coupé introduced to Britain (announced October 1975 in Italy). Available only with 2000 engine. From	Monte Carlo	137ASO	2166

Note: In chassis series, 828 is the generic type, first letter is type (A = first series, B = second series), second letter is body type (B = saloon, C = Coupé, S = Spider, F = estate type), final number represents engine (0 = 1600 c.c., 1 = 2000 c.c., 2 = 1400 c.c., 3 = 1300 c.c.).

Model availability

Year	Saloons					Coupé/Spider			HPE		Monte Carlo
	1300	1400	1600	1800	2000	1300	1600	2000	1600	2000	2000
1973		X	X	X							
1974		X	X	X			X				
1975	X	X	X	X			X				
1976	X		X	X	X		X	X	X	X	
1977	X		X		X	X	X	X	X	X	X
1978	X		X		X	X	X	X	X	X	X

***Note:** 1800 ES saloon, mechanically as 1800, available in 1974/1975/1976. 2000 ES Saloon, mechanically as 2000, available in 1976/1977/1978.*

***Note:** All except the Monte Carlo are based on the same f.w.d. chassis. Saloons and HPEs have a common 8ft 3.5in. wheelbase, Coupés ansd Spiders a shortened 7ft 8.5in. wheelbase. The Monte Carlo is unique, with the Beta power pack mid-mounted behind the seats. Coupé, Spider and HPE share the same nose, scuttle, screen and front-door skins.*

IT IS RARE indeed these days that an all-new car arrives in the market place; the sheer cost of development usually meaning that "new" be a euphamism for some degree of re-designing of an existing model, ranging from comprehensive to the simply cosmetic.

Not so the Lancia Gamma. The Fiat group have lacked a flagship since the ending of the 130. With the concentration of the quality market on to the Lancia part of the group, it was a significat ommission and one very clearly needing to be remedied with a substantial design capable of challenging in this growing market. So the Lancia Gamma is all new,

Lancia Gamma Berlina

New flagship for the whole Lancia-Fiat group
Good performance but poor economy from the unusual "boxer" engine
First class handling and ride allied to excellent power steering
Very roomy interior, but poor ventilation and untidy instruments
An enjoyable car to drive, but spoiled by a lack of the refinement expected at its high price

sharing only concepts with the smaller Beta — front-wheel-drive, MacPherson strut suspension at both ends and a two-box body style. It has been a long time coming to this country; we first described it as a new car in Italy back in *Autocar* 28 June 1976, and at a price of £7,136 the saloon is pitched to compete at the upper end of the executive saloon bracket, with similar new cars like the Rover 3500, Citroen CX Pallas and Peugeot 604 Ti, by whose high standards it must be judged.

The Berlina saloon has distinctive two-box styling, owing slight family resemblance to the Beta, with an excellent drag coefficient of 0.37 — better than the Rover's 0.39 and approaching the CX's 0.34 best for a production saloon. It is a non-hatchback running on a 105-inch wheelbase. The major point of interest centres around the choice of power unit, a flat-four cylinder unit of 2,484 c.c., water-cooled and with overhead camshafts driven by toothed belt. The largest four-cylinder engine in mass production, it is also one of the lightest; being of such compact design and all-alloy, it weighs just 298 lb. Peak power of 140 bhp is developed at 5,400 rpm with maximum torque of 153 lb. ft. at 3,000 rpm.

The MacPherson strut suspension has a separate anti-roll bar at the front and an integral bar as part of the wishbone at the rear. ZF progressive power assistance is fitted as standard to the rack and pinion steering.

The two box, Pininfarina body has an extremely low drag coefficient of ,u low waistline allows good visibility, except in the rear three quarters, where the solid panels impair the view. Slats cover a small window in the boot lid which improves rearward visibility

Below: Twin halogen headlamps give a good spread of light, especially on main beam. The stainless steel bumper wraps around and has a thick rubber insert. The driver's door mirror adjusts by remote control

Performance and economy

Lancia claim a maximum speed of 121 mph for the Gamma and our mean best around the banked MIRA circuit of 118 mph suggests that their claim would be accurate enough over a straight two-way stretch, tyre scrub around the banking accounting for the difference. This maximum speed obtained by us corresponds to 5,620 rpm in fifth gear — which looks very close to the 6,200 rpm red line on the slightly optimistic rev counter. It is an excellent maximum, making the car one of the quickest in its class, and says a good deal for the aerodynamic qualities of the body shape as well as the performance of the engine. It is, however, obtained at the expense of some under-gearing, peak power of course being at 5,400 rpm, and in

A crowded under-bonnet despite the compact dimensions of the flat-four engine. A lot of space is occupied by the air cleaner, carburettor and inlet tracts. But reservoirs for oil, water and battery are accessible, and the plugs can all be reached. Oil level is checked by a facia gauge

view of our experience with economy (of which more later) a rather high top gear that offers more of an overdrive ratio could well be justified and would probably have little effect on outright performance. The present fifth gear — 0.921 to 1 — gives just 21 mph per 1,000 revs, while the well-spaced intermediate ratios provide slightly low maxima of 106, 82, 57 and 35 mph at 6,200 rpm.

Hard though Lancia may have tried, there is no disguising the fact that the Gamma's engine is a flat four and not a six cylinder unit. The distinctive uneven beat of a flat four at low revs that Beetle owners know so well, is allied to a reverberation of the valve gear noise off parked vehicles and walls in narrow roads that can be heard surprisingly loudly with a window open. At higher revs, though, the engine does become nicely smooth and that other flat-four characteristic of a hesitant mid-range throttle response can only be found if really searched for.

Starting from cold holds some perils. Out test car fired up promptly enough once its automatic choke had been primed with a throttle dab, but rattled worryingly at 2,000 rpm for a second or two until the oil ways filled; each fire-up also being accompanied by a cloud of smoke as oil was burned off that had seeped through the valve guides while the engine was stationary. Eventually we took to turning the engine over without the choke to let the pump prime itself at tickover speed.

Outright acceleration is good, though a modest engine capacity and sizeable body weight (27 cwt) are limiting factors. In our standing start acceleration runs, so too was violent scuttle shake, so severe in our usual wheel-spinning starts that we aborted the first take-off for fear of throwing the trembling facia off its mountings.

Slightly less revs (3,500) produced a more tolerable, though still very unpleasant vibration period on starts which gave sufficient wheelspin and left the facia and windscreen in place. A best time to 30 mph of 3.5 sec reflects the starting problem, while the 10.1 sec time to 60 mph includes two gearchanges. It reaches 100 mph in just a fraction over half a minute (30.7 sec) and even in fifth there is only a gradual fall off in power as it pulls steadily on to 110 in 45.1 sec.

Straight line acceleration is on a par with its rivals, but the Gamma feels a lively, crisp car to drive as the lowish intermediate ratios and a flat torque curve give it a lot of flexibility and good pulling power in the gears. For instance acceleration in fourth gear, peaking at 106 mph, gives near-equal 8 sec acceleration times over each 20 mph increment all the way from 30 to 80 mph. This is such a useful ratio, with its balance of flexibility and maximum speed, that it makes an excellent top gear for give-and-take roads and lends a bit more weight to the argument for an overdrive geared fifth. The gearshift itself can only be described as average, for one now expects near perfect changes from the latest generation front-drive cars, especially one with an in-line engine and gearbox. It baulks considerably when cold, often refusing to come out of first and then being equally stubborn about going into second.

The change has a rather dead, linkage-y feel to it. It is accurate, though never especially quick. The lowest four gears are in the usual H pattern, fifth being out on a dog-leg with reverse opposite. Unusually a large chrome ball at the base of the lever is left unshrouded by a gaiter — a fashion resurrected from the pre-war Aprilia, but of dubious value except to those who like the look or feel of grease. The gear lever knob also caused comment in the office; it matches the elaborate styling of the rest of the car, but seems of little ergonomic value, the prominent edges making it uncomfortable to use.

We have already mentioned the question of economy, for this is certainly one of the Gamma's weak points. Our overall consumption figure during the 1,000 miles of testing was 19.1 mpg, a figure which prompts our comments on the gearing. It is below average both for the capacity of car and compared with its rivals. Our intermediate fill-ups showed little deviation from the overall average — ranging from 20.8 mpg down to 16.9 mpg and suggest that there is not a lot of potential economy there to be gained by alternative driving styles.

The steady speed consumption figures in fifth gear are quite modest — 29.3 mpg at a steady 70 mph for example with a progressive deterioration to 18.5 mpg at 100 mph. This suggests carburettor settings chosen to provide the lean mixtures for good steady speed economy, something becoming increasingly commonplace since the inception of "official" fuel consumption figures, at the expense of overall economy, perhaps lost through the need to use large throttle openings in accelerating.

Fuel tank capacity is 13 gallons, a dashboard warning light winking with increasing rapidity and then remaining on as the last two gallons are used. The fuel filler is concealed behind a locking flap, neatly disguised into the bodywork, and filling offers no problems.

Handling and brakes

The light engine of the Gamma is reflected in a front/rear weight distribution of 58.9/41.1 per cent — not perhaps as even a front-to-rear balance as one might have expected with such a light unit, but nonetheless better balanced than front-drive rivals such as the Renault 30TS, which has 63 per cent of its weight over its front wheels.

The good front/rear balance, low engine and all-independent suspension contrive to produce a car that has really excellent roadholding and handling. There is little understeer, even on slow corners, and fast curves are taken in a virtually neutral stance. Body roll is only modest, even at

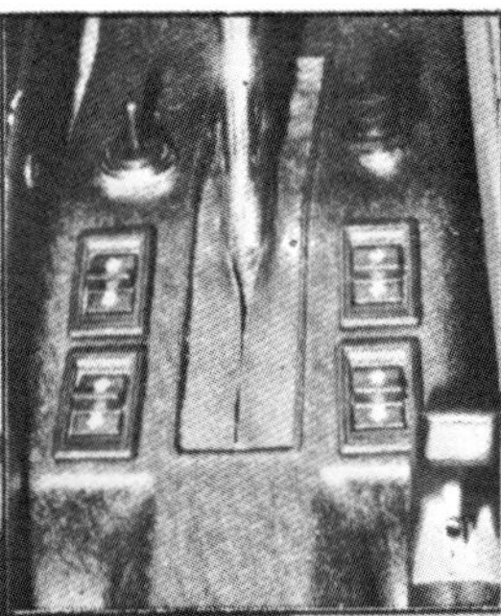

Below left: Front seats, trimmed in optional leather, are large and comfortable. They have a wide range of adjustment, including cushion height/angle on the driver's seat, by the turn-wheel visible at the seat front

Top centre: Between the front seats are switches for the electric windows — there is no over-ride to prevent rear passengers working their windows from their own door mounted switches. To the left of the handbrake is the joy-stick for the remote door mirror; to the right the speaker balance control

Below centre: No child locks are apparent in the rear doors. A red warning light glows in the door edge when the door is opened

Below: In the rear there is very generous legroom and a bench seat wide enough for three adults. Blinds can be pulled up from behind the headrests to relieve glare from the sun

severe cornering attitudes. Releasing the throttle in mid-bend causes only slight tightening of the car's line.

Ultimate cornering grip is high, and the excellent roadholding and balance make the car more enjoyable than many of similar size on cross-country roads. A large part of this enjoyment is contributed by the very excellent ZF power steering. Lancia have gone the correct route with power steering and used it as a means to allow higher gearing — just three turns from lock to lock — which means that the car gives smart response to the wheel. The assistance allows light steering at low speeds which firms up considerably with steering effort and speed to the point where there is sufficient weight and feel for it to be mistaken for a good unassisted system. There is virtually no torque reaction through the wheel, except when making smart getaways with lock applied, and this, along with the neutral handling, could well make the casual driver forget he was in a front-drive car.

The brakes are large, 10in. discs all round, those at the front being ventilated. Such a powerful system naturally showed little or no sign of fade in our 10-stop fade test, though there was some squealing at the half way point and a considerable smell of hot linings towards the end of the testing.

Interestingly, they had a different response to the brakes of the car we tried at the British launch of the Gamma. Those were initially over-sensitive and then required a heavy pressure to stop from high speed, with the rears locking too early. The test car's showed a more even pattern of response, from 20lb pedal pressure which gave 0.35 g retardation to 40lb and 0.77 g and 60lb and 0.85 g. But this low retardation was the best we could achieve before the front brakes locked and the car slid. Even much harder pedal pressures produced only the same result. The system has a load-sensitive brake balance adjusting valve, so we must conclude that there is some variance in the settings.

The handbrake gives the typically moderate response that one has come to expect from disc-braked systems; a 0.28 g stop and the ability just to hold the car on the 1-in-3 slope — from which position it re-started without too much trouble.

Comfort and convenience

The scuttle shake which made itself so violently known during our acceleration tests is a perpetually irritating feature that mars the Gamma's comfort. Some degree of facia rattle is present virtually the whole time and on uneven surfaces or concrete sectioned roads there is considerable vibration and rattling which can be seen and heard in the scuttle and also felt through the steering wheel — suggesting some problem in the mounting of the front sub-frame. Frankly, it is the sort of problem one would have expected to see ironed out between the 1976 launch of the Gamma and now, for it is a considerable spoiling feature. It ruins an otherwise good ride, the Gamma travelling very comfortably at speed with a compliant ride that soaks up bumps without being unduly soggy. At town speeds the ride might be considered slightly knobbly, though this is a reasonable penalty to pay for the taut handling and good high-speed ride.

There is a good deal of engine noise during acceleration — more than one would consider reasonable in a car of this class — but once cruising at motorway speeds the engine becomes quite subdued. Some wind noise can be heard around the pillars from 80mph onwards, but otherwise the Gamma is a quiet cruiser.

Inside the car there is a considerable amount of space for passengers, even by front-wheel-drive saloon standards. Seats in our test car were finished in leather, an optional extra over the standard velour, the rather gaudy material that seems so fashionable these days. They gave an air of quality to the interior that we had felt lacking in earlier, standard trimmed examples tried.

Front seats are large and wide, with well built up sides to cushion and backs, though a few passengers commented on a certain lack of support at the base of the spine over long runs. The driver's seat adjusts in every plane, by a turnwheel backrest angle adjustment and cushion height adjuster which can separately alter the height of front or back of the cushion, and thus its angle, though painfully slowly. The steering column adjusts for angle, though it obscures the minor instruments if lowered more than a small amount, but not telescopically and so there is still a vestige of the "Italian" driving position; stretched arms and cramped legs. A pity, since potential legroom in the front is very good, as is headroom. The rear is spacious by any standards. There is room for three passengers who can stretch their legs out in comfort however far back the front seats have been moved and who will not be short of headroom. If only two are carried, a large central armrest can be folded down between them.

Instrumentation on the dashboard is messy and hard to read. The speedometer and rev counter, sited centrally, both have a confusing amount of calibration while the minor dials around them have virtually none — fuel contents and water temperature are to the left, oil pressure and level to the right. The switches in the centre of the facia are not lit. The vacuum operated heater pushbuttons — for heat, defrost and fresh air can be seen below the (non-standard) cassette player along with the vacuum temperature control slider. They must be set with the engine running. Below the clock is a switch to turn out its illumination as this reflects in the windscreen

Specification

ENGINE	Front; front drive
Cylinders	4, horizontally opposed
Main bearings	3
Cooling	Water
Fan	Electric
Bore, mm (in.)	102 (4.02)
Stroke, mm (in.)	76 (2.99)
Capacity, cc (in.³)	2,484 (151.5)
Valve gear	Ohc
Camshaft drive	Toothed belt
Compression ratio	9.0-to-1
Octane rating	98 RM
Carburettor	Weber 38 ABLD/100 twin choke
Max power	140 bhp (DIN) at 5,400 rpm
Max torque	153 lb ft at 3,000 rpm

TRANSMISSION

Type: Five speed manual all synchromesh

Gear	Ratio	mph/1,000 rpm
Top	0.921	20.9
4th	1.129	17.1
3rd	1.458	13.2
2nd	2.105	9.2
1st	3.462	5.6
Final drive gear		Hypoid bevel
Ratio		3.7-to-1

SUSPENSION	
Front— location	MacPherson struts, lower wishbones
springs	Coil
dampers	Telescopic
anti-roll bar	Yes
Rear— location	MacPherson struts, parallel lower links
springs	Coil
dampers	Telescopic
anti-roll bar	Yes
STEERING	
Type	Rack and pinion
Power assistance	ZF progressive
Wheel diameter	15 in.
BRAKES	
Front	10 in. dia. ventilated disc
Rear	10 in. dia. disc
servo	Yes
WHEELS	
Type	Alloy
Rim width	6½ in.
Tyres—make	Michelin
—type	XAS
—size	185/70HR14
EQUIPMENT	
Battery	12 volt 55 Ah
Alternator	65 amp
Headlamps	110/220 watt total
Reversing lamp	Standard
Hazard warning	Standard
Electric fuses	19
Screen wipers	2-speed plus intermittent
Screen washer	Electric
Interior heater	Air blending
Interior trim	Velour seats, cloth headlining
Floor covering	Carpet
Jack	Scissor type
Jacking points	2 each side
Windscreen	Laminated
Underbody protection	Bitumastic and wax protection
MAINTENANCE	
Fuel tank	13 Imp. galls (59 litres)
Cooling system	16 pints (inc. heater)
Engine sump	11 pints SAE 10W/50
Gearbox and final drive	5.8 pints GX90
Grease	No points
Valve clearance	Inlet 0.012 in. (cold) Exhaust 0.014 in. (cold)
Contact breaker	Electronic ignition
Ignition timing	29 deg BTDC (stroboscopic at 3,000 rpm)
Spark plug—type	Champion N7Y
gap	0.024 in.
Tyre pressures	F 25; R 26 psi (normal driving)
Max payload	992 lb (450 kg)

Maximum Speeds

Gear	mph	kph	rpm
Top (mean)	118	190	5,645
(best)	120	193	5,742
4th	106	171	6,200
3rd	82	132	6,200
2nd	57	92	6,200
1st	35	56	6,200

Acceleration

True mph	Time (secs)	Speedo mph
30	**3.5**	30
40	**5.2**	41
50	**7.3**	50
60	**10.1**	61
70	**13.3**	73
80	**17.5**	82
90	**23.0**	93
100	**30.7**	103
110	**45.1**	114

Standing ¼-mile: **17.5 sec,** 80 mph
kilometre: **32.3 sec,** 102 mph

mph	Top	4th	3rd	2nd
10-30	—	11.1	7.1	4.8
20-40	13.2	9.5	6.2	3.8
30-50	10.6	7.9	5.9	3.9
40-60	10.6	7.6	5.9	—
50-70	10.8	8.1	6.4	—
60-80	11.5	8.8	—	—
70-90	13.0	10.3	—	—
80-100	16.3	13.4	—	—

Consumption

Fuel
Overall mpg: 19.1
(14.8 litres/100km)
Calculated (DIN) mpg: 26.6
(10.6 litres/100km)

Constant speed:

mph	mpg
30	32.1
40	36.0
50	35.0
60	31.5
70	29.3
80	25.8
90	21.8
100	18.5

Autocar formula
Hard driving, difficult conditions
17.2 mpg
Average driving, average conditions
21.0 mpg
Gentle driving, easy conditions
24.8 mpg

Grade of fuel: Premium, 4-star (98 RM)
Mileage recorder: 3 per cent over reading

Official fuel consumption figures
(ECE laboratory test conditions; not necessarily related to Autocar figures):
Urban cycle: 17.1 mpg
Steady 56 mph: 35.3 mpg
Steady 75 mph: 29.1 mpg

Oil
Consumption (SAE 10W/50)
1,000 miles/pint

Brakes

Fade *(from 88 mph in neutral)*
Pedal load for 0.5g stops in lb

	start/end		start/end
1	25-25	6	30-40
2	25-30	7	30-40
3	27-32	8	32-40
4	27-32	9	32-40
5	27-35	10	32-40

Response *(from 30 mph in neutral)*

Load	g	Distance
20lb	0.35	86ft
30lb	0.55	54.7ft
40lb	0.77	39.1ft
50lb	0.80	37.6ft
60lb	0.85	35.4ft
Handbrake	0.28	107.5ft

Max. gradient: 1 in 3

Clutch

Pedal 40lb and 6 in.

Test Conditions

Wind: 10-12 mph
Temperature: 27 deg C (80 deg F)
Barometer: 29.8 in. Hg
Humidity: 40 per cent
Surface: dry asphalt and concrete
Test distance: 1,000 miles

Figures taken at 2,350 miles by our own staff at the Motor Industry Research Association proving ground at Nuneaton.

Regular Service

Change	Interval 6,000	12,000	18,000
Engine oil	Yes	Yes	Yes
Oil filter	Yes	Yes	Yes
Gearbox oil	—	—	Yes
Spark plugs	Yes	Yes	Yes
Air cleaner	Yes	Yes	Yes
Total cost	**£49.96**	**£59.09**	**£53.87**

(Assuming labour at £6.50/hour)

Parts Cost

(including VAT)

Brake pads (2 wheels)—front	£20.30
Brake pads (2 wheels)—rear	£14.80
Exhaust system	£227.99
Tyre—each (typical advertised)	£38.92
Windscreen	£104.47
Headlamp unit	£42.24
Front wing	£37.47
Rear bumper	£100.53

Warranty Period
12 months/unlimited mileage

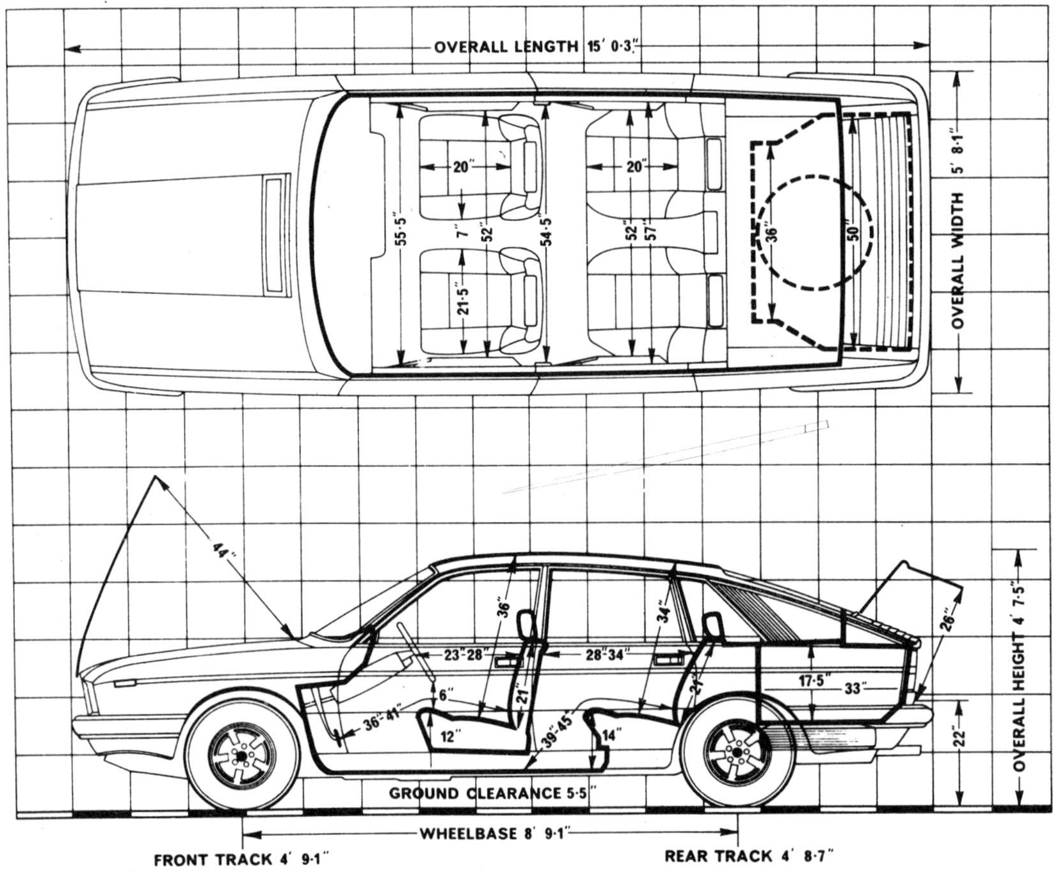

Weight

Kerb:
27.2 cwt/3,052 lb/1,387 kg
(Distribution F/R, 58.9/41.1)
As tested:
30.6 cwt/3,424 lb/1,556 kg

Boot capacity: 17.7 cu.ft.

Turning circles:
Between kerbs:
L, 32ft 3in; R, 34ft 0in.
Between walls:
L, 34ft 6in.; R, 36ft 3in.
Turns, lock to lock: 3.0

Test Scorecard

(Average of scoring by *Autocar* Road Test team)

Ratings: *6 Excellent*
5 Good
4 Above average
3 Below average
2 Poor
1 Bad

PERFORMANCE	4.25
STEERING AND HANDLING	5.13
BRAKES	3.85
COMFORT IN FRONT	4.30
COMFORT IN BACK	4.75
DRIVER'S AIDS *(instruments, lights, wipers, visibility, etc.)*	3.00
CONTROLS	4.20
NOISE	4.10
STOWAGE	3.20
ROUTINE SERVICE *(under-bonnet access: dipstick, etc.)*	4.20
EASE OF DRIVING	4.00

Comparisons

	Price £	max (mph)	0-60 (sec)	overall mpg	capacity (c.c.)	power (bhp)	wheelbase (in.)	length (in.)	width (in.)	kerb weight	fuel (gall)	tyre size
Lancia Gamma Berlina	**7,136**	**118**	**10.1**	**19.1**	**2,484**	**140**	**105.0**	**180.5**	**68.0**	**27.2**	**13**	**185/70HR14**
Rover 3500	7,174	123	8.4	20.5	3,528	155	110.0	185.0	69.8	26.7	14.5	185-14
Citroen CX GTi	6,580	118	10.1	21.6	2,347	128	112.0	181.0	68.0	26.8	15.0	185HR-14
Ford Granada 2.8iS	6,200	117	8.9	20.8	2,792	160	109.0	187.0	70.5	26.5	14.3	190/65HR-390
Audi 100 GLSE†	6,020	109	11.8	23.3	2,144	136	105.5	179.5	69.5	23.5	13.2	185/70HR-14
Peugeot 604 SL	6,611	113	9.4	19.6	2,664	136	110.0	185.5	69.5	27.8	15.5	175-14
Renault 30TS	6,125	117	9.8	18.5	2,664	131	105.0	178.0	68.0	25.5	14.7	175HR14
BMW 525	7,490	117	10.6	23.7	2,494	150	104.0	182.0	66.5	27.8	15.5	195/70HR14

† Performance figures of automatic version

Fixtures and fittings

The interior of the Gamma follows the stylised format of the smaller Beta and is in sharp contrast to the plain simplicity of northern European designs. It is indeed more stylised and ornate than its smaller sister; some will obviously approve, but others of the more puritan natured British, including most of our testers, find it rather kitsch.

But value judgements about the aesthetics of the interior aside, the heavy styling has imposed a number of practical problems for which the Gamma can be criticised. Simply, the instrument panel is a mess. Most of us felt it looked dreadful; the instruments certainly are vague and difficult to read. For instance, the speedometer has three confusing rows of figures in different background colours — mph centrally, with intermediate mph marked around the outside and kph marked inside. Incidentally, both speedometer and rev counter sit off the zero when car and engine are stationary. The minor instruments are similar to those of the Beta, and similarly confusing. They all look the same — red/white/red strips swept by needles, which makes them hard to distinguish quickly and they are individually awkward to read accurately.

Switchgear on the instrument panel is a straightforward set of push buttons — good, except that they are not lit at night until switched on when they self-illuminate, so they must be groped for in the dark. Column stalks are conventional, operating lights, indicators and screen wipers, though these are surprisingly slow in operation — the facia switch for wiper speed selection prompting the joke of "slow or extra slow".

It is in the heating and ventilation system that the pursuit of chic seems to have reached its extreme. The heater controls for the air blending unit are vacuum-operated allowing push button selection of "heat" "defrost" or "fresh air". The temperature selection is by slide, with automatic vacuum over-ride so that it slides back to the off-position when the engine is switched off or "fresh air" selected. Volume is controlled by adjusting the aperture of each individual warm air outlet, at the facia, in the footwells and in the rear passenger compartment. Chic or gimmickry? Who is to say? The fact is that the system does work once understood. What does not work at all well is the ventilation, despite prominent and rather ugly-looking vents. Those in the centre of the facia are linked to the heating system and though they can give fresh air, will give warmed air when the heater is in service. Those at the edges of the facia supply air by ram effect to the interior, but a very poor volume of it, even at high speed, so the car can become stuffy with the heater in use.

The choice and level of equipment on the car also seems somewhat curious, particularly remembering its price. There are a number of fussy details about the interior — such as sun blinds behind the back seats — but one must raise questions over some of the other items fitted, and more importantly, not fitted. Tinted glass is used all round and all the windows have electric window lifters, operated from a central panel between the front seats and individually on each back door. Most oddly there is no over-ride to prevent delighted young children pushing the back windows up and down with potentially dangerous consequences. Pursuing the question of child safety, we were shocked to notice a complete absence of child-proof locks on the rear doors, so if youngsters can't get out of the windows they can try the doors as well.

The boot lid counter-balances in two positions; partly or fully open

Right: The window behind the slats can be seen in the boot lid; it marries up with a glass partition behind the rear seats. Boot space is distinctly small for the overall size of the car, but loading is easy thanks to the lack of a sill. The tool kit includes spare bulbs and a warning triangle

Headlamp angle is automatically adjusted to compensate for load

The fuel filler cap is cleverly hidden away behind this lockable flap

What one discovers about the car is an absence of the sort of refinements found on many similar products; no central locking, no headlamp washers, no sunroof and no radio. There are some nice touches; a load-sensitive automatic headlamp levelling system and a door mirror adjusted by electric remote control from the centre panel by the driver's seat, but one wonders if they are sufficient.

Living with the Lancia Gamma

Despite its two-box styling the Gamma is not a hatchback; its arrival in the executive market carrying on the trend for this body shape but leaving the argument for and against hatchbacks undecided — the Rover and the Renault have them, the Citroën and the Lancia don't.

Although it is a big car, its boot is disappointingly small. Lancia have clearly opted to maximise passenger space, and the petrol tank, sandwiched between rear seat and boot, reduced capacity further. Ease of loading is some compensation, for there is no sill to lift luggage over and the lid has a thoughtful two-position counter-balance. An odd-seeming afterthought of design is the curious double window arrangement used to increase rear visibility. The slats in the boot lid cover a small glass area, which is viewed from inside the car through a small glass panel closing the boot off from the interior. Complex, but giving a useful improvement to what would otherwise be rather restricted straight-back vision. Oddment space inside the car is also rather restricted. There are two small footwell pickets at the front, a modest glovebox and a small console tray — nothing large enough for a road atlas. In the backs of the front seats are pockets for the rear seat passengers' use. The spare wheel lies flat under the boot floor, with jack and tool-kit.

The engine compartment, of course, presents an unusual sight. The "boxer" engine is masked by air cleaner and inlet manifolding, but it is a large engine bay and holds a compact engine so there is plenty of space for under-bonnet servicing.

Conclusion

We were disappointed by the Lancia Gamma. Not simply disappointed because of its faults, but disappointed because these spoil a potentially good car and one which we enjoyed driving.

For as a car to drive the Lancia is delightful; its handling and steering are superb and its performance lively. It is let down by a lack of attention to detail. Lancia just don't seem to have appreciated the refinement needed to compete in this price range; the scuttle shake, the harsh engine noise when revved, the appalling instrumentation, the lack of luxury equipment are all serious debit points. The unusual flat-four engine has presumably been dictated by production considerations, for although by no means a bad engine, it offers no benefits over a six-cylinder — certainly not where it might be expected to score, in fuel consumption.

In the final analysis, it is against its rivals that it must be compared. Quite simply it lacks the solid reassurance of a Rover, the luxury of a Citroën or the comprehensive performance and equipment of a Granada. □

MANUFACTURER:
Lancia SpA,
Via Vincenzo Lancia,
Torino, Italy

UK CONCESSIONAIRES:
Lancia (England) Ltd,
Ealing Road,
Alperton, Middlesex
HAO 1HE

PRICES	
Basic	£6,099.00
Special Car Tax	£508.25
VAT	£528.58
Total (in GB)	**£7,135.83**
Seat Belts	Standard
Licence	£50.00
Delivery charge (London)	Standard
Number plates	£7.50
Total on the Road	
(exc. insurance)	**£7,193.33**
Insurance	Group 7
EXTRAS (inc. VAT)	
*Metallic paint	£221.13
*Leather upholstery	£341.64
Air conditioning	£444.60
Fitted to test car	
TOTAL AS TESTED ON THE ROAD	**£7,756.10**

Long Term Report

Lancia Beta HPE 2000 *(24,000 miles)*

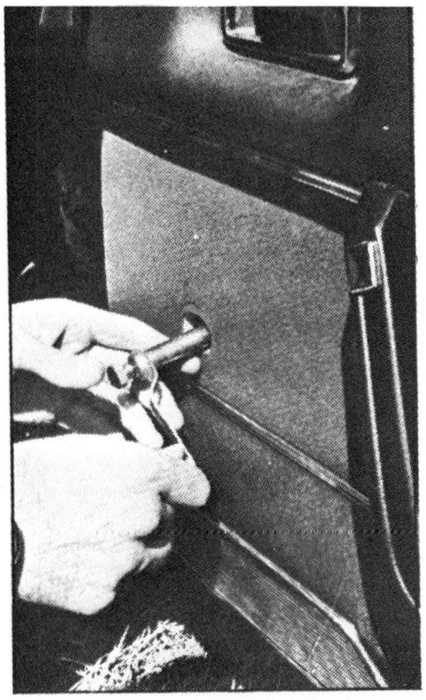

Manual window winding is a chore (left) when electric windows fail even with a helping hand (above). Instrumentation is comprehensive and controls generally well placed (below)

HPE: Handy, Pretty, Enjoyable

By Ray Hutton

IT'S NICE to get back into a car that you have known well and find that it is still as good as you remembered it to be. For various reasons, I haven't been driving "my" HPE very much recently and its last couple of thousand miles have been covered by my advertising colleague Walter Reeves, who will be running the car now that I am about to use a Lotus Eclat for a spell. So a couple of weeks ago it was time for a re-acquaintance, a session at the MIRA Proving Ground to check its performance, and a fresh assessment of how this most elegant of sporting hatchbacks has stood the ravages of 21 months and 24,000 miles.

Not many of *Autocar*'s test staff share my enthusiasm for the HPE or indeed the current series of sporting Lancias. Their criticisms range from a general dislike of front wheel drive in a sporting car, to specific points about noise, finish, instruments and, especially, seats and driving position. I agree with them in some respects but as I was forced to conclude in the last report at 12,000 miles, despite the inherent faults and the many specific problems with our car, the HPE has a character that shows through. It's a driver's car. And when I went back to it after some weeks apart it was like being reunited with an old friend, warts and all.

Regular readers may recall that this car's early life was not without incident. Last summer it was in collision with a galloping horse that did neither the horse nor the front of the Lancia much good. Neither was irreparable and I suspect that nature's bodyshop had the horse back in showground condition before the HPE, which at the time had a busy programme and could not be spared for repairs. The horse's owner accepted responsibility for it escaping from its field and his insurers paid up without question. Eventually after taking advice from Lancia (England) Ltd about the best people to repair and match its light silver paintwork the HPE went to Autodex Ltd in Southall, Middlesex.

A new bonnet and front bumper were needed and a certain amount of re-shaping around the offside front wing. Autodex made an excellent job of the paintwork but we were not impressed by the over-spray on the new bumper when it was collected, nor by the way the headlamp assembly inside the wing came adrift shortly afterwards . . . .

Though it was back in shape, some problems remained. The fact that the offside headlamp was flapping around had nothing to do with its already established appetite for headlamp bulbs. Three within a fortnight, at £3 a time, seemed to confirm that there was a voltage regulation fault — particularly since our old Beta Coupé had a similar bulb consumption. Then there were the electric windows, the blessed electric windows. They hadn't worked properly from the start and I had become resigned to not being able to open the one on the passenger side and, if I persuaded the driver's door window to go down, to expect that it would refuse to go up again. It was not practical to have the car converted to manual windows, though it was significant that the electric winders became optional rather than standard equipment on the 2000HPE at about this time. I was moaning about the windows to our friends at Lancia and they kindly offered to have their own mechanics look at them and the blowing bulb business. They checked the electrical system thoroughly and could find no problem; interestingly, only one bulb has gone in the 8,000 miles since. They also replaced the window motor on the passenger door, fitted new relays and cleaned up the tracks on both sides. The windows worked again — though not as quickly and decisively as those of the 2000ES saloon I was loaned while the work was being carried out.

Alas, only a couple of months later they were giving trouble again. At the time of writing both windows are working, albeit slowly. One of the problems may be the amount of water that can get by the window seal. It is noticeable that the windows are a "loose fit"; the glass is not cleared of moisture by the outside seal. Other occupants of the inside of the doors, the radio speakers that are supplied as standard, also gave up the ghost due, we suspect, to getting wet. Our radio expert, Stuart Bladon, tells me that their location, behind the kick plates at the base of the door, is in any case an "unsound position". Apart from being a ghastly pun this is obviously correct in theory, though since the originals were replaced by Bosch speakers the quality of sound from the Blaupunkt Köln stereo radio has been impressive.

Noise spoils it

A good radio provides a useful yardstick for assessing the noise level of the car itself. It remains a mystery to me why the HPE should be so much noisier, both mechanically and from wind disturbance, than the 1600 Coupé that we had a few years ago. The engine is 2-litres of course, and not over-square like its smaller brother, which accounts for it being rather less refined. Noise levels are such that 80-85 mph is as fast as one can go on a motorway with a hope of enjoying the music at the same time. That's a disappointment — even if it does provide a measure of self-control in this country. . . .

The gearing doesn't help either.

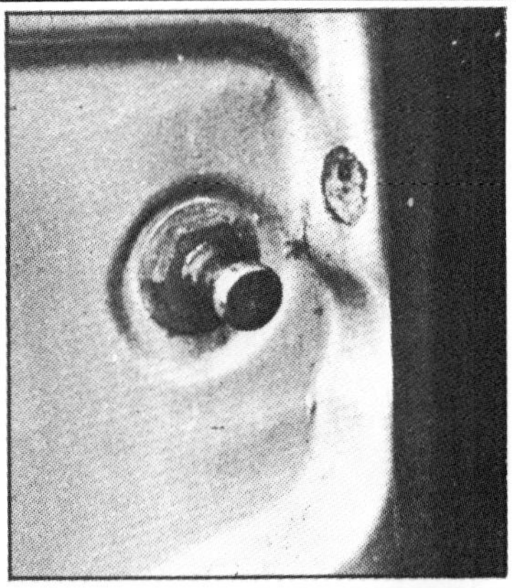

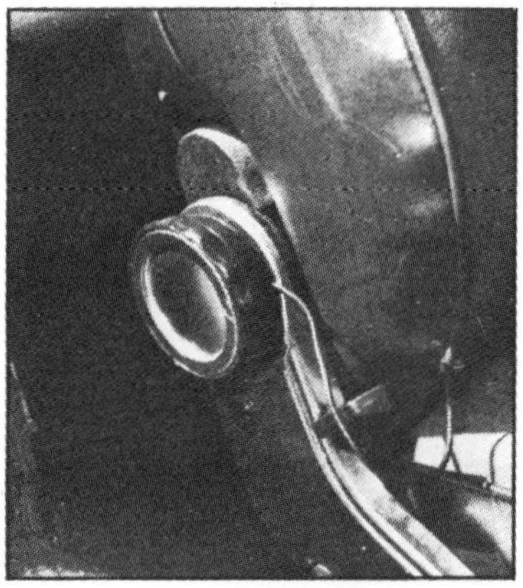

Sunroof (top, far left) is appreciated — and neat. Rust spots have developed particularly on the doors and around the seams (above); trim has generally stood up well though plastic piping on driver's seat has come adrift (top right) due to seat belt chafing. Engine bay (left) is generally accessible. When the tailgate lock fails, it can be opened by a handle within. Roller blind attaches to seat backs to cover luggage (below and right)

As the Technical Editor pointed out a few months ago in the magazine, having five gears does not necessarily provide effortless high speed cruising nor does it guarantee easier driveability with an already torquey engine. The HPE 2000's top gear gives 19.6 mph per 1,000 rpm and could usefully be higher. On paper the ratios of the intermediates look well spaced but in practice both second and third would be better if they were higher. Walter Reeves was disappointed by his commuting fuel consumption —often below 20 mpg — and experimented with using only first, third and fifth. It produced an immediate 15 per cent improvement.

Though it is reluctant when cold, the gearchange is delightfully positive and encourages use on the give-and-take roads that show the car in its best light. The controls generally have that well-developed feel; the steering, lower geared and heavier than one would like around town, has a smooth precision that belies the position of the drive line (in the dry at least); brake pedal effort is light; the clutch take-up, progressive. Altogether, the HPE shows exceedingly good road behaviour that makes the kind of holiday tour that I made in Brittany last September particularly enjoyable.

1,100 miles in a few days proved some points about the accommodation. The split rear seat was ideal for our holiday luggage. With one side down to extend the load platform we were able to carry a large cool box for picnics, etc, while leaving the other seat free for all the bits and pieces that one seems to need at hand when touring in a car. The normal luggage area swallowed two people's luggage without difficulty. With the seat folded down estate-style the handy roller blind luggage cover has to be attached to the top of the slatted sunshade when the car is parked; this helps to keep the inside of the car cool and keeps whatever is stowed in the rear at least partly out of view.

On this occasion the rear seats were not being used for passengers but when they have been, the people concerned have been impressed by the amount of legroom for a car of this type, the clever way in which the side trim has been shaped to provide wrap-round padding, and the fill-in "sausages" that give the fold-up seats extra support between cushion and backrest. There have been a few complaints of lack of headroom and restricted visibility forward from taller passengers.

Seats please some

Those controversial front seats with their boldly shaped but very short backs and narrow head restraints are, for me at least, much more comfortable than they look. I can feel relaxed after a day behind the wheel though my companion in Brittany found that she needed a cushion to fill the gap that is left between the backrest and the cushion; in this the HPE, which has front seats that roll forward when tilted for access to the rear, differs from the equivalent Coupé. Perhaps Walter Reeves' comments on the seat are the most valid: a back-sufferer, he says that it is "the only seat that doesn't give me backache; the back is supported from top to bottom".

Brittany served to emphasize both the good and bad features of the (standard) metal sunroof. Good, because it is easy to open and can be locked in any position from a crack to full open; bad, because a querk of aerodynamics means that it engulfs unpleasant exhaust fumes. With the roof closed, ventilation is not too bad with the fan's low speed assistance; opening the rear quarter windows increases the flow-through but also makes it noisier. More of a problem is the conflict in keeping the car's occupants cool and the windows demisted at the same time during a summer shower. Stuart Bladon had a particular problem with that and solved it by keeping the roof open: "It doesn't let in much rain as long as you keep moving". Whilst on the subject of rain, the wipers could be better. Their primary control is convenient, being a left-hand column stalk giving either continuous or intermittent action. A second speed is available by a push-pull switch on the centre dash panel but is scarcely any faster — and certainly not fast enough to cope with a downpour.

Our holiday journey went well except for the last night when we tried in vain to find a hotel around Mont St Michel. It took over three hours, 100 miles and we lost count of how many *complet* hotels, before we found a welcoming road house at Bayeux well after midnight. Late evening traffic in Brittany in late September is thin. I had not made any effort to adapt the lights for driving on the right but this in itself wasn't a problem. What I did realize was that even with all the bulbs working and the lights set properly, the dipped beam is almost dangerously poor. I went as far as to obtain a pair of auxiliary lamps when I returned but somehow I could never bring myself to spoil the look of the front of the car by fitting them.

Quicker now

The Brittany trip saw an average fuel consumption of 24.6 mpg, slightly better than Walter manages in normal day-to-day running and a good deal better than the 21.5 overall consumption for the first 12,000 miles. The average figure seems to be improving all the time, independent of tricks like the first-third-and-fifth technique. There are probably two reasons for this. For a long time the carburation was not right and the car was plagued with misfire problems; which now seem to have been solved. And, as the performance check shows, in some respects — notably the higher speeds in the gears — the car is actually quicker now than either our original 2000 HPE road test car or the long-term car at 12,000 miles. As it is has aged it has loosened up and the economy has benefited accordingly.

The last serious occurrence of the

WHAT THE LANCIA HAS COST

Total: 12,000 miles/year £1,901.62 **Cost per mile** 15.8p

RUNNING COSTS

Consumable Items:	**Life in miles**	**Unit cost**	**Cost per 12,000 miles**
Fuel: 4-star (gallon)	23.2	0.83	£429.31
Oil: topping-up between changes (litre)	2,000	0.96	£5.76
Brakes:			
Front pads (unit cost = set of 4)	24,000	10.58	£5.29
Rear pads (unit cost = set of 4)	24,000	10.84	£5.42
Tyres: Michelin ZX 175/70-14 (unit cost = single tyre)		28.71	
Front pair	28,000		£24.60
Rear pair	40,000		£17.23
Service and Repairs:			
Manufacturers recommended charges for service at £6.50 per hour (labour only)	6,200 miles		£19.50
	12,400 miles		£21.45
	18,600 miles		£24.70
Service costs incurred with our car in past 12,000 miles (inc. oil and materials)			£162.19
Repair costs incurred			£41.07
Total maintenance costs incurred			£203.26
Total running costs (consumable items, service and repairs)			£406.52

STANDING CHARGES per year

Insurance (see note)	£142.10
Tax	£50.00
Depreciation: Cost of our car when new £4,503; Its estimated value today £3,200; Decline in value over 21 months	£1,303.00
Total standing charges	**£1,495.10**

Fuel consumption

Overall mpg:

12,000 21.5 mpg (13.1 litres/100 km)

24,000 **23.2 mpg** (12.1 litres/100 km)

Fuel tank: 11.4 gal (52 litres)

Range: approx. 250 miles

***24,000** denotes performance figures of our car today. **12,000** figures are taken from **Autocar** long-term report at 12,000 miles published 10 September 1977. Lancia HPE 2000 Autotest published 23 April 1977*

Note: *To put all our cars on equal footing for insurance cost, the figure given above is a typical quotation for a "good risk" driver — with clean record, and car garaged in Oxfordshire, a "middle range" risk area. Full n.c.b. discount has been deducted, as has the saving for £25 excess. The actual figure is the middle one of five quotations ranging from £136 to £289 Source: Quotel Motor Insurance Service.*

Maximum Speeds

Gear	12,000 mph	12,000 rpm	**24,000 mph**	**24,000 rpm**
Top	108	5,300	**108**	**5,300**
4th	101	6,400	**101**	**6,400**
3rd	76	6,400	**76**	**6,400**
2nd	52	6,400	**52**	**6,400**
1st	33	6,400	**33**	**6,400**

Acceleration

FROM REST True mph	Speedo mph	Time (secs) 12,000	**24,000**
30	33	3.3	**3.7**
40	43	5.4	**5.7**
50	53	7.3	**7.6**
60	63	10.2	**10.9**
70	73	13.4	**14.2**
80	83	18.3	**18.8**
90	94	24.7	**25.5**
100	106	37.0	**38.9**

IN THE GEARS

mph	Top 12T	Top **24T**	4th 12T	4th **24T**	3rd 12T	3rd **24T**
10-30	—	—	—	—	5.9	**5.2**
20-40	10.3	**9.5**	7.2	**7.3**	4.7	**4.9**
30-50	8.9	**9.2**	6.2	**6.7**	4.6	**4.5**
40-60	8.7	**8.7**	6.4	**6.4**	4.9	**5.1**
50-70	9.6	**9.0**	7.5	**6.9**	5.9	**6.2**
60-80	11.0	**10.8**	8.3	**7.8**	—	—
70-90	13.2	**13.8**	10.5	**9.1**	—	—
80-100	18.5	**19.3**	18.8	**13.6**	—	—

Standing ¼-mile:
12,000 17.3 sec 78 mph
24,000 18.1 sec 77 mph
Standing kilo:
12,000 32.3 sec 98 mph
24,000 32.7 sec 97 mph

Specification

ENGINE	Front, front drive
Cylinders	In-line, 4-cylinder transverse
Main bearings	5
Fan	Electric
Bore, mm (in)	84 (3.31)
Stroke, mm (in.)	90 (3.54)
Capacity, cc (in.³)	1,995 (122.5)
Valve gear	Dohc
Compression ratio	8.9-to-1
Carburettor	Single twin-choke Weber C34
Max power	119 bhp (DIN) at 5,500 rpm
Max torque	128 lb. ft. at 2,800 rpm

TRANSMISSION

Gear	Ratio	mph/1000rpm
Top	0.925	19.6
4th	1.152	15.8
3rd	1.522	11.9
2nd	2.235	8.1
1st	3.500	5.2
Ratio	3.785 to 1	

SUSPENSION	
Front—location	MacPherson struts
springs	coil
dampers	Telescopic
anti-roll bar	Yes
Rear—location	MacPherson struts, twin links
springs	Coil
dampers	Telescopic
anti-roll bar	Yes
STEERING	
Type	Rack and pinion
Power assistance	No
Turns, lock to lock	3.8
BRAKES	
Front	9.9in dia. disc
Rear	9.9in. dia. disc
Circuits	Twin, split front/front & front/rear
Servo	Yes, vacuum type

MANUFACTURER
Lancia S.p.A.
Casella Postale n.430
10100 Torino, Centro
Italy

Rear seats (above) are comfortable for all but tallest passengers. Sitting position is improved by the use of separate "sausage" cushions provided. Base cushions have to be removed and seat backs folded down to increase rear load area (below). HPE can be used as a three-seater with expanded luggage space

misfire was just after 17,000 miles. It was January and a particularly cold couple of days. At first I put the car's inability to run cleanly down to the temperature and the recalcitrant automatic choke. It always takes a while to warm up and pops and splutters as it does so. But this was serious. The engine would rev but it wouldn't pull, and on a motorway it would suddenly fade. There were all the symptoms of fuel starvation and I suspected some foreign bodies in the fuel system. Accordingly, I took it to DB Autos in Tinworth Street, London SE11 for an early 18,600 mile (30,000 km) service and asked them to check the fuel system thoroughly. They did so, changed every filter in sight, cleaned the carburettor, performed the routine service, and charged £60. Afterwards, it was running better than for some time. Over the next 6,000 miles the engine's tendency to fluff increased and a carburettor clean-up and a new set of sparking plugs seems to be regularly needed to sweeten it again.

Mechanically, the last few thousand miles have been unremarkable. At 19,000 miles the rear silencer box fell off — a rather early casualty surely? — and cost £15 to replace and another £15 to be fitted and have the tail-gate lock fixed after that had stopped working. Fitting the spare wheel after discovering a flat rear tyre (it turned out to be no more than a faulty valve) once again showed the stupidity of having wheel fixing bolts rather than studs and not providing location pegs, while Lancia ought to provide an Allen key in the tool kit to enable one to re-fix the driver's seat when it comes loose — as it seems to every few weeks.

Good impression

The trim has generally stood up well, though the plastic piping round the driver's seat back was an early casualty of seat belt chafing. The novel roller blind has been damaged but through no fault of its design; someone tried to fold down the seat with it still attached. Outwardly, the story is not so good. There are more rust spots and paint blemishes than a car of this class and price deserves after 24,000 miles. The roof has a number of fine scratches, presumably from an automatic car wash.

That's the detail analysis. The overall impression, as the pictures show, is still good. One can forgive the HPE a lot because it looks so nice and because the sporting estate idea has been so well carried out. And despite it all, it has an underlying character too often missing from today's cars — even the apparently sporting ones. Lotus or not, I am sorry that we are parting, my HPE and me. □

The Lancia Range

Above: Interior comfort and a surprising amount of room were combined with front-wheel-drive and a five-speed gearbox and sold at a very reasonable price, helping to make the Beta saloon a financial success for Lancia

Right: The Coupé version of the Beta featured a shorter wheelbase than the saloon and, partly as a result, more agile handling

Below: Already famous for its sporting exploits, the Stratos was sold in very limited numbers as a totally impractical but immensely enjoyable road car. Although Lancia never sold it in Britain, several examples did find their way into the country.

When these pictures were published in *Autocar* in November 1974, the mainstay of the Lancia range was the Beta, then available in saloon and coupé versions with a selection of 1.4, 1.6 and 1.8-litre power units. In addition to the Beta, the first product of the Fiat takeover in 1972, Lancia still manufactured the latest derivatives of their pre-Fiat designs, the Fulvia and the Flavia 2000. 1974 was also the first year the Stratos was listed as a production car, although not freely available.

Beta Monte Carlo

The Lancia Beta Monte Carlo, or Montecarlo as the Italians would have it, was first introduced as a road car in 1975. It was clearly a product of the Fiat takeover: not only was its mid-mounted Beta engine based on a Fiat design, but the whole concept had originated as a bigger version of the Fiat X1/9. The Monte Carlo found immediate favour as one of the very few practical mid-engined designs, but sales were never extensive and the model was re-launched in 1980.

Since their withdrawal from rallying at the end of 1978, Lancia's motor sporting efforts have been concentrated on the World Championship for Makes—effectively the world sports car championship. Lancia succeeded in winning the up-to-2 litres division of this series in 1979 and also finished second in the overall championship, most of the driving having been shared by Italian Formula One star Riccardo Patrese and Fiat rally driver Walter Rohrl.

The Monte Carlo Turbo is, as the name implies, powered by a turbocharged version of the mid-mounted in-line four cylinder engine used in the road car, but its capacity had to be reduced to 1,425c.c. in order to run in the 2-litre Division (the equivalency formula of 1.4:1 gives a 'legal' capacity of 1,995c.c.). For 1979, this unit produced around 370bhp at 8,000rpm.

Considerable improvements during the winter of 1979/80 resulted in the engine producing over 400bhp at 8,800rpm and this, along with suspension and aerodynamic work, made the cars much faster. At the opening race of 1980, the Daytona 24 Hours, Carlo Facetti and Martino Finotto duly won their class; but at the Brands Hatch 6 Hours in March, Patrese and Rohrl (above) won outright. More overall wins and consistent class victories saw Lancia gain the 1980 Championship.

The 1980 engine (below) was a dry sump unit of 82 × 67.5 mm bore and stroke, with a KKK turbocharger and Bosch indirect fuel injection. The car's interior (left) is the spartan affair one has come to expect in a modern racer. The gear lever controls five forward speeds and reverse.

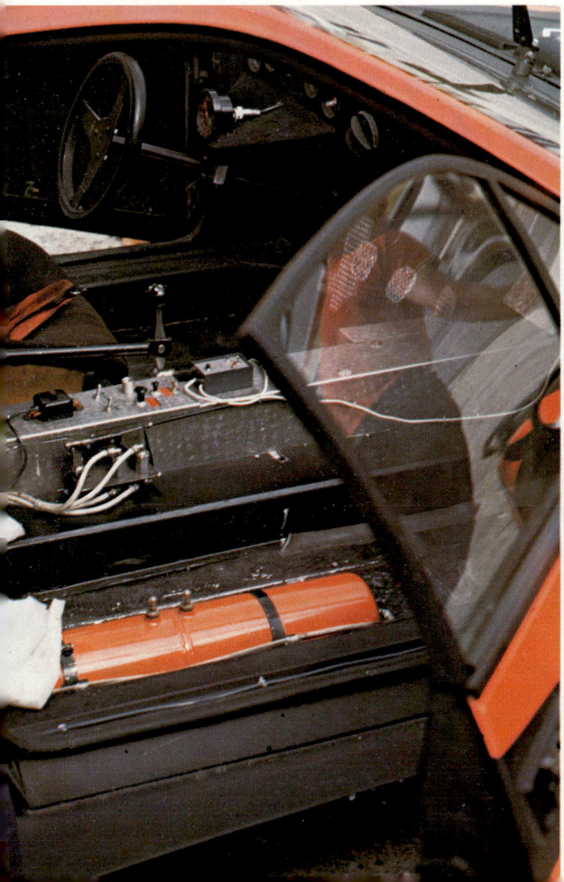

The Stratos is nearing the end of its rallying life, but will always remain a classic and uncompromisingly good looking car.

Radiator cooling air is ducted out via the louvres in the front body section. The occupants get much needed ventilation from the roof centre mounted air vent, while the roof spoiler directs air over the rear body section on to the spoiler. This flow also assists the extraction of air out of the engine compartment through the slatted rear section. The main driving lights are covered by a moulded panel when not in use

Turning in under good conditions it was a case of momentary understeer (main picture) on the way in, and prolonged oversteer (above) on the way out. But like any racing car, the neater you kept it the better it went

Miles Behind the Wheel

Above: *With wide rear tyres fitted inherent dry weather balance is just about neutral*

Stratos on stage

Sampling a stunning rally car before it disappears from world class rallying

LIKE THE drawbacks, some Stratos qualities are plain to see, others are more subtle. Some I probably never found but one way or another there couldn't be any more armchair chat. This was a chance to find out — or at least sample — what rallying this brutal, short, mid-engined masterpiece of a car meant.

There was no advice. Bob Newman of Pirelli kindly provided the spare works car for me to get used to at Donington prior to my running the car there and at Sutton Park in the "early show" before the aces came through on the RAC Rally proper. The mixed loose and tarmac Donington was hopefully going to be no trouble, but the one run over Sutton Park's tarmac would have to be more or less blind.

It was easy to lose sleep thinking about driving the Stratos. Both the previously driven road and Chequered Flag rally cars had been stiffly suspended (*Miles Behind the Wheel* 4 March and 20 May). If the works car was the same, it all seemed like a recipe for skating off on the first corner — after all it was bound to be pouring with rain. I was wrong on the first count, but right on the second.

You soon learn that rallying and Farina-like straight arm driving positions don't go together, so it was one click further forward with the superb seat than I first thought necessary. Securely belted in I gazed at Italian labelled switches, knobs, dials and gauges. The largest knob was the intriguing brake bias control, and if bias to spin was required a sturdy and purposeful-looking handbrake stared from underneath the dash.

Sitting low and enclosed, the initial feeling of claustrophobia soon disappears once on the move. There still isn't much space; conditions must get pretty unpleasant after days of hard work next to your co-driver. On the mixed surfaces of Donington we should have used what Pirelli call "Monte Carlo" pattern tyres (wide racers heavily grooved). Actually Don Fenwick the Chequered Flag's quietly spoken Kiwi mechanic produced some deeply hand cut slicks to run in the dry.

Crashing around with rear wheels scrabbling for grip, the Stratos rides over rutted gravel straight as a die. Long travel "Safari" suspension soaks the deep grooves up, and down goes the power — all of it with a rev counter flicking madly. Here's a car that resents being thrown at a corner. I feel happier trying to get the entry neat and right on the smooth or loose, by braking as far towards the apex as possible — as a racer would — then feeding on the power and opposite lock to rocket out of slow speed corners. Softly set up there is plenty of feel through the chassis; adjusted in the middle the brake balance is right to give plenty of front end bite, and at the same time unsettle the rear enough to kill any initial understeer.

Below: *Bob Newman (on the right) explains some of the tyre combinations that are possible on the day. Between us, what started as a half worn, deeply grooved rear tyre has worn almost to a slick in ten laps*

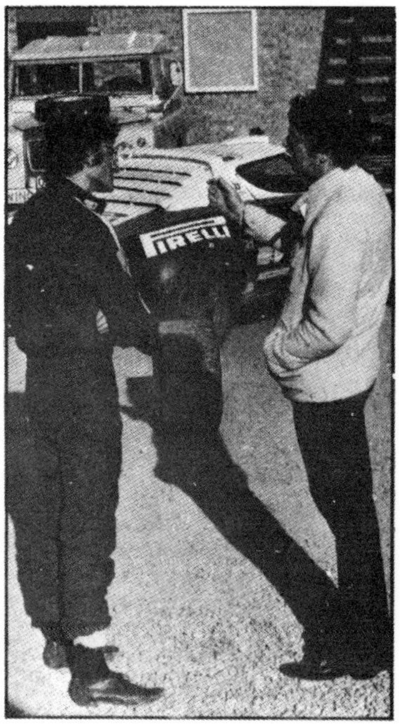

Stratos on stage

Swinging the rear of the Stratos around creepily with the power off and stably with the power on is possible but there seems no need. Once really out of shape a spin is imminent — it's almost certain if you then lift off. It has a Porsche-like weight distribution of 40/60 front to rear, but the mass is concentrated near the middle of the chassis as opposed to behind the rear wheels. There is none of the pendulous slide normally associated with Porsche, Escort, or Chevette with their concentrations of mass at one end. It's like an extension to the body. Racer like, short, responsive, the Stratos does not forgive, but when you get it right on the way out of a corner you know it — the sheer traction makes up for everything.

I don't know how the works have managed to kill potential understeer — all too evident in the road car — but kill it they have. On dry tarmac the chassis moves around, rolling and biting at the front on the turn in, to power neutrally through to Donington's exit of corner kerbs. Later, in the wet, I adjust with difficulty to the amount of power you can get down with only a touch of oversteer on the way out. Some of the adhesion must be down to the super sticky compounds being used nowadays, but balance has been achieved without hard springs. Paradoxically, balance is often what you don't want. A well sorted chassis, low polar moment of inertia, race car suspension geometry, rearward weight distribution, all help to make the limits high. Get it right and the Stratos is difficult to beat for its traction, power (though that's sometimes overrated) and neat cornering, but get it wrong and all the advantages turn and bite. Most of rallying's corners may be as seen but the driver often has to ad lib. The experienced co-driver and driver may know the deceptive ones, but visibility from a low Stratos seat hardly helps you see the road ahead. Sitting low is part of the conception, does it negate most of the potential? The aces have proved not, but their three world Rally Championships have shown a predictable trend toward the car being better where pace notes are used — where the road is known better. There is always an exception. In the 1975 RAC Rally, repairs to replace a broken drive shaft had left Waldegaard over the time limit, he then set the fastest time, stage after stage, in the loose and blind.

Whatever else, it gives the crowds their money's worth in noise, spectacle, and looks. From my position the engine felt glorious, singing round to 8,000 rpm with alarming smoothness — it felt like 6,000 — and giving an urgent 260 bhp. Considering that the hefty gearbox started life in the rear engined Dino over ten years ago the clunkily accurate change isn't bad — better than the ZF box in the Escort, but being like a motorcycle box and almost in unit with the sump the Lancia change becomes harder work as the oil gets hotter.

Of course it's all different on the day, and Sunday's day at Sutton Park was cold, wet, and unfriendly — a throat drying sort of day if you have to take on five miles of daunting, tree lined, leaf covered, often gated, almost unknown tarmac track. Undoubtedly a doddle for the aces, my gentle exploratory road car run at Sutton had me well psyched otherwise. Fast and safe was the brief — nothing too serious. It seemed like a contradiction in terms to me.

My passenger, rally correspondent David Hardcastle sat chatting, ''No I hadn't done this sort of thing before, no I hadn't driven it in the wet.'' Searching for the demister fan and outer headlight switches killed that conversation. We hung around on the starting line.

''When you're ready,'' said one of the multitude of marshals on the stage. I couldn't wait to get the first taste over with. Hardcastle was a good aid — like another pair of eyes — but then he had done this stage several times before. Motioning hands implored on, on, left curve, right curve, sharp left and right. These,and a shouted ''gate gate gate'' said most of it. I didn't believe the arrows — I wanted to see the corner (too conditioned by racing). After the fabulous wets had cut through the first piece of standing water that I had stupidly dabbed the brakes for, things got better. Braking was the problem. It was too early, sometimes stupidly early, like the first lap of practice for a race. Up and down the gearbox, winding in and out. Gates among the trees came up blind — one darkened by overhanging trees gave a foot clearance either side of my precious mount. Left and right, no room to slide wide, trees everywhere, out into the open again and down to first gear, Town Gate, ''watch the posts'' The navigators say you crash on the driver's side, the drivers like it the other way. We were still on the road and on the two mile run home. Fast left, then ''slow, slow tricky one'' (they call it Brookes' corner) scrape through in third gear. Not sure of the road ahead — it's fast but wanders blindly — wish it was dry. Keep in fourth and drone through in the middle of the road, ''bridge, then left left left''. Down to second and away splashing through puddles at the edge. More 100-110 mph fourth and fifth gear nervousness, the last slow esses, then that inconspicuous yellow finish of the stage board.

The feeling of wellbeing that follows the first attempt at something new soon vanished — to be replaced by craving to do the whole thing again. But you can't run again. You are denied the chance to pull back the mass of time you know is lost — there is just the one run. The ad-libbing rally driver might not feel that way, but that's the difference between somebody conditioned to a steady build up, and a real rally driver's instant go, car control, and nerve.

By comparison the three runs at Donington had something of a therapeutic effect. There was the chance to have a look first and then have a go. A new passenger, Mike Stuart, *Cars and Car Conversions* rally championship winner sat back with experienced calm for two runs, then they put a man in with a microphone. Trying to talk coherently and drive made the driving ragged and slower as well. A good illustration of the levels of concentration normally in use.

I probably didn't even scratch the surface, and certainly never flirted with clever stuff like left foot braking, nor did I discover how quickly the Stratos would spin by using the handbrake.

They say that as grip improves driving styles are tending to be neater, so perhaps there is some hope that race and rally driving styles will meet. In the meantime the Stratos is running out of homologation time. Lancia may consider this dramatic machine with its dated mechanical components no longer has marketing relevance or further potential in two valve form at any rate. Possibly so, but dullness threatens. What will replace it from the current model ranges? — perhaps the Monte Carlo? Or horror of horrors, something with front wheel drive. If ever there was an obvious candidate for a number one slot in a collection the Stratos is it. □

Above: A neatly laid out cockpit has all the important gauges nicely positioned. The handbrake can be seen under and below the right hand steering wheel spoke. The large knob under the centre of the dash is the brake bias control, while mounted on the right of the dash are the Halda and exposed fuses. Note the semi circular sliding window adjuster

Right: A massive air filter sits on top of the Lancia neé Ferrari 2.4 litre V6. Pannier tanks carry the fuel. Behind the nearside tank, the drop gear case can be seen (detachable from the back of the clutch housing). Overall ratio changes are relatively easy. Note the hefty chassis frame running around the top of the engine and the tube work that is carried forward.

Automatically Beta

First-time automatic transmission for Lancia, developed from AP's four-speed transverse engine unit originally used in the Mini

By Martin Lewis

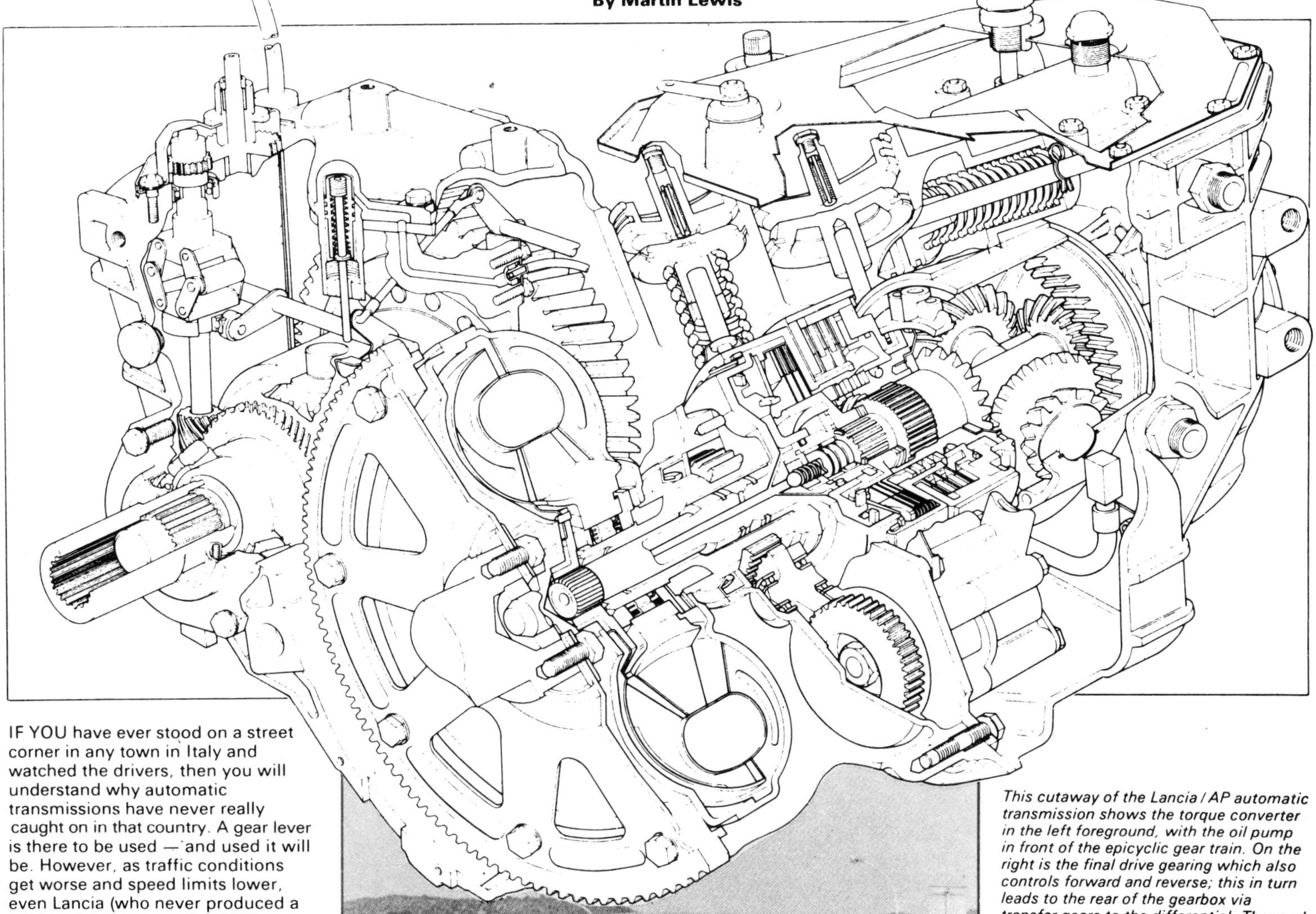

This cutaway of the Lancia/AP automatic transmission shows the torque converter in the left foreground, with the oil pump in front of the epicyclic gear train. On the right is the final drive gearing which also controls forward and reverse; this in turn leads to the rear of the gearbox via transfer gears to the differential. The road speed detection governer is driven from an output on the left-hand side of the differential, alongside the dipstick

Left: The principle external change for the new model is the extension of the roof gutter down the quarter panel to the rear lamp cluster. Below: To distinguish the automatic versions, the word is added alongside the car's capacity designation

IF YOU have ever stood on a street corner in any town in Italy and watched the drivers, then you will understand why automatic transmissions have never really caught on in that country. A gear lever is there to be used — and used it will be. However, as traffic conditions get worse and speed limits lower, even Lancia (who never produced a left-hand drive car until 1952) saw the sense in providing a driver with a transmission which will save wear and tear on the car, do away with the clutch and at the same time give the sort of performance expected of the *marque*.

The story of Lancia's venture into automatic transmission goes back about six years, when they approached Automotive Products with a view to setting up a joint project. AP are the company who made the four-speed automatic used in the Mini, 1100/1300 and Allegro, thus breaking into the Borg-Warner stronghold. The compact, transverse engine layout seemed ideal for application to Lancia's new transverse engine Beta range and for a time things progressed well. Then AP decided that they were going to get out of the market, thus threatening to leave Lancia suspended in mid-air, with a half-developed transmission and no technical backup. AP were persuaded to continue with the development, and the three-speed automatic for the Beta was able to go ahead.

To produce the transmission, Lancia have built an entirely new factory at Verrone, making all the components with the exception of the torque converter and control valves, which are supplied from Britain by AP. With development of the three-speed unit for the Beta range now complete, Lancia are concentrating on a four-speed automatic for the Gamma range, and this will probably come into production in the autumn of 1979.

Although the engine layout in the Beta range is transverse, the gearbox is in line with the crankshaft, to the right of the block. The starter ring gear and torque converter take the place of the flywheel on the manual transmission cars; on the 1995 c.c. Beta, the converter ratio is 1.95 to 1, while on the smaller-engined models it is 2.05 to 1. Two main control valves govern the car's direction. The primary one gives forward motion, while the secondary one acts in conjunction with the first to give direct top (with no relative movement of the epicyclic gear trains), and on its own to give reverse. The gears are selected by three sets of brake bands working on the epicyclic gear clusters.

Unlike the original four-speed AP transmission, which was operated and lubricated with the oil shared by the engine, the Lancia version is separate, using automatic transmission fluid. The pump is driven from the rear of the torque converter, with straight-cut gears, plus an idler, transmitting the power. The pump is located on the forward face of the box, and a separate heat exchanger is fitted to keep fluid temperatures within limits, especially when the car is being used for towing.

From the output end of the gear train, a pair of transfer gears take the drive to the rear of the gearbox, to the final drive. On the 1600 cars, the reduction is 1.17 to 1, while on the 2000 models, it is 1.24 to 1. The gear ratios and final drive ratio are common to both models: first gear is 2.346 to 1, and second 1.402 to 1, with a 4.38 to 1 final drive ratio. For the 2000 model, this gives a top gear figure of 19.5 mph/1000 rpm, against the 19.7 mph/1000 rpm of the five-speed manual transmission model.

The gear selector follows the conventional P-R-D-2-1 pattern, with free movement between D and 2; a press-down catch on top of the selector knob allows other positions to be reached. Unlike most other automatics, when 2 is selected, the car starts in that gear and stays there, with no kick down to first. This is useful in town driving, preventing uncomfortable hunting up and down between gears, but it can also lead to the driver being caught out at times when full acceleration is needed to get from oncoming traffic at a junction, for instance.

Left: The transmission seen from the rear, showing the transfer gearing and shaft which takes power to the differential

Lancia have built in a nice refinement to compensate for the load imposed by the torque converter when the car is stationary in traffic. To prevent tick-over from becoming lumpy, a bleed valve from the brake servo vacuum system slightly raises the revs when the brake pedal is pressed. This system operates both when the car is in gear or neutral, and appears to have no adverse effect on behaviour when, for instance, braking for a corner.

Improving the Beta

Several of the forthcoming improvements to the Beta range were seen on the cars shown at last month's Motor Show, although they will be introduced only gradually onto the cars coming into Britain. Initially, the automatic transmission will be available only on the 2000ES, when sales start early in the New Year. This will be followed by the 1600 and basic 2000 models (probably in April) and finally by the coupé and HPE versions.

For the engine, electronic ignition is now fitted, with the power pack bolted to the lefthand suspension turret. On the carburettor, a power valve is being used to automatically enrich mixture as the second choke comes into operation. A thermostatically controlled device is now used on the carburettor air intake to give a better warm-up and smoother running.

Inside, a new cloth trim is used on the seats and headlining, and the boot is now fully carpeted. Externally, the only major change is the extension of the roof guttering down the quarter panel to give a better line and to prevent rain streaking on the coachwork. Unfortunately, power steering, which is available on left-hand drive cars, cannot be fitted to those with right-hand drive.

Road impressions

With the very good selector arrangement, the Beta automatic is a car which can be driven equally well as a manual gearshift car — thus preserving to some extent the Italian's love affair with the gear lever. However, this is an automatic transmission first and foremost, and as such is not quite as refined as some of the more conventional designs. Nevertheless, it matches the Beta's lively performance and handling well.

In Drive, and under full throttle, upward changes occur at 6000 rpm from first to second, equivalent to 50 mph. The second to top change on the car which we drove took place some 200 rpm lower down the scale, at 5800 rpm — or 81 mph. The transmission kicked down from top to second at under 72 mph, and from second to first at under 40 mph. There is also a part-throttle kick down facility, depending on road speed and load.

Initially the transmission seemed a little too eager to change down from top to first if left in Drive when being used in busy traffic conditions, and if general speeds were in the 30 to 40 mph region, engine revs and gear ratios could be sent all over the place when overtaking, as the transmission went from top to first at full throttle, then into second and top again as the manouvre was completed. Experience taught that unless this full-bore type of acceleration is needed, it is far better to snick the selector back into second, thus preventing the kick down into first.

Full-throttle upward changes can produce a noticeable thump, due mainly to the very short drive line which has little torsional flexibility. At part throttle, and especially if one lifts off fractionally to "fool" the transmission, changes are far smoother.

As we have said, care must be taken not to get caught out with the selector in second when full acceleration is needed to avoid a potentially dangerous situation. The remedy is to either put the selector forward into Drive, and let the transmission make its own decisions, or to revert to the semi-automatic mode, and drop down manually into first. The transmission is not particularly quiet, especially in the intermediate gears, where a degree of whining can be heard.

The test cars had hardly completed sufficient distance to be considered fully run in, but as a rough comparison, a 0 to 100 kph (62 mph) time of 13.6 sec was achieved, against the 10.1 sec for the 0 to 60 mph (true) time reached with the *Autotest* 2000 of 25 September 1976. A top speed of 175 kph (109 mph) was reached on a speedometer reading; again, the 2000 manual transmission car had a true maximum of 110 mph. Although no on-the-road fuel consumption figures could be taken, the DoE figures may provide a measure of comparison. In the urban driving cycle, the automatic 2000ES returns 23.9 mpg against 21.7 for manual, while at a constant 56 mph, the figures are 31.7 against 37.7, while at a constant 75 mph, the automatic gives 25.5 compared to the manual car's 30.7 mpg.

The price of the automatic transmission will add £394.29, including Special Car Tax and VAT, to the price of the 2000ES when it becomes available in January. □

Changes to the engine include electronic ignition, with the "black box" located on the right-hand suspension turret, and a new thermostatically-controlled carburettor air intake system

More lovable Lancias

By Stuart Bladen

Refinements for Beta Coupé and HPE

MANY drivers find it difficult to understand the special appeal of a Lancia with its numerous slightly dated features, but the attraction is very much in the way the cars behave on the road. This aspect has been left largely unchanged in the newly-announced revisions for the Coupé and HPE models, and instead concentration has been put on eliminating some of the more common causes of criticism.

Thus there is a re-designed facia panel, minor controls are improved, and new seats are fitted having a better shape and featuring woollen cloth upholstery. The instrument panel is now formed in a one-piece plastic moulding with prominent upper and lower lips, and includes housing for a radio, which always seemed rather forgotten on previous models. A new style of steering wheel, with inverted V-shaped spokes, blends well with the new facia material, and has a considerably larger central horn boss. The facia layout is a great deal tidier than before, though some will no doubt still regret that the opportunity was not taken to fit clearer and more modern-looking instruments. Deletion of the former wood panel from the facia has bettered, rather than detracted from, the appearance.

The wiper control is now on the column, giving choice of intermittent, slow or fast, and the separate facia knob for controlling wiper speed has also gone. Column switches are now symbol-labelled. The facia clock is replaced by a neat little digital clock of the same type as that on the Fiat Ritmo.

The heater has been modified to a new air blending type with more understandable sliding controls now higher up in the centre of the facia, and illuminated at night.

Other additions include internally adjustable door mirrors — two for the HPE, one on the Coupé — plastic mud shields in the front wheel arches, and halogen headlamps. In revising the seats, access to the rear compartment has been made easier by arranging the seat cushion to slide forward when the backrest is tipped forward. The former release lever at the lower edge of the seat, which one can easily operate with the foot, is retained and in addition there is a central release button just below the headrest on the back of each seat, making it easier for anyone in the back to tip the seat forward to get out.

As predicted when we reported on the new automatic version in November last year, Bosch electronic ignition is now fitted. There is also a thermostatic control to maintain air flow into the carburettor at a constant 25 deg C. A change on the Coupé 1300 is a tiny increase in bore diameter to take it over 1300 c.c. instead of just under, qualifying for the upper speed limit of 87 mph in Italy. No power output changes are made, except that the 2000 engine has decreased slightly from 119 to 115 bhp.

Tried in rather cold weather last week, some aspects of the new models proved a little disappointing. Thus, the heater, although more controllable than ever before, proved very lacking in output; and the engine changes have not cured the hesitant and snatchy running during warm-up. Not a great deal of thought seems to have gone into the revised facia panel because it still has instrument lighting that is inadequate at night, and the new digital clock is so buried away that the driver has to bend to peer at it.

In some other matters, though, there has been useful improvement, notably the much better headlamps, the improved rear access, and the more comfortable seating. It was certainly a pleasure to sit on the warm woollen seats after the car had stood out in sub-zero overnight air. They should also prove comfortable in hot weather. □

Prices are unchanged, and the Coupé is available as before with choice of 1300, 1600 or 2000 engine. The three-door HPE is available with 1600 or 2000 engine. Redesigned seats are now upholstered in woollen cloth material, and the facia panel has been completely re-shaped for neater appearance

AutoTEST

Lancia Beta 1600 HPE

Better, but still far from perfect

Lancia Beta HPE 1600
Much improved version of Lancia hatchback with better-finished interior. Original layout largely unchanged as first introduced in 1975 at the Geneva Show, with transverse dohc four-cylinder engine. 1600 version tested has the smaller of two engine sizes available for the HPE. Car tested has standard five-speed manual gearbox, but automatic transmission will be available for the HPE later this year. Engine improved by changes to carburation and introduction of electronic ignition, but problems of warm-up hesitance remain.

PRODUCED BY:

Fiat Auto SpA, Lancia-Sede Centrale, Viv V. Lancia 27, 10141 Torino, Italy.

SOLD IN THE UK BY:

Lancia (England) Ltd., Ealing Road, Alperton, Middlesex.

REVISED versions of the Coupé and HPE Lancia Beta models were announced in February, promising a number of improvements. During our *Autotest* we have found the extent of the changes to be less than had been hoped for, and some areas that should have been made better remain a problem. Despite all this, the picture emerges of a car that is very much aimed at the enthusiast, which provides great enjoyment for the driver who takes a pride in his skill at the wheel, and which is liked in spite of its faults.

This is our first test of the HPE in 1600 form, previously we have tested the very comparable Coupé 1600, and both Long Term and *Autotest* reports were published on the HPE 2000. Chief changes are to the interior fittings and trim, but the engine now has electronic ignition.

Basic mechanical details and layout of the car are unchanged, and the formula is very attractive, presenting the rather unusual combination of high performance machinery in a semi-estate car of compact dimensions. In the 1600, the engine is a short stroke unit with relatively high compression at 9.4-to-1, and it develops a creditable 100bhp at 5,800rpm. As for all Lancias, it has belt-driven twin overhead camshafts. The engine is transverse mounted and drives the front wheels through a five-speed manual gearbox. There is no automatic option, though as we have already announced, the Automotive Products-designed automatic is to become available later this year.

The engine for both models was substantially altered in 1976 when bore and stroke were increased to produce the 1,995 c.c. 2-litre model. The 1600 has the same bore diameter of 84mm, and only the stroke and compression are different. The 1600 is thus quite different from the former 1600 which was an exactly "square" engine and developed eight bhp more.

Performance
Seems quicker than it is

When driving the 1600, the engine is so lively and responsive that the impression given is of a high-efficiency unit giving really vigorous performance. When it comes to measuring the acceleration against the stop watch, the figures perhaps come as a slight disappointment, and no one is going to get very excited over a time of 11.3sec to reach 60mph from rest, and a standing quarter-mile in 18.0sec.

It is a very eager and high revving engine, which produces an angry snarl when accelerating hard that adds to the responsive nature implied by the High Performance Estate name of the car. The engine soars through the rev range without any vibration periods but it could never be called smooth. It is the sort of engine in which the harshness of the combustion is such that you could never fail to know about it if the engine ever "missed a beat". At the top end there is no thrash, and it reaches the indicated rev limit at 6,500rpm while still pulling strongly.

External appearance is largely unchanged from the previous HPE. Side and indicator lamps are recessed into the bumper, protected by the rubber facing

At lower revs the engine is rather intractible and gives a lot of vibration if it is made to pull in fifth gear from anything less than about 30mph. It is interesting to note, too, that more fuel was taken at 30mph in fifth than at 50mph, confirming that the driver is well-advised to make free use of the indirect gears. Fifth gear is not as high as it seems to be, giving only 18.5mph per 1,000rpm, but the engine is apparently quite unstressed when sustaining just under 5,000rpm which provides a 90mph cruising speed.

Testing has not been easy this winter, and we had to abandon performance figures on one day with the Lancia when the wind was gusting to 50mph. When we ran repeat tests the wind was still fairly brisk at 15mph and the car was unfortunate in having the direction of the gusts absolutely down the test track, so that one way it was a head wind. This had some effect, inevitably, on the performance figures, which are not as good as they might be at the top end, though to reach 90mph in 32.3sec is not unreasonable for a 1600. We were also able, even under these conditions, to shave a fraction off the official Lancia times for the car.

Maximum speed runs also suffered slightly, and against the wind the 1600 was not quite able to reach 100mph. However, a best of 106 with the wind behind it gave a mean top speed of 102mph. This is a long way down from the 113 achieved by the previous 1600 in the Coupé body, but with more size and less power it is the inevitable result.

One of the changes to the new engine is provision of thermostatic control for the air fed to the carburettor, but sadly we have to report no improvement in the poor cold running behaviour. The engine starts promptly enough but runs with a lot of snatch and hesitance for at least the first mile. Enrichment is automatic but it just does not cope adequately with a cold weather start, and the Lancia engineers would be well advised to examine the latest trends to electrically heated hot spots in a bid to remedy this problem.

Clutch take-up is smooth, with plenty of bite to spin the wheels when making standing start tests. Most cars cope so easily with the 1 in 3 test hill restart these days that we often do not comment on it, but the Lancia found this decidedly difficult. The engine lacked the torque to pull away in first gear, and the clutch did not like the prolonged slip necessary to get going. The only satisfactory technique proved to be deliberate abrupt clutch release to cause wheelspin, and then it would just cope.

Once thoroughly warmed through, the gear change is reasonably good although tending to notchiness; at least the positions are well defined and the lever has sturdy, positive feel to it. The change up into fifth, offset alongside third gear position, is particularly satisfying. When the unit is cold, however, the change is very reluctant and it sometimes proved almost impossible to get into second gear in the morning at the first try.

The revised facia layout is much more logical than before, and the instruments are better positioned, but they are still rather lacking clarity. Minor instruments have no calibration. A digital clock is recessed to the left of the steering-wheel and lights up only when the ignition switch is turned to the accessories position. It is rather concealed to be read clearly. Column mounted controls are the indicator's lever on the right and multi-control for windscreen wipers and washers on the left. The third lever controls the lamps, which is both rotated and moved in the vertical plane. The horns are sounded by pressing the steering-wheel boss

Economy
Good potential

At this stage we should emphasize that, despite inevitable criticisms, we really enjoyed driving this little Lancia. It is the sort of car that seems to urge the driver on and he finds himself pushing it hard just for the fun of it. The outcome, of course, is that we have run through quite a lot of fuel, but perhaps the overall figure of 25.4mpg is fair enough for a spiritedly driven and quite roomy four-seater. In particular, the efficient engine and quite good body shape give satisfactory potential for economy and the owner will easily find that moderate restraint will enable him to keep on the right side of 30mpg. We exceeded 27mpg on runs which included a lot of cruising at 90mph and above.

A rather bigger fuel tank than the 10.8-gallon one fitted would also be appreciated. Once or twice we ran the car until the fuel warning light had been on for a worryingly long time but still had covered only 260 miles since the last fill-up.

As explained already, the engine does not take kindly to low revs, and it seems to come very much "on song" for efficiency at about 60–80mph in fifth, and does not drop too rapidly when sustaining 90mph. The extra to maintain 100mph is relatively extravagant.

There was no measurable drop in oil level during the test, and we appreciated the fitting of a remote oil level check button. On the right of the facia, it is pressed in and gives an indication of level on a separate gauge. The reading can be taken only when the engine is at rest, but one tends to get into the habit of pressing the button whenever the car is on level standing, before starting up.

Road behaviour
Sheer fun

It is in the way that the Lancia HPE handles and responds that goes with the responsive nature of the power unit to make it a very rewarding car to drive. It sits down square and sure on the road and flies round with no protest from the tyres and absolutely minimal roll. In extreme conditions the driver gets more and more aware of the understeer, and there is a safety factor in the way in which it tucks in more tightly if the throttle is eased in mid-corner.

Suspension is independent front and rear by coil springs and MacPherson struts, and the impression given is that it is very heavily damped. Severe undulations are swallowed up at almost any speed without any violent reaction, but ordinary surface irregularities are all transmitted to the body as a constant joggy vertical movement. It is not at all upsetting for the occupants, indeed many prefer a rather firm ride such as this to one that is looser and more prone to float.

As already mentioned, we were driving the HPE on some days in conditions of very high wind. On these occasions it was always a surprise to arrive and get out to find the wind blowing as strongly as it was, as the car remains so stable and easily controllable in cross winds that it disguises the severity of the weather. The rack and pinion steering is fairly low-geared taking nearly four turns between the extremes of quite modest locks, but it gives very good response with no detectable lost movement.

In hard cornering the extra steering load tells the driver how hard he is pushing the car without getting objectionably heavy. However, at low speeds the steering toughens up considerably and becomes fairly hard work.

Ordinary impressions of the brakes on the road are of good response in nice progression with extra load on the pedal, and the car stops very well without fuss from high speed — the sort of braking one has to do when slowing from 90mph to take a roundabout. When it came to actually testing the brakes against a deceleration meter it was disappointing to find that we could not achieve more than 82 per cent g without locking the front wheels and leaving heavy black lines on the road.

It was suspected that the pressure limiting valve in the line to the rear brakes was doing more work than it should, and we confirmed this by improving the figure to 95 per cent when we used the handbrake in conjunction with the foot brake. The handbrake gives good leverage and holds firmly — given a strong pull up — on the 1 in 3 test hill; but one cannot expect the driver to remember to use the handbrake as well in case of emergency.

The front-hinged bonnet gives good access to the engine compartment, but the space is very crowded for anything other than routine work

Behind the wheel
Still some grumbles

One needs to know what a strange old jumble the former Lancia HPE facia design was, to appreciate the improvements in the new one. It is, in fact, much better, but newcomers to the marque will be rather dismayed at the weirdly marked symbols and vague instruments. There is no calibration on the instruments, and it takes a little thought to work out what is a high reading and what is low. In fact, all but the voltmeter have the danger limit in red, and the voltmeter has both ends of the scale in red. The strange symbols are so bizarre that it could almost be a guessing game to identify some of them. The owner will eventually learn what they all mean, but this still does not forgive poor design.

A digital clock is fitted, which lights up only when the ignition is turned to the accessories position. It keeps excellent time, but unfortunately is so buried away in a narrow slot in the lower edge of the facia panel that the driver has to bend down to see it at all, and even then is liable to lose the tops of the figures and mistake a 7 for a 1.

One of the significant improvements made to the Lancia is a redesign of its heating and ventilation. Unfortunately they still have not made a very good job of it, and it is the only car we can think of having an air blending heater in which response to the temperature control is so abrupt as to make it difficult to adjust. In fact, the output of the heater is decidedly limited and one can run for about the first half hour of a winter morning with the heater full on before it gets uncomfortably warm in the car. On the credit side, it is true that very careful adjustment of the temperature lever over about a half inch of its travel does give a possibility of obtaining the desired temperature. Ram effect is poor so that the fan has to be on most of the time for adequate output, and it tends to be very noisy even on the slowest of its three speeds.

For warm weather there is good output from directional centre outlets and there will then be much less cause for criticism. The car can also be ordered with a sliding steel sunroof, though this was not fitted to the test car.

One of the most significant changes in the new Lancia is complete redesign of the seating, which is now upholstered in woollen cloth claimed to be warm in winter — which it certainly was — and should also be pleasantly free from stickiness or clamminess in summer. The seats are well shaped and give excellent lateral and small of the back support. There is adequate rearward seat adjustment to cope with long-legged drivers, and the backrests have infinitely variable rake adjustment by means of a hand wheel. Headrests are standard, which can be pulled upwards to position correctly behind the head. When pushed fully down they are low enough not to be too obstructive of vision, but if need be, they are readily removed.

A release lever which one would normally operate with the foot is provided at the lower outer edge of each front seat, to enable it to tip forward for access to the rear compartment. When it does so, the seat cushion also slides forward which makes it particularly easy to get in and out. On the test car, the release lever on the driving seat was not working, but an additional

Doors open wide for good access, and a lever on the side of the seat can be pressed down with the foot to allow the back-rest to tip forward

release for use by the rear passengers is fitted in the centre of the seat backrest, just below the headrest. This *was* working, and enabled us to move the driving seat forward for access as well. Rear windows open outwards with an over-centre catch on each side.

Accommodation for those in the back is snug and comfortable, with adequate legroom. Those who remember the removable bolsters of the former model thought it a pity that these had been deleted, but there are still no grounds for complaint about the standards of front and rear comfort offered.

In particular, the driving position is very suitable, with the steering wheel at good arm's length, adequate legroom and thigh support, and very fair visibility. The more usual complaint of design for the short-legged Italian does not apply to the HPE.

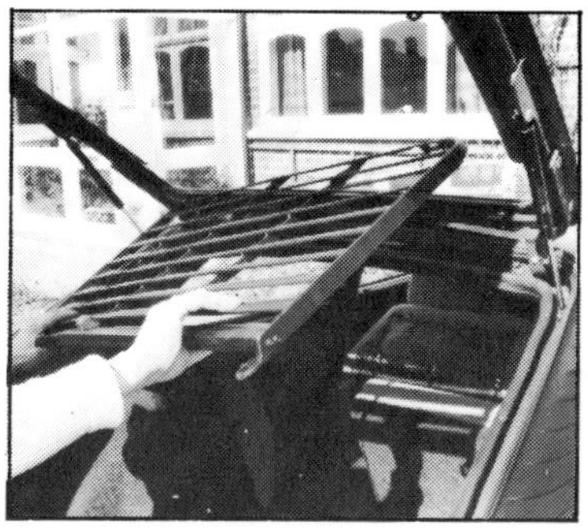

Above: Rear vision is seriously obstructed by the rear window slats, but this panel is quite readily removed

Left: A rear window wiper is fitted, but there is no provision for rear window washing

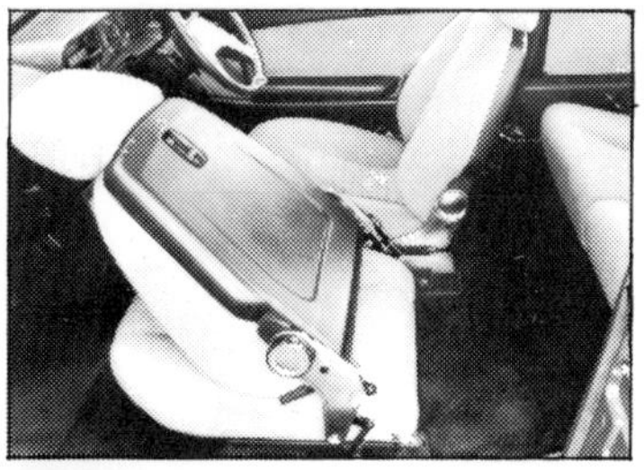

Above: The rear compartment gives comfortable accommodation for two and can take an occasional third passenger

Right: In addition to the side-lever release, there is a release button beneath the head-rest which makes it easy for the back seat passengers to let themselves out

Below: There is neat provision of a roller blind to cover luggage and possessions in the rear load space. Either half of the back seat can be tipped forward for extra luggage space

Living with the HPE

Special appeal of the HPE is its versatile body. Among other things, we used it to transport a large sheet of glass, which certainly would not have been possible in a more conventional design saloon. A release catch at the top edge of each rear seat allows the backrest to be pushed forward to increase the already quite generous load space. First, the seat cushion must be pulled up and tipped forward. It is convenient that either or both seats may be moved forward in this way, so that there is still possibility of generous luggage space with three occupants on board. A hinged panel at the back of each rear seat can be pushed up to the vertical as a bulkhead against forward movement of luggage. We found the release catches rather difficult to operate without actually climbing into the rear load space first, but the arrangement and resulting space are good.

The tailgate is released by the same strange key — flat but with multi-drillings, making it difficult for thieves to force the lock — that is used for the doors. We admired the way in which the tailgate lock is a pushbutton release until it is locked, when the button retreats into its hole so it cannot be forced. The door locks have vertical lock buttons which blend into the surrounding trim.

Halogen headlamps are fitted, and they give good range on main or dipped beams, with sharp cut-off when dipped. Automatic height adjustment is provided with load, and we found this worked unobtrusively and effectively. The light switch is a column mounted lever which is turned once to put the side lamps on. It then gives side or dipped when moved up or down. A further rotation of the lever changes this function to dipped or main beam, and there is an inter-lock so that you cannot turn off the lamps without moving the lever first to the upper position. This arrangement proved very convenient to use.

We also appreciated the unusual feature — on a foreign car — that the indicators lever was on the right — which is still where most British drivers expect to find it, although there are moves to bring us in line with Europe, and have the indicators stalk on the left. It is also unusual that the indicators lever has no other function. The pleasing shrill tone horns are sounded by the inverted centre part of the steering wheel.

A third column lever on the left operates the windscreen washers when pulled toward the driver — but without any inter-linked wiper function; in the vertical plane it gives choice of slow, fast or intermittent wiper operation. A rocker switch beside the heater controls turns on the heated rear window, with tell-tale warning light, and an adjacent one works the rear window wiper. This is a single one-press one-wipe switch, and there is no provision for constant rear window wiping, but except at low speeds it keeps clear. There is also no provision for rear window washing, nor did we find any need for this.

Under the bonnet the layout is almost frighteningly crowded, but in fact, access to anything requiring regular attention is easy enough. It is in all respects a complex car, not without a number of faults that could easily and inexpensively be remedied; but anyone who knew the HPE before will find the new one a big improvement, and will enjoy living with the HPE for its sheer vitality and fun and will learn to accept its numerous faults.

The Lancia Beta Range

Betas come in three body styles — the saloon, the two-door coupé and three-door HPE hatchback. The four-door saloons and the coupé come with choice of 1300, 1600 or 2000 engine. For the HPE, there is just a choice of two models — the 1600, as tested, and the 2000. The essential difference is extension of the stroke on the 2000 engine from 71.5 to 90mm, and the 2000 is also slightly higher-geared, having a 3.785-to-1 final drive ratio instead of the 4.07 ratio of the 1600.

HOW THE LANCIA BETA HPE 1600 PERFORMS

MAXIMUM SPEEDS

Gear	mph	kph	rpm
Top (mean)	102	164	5,570
(best)	106	171	5,800
4th	96	155	6,500
3rd	72	116	6,500
2nd	49	79	6,500
1st	31	50	6,500

TEST CONDITIONS:

Wind: 10-15 mph
Temperature: 4 deg C (40 deg F)
Barometer: 29.5 in. Hg (1,000 mbar)
Humidity: 40 per cent
Surface: dry asphalt and concrete
Test distance: 1,050 miles

Figures taken at 2,700 miles by our own staff at the Motor Industry Research Association proving ground at Nuneaton.

ACCELERATION

FROM REST

True mph	Time (sec)	Speedo mph
30	3.9	32
40	5.7	42
50	8.4	52
60	11.3	63
70	15.3	74
80	21.7	85
90	32.3	96
100	—	107

Standing ¼-mile: 18.0 sec, 73 mph
Standing km: 33.6 sec, 91 mph

IN EACH GEAR

mph	Top	4th	3rd	2nd
10-30	—	—	6.7	4.3
20-40	13.5	8.8	5.8	3.9
30-50	12.2	8.0	5.7	—
40-60	12.2	8.4	5.8	—
50-70	13.1	8.8	6.5	—
60-80	15.2	10.1	—	—
70-90	19.6	13.7	—	—

FUEL CONSUMPTION

Overall mpg;
25.4 (11.1 litres/100 km)

Constant speed:

mph	mpg	mph	mpg
30	35.4	70	29.0
40	41.4	80	24.2
50	39.2	90	19.8
60	32.8	100	16.5

Autocar formula: Hard 22.9 mpg
Driving and conditions: Average 27.9 mpg; Gentle 33.0 mpg

Grade of fuel: Premium, 4-star (98 RM)
Fuel tank: 10.8 Imp. galls (49 litres)
Mileage recorder: 4 per cent long

Official fuel consumption figures
(ECE laboratory test conditions; not necessarily related to Autocar figures)
Urban cycle: 24.6 mpg
Steady 56 mph: 44.1 mpg
Steady 75 mph: 30.7 mpg

OIL CONSUMPTION

(SEA 10W/50) negligible

BRAKING

Fade *(from 73 mph in neutral)*
Pedal load for 0.5g stops in lb

	start/end		start/end
1	30/20	6	25/45
2	30/30	7	30/45
3	35/25	8	30/45
4	30/40	9	30/45
5	30/40	10	30/40

Response *(from 30 mph in neutral)*

Load	g	Distance
20 lb	0.31	97 ft
40 lb	0.62	49 ft
60 lb	0.80	38 ft
65 lb	0.82	36.6 ft
Handbrake	0.32	94 ft

Max. gradient: 1 in 3

CLUTCH

Pedal 30 lb; Travel 6 in.

WEIGHT

Kerb, 20.3 cwt/2,270 lb/1,030 kg
(Distribution F/R, 57.9/42.1)
Test, 23.3 cwt/2,610 lb/1,186 kg
Max. payload 1,100 lb/500 kg

DIMENSIONS

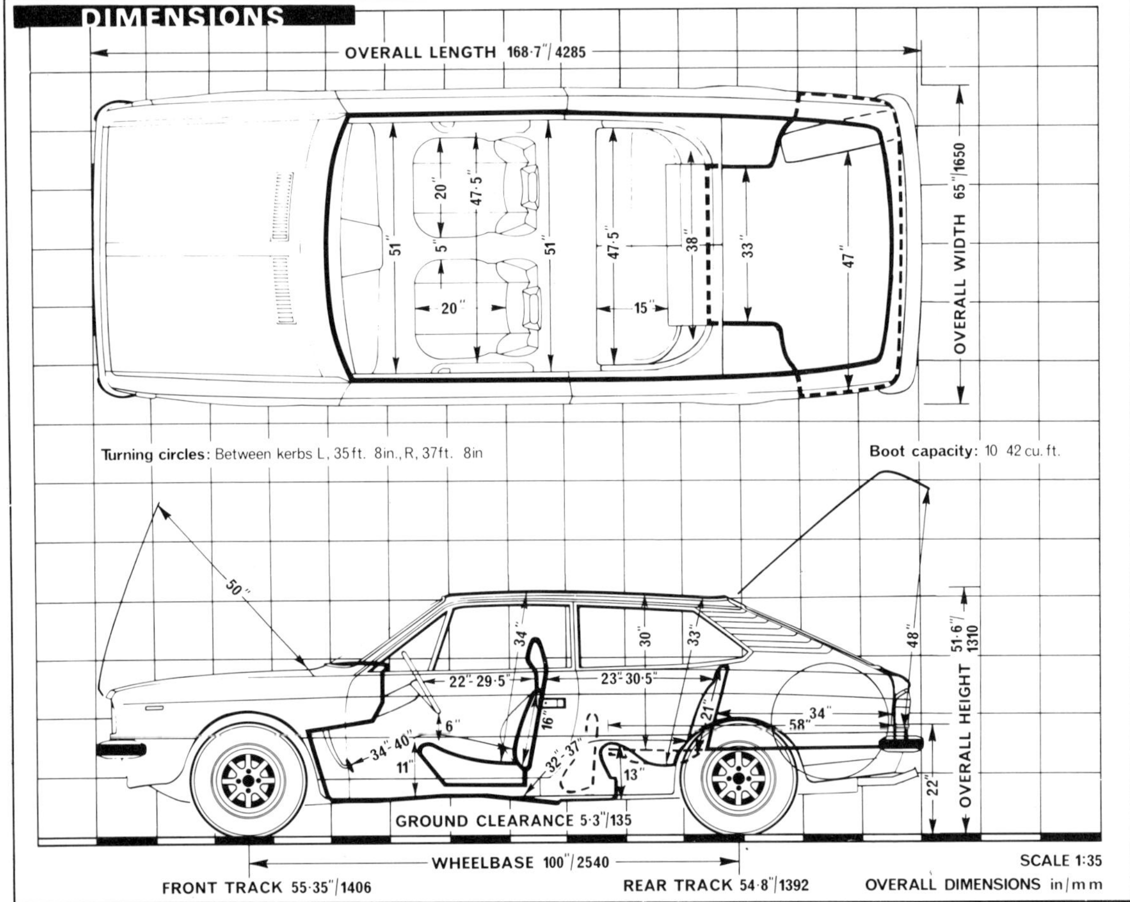

PRICES

Basic	£4,735.00
Special Car Tax	£394.58
VAT	£410.37
Total (in GB)	**£5,539.95**
Seat Belts	Standard
Licence	£50.00
Delivery charge	Included
Number plates	£12.00
Total on the Road (exc. insurance)	**£5,601.95**
EXTRAS (inc. VAT)	
*Metallic paint	£181.35
*Electric windows	£149.78

**Not on test car*

TOTAL AS TESTED ON THE ROAD	**£5,601.95**
Insurance	Group 6

SERVICE & PARTS

Interval			
Change	**6,000**	**12,000**	**18,000**
Engine oil	Yes	Yes	Yes
Oil filter	Yes	Yes	Yes
Gearbox oil	No	No	Yes
Spark plugs	Yes	Yes	Yes
Air cleaner	Yes	Yes	Yes
Total cost	£17.52	£36.70	£21.34

(Assuming labour at £6.50/hour)

PARTS COST *(including VAT)*

Brake pads (2 wheels)—front	£10.02
Brake pads (2 wheels)—rear	£9.36
Exhaust complete	£113.90
Tyre—each (typical advertised)	£30.84
Windscreen	£48.69
Headlamp unit	£5.30
Front wing	£39.49
Rear bumper	£52.49

WARRANTY

12 months/unlimited mileage

SPECIFICATION

ENGINE

ENGINE	Front, front drive
Head/block	Aluminium alloy/cast iron
Cylinders	4 in line, transverse
Main bearings	5
Cooling	Water
Fan	Electric
Bore, mm (in.)	84 (3.3)
Stroke, mm (in.)	71.5 (2.81)
Capacity, cc (in³)	1,585 (96.7)
Valve gear	Dohc
Camshaft drive	Toothed belt
Compression ratio	9.4-to-1
Ignition	Breakerless
Carburettor	Weber 34 DAT 1/250
Max power	100 bhp (DIN) at 5,800 rpm
Max torque	99 lb ft at 3,000 rpm

TRANSMISSION

Type		Five-speed all-synchromesh
Clutch		S.d.p. 200 mm
Gear	Ratio	mph/1000 rpm
Top	0.93	18.3
4th	1.15	14.7
3rd	1.52	11.12
2nd	2.24	7.57
1st	3.50	4.83
Final drive gear		Helical spur
Ratio		4.07-to-1

SUSPENSION

Front—location	MacPherson struts
springs	Coil
dampers	Telescopic
anti-roll bar	Yes
Rear—location	MacPherson strut
springs	Coil
dampers	Telescopic
anti-roll bar	Yes

STEERING

Type	Rack and pinion
Power assistance	No
Wheel diameter	14.8 in.
Turns lock to lock	3.8

BRAKES

Circuits	Two (one front, and one all four)
Front	9.9 in. dia. disc
Rear	9.9 in. dia. disc
Servo	Yes
Handbrake	Centre lever operating rear discs

WHEELS

Type	Alloy
Rim Wdith	5½J
Tyres—make	Michelin
—type	ZX
—size	175/70 SR 14
—pressures	F27, R27 psi (normal driving)

EQUIPMENT

Battery	12V 45Ah
Alternator	55A
Headlamps	110W
Reversing lamp	Standard
Hazard warning	Standard
Electric fuses	16
Screen wipers	2-speed, plus intermittent
Screen washer	Electric
Interior heater	Air blending
Air conditioning	Not available
Interior trim	Woollen cloth seats, and headlining
Floor covering	Carpet
Jack	Screw pillar with winding handle
Jacking points	1 each side
Windscreen	Laminated
Underbody protection	Electrophoretic phosphate and tectile cavity injection

HOW THE LANCIA BETA HPE 1600 COMPARES

Lancia Beta HPE 1600 — £5,540

Front engine, front drive

Capacity 1,585 c.c.

Power 100 bhp (DIN) at 5,800 rpm

Weight 2,270 lb / 1,030 kg

Autotest 21 April 1979

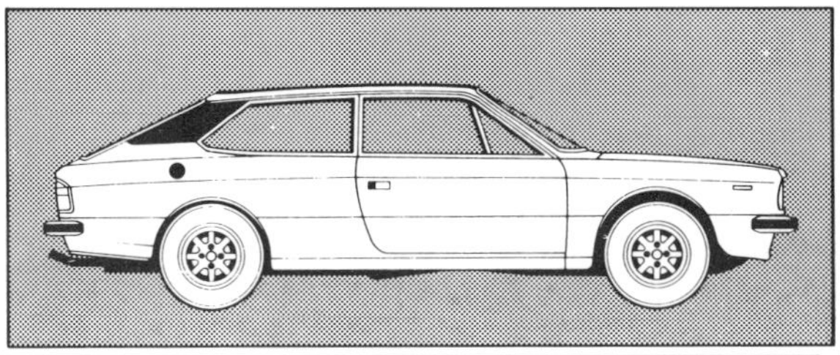

BMW 320 — £5,797

Front engine, rear drive

Capacity 1,990 c.c.

Power 122 bhp (DIN) at 6,000 rpm

Weight 2,390 lb / 1,090 kg

Autotest 19 November 1977

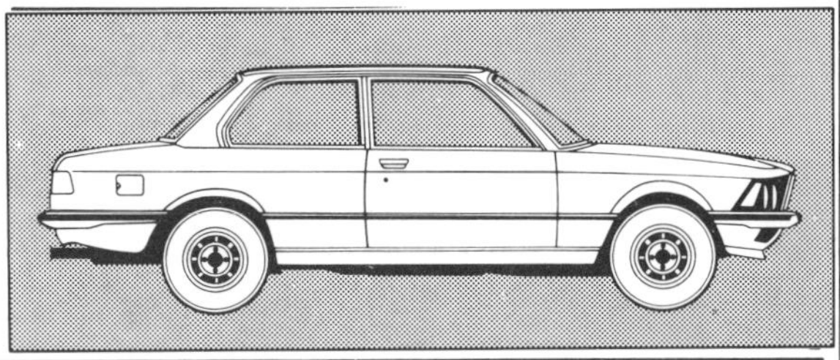

Colt Sapporo 2000 GSR — £5,899

Front engine, rear drive

Capacity 1,995 c.c.

Power 98 bhp (DIN) at 5,500 rpm

Weight 2,525 lb / 1,145 kg

Autotest 20 May 1978

Ford Capri 3000S — £4,839

Front engine, rear drive

Capacity 2,994 c.c.

Power 138 bhp (DIN) at 5,000 rpm

Weight 2,574 lb / 1,168 kg

Autotest 13 November 1976

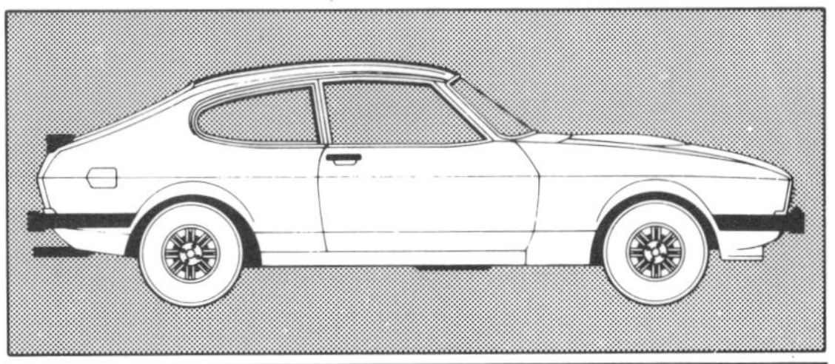

Toyota Celica 2000GT — £5,417

Front engine, rear drive

Capacity 1,968 c.c.

Power 118 bhp (DIN) at 5,800 rpm

Weight 2,333 lb / 1,058 kg

Autotest 18 March 1978

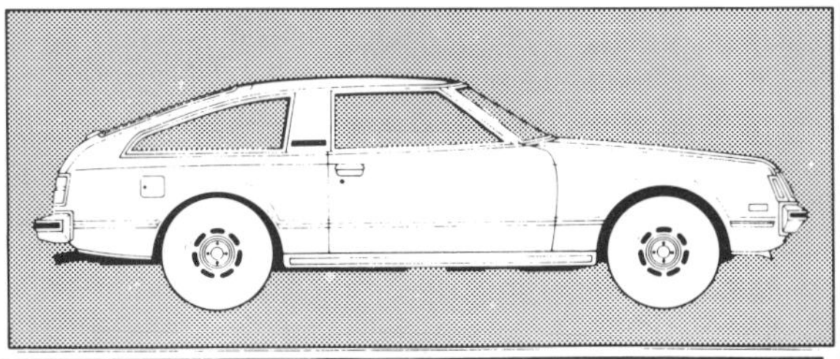

Triumph Dolomite Sprint — £5,408

Front engine, rear drive

Capacity 1,998 c.c.

Power 127 bhp (DIN) at 5,700 rpm

Weight 2,214 lb / 1,005 kg

Autotest 26 July 1973

MPH & MPG

Maximum speed (mph)

Ford Capri 3000S	117
Triumph Dolomite Sprint	115
BMW 320	111
Toyota Celica 2000GT	111
Colt Sapporo 2000SR	102
Lancia Beta HPE 1600	102

Acceleration 0-60 (sec)

Triumph Dolomite Sprint	8.7
Toyota Celica 2000GT	8.8
Ford Capri 3000S	9.0
BMW 320	9.8
Lancia Beta HPE 1600	11.3
Colt Sapporo 2000GSR	12.7

Overall mpg

Lancia Beta HPE 1600	25.4
BMW 320	24.6
Toyota Celica 2000GT	23.9
Triumph Dolomite Sprint	23.6
Ford Capri 3000S	23.1
Colt Sapporo 2000GSR	20.8

Only two of the cars chosen for comparison with the Lancia HPE are hatchbacks — the Ford Capri and Toyota Celica, but the others, we feel, are decidedly in the same sector of the market. We are looking at cars of distinctive appeal and rather sporting pretentions. But it could certainly be claimed that while they are all in the same sort of price league — except the very good value Ford Capri 3000S — the 2000 model of the Lancia Beta HPE could well be there as well since its price does not exceed £6,000. In 1600 form it is rather out-classed, which simply emphasises the undoubted fact that it is expensive in relation to its engine capacity.

While the HPE 1600 is well behind most of its competitors on top speed and acceleration, it appropriately heads the fuel economy list, and many might consider it offers a fair enough compromise for these two conflicting needs. A particularly good showing is made by the Triumph Dolomite Sprint, reflecting the efficiency of its engine, and the Capri 3000S also offers leisurely performance without taking too much fuel in the process. The Toyota Celica and BMW 320 give a good showing on both counts. In summary, the Lancia HPE 1600 holds its head up well in spite of having by far the smallest engine in the group.

ON THE ROAD

Much of the fun of driving the little Lancia is owed to its superb road behaviour, with impeccable and always entirely predictable handling. The way in which it sits down all square on the road and flies round tight bends is really delightful and it certainly has the lead on its rivals here in this respect. In terms of ride comfort it will appeal to those who like a very firmly damped suspension, but more comfort would be found in any of the other five cars, especially the BMW 320, and the Triumph Dolomite. These two are also its closest rivals for steering precision and security in fast cornering. The ride and handling are not the most outstanding features of the two Japanese contenders, and although predictable enough, the Capri 3000S is rather too nose heavy to score well here.

On the important matter of brakes for fast driving, the Lancia needs to be a good deal better. The Dolomite Sprint proved to have the best brakes of the group, followed by the BMW 320 and the Toyota Celica. The Capri stops well enough in the dry, but is prone to lock its front wheels in the wet.

For simplicity and excellence of engine design it is difficult to pick the winner of the group, except to say that the BMW 320 has a superb engine, while in all the others, from the lusty 3-litre V6 of the Capri, through the 16-valve Dolomite unit, to the overhead cam Colt and dohc Toyota, an outstandingly good engine is a major part of the car's special appeal. So it is indeed, with the Lancia, but engine behaviour, with its warm-up problems and the suggestion of harshness, is not quite in the same league as its rivals, while rather low overall gearing even in fifth makes it a little too fussy at speed.

SIZE & SPACE

Legroom front / rear (in)
(seats fully back)

BMW 320	41/37
Ford Capri 3000S	40/36
Triumph Dolomite Sprint	38/38
Colt Sapporo 2000GSR	37/37
Lancia HPE 1600	40/32
Toyota Celica 2000GT	39/33

Dimensions are not the full story when interior roominess is being discussed, and personal experience of the cars considered here leads to the conclusion that the Ford Capri offers the best compromise of front and rear legroom, even though the BMW on paper comes out with a couple of inches more room. The Triumph Dolomite Sprint is about the same as the BMW, but gives more legroom in the back. Both the Japanese cars are a little lacking in front space, and the Lancia makes its rear passengers suffer a rather cramped ride.

VERDICT

When a logical comparison is made between the Lancia Beta HPE 1600 and similar cars on appeal and price, it is rather difficult to justify its choice. Other cars do the job better, and do not suffer from some of its silly problems such as the disappointing ventilation. Any of the cars being considered against the Beta would offer more comfort, with the BMW 320 perhaps coming out on top, closely rivalled by the Dolomite Sprint, while the Ford Capri 3000S would win if we were looking for relaxed fast journey transport. But what one cannot argue against is the special appeal of the Lancia due to its responsive and spirited character; in these respects it is in a class of its own.

NEW

The bumpers front and rear are moulded in glass fibre and designed to survive parking impacts of up to 2½mph

Driving the Delta

Big car standards from Lancia's new small car — but you can't buy one until next year

By Ray Hutton

IN THIS AGE of rationalization and standardization it is encouraging to find that the big wheels of the European motor industry can still produce cars of distinctive character. Fiat Auto was set up to bring the Group's car manufacturing under the same umbrella and could easily have resulted in badge engineered or simply reskinned versions of Fiats to be sold as Lancias. But like Citroen, Peugeot and Talbot in the PSA Group, the influence of the corporation on the individual companies is subtle. Lancia, always fiercely independent in engineering, have to draw from a Fiat components "pool" but continue with their own design team. They wanted a small car, to slot into their range below the Beta and play the role of the Aprilia, Appia and Fulvia of the past. It could have been a Ritmo-Strada by a different name but it isn't.

When you look round the Lancia Delta there are a number of familiar bits. Under the bonnet there is a familiar engine, though with something different in the way of carburettors from the Ritmo original. It is even made in a Fiat factory — Lingotto. But there the resemblance ends.

Lancia describe their role within Fiat as "producing the elite cars" of the Group. They are tooling up for 40 per cent increase in output, and 200,000 sales next year. The high-specification, luxury small car is they say "the car of the moment." It is a social thing; an awareness perhaps that it is unnecessarily wasteful to have a car bigger than you need. If the same luxury, the same equipment, the same aura, can come from something smaller, people will convert to it. A small car needn't be cheap, noisy or unrefined. That is the premise on which the Delta was based. They admit that its lines and its design are conservative (particularly by comparison with the cubist-modern Ritmo) but believe that too is right for its market. It is perhaps what the Triumph Dolomite of the 1980s should be.

The Delta was described in detail in *Autocar* 8 September. 153in. long, or about the size of an Alfasud, it has a body by Guigaro's Ital-Design. Clean and tidy in modern five-door hatchback style, it has affinities with several others of its type (not surprising in view of Ital's work for other clients) and is distinguished by a version of the traditional Lancia grille, neatly integrated with the front lamp units. Given the desire to keep the overall size down, the uniformity of its shape with similar cars is understandable; it unfortunately shares with some others a high-set rear window which seriously limits rear vision when parking.

In summary, it has transverse-mounted, four cylinder engines of 1,301 and 1,498 c.c. with twin-choke carburettors and maximum power of 75 and 85 bhp respectively, 10 more than two versions of the Ritmo. There are three different gear-sets: a basic four-speeder that goes with the smaller engine in the base model, and a five-speed gearbox with overdrive fifth for the 1300 and almost direct fifth (plus different fourth and third ratios) for the 1500. Suspension is by MacPherson struts front and rear, but unlike the Ritmo (which has a transverse leaf spring) the Delta has long transverse arms at the rear and coil springs. There are anti-roll bars front and rear. Brakes are servo-assisted disc front, drum rear, with a diagonal split system.

Particular importance has been placed on ride comfort and running quietness. This is reflected in suspension bushes and mountings, the "independent" mounting of the gear-lever and the extra bulkhead in the engine compartment (compared with the Ritmo). Outwardly the cars still have something of the traditional Lancia exhaust "rasp" but inside they are commendably quiet at touring speeds, as we found out last week when British journalists had the first opportunity to drive the Delta.

Below: Rear wash-wipe systems are standard on all models

Right: Giugiaro's Ital Design five-door body styling gives the Delta a length of just under 13ft. The optional alloy wheels on the car in the background look rather like steel ones with alloy centre caps

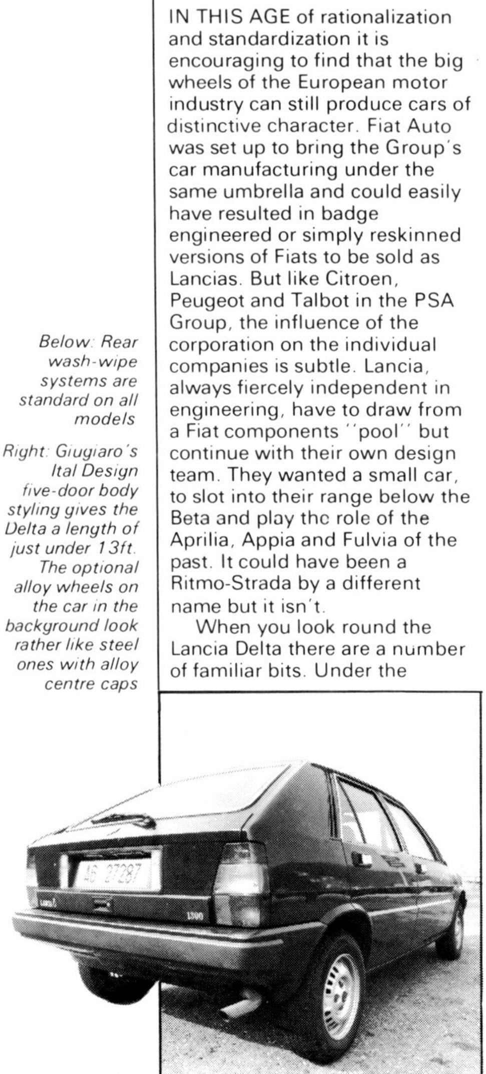

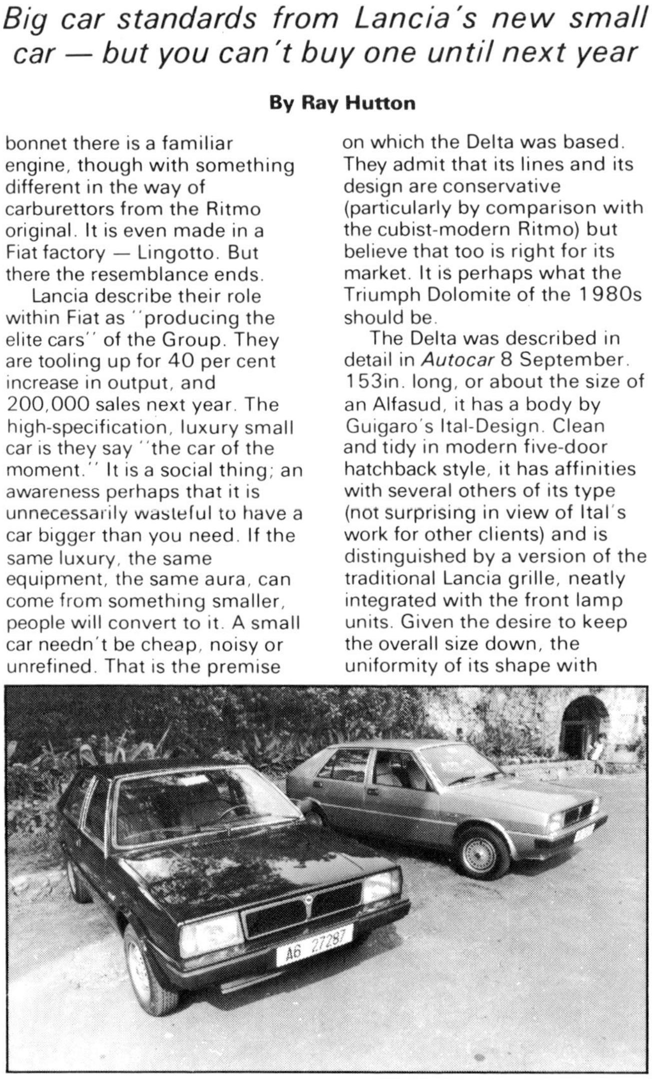

Welcoming

As our Italian correspondent said at the time of our description, first impressions of the Delta are good. The seats are comfortable, the surroundings inside nicely toning and pleasingly designed. The trim is nicely finished and the facia and controls neatly integrated; there is an air of thoroughness, of quality. The driving position is not of the worst Italian kind. The steering column can be adjusted up and down through 2½in. and unlike in some of the Betas, this driver did not find himself driving the Delta knees-splayed.

On the move, the steering immediately impresses. Lancias generally have nice steering and the Delta is no exception. Sweet through 3.8 turns from lock to lock, it is remarkably light by the standards of its class — and much lighter than the Ritmo. Other controls are similarly light and easy in operation — some thought the brakes rather too light and easy in operation — but, like the Beta, the quality of the gear change seemed to vary from car to car. At its best, the Delta gearchange is no better than average. Some we tried baulked on the third-to-second downchange and had an awkward movement into and out of fifth. Right-hand-drive cars may feel different again.

We tried a 1300 five-speed first. Its performance is adequate without being quick. It is around 1 cwt heavier than the Ritmo and would seem to be slightly slower than our long term Strada 75 with the same power output. On the *autostrada,* running through the tunnels and galleries of the mountains behind the Italian Riviera, the 1300 needed fourth rather than fifth gear most of the time to keep up with the higher speed traffic. Like the Ritmo, whose ratios it shares, this version has a high overdrive top gear (0.863 to 1) and achieves its maximum speed of something over 90 mph in fourth gear which is almost direct. The four-speed 1300 Delta tried briefly later has the same four ratios without the overdrive and for the driver who isn't in a hurry would not be expected to produce the same kind of fuel consumption figures as the five-speed. The Italian Official Fuel Consumption figures at 56 mph are 44.1 mpg for the five-speed and 40.9 for the four-speed.

The 1500 is immediately more lively, not only because of its extra power but also because it has a "sports-type" five-speed with top at 0.959 to 1 and proportionally lower fourth and third. The effect, however, is to improve performance (100 mph and 0.60 mph in 12.5 sec are claimed) *and* noise levels, though all the cars have a fair amount of transmission whine in the lower gears.

Twisting mountain roads confirmed the precision of the steering, the effectiveness of the brakes and the small amount of body roll. This is a car of particularly good road manners from a group (of small front-drive saloons) which are generally safe and predictable. Throttle-off mid-corner evokes little adverse reaction and the ride is impressive. Regular undulations, like cobbles, can set some vibrations through the facia but otherwise the efforts at insulating the suspension from the cabin seem to have paid off.

Inside, the Delta is comfortable for four. The seat cushions and backs are unusual in not having seams at their edges but being stitched in square panels and pulled over the foam structure and tightened with a draw-string. Rear leg-room is good considering the size of car and at six foot I could sit behind the driver's seat as set for me — though headroom is marginal. The heating and ventilating system is the first technical outcome of Lancia's links with Saab (who will call the Delta their own in Sweden), is adaptable and has good output, though last week's weather didn't provide much of a test for this. The facia is neatly done and incorporates a padded knee roll which forms an oddments shelf across the full width (but as with all facia-top trays, contents reflect in the screen). The instrument warning lights and switchgear all have their specific place and Lancias are helped here by all versions having the same high level of equipment and so they do not have to leave the "blanks" which are such an unsightly feature of the cheaper models of some other people's ranges. The cheapest four-speed 1300 has a clock instead of the rev counter matching the speedometer and does not have the LED-display digital clock (with stopwatch facility) that sits above the rear-view mirror in the other models.

The switchgear is arranged so that essential items are on column-mounted stalks and the less often used controls are on a push button panel at the facia centre. The main light switch is a square section column stalk which could do with some more obvious indication that it is designed to be twisted.

The attention to interior detail with such things as grab handles that recess into the cant-rail, and a service reminder panel above the mirror is as one would expect from an up-market Lancia. The easily folded-down rear seat and resulting flat luggage area is a useful utility borrowed from less elaborate cars. A split rear seat can be specified as an option, as can headlamp wiper/washers, electric front windows, sunroof, light alloy wheels and even air conditioning on the 1500.

The Delta goes on sale in Italy on 5 November and as we went to press the domestic prices had not been revealed. For a car of its size and type it will not be cheap. We were told the price would be in the 8-8.5 million lire range (£4,500-4,800) or about equivalent to the Audi 80 and Alfa Romeo Giulietta. That suggests that the Beta 1300 will eventually be displaced by the newcomer at the bottom of the Lancia range. On past form, there will be high performance and an ES-type "fully loaded" model in time. But no Deltas will be coming to Britain until well into next year — perhaps not until the summer. By then the luxury small car may be even more in vogue than it is now. □

The transverse engine carries the name Lancia rather than Fiat on it. The distributor is driven from the end of the camshaft. Note the dual bulkheads, to reduce internal noise levels

Far left: Seats have moulded backs, with cloth drawn over them without conventional seam edges

Left: There are three separate instrument panels, with speedometer and rev counter in the largest. Row of press button switches are above the heating and ventilation controls in the centre

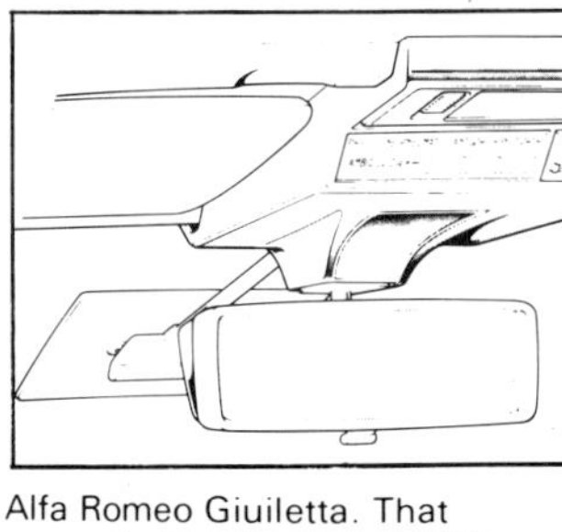

Console above rear view mirror carries the interior lamp, digital clock, with stopwatch facility, and wipe-clean "note pad" to jot down tyre pressures. Italian cars also have integral licence holder

AutoTEST Lancia Beta 2000 Automatic

A sports saloon with a little British knowhow

Lancia Beta 2000 Automatic

Automatic version of Lancia's successful front wheel drive sports saloon. Uses a three-speed automatic gearbox developed in conjunction with Automotive Products that still puts the Beta ahead of many of its manual gearbox rivals. Excellent handling, good brakes, and sound finish are marred by heavy steering, but power assistance for rhd models should be available in mid-1980.

PRODUCED BY:
Lancia & C, Via Vincenzo Lancia 27
Turin, Italy

SOLD IN THE UK BY:
Lancia (England) Ltd,
Ealing Road, Alperton,
Middlesex, HA0 1HE

THE MOST surprising aspect about Lancia's Beta Automatic is that it is the first production model from this prestigious Italian manufacturer to be fitted with an automatic gearbox in the company's 70 year history. That it comes within five years of Lancia's successful takeover by Fiat can surely be no coincidence. Many people feared that the much respected marque would simply be absorbed by the Fiat combine and take the path to oblivion that is being followed by our own MG, but fortunately, this is not the case. Indeed, Lancia seem (outwardly at least) to have been allowed to continue very much in the direction that they wanted to — the difference now being that they have far stronger financial support and ready access to Fiat's vast resources, in terms of both management and engineering.

For decades Lancia had reasoned that it would be anathema to have the option of an automatic gearbox for any of their sporting models. Apart from the handicap of additional weight, the argument went, the cost in terms of loss of performance would be intolerable; big capacity cars like those from Jaguar could overcome the problem, but it would be disaster for the smaller capacity range offered by Lancia to go the same way. A new argument appeared over the past two decades: the cost of development of a reliable lightweight sports auto box would be prohibitively expensive.

This is where Automotive Products come in. The fitting of an automatic gearbox to the diminutive Mini with little of the adverse effects propounded by the antis proved to the world both AP's expertise and that some of the old arguments against the auto box were no longer absolute truths. So it is not surprising, therefore, that in the change of climate and their own fortunes, Lancia approached AP for co-operation in the long-awaited development of an automatic gearbox for their marque.

All of the 1.6 and 2.0 litre Beta range (with the exception of the Spyder) will be available fitted with the AP box, built at Lancia's new factory at Verrone in the industrial north of Italy.

The new gearbox offers no surprises in terms of design. It is coupled to the engine by a high maximum torque multiplication torque converter and the three-speed gear selection (with manual override) is effected by two sets of hydraulic clutches and three servo-operated brake bands. In common with the four-speed AP box found on the Mini (and of course most conventional automatics), epicyclic gears are used in preference.

Until next month, only the Beta 2000 and 2000 ES saloons are available with the automatic

gearbox option, and so the car that we have chosen to evaluate is the ordinary Beta 2000 Automatic. Our last test of the Beta 2000 saloon was in 1976, and since then the only real change has been alteration to the Weber twin choke carburetion which has resulted in a 2 lb ft increase in torque to 129 lb. ft. at 2,800 rpm, but a decrease in bhp from 119 to 115 bhp at 5,500 rpm. The engine is the proven 1,995 c.c. four cylinder in-line unit with belt-drive double overhead camshaft, transversely mounted and driving the front wheels.

Performance

What a pleasant surprise

In spite of the decrease in bhp, a comparison of the figures between today's automatic and the manual version of 1976 throws an intriguing light on the pros and cons of automatic gearboxes. In terms of top speed, the automatic grudgingly gives away a mere 3 mph to the manual version, with a mean of 107 mph against 110 mph. In standing start acceleration, exactly one second is lost in the time to 30 mph with 4.3 sec against 3.3 sec. Leaving the gear selector in Drive on the flat-out run means automatic upchanges at 38 mph (4,500 rpm) and 70 mph (5,250), and a 2½ sec gap by 60 mph at 12.6 sec (10.1 sec for the manual Beta). At 80 mph, this gap widens to 5.7 sec at 23.2 sec (17.5 sec) and the manual progressively increases the distance between the two. However, by over-riding the automatic upchanges and holding the Lancia to change up at 6,000 rpm (50 mph and 80 mph), the automatic saloon loses only 1.3 sec to 60 mph with 11.4 sec, and 2.8 sec to 80 mph with 20.3 sec. Such a relationship between manual and automatic performance is typical — if acceptable to those who want the ease of two-pedal motoring — of the way in which torque converters sap something of a car's vitality.

The gear selector follows AP's design for the Mini auto in its sensible method of operation: a button on top of the gear lever knob is used to overcome the lock to prevent the driver inadvertently selecting neutral or first while on the move. The gate movement is not blocked between second and drive, which enables the driver to flick the lever into second for better control into corners, and back into D without the continual threat of either engaging first at too high a speed or freewheeling in neutral.

The Beta changes up in Drive relatively early on part throttle into second from first, and the upchange from second into top occurs almost immediately. This is not a criticism, merely a comment, as the Lancia has ample torque, and this probably combines with the early and close light throttle upchanges to give greater economy. The smoothness of the gearchanges is difficult to fault, though understandably not in the same class as on the large capacity Jaguars and American saloons.

An interesting, possibly unique characteristic of the AP box is for the revs to increase in idling speed when the car is taken out of neutral, the idea being to avoid any possibility of hesitation or risk of stalling. On the test car, it was not altogether successful. The Beta automatic's cold starting on two cold mornings, was more than hesitant when it stalled after running for five minutes and a couple of miles; driveaway tends to be lumpy.

The Beta's new transmission selector is an example of how to arrange the controls of an automatic properly; changes between Drive and second are unhindered, but the button has to be depressed for engaging neutral or first — this avoids accidental freewheeling or over revving

Economy

Good for an automatic

When one considers that much of the test Lancia's mileage was covered at a brisk pace and that the manual returned an overall fuel consumption which is only 0.9 mpg better, all credit is due to the car for managing 23.1 mpg, an overall figure that would not be out of place amongst manual gearbox rivals. Over a two hundred mile trip of motorway driving at high speed, the Lancia managed to return 23.2 mpg, which would enable it to travel about 260 miles on its 11.4 gallon tank — provided of course that you have the patience to fill the tank to the utmost, as the Beta is not the easiest car to brim.

Noise

Typically Italian

Engine noise is at the sort of level that one might expect to find in a sports car rather than a saloon — rarely annoying, simply noticeable. Until, that is, one gets to between 70 and 80 mph, where there appears a frustrating boom period that makes one want to go faster or slower to avoid a headache. Engine apart, though, the Lancia is fairly quiet as road noise is kept to a reasonable level and wind roar is virtually non-existent until really high speed.

The bonnet hinges forward onto a self propping stay to reveal the dohc two litre engine, which is inclined backwards at 20 deg. This makes the spark plugs a little difficult to get at, but access to all of the ancillary service items is very good

The clean stylish lines of the Lancia Beta Saloon make it immediately identifiable. The roof pillars, even those at the rear, are sufficiently narrow so as not to create any bad blind spots, and the light clusters at the rear look remarkably tidy

Road Behaviour
Matches the performance

The Beta's suspension has been designed to meet the needs of a sports saloon without adversely affecting ride, something that in practice can be very difficult to achieve, especially with a front-engined, front-wheel-drive layout. In the original 1972 design, Lancia opted for independent suspension, using MacPherson struts all round, with anti-roll bars at front and rear reducing corner roll to an acceptable level. We noted in our Autotest of the manual transmission Beta 2000 that strong acceleration whilst cornering tends to accentuate the Lancia's mild basic understeer — using kickdown on the automatic produces the same characteristic to a lesser degree. Lifting off in the corner merely induces a safe gentle tightening of the line, which is due to the nature of the torque converter which has a cushioning effect on the interaction between engine and suspension.

The steering is the most disappointing area in the Beta's design. With low gearing of 4.1 turns lock to lock, it is surprising to find that the steering is still unreasonably heavy for low speed manouevreing in car parks and when turning round. The main reason for the unfortunate combination of arm-flailing contortions and heavy load is the high bias of weight over the front wheels. We understand that power steering is fitted as standard on left-hand-drive models, and transforms the car, but it is not at present available for right-hand-drive versions as the transition from left to right leaves little room for the box and places it too close to the hot engine, causing overheating problems.

Lancia say that they are working on the problem and that power assistance for right-hand-drive models should be available in mid-1980. Ride is what one would expect from Lancia; it's got that sporty firmness to aid handling without going overboard to detract from the comfort to be expected from a two litre saloon. At low speeds, small surface irregularities such as minor pot holes and raised scars from road repairs are noticeable and accompanied by a degree of bump thump. At speed, the Lancia is much better behaved, the effectiveness of the good damping becoming more apparent, coping well with the roughest of A class roads. Straight line stability is very good, and the Beta seems little affected by strong side winds.

The brakes, 9.9in. dia discs front and rear, are servo-assisted and provide good stopping power, which is perhaps all the more essential in a saloon fitted with an automatic gearbox, as the retardant effect of engine braking is greatly reduced in D. The response is progressive — 40 lb pressure on the wide brake pedal gives better than 0.5g whilst the best stop of just over 1g is achieved at a rather heavy-footed 100 lb pressure, which goes to prove that servo systems need not make braking feather-light and prone to locking in a panic stop. The Lancia's brakes allow one to go right to just below the limits of adhesion with a reassuringly hard shove of the foot and not overdo it. Stopping using the handbrake only gave a reasonable 0.38g retardation. Our ten 0.5g stop fade test from the Beta 2000 Automatic's reasonably quick standing quarter speed of 77 mph showed that the Lancia kept to within acceptable limits, though the last four stops required a final pedal effort of 60 lb, and was accompanied by smoke from the pads. After the tenth stop, the discs glowed warm red, but radiated the heat and recovered quickly.

Behind The Wheel
Function with taste

With the exception of the steering, as already discussed, the Lancia is well sorted out and this is reflected in the interior. The seats are well padded, with the cushions nicely extended forward to give good support to the thighs, and a well-designed back that is sufficiently rounded to give reasonable lateral support without encouraging or enforcing the round-shouldered stance that some luxury "racing" seats impose. Well padded headrests are fitted, but can be removed to improve visibility. Seat adjustment could be improved, as the rotary handwheel which raises the reclining backrest is located on the outer edge and is rather small in diameter and difficult to reach. Rear seat legroom is sensibly generous, and to add to rear passenger comfort, take off from the heater vents into the rear compartment through separately adjustable outlets. All of the seating is covered in a really comfortable soft fabric which is used to cover much of the interior up from the carpetted floor, on the door panels, along all of the pillars and overhead as the roof trim. It even covers the broad sun visors which, incidentally, work very well — they will unclip and pivot to the side windows without catching your head. The overall effect of the cloth trim, with its conservative pattern, is very pleasing and gives the Beta a very warm, luxuriously cosy feeling. What is left is a plastic trim that might look cheap if used in conjunction with another type of interior covering, but on the Beta it remains unobtrusive, thankfully without any pretence to be leather.

Visibility is good all round — although the Lancia saloon has a

Conservative styling suits the Lancia well. The facia is nicely thought out. Gauges between the speedo and rev counter are for temperature and oil pressure. Clock and fuel gauge are located to the left of the speedometer. Left hand stalk on the steering column operates the two speed / intermittent wiper and wash; indicators and lights are controlled by two right hand stalks. Horn is gratifyingly mounted as a broad bar on the steering wheel

Seats are very comfortable and legroom is more than adequate for front and rear passengers. We particularly like the interior finish and seat covering, which is one of the most attractive around and uses a soft, presumably hard wearing cloth

sloping rear design, the pillars are pleasingly thin and there are no really bad blind spots. Driver's door mirror and rear view mirror provide good rearward vision, and interestingly, the rear view mirror dips not by pushing or pulling a terestingly, the rear view mirror dips not by pushing or pulling a stubby lever mounted at the base as on other cars, but by a knob which slides sideways — a simple idea that avoids the possibility of pushing the mirror out of alignment when dipping at night.

The accelerator and large brake pedals will feel strange to those unaccustomed to driving automatics, but our only criticism is the effort needed to work the throttle which we are told is due to the heavy springs used in the linkage between throttle and gearbox. After a hundred miles of driving, the driver adapts to this and the heaviness becomes virtually unnoticeable. The steering column has a vertical adjustment, but really needs fore and aft movement as well in order to eliminate the vestiges of the Italian Ape driving position that have remained with this car over the years.

Minor controls are operated by three stalks located on the steering column. The right hand stalk nearest to the driver activates the indicators whilst the other operates the lights — rotating the knob switches on side and then dip, lowering the stalk turns on dip if the side lights are on and beam if dip is in use. The stalk on the left of the wheel operates the two-speed/intermittent wiper, the pattern of which is set for rhd, but leaves a vertical band on the driver's side next to the pillar which could in really foul weather develop into a blind spot. The horn control is right where it should be — in the centre of the steering wheel; the horn itself emits a reassuringly loud note.

The facia layout has an attractive old-fashioned appearance that seems to have been culled from the decayed *art nouveau* style of the late thirties; on the far left of the panel is a clock; moving to the right, there is a fuel gauge and handbrake warning light which flashes on and off and makes quite a loud clicking sound that distracts when waiting at traffic lights. To the right of that is the more useful fuel warning light which comes on when there is 1¾ gallons of fuel left in the tank. Sitting between the speedometer (calibrated to 120 mph) and the rev counter (calibrated to 7,000 rpm with a 6,500 red line) lies an array of temperature gauge, oil pressure gauge and warning lamps for both, with others for indicators, high beam and dipped headlights. Rheostat knob for the panel lights and resettable trip knob are located neatly on either side of the steering column axis. In fact, the overall layout of the dashboard is one of the tidiest around, and the thirties style appearance really becomes noticeable at night when the panel lights illuminate the off whites and greys in a creamy glow. Heating and ventilation have not changed, and work adequately, once one has mastered the sliding controls. Outlets seem well located and as mentioned, there is separate venting for the rear passengers.

Living with the Lancia Beta 2000 Automatic

For all its good points, the Beta does have a few areas which could be improved, and one — the heavy steering — which *should* be improved. Stowage space is reasonable, there are map pockets ahead of the front doors — these could ideally be a little larger — and a well-designed parcel shelf behind the rear seat that really is big enough to carry parcels; it is sufficiently below the top edge of the rear seat so that loose pens or packets are unlikely to hit passengers in the neck in the event of a rapid stop.

One key opens all doors, boot and fuel cap lock, and is easily distinguishable from the ignition key due to its unusual design. Opening the L shaped boot lid reveals a cavernous luggage area that is only marred by the body line of the car, which requires a stooped approach to loading and unloading cases.

Opening the bonnet to inspect the engine reveals that Lancia have thoughtfully installed a bonnet release lever on the right hand driver's side — something that many other foreign (and curiously some UK) manufacturers fail to provide. At night, a fixed lamp illuminates the underbonnet area, which is well laid out, with all the "filler" items located on the near side of the engine, and a centrally located fuse box covered with a marked transparent top. Our road test model mysteriously died on return to Lancia after the end of our 1,000 mile test. It transpires that the electronic ignition black box had failed — just "one of those things" that is a disquieting facet of the supposed advance towards more electronics in cars. The self levelling headlamps are a good idea but the cut-off on dip was too low on our car. Adjustment is possible by "authorised personnel" and we would think that a little alteration would improve matters without raising the beam too high.

Cavernous 17.6 cu. ft. boot has plenty of room for a family's holiday luggage and has box-like dimensions. Removing gear from the depths of the boot may annoy a back sufferer, though, as he will have to crouch

The Beta Range

There are ten Betas in the Lancia line-up, ranging from the 1300 c.c. Beta saloon at £4,252 to the £6,789 Spyder which, by the way, is the only Beta that will not have the option of the AP auto box at an extra £455. The saloon and coupés are available in 1.3, 1.6 and 2.0 litre versions. The two litre saloon is also available in ES form which differs from our standard road test model in having a sliding sunroof and alloy wheels. Prices for the Automatic versions of the 2000 and 2000 ES saloons are £5,832 and £6,212 respectively.

HOW THE LANCIA BETA 2000 AUTOMATIC PERFORMS

Figures taken at 2,500 miles by our own starf at the Motor Industry Research Association proving ground at Nuneaton.

TEST CONDITIONS:
Wind: 0-15 mph
Temperature: 4.5 deg C (40 deg F)
Barometer: 30.0in. Hg (1017 mbar)
Humidity: 98 per cent
Surface: damp asphalt and concrete
Test distance: 1,016 miles

MAXIMUM SPEEDS

Gear	mph	kph	rpm
Top (mean)	**107**	172.2	5,720
(best)	**109**	175.4	5,830
2nd	**88**	141.6	6,500
1st	**53**	85.3	6,500

ACCELERATION

True mph	Time (sec)	Speedo mph
30	**4.3**	32
40	**6.2**	42
50	**8.3**	53
60	**11.4**	62
70	**15.1**	72
80	**20.3**	82
90	**30.3**	92
100	**49.4**	109

Standing ¼-mile: 18.6 sec, 76 mph
Standing km: 34.5 sec, 90 mph

IN EACH GEAR

mph	Top	2nd	1st
0-20	—	4.1	2.7
10-30	—	4.8	3.5
20-40	—	5.6	3.8
30-50	—	6.2	4.2
40-60	—	6.5	—
50-70	—	7.3	—
60-80	—	8.5	—
70-90	15.9	—	—
80-100	26.6	—	—

FUEL CONSUMPTION

Overall mpg:
23.1 (12.2 litres/100km)

Constant speed:

mph	mpg	mph	mpg
30	40.6	70	26.7
40	37.7	80	22.4
50	33.8	90	18.4
60	24.3	100	15.1

Autocar formula: Hard 20.8 mpg
Driving and conditions: Average 25.4 mpg, Gentle 30.0 mpg

Grade of fuel: Premium, 4-star (98 RM)
Fuel tank: 11.4 Imp galls (51.8 litres)
Mileage recorder: 4 per cent long

Official fuel consumption figures
(ECE laboratory test conditions; not necessarily related to Autocar figures)

Urban cycle: 23.9 mpg
Steady 56 mph: 31.7 mpg
Steady 75 mph: 25.4 mpg

OIL CONSUMPTION

(SAE 20/50) Negligible

BRAKING

Fade *(from 30 mph in neutral)*
Pedal load for 0.5g stops in lb

	start/end		start/end
1	20-12	6	20-44
2	20-28	7	20-60
3	20-38	8	20-58
4	20-38	9	20-60
5	20-40	10	20-60

Response *(from 30 mph in neutral)*

Load	g	Distance
20lb	0.38	79ft
40lb	0.54	56ft
60lb	0.80	38ft
80lb	0.90	33ft
100lb	1.05	29ft
Handbrake	0.38	79ft

Max. gradient: 1 in 3

WEIGHT

Kerb, 23.2 cwt/2,599lb/1,179kg
(Distribution F/R, 60/40)
Test, 26.7/2,989lb/1,355kg

DIMENSIONS

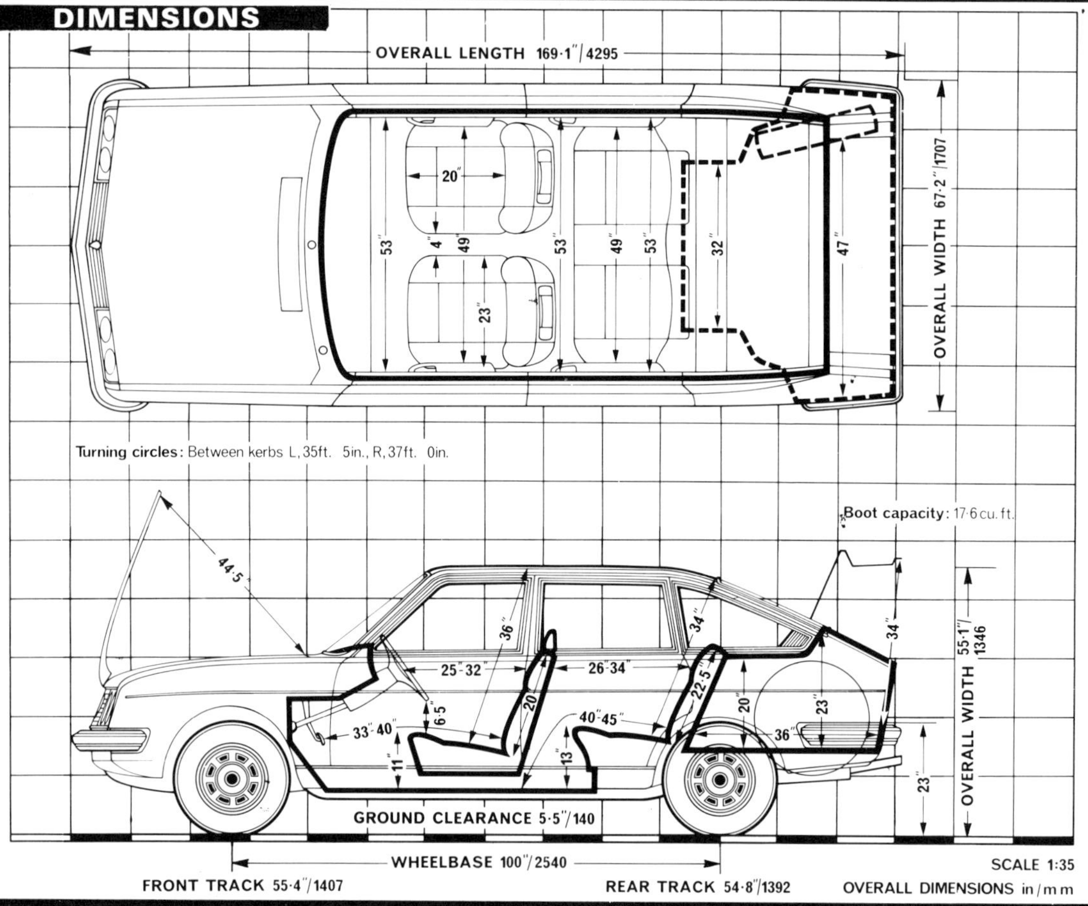

PRICES

Basic	£4,681.00
Special Car Tax	£390.09
VAT	£760.85
Total (in GB)	**£5,831.94**
Seat Belts	Inertia reel standard
Licence	£50.00
Delivery charge (London)	included
Number plates	£8.00
Total on the Road (exc insurance)	**£5,889.94**

EXTRAS (inc VAT)

Metallic paint	£206.80

**Fitted to test car*

TOTAL AS TESTED ON THE ROAD	**£5,889.94**
Insurance	Group 6

SERVICE & PARTS

Change	Interval 6,000	12,000	18,000
Engine oil	Yes	Yes	Yes
Oil filter	Yes	Yes	Yes
Gearbox oil	No	Yes	Yes
Spark plugs	Yes	Yes	Yes
Air cleaner	No	Yes	Yes
Total cost	17.46	52.81	27.21

(Assuming labour at £8.00/hour)

PARTS COST *(including VAT)*

Brake pads (2 wheels) — front	£12.27
Brake pads (2 wheels) — rear	£11.47
Exhaust complete	£153.28
Tyre — each (typical	£39.11
Windscreen (laminated)	£49.23
Headlamp unit	£49.68
Front wing	£71.70
Rear bumper	£64.89

WARRANTY

12 months/unlimited mileage

SPECIFICATION

ENGINE

Head/block	Front, front drive Alloy/cast iron
Cylinders	4, in line, transversely inclined rearwards at 20 degrees
Main bearings	4
Cooling	Water
Fan	Electric
Bore, mm (in.)	84 (3.31)
Stroke, mm (in.)	90 (3.54)
Capacity, cc (in³)	1,995 (122)
Valve gear	Dohc
Camshaft drive	Toothed belt
Compression ratio	8.9-to-1
Ignition	Breakerless
Carburettor	Weber 34DATR
Max power	115 bhp (DIN) at 5,500 rpm
Max torque	129 lb ft at 2,800 rpm

TRANSMISSION

Type: 3-speed automatic with torque converter

Gear	Ratio	mph/1000 rpm
Top	1.0-2.4	18.7
2nd	1.402-3.36	13.3
1st	2.346-5.63	8.0
Final drive gear		Helical spur
Ratio	4.38	

SUSPENSION

Front — location	MacPherson struts
springs	Coil
dampers	Telescopic
anti-roll bar	Yes
Rear — location	MacPherson struts
springs	Coil
dampers	Telescopic
anti-roll bar	Yes

STEERING

Type	Rack and pinion
Power assistance	NA
Wheel diameter	15.25 in.
Turns lock to lock	4.1

BRAKES

Circuits	Dual
Front	9.9 in. dia disc
Rear	9.9 in. dia disc
Servo	Vacuum
Handbrake	Front wheels

WHEELS

Type	Pressed steel
Rim width	5J
Tyres — make	Pirelli
— type	P3
— size	175/70 SR14
— pressures	F: 25; R: 28 psi (normal driving)

EQUIPMENT

Battery	12V 45 Ah
Alternator	750 watt
Headlamps	110W
Reversing lamp	Standard
Hazard warning	Standard
Electric fuses	10
Screen wipers	2-speed
Screen washer	Electric
Interior heater	Water valve
Interior trim	Cloth seats, cloth headlining
Floor covering	Carpet
Jack	Screw pillar
Jacking points	One each side, under front door
Windscreen	Laminated
Underbody protection	Electrophoretic treatment prior to painting; sealant after painting

HOW THE LANCIA BETA 2000 AUTOMATIC COMPARES

Lancia Beta 2000 Automatic — £5,892

Front engine
front drive

Capacity
1,995 c.c.

Power
115 bhp (DIN)
at 5,500 rpm

Weight
2,599 lb / 1,179 kg

Autotest
22 December 1979

Audi 100 GL 5E (A) — £8,080

Front engine
front drive

Capacity
2,144 c.c.

Power
136 bhp (DIN)
at 5,700 rpm

Weight
2,632 lb / 1,194 kg

Autotest
6 August, 1977

Citroen CX Pallas Injection (A) — £7,799

Front engine
front drive

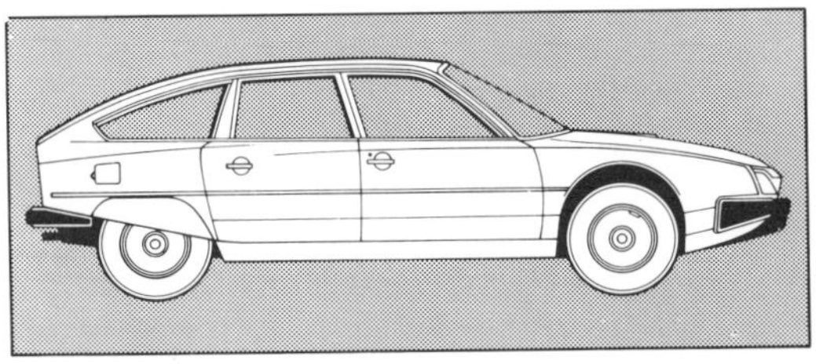

Capacity
2,347 c.c.

Power
128 bhp (DIN)
at 4,800 rpm

Weight
3,073 lb / 1,395 kg

Autotest
5 August, 1978

Mercedes 230 (A)* — £8,965

Front engine
rear drive

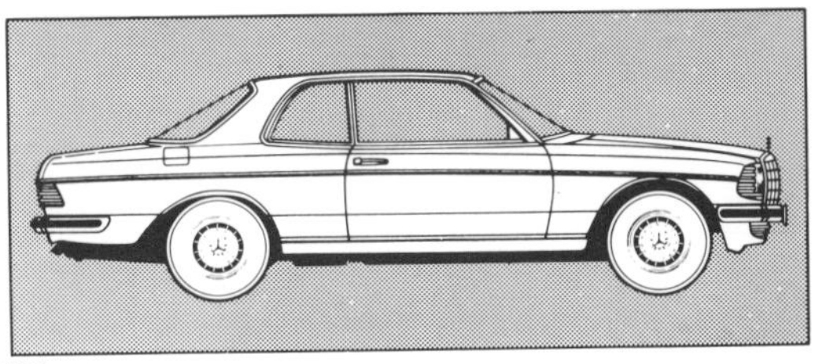

Capacity
2,307 c.c.

Power
109 bhp (DIN)
at 4,800 rpm

Weight
3,070 lb / 1,390 kg

Autotest
29 October, 1977

Performance figures for heaver 230C

Princess 2200 HLS (A) — £6,452

Front engine
front drive

Capacity
2,227 c.c.

Power
110 bhp (DIN)
at 5,250 rpm

Weight
2,677 lb / 1,214 kg

Autotest
6 March, 1976

Renault 20 TS (A) — £6,739

Front engine
front drive

Capacity
1,995 c.c.

Power
110 bhp (DIN)
at 5,500 rpm

Weight
2,754 lb / 1,252 kg

Autotest
26 November, 1977

MPH & MPG

Maximum speed (mph)	
Citroen CX Pallas injection (A)	111
Audi 100 GL 5E (A)	109
Lancia Beta 2000 (A)	107
Renault 20 TS (A)	100
Mercedes 230 (A)*	99
Princess 2200 HLS (A)	98

Acceleration 0-60 (sec)	
Lancia Beta 2000 (A)	11.4
Audi 100 GL 5E (A)	11.8
Citroen CX Pallas Injection (A)	12.2
Mercedes 230 (A)*	14.0
Princess 2200 HLS (A)	14.2
Renault 20 TS (A)	14.8

Overall mpg	
Audi 100 GL 5E (A)	23.3
Lancia Beta 2000 (A)	23.1
Renault 20 TS (A)	22.9
Princess 2200 HLS (A)	21.8
Citroen CX Pallas Injection (A)	20.9
Mercedes 230 (A)*	18.7

The five automatic rivals that we have chosen from our Road Test files for comparison may surprise some, not least because of the massive price range between the models. The Lancia is by far the cheapest, being £620 less than the Princess and £905 cheaper than the Renault 20 TS — demolishing a commonly held misconception that Lancias are an expensive luxury. Other two litre saloons with auto boxes that have not been included in the line-up but are worthy of note due to reasons of performance and/or price are the BMW 520 (£8,209), Fiat 132 2000 (£6,083), Ford Cortina 2000 GL (£4,959) and the excellent Vauxhall Cavalier 2000, which at £5,124 is not only cheap, but also a match for the rivals in both handling and performance.

Looking at the performance figures for the Lancia's rivals, it is obvious that the Beta has a lot going for it — well up the field in top speed, fastest in acceleration amongst the automatics with a manual-like 11.4 sec to 60 mph, all with the unlikely accompaniment of good fuel economy. Fuel injection sets the Audi and Citroen at the top in maximum speed as they respectively have a 21 and 13 bhp advantage over the Lancia, but it would seem that AP has the better gearbox for acceleration.

ON THE ROAD

All independent suspension is common to each rival and all but the Mercedes are front-wheel-drive saloons. But a more interesting division can be found by splitting the cars into soft and hard suspension characteristics. Into the former category falls the Princess with its Hydragas suspension, and not surprisingly, the two French cars — the Renault and the Citroen, which in our opinion offers the very best in medium car ride comfort as only the French know how. Into the latter, firm ride category fall the Lancia and the two cars from Germany. None of these are uncomfortable in ride, but the lack of body roll when cornering and the consistently taut feel of the cars underline a greater emphasis on sporty handling than the others. Although the Merc is the only car with rear wheel drive, understeer is the predominant characteristic of this rather heavy beast and oversteer is only likely to be encountered under hard acceleration out of a rainswept corner, or if one provokes the semi-trailing arm rear end by decelerating abruptly. The Audi and Lancia feel much more nimble, being lighter, and they offer the additional advantage of having rack and pinion steering though, as we have mentioned, the Beta suffers badly from heavy steering to the extent that the Audi is more enjoyable to drive. Now, it may be a different matter when rhd Betas are available with power assisted steering . . . .

SIZE & SPACE

Legroom front/rear (in)	
(Seats fully back)	
Audi 100 GL 5E (A)	42/39
Lancia Beta 2000 (A)	40/40
Citroen CX Pallas Injection (A)	41/39
Mercedes 230 (A)	41/38
Princess 2200 HLS (A)	40/38
Renault 20TS (A)	39.5/34

The Renault 20 TS fares least well in the legroom stakes but does have the versatile advantage over the others of a hatchback body. None of the rest do, though the Princess, Citroen and Lancia all look as though they should, with their sloping rear bodies. The shape does at least enhance the luggage capacity of their boots, and in spite of awkward L shaped boot lids, these three can take a surprising amount of baggage.

None of these cars are really short on room, but the Princess' dimensions for legroom belie the actual space available for rear passengers, and we would rate it as generous in proportion as the Audi.

VERDICT

On price and performance, the Lancia obviously offers much. The others are more expensive, and in most instances the extra cost is justified by a greater degree of sophistication and level of finish, but one wonders if this can be seriously applied to the Princess which, even though it has the benefit of power steering, cannot be considered to be as superior to the Lancia as its extra cost would suggest. In terms of comfort, as already mentioned, the Renault and Citroen are hard to beat and so a potential buyer considering the six car line-up should decide on how much emphasis to assign to comfort or to handling and performance. If he is prepared to sacrifice an edge in comfort for the other two, then the Audi and Lancia should vie very closely in his final considerations. Until power steering is employed to improve the Lancia's heavy steering, as will hopefully soon be the case, we would move in favour of the Audi.

12 years of AP automaticity

The latest Automotive Products design for Lancia and its Mini forebear

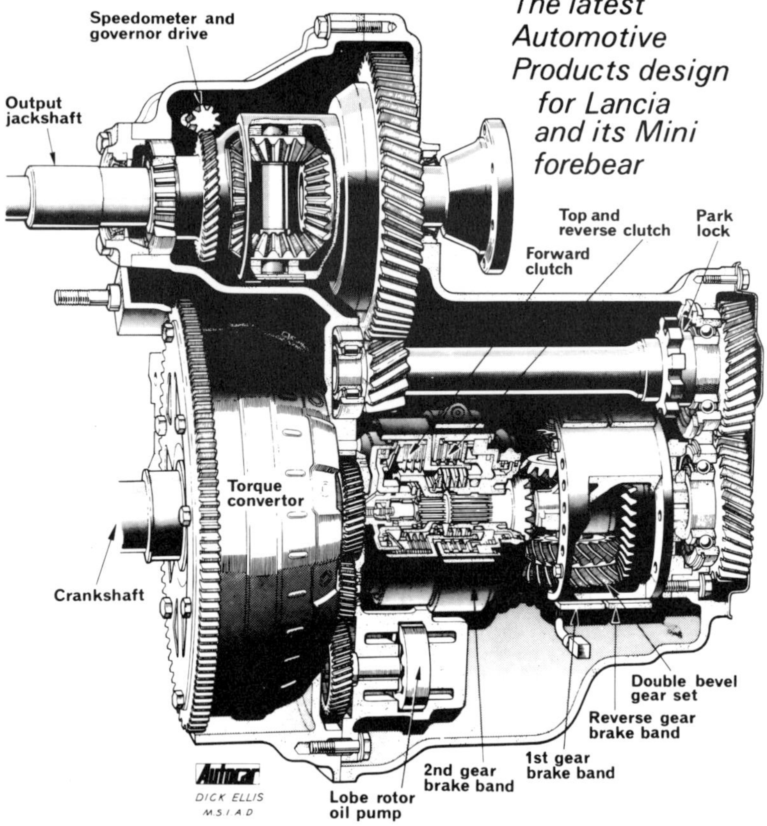

Above: The AP three-speed automatic for the Lancia Beta saloons. Right: The 1967 four-speed Mini box

THE AUTOMOTIVE Products four-speed automatic originally designed for and used in the Mini and Austin/Morris 1100 in 1967 is very much parent to the AP-originated three-speed automatic offered in 1600 (not in Britain) and 2000 Beta saloons this year. The Mini AP box, still in production for a number of BL's transverse front-drive cars, was a brilliant achievement for its time. Contriving to squeeze automatic transmission into the only slightly expanded confines of a Mini gear case was remarkable, and to do so offering four speeds which could be either automatically or individually selected was unusual. The change quality was certainly rather jerky, which wasn't unexpected given the relatively very low jerk-absorbing mass of the car compared to most automatic models — but it was delightfully fast and responsive, particularly for 1967 and after a midly problematic start, the box was seen to work; its comparatively high add-on price for the class restricted sales however.

Most radical distinction of the AP transmission in both Mini and latest Lancia form is the use not of the various sorts of conventional epicyclic gearing, in which spur gears are used for sun, planet and ring gear, but of a variant of the Humpage gear principle, which depends on differential gears. This makes for a more compact gear arrangement for a given size (and therefore strength) of tooth. In the Mini box there are in fact two co-axial differential trains, one inside the other, with their planet wheels cut on the same shaft. Different ratios are provided by (using brake bands or multi-plate clutches) driving through all differential gears (first), locking one of the innermost diff's output gears (second), or the same side output gear of the second diff (third), or locking both sides of the innermost diff to each other (direct drive top), or holding the outer casing still and taking the drive out from the opposite side of the innermost diff (reverse). The diff housing runs on a sprag clutch (in effect a freewheel), which reminds the driver of its existence in first gear where there is no over-run braking. Another distinction of the Mini box was its ability to allow a tow start, thanks to an additional auxiliary oil pump (normal brake cum clutch servo pressure was supplied by an enlarged version of the engine oil pump).

Comparison

Lawrence Watts' 1967 drawing of the Mini box included all ancillaries — most important of which are the servo assembly and valve chest; Dick Ellis's Lancia AP box omits these items for clarity.

Comparison of the two shows that there are a number of differences. The Lancia one runs on its own oil, unshared with the engine. Its own supply of hydraulic pressure is provided by a lobe pump driven by a helical gear train off the output of the torque converters. There is no freewheeling in any gear, but a park lock is provided (not seen on the AP box for the Mini but now incorporated on the larger engine applications). The layout, aside from the fact that this is a three-speed instead of a four, is different even though it centres on a similarly ingenious differential principle. In the Mini box, final drive is taken off between the differential change-speed gearing unit and the forward clutch, which is on the far side at the opposite end to the torque converter. The gearbox output is taken out by the spur output set at the right hand end and back across the box again to the final drive. As far as the change speed arrangement itself is concerned, it could really be described as seven eighths of the Mini box, needing only one complete differential (the inner one). It has a narrower maximum span of ratio — first (and reverse, which in these arrangements must have the same numerical ratio) on the Mini box is 2.69 to 1; on the Lancia one it is 2.346, any necessary difference due to this and the larger maximum ratio step being more than bridged by the Italian car's appreciably higher maximum converter torque multiplication which at 2.4 to 1 is 20 per cent bigger than the Mini's. □

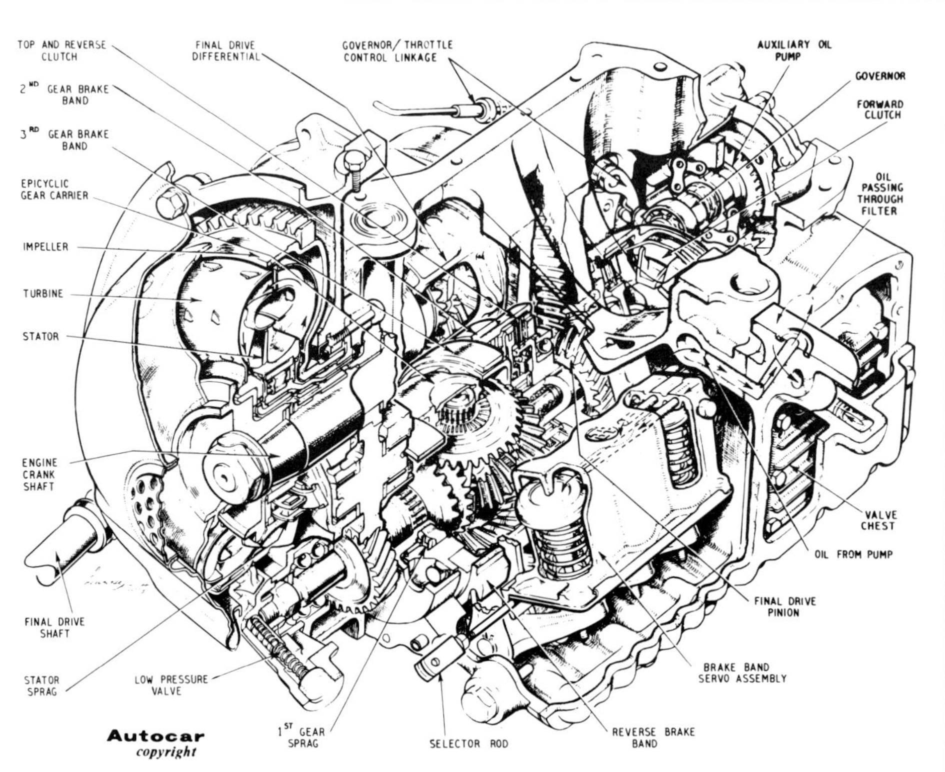

Italy's Car of the Year

Lancia Delta — a new kind of small car?

THIS THURSDAY, Fiat-Lancia will receive the coveted Car of the Year trophy to celebrate the new Lancia Delta's success in last autumn's judging by 52 European motoring journalists.

The Delta is Car of the Year 1980. It scored a clear victory over the Opel Kadett and many of the judges thought that it showed the way to a new kind of small car, with big car values in terms of comfort, accommodation and equipment. But is the Delta something new? Does it represent a step into a new motoring world? No. It is perhaps the Triumph Dolomite of the new decade; the small car designed for the person who would have but doesn't need a bigger one. It was planned that way from the outset so it is not a dressed up and well insulated version of something more prosaic. Yes, the Delta uses the Ritmo-Strada engines and a lot of parts from the Fiat Group's common pool but it remains a very distinctive car in the Lancia tradition. In the marque's terms, it follows the illustrious line from the Aprilia and Ardea to the Appia and Fulvia.

The Delta comes in three versions at present though there are likely to be others in the future. There is a 75 bhp 1300 and an 85 bhp 1500. The former comes with either a four-speed or five-speed gearbox, the latter with overdrive fifth. The 1500 has five speeds but with "sports" ratios. There is therefore a considerable difference in the performance and character of the two versions. Independent sources in Italy give the maximum speed of the two five-speeders as 99 and 103 mph respectively and 0-100 kph (62.5 mph) as 12.8 and 11.7 sec*.

All versions have the same high level of fittings and comfort; there are few options as most "extras" are standard. Giugiaro's Ital Design did the body design which is neat without being particularly distinguished and has only poor rear visibility and a relatively small boot as disadvantages.

The Delta is expected to cost between £4,200 and £4,800 when it arrives in Britain later this year. It is also expected to oust the 1300 version of the Beta, falling into place below the Beta 1600 with the new grille which gives that a family resemblance to its new and celebrated smaller brother. □

*Quattroruote

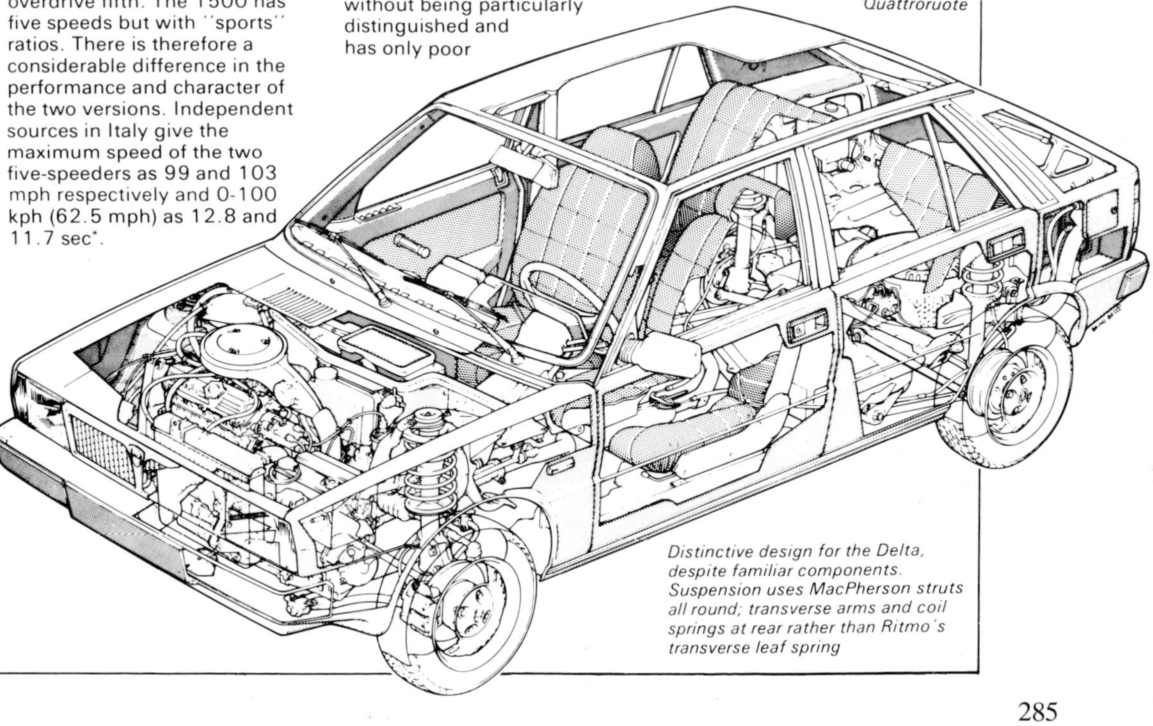

Distinctive design for the Delta, despite familiar components. Suspension uses MacPherson struts all round; transverse arms and coil springs at rear rather than Ritmo's transverse leaf spring

Lancia 1980

THEIR advertising calls them "the most Italian car" but in fact Lancia's relationship with their Fiat owners has become closer in the past year, both in Italy and in this country where the two importers have merged. Rationalisation with Fiat models does not show much in the range. The Betas are front-wheel drive and up-market from their 1,600 and 2,000 c.c. Fiat counterparts. A nice group, this, with saloons, coupés, a convertible and the sports-estate HPE all using the same running gear; it is turned round the other way for the mid-engined Monte Carlo which should be returning to the market soon. Lancia's — and Fiat's — prestige car, the Gamma, is a curiosity; very good in some respects but not universally admired. The Delta, extending the range at the lower end, promises well but production is slow getting under way and it won't be here until late summer.

Above: **Lancia Beta Spyder 2000** — *very attractive roll-barred convertible version of Lancia's excellent front-drive saloon*
Left and below: **Lancia Beta HPE** — *Turin's take-up of the sporting estate car theme invented by Tom Karen's Scimitar GTE*

Left: **Lancia Beta Coupe 1600** — *basic sporting Lancia with same mechanicals as the saloon but shorter wheelbase. Below:* **Lancia Beta Saloon** *comes in three models, now that 1300 has given way to new Delta.*

Right: **Lancia Gamma saloon** — *Italian elegance and the best of big front-drive road behaviour spoiled by the understandable roughness of that big 2½-litre flat four*
Above: **Lancia Gamma Coupé:** *in many opinions, a stunningly tasteful and good looking piece of styling, even by its creator Pininfarina's high standards. Revised Gammas are expected soon with a styling resemblance to the Beta and Delta around the front*

Specifications of Major Production Models

Year	*Model*	*Type or chassis number*	*No. and configuration of cylinders*	*Bore × stroke in mm*	*Capacity in cc*	*Bhp @ rpm*	*Track F/R in cm*	*Wheelbase in cm*
1908	Alpha (18–24 hp)	51	4	90 × 100	2543	53 @ 1800	133/133	282
1908	Dialpha (30 hp)	53	6	90 × 100	3815	—	133/133	323
1909	Beta (20 hp)	54	4	95 × 110	3120	—	133/133	293
1910	Gamma (24 hp)	55	4	100 × 110	3460	—	133/133	293
1911	Delta	56	4	100 × 130	4080	—	133/133	293
1911	Epsilon	58	4	100 × 130	4080	—	133/133	323
1911	Eta	60	4	100 × 160	5030	—	133/133	277
1913	Theta (35 hp)	61	4	110 × 130	4940	70 @ 2200	133/133	338
1919	Kappa (35 hp)	64	4	110 × 130	4940	70 @ 2200	133/133	339
1921	Dikappa (35 hp)	66	4	110 × 130	4940	87 @ 2300	136/137	339
1922	Trikappa (28–80 hp)	68	V8	75 × 130	4594	98 @ 2500	136/137	338
1923	Lambda 214 (14–60 hp)	67	V4	75 × 120	2120	49 @ 3250	{133/136 140/143}	310
1925	Lambda 216 (14–60 hp)	67	V4	75 × 120	2120	49 @ 3250	140/143	342
1926	Lambda 216 bis (16 hp)	78	V4	79 × 120	2370	59 @ 3250	140/143	342
1927	Lambda 218 (16 hp)	78	V4	79 × 120	2370	59 @ 3250	140/143	310
1928	Lambda 223 (17 hp)	79	V4	83 × 120	2570	69 @ 3500	140/143	310
1928	Lambda 224 (17 hp)	79	V4	83 × 120	2570	69 @ 3500	140/143	342
1928	Dilambda 227	81	V8	79 × 100	3960	100 @ 3800	146/148	347
1930	Lambda 221A	79	V4	83 × 120	2570	69 @ 3500	140/143	310
1930	Lambda 222A	79	V4	83 × 120	2570	69 @ 3500	140/143	342
1930	Dilambda 229 (30 hp)	81A	V8	79 × 100	3960	100 @ 3800	142/144	329
1931	Astura 230 (20 hp)	85	V8	70 × 85	2604	73 @ 4000	137/140	318
1931	Artena 228 (15 hp)	84	V4	83 × 90	1925	55 @ 4000	137/140	299
1932	Dilambda 232 (31.2 hp)	81A	V8	79 × 100	3960	100 @ 3800	142/144	347
1933	Augusta 231 (11.9 hp)	88	V4	70 × 78	1196	35 @ 4000	{120/121 121/122}	265
1934	Astura 233–233C (27.6 hp)	91	V8	75 × 85	2972	82 @ 4000	137/140	333/310
1934	Artena 228A & C (17 hp)	84	V4	83 × 90	1925	55 @ 4000	137/140	318/295
1937	Aprilia 238 (12.9 hp)	97	V4	72 × 83	1352	48 @ 4300	{124/127 126/129}	275
1939	Aprilia 438	99	V4	75 × 85	1486	48 @ 4300	126/129	275
1939	Aprilia 439	99	V4	75 × 85	1486	48 @ 4300	126/129	285
1939	Ardea 250	100–100A	V4	65 × 68	903	29 @ 4600	116/118	244
1946	Aprilia 539, 539/2	99	V4	75 × 85	1486	48 @ 4300	126/132	295
1948	Ardea (3rd Series) 250	100A	V4	65 × 68	903	29 @ 4600	116/118	244
1949	Ardea (4th Series) 250	100B	V4	65 × 68	903	30 @ 4600	116/118	244
1950	Aurelia	B10	V6	70 × 76	1754	57 @ 4700	128/130	286
1951	Aurelia	B21, B21S	V6	72 × 82	1991	70 @ 4800	128/130	286
1951	Aurelia GT	B20	V6	72 × 82	1991	80 @ 5000	128/130	266
1952	Aurelia	B15, B15S	V6	72 × 82	1991	64 @ 4800	130/132	325
1952	Aurelia	B22, B22S	V6	72 × 82	1991	90 @ 5000	128/130	286
1953	Aurelia GT2500	B20	V6	78 × 86	2451	116 @ 5200	128/130	266
1953	Appia	C10, C10S	V4	68 × 75	1090	38 @ 4800	118/118	248
1954	Aurelia (2nd Series)	B12, B12S	V6	75 × 86	2266	85 @ 4800	128/130	285
1955	Aurelia Spider	B24, B24S	V6	78 × 86	2451	116 @ 5000	129/130	245
1956	Appia (2nd Series)	C10, C10S	V4	68 × 75	1090	44 @ 4800	118/118	251
1956	Aurelia GT2500	B20, B20S	V6	78 × 86	2451	110 @ 5300	128/130	265
1956	Aurelia Convertible	B24S	V6	78 × 86	2451	110 @ 5300	128/130	245
1957	Aurelia GT2500	B20, B20S	V6	78 × 86	2451	112 @ 5300	128/130	265
1957	Aurelia Convertible	B24S	V6	78 × 86	2451	112 @ 5300	128/130	245
1957	Flaminia	813.00	V6	80 × 82	2458	100 @ 4800	137/137	287
1959	Appia 3S	808.07	V4	68 × 75	1090	48 @ 5200	118/118	251
1959	Flaminia Coupé	824.00	V6	80 × 82	2458	119 @ 5100	137/137	275
1959	Flaminia GT Touring	824.00	V6	80 × 82	2458	119 @ 5100	137/137	252
1959	Flaminia Sport Zagato	824.00	V6	80 × 82	2458	119 @ 5100	137/137	252
1960	Flaminia GT Convertible	824.04	V6	80 × 82	2458	119 @ 5100	137/137	252
1960	Flavia Saloon (1st Series)	815.00	F4	82 × 71	1500	78 @ 5400	130/128	265
1960	Appia 3S Giardinetta	808.21	V4	68 × 75	1090	48 @ 5200	118/118	251
1961	Appia Sport	812.05	V4	68 × 75	1090	60 @ 5400	118/118	235
1961	Flaminia	813.10	V6	80 × 82	2458	110 @ 5200	137/137	287
1961	Flaminia GT	824.10	V6	80 × 82	2458	140 @ 5600	137/137	252
1961	Flaminia Sport	824.13	V6	80 × 82	2458	140 @ 5600	137/137	252
1961	Flaminia Convertible	824.14	V6	80 × 82	2458	140 @ 5600	137/137	252
1962	Flaminia Speciale	813.12	V6	80 × 82	2458	140 @ 5600	137/137	287
1962	Flavia Coupé	815.130	F4	82 × 71	1500	90 @ 5800	130/128	248
1962	Flavia Sport	815.132	F4	82 × 71	1500	90 @ 5800	130/128	248
1962	Flaminia Coupé	823.02	V6	80 × 82	2458	128 @ 5600	137/137	275
1962	Flavia Convertible	815.134	F4	82 × 71	1500	90 @ 5800	130/128	248
1963	Fulvia Sedan	818.000	V4	72 × 67	1091	58 @ 6000	130/128	248
1963	Flavia 1.8 Saloon (2nd Series)	815.300	F4	88 × 74	1800	86 @ 5500	130/128	265
1963	Flavia 1.5 Saloon (2nd Series)	815.200	F4	80 × 74	1488	75 @ 5600	130/128	265
1963	Flavia Coupé 1.8	815.330	F4	88 × 74	1800	88 @ 5650	130/128	248
1963	Flavia Convertible 1.8	815.334	F4	88 × 74	1800	88 @ 5650	130/128	248
1963	Flavia Sport	815.532	F4	88 × 74	1800	95 @ 6000	130/128	248
1963	Flaminia 2.8	826.000	V6	85 × 82	2775	125 @ 5300	137/137	287
1963	Flaminia Coupé 2.8	826.030	V6	85 × 82	2775	136 @ 5450	137/137	275

Year	Model	Type or chassis number	No. and configuration of cylinders	Bore × stroke in mm	Capacity in cc	Bhp @ rpm	Track F/R in cm	Wheelbase in cm
1963	Flaminia Zagato Sport 2.8	826.132	V6	85×82	2775	146@5600	137/137	252
1963	Flaminia Convertible 2.8	826.134	V6	85×82	2775	146@5600	137/137	252
1963	Flaminia GT 2.8	826.138	V6	85×82	2775	146@5600	137/137	252
1963	Flaminia GTL 2.8	826.140	V6	85×82	2775	146@5600	137/137	260
1964	Fulvia Sedan 2C	818.100	V4	72×67	1091	71@6200	130/128	248
1964	Flaminia Super Sport	826.232	V6	85×82	2775	148@5900	137/137	252
1965	Fulvia Coupé	818.130	V4	76×67	1216	80@6200	130/128	233
1965	Flavia Berlina	815.400	F4	88×74	1800	102@5800	130/128	265
1965	Flavia Coupé	815.430	F4	88×74	1800	102@5800	130/128	248
1965	Flavia Sport	815.432	F4	88×74	1800	102@5800	130/128	248
1965	Flavia Convertible	815.434	F4	88×74	1800	102@5800	130/128	248
1965	Fulvia Sport	818.132	V4	76×67	1216	80@6200	130/128	233
1966	Fulvia Coupé HF	818.140	V4	76×67	1216	88@6200	130/128	233
1967	Fulvia Sedan GT	818.200	V4	76×67	1216	80@6200	130/128	248
1967	Fulvia Coupé Rallye 1.3	818.330	V4	77×70	1298	87@6200	130/128	233
1967	Fulvia Sport 1.3	818.332	V4	77×70	1298	87@6200	130/128	233
1967	Fulvia Coupé Rallye 1.3 HF	818.340	V4	77×70	1298	101@6500	130/128	233
1967	Fulvia Sedan GT	818.200	V4	75×70	1231	80@6200	130/128	248
1967	Fulvia Coupé	818.130	V4	75×70	1231	80@6200	130/128	233
1967	Flavia 1.5 Saloon	819.200	F4	80×74	1488	80@5600	132/128	265
1967	Flavia 1.8 Saloon	819.300	F4	88×74	1800	92@5700	132/128	265
1967	Flavia 1.8 Saloon	819.400	F4	88×74	1800	102@5800	132/128	265
1968	Fulvia Sedan GTE	818.300	V4	77×70	1298	87@6200	130/128	248
1968	Fulvia Coupé Rallye 1.3S	818.360	V4	77×70	1298	103@6200	130/128	233
1968	Fulvia Sedan	818.282	V4	74×70	1199	87@6200	130/128	248
1968	Fulvia Sport 1.3S	818.362	V4	77×70	1298	103@6200	130/128	233
1969	Flavia 1.5 Saloon	819.200	F4	77×80	1490	84@5600	132/128	265
1969	Flavia 1.8 Saloon	819.300	F4	85×80	1816	96@5700	132/128	265
1969	Flavia Coupé	820.030	F4	89×80	1991	131@5800	132/128	248
1969	Flavia 2000 Saloon	819.610	F4	89×80	1991	131@5800	132/128	265
1969	Fulvia Coupé Rallye 1.6HF	818.540	V4	82×75	1584	130@6500	139/133	233
1969	Fulvia Sedan (2nd Series)	818.610	V4	77×70	1298	95@6200	130/128	250
1969	Flavia Coupé	820.430	F4	89×80	1991	140@5800	132/128	248
1969	Flavia 2000 Saloon	819.810	F4	89×80	1991	140@5800	132/128	265
1969	Fulvia Sedan (2nd Series)	818.692	V4	74×70	1199	87@6200	130/128	250
1970	Fulvia Coupé (2nd Series)	818.630	V4	77×70	1298	90@6200	130/128	233
1970	Fulvia Sport (2nd Series)	818.650	V4	77×70	1298	90@6200	130/128	233
1970	Fulvia Coupé HF	818.740	V4	82×75	1584	114@6500	139/133	233
1970	Fulvia Sedan (2nd Series)	818.612	V4	77×70	1298	85@6200	130/128	250
1970	Fulvia Sedan (2nd Series)	818.694	V4	74×70	1199	78@6200	130/128	250
1971	Flavia 2000 Saloon	820.010	F4	89×80	1991	114@5800	132/128	265
1971	Flavia 2000 S1 Saloon	820.410	F4	89×80	1991	131@5800	132/128	265
1971	Lancia 2000 Sedan	820.210	F4	89×80	1991	115@6000	133/129	265
1971	Lancia 2000 Coupé	820.230	F4	89×80	1991	115@6000	133/129	248
1971	Fulvia Sport 1600 (2nd Series)	818.750	V4	82×75	1584	114@6500	130/128	233
1971	Lancia Coupé HF	820.436	V4	89×80	1991	125@6000	133/129	248
1972	Lancia 2000 Sedan IE	820.416	F4	89×80	1991	125@6000	133/129	265
1972	Fulvia Coupé 1.3 Monte Carlo	818.630	V4	77×70	1298	90@6200	130/128	233
1972	Beta 1600 Saloon	828 AB.0	4	80×79	1592	100@6400	141/139	254
1972	Beta 1800 Saloon	828 AB.1	4	84×79	1756	110@6400	141/139	254
1973	Beta 1400 Saloon	828 AB.2	4	80×72	1438	90@6400	141/139	254
1974	Beta 1600 Coupé	828 AC.0	4	80×79	1592	106@6400	141/139	235
1974	Beta 1800 Coupé	828 AC.1	4	84×79	1756	120@6400	141/139	235
1974	Stratos	829 AR.0	V6	93×60	2418	190@7800	143/146	218
1974	Beta Spyder	828 AS.0	4	80×79	1592	106@6400	141/139	235
1974	Beta Spyder	828 AS.1	4	84×79	1756	120@6400	141/139	235
1975	Beta 1300 Saloon	828 BB.3	4	76×72	1297	82@6400	141/139	254
1975	H.P.E. 1600	828 AF.0	4	84×72	1585	100@6400	141/139	254
1975	H.P.E. 1800	828 AF.1	4	84×90	1756	119@6400	141/139	254
1975	Beta 1600 Saloon	828 CB.0	4	84×72	1585	100@6400	141/139	254
1975	Beta 2000 Saloon	828 CB.1	4	84×90	1995	119@6400	141/139	254
1975	Beta 1300 Coupé	828 BC.3	4	76×72	1297	82@6400	141/139	254
1975	Beta 1600 Coupé	828 BC.0	4	84×72	1585	100@6400	141/139	235
1975	Beta 2000 Coupé	828 BC.1	4	84×90	1995	119@6400	141/139	235
1975	Beta Spyder	828 BS.0	4	84×72	1585	100@6400	141/139	235
1975	Beta Spyder	828 BS.1	4	84×90	1995	119@6400	141/139	235
1975	H.P.E. 1600	828 BF.0	4	84×72	1585	100@6400	141/139	254
1975	H.P.E. 2000	828 BF.1	4	84×90	1995	119@6400	141/139	254
1975	Beta Monte Carlo	137 AS	4	84×90	1995	120@6000	141/146	230
1978	Gamma Sedan	830 AB.0	4	102×76	2484	140@5400	145/144	267
1978	Gamma Coupé	830 AC.0	4	102×76	2484	140@5400	145/144	255
1979	Delta	831 AB.0/5	4	86.4×55.5	1301	75@5800	140/140	247
1979	Delta	831 AB.0/1	4	86.4×63.9	1498	85@5800	140/140	247
1980	Beta Trevi	828 DB.0/3	4	84×90	1995	122@5500	141/139	254

The above details were supplied by the Lancia Company and may differ in some minor respects from those quoted in the contemporary *Autocar* material.

Figures in brackets after the names of pre-1939 models show the RAC horsepower rating, which is commonly used to identify those models in the *Autocar* articles. This figure is only given for models which were imported into the United Kingdom.